D1592241

This work was funded by a grant from the Iraq Afghanistan Deployment Impact Fund, which is administered by the California Community Foundation. The study was conducted jointly under the auspices of the Center for Military Health Policy Research, a RAND Health center, and the Forces and Resources Policy Center of the National Security Research Division (NSRD).

Library of Congress Cataloging-in-Publication Data

Tanielian, Terri L.
    Invisible wounds of war : psychological and cognitive injuries, their consequences, and services to assist recovery / Terri Tanielian, Lisa H. Jaycox.
        p. ; cm.
    Includes bibliographical references.
    ISBN 978-0-8330-4454-9 (pbk. : alk. paper)
        1. Post-traumatic stress disorder—United States. 2. Brain—Wounds and injuries—United States. 3. Depression—United States. 4. Veterans—Mental health—United States. 5. Iraq war, 2003-—Psychological aspects. 6. Afghan war, 2001-—Psychological aspects. 7. War on terrorism, 2001-—Psychological aspects. 8. War—Psychological aspects. I. Jaycox, Lisa. II. Rand Corporation. III. Title.
        [DNLM: 1. Combat Disorders. 2. Brain Injuries. 3. Depressive Disorder. 4. Iraq War, 2003- . 5. Stress Disorders, Post-Traumatic. 6. Veterans—psychology. WM 184 T164i 2008]

    RC552.P67T34 2008
    362.196'85212—dc22

                                                                          2008008840

The RAND Corporation is a nonprofit research organization providing objective analysis and effective solutions that address the challenges facing the public and private sectors around the world. RAND's publications do not necessarily reflect the opinions of its research clients and sponsors.

RAND® is a registered trademark.

Cover design by Eileen Delson La Russo
Cover photo: U.S. Army photo by SPC Eric Jungels

Published 2008 by the RAND Corporation
1776 Main Street, P.O. Box 2138, Santa Monica, CA 90407-2138
1200 South Hayes Street, Arlington, VA 22202-5050
4570 Fifth Avenue, Suite 600, Pittsburgh, PA 15213-2665
RAND URL: http://www.rand.org/
To order RAND documents or to obtain additional information, contact
Distribution Services: Telephone: (310) 451-7002;
Fax: (310) 451-6915; Email: order@rand.org

Preface

Since October 2001, approximately 1.64 million U.S. troops have been deployed for Operations Enduring Freedom and Iraqi Freedom (OEF/OIF) in Afghanistan and Iraq. Early evidence suggests that the psychological toll of these deployments—many involving prolonged exposure to combat-related stress over multiple rotations—may be disproportionately high compared with the physical injuries of combat. In the face of mounting public concern over post-deployment health care issues confronting OEF/OIF veterans, several task forces, independent review groups, and a President's Commission have been convened to examine the care of the war wounded and make recommendations. Concerns have been most recently centered on two combat-related injuries in particular: post-traumatic stress disorder and traumatic brain injury. Many recent reports have referred to these as the signature wounds of the Afghanistan and Iraq conflicts. With the increasing incidence of suicide and suicide attempts among returning veterans, concern about depression is also on the rise.

The study discussed in this monograph focuses on post-traumatic stress disorder, major depression, and traumatic brain injury, not only because of current high-level policy interest but also because, unlike the physical wounds of war, these conditions are often invisible to the eye, remaining invisible to other servicemembers, family members, and society in general. All three conditions affect mood, thoughts, and behavior; yet these wounds often go unrecognized and unacknowledged. The effect of traumatic brain injury is still poorly understood, leaving a large gap in knowledge related to how extensive the problem is or how to address it.

RAND conducted a comprehensive study of the post-deployment health-related needs associated with post-traumatic stress disorder, major depression, and traumatic brain injury among OEF/OIF veterans, the health care system in place to meet those needs, gaps in the care system, and the costs associated with these conditions and with providing quality health care to all those in need. This monograph presents the results of that study. These results should be of interest to mental health treatment providers; health policymakers, particularly those charged with caring for our nation's veterans; and U.S. service men and women, their families, and the concerned public. All the research products from this study are available at http://veterans.rand.org.

Data collection for this study began in April 2007 and concluded in January 2008. Specific activities included a critical review of the extant literature on the prevalence of post-traumatic stress disorder, major depression, and traumatic brain injury and their short- and long-term consequences; a population-based survey of servicemembers and veterans who served in Afghanistan or Iraq to assess health status and symptoms, as well as utilization of and barriers to care; a review of existing programs to treat servicemembers and veterans with post-traumatic stress disorder, major depression, and traumatic brain injury; focus groups with military servicemembers and their spouses; and the development of a microsimulation model to forecast the economic costs of these conditions over time.

Interviews with senior Office of the Secretary of Defense (OSD) and Service (Army, Navy, Air Force, Marine Corps) staff within the Department of Defense and within the Veterans Health Administration informed our efforts to document the treatment and support programs available to this population. Note, however, that the views expressed in this monograph do not reflect official policy or the position of the U.S. government or any of the institutions we included in our interviews.

This work was funded by a grant from the Iraq Afghanistan Deployment Impact Fund, which is administered by the California Community Foundation. The fund had no role in the design and conduct of this study; collection, management, analysis, or interpretation of data; or in the preparation of this document. The study was conducted jointly under the auspices of the Center for Military Health Policy Research, a RAND Health center, and the Forces and Resources Policy Center of the National Security Research Division (NSRD). The principal investigators are Terri Tanielian and Lisa H. Jaycox. More information about RAND is available at www.rand.org.

Study Directors
Terri Tanielian
Lisa H. Jaycox

Management Team

Terri Tanielian	Lisa S. Meredith
Lisa H. Jaycox	Christine Eibner
M. Audrey Burnam	Jeanne S. Ringel
Terry L. Schell	Karen N. Metscher
Grant N. Marshall	Gail Fisher
Benjamin R. Karney	

Survey Team
Terry L. Schell[a]
Grant N. Marshall[a]
Jeremy N. V. Miles
Gail Fisher
Karen N. Metscher
Lisa H. Jaycox
Terri Tanielian

Economics/Costs
Christine Eibner[a]
Jeanne S. Ringel[a]
Beau Kilmer
Rosalie Liccardo Pacula
Claudia Diaz
Regina A. Shih

Literature Review of Consequences
Benjamin R. Karney[a]
Rajeev Ramchand
Karen Chan Osilla
Leah Barnes Calderone
Rachel M. Burns

Systems of Care
M. Audrey Burnam[a]
Lisa S. Meredith[a]
Elizabeth D'Amico
Todd C. Helmus
Robert A. Cox
Laurie T. Martin
Diane C. Schoeff
Rachel M. Burns
Kayla M. Williams
Michael R. Yochelson
Ellen Burke Beckjord
Andrew M. Parker
Manan M. Trivedi
Sarah Gaillot

Communications Support
Mary E. Vaiana[a]
David M. Adamson
Jerry M. Sollinger

Administrative Support
Samantha Abernethy
Catherine Chao
Taria Francois
Stacy Fitzsimmons
Michael Woodward

[a] Denotes team leader.

Contents

Figures

Tables

Summary

Since October 2001, approximately 1.64 million U.S. troops have deployed as part of Operation Enduring Freedom (OEF; Afghanistan) and Operation Iraqi Freedom (OIF; Iraq). The pace of the deployments in these current conflicts is unprecedented in the history of the all-volunteer force (Belasco, 2007; Bruner, 2006). Not only is a higher proportion of the armed forces being deployed, but deployments have been longer, redeployment to combat has been common, and breaks between deployments have been infrequent (Hosek, Kavanagh, and Miller, 2006). At the same time, episodes of intense combat notwithstanding, these operations have employed smaller forces and have produced casualty rates of killed or wounded that are historically lower than in earlier prolonged wars, such as Vietnam and Korea. Advances in both medical technology and body armor mean that more servicemembers are surviving experiences that would have led to death in prior wars (Regan, 2004; Warden, 2006). However, casualties of a different kind are beginning to emerge—invisible wounds, such as mental health conditions and cognitive impairments resulting from deployment experiences. These deployment experiences may include multiple deployments per individual servicemember and exposure to difficult threats, such as improvised explosive devices (IEDs).

As with safeguarding physical health, safeguarding mental health is an integral component of the United States' national responsibilities to recruit, prepare, and sustain a military force and to address Service-connected injuries and disabilities. But safeguarding mental health is also critical for compensating and honoring those who have served our nation.

Public concern over the handling of such injuries is running high. The Department of Defense (DoD), the Department of Veterans Affairs (VA), Congress, and the President have moved to study the issues related to how such injuries are handled, quantify the problems, and formulate policy solutions. And they have acted swiftly to begin implementing the hundreds of recommendations that have emerged from various task forces and commissions. Policy changes and funding shifts are already occurring for military and veterans' health care in general and for mental health care in particular.

However, despite widespread policy interest and a firm commitment from DoD and the VA to address these injuries, fundamental gaps remain in our knowledge about the mental health and cognitive needs of U.S. servicemembers returning from Afghanistan and Iraq, the adequacy of the care systems available to meet those needs, the experience of veterans and servicemembers who are in need of services, and factors related to whether and how injured servicemembers and veterans seek care.

To begin closing these gaps, RAND undertook this comprehensive study. We focused on three major conditions—post-traumatic stress disorder (PTSD), major depressive disorder and depressive symptoms, and traumatic brain injury (TBI)—because these are the conditions being assessed most extensively in servicemembers returning from combat. In addition, there are obvious mechanisms that might link each of these conditions to specific experiences in war—i.e., depression can be a reaction to loss; PTSD, a reaction to trauma; and TBI, a consequence of blast exposure or other head injury. Unfortunately, these conditions are often invisible to the eye. Unlike the physical wounds of war that maim or disfigure, these conditions remain invisible to other servicemembers, to family members, and to society in general. All three conditions affect mood, thoughts, and behavior; yet these wounds often go unrecognized and unacknowledged. The effects of traumatic brain injury are still poorly understood, leaving a large gap in knowledge related to how extensive the problem is or how to handle it.

The study was guided by a series of overarching questions:

- **Prevalence:** What is the scope of mental health and cognitive conditions that troops face when returning from deployment to Afghanistan and Iraq?
- **Costs:** What are the costs of these conditions, including treatment costs and costs stemming from lost productivity and other consequences? What are the costs and potential savings associated with different levels of medical care—including proven, evidence-based care; usual care; and no care?
- **The care system:** What are the existing programs and services to meet the health-related needs of servicemembers and veterans with post-traumatic stress disorder, major depression, or traumatic brain injury? What are the gaps in the programs and services? What steps can be taken to close the gaps?

To answer these questions, we reviewed the existing literature on the prevalence of PTSD, major depression, and TBI among OEF/OIF veterans. We also fielded a survey of 1,965 servicemembers and veterans to provide data on levels of probable PTSD, major depression, and TBI, as well as on self-reported use of and barriers to health care. We examined the scientific literature on the short-term and long-term consequences associated with psychological and cognitive injuries. We developed a microsimulation model to estimate the individual and societal costs of these conditions in expenditures for treatment and lost productivity. We assessed the systems of care designed to provide treatment for these conditions, evaluated the evidence supporting the services being offered, and identified gaps in access to and quality of care being provided. We supplemented that information by conducting focus groups with military servicemembers and their families and by interviewing key administrators and providers. We integrated our findings to offer recommendations for addressing these gaps and improving quality.

Key Findings

Prevalence of Mental Health Conditions and TBI

What is the scope of mental health and cognitive issues faced by OEF/OIF troops returning from deployment? Most of the 1.64 million military servicemembers who have deployed in support of OIF or OEF will return home from war without problems and readjust successfully, but many have already returned or will return with significant mental health conditions. Among OEF/OIF veterans, rates of PTSD, major depression, and probable TBI are relatively high, particularly when compared with the general U.S. civilian population. A telephone study of 1,965 previously deployed individuals sampled from 24 geographic areas found substantial rates of mental health problems in the past 30 days, with 14 percent screening positive for PTSD and 14 percent for major depression. A similar number, 19 percent, reported a probable TBI during deployment. Major depression is often not considered a combat-related injury; however, our analyses suggest that it is highly associated with combat exposure and should be considered as being along the spectrum of post-deployment mental health consequences. Although a substantial proportion of respondents had reported experiencing a TBI, it is not possible to know from the survey the severity of the injury or whether the injury caused functional impairment.

Assuming that the prevalence found in this study is representative of the 1.64 million servicemembers who had been deployed for OEF/OIF as of October 2007, we estimate that approximately 300,000 individuals currently suffer from PTSD or major depression and that 320,000 individuals experienced a probable TBI during deployment. About one-third of those previously deployed have at least one of these three conditions, and about 5 percent report symptoms of all three. Some specific groups, previously understudied—including the Reserve Components and those who have left military service—may be at higher risk of suffering from these conditions.

Seeking and Receiving Treatment. Of those reporting a probable TBI, 57 percent had not been evaluated by a physician for brain injury. Military servicemembers with probable PTSD or major depression seek care at about the same rate as the civilian population, and, just as in the civilian population, many of the afflicted individuals were not receiving treatment. About half (53 percent) of those who met the criteria for current PTSD or major depression had sought help from a physician or mental health provider for a mental health problem in the past year.

xxii Invisible Wounds of War

Getting Quality Care. Even when individuals receive care, too few receive quality care. Of those who have a mental disorder and also sought medical care for that problem, just over half received a minimally adequate treatment. The number who received *quality* care (i.e., a treatment that has been demonstrated to be effective) would be expected to be even smaller. Focused efforts are needed to significantly improve both accessibility to care and quality of care for these groups. The prevalence of PTSD and major depression will likely remain high unless greater efforts are made to enhance systems of care for these individuals.

Survey respondents identified many barriers that inhibit getting treatment for their mental health problems. In general, respondents were concerned that treatment would not be kept confidential and would constrain future job assignments and military-career advancement. About 45 percent were concerned that drug therapies for mental health problems may have unpleasant side effects, and about one-quarter thought that even good mental health care was not very effective. These barriers suggest the need for increased access to confidential, evidence-based psychotherapy, to maintain high levels of readiness and functioning among previously deployed service-members and veterans.

Costs

What are the costs of these mental health and cognitive conditions to the individual and to society? Unless treated, each of these conditions has wide-ranging and negative implications for those afflicted. We considered a wide array of consequences that affect work, family, and social functioning, and we considered co-occurring problems, such as substance abuse, homelessness, and suicide.

The presence of any one of these conditions can impair future health, work productivity, and family and social relationships. Individuals afflicted with any of these conditions are more likely to have other psychiatric diagnoses (e.g., substance use) and are at increased risk for attempting suicide. They have higher rates of unhealthy behaviors (e.g., smoking, overeating, unsafe sex) and higher rates of physical health problems and mortality. Individuals with any of these conditions also tend to miss more days of work or report being less productive. There is also a possible connection between having one of these conditions and being homeless.

Suffering from these conditions can also impair relationships, disrupt marriages, aggravate the difficulties of parenting, and cause problems in children that may extend the consequences of combat experiences across generations.

Associated Costs. In dollar terms, the costs associated with mental health and cognitive conditions stemming from the conflicts in Afghanistan and Iraq are substantial. We estimated costs using two separate methodologies. For PTSD and major depression, we used a microsimulation model to project *two-year costs*—costs incurred within the first two years after servicemembers return home. Because there were insufficient data to simulate two-year-cost projections for TBI, we estimated one-year costs for TBI using a standard, cost-of-illness approach. On a per-case basis, two-year costs associated with PTSD are approximately $5,904 to $10,298, depending on whether we include the cost of lives lost to suicide. Two-year costs associated with major depression are approximately $15,461 to $25,757, and costs associated with co-morbid PTSD and major depression are approximately $12,427 to $16,884. One-year costs for service-members who have accessed the health care system and received a diagnosis of trau-matic brain injury are even higher, ranging from $25,572 to $30,730 in 2005 for mild cases ($27,259 to $32,759 in 2007 dollars), and from $252,251 to $383,221 for moder-ate or severe cases ($268,902 to $408,519 in 2007 dollars).

However, our cost figures omit current as well as potential later costs stemming from substance abuse, domestic violence, homelessness, family strain, and several other factors, thus understating the true costs associated with deployment-related cognitive and mental health conditions.

Translating these cost estimates into a total-dollar figure is confounded by uncer-tainty about the total number of cases in a given year, by the little information that is available about the severity of these cases, and by the extent to which the three con-ditions co-occur. Given these caveats, we used our microsimulation model to predict two-year costs for the approximately 1.6 million troops who have deployed since 2001. We estimate that PTSD-related and major depression–related costs could range from $4.0 to $6.2 billion over two years (in 2007 dollars). Applying the costs per case for TBI to the total number of diagnosed TBI cases identified as of June 2007 (2,726), we estimate that total costs incurred within the first year after diagnosis could range from $591 million to $910 million (in 2007 dollars).

These figures are for diagnosed TBI cases that led to contact with the health care system; they do not include costs for individuals with probable TBI who have not sought treatment or who have not been formally diagnosed. To the extent that additional troops deploy and more TBI cases occur in the coming months and years, total costs will rise. Because these calculations include costs for servicemembers who returned from deployment starting as early as 2001, many of these costs (for PTSD, depression, and TBI) have already been incurred. However, if servicemembers continue to be deployed in the future, rates of detection of TBI among servicemembers increase, or there are costs associated with chronic or recurring cases that linger beyond two years, the total expected costs associated with these conditions will increase beyond the range.

Lost Productivity. Our findings also indicate that lost productivity is a key cost driver for major depression and PTSD. Approximately 55 to 95 percent of total costs can be attributed to reduced productivity; for mild TBI, productivity losses may account for 47 to 57 percent of total costs. Because severe TBI can lead to death, mor-tality is the largest component of costs for moderate to severe TBI, accounting for 70 to 80 percent of total costs.

Evidence-Based Treatment. Certain treatments have been shown to be effective for both PTSD and major depression, but these *evidence-based treatments* are not yet available in all treatment settings. We estimate that evidence-based treatment for PTSD and major depression would pay for itself within two years, even without considering costs related to substance abuse, homelessness, family strain, and other indirect consequences of mental health conditions. Evidence-based care for PTSD and major depression could save as much as $1.7 billion, or $1,063 per returning veteran; the savings come from increases in productivity, as well as from reductions in the expected number of suicides.

Given these numbers, investments in evidence-based treatment would make sense from DoD's perspective, not only because of higher remission and recovery rates but also because such treatment would increase the productivity of servicemembers. The benefits to DoD in retention and increased productivity would outweigh the higher costs of providing evidence-based care. These benefits would likely be even stronger (higher) had we been able to capture the full spectrum of costs associated with mental health conditions. However, a caveat is that we did not consider additional implementation and outreach costs (over and above the day-to-day costs of care) that might be incurred if DoD and the VA attempted to expand evidence-based treatment beyond current capacity.

Cost studies that do not account for reduced productivity may significantly understate the true costs of the conflicts in Afghanistan and Iraq. Currently, information is limited on how mental health conditions affect career outcomes within DoD. Given the strong association between mental health status and productivity found in civilian studies, research that explores how the mental health status of active duty personnel affects career outcomes would be valuable. Ideally, studies would consider how mental health conditions influence job performance, promotion within DoD, and transitions from DoD into the civilian labor force (as well as productivity after transition).

Systems of Care

What are the existing programs and services to meet the health-related needs of servicemembers with PTSD or major depression? What are the gaps in the programs and services? What steps can be taken to close the gaps? To achieve the cost savings outlined above, servicemembers suffering from PTSD and major depression must be identified as early as possible and be provided with evidence-based treatment. The capacity of DoD and the VA to provide mental health services has been increased substantially, but significant gaps in access and quality remain.

A Gap Between Need and Use. For the active duty population in particular, there is a large gap between the need for mental health services and the use of such services—a pattern that appears to stem from structural aspects of services (wait times, availability of providers) as well as from personal and cultural factors. Institutional and cultural barriers to mental health care are substantial—and not easily surmounted.

Military servicemembers expressed concerns that use of mental health services will negatively affect employment and constrain military career prospects, thus deterring many of those who need or want help from seeking it.

Institutional barriers must be addressed to increase help-seeking and utilization of mental health services. In particular, the requirement that service usage be reported may be impeding such utilization. In itself, addressing the personal attitudes of service-members about the use of mental health services, although important, is not likely to be sufficient if the institutional barriers remain in place.

Quality-of-Care Gaps. We also identified gaps in organizational tools and incentives that would support the delivery of high-quality mental health care to the active-duty population, and to retired military who use TRICARE, DoD's health insurance plan. In the absence of such organizational supports, it is not possible to provide oversight to ensure *high quality of care*, which includes ensuring both that the treatment provided is evidence-based and that it is patient-centered, efficient, equitable, and timely. DoD has initiated training in evidence-based practices for providers, but these efforts have not yet been integrated into a larger system redesign that values and provides incentives for quality of care. The newly created Defense Center of Excellence for Psychological Health and Traumatic Brain Injury, housed within DoD, represents a historic opportunity to prioritize a system-level focus on monitoring and improving quality of care; however, continued funding and appropriate regulatory authority will be important to sustain this focus over time.

The VA provides a promising model of quality improvement in mental health care for DoD. Significant improvements in the quality of care the VA provides for depression have been documented, and efforts to evaluate the quality of care provided within the VA for PTSD remain under way. However, it too faces challenges in providing access to OEF/OIF veterans, many of whom have difficulty securing appointments, particularly in facilities that have been resourced primarily to meet the demands of older veterans. Better projections of the amount and type of demand among the newer veterans are needed to ensure that the VA has the appropriate resources to meet the potential demand. At the same time, OEF/OIF veterans report feeling uncomfortable or out of place in VA facilities (some of which are dated and most of which treat patients who are older and chronically ill), indicating a need for some facility upgrades and newer approaches to outreach.

Going Beyond DoD and the VA. Improving access to mental health services for OEF/OIF veterans will require reaching beyond DoD and VA health care systems. Given the diversity and the geographic dispersal of the OEF/OIF veteran population, other options for providing health services, including Vet Centers, nonmedical centers that offer supportive counseling and other services to veterans (see Chapter Seven), and other community-based providers, must be considered. Vet Centers already play a critical role and are uniquely designed to meet the needs of veterans. Further expansion of Vet Centers could broaden access, particularly for veterans in underserved areas. Networks of community-based mental health specialists (available through private, employer-based insurance, including TRICARE) may also provide an important opportunity to build capacity. However, taking advantage of this opportunity will require critical examination of the TRICARE reimbursement rates, which may limit network participation.

Although Vet Centers and other community-based providers offer the potential for expanded access to mental health services, ways to monitor performance and quality among these providers will be essential to ensuring quality care. Although ongoing training for providers is being made broadly available, it is not supported with a level of supervision that will result in high-quality care. Systems for supporting delivery of high-quality care (information systems, performance feedback) are currently lacking in these sectors. Commercial managed health care organizations have some existing approaches and tools to monitor quality that may be of value and utility, but many of the grassroots efforts currently emerging to serve OEF/OIF veterans do not.

What are existing programs and services to meet the health-related needs of those with traumatic brain injuries? What are the gaps in care? What steps can be taken to close those gaps? The medical science for treating combat-related traumatic brain injury is in its infancy. Research is urgently needed to develop effective screening tools that are both valid and sensitive, as well as to document what treatment and rehabilitation will be most effective.

For mild TBI, a head injury that may or may not result in symptoms and long-term neurocognitive deficits, we found gaps in access to services stemming from poor documentation of blast exposures and failure to identify individuals with probable TBI. These gaps not only hamper provision of acute care but may also place individuals at risk of additional blast exposures.

Servicemembers with more-severe injuries face a different kind of access gap: lack of coordination across a continuum of care. Because of the complex nature of health care associated with severe combat injuries, including moderate and severe TBI,[1] an individual's need for treatment, as well as for supportive and rehabilitative services, will change over time and involve multiple transitions across systems. Task forces, commissions, and review groups have already identified multiple challenges arising from these complexities; these challenges remain the focus of improvement activities in both DoD and the VA.

---

[1]   Classification of TBI is based on a combination of the cause of the injury and the level of deficits suffered as a result. See Chapter Seven.

Recommendations

Current concern about the invisible wounds of war is increasing, and many efforts to identify and treat those wounds are already under way. But more is needed to ensure equitable and sustainable solutions. Our data show that these mental health and cognitive conditions are widespread; in a cohort of otherwise-healthy, young individuals, they represent the primary type of morbidity in coming years. What is most worrisome is that these problems are not yet fully understood, particularly TBI, and systems of care are not yet fully available to assist recovery for any of the three conditions. Thus, these invisible wounds of war require special attention and high priority. An exceptional effort will be needed to ensure that they are appropriately recognized and treated.

Looking across the dimensions of our analysis, and in light of the strengths and limitations of our methodology, we offer four specific recommendations that we believe will improve the understanding and treatment of PTSD, major depression, and TBI among military veterans. We briefly describe each recommendation, and then discuss some of the issues that would need to be addressed for successful implementation. We believe efforts to address these recommendations should be standardized to the greatest extent possible within DoD (across Service branches, with appropriate guidance from the Assistant Secretary of Defense for Health Affairs) and within the VA (across health care facilities and Vet Centers), and across these systems and extended into the community-based civilian sector. These policies and programs must be consistent within and across these sectors before they can have the intended effect on care-seeking and improvements in quality of care for our nation's veterans.

1. **Increase the cadre of providers who are trained and certified to deliver proven (evidence-based) care, so that capacity is adequate for current and future needs.**

There is substantial unmet need for treatment of PTSD and major depression among servicemembers following deployment. Both DoD and the VA have had difficulty in recruiting and retaining appropriately trained mental health professionals to fill existing *or* new slots. With the possibility of more than 300,000 new cases of mental health conditions among OEF/OIF veterans, a commensurate increase in treatment capacity is needed. Increased numbers of trained and certified professionals are needed to provide high-quality care (evidence-based, patient-centered, efficient, equitable, and timely care) in all sectors, both military and civilian, serving previously deployed personnel. Such professionals would include providers not just in specialty mental health settings but also those embedded in settings such as primary care where servicemembers already are served. Stakeholders consistently referred to challenges in hiring and retaining trained mental health providers. Determining the exact number of providers will require further analyses of demand projections over time, taking into account the expected length of evidence-based treatment and desired utilization rates.

Although the precise number of newly trained providers required is not yet known, it is likely to be in the thousands. Additional training in evidence-based treatment for trauma will also be required for tens of thousands of existing providers. Moreover, since the dramatic increase in need for services exists now, the required expansion in trained providers is already several years overdue.

This large-scale training effort necessitates substantial investment immediately, and that investment could be facilitated by several strategies, including the following:

- Adjusting financial reimbursement for providers to offer appropriate compensation and incentives to attract and retain highly qualified professionals and ensure motivation for delivering quality care.
- Developing a certification process to document the clinical qualifications of providers. Providers would also be required to demonstrate requisite knowledge of unique military culture, military employment, and issues relevant to veterans.
- Expanding existing training programs for psychiatrists, psychologists, social workers, marriage and family therapists, and other counselors to include in their curricula and practice settings training in specific therapies related to trauma and military culture.
- Establishing regional training centers for joint training of DoD, VA, and civilian providers in evidence-based care for PTSD and major depression. The centers should be funded federally, possibly outside of DoD and VA budgets.
- Linking certification to training to ensure that providers not only receive required training but also are supervised and monitored to verify that quality standards are met and maintained over time.
- Retraining or expanding the number of existing providers within DoD and the VA (e.g., military community-service-program counselors) to include delivery or support of evidence-based care.
- Evaluating training efforts as they are rolled out, so that we understand how much training is needed and of what type, thereby ensuring delivery of effective care.

2. Change policies to encourage active duty personnel and veterans to seek needed care.

Creating an adequate supply of well-trained professionals to provide care is only one facet of ensuring access to care. Strategies must also increase demand for necessary services. Many servicemembers are reluctant to seek services for fear of negative career repercussions. Policies must be changed so that there are no perceived or real adverse career consequences for individuals who seek treatment, except when functional impairment (e.g., poor job performance or being a hazard to oneself or others) compromises fitness for duty. Primarily, such policies will require creating new ways for servicemembers and veterans to obtain treatments that are confidential, to operate in parallel with existing mechanisms for receiving treatment (e.g., command referral, unit-embedded support, or self-referral).

We are not suggesting that the confidentiality of treatment should be absolute; since both military and civilian treatment providers already have a legal obligation to report to authorities/commanders any patients who represent a threat to themselves or others. Information about being in treatment is currently available to command staff, although treatment itself is not a sign of dysfunction or poor job performance and may not have any relationship to deployment eligibility. Providing an option for confidential treatment has the potential to increase total-force readiness by encouraging individuals to seek needed health care before problems accrue to a critical level. In this way, mental health treatment would be appropriately used by the military as a tool to avoid or mitigate functional impairment, rather than as evidence of functional impairment. We believe this would ultimately lead to better force readiness and retention, thus being a beneficial change both for the organization and for the individual.

This recommendation would require resolving many practical challenges, but it is vital for addressing the mental health problems of those servicemembers who are not seeking care out of concern for their military careers.

Specific strategies for facilitating care-seeking include the following:

- Developing strategies for early identification of problems that can be confidential, so that problems are recognized and care sought early, before problems lead to impairments in daily life, including job functioning or eligibility for deployment.
- Developing ways for servicemembers to seek mental health care voluntarily and off-the-record, including ways to allow servicemembers to seek this care off-base if they prefer and ways to pay for confidential mental health care (that is not necessarily tied to an insurance claim from the individual servicemember). Thus, the care would be offered to military personnel without mandating disclosure, unless the servicemember chooses to disclose use of mental health care or there is a command-initiated referral to mental health care.
- Separating the system for determining deployment eligibility from the mental health care system. Doing so may require the development of new ways to determine fitness for duty and eligibility for deployment that do not include information about mental health service use.
- Making the system transparent to servicemembers so that they understand how information about mental health services is and is not used. This may help mitigate servicemembers' concerns about detriments to their careers.

3.   Deliver proven, evidence-based care to servicemembers and veterans whenever and wherever services are provided.

Our extensive review of the scientific literature documented that treatments for PTSD and major depression vary substantially in their effectiveness. In addition, the 2007 report from the Institute of Medicine shows reasonable evidence for treatments for PTSD among military servicemembers and veterans. Our evaluation shows that the most effective treatments are being delivered in some sectors of the care system for military personnel and veterans, but that gaps remain in systemwide implementation. Delivery of evidence-based care to all veterans with PTSD or major depression would pay for itself within two years, or even save money, by improving productivity and reducing medical and mortality costs. Providing evidence-based care is not only the humane course of action, it is also a cost-effective way to retain a ready and healthy military force for the future. The VA, which provides one model, is at the forefront of initiatives to ensure delivery of evidence-based care, but it has not yet fully evaluated the success of these initiatives across the entire system.

We suggest requiring that all providers who treat military personnel use treatment approaches empirically demonstrated to be the most effective. This requirement would include uniformed providers in theater and providers embedded in active duty units. It would also involve primary and specialty care providers in military health facilities, VA health care facilities, and Vet Centers, and civilian providers who serve military personnel when they return home. In addition to mental health providers, evidence-based care needs to be enforced among informal providers, to bolster promising prevention efforts pre-deployment, noncommissioned-officer support models in theater, and the work of chaplains and family-support providers. The goal of this requirement is not to stifle innovation or prevent tailoring of treatment to individual needs, but to ensure that individuals who have been diagnosed with PTSD or major depression are provided the most effective evidence-based treatment available.

Key transformations may be required to achieve this improvement in quality of care:

- The "black box" of psychotherapy delivered to veterans must be made more transparent, so that providers are accountable for their services. Such accountability might require that TRICARE and the VA implement billing codes to indicate the specific type of therapy delivered, documentation requirements (i.e., structured medical note-taking that needs to accompany billing), and the like.
- TRICARE and the VA should require that all patients be treated by therapists who are certified to handle the diagnosed disorders of those patients.
- Veterans should be empowered to seek appropriate care by being informed about what types of therapies to expect, the benefits of those treatments, and how to evaluate whether they are receiving quality care.

- A monitoring system should be used to ensure sustained quality and coordination of care and quality improvement. Transparency, accountability, and training/certification would facilitate monitoring. Additionally, linking performance measurements to reimbursement and incentives for providers may also promote delivery of quality care.

4. Invest in research to close information gaps and plan effectively.

In many respects, this study raises more research questions than it provides answers. Our nation urgently needs a better understanding of the full range of problems (emotional, economic, social, health, and other quality-of-life deficits) that confront individuals with post-combat PTSD, major depression, and TBI. Such knowledge is required both to enable the health care system to respond effectively and to calibrate how disability benefits are ultimately determined. We also need to understand who is at risk for developing mental health problems and who is most vulnerable to relapse, and how to target treatments for these individuals.

We need to be able to accurately measure the costs and benefits of different treatment options so that fiscally responsible investments in care can be made. We need to document how these mental health and cognitive conditions affect the families of servicemembers and veterans so that appropriate support services can be provided. We need sustained research into the effectiveness of treatments, particularly treatments that can improve the functioning of individuals who do not improve from the current evidence-based therapies. Finally, we need research that evaluates how policy changes implemented to address the needs of OEF/OIF veterans affect their health and well-being, the costs to society, and the state of military readiness and effectiveness.

Addressing these vital questions will require a substantial, coordinated, and strategic research effort. Further, to adequately address knowledge gaps will require funding mechanisms that encourage longer-term research examining a broader set of issues than can be financed within the mandated priorities of existing funders or agencies. Responsibility for conducting this research should not fall just to DoD and the VA; other federal agencies should be engaged, including the National Institutes of Health, the Substance Abuse and Mental Health Services Administration, the Centers for Disease Control and Prevention, and the Agency for Healthcare Research and Quality. These agencies already have limited research activities relevant to military and veterans populations, but these populations have not always been prioritized within their programs. Initial strategies for implementing this national research agenda include the following:

- Launching a large, longitudinal study on the natural course of these mental health and cognitive conditions, including predictors of relapse and recovery, among OEF/OIF veterans. Ideally, such a study would gather data pre-deployment, during deployment, and at multiple time points post-deployment. It should also be designed so that the findings can be generalized to all deployed servicemembers while still facilitating identification of those at highest risk, and should focus on examining the causal links between deployment and mental health conditions and the effects of the disorders on the families of servicemembers and veterans. A longitudinal approach, using proven techniques for achieving high response rates, would make it possible to evaluate how use of health care services affects symptoms, functioning, physical health, economic productivity, and social functioning over time. The resulting data would inform the arraying of services to meet evolving needs of OEF/OIF veterans and suggest what fiscally responsible investments in treatment and prevention programs should be made. Studies that are currently under way are not sufficient to answer the necessary questions.

- Continuing to aggressively support research to identify the most effective treatments and approaches, especially regarding TBI care and rehabilitation. Although many studies are already under way or under review (as a result of the congressional mandate over the past year for more research on PTSD and TBI), a strategic analysis of research needs could add value to the current programs by informing the overall research agenda and creating new program opportunities in areas in which research may be lacking or needed. More research is also needed to evaluate innovative treatment methods, since not all individuals benefit from the currently available treatments.

- Evaluating new initiatives, policies, and programs. Many new initiatives and programs designed to address psychological and cognitive injuries have been put into place, ranging from screening programs and resiliency trainings, to use of care managers and recovery coordinators, to implementation of new therapies. Each of these efforts should be evaluated carefully to ensure that it is effective and is improving over time. Only programs that demonstrate effectiveness should be maintained and disseminated.

Treating the Invisible Wounds of War

Addressing PTSD, depression, and TBI among those who deployed to Afghanistan and Iraq is a national priority. But it is not an easy undertaking. The prevalence of such wounds is high and may grow as the conflicts continue. And long-term negative consequences are associated with these conditions if they are not treated with evidence-based, patient-centered, efficient, equitable, and timely care. The systems of care available to address these wounds have been improved significantly, but critical gaps remain.

The nation must ensure that quality care is available and provided to military veterans now and in the future. As a group, the veterans returning from Afghanistan and Iraq are predominantly young, healthy, and productive members of society. However, about a third are currently affected by PTSD or depression, or report exposure to a possible TBI while deployed. Whether the TBIs will translate into any lasting impairments is unknown. In the absence of knowing, these injuries cause great concern for servicemembers and their families. These veterans need our attention now to ensure successful adjustment post-deployment and full recovery.

Meeting the goal of providing care for these servicemembers will require system-level changes, which means expanding the nation's focus to consider issues not just within DoD and the VA, from which the majority of veterans will receive benefits, but also across the overall U.S. health care system, in which many will seek care through other, employer-sponsored health plans and in the public sector (e.g., Medicaid). System-level changes are essential if the nation is to have the resources it needs to meet its responsibility not only to recruit, prepare, and sustain a military force but also to address Service-connected injuries and disabilities.

References

Belasco, A. *The Cost of Iraq, Afghanistan, and Other Global War on Terror Operations Since 9/11.* Washington, D.C.: Congressional Research Service, 2007.

Bruner, E. F. *Military Forces: What Is the Appropriate Size for the United States?* Washington, D.C.: Congressional Research Service, 2006.

Hosek, J., J. Kavanagh, and L. Miller. *How Deployments Affect Service Members.* Santa Monica, Calif.: RAND Corporation, MG-432-RC, 2006. As of March 13, 2008: http://www.rand.org/pubs/monographs/MG432/

Institute of Medicine, Committee on Treatment of Posttraumatic Stress Disorder, Board on Population Health and Public Health Practice. *Treatment of Posttraumatic Stress Disorder: An Assessment of the Evidence.* Washington, D.C.: National Academies Press, 2007.

Regan, T. Report: High survival rate for US troops wounded in Iraq. *Christian Science Monitor,* November 29, 2004.

Warden, D. Military TBI during the Iraq and Afghanistan wars. *Journal of Head Trauma Rehabilitation,* Vol. 21, No. 5, 2006, pp. 398–402.

Acknowledgments

The authors acknowledge several individuals without whom this study and monograph would not be possible. We thank Susan Hosek, James Hosek, Margaret Harrell, Suzanne Wenzel, and Paul Koegel for their guidance and advice throughout this project. We thank LTC David Benedek, Howard Goldman, Cathy Sherbourne, LTG Ronald Blanck (Ret.), Thomas Garthwaite, and Carole Gresenz for their careful review and comments on the earlier drafts of this monograph. We are also indebted to Marian Branch, James Torr, and Christina Pitcher for their editorial assistance, and to Steve Oshiro for managing production. We thank COL Charles C. Engel and the staff of the Deployment Health Clinical Center for providing us with feedback and inspiration. We are grateful to the many military and veteran service organizations that offered access to their membership and provided valuable feedback on the needs of this population. We are also grateful for the funding support provided by the Iraq Afghanistan Deployment Impact Fund, which is administered by the California Community Foundation.

We acknowledge the many RAND staff who contributed to the successful completion of this work—most notably, Samantha Abernethy and Taria Francois for their able administrative assistance and Diane Schoeff for her coordination of our many data-collection activities. We would also like to acknowledge the outstanding work of Robert Magaw and Lisa Gowing from SRBI in managing data collection. Finally, we thank the men and women of the United States armed forces, particularly those veterans of Operations Enduring Freedom and Iraqi Freedom who participated in this study and who serve our country each day.

Abbreviations

ADL	activities for daily living
AF	Air Force
AHLTA	Armed Forces Health Longitudinal Technology Application
AMEDD	Army Medical Department
ASA	acetylsalicylic acid (or aspirin)
ASD/HA	Assistant Secretary of Defense for Health Affairs
ASER	*Army Suicide Event Report*
ASR	Acute Stress Reaction
AT	assertiveness training
BA	behavioral activation
BCT	Brigade Combat Team
BDZ	benzodiazepine
BI	battle injury
BIO	biofeedback
BPD	borderline personality disorder
BTBIS	Brief Traumatic Brain Injury Screener
BUMED	Bureau of Medicine and Surgery (Navy)
CAPS	clinician-administered PTSD Scale
CAPS-D	CAPS Criterion D (hyperarousal)
CBHCO	Community Based Health Care Organization
CBO	Congressional Budget Office
CBT	cognitive-behavioral therapy

CCF	California Community Foundation
CDC	Centers for Disease Control and Prevention
CESD	Center for Epidemiologic Studies Depression Inventory
CEU	continuing education unit
CLFS	civilian labor force status
CGI-S	Clinical Gobal Impression Scale-Severity
CHD	coronary heart disease
CI	confidence interval
CISD	critical-incident stress debriefing
CISM	critical-incident stress management
CME	continuing medical education
CNA	Center for Naval Analyses
COI	cost of illness
COSR	Combat or [Ongoing Military] Operational Stress Reaction
CPI	Consumer Price Index
CPP	cerebral perfusion pressure
CPRS	computerized patient record system
CPS	Current Population Survey
CPT	cognitive processing therapy
CT	computerized tomography; cognitive therapy
DBT	dialectical behavior therapy
DEERS	Defense Eligibility Enrollment System
DHCC	Deployment Health Clinical Center–DoD
DHHS	Department of Health and Human Services
DMDC	Defense Manpower Data Center
DMRR	*Defense Manpower Requirements Report*
DNBI	Disease or Non-Battle Injury
DoD	Department of Defense
DOW	died of wounds
DRG	Diagnosis-Related Group

DSHRB	Defense Survey of Health Related Behaviors
DSM-IV	*Diagnostic and Statistical Manual–Version 4*
DVBIC	Defense and Veterans Brain Injury Center
DVT	deep vein thrombosis
EAP	employee assistance professional
ECT	electroconvulsive therapy
EEG	electroencephalogram
EMDR	eye-movement desensitization and reprocessing
EMR	electronic medical record
EX	exposure therapy
FFS	fee for service
FHP&R	Force Health Protection and Readiness
FI	functional impairment
FY	fiscal year
GAO	Government Accountability Office
GCS	Glasgow Coma Scale
GT	group therapy
GWOT	Global War on Terror
HAM-A	Hamilton Rating Scale for Anxiety
HART	Helping Airmen Recover Together
HCUP	Healthcare Cost and Utilization Study
HEDIS	Healthcare Effectiveness Data and Information Set
HIV	human immunodeficiency virus
HMO	health maintenance organization
HPAE	Health Program Analysis and Evaluation
IADIF	Iraq Afghanistan Deployment Impact Fund
ICD-9-CM	*International Classification of Diseases*, Ninth Edition, *Clinical Modification*
ICIC	Improving Chronic Illness Care
ICICE	Improving Chronic Illness Care Evaluation
ICP	intracranial pressure

ICU	intensive care unit
IED	improvised explosive device
IMR	Individual Medical Readiness
IOM	Institute of Medicine
IPT	interpersonal therapy
IRB	Institutional Review Board
IRG	Independent Review Group
IRT	image rehearsal therapy
JCAHO	Joint Commission for the Accreditation of Healthcare Organizations
KIA	killed in action
LL	lower limit
LOC	loss of consciousness
MA	master of arts
MAOI	monoamine oxidase inhibitor
MCSC	Managed Care Support Contractor
MDD	major depressive disorder
MFT	marital and family therapy
MH	mental health
MHAT	Mental Health Advisory Team
MHC	mental health condition
MHS	Military Health System
MI	myocardial infarction
MRI	magnetic resonance imaging
MSMR	*Medical Surveillance Monthly Report*
MTF	Military Treatment Facility
MVAMC	Minneapolis VA Medical Center
NACBT	National Association of Cognitive-Behavioral Therapists
NAS	Naval Air Station
NCA	National Cemetery Association
NCO	noncommissioned officer

NCPTSD	National Center for Post Traumatic Stress Disorder
NCQA	National Committee for Quality Assurance
NCS	National Compensation Survey
NCS-R	National Comorbidity Survey Replication
NDAA	National Defense Authorization Act
NESARC	National Epidemiologic Survey of Alcohol and Related Conditions
NIH	National Institutes of Health
NIMH	National Institute of Mental Health
NIS	National Inpatient Sample
NJ-WRIIC	New Jersey War-Related Injury and Illness Center
NNMC	National Naval Medical Center (in Bethesda, MD)
NSAID	nonsteroidal anti-inflammatory drug
NSRD	National Security Research Division
NSVG	National Survey of the Vietnam Generation
NVVRS	National Vietnam Veterans Readjustment Study
OEF	Operation Enduring Freedom (Afghanistan)
OIF	Operation Iraqi Freedom (Iraq)
OSCAR	Operational Stress Control and Readiness
OTSG	Office of the Surgeon General
OUSDPR	Office of the Under Secretary of Defense for Personnel and Readiness
PANSS-P	Positive and Negative Syndrome Scale–Positive Subscale
PC-PTSD	primary care PTSD screen
PCCWW	President's Commission on Care for America's Returning Wounded Warriors
PCL	PTSD Checklist
PCP	primary care provider
PD	psychological debriefing
PDHA	Post-Deployment Health Assessment
PDHRA	Post-Deployment Health Re-Assessment

xlii   Invisible Wounds of War

PE	prolonged exposure
PHQ-9	Patient Health Questionnaire–9 items
PL	placebo
PM&R	Physical Medicine and Rehabilitation
PPO	preferred provider organization
PR	psychosocial rehabilitation
PSS	PTSD Symptom Scale
PST	problem-solving therapy
PT	psychodynamic therapy
PTA	post-traumatic amnesia
PTS	post-traumatic seizure
PTSD	post-traumatic stress disorder
QI	quality improvement
Q-LES-Q	Quality of Life Enjoyment and Satisfaction Questionnaire
QOL	quality of life
QUERI	Quality Enhancement Research Initiative
RCT	randomized clinical trial
RDD	random digit dialing
RESPECT	Re-Engineering Systems for Primary Care Treatment of Depression Project
RR	risk ratio
RT	relaxation training
RTD	Return to Duty
SADR	Standard Ambulatory Data Record
SCID	structured clinical interview–diagnostic
SD	systematic desensitization
SDS	Sheehan Disability Scale
SES	socioeconomic status
SIT	stress inoculation training
SNRI	serotonin-noradrenaline reuptake inhibitors

SOFA	Support Our Family in Arms
SOFAR	Strategic Outreach to Families of All Reservists
SPTSS	Screen for Posttraumatic Stress Symptoms
SSRI	selective serotonin reuptake inhibitor
TBI	traumatic brain injury
TCA	tricyclic antidepressant
TF	Task Force
TMA	TRICARE Management Activity
TMS	Transcranial Magnetic Stimulation
TOP-8	Treatment Outcome for PTSD–8 items
TRICARE	Department of Defense's Managed Care Program
UK	United Kingdom
UL	upper limit
USAMRMC	U.S. Army Medical Research and Materiel Command
USDPR	Under Secretary of Defense for Personnel and Readiness
USUHS	Uniformed Services University for the Health Sciences
VA	Department of Veterans Affairs
VBA	Veterans Benefits Administration
VHA	Veterans Health Administration
VISN	Veterans Integrated Service Network
WIA	wounded in action
WRAMC	Walter Reed Army Medical Center
YOS	years of service

Part I: Introduction, Current Policy Context, and Historical Perspective

Chapter One briefly describes the psychological and cognitive injuries associated with combat, discusses the unique features associated with the current deployments, introduces the issues surrounding caring for servicemembers with these invisible wounds, and provides an overview of RAND's study on these topics and the scope of this monograph.

Chapter Two provides a thumbnail sketch of the conflicts in Afghanistan and Iraq, describing the composition of the U.S. forces in terms of both demographic components and their organizational affiliations in the Active and Reserve Components; placing the conflicts in perspective, comparing them with other wars the United States has fought; showing the history of troop deployments in the war on terrorism and arraying them against signal events that have occurred in Operation Enduring Freedom (OEF) and Operation Iraqi Freedom (OIF); discussing the casualties sustained in Iraq in terms of killed in action (KIA) and wounded in action (WIA) in Iraq for ground forces—that is, the predominantly Active and Reserve forces of the Army and the Marine Corps—and showing the numbers who have died as a result of improvised explosive devices (IEDs); and providing a brief overview of the health care systems that serve OEF/OIF veterans.

Introduction

Terri Tanielian, Lisa H. Jaycox, David M. Adamson, and Karen N. Metscher

Signature Wounds

Since October 2001, approximately 1.64 million U.S. troops have deployed as part of Operation Enduring Freedom (OEF, Afghanistan) and Operation Iraqi Freedom (OIF, Iraq). These operations have employed smaller forces and (notwithstanding episodes of intense combat) have produced casualty rates of killed or wounded that are historically lower than in earlier prolonged conflicts, such as Vietnam and Korea. However, casualties of a different kind—invisible wounds, such as mental health conditions and cognitive impairments resulting from deployment experiences—are just beginning to emerge. Recent reports and increasing media attention have prompted intense scrutiny and examination of these injuries. As a grateful nation seeks to find ways to help those with injuries recover, research and analysis of the scope of the problem are ongoing, and there is limited evidence to suggest how best to meet the needs of this population.

The majority of servicemembers deployed to Afghanistan and Iraq return home without problems and are able to readjust successfully; however, early studies of those returning from Afghanistan and Iraq suggest that many may be suffering from mental disorders. Upward of 26 percent of returning troops may have mental health conditions (applying broad screening criteria for post-traumatic stress disorder, anxiety disorder, or depression), and the frequency of diagnoses in this category is increasing while rates for other medical diagnoses remain constant (Hoge et al., 2004). The most common diagnoses are post-traumatic stress disorder (PTSD), an anxiety disorder that can develop after direct or indirect exposure to a terrifying event or ordeal in which grave physical harm occurred or was threatened; major depression; and generalized anxiety (National Institute of Mental Health Web site, Mental Health Topics page).

Recent data available from the Department of Defense (Hoge et al., 2004; Milliken, Auchterlonie, and Hoge, 2007; Smith et al., 2008) provide both pre-deployment and post-deployment data for these conditions. For example, Hoge et al. (2004) examined Army and Marine Corps personnel both before and after deployment, as well as their peers who were not deployed. Results showed that 16 to 17 percent of those returning from Iraq met strict screening criteria for mental health conditions. About 11 percent of servicemembers returning from Afghanistan reported symptoms consistent with a mental health condition, compared with about 9 percent of those not deployed, suggesting that the nature of the exposures in Iraq may be more traumatic (Hoge et al., 2004).

In today's battlefields, the use of improvised explosive devices (IEDs) has made traumatic brain injury (TBI) a major concern for servicemembers. According to the Defense Veterans Brain Injury Center, approximately 2,700 U.S. troops have suffered a traumatic brain injury, and potentially hundreds of thousands more (at least 30 percent of troops engaged in active combat in Afghanistan and Iraq for four months or more) may have suffered a mild TBI as a result of IED blast waves (Glasser, 2007; Hoge et al., 2007; Hoge et al., 2008). There is some indication that TBI and PTSD have overlapping symptoms. For example, Hoge et al. (2008) suggest that, once PTSD symptoms are taken into account, linkages between a mild TBI and current symptoms or physical health outcomes are no longer significant, except for headache, indicating that some of the experience of such problems may be attributable to PTSD rather than to the injury itself. These high rates of mental health conditions and TBI among post-deployment servicemembers and veterans have led some to refer to PTSD and traumatic brain injury as the "signature wounds" of Operation Enduring Freedom and Operation Iraqi Freedom (Altmire, 2007).

The psychological wounds of war are nothing new. The risk for mental health conditions and the need for mental health services among military servicemembers are greater during wars and conflicts (Milliken, Auchterlonie, and Hoge, 2007; Rosenheck and Fontana, 1999; and Marlowe, 2001). Combat stress (historically termed soldier's heart, shell shock, or battle fatigue) is a known and accepted consequence of warfare. Although diagnoses such as PTSD were not formally defined and adopted until the 1970s, the existence of psychiatric casualties in war undoubtedly goes back as far as warfare itself (Rosenheck and Fontana, 1999; Marlowe, 2001).

The U.S. military has tracked and planned for mental health casualties at least since World War II. Among the 16.1 million U.S. troops who served in that war, medical estimates indicate that the incidence of psychiatric-related casualties ranged between 28 per 1,000 and 101 per 1,000, depending on assignment (Dean, 1997). In the Korean War (1950–1953), 5.7 million U.S. troops deployed and the incidence was reported to be at the 37 per 1,000 mark (Dean, 1997; Jones and Palmer, 2000). In Vietnam (1960–1975), 3.4 million served in theater, with a reported incidence rate of 12 per 1,000 (Dean, 1997; Jones and Palmer, 2000). Many scholars believe that these figures may be understated due to the lack of uniform evaluation and diagnosis, inaccurate recording during these earlier times, and the documentation of only rates on the battlefield (that is, these estimates do not include conditions that may have developed post-combat) (Dean, 1997; Jones and Palmer, 2000; U.S. Census Bureau, 1999). Over the years, the Department of Defense has made efforts to improve evaluation, diagnosis, and recording of psychiatric casualties. However, the changing definitions and measures of combat-related mental health conditions make it difficult to compare incidence rates across different conflicts.

During the Vietnam War, the medical system created a more formal infrastructure in which to diagnose and treat what would later be termed post-traumatic stress disorder and related mental health problems. With the more in-depth monitoring and study during this conflict, analysis found that incidence varied significantly according to characteristics of combat exposure. High-intensity combat produced a higher incidence of psychiatric casualties, and the infantry was disproportionately affected (Dean, 1997; Jones and Palmer, 2000; Newman, 1964).

In the midst of the Vietnam War, there was also concern about readjustment difficulties that veterans were facing on returning home. For the first time, the nation expressed a collective concern about the mental health of returning veterans. In 1970, Congress conducted the first hearing to address these issues (Rosenheck and Fontana, 1999). Following return from the combat zone, servicemembers reported psychological problems, including anxiety, depression, nightmares, and insomnia. The Vietnam era was a turning point in the assessment and treatment of combat-related psychological distress. PTSD was officially defined as a mental disorder in 1979, in recognition of the potentially disabling mental health challenges confronting veterans returning from the war: "The most lasting contribution of Vietnam to the history of battle trauma is the legacy of post-traumatic stress disorder (PTSD)" (Helmus and Glenn, 2005). The National Vietnam Veterans Readjustment Study (NVVRS) estimated that, in 1998, 15 percent (472,000) of those who had served in Vietnam met the criteria for active PTSD (Rosenheck and Fontana, 1999).

Unique Features of the Current Deployments

While stress has been a fact of combat since the beginning of warfare, three novel features of the current conflicts may be influencing rates of mental health and cognitive injuries at present: changes in military operations, including extended deployments; higher rates of survivability from wounds; and traumatic brain injuries.

Changes in Military Operations, Including Extended Deployments

The campaigns in Afghanistan and Iraq represent the most sustained U.S. combat operations since the Vietnam War. The number of military deployments has increased exponentially in recent years (Belasco, 2007; Bruner, 2006; Serafino, 2003). Troops are seeing more-frequent deployments, of greater lengths, with shorter rest periods in between—factors thought to create a more stressful environment for servicemembers. The day-to-day activities of troops in combat vary widely, but some common stressors in the current conflicts have been identified as roadside bombs, IEDs, suicide bombers, the handling of human remains, killing an enemy, seeing fellow soldiers and friends dead or injured, and the helplessness of not being able to stop violent situations (Hoge et al., 2004). Because of the nature of these current conflicts, a high proportion of deployed soldiers are likely to experience one or more stressors.

At the same time, doctrinal changes have influenced the way in which the United States employs, deploys, and supports its armed forces, as well as how the military approaches combat operations and operations other than war (see Chapter Two). Even though many recent military operations have been characterized as peacekeeping missions or stability operations, many of these efforts may share the same risks and stressors inherent in combat—exposure to hostile forces, injured civilians, mass graves, and land mines, for example.

Higher Rates of Survivability from Wounds

The current conflicts have witnessed the highest ratio of wounded to killed in action in U.S history. As of early January 2008, the Department of Defense (DoD) reports a total of 3,453 hostile deaths and over 30,721 wounded in action in Afghanistan and Iraq (see DoD Personnel & Procurement Statistics, Military Casualty Information page). Although a high percentage of those wounded is returned to duty within 72 hours, a significant number of military personnel are medically evacuated from theater (including approximately 30,000 servicemembers with nonhostile injuries or other medical issues/diseases). Approximately 3,000 servicemembers returned home from Iraq or Afghanistan with severe wounds, illnesses, and/or disabilities, including amputations, serious burns, spinal-cord injuries, blindness, and traumatic brain injuries (President's Commission on Care for America's Returning Wounded Warriors, 2007). The ratio of wounded to killed is higher than in previous conflicts as a result of advances in combat medicine and body armor. Wounded soldiers who would have likely died in previous conflicts are instead saved, but with significant physical, emotional, and cognitive injuries. Thus, caring for these wounded often requires an intensive mental-health component in addition to traditional rehabilitation services.

Traumatic Brain Injuries

Also gaining attention recently are cognitive injuries in returning troops. In particular, traumatic brain injury in combat veterans is getting increasing consideration in the wake of the current military conflicts. TBI is associated with decreased levels of consciousness, amnesia, and other neurological abnormalities; skull fracture; and intracranial lesions; and it can lead to death (Thurman et al., 1995). Blasts are the primary cause of TBI for active duty military personnel in war zones (Defense and Veterans Brain Injury Center, 2005). TBI diagnoses can range from mild to severe. In its milder forms, TBI can resolve quickly (often within three months of the injury), and it can be difficult to diagnose and distinguish from psychological co-morbidities.

The term *traumatic brain injury* appears in the medical literature at least as far back as the 1950s, but its early use is almost exclusively in reference to relatively severe cases of brain trauma.[1] Its application to mild concussive injuries, which are now a major focus of military medicine, begins to appear in the medical literature in the 1990s, with a significant increase in usage since the onset of the current conflicts. However, the exact nature of any emotional or cognitive deficits or demonstrable neuropathology resulting from exposure to a blast has not been firmly established (Hoge et al., 2008), leaving open many questions about the extent of problems that might be expected from servicemembers who have been exposed.

Caring for Invisible Wounds

Rates of PTSD and concerns about mild TBI among those returning from Afghanistan and Iraq have sparked media attention and additional health assessments of servicemembers three to six months after they redeploy. However, the extent to which mental health and cognitive problems are being detected and appropriately treated in this population remains unclear. Unlike the physical wounds of war that maim or disfigure, PTSD, major depression, and TBI are often invisible to other servicemembers, family members, the military, and the broader society.

For instance, although the military does screen for post-deployment health issues, health officials have speculated that soldiers leaving the war zone often minimize or fail to disclose mental health symptoms for fear that admitting any problem could delay their return home. And even if risk of a mental health problem is detected among those returning home, whether effective treatment is delivered is uncertain. The Government Accountability Office (GAO) (2006) noted concern about adequate follow-up and treatment, citing low rates of referrals for mental health treatment among those screening positive for post-traumatic stress.

In addition, only a small proportion of those returning from deployment who experience symptoms seeks mental health care, according to early studies (GAO, 2006; Hoge, Auchterlonie, and Milliken, 2006; Milliken, Auchterlonie, and Hoge, 2007). For example, Hoge et al. (2004) found that only 23–40 percent of those who met their strict criteria for a mental health problem reported receiving professional help in the past year. Changes in utilization rates of mental health services as a result of current combat operations are also documented. From 2000 to 2004, the number of active duty marines and soldiers accessing mental health care increased from 145.3 to 222.3 per 1,000 (Hoge, Auchterlonie, and Milliken, 2006). All categories of recent combat veterans show increasing utilization rates, but veterans returning from Iraq are accessing care at a much higher rate than those returning from Afghanistan or those in any other category (Hoge, Auchterlonie, and Milliken, 2006). However, there are still "no

---

[1]   Query conducted through PubMed database, National Center for Biotechnology Information, August 2007.

systematic studies of mental health care utilization among these veterans after deployment" (Hoge, Auchterlonie, and Milliken, 2006). In addition, although utilization rates for mental health services are increasing, those who are accessing care and those who are identified as needing care are not necessarily the same people.

The federal system of medical care for this population spans the Departments of Defense and Veterans Affairs. OEF/OIF veterans are eligible to receive care through the Department of Defense (while they are on active duty or covered by TRICARE) and the Veterans Health Administration (all OEF/OIF veterans are eligible for five years following military discharge). The Department of Defense does not have a unified mental health program, but a fairly comprehensive array of mental health services is available through the Services, military hospitals, and the TRICARE network, and programs typically are designed and implemented at the local level (Defense Health Board Task Force on Mental Health, 2007). As a result, the mental health services provided across the system vary considerably (Defense Health Board Task Force on Mental Health, 2007). The DoD mental health providers also collaborate with nonmedical support systems, which include Family Support Centers, chaplains, civilian support organizations, and the Department of Veterans Affairs (VA).

Since 1930, the VA has provided primary care, specialized care, and related medical and social support services for veterans of the U.S. military (Department of Veterans Affairs, 2007). The VA operates the largest integrated health care system in the United States. Veterans are eligible to receive care from the VA through a priority system, which is based on the severity of military service–connected disability and financial need. Mental health services are primarily delivered through ambulatory settings—outpatient and community-based clinics, with several specialized programs for PTSD.

The VA has been a leader in promoting quality care in the United States. The VA's National Center for PTSD has been a recognized national leader in conducting research and promoting appropriate treatment for veterans suffering from PTSD. The VA's polytrauma system of care has rapidly evolved to expand services for TBI among returning veterans as well. However, not all veterans receive their care through the VA.

Over the past year, both DoD and the VA have come under congressional and public scrutiny regarding their capacity to address PTSD and TBI. Congress has directed billions of dollars to address perceived capacity constraints, whether on human resources or financial resources; however, little is known to date about the capacity requirements for addressing the needs of the newest veteran population.

Direct medical costs of treatment are only a fraction of the total costs related to psychological and cognitive injuries. Indirect, long-term individual and societal costs stem from lost productivity, reduced quality of life, homelessness, domestic violence, the strain on families, and suicide. Delivering effective mental health care and restoring veterans to full mental health has the potential to reduce these longer-term costs significantly. Therefore, it is important to consider the direct costs of care in the context of the potentially higher indirect, long-term costs of providing no care or inadequate care. Unfortunately, data on these longer-term costs among the military population are sparse at best and largely unavailable. For this reason, most of the national discussion of resources has focused on direct medical costs to the government.

Increasing numbers of veterans are also seeking care in the private, community sector, outside the formal military and veterans health systems. Yet, we have very little systematic information about the organization and delivery of services for veterans in the non-federal sector, particularly with respect to access and quality.

Ongoing advances in treatment provide hope for a new generation of servicemembers suffering the psychological effects of warfare. Medical science provides a better understanding than ever before of how to treat the psychological effects of combat. With *evidence-based interventions*, treatments that have been proven to work, "complete remission can be achieved in 30–50 percent of cases of PTSD, and partial improvement can be expected with most patients" (Friedman, 2006, p. 592). Studies continue to raise a "hopeful possibility that PTSD may be reversible if patients can be helped to cope with stresses in their current life" (Friedman, 2004, p. 76). Similarly, effective treatments for major depression are available and may be appropriate for this population (APA, 2000). However, treatment for traumatic brain injury among combat veterans is still in the early stages of development and evaluation; experts indicate that, with appropriate rehabilitation and treatment, those suffering from TBI can regain functioning.

The Current Policy Context

Public concern over these issues is running high, as reflected in the activity of policy leaders at all levels of government and throughout many government agencies. The Department of Defense, the Department of Veterans Affairs, Congress, and the President have moved to study the issues, quantify the problems, and formulate policy solutions, producing rapid recommendations for changes and expansion of services designed to detect and treat these problems. For instance, immediately following coverage of conditions at Walter Reed, Defense Secretary Robert Gates formed an Independent Review Group to Conduct an Assessment of Outpatient Treatment at Walter Reed Army Medical Center (WRAMC) and the National Naval Medical Center (NNMC). Tasked with identifying critical shortcomings, suggesting opportunities to improve care and quality of life for injured and sick servicemembers, and making recommendations for corrective actions, the group cited concerns about coordination across the continuum of care for injured servicemembers and recommended the establishment of a center of excellence for TBI and PTSD treatment, research, and training (Independent Review Group to Conduct an Assessment of Outpatient Treatment at Walter Reed Army Medical Center [WRAMC] and the National Naval Medical Center [NNMC], 2007).

Also in the wake of the Walter Reed press coverage, President Bush established the President's Commission on Care for America's Returning Wounded Warriors to review all health care for wounded servicemembers. Their July 2007 report called for radical changes in the coordination of care for severely injured servicemembers and the disability evaluation and compensation system, but also highlighted the special challenges associated with PTSD and TBI. The report also included a recommendation to enable all OEF/OIF veterans who need care for PTSD to receive it from the VA. This recommendation remains under policy consideration at the time of this writing.

In conjunction with the President's Commission to look at the military system, President Bush also directed Department of Veterans Affairs Secretary Jim Nicholson to establish an Interagency Task Force on Returning Global War on Terror Heroes. In this task force, solutions were identified within existing funding levels and included a governmentwide action plan. Specific changes for DoD and the VA in response to these groups included the joint assignment of disability ratings and co-management for continuity of care.

The work on these issues was also informed by a congressionally mandated DoD Task Force on Mental Health, which operated as a subcommittee of the Defense Health Board to examine matters relating to mental health and the armed forces. Its report, released in May 2007, called for major changes in the culture for psychological health within the military, the provision of additional resources to meet requirements, and enhancements to the provision of the full continuum of excellent care.

The President, Congress, DoD, and the VA have acted swiftly to pursue implementation of the hundreds of recommendations emerging from the task force and commission reports. As a result, policy changes and funding shifts are already occurring for military and veterans' health care in general and mental health services in particular. Several new programs and expansions of treatment and support services have already been established or are under development. Both DoD and the VA have taken steps to increase the number of mental health providers; instituted broad-based screening for mental health and cognitive conditions among OEF/OIF veterans within their primary care settings; expanded training in the provision of care and screenings for servicemembers, military leaders, and providers; and created new resources for servicemembers and veterans, in the form of hotlines and online resources. Most recently, the Office of the Secretary of Defense for Health Affairs announced the establishment of the Defense Center of Excellence for Psychological Health [PH] and Traumatic Brain Injury (DCoE). In collaboration with the VA, the DCoE plans to lead a national collaborative network to advance and disseminate knowledge about psychological health and TBI, enhance clinical and management approaches, and facilitate other vital services to best serve the urgent and enduring needs of servicemembers and veterans families.

Through these ongoing efforts, the VA, DoD, and the armed services have attempted to improve the care and support provided to veterans, servicemembers, and their families facing mental, emotional, and cognitive challenges as a result of their deployments to Afghanistan and Iraq. To build an evidence base for future quality improvement, a rigorous evaluation of the effect of current and future programs is an essential element of the policy and programming.

Given the effort and energy that has been channeled and is being channeled into improving care for veterans and servicemembers who have suffered mental health or cognitive injuries in Afghanistan and Iraq, there will continue to be a great need for information to help inform these decisions, both for the current conflict and for the future.

The Purpose of the RAND Study

Despite the widespread policy interest and a committed response from DoD and the VA, fundamental gaps remain in our knowledge about the mental health needs of U.S. servicemembers returning from deployment to Afghanistan and Iraq, the adequacy of the care system that exists to meet those needs, and how veterans and servicemembers fare in that system. To address this gap and generate objective data to inform policies and programs for meeting these needs, RAND undertook the first comprehensive, independent study of these issues. The study was guided by a series of overarching questions:

- **Prevalence:** What is the scope of mental health and cognitive conditions that troops face when returning from deployment to Afghanistan and Iraq?
- **Costs:** What are the costs of these conditions, including treatment costs and costs stemming from lost productivity and other consequences? What are the costs and potential savings associated with different levels of medical care—including proven, evidence-based care; usual care; and no care?
- **The care system:** What are the existing programs and services to meet the health-related needs of servicemembers and veterans with post-traumatic stress disorder, major depression, or traumatic brain injury? What are the gaps in the programs and services? What steps can be taken to close the gaps?

To answer these questions, we designed a series of data-collection activities to accomplish four aims:

1. Identify and assess current mental health and cognitive conditions among military servicemembers and veterans who served in Afghanistan or Iraq.
2. Identify the short- and long-term consequences of untreated psychological and cognitive injuries (i.e., PTSD, major depression, TBI).

3. Document and assess the availability, accessibility, and capacity of existing programs and services to meet short- and long-term mental health and cognitive needs, as well as brain injuries, in injured servicemembers.
4. Evaluate aids and barriers to seeking care and to using services.

Scope of the Monograph

This monograph discusses the psychological and cognitive injuries associated with military deployment. It does not cover issues related to treating or caring for those individuals who suffer other combat-related physical injuries; such issues have been documented and covered by other recent task forces, commissions, and review groups. Note, however, that individuals with severe physical injuries may be at risk for developing post-deployment mental health or cognitive conditions; for this reason, this monograph will also be relevant in considering the overall care system for the severely wounded.

In this monograph, we focus on three specific post-deployment conditions: post-traumatic stress disorder, major depression, and traumatic brain injury. These conditions were chosen because of their clear link to servicemember exposures in a combat theater. PTSD is defined by its linkage to exposure to traumatic or life-threatening events, such as combat. Major depression is often linked to grief and loss, which can be salient for servicemembers who lose their comrades. TBI is the result of a service- or combat-related injury to the brain. In addition, PTSD and TBI are among the signature injuries for U.S. troops who served in Afghanistan and Iraq (President's Commission on Care for America's Returning Wounded Warriors, 2007), and concerns about suicide risk make major depression very important to study. We define each of these conditions in turn.

Post-traumatic stress disorder, or PTSD, is an anxiety disorder that occurs after a traumatic event in which a threat of serious injury or death was experienced or witnessed, and the individual's response involved intense fear, helplessness, or horror. In addition, the disorder is marked by the following symptoms occurring for more than one month and causing significant distress and/or impairment: re-experiencing the event, avoidance of stimuli relating to the event, numbing of general responsiveness, and hyperarousal (APA, 2000). A further distinction is sometimes made between PTSD and Acute Stress Reaction (ASR) and Combat (or Ongoing Military) Operational Stress Reaction (COSR). ASR is a severe but transient disorder that develops in an individual in response to exceptional physical or mental stress. Symptoms are usually minimal after about three days. COSR, also known as battle fatigue or battle shock, is any response to battle stress that renders a soldier (servicemember) transiently unable to remain on duty. COSR is distinguished from DSM-IV (*Diagnostic and Statistical Manual–Version Four*) mental disorders in that the former is by definition transient and preferably managed conservatively in the operational theater (via principles of proximity, immediacy, expectancy, and simplicity) and do not generally require traditional psychiatric management, such as ongoing psychotherapy or psychopharmacologic treatment. We focus specifically on PTSD, which is diagnosed only after symptoms have persisted for more than 30 days post-exposure.

Depression, or major depressive disorder (MDD), is a mood disorder that interferes with an individual's everyday functioning. Individuals with MDD have a persistent constellation of symptoms, including depressed mood, inability to experience pleasure, or loss of interest in almost all activities, that occur almost every day for two weeks (APA, 2000). Other symptoms can include significant weight loss or gain or a decrease in appetite; insomnia or hypersomnia; psychomotor agitation or retardation; fatigue or loss of energy; feelings of worthlessness or excessive or inappropriate guilt; diminished ability to think or concentrate or significant indecisiveness; and recurrent thoughts of death, suicidal ideation, or suicidal attempts or plans. In this monograph, we use the term *depression* to indicate major depressive disorder or symptoms of this disorder that may not meet full diagnostic criteria.

Traumatic brain injury, or TBI, is a trauma to the head that either temporarily or permanently disrupts the brain's function (Centers for Disease Control and Prevention, 2008). Disruptions in brain functioning can include a decreased level of consciousness, amnesia, or other neurological or neuropsychological abnormalities. TBI can also be marked by skull fracture or intracranial lesions (Thurman et al., 1995). Brain injuries can be caused by an object that pierces the skull and enters brain tissue, which is defined as a *penetrating injury*, or when the head hits an object but the object does not break through the skull, resulting in rapid acceleration-deceleration of the brain, which is defined as a *closed head injury*. Injuries from exposures to blasts cause a non-penetrating injury as well; however, it is a result of a blast wave being transmitted through the brain rather than acceleration-deceleration or an external impact to the skull itself (National Institute of Neurological Disorders and Stroke, 2002; Warden, 2006). Moreover, depending on the proximity of the servicemember to the blast, there may be associated brain trauma from the person being thrown into an object and/or objects acting as missiles that hit or penetrate the skull. Therefore, there may be multiple causes of brain injury resulting from a blast injury. The term TBI itself refers simply to the injury to the brain, whether or not it is associated with lasting functional impairment. The exact nature of the symptoms depends upon the type and severity of the injury. Measures of TBI severity include the Glasgow Coma Scale (which is scored by assessing a patient's eye-opening, motor, and verbal responses), length of loss of consciousness, and length of post-traumatic amnesia; about 80 percent of patients with known TBIs are categorized as "mild TBI" (see Chapter Seven, Appendix 7.C). However, to date there is still much ambiguity in definitions and in understanding of the possible long-term repercussions of exposure to blast, leaving large gaps in knowledge.

Each of these conditions affects mood, thoughts, and behavior, bringing with it a host of difficulties in addition to the symptoms themselves. Previous research has demonstrated significant impairments in daily lives, as well as linkages with suicide, homelessness, and substance abuse, even when a mental disorder is not diagnosed (see Chapter Five). Thus, it is important to consider the full spectrum of issues related to how the OEF/OIF veterans are transitioning back into home life and how they will fare in the years to come.

Organization of This Monograph

This volume is organized into several parts. Recognizing that some audiences will be interested in specific parts, we have made some chapters more technical than others, and we repeat main findings in each as well as in Chapter Eight, which summarizes the findings of the entire project. In the remainder of the first part (Chapter Two), we describe the population of U.S. forces serving, including those serving in Afghanistan and Iraq, and provide a brief description of the Operations. Part II details the research literature on the prevalence of mental health and cognitive conditions among OEF/OIF veterans (Chapter Three), including findings from our own survey of veterans and servicemembers to provide data on current health status, levels of probable PTSD, major depression, and TBI, as well as self-reported use of and barriers to health care (Chapter Four). In Part III, we summarize the available literature on the short- and long-term consequences associated with psychological and cognitive injuries. Part IV uses a modeling approach to estimate the costs of these conditions—in medical costs required to provide treatment and the employment effects of different outcomes, ranging from a full return to mental health to death via suicide. Part V provides an overview of the systems of care designed to treat these conditions and evaluates existing programs according to the evidence supporting the services offered within each. Part VI presents conclusions and offers recommendations for programs and policies aimed at filling gaps and improving treatment.

References

Altmire, J. *Testimony of Jason Altmire*, Hearing Before the Subcommittee on Health of the House Committee on Veterans' Affairs. Washington, D.C., 2007.

American Psychiatric Association. *Diagnostic and Statistical Manual—Version Four*. Washington, D.C., 2000.

American Psychological Association (APA). Practice guideline for the treatment of patients with major depressive disorder (revision). *American Journal of Psychiatry,* Vol. 157, No. 4 Suppl., April 2000, pp. 1–45.

Belasco, A. *The Cost of Iraq, Afghanistan, and Other Global War on Terror Operations Since 9/11.* Washington, D.C.: Congressional Research Service, 2007.

Bruner, E. F. *Military Forces: What Is the Appropriate Size for the United States?* Washington, D.C.: Congressional Research Service, 2006.

Centers for Disease Control and Prevention, National Center for Injury Prevention and Control Web site. Traumatic Brain Injury page, 2008. As of January 25, 2008: http://www.cdc.gov/ncipc/factsheets/tbi.htm

Dean, E. T., Jr. *Shook Over Hell—Post-Traumatic Stress, Vietnam, and the Civil War.* Cambridge, Mass.: Harvard University Press, 1997.

Defense and Veterans Brain Injury Center. A Congressional Program for Servicemembers and Veterans with Traumatic Brain Injury and Their Families, Informational Brochure, Washington, D.C., Walter Reed Army Medical Center, 2005.

Defense Health Board Task Force on Mental Health. *An Achievable Vision: Report of the Department of Defense Task Force on Mental Health.* Falls Church, Va.: Defense Health Board, 2007.

Department of Veterans Affairs Web site. Health Care—Veterans Health Administration page. As of July 2007: http://www1.va.gov/health/gateway.html

DoD Personnel and Procurement Statistics. Military Casualty Information page. As of December 8, 2007: http://siadapp.dmdc.osd.mil/personnel/CASUALTY/castop.htm

Friedman, M. J. Acknowledging the psychiatric cost of war. *The New England Journal of Medicine,* Vol. 351, No. 1, July 1, 2004, pp. 75–77.

———. Posttraumatic stress disorder among military returnees from Afghanistan and Iraq. *The American Journal of Psychiatry,* Vol. 163, No. 4, April 2006, pp. 586–593.

Glasser, R. A shock wave of brain injuries. *The Washington Post,* April 8, 2007. http://www.washingtonpost.com/wp-dyn/content/article/2007/04/06/AR2007040601821.html

Government Accountability Office (GAO). *Posttraumatic Stress Disorder: DoD Needs to Identify the Factors Its Providers Use to Make Mental Health Evaluation Referrals for Service Members.* Washington, D.C., 2006.

Helmus, T. C., and R. W. Glenn. *Steeling the Mind: Combat Stress Reactions and Their Implications for Urban Warfare.* Santa Monica, Calif.: RAND Corporation, MG-191-A, 2005. As of March 4, 2008: http://www.rand.org/pubs/monographs/MG191/

Hoge, C. W., J. L. Auchterlonie, and C. S. Milliken. Mental health problems, use of mental health services, and attrition from military service after returning from deployment to Iraq or Afghanistan. *JAMA,* Vol. 295, No. 9, March 1, 2006, pp. 1023–1032.

Hoge, C. W., C. A. Castro, S. C. Messer, D. McGurk, D. I. Cotting, and R. L. Koffman. Combat duty in Iraq and Afghanistan, mental health problems, and barriers to care. *New England Journal of Medicine,* Vol. 351, No. 1, July 2004, pp. 13–22.

Hoge, C. W., S. E. Lesikar, R. Guevara, J. Lange, J. F. Brundage, Jr., C. C. Engel, S. C. Messer, and D. T. Orman. Mental disorders among U.S. military personnel in the 1990s: Association with high levels of health care utilization and early military attrition. *The American Journal of Psychiatry,* Vol. 159, No. 9, September 2002, pp. 1576–1583.

Hoge, C. W., D. McGurk, J. L. Thomas, A. L. Cox, C. C. Engel, and C. A. Castro. Mild traumatic brain injury in U.S. soldiers returning from Iraq. *New England Journal of Medicine,* Vol. 358, No. 5, January 31, 2008, pp. 453–463.

Hoge, C. W., A. Terhakopian, C. A. Castro, S. C. Messer, and C. C. Engel. Association of posttraumatic stress disorder with somatic symptoms, health care visits, and absenteeism among Iraq war veterans. *American Journal of Psychiatry,* Vol. 164, No. 1, January 2007, pp. 150–153. As of January 23, 2008:
http://www.ncbi.nlm.nih.gov/entrez/query.fcgi?cmd=Retrieve&db=PubMed&dopt=Citation&list_uids=17202557

Independent Review Group to Conduct an Assessment of Outpatient Treatment at Walter Reed Army Medical Center (WRAMC) and the National Naval Medical Center (NNMC). *Rebuilding the Trust.* Washington, D.C., 2007.

Jones, E., and I. P. Palmer. Army psychiatry in the Korean War: The experience of 1 Commonwealth Division. *Military Medicine,* Vol. 165, No. 4, April 2000, pp. 256–260.

Marlowe, D. H. *Psychological and Psychosocial Consequences of Combat and Deployment, with Special Emphasis on the Gulf War.* Washington, D.C.: The RAND Corporation, MR-1018/11-OSD, 2001. As of March 4, 2008:
http://www.rand.org/pubs/monograph_reports/MR1018.11/

Milliken, C. S., J. L. Auchterlonie, and C. W. Hoge. Longitudinal assessment of mental health problems among Active and Reserve Component soldiers returning from the Iraq War. *Journal of the American Medical Association,* Vol. 298, No. 18, 2007, pp. 2141–2148.

National Institute of Mental Health Web site, Mental Health Topics page. As of March 28, 2008:
http://www.nimh.nih.gov/health/topics

National Institute of Neurological Disorders and Stroke. *Traumatic Brain Injury: Hope Through Research.* NIH Publication No. 02-158, 2002. As of January 30, 2008:
http://www.ninds.nih.gov/disorders/tbi/detail%5Ftbi.htm

Newman, R. A. Combat fatigue: A review of the Korean Conflict. *Military Medicine,* Vol. 129, 1964, pp. 921–928.

President's Commission on Care for America's Returning Wounded Warriors. *Serve, Support, Simplify: Report of the President's Commission on Care for America's Returning Wounded Warriors.* Washington, D.C., July 2007. As of January 23, 2008:
http://www.pccww.gov/index.html

PubMed database, National Center for Biotechnology Information. As of August 2007:
http://www.pubmed.gov

Rosenheck, R., and A. Fontana. Changing patterns of care for war-related post-traumatic stress disorder at Department of Veterans Affairs Medical Centers: The use of performance data to guide program development. *Military Medicine,* Vol. 164, No. 11, November 1999, pp. 795–802.

Serafino, N. M. *Peacekeeping: Issues of U.S. Military Involvement.* Washington, D.C.: Congressional Research Service, 2003.

Smith, T. C., M. A. K. Ryan, D. L. Wingard, D. J. Slymen, J. F. Sallis, D. Kritz-Silverstein, for the Millenium Cohort Study Team. New onset and persistent symptoms of post-traumatic stress disorder self reported after deployment and combat exposures: Prospective population based US military cohort study. *British Medical Journal* online, downloaded on January 16, 2008.

Thurman, D. J., J. E. Sniezek, D. Johnson, A. Greenspan, and S. M. Smith. *Guidelines for Surveillance of Central Nervous System Injury.* Atlanta, Ga.: Centers for Disease Control and Prevention, 1995.

U.S. Census Bureau. Population estimates for counties by race and Hispanic origin, 1999. As of June 2007:
http://www.census.gov/population/estimates/county/crh/crhga99.txt

Warden, D. Military TBI during the Iraq and Afghanistan wars. *Journal of Head Trauma Rehabilitation,* Vol. 21, No. 5, 2006, pp. 398–402.

CHAPTER TWO

The Wars in Afghanistan and Iraq—An Overview

Jerry M. Sollinger, Gail Fisher, and Karen N. Metscher

This chapter provides a thumbnail sketch of the conflicts in Afghanistan and Iraq. The first section describes the composition of the U.S. forces by demographic components and organizational affiliations in the Active and Reserve Components. The second section places the conflicts in perspective, comparing them with other wars the United States has fought. The third section shows the history of troop deployments in the war on terrorism and arrays those deployments against significant events that have occurred in Operation Enduring Freedom (OEF) and Operation Iraqi Freedom (OIF). The third section also discusses the casualties for ground forces sustained in Iraq—those killed in action (KIA) and wounded in action (WIA)—that is, the predominantly Active and Reserve forces of the Army and the Marine Corps. It also shows the numbers who have died as a result of improvised explosive devices. The fourth section provides a brief overview of the health care systems that serve the OEF/OIF veterans.

What the Current Fighting Force Looks Like

In 2007, Congress authorized the total U.S. military force at approximately 2.2 million servicemembers (Department of Defense [DoD], 2008). Of that total, approximately 47 percent of the all-volunteer force[1] was authorized for the Army, 25 percent for the Air Force, 19 percent for the Navy, and the remaining 10 percent for the Marine Corps (Department of Defense, 2008). Each military service has personnel in two components: Active and Reserve. The Active Component includes personnel who are full-time, active duty forces. The Reserve Component includes Reserve (Army, Navy, and Marine Corps) and National Guard (Army, Air Force) forces. In this monograph, we use the term Reserve Component to include Guard personnel.

In 2007, the Army had 47 percent of its authorized force in the Active Component; the Air Force had 65 percent; the Navy, 83 percent; and the Marine Corps, 82 percent[2] (DoD, 2008). Table 2.1 shows that the military has more Blacks than does the

---

[1] Conscription (the draft) ended in 1973; since that time, the U.S. military is an all-volunteer force.

[2] These figures do not include Reserve Component members serving on active duty.

Table 2.1
Percentage of Race/Ethnicity, by Service, 2004

	White	Black	Hispanic	Asian/ Pacific Islander	Indian/ Alaskan Native	Other
Army						
Active Army	60	23	10	3	1	3
Army Reserve	60	24	11	4	1	1
Army National Guard	74	14	7	2	1	2
Navy						
Active Navy	62	19	8	6	3	3
Navy Reserve	64	15	9	4	1	7
Marine Corps						
Active Marine Corps	66	12	14	2	1	5
Marine Corps Reserve	68	9	14	4	1	5
Air Force						
Active Air Force	72	15	6	2	<1	4
Air National Guard	80	9	6	2	1	2
Air Force Reserve	72	16	7	2	<1	4
Total Military	67	17	9	3	1	3
Civilian Work Force	71	11	11	5	<1	1

SOURCE: Government Accountability Office (GAO), *Military Personnel: Reporting Additional Servicemember Demographics Could Enhance Congressional Oversight.* Washington, D.C., 2005, p. 22.

civilian workforce, and fewer Hispanics, Whites, and Asian Americans/Pacific Islanders. Also, military servicemembers tend to be younger than the civilian population: Approximately 47 percent of the active duty enlisted force is between 17 and 24 years old, whereas only about 14 percent of the civilian labor force is in that age group (Office of the Under Secretary of Defense for Personnel and Readiness, 2007).

Additionally, the Reserve Components tend to be older than the Active Component, and in 2004 the GAO reported that the Reserve Components had five times the proportion of servicemembers age 45 and older of the Active Components (GAO, 2005). Further, women accounted for approximately 14 percent of the total military force in 2007 (Office of the Under Secretary of Defense for Personnel and Readiness, 2007), whereas approximately 51 percent of the U.S. population is women (U.S. Census Bureau, 2006).

In 2004, approximately 52 percent of the total force was married (Office of the Under Secretary of Defense for Personnel and Readiness, 2005), and proportionally more servicemembers had at least a high school diploma (or an equivalent) than the U.S. population 18 years and older (GAO, 2005).

Troops Deployed to OEF/OIF

As of October 31, 2007, 1,638,817 servicemembers have been deployed to the theaters of operation for Afghanistan (OEF) or Iraq (OIF) since the hostilities began.[3] Of these, approximately, 1.2 million were active component, with 455,009 from the reserve forces (Office of the Under Secretary of Defense, 2007). Reserve participation in both operations has been historically high, particularly for the Army and the Marine Corps as seen in Table 2.2.

To provide some perspective on the scope of current military operations, we give statistics on the Vietnam War: Approximately 3.4 million servicemembers, about one-third of them drafted, were deployed to Southeast Asia in support of that war (Department of Veterans Affairs, Public Affairs). Eighty-eight percent was White, 11 percent was Black, and 1 percent belonged to other races. Demographically, the troops were younger than the current force (average age of 19), less likely to be married, and almost all male (only 7,494 women served in Vietnam) (Summers, 1985).

The Conflicts in Perspective

The conflicts in Afghanistan and Iraq can be seen as extensions of a larger struggle against global terrorism. While they have absorbed the national attention, it is useful to place them in a larger historical perspective. They are not the longest, the largest, or the bloodiest of the conflicts that the United States has fought. To date, Vietnam is the longest conflict, lasting 13 years if the fall of the U.S. Embassy in Saigon in April 1975 is seen as the end point, or 11 years if departure of the last combat troops is used as the termination. Of the 3.4 million U.S. servicemembers involved in the conflict, 47,424 were killed in battle and 153,303 were wounded (Department of Veterans Affairs, Public Affairs). Although it lasted less than four years, World War II was the largest conflict, involving over 16.1 million U.S. military personnel. Some 405,000 military personnel died in the conflict, and 671,846 were wounded (Department of Veterans Affairs, Public Affairs). The bloodiest war the United States ever fought was the Civil War, in which 324,511 soldiers of about 2.2 million serving in the Union forces died (DoD, 2007). By contrast, 4,357 U.S. military personnel have died in Afghanistan and Iraq (both hostile and nonhostile deaths) and 30,613 have been wounded to date (DoD, 2007).

---

[3]   References to servicemembers serving in Iraq and Afghanistan include all U.S. forces serving in those theaters of operation.

Table 2.2
Deployed Force Composition as of October 31, 2007

	Members Ever Deployed in Support of OIF/OEF
Army	
Active Duty	494,465
National Guard	196,052
Reserve	110,164
Total	800,681
Navy	
Active Duty	276,926
Reserve	27,456
Total	304,382
Air Force	
Active Duty	234,084
National Guard	58,094
Reserve	32,845
Total	325,023
Marine Corps	
Active Duty	178,333
Reserve	30,398
Total	208,731
DoD	
Active Duty Total	1,183,808
National Guard Total	254,146
Reserve Total	200,863
DoD Total	1,638,817

SOURCE: Department of Defense Public Affairs Office.
Number of members deployed by service component and
month/year (based on the Contingency Tracking System),
2007.

What Makes the Conflicts in Afghanistan and Iraq Different?

Each conflict has its own distinguishing characteristics beyond size and location. Probably the signal difference of the conflicts in Afghanistan and Iraq is that they mark the first time that the United States has attempted to fight an extended conflict with a post–Cold War all-volunteer force. Operation Desert Storm also drew on volunteer forces, but that operation lasted only a matter of months. But today, the Services have no easily accessible personnel pool to draw on to expand their ranks, as was the case during the Vietnam War, when hundreds of thousands of draftees were called up to serve. Active duty forces in fiscal year 2007, which for the Army numbered about 482,000 and for the Marine Corps, about 180,000 (DoD, 2008), are the most available source of troops, followed by the Reserve Component forces, which totaled about 550,000 for the Army National Guard and the Army Reserve combined in 2007 (Office of the Assistant Secretary of the Army, 2007), and 39,600 for the Marine Corps (Department of the Navy, 2007). The thought underpinning the creation of the all-volunteer force was that it would be smaller but highly professional and capable of deploying worldwide and winning conflicts in a relatively short time. Operation Desert Storm seemed to bear out that thinking, when U.S. and coalition forces crushed Iraqi forces in a matter of a few months.

However, the extended nature of the conflicts in Afghanistan and Iraq has subjected the U.S. military to demands that, arguably, it was not sized, resourced, or configured to meet at the time. The ground forces, composed predominantly of personnel from both the Army and the Marine Corps, have borne the brunt of the conflict in casualties and wounded in action. To meet the demands of both conflicts, DoD has devised rotational policies that cycle forces and equipment through both conflicts. In a memorandum from January 2007, the Secretary of Defense announced benchmarks of one year of deployment to a combat theater for every two years outside of combat (i.e., training and re-equipping) for the Active Components of all Services, and one year of deployment to a theater of war to five years nondeployed for the Reserve Components (Office of the Under Secretary of Defense, 2007).

Although the Army policy is clear on both the length of deployment and the amount of time back in the States before another deployment, the demands of the conflicts in Afghanistan and Iraq have made implementation of this new policy difficult (GAO, 2007). The Congressional Budget Office (2005) offers evidence, in fact, that some combat units are spending much less time back in the United States between deployments; even when they are in the United States, the units are preparing for their next deployment by training away from their home stations. Further, the demands of the Iraq conflict have prompted the Army to extend the deployments of some units from 12 to 15 months.

Operation Enduring Freedom

At its inception in October 2001, Operation Enduring Freedom was unique in that it struck against the Taliban, which harbored al Qaeda, with the goal of denying continuance of that relationship, while providing humanitarian relief to the people of Afghanistan, (Johnson, 2007). Much of the initial fighting in Afghanistan was done by indigenous forces supported by Special Operations Forces from all three U.S. military Services and several coalition partners, including Great Britain, France, and Australia. These forces accompanied indigenous forces, most from the Northern Alliance, which had been fighting the Taliban for more than five years. The goal of the Bush administration was to keep the ground-force presence relatively small inside Afghanistan. The U.S. Navy provided initial air support, flying from carriers in the Indian Ocean, from Diego Garcia, or from bases outside Afghanistan. Eventually, the Navy, along with the Air Force, flew from bases adjacent to or inside Afghanistan—most notably, Baghram Air Base.

The combination of air strikes guided by controlling ground forces proved overwhelming to the Taliban forces. The use of technology to target air strikes was not new, but the use of a small number of Special Operations Forces on the ground maximized the delivery of airpower for the first time. The Taliban essentially had no air defenses, allowing the coalition forces nearly unchallenged control of the battlespace. In addition to the powerful control of the battle, the simultaneous humanitarian relief is attributed with producing an Afghan perception that the United States' power was being used to liberate rather than invade (Lambeth, 2005). The war against the Taliban lasted approximately two and a half months, ending in mid-December 2001 (Lambeth, 2005). U.S. ground forces played no direct combat role in Afghanistan until March 2002, when the U.S. strategy turned toward rooting out remaining Taliban and al Qaeda fighters (Johnson, 2007).

With the installation of a new Afghan government, U.S. efforts turned to stability operations, which have continued to this day (Lambeth, 2005). Since the end of major combat operations and the initiation of stability operations, the United States has maintained approximately 15,000 to 20,000 personnel in the Afghan theater, most of whom are ground forces (Congressional Budget Office, 2005).

Operation Iraqi Freedom

Troop deployments that began in late 2002 reflect the run-up to Operation Iraqi Freedom, which began in March 2003. Major combat operations were anticipated to be short and turned out to be even shorter than anticipated, beginning on March 21, 2003, ending with the fall of Baghdad on April 9. Coalition forces occupied Tikrit, Saddam Hussein's hometown, on April 15, effectively ending organized Iraqi resistance. Prewar estimates were for major combat to last between 90 and 125 days. Iraqi resistance collapsed in just over three weeks. As with Operation Desert Storm (147 battle deaths), casualties were light, with 139 killed and 429 wounded.[4] In May 2003, on the deck of the carrier *Abraham Lincoln*, which had just returned from the Persian Gulf, President Bush publicly declared an end to major combat operations. With the end of major combat operations, the United States turned toward the tasks of providing security while building and supporting a new civil government. As the Sunni and Shiite (and other secular) factions fought for power, security deteriorated around the country, requiring ongoing combat operations, albeit against insurgents rather than uniformed forces.

In June 2004, the coalition authorities handed the sovereignty of Iraq to an interim government, and in December 2005, the Iraqis went to the polls for the first

---

[4]   Figures for wounded are for those who did not return to duty and are from the Department of Defense Personnel & Procurement Statistics Web site.

free election in 50 years. The elections appeared to be a success, with a turnout of about 70 percent and markedly little violence. Results generally went along religious and sectarian lines. Violence continued between factions seeking power; attacks on reconstruction projects were aimed at discrediting the coalition and the Iraqi government.

In February 2006, insurgents dressed as Iraqi police officers seized the al Askariya mosque, also known as the Golden Dome and one of the holiest sites in Shia Islam, and detonated two bombs inside, causing catastrophic damage to the 1,000-year-old structure. Immediate and violent reprisals ensued. Ordinary Shiites attacked Sunnis at random. The violence was especially severe in Baghdad. Every morning, authorities would discover tortured and executed bodies from one group or another. Even by the most optimistic assessments, the country was teetering on the brink of all-out civil war.

In December 2006, the Iraq Study Group released its report, noting a grave and deteriorating situation in Iraq. The report argued for increased involvement of other nations in the Persian Gulf region, to include Iran and Syria, and recommended substantial increases in the support provided to the Iraqi security forces.

In January 2007, President Bush announced plans to increase the number of U.S. forces in Iraq. The increase was to be temporary and done with the goal of stabilizing the situation, particularly in Baghdad, until the Iraqi government could establish better control. The surge was accompanied by a change of military command, with General David Petraeus taking over from General George Casey. In contrast to the conflict in Afghanistan, the conflict in Iraq has required a commitment of approximately 160,000 to 180,000 military personnel (Congressional Budget Office, 2005).

Casualties and Improvised Explosive Devices

Figure 2.1 charts the casualties in Iraq by those killed in action (KIA; middle curve) and wounded in action (WIA; top curve). The bottom-most curve indicates the numbers that have been killed as a result of what has become the weapon of choice in Iraq for attacking coalition forces: the improvised explosive device, or IED. The data represent wounded and fatalities for Army and Marine Corps forces deployed in Iraq. Three aspects warrant comment. First, the curves show a sharp falloff in casualties following the major combat operations, a period during which the country was chaotic and the insurgency had not yet begun to take hold. After that, casualties, particularly the wounded, spike, only to decline again in 2005, surging again starting in 2006. They remained high until the sharp decline seen at the end of 2007.

Second, beginning in 2005, IEDs account for an increasing share of those killed, and the proportion remains high until late in 2007 (last data are for September). Third, the ratio of wounded to fatalities is relatively high. For every nine wounded, there

Figure 2.1
Marine Corps and Army Wounded and Killed in Action, Iraq, March 2003–September 2007

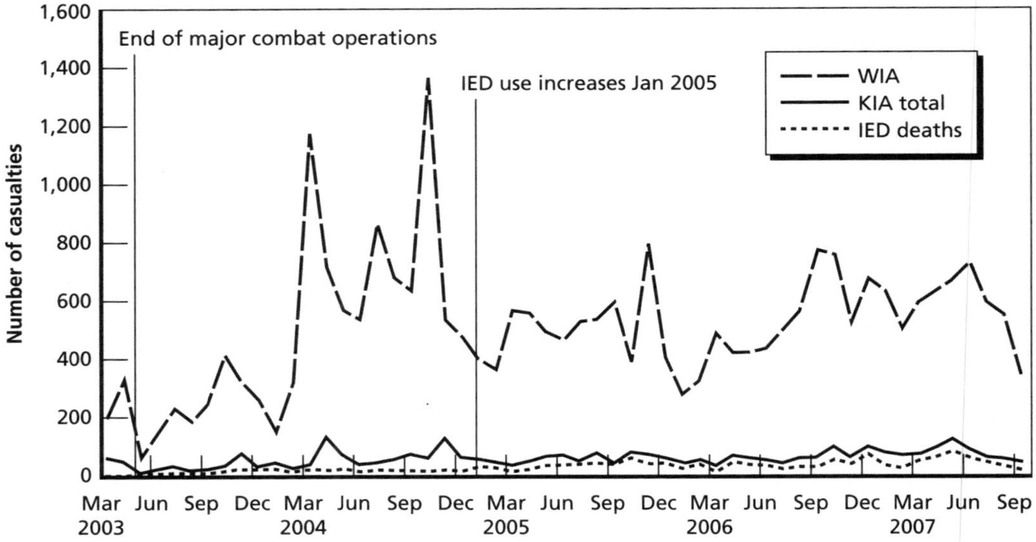

SOURCE: Casualty data are from http://siadapp.dmdc.osd.mil/personnel/CASUALTY/ and
www.brookings.edu/iraqindex for IED deaths.
RAND MG720-2.1

is only about one fatality.[5] The ratio in World War II for battle deaths to wounded was 1:2.4, and the fatality-to-wounded ratio in Vietnam was 1:3 (Fischer, Klarman, and Oboroceanu, 2007). Although the survivability rate is higher, wounds resulting from IED blasts often cause multiple wounds and usually involve severe injuries to extremities.

IEDs have evolved from relatively crude devices detonated by such simple mechanisms as garage-door openers to larger and increasingly sophisticated weapons triggered by cell phones, infrared signals, or pressure plates. Their use imposes few risks on the insurgents, and they have proven to be devastatingly effective against U.S. forces. By some estimates, they account for about 40 percent of all casualties (Brookings Institution, 2007).

The "IED fight" has been marked by a series of moves and countermoves as each side adapts to the latest innovation by the other. As Figure 2.1 shows, IEDs were not used during the first months following the end of major combat operations. Once they started to be used, U.S. forces initially responded by increasing the amount of armor

---

[5]   The wounded-to-fatality rates for OIF and OEF have become the source of some controversy because of the nature of the counts. Some sources count all wounds, whether they were incurred by hostile action or not, as well as all deaths, which can skew the ratio to approximate 7 wounded to 1 fatality (Goldberg, 2007). Others count only the wounded unable to return to duty compared with the number of deaths due to hostilities, which produces a ratio of approximately 4 to 1 (Goldberg, 2007).

protection afforded the troops, which included adding armor plate and shatter-resistant glass to the High Mobility Multipurpose Wheeled Vehicle and patrolling in Bradley fighting vehicles. Insurgents responded with larger and more-deadly devices—most notably, the explosively forged penetrator, which ejects a high-velocity jet of molten metal that can penetrate the armor of an M-1 Abrams tank, the Army's heaviest combat vehicle. In addition to employing increasingly sophisticated jammers that block the signals used for remote detonation, U.S. forces have focused on disrupting the sequence of material collection, and bomb construction and implanting.

The low KIA rates stem not only from the improved body armor given to all the forces in Afghanistan and Iraq but also from improved delivery of emergency medical care in theater, along with swift evacuation to full-treatment trauma centers outside the conflict zone. Servicemembers experiencing trauma in either Iraq or Afghanistan can be evacuated to a trauma center in Landstuhl, Germany, within 24 hours of their injury, and they can reach facilities in the United States within another 24 hours via the Air Forces' Critical Care Air Transport Teams, which are essentially flying intensive care units (Cullen, 2006; Moore et al., 2007). By contrast, during the Vietnam War, it took approximately 45 days to move servicemembers from the battlefield to a U.S. hospital (Cullen, 2006).

The many improvements in technology and evacuation assets have enabled the military health system to deliver urgent care from the point of injury on the battlefield, as well as both short- and long-term rehabilitative care through U.S.-based facilities. Through the Department of Defense, the military health system offers a broad array of health care services, ranging from preventative services to sophisticated trauma care and rehabilitation (e.g., for severe combat-related injuries). Servicemembers injured during combat flow through this system of care, but their health care does not necessarily end within DoD. Some severely wounded servicemembers will be treated by VA facilities, depending on the nature of their injuries. These systems of care are briefly described in the following section.

The Military and Veterans Health Systems

DoD's health care system is commonly referred to as the military health system (MHS). Over 9 million individuals are eligible to receive care within the MHS, including all Active Component servicemembers and their dependents; Reserve Component members and their dependents when they are on active duty for at least 30 days; and some military retirees and their dependents. The MHS provides this support via 70 hospitals and 400 clinics, known as the direct care system (Office of Health Affairs Web site). The MHS-provided direct care services are supplemented by a network of civilian providers (often referred to as *purchased care*) under an umbrella health plan of TRICARE.

The Department of Veterans Affairs' (VA's) health care system is organized into a system of 21 Veterans Integrated Service Networks (VISNs). The majority of services provided by the VA are delivered in facilities owned and maintained by the VA and staffed by VA employees. The balance, referred to as *purchased services*, is paid for on a fee-for-service basis. Currently, all veterans with at least 24 months of continuous active duty military service and an "other-than-dishonorable" discharge are eligible to receive care from the VA through a priority-based enrollment system. Veterans are prioritized for enrollment according to eight tiers: those with Service-connected disabilities (priority levels 1 through 3); prisoners of war and recipients of the Purple Heart (priority 3); veterans with catastrophic disabilities unrelated to service (priority 4); low-income veterans (priority 5); veterans who meet specific criteria, such as having served in the first Gulf War (priority 6); and higher-income veterans who do not qualify for other priority groups (priorities 7 and 8). Enrollment is currently suspended for priority group 8 to ensure that the VA can meet the needs of its higher-priority enrollees.

For servicemembers serving in Afghanistan or Iraq at the time of injury detection, health care is provided by DoD military facilities in theater. In the event of traumatic injury or illness, evacuation is done by military airlift to a large military hospital in Germany. Depending on the severity of injury or illness and their care needs, servicemembers may be treated and returned to duty or they may be evacuated to the United States to one of a few very large military hospitals. As care and rehabilitation for servicemembers progresses, the injured may move from inpatient to outpatient at the same military hospital, or they may be moved to other facilities, including VA facilities.

If servicemembers separate from active duty (a complex decision process based on medical and disability criteria, personal choice, and other factors), they may be eligible to enroll in the VA health care system. Servicemembers who continue on active duty will continue to receive their health care benefits from the Department of Defense. Reserve Component members who return and are released from active duty may also enroll in TRICARE or return to their civilian health care providers and/or insurance. Within five years of their return from combat, Reserve Component members who are combat veterans are also eligible to access the VA health care system.

Therefore, Active and Reserve Component military members returning from Afghanistan and Iraq have access to a number of health care resources, through DoD, the VA, and beyond. Each health system purchases some care from civilian providers. Within DoD, civilian providers are contracted and reimbursed through the TRICARE system. Care may even extend beyond TRICARE to purely civilian health insurance and health networks for Reserve Component members or for servicemembers leaving the military who do not use their VA health benefits or use their civilian-employment benefits. Many factors drive eligibility and access to these systems for servicemembers and veterans.

These issues, along with a discussion of the specific programs and services for meeting the health care needs of servicemembers and veterans with post-traumatic stress disorder, major depression, or traumatic brain injury, are discussed in Chapter Seven.

Concluding Comments

The United States finds itself nearing its eighth year of continuous combat, and U.S. forces could be engaged at some level in both Afghanistan and Iraq for years. Although the United States has modified its tactics and appears to have made progress in Iraq, a resurgent Taliban is threatening gains made in Afghanistan. The nation is fighting this war with an all-volunteer force, which has, by most accounts, performed exceptionally well.

Even if the United States is able to scale back its commitments in the two countries, gauging the long-term effects on the forces from other perspectives, such as morale, mental stress, and the willingness to face repetitive combat tours, is difficult.

Any war exacts a human toll. The psychological toll of the current conflicts on the force is not a factor to be dismissed—particularly in light of the ongoing demand for battle-ready soldiers, sailors, airmen, and marines. Understanding the nature of the psychological toll is critical to an effective strategy for maintaining or even improving the health of that fighting force.

In the next part of this monograph, we provide an overview of the research literature on the prevalence of mental and cognitive injuries among OEF/OIF veterans (Chapter Three), including findings from our own survey of veterans and servicemembers to provide data on current health status, levels of probable post-traumatic stress injury, major depression, and traumatic brain injury, as well as self-reported use of and barriers to health care (Chapter Four)

References

Brookings Institution, Saban Center for Middle East Policy. Iraq index: Tracking variables of reconstruction and security in post-Saddam Iraq. October 1, 2007. As of January 22, 2008: www.brookings.edu/iraqindex

Congressional Budget Office. *An Analysis of the U.S. Military's Ability to Sustain an Occupation in Iraq: An Update.* Washington, D.C.: Congress of the United States, 2005.

Cullen, K. A trip from Iraq aboard a flying ICU. *The Boston Globe*, 2006, p. A1.

Department of Defense. Military Casualty Information Web site. 2007. As of January 3, 2008: http://siadapp.dmdc.osd.mil/personnel/CASUALTY/castop.htm

Department of Defense, Public Affairs Office. Number of members deployed by service component and month/year (based on the contingency tracking system), 2008.

Department of the Navy, FY 2008/FY 2009 President's budget: Personnel appropriations. 2007. As of January 3, 2008: http://www.finance.hq.navy.mil/fmb/08pres/PERS.htm

Department of Veterans Affairs, Office of Public Affairs, America's wars. As of January 23, 2008: http://www1.va.gov/opa/fact/docs/amwars.pdf

Fischer, H., K. Klarman, and M.-J. Oboroceanu. *American War and Military Operations Casualties: Lists and Statistics.* Washington, D.C.: Congressional Research Service, June 2007.

Goldberg, M. S., Deputy Assistant Director for National Security. *Projecting the Costs to Care for Veterans of U.S. Military Operations in Iraq and Afghanistan, Statement Before the Committee on Veterans' Affairs.* Washington, D.C.: U.S. House of Representatives, October 17, 2007. As of January 23, 2008: http://veterans.house.gov/hearings/Testimony.aspx?TID=7260

Government Accountability Office (GAO). *Military Personnel: Reporting Additional Servicemember Demographics Could Enhance Congressional Oversight.* Washington, D.C., 2005.

———. *Military Personnel, DoD Lacks Reliable Personnel Tempo Data and Needs Quality Controls to Improve Data Accuracy.* Washington, D.C., 2007.

Iraq Study Group Report. As of January 25, 2008: http://www.usip.org/isg/iraq_study_group_report/report/1206/iraq_study_group_report.pdf

Johnson, D. E. *Learning Large Lessons: The Evolving Roles of Ground Power and Air Power in the Post–Cold War Era.* Santa Monica, Calif.: RAND Corporation, MG-405-1-AF, 2007. As of March 4, 2008: http://www.rand.org/pubs/monographs/MG405-1/

Lambeth, B. S. *Air Power Against Terror: America's Conduct of Operation Enduring Freedom*, Santa Monica, Calif.: RAND Corporation, MG-166-CENTAF, 2005. As of March 4, 2008: http://www.rand.org/pubs/monographs/MG166/

Moore, E. E., M. Knudson, C. W. Schwab, D. Trunkey, J. A. Johannigman, and J. B. Holcomb. Military-civilian collaboration in trauma care and the Senior Visiting Surgeon Program. *New England Journal of Medicine,* Vol. 357, No. 26, December 27, 2007, pp. 2723–2727.

National Institute of Mental Health, Mental Health Web site. Topics page. As of January 23, 2008: http://www.nimh.nih.gov/health/topics/

Office of Health Affairs Web site. As of January 20, 2008: http://mhs.osd.mil/aboutMHS.jsp

Office of the Assistant Secretary of the Army, Financial Management and Comptroller. FY 2008/ FY 2009 budget materials. 2007. As of January 3, 2008: http://www.asafm.army.mil/budget/fybm/fybm.asp

Office of the Under Secretary of Defense. *DoD News Briefing with Under Secretary of Defense David Chu, Lt. Gen. Stephen Speakes, and Lt. Gen. Emerson Gardner from the Pentagon.* Washington, D.C.: U.S. Department of Defense, 2007.

Office of the Under Secretary of Defense (Comptroller). Defense Budget Materials. Army, Air Force, and Navy 2008 budget estimations justification books. 2008. As of January 3, 2008: http://www.defenselink.mil/comptroller/defbudget/fy2008/index.html

Office of the Under Secretary of Defense for Personnel and Readiness. *Population Representation in the Military Services: Executive Summary.* Washington, D.C., 2007.

————. *Population Representation in the Military Services: Fiscal Year 2005.* Washington, D.C., 2005.

Summers, Harry G. *The Vietnam War Almanac.* New York: Facts on File Publications, 1985.

U.S. Census Bureau. U.S. Census Bureau fact finder for 2006. 2006. As of January 2, 2008: http://factfinder.census.gov

Part II: The Nature and Scope of the Problem

This part of the monograph reviews information about the prevalence of post-traumatic stress disorder, depression, and traumatic brain injury among troops deployed to either Afghanistan (as part of Operation Enduring Freedom) or Iraq (as part of Operation Iraqi Freedom). The first chapter, Chapter Three, provides a systematic review of the existing studies of OEF/OIF troops. Chapter Four describes our own survey of those who have been deployed for OEF/OIF.

Prevalence of PTSD, Depression, and TBI Among Returning Servicemembers

Rajeev Ramchand, Benjamin R. Karney, Karen Chan Osilla, Rachel M. Burns, and Leah Barnes Calderone

As Kessler (2000) has noted: "Any assessment of the societal impact of a disorder must begin with a consideration of prevalence" (p. 4). By critically reviewing the current epidemiological studies on post-traumatic stress disorder (PTSD), depression, and traumatic brain injury (TBI) following deployment to Afghanistan and Iraq, we aim specifically to address several questions of both scientific and political importance, including: How widespread are mental health and cognitive conditions in the military currently? How do rates of mental health and cognitive conditions differ among troops deployed to Afghanistan, those deployed to Iraq, and nondeployed troops? How long do conditions and associated symptoms last? How are conditions distributed across the services of the military? Are there differences by gender, ethnicity, rank, or service?

This chapter reviews and describes the best available data on the prevalence of mental health and cognitive conditions endured by servicemembers in the current conflicts. Unlike previous conflicts, such as the Vietnam War or Gulf War, on which prevalence studies were generally conducted years after servicemembers returned home, in the current conflicts epidemiologic studies are being conducted throughout the course of the deployment cycle—i.e., a week before being deployed, while troops are in theater, and immediately upon their return. Comparisons of prevalence rates obtained across these assessments may provide unique insights into mental health and cognitive conditions in the military in general and how the experience of these conditions may be related to deployment. In sum, this chapter describes the current landscape of mental health and cognitive conditions among servicemembers of the military deployed to Afghanistan and Iraq, in hopes of highlighting where future problems, vulnerabilities, and resource needs may lie.

Methods

Epidemiologic studies addressing the prevalence of PTSD, major depression, and TBI among servicemembers deploying or deployed to Afghanistan and Iraq were identified by searching peer-reviewed journals for relevant articles, using systematic search approaches on PubMed and PsycINFO databases. Search terms included Military, War, Veterans, Combat, Operation Enduring Freedom (OEF), Operation Iraqi Freedom (OIF), Afghanistan, Iraq, Prevalence, PTSD (Stress disorders, Post-Traumatic), Depression/Depressive disorder, Traumatic Brain Injury, Mental disorders, and Mental health. Keywords were used to search titles, abstracts, and the text of articles, and there were no publication-year restrictions. When more than one article presented prevalence information on the same sample, we chose the earliest-published article. Reference lists of pertinent articles identified in database searches were examined in a cited reference search that identified government reports as well as other peer-reviewed articles. Studies were considered eligible for inclusion only if the study population included U.S. military populations deployed to Afghanistan and Iraq (although we included two studies of servicemembers from corresponding United Kingdom [UK] and Dutch deployments), and if the reported study outcomes included prevalence figures for PTSD, depression, or TBI before deployment, in theater, or post-deployment.

Results

In total, we identified 22 independent studies that have provided specific evidence of the prevalence of PTSD, major depression, and/or brain injury among troops deployed or deploying to Afghanistan and/or Iraq. Tables 3.2 through 3.23 summarize the characteristics and results of each of these studies. Before reviewing the results from these studies, we first discuss the methods that these studies used to identify cases of PTSD, major depression, and/or TBI. Knowing the methods used to identify cases is important for understanding how to interpret study results. We then provide an overview of the prevalence estimates from studies that have assessed servicemembers before deployment, in theater, and upon returning from deployment. We proceed to then identify and elaborate upon themes that emerged from an analysis of the group of studies as a whole.

Screening for PTSD, Depression, and TBI in Epidemiological Surveys

In psychiatric epidemiology, three methods are commonly used to identify "caseness" (i.e., who has a disease or disorder, referred to as *cases*, and who does not): diagnostic codes from case registries among individuals in *treatment contact* (i.e., receiving some type of medical care); screening tools that identify persons with probable disorders; and diagnostic interviews that assign actual diagnoses based on criteria set forth in the *Diagnostic and Statistical Manual of Mental Disorders* (DSM) [American Psychiatric Association, 2000] or *International Classification of Diseases* (ICD). Diagnostic interviews may be either fully structured (administered by trained lay interviewers) or semi-structured (administered by clinicians) (Jablensky, 2002). Each method varies in its *validity*, or its ability to distinguish who has a particular disorder and who does not. The validity of a screening tool can be measured by its *sensitivity*, or the proportion of persons with a given condition correctly identified by the screening tool as having the condition, and its *specificity*, or the proportion of persons without a condition correctly identified by the screening tool as not having the condition.

For most screening tools, there is typically a trade-off between sensitivity and specificity, and choosing one tool over another should be based on the ultimate goal of the research. A highly sensitive tool with lower specificity will detect most true cases, but some of those individuals without the disorder will be incorrectly identified as "positive." A highly specific tool with low sensitivity might detect fewer actual cases, but the cases detected are almost certain to be true cases. Thus, researchers need to decide whether the goal of their research is to identify all possible cases or only to identify true cases, or something in between the two.

Defining a Case

Since the methods of detection vary across studies, it is important to understand the way each defines a *case* in order to be able to interpret the results appropriately. Thus, we explain the different screening methods before presenting results.

Diagnostic Interviews. Diagnostic interviews are typically considered the gold standard, the most accurate way to identify cases (Jablensky, 2002). In the studies we identified, diagnostic interviews have not been used, with the exception of one study of Dutch Army troops deployed to Iraq (Engelhard et al., 2007). No studies of U.S. servicemembers have used structured diagnostic interviews. Nineteen studies used screening tools, and three relied on diagnostic codes or other types of information from medical records. Table 3.1 lists the method each study used to identify cases of PTSD, depression, and TBI.

PTSD Checklist. To assess post-traumatic stress disorder, 14 studies used the 17-item PTSD Checklist (PCL) (Weathers et al., 1993). The scale contains 17 questions corresponding to the three clusters of DSM-IV symptoms (American Psychiatric Association, 2000): re-experiencing the event; avoiding stimuli related to the event; and *hyperarousal*, which is defined as increased arousal, such as difficulty falling or staying asleep or hypervigilance. Respondents were asked to rate the degree to which they were bothered by each symptom on a scale from 1 (not at all) to 5 (extremely) for a specified period of time, typically, over the past 30 days. Thus, the total scale value ranged from 17 to 85. There are various ways in which the scale can be used to identify respondents as likely to have PTSD, and each scoring method varies in ability to detect a case of PTSD. In our review, 11 studies required that subjects meet DSM-IV diagnostic symptom criteria: experiencing at least one intrusion (re-experiencing) symptom, three or more avoidance symptoms, and at least two hyperarousal symptoms. Symptoms were considered to have been experienced if respondents indicated that they had been bothered by each to a moderate degree. This scoring approach, which is

Table 3.1
Methods Used to Define Cases of PTSD, Depression, and TBI, by Study

Study (Table Number)	PTSD Measure	Depression Measure	TBI Measure
Hoge et al., 2004 (Table 3.2)	PCL-DSM PCL-DSM-50	PHQ-DSM PHQ-DSM+FI	
Hoge, Auchterlonie, and Milliken, 2006 (Table 3.3)	PC-PTSD	PHQ-2	
Hotopf et al., 2006 (Table 3.4)	PCL≥50		
Vasterling et al., 2006 (Table 3.5)	PCL-DSM-50	CES-D-9	a
Grieger et al., 2006 (Table 3.6)	PCL-DSM-50	PHQ-DSM	
Hoge et al., 2007 (Table 3.7)	PCL-DSM-50		
Seal et al., 2007 (Table 3.8)	ICD-9-CM	ICD-9-CM	
Erbes et al., 2007 (Table 3.9)	PCL≥50		
Kolkow et al., 2007 (Table 3.10)	PCL-DSM-50	PHQ-DSM	
Helmer et al., 2007 (Table 3.11)	Chart Abstract		
Engelhard et al., 2007 (Table 3.12)	SCID PSS		
Martin, 2007 (Table 3.13)	PC-PTSD		
Milliken, Auchterlonie, and Hoge, 2007 (Table 3.14)	PC-PTSD	PHQ-2	
Rosenheck and Fontana, 2007 (Table 3.15)	ICD-9-CM		
Lapierre, Schwegler, and LaBauve, 2007 (Table 3.16)	SPTSS	CES-D-20	
Smith et al., 2008 (Table 3.17)	PCL-DSM PCL-DSM-50		
Hoge et al., 2008 (Table 3.18)	PCL-DSM-50	PHQ-DSM+FI	b
U.S. Department of the Army, Office of the Surgeon General (MHAT-I), 2003 (Table 3.19)	N/A	N/A	
U.S. Department of the Army, Office of the Surgeon General (MHAT-II), 2005 (Table 3.20)	PCL-DSM-50	PHQ-DSM+FI	
U.S. Department of the Army, Office of the Surgeon, Multinational Force–Iraq and Office of the Surgeon General, U.S. Army Medical Command (MHAT-III), 2006a (Table 3.21)	PCL-DSM-50	PHQ-DSM+FI	

Table 3.1—Continued

Study (Table Number)	PTSD Measure	Depression Measure	TBI Measure
U.S. Department of the Army, Office of the Surgeon, Multinational Force–Iraq and Office of the Surgeon General, U.S. Army Medical Command (MHAT-IV), 2006b (Table 3.22)	PCL-DSM-50	PHQ-DSM+FI	
Abt Associates, 2006 (Table 3.23)	PCL-DSM		

[a] Self-report of a head injury with loss of consciousness lasting more than 15 minutes.

[b] Self-report of a head injury with either (1) loss of consciousness, (2) being dazed, confused, or "seeing stars," or (3) not remembering the injury.

N/A = MHAT-I does not provide precise detail on the method used to define cases of PTSD and depression (see Table 3.19).

Outcome Measures for PTSD

PCL-DSM: Reporting at least 1 intrusion symptom, 3 avoidance symptoms, and 2 hyperarousal symptoms at the moderate level on PTSD Checklist.

PCL-DSM-50: PCL-DSM + total score of at least 50 (range: 17–85) on PTSD Checklist.

PCL≥50: Total score of at least 50 on PTSD Checklist.

PC-PTSD: Reporting 2 or more of 4 items on Primary Care–PTSD Screen.

SPTSS: An average total score of 4 or more (range: 0–10) on the Screen for Posttraumatic Stress Symptoms.

PSS: Total score of 14 (range: 0–51) on the PTSD Symptom Scale.

SCID: Structured Clinical Interview for DSM Disorders (semi-structured diagnostic interview).

ICD-9-CM: Diagnostic code of PTSD from medical records (*International Classification of Diseases*, Ninth Revision, *Clinical Modification*).

Outcome Measures for Depression

PHQ-DSM: Reporting 5 or more of 9 symptoms "more than half the day" or "nearly every day" in the specified time period and the presence of depressed mood or anhedonia among those symptoms on the PHQ-9.

PHQ-DSM + FI: PHQ-DSM on the PHQ-9 + self-reported functional impairment.

PHQ-2: Positive response to question on depressed mood or anhedonia.

CES-D-20: Averaged score across 20 depressive symptoms >16 (range: 0–20) on Center for Epidemiologic Studies Depression Inventory, 20-item version.

CES-D-9: Summed score across 9 depressive symptoms >4 (range: 0–9) on Center for Epidemiologic Studies Depression Inventory, 9-item version.

termed the *symptom-cluster method* (Brewin, 2005), has resulted in a sensitivity of 1.00 and specificity of 0.92, meaning that all cases of PTSD are correctly identified, but 8 percent of persons without PTSD are identified as having the disorder (Manne et al., 1998). To meet screening criteria, all but one of these studies also required that the total score be at least 50 on the entire PCL scale, raising the threshold for detecting a case considerably. Adding this latter criterion to the symptom-cluster method of scoring has not been validated against clinician diagnoses of PTSD, although its validity has been evaluated by itself. Having a total score of at least 50 on the PCL scale has a sensitivity=0.60, meaning that 60 percent of PTSD cases are identified by the test, and a specificity=0.99, meaning that 1 percent of those without the disorder are incorrectly identified as having PTSD (Andrykowski et al., 1998). Thus, this method is more specific but less sensitive than the symptom-cluster approach, missing many cases of PTSD, and when added to the symptom-cluster approach would make the combined approach more specific but less sensitive as well.

Patient Health Questionnaire. Out of 13 studies that have assessed major depression, seven used servicemembers' self-reports on the Patient Health Questionaire-9 (PHQ-9). The PHQ-9 is a 9-item questionnaire that asks respondents how often they have been bothered by each of nine symptoms of depression (e.g., trouble falling or staying asleep, or sleeping too much). Response options include not at all (=0), several days (=1), more than half the days (=2), or nearly every day (=3) during a specified period of time, typically in the past two weeks. Cases of major depression can be identified when respondents report five or more of the nine items as occurring more than half the days or nearly every day, including reports of either depressed mood or *anhedonia* (defined as loss of pleasure in once-pleasurable activities). This criterion correctly identifies 73 percent of persons with major depression and 94 percent of those without major depression (Spitzer, Kroenke, and Williams, 1999) and was the scoring method used for each of the seven studies that used the PHQ-9. In addition, five of these studies required that respondents also report *functional impairment* (FI), which is defined as impairment in work, at home, or in interpersonal functioning, to be identified as cases of depression. Imposing the functional-impairment requirement in addition to reporting five or more symptoms has not been validated against clinical interviews. It is virtually inevitable, however, that these screening criteria would be less sensitive, although they may be more specific, because they raise the threshold for detecting a case. Thus, this approach would not identify a substantial number of persons with major depression, meaning that they would be excluded from prevalence estimates.

An alternative approach for using the PHQ-9 to identify cases of major depression is to require a total score of ten or above across all nine items. Using this approach, nearly all actual cases of major depression are correctly identified as having the disorder (sensitivity >0.99), although approximately 9 percent of persons without major depression are incorrectly identified as having the disorder (specificity=0.91; Kroenke and Spitzer, 2002). In our review, no studies used this more-sensitive, but less-specific, approach.

Other Instruments. In a few studies, other instruments were used to identify cases of PTSD and depression. For PTSD, Lapierre, Schwegler, and LaBauve (2007) used the Screen for Posttraumatic Stress Symptoms (SPTSS), which is rarely used and has only been validated once (established sensitivity=0.94; specificity=0.60) (Carlson, 2001). In addition to their structured diagnostic interview, Engelhard et al. (2007) used a cutoff score of 14 on the PTSD Symptom Scale (PSS) (established sensitivity=0.91; specificity=0.62; Coffey et al., 2006). While both of these tools are very sensitive, meaning that they are identifying most people with PTSD correctly, the low specificities indicate that a substantial number of those without the disorder are being classified as having PTSD. For depression, one study (Vasterling et al., 2006) used the 9-item and one study (Lapierre, Schwegler, and LaBauve, 2007) used the 20-item versions of the Center for Epidemiologic Studies Depression Inventory (CES-D). The scoring methods used for both scales correctly identify the same proportion of persons with depression (established sensitivities=0.72), although the scoring method for the 9-item CES-D is better at correctly identifying persons without depression than the scoring method used with the 20-item CES-D (established specificity for 9-item CES-D=0.86; established specificity for 20-item CES-D=0.71; Santor and Coyne, 1997). Finally, one government study of Army soldiers assessed in theater does not contain the definitional criteria that would typically be included in scientific studies (Mental Health Advisory Team 1 [MHAT-I]). However, in this study, the authors write that persons had to report experiencing "several" items on the PHQ *and* report that symptoms caused functional impairment (e.g., symptoms affected their work).

Post-Deployment Health Assessment. Three studies analyzed data from the Post-Deployment Health Assessment (PDHA) and/or Post-Deployment Health Re-Assessment (PDHRA) (we define these assessments in more detail further below) (Hoge et al., 2007; Martin, 2007; Milliken, Auchterlonie, and Hoge, 2007). To identify cases of PTSD, both the PDHA and PDHRA assessments contain the Primary Care–PTSD (PC-PTSD), which is a 4-item subscale of the PCL with yes/no response options. Reporting "yes" to two of the four items can be used to identify cases with a sensitivity of 0.91 and specificity of 0.72, meaning that 91 percent of cases of PTSD are correctly identified, although 28 percent of those without PTSD screen positive for the disorder (Prins et al., 2004). The PDHA and PDHRA also contain the PHQ-2, which is a subscale of the PHQ-9, containing the two questions relating to depressed mood and anhedonia. A positive response to one of these questions is valid for identifying cases of major depression with a sensitivity of 0.83 and specificity of 0.92, meaning that 83 percent of cases of major depression are correctly identified, and 8 percent of those without the disorder screen positive for it (Kroenke, Spitzer, and Williams, 2003).

Self-Reports of Head Injury. Two studies estimated the prevalence of mild traumatic brain injury. The first (Vasterling et al., 2006) used a question that asked whether the respondent had suffered a prior head injury with loss of consciousness lasting longer than 15 minutes. The other (Hoge et al., 2008) identified respondents as having mild TBI if they reported a head injury and one of the following three conditions: (1) loss of consciousness; (2) being dazed, confused, or "seeing stars"; or (3) not remembering the injury. While some preliminary evidence suggests that these screening criteria are valid for identifying cases of mild TBI (Schwab et al., 2007), more thorough validation of these tools is needed.

Mental and Cognitive Conditions Pre-Deployment

To better interpret post-deployment mental health and cognitive conditions, it is helpful to understand the rates of mental and cognitive conditions among military personnel before their deployment. Three studies have assessed the prevalence of PTSD, depression, and/or TBI among servicemembers before their deployment to Iraq. Vasterling et al. (2006) found that approximately 75 days prior to deployment, the mean score on the PCL was 29, which is significantly lower than those cutoff values recommended to classify individuals with and without PTSD (Blanchard et al., 1996). This study did not present the percentage who met criteria for probable PTSD or depression. These authors also showed that, prior to deployment, there was no difference in the prevalence of *mild TBI*, which they defined as a head injury with loss of consciousness for more than 15 minutes, between servicemembers who later were deployed and a comparison group that were not deployed, with an estimated prevalence of mild TBI around 5 percent.

Hoge et al. (2004) assessed 2,530 Army soldiers one week before their deployment and reported that 9 percent screened positive for PTSD using the symptom-cluster method and 11 percent screened positive for depression regardless of functional impairment. Finally, in a random sample of servicemembers across the United States that excluded anyone who had already deployed to Afghanistan/Iraq, as well as those who responded to the baseline or follow-up questionnaires during deployment, 5 percent met criteria for PTSD using the symptom-cluster method of scoring the PCL prior to being deployed, although only approximately one-quarter of this sample was eventually deployed (Smith et al., 2008).

Mental and Cognitive Conditions in Theater

In July 2003 and three times thereafter (July 2004, 2005, and 2006), the U.S. Army Surgeon General chartered Mental Health Advisory Teams to produce reports on mental health issues related to deployment to Iraq. Although in the rest of the review we rely primarily on peer-reviewed publications, we include these reports also because they are the only ones that assessed the prevalence of PTSD and depression among servicemembers in theater. Note, however, that over the course of these multiple assessments in theater, the nature of the conflicts changed. As we described in Chapter Two, the first phase of OIF involved troop buildup and major combat operations, which was followed by a period of relative calm before a growth in insurgency. Thus, the nature of the risks confronting a servicemember during this conflict changed over time. The MHAT reports specifically focused on *Army brigade combat teams* in Iraq; the first two of these reports also included soldiers in Kuwait in areas with high levels of occupational stress, and the final report also included a sample of marines who served with regimental combat teams in Iraq. The MHAT reports use the PCL to identify cases of what the authors term "acute stress"—but not PTSD—to describe PTSD-like symptoms reported in a combat zone. Prevalence estimates of acute stress were around 15 percent across all MHAT assessments, except when data were collected in 2004 (MHAT-II), when the prevalence of acute stress was around 10 percent. Rates of depression, measured with the PHQ-9, in theater also were relatively constant across the MHAT samples, with between 5 and 9 percent of troops meeting probable diagnostic criteria. Although the MHAT studies provide estimates of stress reactions experienced by servicemembers in theater, it is unclear how they relate to symptoms that emerge or continue when servicemembers are removed from the combat environment (U.S. Department of the Army, Office of the Surgeon General, 2003, 2005; U.S. Department of the Army, Office of the Surgeon, Multinational Force–Iraq and Office of the Surgeon General, U.S. Army Medical Command, 2006a, 2006b).

Mental and Cognitive Conditions Post-Deployment

The remaining studies estimated the prevalence of mental health and cognitive conditions post-deployment, but they varied with respect to the average interval between returning from deployment and assessment. Together, these studies generally reveal that the estimated prevalence of PTSD and depression increases as the time from returning from deployment increases. In addition, there are few peer-reviewed studies on TBI, leaving much unknown about the prevalence of this condition.

Prevalence estimates of PTSD and depression are available for servicemembers immediately upon their return from deployment. In April 2003, the Department of Defense (DoD) mandated that, immediately upon returning from deployment, all servicemembers complete a Post Deployment Health Assessment questionnaire. Servicemembers generally fill out these questionnaires before leaving the country in which they are deployed or within two weeks of returning home (Hoge, Auchterlonie, and Milliken, 2006). The PDHA uses the PC-PTSD and PHQ-2, which have low specificities and are therefore likely to incorrectly screen positive for PTSD and depression, respectively, many persons who do not actually have these conditions.

Three studies used data from samples that were assessed with the PDHA (Hoge, Auchterlonie, and Milliken, 2006; Martin, 2007; Milliken, Auchterlonie, and Hoge, 2007). Only one study included servicemembers returning from Afghanistan. It estimated that 5 percent of servicemembers returning from Afghanistan screened positive for PTSD (Hoge, Auchterlonie, and Milliken, 2006). All three studies indicated that approximately 10 percent of those returning from Iraq screened positive for PTSD. For depression, one study indicated that 3 percent of those returning from Afghanistan and 5 percent of those returning from Iraq screened positive on the PDHA (Hoge, Auchterlonie, and Milliken, 2006); a separate study indicated that 4 percent of the Army National Guard and reservists returning from Iraq and 5 percent of Army soldiers from the Active Component screened positive for depression on the PDHA (Milliken, Auchterlonie, and Hoge, 2007).

When troops return home, there may be a disincentive for reporting mental health symptoms on the PDHA. For example, servicemembers may worry that answering "yes" to questions about mental health problems may delay their return to their family and friends. In addition, many symptoms of psychiatric disorders may develop over time and not be present immediately upon returning. Because of this situation, in 2006 DoD began reassessing returning servicemembers three to six months after returning from deployment, using a tool similar to the PDHA, the Post-Deployment Health Reassessment. Among one cohort of 88,235 Army soldiers who completed both the PDHA and PDHRA, a greater proportion screened positive for PTSD on the PDHRA (17 percent of the Active Component and 25 percent of the Reserve Component) than on the PDHA (12 percent of the Active Component and 13 percent of the Reserve Component). The proportion screening positive for depression among this cohort also increased from 5 percent to 10 percent among Active Component Army soldiers and from 4 percent to 13 percent among members of the Army Reserve Component (Milliken, Auchterlonie, and Hoge, 2007). In separate analyses using the PDHRA, 16 percent of 96,934 servicemembers screened positive for PTSD (Martin, 2007). In this study, approximately 94 percent of those who had PDHRA assessments had PDHAs: Of those who screened positive for PTSD on the PDHRA, 30 percent had screened positive for PTSD on the PDHA. These findings mean that approximately two-thirds of persons screening positive for PTSD on the PDHRA were new cases (Martin, 2007).

In addition to those studies that used the PDHRA, two additional studies assessed the same cohort of servicemembers at multiple times post-deployment (i.e., longitudinal studies). Grieger et al. (2006) followed a cohort of wounded soldiers evacuated from combat between March 2003 and September 2004. At one month post-injury, 4 percent met criteria for PTSD and a similar proportion met criteria for depression; 2 percent met criteria for co-morbid PTSD and depression. At four months, the proportion of persons meeting criteria for PTSD and depression increased to 12 percent and 9 percent, respectively; 8 percent met criteria for co-morbid PTSD and depression, estimates that remained relatively unchanged at seven months (Grieger et al., 2006). The other longitudinal study was of soldiers from three Dutch infantry army battalions assessed at five and 15 months after returning from Iraq. In this sample, the mean level of depression was stable at both assessments, whereas the mean level of PTSD symptoms tended to be lower at 15 months than at five months (Engelhard et al., 2007).

Three post-deployment studies employed *cross-sectional survey designs*, in which subjects were interviewed only once within six months from servicemembers' returning from deployment. Hoge et al. (2004) studied the prevalence of PTSD and depression among an Army sample three or four months after returning from deployment to Afghanistan, and separate Army and Marine Corps samples three or four months after returning from deployment to Iraq. When using the symptom-cluster method to identify cases, they found that 12 percent of Army soldiers returning from Afghanistan met criteria for PTSD and 14 percent met criteria for depression, regardless of functional status. Using the same case definitions, they found that 18 percent of the

Army sample met criteria for PTSD upon returning from Iraq and 15 percent met criteria for depression; among marines, 20 percent met criteria for PTSD and 15 percent met criteria for depression upon returning from Iraq. Vasterling et al. (2006) indicate that the mean time interval between returning from deployment and assessment was 73 days, and most intervals ranged between 58 and 84 days. In this study, 12 percent met criteria for PTSD using a cutoff point of 50 in addition to the symptom-cluster scoring, and 25 percent met criteria for depression. In a separate study of Army soldiers attending a reintegration program five to eight weeks after returning from deployment, Lapierre, Schwegler, and LaBauve (2007) estimated that the prevalence of PTSD was 31 percent among those returning from Iraq and 30 percent among those returning from Afghanistan. However, as mentioned earlier in this chapter, the screening tool these researchers used includes a large number of people screening positive for PTSD who do not actually have the disorder.

The remaining studies generally assessed symptoms around one year after servicemembers' returned from deployment. When assessed at least one year after returning from Iraq and neighboring areas, 4 percent of UK servicemembers met criteria for PTSD using a cutpoint of 50 on the PCL and 20 percent met criteria for an "unspecified" [sic] common mental health condition (Hotopf et al., 2006). Studies of U.S. troops, however, produce much larger estimates. Hoge et al. (2007) found that 17 percent of Army soldiers met criteria for PTSD one year after returning home, using a cutpoint of 50, in addition to the symptom-cluster method on the PCL. Abt Associates mailed surveys between July and December 2004 to military personnel in the Active Component who had deployed to Iraq on or after January 2003 and returned from theater by February 2004, meaning that assessments generally occurred between six and 12 months after returning from deployment. Among the 43 percent of 3,329 deployed servicemembers who responded to the survey, 7 percent met screening criteria for PTSD using the symptom-cluster scoring method alone. Taken together, these studies reveal that the prevalence of both PTSD and depression seems to increase as the time from returning from deployment increases.

Three studies identified PTSD cases using medical records among U.S. veterans who served in Afghanistan or Iraq and sought medical care at the Veterans Administration (VA), a patient population likely to include servicemembers with widely ranging intervals since returning from Afghanistan or Iraq. Seal et al. (2007) reviewed records of veterans specifically from Afghanistan and Iraq who sought any type of inpatient or outpatient care at a VA health care facility between September 2001 and September 2005. Among 103,788 veterans with VA records, 13 percent had a diagnosis code for PTSD and 5 percent had a diagnosis code for depression. Helmer and colleagues (2007) reviewed charts from 56 veterans seeking care at the New Jersey War-Related Injury and Illness Center (NJ-WRIIC) from June 2004 to January 2006; definite or probable PTSD diagnoses were documented in the final impression sections of 45 percent of the abstracted charts. Rosenheck and Fontana (2007) also reviewed VA records but were not able to specifically identify those who were veterans from Afghanistan and Iraq. Instead, their sample termed probable OEF/OIF veterans as individuals born after 1972 who had their first VA outpatient encounter occur in 1991 or after. Among these individuals, there was a 232-percent increase in PTSD diagnoses between 2003 and 2005.

The remaining four studies do not indicate when their assessments took place with respect to servicemembers' return from deployment. As with those studies using medical records, these studies are also likely to include servicemembers with widely ranging intervals since returning. Erbes et al. (2007) surveyed OEF/OIF veterans who enrolled for care at the Minneapolis VA Medical Center (MVAMC) and who were not already accessing mental health care at the VA: Of those who responded, 12 percent screened positive for PTSD. Smith et al. (2008) assessed their cohort of servicemembers twice, roughly three years apart, but they do not explicitly present the proportion of servicemembers who deployed and developed PTSD between the two assessments. Instead, they report that, among those who did not have PTSD symptoms at baseline and deployed to Afghanistan or Iraq, 9 percent of those who reported combat exposure and 2 percent of those who did not report combat exposure developed PTSD. Among those who screened positive for PTSD at baseline and were deployed, 48 percent of those who reported combat exposure met criteria for PTSD, as did 22 percent of those without combat exposure. Kolkow et al. (2007) assessed military health care workers at a Naval Medical Center, 9 percent of whom met criteria for PTSD and 5 percent of whom met criteria for depression.

Our review identified only two *peer-reviewed studies* (i.e., studies that have been subjected to review by experts in the field before they are published) that attempted to estimate the prevalence of TBI. Vasterling et al. (2006) asked respondents whether they suffered a head injury with a related loss of consciousness lasting more than 15 minutes. When assessed in 2005 at around 2.5 months after returning from deployment, 8 percent of deployed troops reported having such an injury over a period that included the duration of their deployment compared with a prevalence of 4 percent among nondeployed servicemembers over a corresponding interval. Hoge et al. (2008) estimated that, in 2006, three or four months after returning from Iraq, 15 percent of Army soldiers reported a head injury during deployment that was accompanied by loss of consciousness or altered mental status (i.e., being dazed, confused, or "seeing stars," or not remembering the injury).

The only other reference we found that indicated the prevalence of TBI among deployed servicemembers was taken from reports that document reasons for medical evacuations from Afghanistan and Iraq (Fischer and Library of Congress, 2006). As of March 31, 2006, there were 1,179 TBIs among evacuees, 96 percent of which were sustained in Iraq and 4 percent, in Afghanistan. This report, published by the Congressional Research Service, provides no information on how it defines TBI and whether these numbers represent cases of mild TBI.

The other source of information on the prevalence of TBI comes from post-deployment screenings performed at select military bases. To our knowledge, those estimates have not yet been presented in peer-reviewed publications and thus may be less reliable. According to a report described in *USA Today*, 10 percent of 7,909 marines with the 1st Marine Division at Camp Pendleton, California, suffered brain injuries and 84 percent of 500 troops who suffered concussions were still suffering symptoms an average of ten months after the injury (Zoroya, 2006). At Fort Irwin, also in California, 1,490 soldiers were screened, and almost 12 percent suffered concussions during their combat tours (Zoroya, 2006).

Emergent Themes

We identified a number of emergent themes from this literature. We discuss each below.

- *There is limited research on the prevalence of traumatic brain injury, owing to assessment difficulties, case definitions, and restrictions on the release of such information.*

Research on the prevalence of traumatic brain injury among returning troops is sparse. This may be due in part to methodological constraints that hinder efforts to estimate the prevalence of TBI in epidemiological surveys. Although identifying penetrating brain injuries is a relatively straightforward procedure, estimating the prevalence of closed head injuries (when an object hits the head but does not break the skull) and primary blast injuries (injuries caused by wave-induced changes in atmospheric pressure) is difficult, even though such injuries are anecdotally noted as extremely prevalent among returning servicemembers (Warden, 2006; Murray et al., 2005). In addition, definitions for TBI subtypes, particularly mild TBI, are relatively broad. In the two peer-reviewed studies we found that examined prevalence of brain injury, Vasterling et al. (2006) identified those with a head injury with loss of consciousness for more than 15 minutes, whereas Hoge et al. (2008) used a definition that could include loss of consciousness or altered mental status. In addition, symptoms of mild TBI often overlap with those of other conditions, including PTSD (Colarusso, 2007).

Current TBI-screening initiatives will provide useful information on the prevalence of this condition among servicemembers returning from Afghanistan and Iraq. Most notably, as of December 2007 the PDHA and PDHRA include questions regarding symptoms of mild TBI. In addition, routine TBI screenings are conducted in theater among all Army soldiers exposed to a blast, at Landstuhl Regional Medical Center in Germany among all servicemembers medically evacuated from Afghanistan or Iraq when the reason for evacuation is something other than a psychiatric diagnosis, and at Walter Reed Army Medical Center among anyone medically evacuated due to an injury caused by a blast, motor vehicle accident, fall, or gunshot wound to head or neck (The Traumatic Brain Injury Task Force, 2007; Warden, 2006). In addition, uniform screenings are being conducted among all those returning to Fort Carson in Colorado from deployment. When released, the results of these screenings will be important sources of data, although some may have limited utility. Prevalence estimates based on screenings conducted among those who have been medically evacuated may overlook persons with mild-to-moderate closed head injuries (Warden, 2006), and those conducted among servicemembers returning to Fort Carson may not be generalizable to personnel returning to other military bases.

- *Most existing studies define cases of PTSD and depression using criteria that have not been validated, that are not commonly used in population-based studies of civilians, and that are likely to exclude a significant number of servicemembers who have these conditions.*

The majority of studies identify cases of PTSD and depression using methods that Hoge et al. (2004) term "strict" criteria but that have not been validated against clinical diagnoses. For PTSD, studies applied a combination of two approaches that have been validated independently of one another (i.e., meeting symptom-cluster criteria and requiring a total score above 50 on the PCL). As stated earlier in this chapter, imposing a cutpoint of 50 on the PCL alone correctly identifies only around 60 percent of persons who have PTSD (Andrykowski et al., 1998). For depression, most studies required that respondents report significant functional impairment in addition to DSM-IV depressive symptoms on the PHQ-9; however, even without requiring significant functional impairment, this method identifies only 73 percent of depressed cases (Spitzer, Kroenke, and Williams, 1999). The failure of these criteria alone to identify a substantial number of individuals with these two conditions who may need treatment and other services is why most epidemiological studies of civilians use criteria that is more sensitive but less specific, such as symptom-cluster criteria (e.g., Jaycox, Marshall, and Schell, 2004) or a total-score cutpoint of 44 (e.g., Zatzick et al., 2002; Walker et al., 2003) on the PCL to identify cases of PTSD, and a total cutpoint of 10 on the PHQ-9 to identify cases of probable depression (e.g., Ruo et al., 2003).

By imposing additional requirements on tools that already miss a substantial number of actual cases, we can surmise that estimates of PTSD and depression from these studies are likely underestimating the actual prevalence of these conditions. Two studies that apply two sets of criteria for identifying PTSD and one study that applies two sets of criteria for identifying cases of depression show such underestimation empirically. Using the symptom-cluster method only, Hoge et al. (2004) estimate that the post-deployment prevalence of PTSD among Army soldiers is 18 percent; it is 13 percent using the symptom-cluster method plus the 50-point cutoff. Among the same group, estimates of depression are 15 percent without and 8 percent with the functional-impairment requirement. Smith and colleagues (2008) also report both sets of numbers for PTSD: When a cutoff score of 50 is required in addition to symptom-cluster criteria, they estimate that 8 percent of those deployed with combat exposure develop PTSD; however, when this cutoff is not required, 9 percent of those without are estimated to develop PTSD. Stringent screening criteria will miss not only actual cases of PTSD and depression but also *subthreshold cases*, individuals with symptoms of PTSD or depression who do not meet the established case definition yet who experience significant impairment. Identifying subthreshold cases of PTSD and depression is important, since interventions and treatment aimed at these cases can reduce symptomatology and prevent progression to full diagnoses (Cuijpers, Smit, and van Straten, 2007; Marshall et al., 2001).

- *Army soldiers were the most-frequently sampled servicemembers, although most studies employed convenience samples, which are not generalizable to the total deployed force.*

Army soldiers make up the largest share of military personnel in Afghanistan and Iraq (O'Bryant, 2006, 2007) and also are the servicemembers most frequently studied with respect to deployment-related mental and cognitive health. Among studies of U.S. servicemembers, almost half focused exclusively on Army soldiers (i.e., Grieger et al., 2006; Vasterling et al., 2006; Hoge et al., 2007; Milliken, Auchterlonie, and Hoge, 2007; Lapierre, Schwegler, and LaBauve, 2007; Hoge et al., 2008; and U.S. Department of the Army, Office of the Surgeon General, 2003, 2005; U.S. Department of the Army, Office of the Surgeon, Multinational Force–Iraq, and Office of the Surgeon General, U.S. Army Medical Command, 2006a). Three studies focused on samples of only Army soldiers and marines (Hoge et al. 2004; Hoge, Auchterlonie, and Milliken; and U.S. Department of the Army, Office of the Surgeon, Multinational Force–Iraq, and Office of the Surgeon General, 2006b). The remaining seven studies either examined medical records or drew samples from all deployed armed-forces personnel accessing medical care in the VA (Seal et al., 2007; Rosenheck and Fontana, 2007; Erbes et al., 2007; Helmer et al., 2007) or were samples that contained members from all services (Martin, 2007; Smith et al., 2008; Abt Associates, 2006).

With respect to military component, most studies contained a mix of servicemembers from the Reserve and Active Components, although the Reserve Component was generally underrepresented with respect to the total deployed force. One study (Abt Associates, 2006) sampled only members of the Active Component; we suspect that four additional studies restricted their samples to members of the Active Component, although the authors did not provide specific information to make this distinction (Hoge et al., 2004; Vasterling et al., 2006; Hoge et al., 2007; Lapierre, Schwegler, and LaBauve, 2007). Two of these indicated that they sampled "active duty" soldiers (Vasterling et al., 2006; Lapierre, Schwegler, and LaBauve, 2007); however, because

Reserve/National Guard personnel are considered "activated" and therefore on "active duty" when deployed, these terms are ambiguous for making this distinction.

Only a handful of studies can be considered generalizable to all troops deployed to Afghanistan or Iraq. Studies that used the PDHA (Hoge, Auchterlonie, and Milliken, 2006) or the PDHA combined with the PDHRA (Martin, 2007; Milliken, Auchterlonie, and Hoge, 2007) should be generalizable to the larger population of servicemembers they represent, because completion of these assessments is required by DoD. However, Martin (2007) could only identify 77 percent of PDHAs among servicemembers returning from Iraq in 2005, and that fewer males, servicemembers of younger ages, members of the Marine Corps and Navy/Coast Guard, and members of the Active Component completed these assessments than did their counterparts.

Three studies used surveys administered to random samples of servicemembers: U.S. military personnel from the Active Component (Abt Associates., 2006), UK servicemembers (Hotopf et al., 2006), and all U.S. military personnel (Smith et al., 2008). Each of these population-based studies of servicemembers suffers from low participation rates (49 percent in the study by Abt Associates, 2006; 61 percent in Hotopf et al., 2006; and 36 percent in Smith et al., 2008). In the UK sample (Hotopf et al., 2006), younger servicemembers, males, members of the Air Force and Navy, noncommissioned officers, reservists, and non-Whites were less likely to respond than were their counterparts; however, these authors adjusted for these differential response rates when presenting their results. In contrast, the study of all U.S. military personnel (Smith et al., 2008) oversamples females, those previously deployed, and Reserve/National Guard personnel, and also overrepresents Air Force personnel relative to the actual deployed U.S. force; in presenting their results, the authors make no efforts to adjust for this sampling design.

Most of the other studies used convenience samples or reviewed the medical records of those in treatment contact, two methods that systematically exclude important segments of the population. For instance, samples were focused on specific military *units* that were scheduled to be deployed or likely to be deployed (Hoge et al., 2004; Vasterling et al., 2006), were deployed with a high likelihood of combat exposure or operational stress (MHATs I–IV, U.S. Department of the Army, Office of the Surgeon General, 2003, 2005; U.S. Department of the Army, Office of the Surgeon, Multinational Force–Iraq, and Office of the Surgeon General, U.S. Army Medical Command, 2006a, 2006b), or had returned from deployment (Hoge et al., 2004; Hoge et al., 2007; Lapierre, Schwegler, and LaBauve, 2007). Studying military units post-deployment is likely to exclude servicemembers who are at highest risk for mental health problems, such as those with severe injuries or those who have separated from military service. In addition, Hotopf et al. (2006) hypothesize that sampling procedures may be the underlying reason why rates of PTSD in the UK sample are so much lower than among the U.S. samples. They suggest that the U.S. samples may focus on troops more likely to have combat roles than a random sample of all servicemembers that encompasses those in both combat service and combat service support (units that provide operational and logistical support, respectively, to combat elements) (Hotopf et al., 2006). Studies relying on chart reviews or samples drawn from servicemembers seeking treatment in the VA also have limited generalizability because they do not include veterans who do not seek care at the VA.

In addition to these studies' limited generalizability, most studies suffer from other limitations common to many epidemiological studies. For example, for all of the post-deployment studies, individuals with the most significant mental health problems may be unavailable, unable, or unwilling to participate in the survey, a bias that leads to more-conservative estimates of prevalence than is actually the case. On the other hand, the healthiest servicemembers may be those who are deployed more than once, and therefore less likely to be surveyed during a post-deployment assessment. If this is the case, these studies would yield overestimates of the prevalence of these conditions.

The same problem applies to longitudinal studies, for which those persons lost to follow-up are likely to be systematically different from those who participated in follow-up assessments. Both studies that analyzed data from the PDHRA present the proportion of those with PDHRAs who had completed PDHAs, but neither presents the proportion of those with PDHAs who are missing PDHRAs, and it is unclear who is being missed in the PDHRA (Martin, 2007; Milliken, Auchterlonie, and Hoge, 2007). Other longitudinal studies also suffered from attrition. Only 72 percent of deployed soldiers participated in the second wave of the study of post-deployment neuropsychological outcomes by Vasterling et al. (2006). Separation from military service was the most common reason for nonresponse in that sample; also, many did not respond because they were redeployed or on leave. In the sample of wounded servicemembers, 72 percent of those interviewed at wave 1 were assessed at wave 2 (four months), 61 percent were assessed at wave 3 (seven months), and only 50 percent were interviewed at all three assessments; the authors report no differences in probable PTSD or depression at one month among those lost to follow-up (Grieger et al., 2006). Finally, in the cohort study by Smith and colleagues (2008), more than 25 percent of the study sample was lost to follow-up at the year 3 assessment.

- *Regardless of the sample, measurement tool, or time of assessment, combat duty and being wounded were consistently associated with positive screens for PTSD.*

Many studies asked servicemembers about combat exposure, such as having been shot at, handling dead bodies, knowing someone who was killed, killing enemy combatants, or discharging one's weapon. When measures such as these were included in multivariate regression models, they were consistently associated with increased likelihood of screening positive for PTSD (Grieger et al., 2006; Hoge, Auchterlonie, and Milliken, 2006; Hoge et al., 2004; Hotopf et al., 2006; Kolkow et al., 2007; U.S. Department of the Army, Office of the Surgeon, Multinational Force–Iraq, 2006b).

In addition, Smith et al. (2008) found that, for persons without PTSD at baseline who were deployed, 9 percent of those who were exposed to combat reported symptoms of PTSD at follow-up versus 2 percent of those who did not report combat exposures. Given the changing nature of risks confronting servicemembers during these conflicts (see Chapter Two), servicemembers from different deployment cycles may report different exposures and rates of PTSD.

The longitudinal study of wounded soldiers indicates, however, that the effect of combat exposure on PTSD may vary as the time from returning from deployment increases, because combat exposure was associated with PTSD one month after injury but not at four or seven months (Grieger et al., 2006). Similarly, combat exposure may differ by deployment to Afghanistan or Iraq: Hoge, Auchterlonie, and Milliken (2006) found that combat experience was only associated with PTSD in the sample of servicemembers deployed to Iraq but not Afghanistan. In contrast, combat exposure was only associated with depression in one of 11 studies that contained measures of depression (U.S. Department of the Army, Office of the Surgeon, Multinational Force–Iraq, 2006b). Having suffered an injury or being wounded was also associated with an increased likelihood of PTSD across studies (Hoge, Auchterlonie, and Milliken, 2006; Hoge et al., 2004; Hoge et al., 2007). Among soldiers who were wounded, those with more severe physical symptoms were most likely to have PTSD and depression at four and seven months post-injury, and more severe physical symptoms at one month predicted PTSD at seven months (Grieger et al., 2006).

Aside from these consistent correlates of PTSD, studies also highlighted features that appeared to increase the risk of PTSD or depression among their samples. Young age, such as being under 25, was associated with PTSD in two studies (Grieger et al., 2006; Seal et al., 2007), although those younger than 20 were *least likely* to screen positive for PTSD in analyses using the PDHA (Martin, 2007). In MHAT-I (U.S. Department of the Army, Office of the Surgeon General, 2003) and in the study by Abt Associates (2006), reports of low personal and unit morale and lower unit cohesion were linked to increased reports of PTSD symptoms. Some studies that examined differences by component found that reservists often were more likely to report symptoms of PTSD than members of the Active Component (Milliken, Auchterlonie, and Hoge, 2007; Martin, 2007; Helmer et al., 2007). Junior enlisted servicemembers may also be at increased risk for PTSD (Martin, 2007; Smith et al., 2008) and TBI (Hoge et al., 2008) relative to more senior ranking servicemembers. In one study, medical officers faced an increased risk of developing PTSD (Martin, 2007). Finally, having been deployed more than once was associated with acute stress in the two later MHAT reports, when data were collected in 2005 and 2006; multiple deployments were associated with depression in the MHAT-III report (data collected in 2005); and being deployed for more than six months was associated with both acute stress and depression in the final MHAT report, conducted in fall 2006 (U.S. Department of the Army,

Office of the Surgeon, Multinational Force–Iraq, and Office of the Surgeon General, U.S. Army Medical Command, 2006a, 2006b).

• *When comparisons are available, servicemembers deployed to Iraq appear to be at higher risk for PTSD than servicemembers deployed to Afghanistan.*

Many studies attempted to draw comparisons between groups of servicemembers to identify variables associated with differences in the prevalence of disorders across groups. In studies that included servicemembers deployed to Afghanistan, Iraq, or another location, those deployed to Iraq were consistently more likely to report PTSD, although such reports are likely due to the increased likelihood of combat exposure among servicemembers in Iraq (Abt Associates, 2006; Hoge, Auchterlonie, and Milliken, 2006; Hoge et al., 2004; Lapierre, Schwegler, and LaBauve, 2007; U.S. Department of the Army, Office of the Surgeon General, 2005). The results of the MHAT reports were compared with each other to discern whether, over the period in which the four studies were conducted, rates of PTSD and depression increased or decreased among servicemembers in theater. Among Army soldiers interviewed in 2004 (MHAT-II) rates of PTSD were lower than they were when interviewed in 2003 (MHAT-I), although rates of depression were not significantly different. There were no differences between rates of either PTSD or depression in MHAT-I and MHATs III and IV.

Other studies attempted to investigate whether deployment has a *causal* influence on PTSD and depression. To properly conduct such an assessment would involve a longitudinal study among a cohort of soldiers assessed both before and after deployment, and preferably a control group that did not deploy, to ensure that there is no effect unrelated to deployment over the specified interval. Only two studies were designed in this way. One of them (Vasterling et al., 2006) did not present whether the prevalence of PTSD or depression increased among the sample post-deployment. Smith et al. (2008), on the other hand, did show that, among those who did not have PTSD at baseline, those who deployed were three times more likely to develop PTSD than those who did not deploy.

Other studies have compared rates of PTSD and depression across different samples to assess whether rates of these outcomes are different among those who have served in Afghanistan or Iraq and those about to be deployed (Hoge et al., 2004), or among servicemembers who were not deployed at the same time (Abt Associates, 2006; Hotopf et al., 2006). Hoge et al. (2004) found that Army and Marine Corps units assessed after returning from deployment to Iraq had higher rates of PTSD and depression than an Army unit scheduled to deploy to Iraq in one week's time. The Abt Associates study (2006) found that 7 percent of deployed military personnel from the Active Component screened positive relative to 4 percent of nondeployed Active Component personnel, and that the average value across all items on the PCL was also higher among deployed servicemembers than among the nondeployed group. On the other hand, Hotopf and colleagues (2006) found no difference in PTSD or other mental health outcomes among deployed and nondeployed servicemembers from the United Kingdom. None of these studies adjusted for differing baseline characteristics, which may make one group more likely than the other to report mental health or cognitive conditions. Thus, although the studies have provided evidence that the prevalence of PTSD and depression is greater post-deployment, no study has yet been able to provide evidence of a causal relationship.

Discussion

Assembling and critically reviewing the existing epidemiological studies that have examined mental and cognitive conditions among servicemembers deployed to Afghanistan and Iraq allowed us to address several specific objectives of the current chapter. Below, we describe consistencies and inconsistencies across studies, identify the strengths and weaknesses of the studies, and conclude by proposing future research directions.

Consistencies and Inconsistencies Across Studies

The assembled research to date on the prevalence of post-combat mental health and cognitive conditions among servicemembers deployed to Afghanistan and Iraq supports five broad generalizations.

First, PTSD is more prevalent than depression among deployed servicemembers, and it affects roughly 5 to 15 percent of servicemembers, depending on who is assessed and when they are assessed; the prevalence of depression among servicemembers ranges from 2 to 10 percent, also depending on when assessment occurs and who is assessed. We acknowledge that some studies have yielded prevalence estimates that extend beyond these intervals and have chosen these intervals from the group of studies as a whole, relying more heavily upon those that we consider most representative of the deployed population and considering carefully the methods that study authors used to identify cases. Second, many studies employ the same screening tools, making prevalence estimates across studies generally comparable. Therefore, variability across studies is likely due to differences in study samples or the time of assessment. However, the criteria used across most of these studies to identify PTSD and depression have not been validated and do not identify a substantial portion of those who actually have these conditions. Third, because different studies have been conducted at different periods during deployment and post-deployment, comparing across studies suggests that the prevalence of PTSD and depression increases as the time since returning from deployment increases. Fourth, across studies, servicemembers who experience combat exposure and who have been wounded are more likely to meet criteria for PTSD. Fifth, servicemembers deployed to Afghanistan and Iraq are more likely to meet criteria for PTSD and depression than nondeployed troops, although those deployed to Iraq have higher rates of PTSD and depression than those deployed to Afghanistan.

For the purposes of allocating funds and services, policymakers will want to know how many returning servicemembers will likely meet diagnostic criteria for PTSD, depression, and TBI by the end of OEF and OIF, and whether or not these individuals sought treatment or can be persuaded to seek treatment. This number will help inform projections of workforce and capacity requirements for meeting potential demand. Providing this number, however, is difficult, owing to the methodological limitations of the epidemiological studies we have reviewed. Studies with the most-sensitive screening criteria have not been conducted among samples representative of the entire deployed population, and those studies that are most generalizable (Hoge, Auchterlonie, and Milliken, 2006; Martin, 2007; Milliken, Auchterlonie, and Hoge, 2007) use a screening tool that is likely to incorrectly identify some persons without PTSD or depression as having these conditions.

If we apply the range of prevalence estimates for PTSD (5 to 15 percent) and depression (2 to 10 percent) to the 1.64 million servicemembers who have already been deployed, we can estimate that the number of servicemembers returning home with PTSD will range from 75,000 to 225,000 and with depression, from 30,000 to 150,000. The precise number depends on how many of all deployed servicemembers are at increased risk for these outcomes—specifically, the percentage of those deployed with direct combat experience, those who have been wounded, and the military service of which they are a part. Note, however, that the most-generalizable studies estimated that the prevalence of PTSD fell almost midway in this range and at the lower end of the range for depression. If we were to use the median value between the range of servicemembers likely to have PTSD, we would arrive at a figure of 150,000. As we reiterate throughout this chapter, we do not yet have a sound basis for estimating numbers for TBI.

Strengths and Limitations of the Existing Studies

From a methodological perspective, these studies all have strengths that should be noted and replicated in future studies. As mentioned above, researchers often use the same screening tools and screening criteria, enabling comparisons across samples. Thus, although samples differ, we can examine studies collectively and draw general conclusions (e.g., that the prevalence of disorders increases over time or is greater for one group than for another). In addition, the current research tends to focus on combat troops. This group may warrant special attention to the extent that it has disproportionately higher levels of combat exposure: Studies from broader deployed populations indicate that those with combat exposure are more likely to have PTSD and may be more likely to have depression. However, focusing exclusively on combat troops is also a limitation. First, as argued by Hotopf et al. (2006), sampling combat troops creates samples that are not representative of the entire deployed force; if combat exposure is higher among this group, such sampling can yield estimates of PTSD and depression that are inflated. On the other hand, combat exposure can include being caught in an ambush or handling dead bodies, which may be just as prevalent, if not more so, among supply personnel or combat medics, respectively.

Despite these strengths, if the reviewed studies are to guide the allocation of mental health services for military personnel in the United States it is imperative that two common limitations of these studies, and the implications that these limitations have on prevalence estimates, be recognized. First, in all but a handful of studies (Abt Associates, 2006; Martin, 2007; Milliken, Auchterlonie, and Hoge, 2007; Hoge, Auchterlonie, and Milliken, 2006; Hotopf et al., 2006), generalizability is weak. This weakness means that prevalence estimates are specific to the servicemembers in the respective samples. The current samples, including longitudinal assessments that are considered to be the most generalizable (Martin, 2007; Milliken, Auchterlonie, and Hoge, 2007), are likely to exclude servicemembers with the highest likelihood of mental problems, such as those with serious injuries or those who have separated from military service. This type of bias is likely to yield *lower* prevalence estimates than are actually the case. On the other hand, the healthiest troops may be systematically excluded from some surveys because they are being deployed multiple times and may therefore not be included in post-deployment samples. In addition, by focusing on troops most likely to be in combat situations, current studies may also be systematically excluding those servicemembers deployed but serving in combat support or combat services support roles. These other biases may therefore yield prevalence estimates *higher* than are actually the case. We discuss below one strategy for addressing these types of biases: surveying a random sample of all deployed servicemembers.

Second, most of the current studies used screening tools to measure the prevalence of mental health and cognitive conditions. Screening tools are typically short and simple to administer, but they are not equivalent to diagnostic procedures. The methods used to identify cases of PTSD, depression, and TBI with these screening tools in most studies have not been validated, and they miss a significant number of those persons with these mental and cognitive conditions, thereby producing estimates that could potentially underestimate the actual prevalence of these conditions. While fully or semi-structured diagnostic instruments are improvements upon screening tools for diagnosing individuals with disorders, these methods may also have problematic sensitivity and specificity (Kendler et al., 1996). They may also be impractical for community-based epidemiological surveys, although they can be used as the second stage of a two-phased design for those persons identified as probable cases via a screening tool (Jablensky, 2002).

Future Research Directions

We have reviewed what we believe to be the "first wave" of epidemiological studies designed to assess psychological problems among servicemembers in theater, immediately upon their return, and closely thereafter. These studies are a significant advance in both psychiatric epidemiology and military medicine. Future studies should use them to guide their research designs, but they also should improve upon them by addressing the limitations noted above. Specifically, epidemiologists and those conducting epidemiological studies should address four specific gaps in the current research:

1. **Epidemiological studies should employ random-sample designs to generalize to all deployed servicemembers.**

    Targeted research on troops engaged in combat is warranted and important. However, research on representative samples of all deployed servicemembers, regardless of their duties during deployment is encouraged to provide prevalence estimates that can be generalized to all deployed servicemembers. These studies should be designed to accurately measure differences in outcomes across relevant subgroups (e.g., those in the Active and Reserve Components). Sufficient attention should be paid to, for example, characteristics of nonresponders, so that the researchers understand who they are excluding from their study and how such individuals differ from their study sample. In addition, study samples should be compared with the larger populations they are designed to represent, and researchers should use the appropriate statistical methods to ensure that their samples and the estimates they publish are not biased by their study designs.

    From a policy perspective, these advancements will aid in the correct allocation of mental health services for military personnel. In addition, future research should make targeted efforts to engage deployed servicemembers who are no longer active in the military, including those who have separated and those who have suffered significant wounds. Together, these efforts will confront those issues that are likely to yield biased estimates among the extant studies.

2. **Researchers should use caution when defining cases to ensure that their case definition serves the larger purpose of the study.**

    From a public health perspective, epidemiological studies of prevalence help guide the allocation of resources to ensure that care and support are available at the level at which it is needed. Highly specific screening tools are attractive because most people without a given disorder are correctly identified as such. But for PTSD and depression, highly specific tools often come at the cost of low sensitivity. As a result, many persons who actually have PTSD or depression are not correctly classified as having these disorders. Researchers should think critically about the method they use to define cases and choose a technique that is in line with the ultimate goal of their research.

3. Research should address causal associations between deployment and subsequent mental health problems.

Studies have been conducted on servicemembers pre-deployment, in theater, and post-deployment, and some have compared rates of mental health problems at these different stages of service. Two studies (Vasterling et al., 2006; Smith et al., 2008) examined cohorts of servicemembers from a period pre-deployment to post-deployment, but both have significant limitations. A quasi-experimental research design that assesses the same servicemembers prior to deployment and post-deployment and an adequately defined control group will aid in determining the extent to which the risk of developing adverse mental and cognitive outcomes increases after serving in a conflict. Results of studies of servicemembers in theater indicate that multiple deployments and length of deployment may be associated with acute stress reactions. To reflect this situation, future studies should be designed to investigate whether these factors also increase the risk of PTSD, depression, or TBI when servicemembers return from being deployed.

4. Research should directly examine the prevalence of traumatic brain injury and its associated impairments.

Finally, although traumatic brain injury has been deemed a "signature" wound of the current conflicts, data on the prevalence of traumatic brain injury are lacking. Results from screenings at Camp Pendleton and Fort Irwin have not been subjected to the peer-review process, and it is not clear how these samples generalize to other servicemembers. Researchers should agree on a standardized definition of TBI or subtypes of TBI, such as mild TBI, investigate the psychometric properties of screening instruments used to identify these cases, and discern whether they are reliable and valid. Significant efforts are needed to identify cases of TBI—particularly mild TBI—in epidemiological surveys, as well as to identify ways to assess any impairments that result from TBI. Analysis and publication of prevalence data from TBI screens among servicemembers returning from deployment will be crucial for understanding the burden that brain injury poses on the U.S. military and society at large.

Conclusion

The studies identified in this critical review represent substantial advances in our understanding of PTSD and depression among servicemembers immediately after serving in war. Mental-health outreach and service allocation for deployed troops should occur both in theater and immediately upon the troops' return home, given the relatively high rates of problems shown here. Targeted interventions should focus on those who served in combat roles and those who are physically wounded. In addition, research conducted many years after previous conflicts, such as Vietnam (Dohrenwend et al., 2006) and the first Gulf War (Stimpson et al., 2003), have produced prevalence estimates equal to if not higher than those presented here, which may be due to the emergence of symptoms over time (i.e., a "delayed onset" PTSD) or increases in treatment-seeking behaviors. We hypothesize that, regardless of its cause, the need for mental health services for servicemembers deployed to Afghanistan and Iraq will increase over time, given the prevalence of information available to date and prior experience with Vietnam. Policymakers may therefore consider the figures presented in these studies to underestimate the burden that PTSD, depression, and TBI will have on the agencies that will be called upon to care for these servicemembers now and in the near future.

Table 3.2
Studies of Mental and Cognitive Conditions Among Servicemembers Returning from Afghanistan and Iraq: Hoge et al., 2004

Hoge C. W., C. A. Castro, S. C. Messer, D. McGurk, D. I. Cotting, and R. L Koffman. Combat duty in Iraq and Afghanistan, mental health problems, and barriers to care. *New England Journal of Medicine*, Vol. 351, No. 1, 2004, pp. 13–22.
Type of Report (e.g., peer-reviewed, government report): Peer-reviewed
N: 6,201
Design (e.g., cross-sectional, longitudinal, medical-record review): Cross-sectional
Conditions Studied: PTSD, Depression

Sample which Service (e.g., Army, Navy)	Assessment (e.g., survey, medical record)	Outcome Measures	Results	Correlates of Mental Health Conditions	Comparisons	Critique
Convenience sample of 3 Army units and 1 Marine Corps unit in 2003	Anonymous survey administered to: 1 Army unit 1 week before deployment to Iraq (n=2,530); 1 Army unit 3–4 months after deployment to Iraq (n=894); 1 Marine Corps Unit 3–4 months after deployment to Iraq (n=815); 1 Army unit 3–4 months after deployment to Afghanistan (n=1,962)	**PTSD:** PCL-DSM[a] PCL-DSM-50[a] **Depression:** PHQ-DSM[b] PHQ-DSM+FI[b] **Other:** Current stress, emotional problems, alcohol misuse, family problems, use of professional mental health services in the past month or year, barriers to mental health treatment	**PTSD:** (DSM %/DSM-50 %) Pre-Iraq Army: 9.4/5.0 Post-Iraq Army: 18.0/12.9 Post-Iraq Marine Corps: 19.9/12.2 Post-Afghanistan Army: 11.5/6.2 **Depression:** (DSM %/DSM-50 %) Pre-Iraq Army: 11.4/5.3 Post-Iraq Army: 15.2/7.9 Post-Iraq Marine Corps: 14.7/7.1 Post-Afghanistan Army: 14.2/6.9	**Combat experience** (being shot at, handling dead bodies, knowing someone who was killed, or killing enemy combatants) was strongly correlated with PTSD **Being wounded** or injured was positively associated with rates of PTSD	Units assessed after deploying to Iraq were significantly more likely to report experiencing PTSD and depression than units assessed before deploying to Iraq and units assessed after deploying to Afghanistan	**Comparison groups:** Pre-deployed and post-deployed groups are different samples; baseline distress may be heightened immediately before deployment **Generalizability:** Sample excludes severely wounded or those who may have been removed from units; not randomly selected **Outcomes:** Self-report

[a] PCL-DSM—Reporting at least 1 intrusion symptom, 3 avoidance symptoms, and 2 hyperarousal symptoms at the moderate level on PTSD Checklist. PCL-DSM-50—PCL-DSM + total score of at least 50 (range: 17–85) on the PTSD Checklist.

[b] PHQ-DSM—Reporting 5 or more of 9 symptoms "more than half the day" or "nearly every day" in the specified period and the presence of depressed mood or anhedonia among those symptoms on the PHQ-9.

PHQ-DSM+FI—PHQ-DSM on the PHQ-9 + self-reported functional impairment.

Table 3.3
Studies of Mental and Cognitive Conditions Among Servicemembers Returning from Afghanistan and Iraq: Hoge, Auchterlonie, and Milliken, 2006

Hoge, C. W., J. L. Auchterlonie, C. S. Milliken. Mental health problems, use of mental health services, and attrition from military service after returning from deployment to Iraq or Afghanistan. *Journal of the American Medical Association,* Vol. 295, No. 9, 2006, pp. 1023–1032.
Type of Report (e.g., peer-reviewed, gov't report): Peer-reviewed
N: 303,905
Design (e.g., cross-sectional, longitudinal, medical-record review): Cross-sectional
Conditions Studied: PTSD, Depression

Sample which Service (e.g., Army, Navy)	Assessment (e.g., survey, medical record)	Outcome Measures	Results	Correlates of Mental Health Conditions	Comparisons	Critique
All Army and Marine Corps units who returned from deployment from Afghanistan, Iraq, or other locations between May 1, 2003, and April 30, 2004	Survey and administrative records: PDHA linked with administrative data on health care visits among military personnel who served in Afghanistan (n=16,318), Iraq (n=222,620), and other locations (n=64,967)	**PTSD:** PC-PTSD[a] **Depression:** PHQ-2[b] **Other:** Other mental health problem (from PDHA), referral for an MH reason (from PDHA), health care utilization (from administrative records), attrition from military service (administrative records)	**PTSD:** Iraq: 9.8 Afghanistan: 4.7 Other: 2.1 **Depression:** (% report 1 item/ % report both items) Iraq: 4.5/1.6 Afghanistan: 2.5/1.0 Other: 1.9/0.8	**Combat experience** (witnessing person being wounded or killed or engaging in direct combat during which they discharged their weapon) was positively associated with PTSD among OIF veterans **Hospitalization** during deployment was associated with a mental health problem **Female** OIF veterans were slightly more likely to report a mental health concern	Deployment to Iraq rather than to Afghanistan or other locations was associated with increased odds of reporting any mental health concern	**Outcomes:** Self-report, and screening tools with low specificity **Generalizability:** Unknown

NOTES: MH—mental health; PDHA—Post-Deployment Health Assessment (survey for all military personnel conducted immediately upon returning from any deployment.
[a] PC-PTSD—Reporting 2 or more of 4 items on Primary Care–PTSD (PC-PTSD) Screen.
[b] PHQ-2—Positive response to question on depressed mood or anhedonia.

Table 3.4
Studies of Mental and Cognitive Conditions Among Servicemembers Returning from Afghanistan and Iraq: Hotopf et al., 2006

Hotopf, M., L. Hull, N. T. Fear, T. Browne, O. Horn, A. Iversen, M. Jones, D. Murphy, D. Bland, M. Earnshaw, N. Greenberg, J. H. Hughes, A. R. Tate, C. Dandeker, R. Rona, and S. Wessely. The health of UK military personnel who deployed to the 2003 Iraq war: A cohort study. *Lancet*, Vol. 367, No. 9524, 2006, pp. 1731–1741.
Type of Report (e.g., peer-reviewed, gov't report): Peer-reviewed
N: 10,272
Design (e.g., cross-sectional, longitudinal, medical-record review): Cross-sectional
Conditions Studied: PTSD

Sample which Service (e.g., Army, Navy)	Assessment (e.g., survey, medical record)	Outcome Measures	Results	Correlates of Mental Health Conditions	Comparisons	Critique
UK armed forces personnel (Royal Navy including Royal Marine Corps, Army, Royal Air Force) who served in Iraq or surrounding areas between January 18 and June 28, 2003, and a comparison group of nondeployed servicemembers on March 31, 2003	Questionnaire administered to a random sample of regular servicemembers and reservists: Deployed sample (n=4,722) Nondeployed sample (n=5,550)	**PTSD:** PCL≥50[a] **Unspecified mental health condition:** Score of 4 or greater on the General Health Questionnaire-12 **Other:** Alcohol-use disorders; service information; experiences before, on, and after deployment; current health; background info (including past med history and adversity in early life)	**PTSD** Deployed: 4% Nondeployed: 4% **Common mental health condition** Deployed: 20% Nondeployed: 20%	**Combat duties** were associated with increased rates of PTSD symptoms No evidence that later deployments, which were associated with escalating insurgency and UK casualties, were associated with poorer MH outcomes	In general, there were no significant differences in PTSD and other mental health outcomes for deployed and nondeployed servicemembers **Reservist status** modified the effect of deployment: Deployed reservists were more likely to report common mental health conditions and fatigue than were nondeployed reservists, although this difference was not seen for regular servicemembers	**Outcomes:** Self-report **Response rate:** 61%; response rates were lower for those who were younger, male, non-officers, reservists, and nondeployed

[a] PCL≥50—Total score of at least 50 on the PTSD Checklist.

Table 3.5
Studies of Mental and Cognitive Conditions Among Servicemembers Returning from Afghanistan and Iraq: Vasterling et al., 2006

Vasterling, J. J., S. P. Proctor, P. Amoroso, R. Kane, T. Heeren, R. F. White. Neuropsychological outcomes of Army personnel following deployment to the Iraq war. *Journal of the American Medical Association*, Vol. 296, No. 5, 2006, pp. 519–529.
Type of Report (e.g., peer-reviewed, gov't report): Peer-reviewed
N: 1,457
Design (e.g., cross-sectional, longitudinal, medical-record review): Longitudinal
Conditions Studied: PTSD, Depression, TBI

Sample which Service (e.g., Army, Navy)	Assessment (e.g., survey, medical record)	Outcome Measures	Results	Correlates of Mental Health Conditions	Comparisons	Critique
Random sample of soldiers of Army battalion–level units originating in Fort Hood, Texas, and Fort Lewis, Washington, assessed before deployment to Iraq (April–December 2003) and post-deployment (January–May 2005) and a nondeployed comparison group assessed at the same times	Assessments conducted by a civilian examiner team at military installations at two time points: Before deployment to Iraq (n=1,368), after deployment to Iraq (n=1,028). After exclusions, total n=961 (654 categorized as deployed and 307 categorized as nondeployed)	**PTSD:** PCL-DSM-50[a] **Depression:** Center for Epidemiological Studies Depression Inventory, 9-item version (CES-D-9)[b] **TBI:** Self-reported head injury with a loss of consciousness lasting more than 15 minutes **Other:** Functional neurocognitive health, deployment experiences, state affect, performance-based neuropsychological tests	**PTSD** Deployed: 11.6% **Depression** Deployed: 25.0% **Head injury with related loss of consciousness** Deployed: 7.6% Nondeployed: 3.9%	N/A	N/A	**Comparison groups:** Rates of PTSD and depression not presented for nondeployed **Outcomes:** Self-report; validity of measure for TBI does not include nonconcussive blast exposures **Retention:** Most of those lost to follow-up had separated from military service and may be more likely to have mental or cognitive conditions

NOTE: N/A—not available.

[a] PCL-DSM-50—PCL-DSM + total score of at least 50 (range: 17–85) on the PTSD Checklist.

[b] CES-D-9—Summed score across 9 depressive symptoms >4 (range: 0–9) on Center for Epidemiologic Studies Depression Inventory, 9-item version.

Table 3.6
Studies of Mental and Cognitive Conditions Among Servicemembers Returning from Afghanistan and Iraq: Grieger et al., 2006

Grieger, T. A., S. J. Cozza, R. J. Ursano, C. Hoge, P. E. Martinez, C. C. Engel, H. J. Wain. Posttraumatic stress disorder and depression in battle-injured soldiers. *American Journal of Psychiatry*, Vol. 163, No. 10, 2006, pp. 1777–1783.
Type of Report (e.g., peer-reviewed, gov't report): Peer-reviewed
N: 613
Design (e.g., cross-sectional, longitudinal, medical-record review): Longitudinal
Conditions Studied: PTSD, Depression

Sample which Service (e.g., Army, Navy)	Assessment (e.g., survey, medical record)	Outcome Measures	Results	Correlates of Mental Health Conditions	Comparisons	Critique
Convenience sample of Army soldiers wounded in combat and evacuated to Walter Reed Army Medical Center between March 2003 and September 2004	Survey administered to the same cohort three times after the injury: 1 month (n=613); 4 months (n=395); 7 months (n=301). 243 (50%) soldiers completed all three assessments.	**PTSD (past month):** PCL-DSM-50[a] **Depression (past 2 weeks):** PHQ-DSM[b] **Other:** War exposure, deployment length, somatic-symptom severity	**PTSD** 1 month: 4.2% 4 months: 12.2% 7 months: 12.0% **Depression** 1 month: 4.4% 4 months: 8.9% 7 months: 9.3% **PTSD + Depression** 1 month: 2.0 4 months: 7.6% 7 months: 6.3% In the longitudinal cohort, 78.8% (26 of 33) of those positive for PTSD or depression at 7 months screened negative for both conditions at 1 month	At 1 month: **Under age 25** more likely to meet PTSD and depression criteria than over 25; **married** soldiers more likely to meet criteria for PTSD and depression than unmarried; **high combat exposure** more likely to meet PTSD criteria, not depression **High levels of physical problems** were associated with increased odds of PTSD and depression at 1 month, 4 months, and 7 months Sociodemographics and combat exposure not associated with PTSD or depression at 4 or 7 months Longitudinal sample: Among those without PTSD/depression at 1 month, **high levels of physical problems** at 1 month predicted PTSD and depression at 7 months	N/A	**Generalizability:** Sample is severely injured, with low numbers of female soldiers and exclusion of patients with low cognitive abilities **Retention:** 72% at 4 months, 60% at 7 months. Bias if nonrespondents/those lost to follow-up are significantly different from those who were assessed **Outcomes:** Self-report

NOTE: N/A—not available.

[a] PCL-DSM-50—PCL-DSM + total score of at least 50 (range: 17–85) on the PTSD Checklist.

[b] PHQ-DSM—Reporting 5 or more of 9 symptoms "more than half the day" or "nearly every day" in the specified period and the presence of depressed mood or anhedonia among those symptoms on the PHQ-9.

Table 3.7
Studies of Mental and Cognitive Conditions Among Servicemembers Returning from Afghanistan and Iraq: Hoge et al., 2007

Hoge, C. W., A. Terhakopian, C. A. Castro, S. C. Messer, and C. C. Engel. Association of posttraumatic stress disorder with somatic symptoms, health care visits, and absenteeism among Iraq war veterans. *American Journal of Psychiatry*, Vol. 164, No. 1, 2007, pp. 150–153.
Type of Report (e.g., peer-reviewed, gov't report): Peer-reviewed
N: 2,863
Design (e.g., cross-sectional, longitudinal, medical-record review): Cross-sectional
Conditions Studied: PTSD

Sample which Service (e.g., Army, Navy)	Assessment (e.g., survey, medical record)	Outcome Measures	Results	Correlates of Mental Health Conditions	Comparisons	Critique
Convenience sample of 4 Army combat infantry brigades deployed to Iraq	Anonymous survey administered 1 year after returning from deployment to Iraq	**PTSD (past month):** PCL-DSM-50[a] **Other:** Alcohol misuse, self-rated health status, sick-call visits, missed workdays, somatic symptoms	**PTSD:** 16.6%	Injury was associated with higher rate of PTSD	PTSD was associated with lower perceptions of general health, more sick-call visits, missed workdays, more physical symptoms, and higher somatic-symptom severity	**Outcomes:** Self-report **Generalizability:** Sample based only on soldiers from combat infantry units; sample not randomly selected and may, by design, exclude severely injured/medically ill

[a] PCL-DSM-50—PCL-DSM + total score of at least 50 (range: 17–85) on the PTSD Checklist.

Table 3.8
Studies of Mental and Cognitive Conditions Among Servicemembers Returning from Afghanistan and Iraq: Seal et al., 2007

Seal, K. H., D. Bertenthal, C. R. Miner, S. Sen, and C. Marmar. Bringing the war back home: Mental health disorders among 103,788 US veterans returning from Iraq and Afghanistan seen at Department of Veterans Affairs facilities. *Archives of Internal Medicine*, Vol. 167, No. 5, 2007, pp. 476–482.
Type of Report (e.g., peer-reviewed, gov't report): Peer-reviewed
N: 103,788
Design (e.g., cross-sectional, longitudinal, medical-record review): Medical-record review
Conditions Studied: PTSD, Depression

Sample which Service (e.g., Army, Navy)	Assessment (e.g., survey, medical record)	Outcome Measures	Results	Correlates of Mental Health Conditions	Comparisons	Critique
OEF/OIF Afghanistan/Iraq veterans receiving care in the VA between September 30, 2001, and September 30, 2005	Medical-record review of new users of the VA health care system included in the VA OEF/OIF roster database; thus, all participants have been separated from service in Afghanistan/Iraq, adjusted to maximize likelihood that VA visit occurred post-deployment	ICD-9-CM[a] mental health diagnoses codes	**PTSD:** 13% **Depression:** 5% **Other:** 25% received mental health diagnosis(es), 56% of whom had ≥2 distinct MH diagnoses	**Younger** OEF/OIF Afghanistan/Iraq veterans were at greater risk for receiving MH/PTSD diagnoses than were veterans ≥40 yrs (i.e., 18–24-year-olds more likely to receive 1 or more mental health diagnoses and PTSD diagnosis).	N/A	**Generalizability:** Sample restricted to only veterans who have left the Service and sought treatment at VA

NOTE: N/A—not available.

[a] ICD-9-CM (*International Classification of Diseases, Ninth Revision, Clinical Modification*)—Diagnostic code of PTSD from medical records.

Table 3.9
Studies of Mental and Cognitive Conditions Among Servicemembers Returning from Afghanistan and Iraq: Erbes et al., 2007

Erbes, C., J. Westermeyer, B. Engdahl, and E. Johnsen. Post-traumatic stress disorder and service utilization in a sample of service members from Iraq and Afghanistan. *Military Medicine*, Vol. 172, No. 4, 2007, pp. 359–363.
Type of Report (e.g., peer-reviewed, gov't report): Peer-reviewed
N: 120
Design (e.g., cross-sectional, longitudinal, medical-record review): Cross-sectional
Conditions Studied: PTSD

Sample *which Service (e.g., Army, Navy)*	Assessment *(e.g., survey, medical record)*	Outcome Measures	Results	Correlates of Mental Health Conditions	Comparisons	Critique
Servicemembers returning from Iraq or Afghanistan who enrolled for care at the Minneapolis VA Medical Center (MVAMC), excluding those receiving mental health services at the VA between February 2005 and time of publication	Mailed survey	**PTSD:** PCL≥50[a] **Depression:** BDI[b] **Other:** Alcohol use/ hazardous drinking,[c] quality of life, mental health service utilization	**PTSD:** 12%	Half of those screening positive for PTSD also screened positive for **hazardous drinking**		**Generalizability:** Sample restricted to only veterans who sought treatment at MVAMC **Outcomes:** Self-report **Retention:** 55% response rate; persons receiving treatment for mental health were excluded **Small sample size:** Power to detect only large differences

[a] PCL≥50—Total score of at least 50 on the PTSD Checklist.

[b] BDI—7 items from the Beck Depression Inventory (no further information provided).

[c] Total score of at least 8 on a scale ranging from 0 to 40 across 10 items from the Alcohol Use Disorders Identification Test.

Table 3.10
Studies of Mental and Cognitive Conditions Among Servicemembers Returning from Afghanistan and Iraq: Kolkow et al., 2007

Kolkow, T. T., J. L. Spira, J. S. Morse, and T. A. Grieger. Post-traumatic stress disorder and depression in health care providers returning from deployment to Iraq and Afghanistan. *Military Medicine*, Vol. 172, No. 5, 2007, pp. 451–455.
Type of Report (e.g., peer-reviewed, gov't report): Peer-reviewed
N: 102
Design (e.g., cross-sectional, longitudinal, medical-record review): Cross-sectional
Conditions Studied: PTSD, Depression

Sample *which Service (e.g., Army, Navy)*	Assessment *(e.g., survey, medical record)*	Outcome Measures	Results	Correlates of Mental Health Conditions	Comparisons	Critique
U.S. Military Health Care Providers previously deployed to Afghanistan or Iraq, assessed in 2004	Anonymous, Internet-based survey administered to military personnel "on staff" at Naval Medical Center San Diego	**PTSD (past month):** PCL-DSM-50[a] **Depression:** PHQ-DSM[b] **Other:** Direct exposure, perceptions of threat during deployment, mental health service use, severity of physical problems	**PTSD:** 9% **Depression:** 5%	**Non-White race** was associated with PTSD and depression **Frequent personal engagement in direct combat** or **being fired upon by opposition forces** was associated with PTSD **Threat perception** (frequent concern regarding being in danger) had greater risk of PTSD	N/A	**Generalizability:** Sample restricted to health care providers or staff at Naval Medical Center San Diego **Response rate:** 36% among those recently deployed to combat areas, based on hospital personnel records; may exclude severely wounded/medically ill **Outcomes:** Self-report **Small sample size:** Power to detect only large differences

NOTE: N/A—not available.

[a] PCL-DSM-50—PCL-DSM + total score of at least 50 (range: 17–85) on the PTSD Checklist.

[b] PHQ-DSM—Reporting 5 or more of 9 symptoms "more than half the day" or "nearly every day" in the specified period and the presence of depressed mood or anhedonia among those symptoms on the PHQ-9.

Table 3.11
Studies of Mental and Cognitive Conditions Among Servicemembers Returning from Afghanistan and Iraq: Helmer et al., 2007

Helmer, D. A., M. Rossignol, M. Blatt, R. Agarwal, R. Teichman, and G. Lange. Health and exposure concerns of veterans deployed to Iraq and Afghanistan. *Journal of Occupational and Environmental Medicine*, Vol. 49, No. 5, 2007, pp. 475–480.
Type of Report (e.g., peer-reviewed, gov't report): Peer-reviewed
N: 56
Design (e.g., cross-sectional, longitudinal, medical-record review): Medical-record review
Conditions Studied: PTSD

Sample which Service (e.g., Army, Navy)	Assessment (e.g., survey, med record)	Outcome Measures	Results	Correlates of Mental Health Conditions	Comparisons	Critique
Consecutively evaluated veterans at the New Jersey War-Related Injury and Illness Center (NJ-WRIIC) between June 2004 and January 2006	Chart review	**PTSD:** Definitive or probable diagnosis of PTSD in the final-impression section of the clinical notes	**PTSD:** 45%	N/A	No difference between Active Component and Reserve Component veterans	**Generalizability:** Sample restricted to only veterans who have sought treatment at NJ-WRIIC
						Small sample size: Power to detect only large differences

NOTE: N/A—not available.

Table 3.12
Studies of Mental and Cognitive Conditions Among Servicemembers Returning from Afghanistan and Iraq: Engelhard et al., 2007

Engelhard, I. M., M. A. Van Den Hout, J. Weerts, A. Arntz, J. J. C. M. Hox, and R. J. McNally. Deployment-related stress and trauma in Dutch soldiers returning from Iraq. *British Journal of Psychiatry*, Vol. 191, 2007, pp. 140–145.
Type of Report (e.g., peer-reviewed, gov't report): Peer-reviewed
N: 479
Design (e.g., cross-sectional, longitudinal, medical-record review): Longitudinal
Conditions Studied: PTSD

Sample *which Service (e.g., Army, Navy)*	Assessment *(e.g., survey, medical record)*	Outcome Measures	Results	Correlates of Mental Health Conditions	Comparisons	Critique
Dutch Army troops from 3 successive 4-month rotations between March 2005 and March 2006 (an Armored Infantry Battalion and 2 battalions of the Air Assault Brigade)	Survey and Structured Clinical Interview for the DSM-IV (SCID) administered at Baseline (479 surveys) 5 months post-deployment (382 surveys/331 SCID) 15 months post-deployment (331 surveys/203 SCID)	**PTSD:** PSS[a] SCID[b]	**PTSD (PSS/SCID) 5 months** 12%/7%	**Pre-deployment symptoms** and **harmful exposures in Iraq** explained higher rates of PTSD among Armored Infantry Battalion	Higher prevalence of PTSD among Armored Infantry Battalion	**Retention:** 80%/71% (survey/SCID) response rate at 5 months; 69%/42% (survey/SCID) response rate at 15 months. Bias if nonrespondents/those lost to follow-up were significantly different from respondents.

[a] PSS—Total score of 14 (range: 0–51) on the PTSD Symptom Scale.

[b] SCID—Structured Clinical Interview for the DSM-IV (semi-structured diagnostic interview).

Table 3.13
Studies of Mental and Cognitive Conditions Among Servicemembers Returning from Afghanistan and Iraq: Martin, 2007

Martin, C. B. Routine screening and referrals for PTSD after returning from Operation Iraqi Freedom in 2005, U.S. Armed Forces. *MSMR: Medical Surveillance Monthly Report*, Vol. 14, No. 6, 2007, pp. 2–7.
Type of Report (e.g., peer-reviewed, gov't report): Publication of the Army Forces Health Surveillance Center
N: 91,408
Design (e.g., cross-sectional, longitudinal, medical-record review): Longitudinal
Conditions Studied: PTSD

Sample which Service (e.g., Army, Navy)	Assessment (e.g., survey, medical record)	Outcome Measures	Results	Correlates of Mental Health Conditions	Comparisons	Critique
U.S. armed forces returning from OIF in 2005	PDHA linked, when possible, to the PDHRA	**PTSD:** PC-PTSD[a]	**PTSD:** OIF: 10.5%	Those in **medical service occupations** were most likely to screen positive for PTSD **Reservists** and **junior enlisted** were more likely to screen positive for PTSD Military servicemembers in the **Army** were more likely to screen positive for PTSD **Younger** military members (<20 years) and older (>35 years) were the least likely to screen positive for PTSD	48.1% of those who received clinical diagnoses of PTSD within 6 months of returning from OIF deployment screened positive on the PDHA 29.9% of those who screened positive on the PDHRA screened positive on the PDHA	**Quality control:** Not peer-reviewed **Generalizability:** Unknown **Outcomes:** Self-report, and screening tools with low specificity **Retention:** 24% of returning servicemembers did not have a PDHA; the proportion of those with a PDHA who had a PDHRA is not disclosed. Differences between those who complete follow-up and those who do not are not addressed.

NOTES: PDHA—Post-Deployment Health Assessment (survey for all military personnel conducted immediately upon returning from any deployment); PDHRA—Post-Deployment Health Reassessment (survey for all military personnel conducted 3–6 months after returning from any deployment).

[a] PC-PTSD—Reporting 2 or more of 4 items on Primary Care–PTSD (PC-PTSD) Screen.

Table 3.14
Studies of Mental and Cognitive Conditions Among Servicemembers Returning from Afghanistan and Iraq: Milliken, Auchterlonie, and Hoge, 2007

Milliken, C. S., J. L. Auchterlonie, C. W. Hoge. Longitudinal assessment of mental health problems among Active and Reserve Component soldiers returning from the Iraq war. *Journal of the American Medical Association*, Vol. 298, No. 18, 2007, pp. 2141–2148.
Type of Report (e.g., peer-reviewed, gov't report): Peer-reviewed
N: 88,235
Design (e.g., cross-sectional, longitudinal, medical-record review): Longitudinal
Conditions Studied: PTSD, Depression

Sample *which Service (e.g., Army, Navy)*	Assessment *(e.g., survey, medical record)*	Outcome Measures	Results	Correlates of Mental Health Conditions	Comparisons	Critique
Army soldiers returning from OIF between June 1, 2005, and December 31, 2006	PDHRA linked to PDHA and administrative records on use of medical services	**PTSD:** PC-PTSD[a] **Depression:** PHQ-2[b] **Other:** Other mental health problem, referral for an MH reason, suicidal ideation, alcohol-use disorder	**PTSD** PDHA Active: 11.8% Reserve: 12.7% PDHRA Active: 16.7% Reserve: 24.5% **Depression** PDHA Active: 4.7% Reserve: 3.8% PDHRA Active: 10.3% Reserve: 13.0%	N/A	Higher rates among National Guard and Reserve More than 2 times as many new PTSD cases on PDHRA (at 6 months) as on PDHA (at 1 month)	**Generalizability:** Excludes those who did not complete the PDHRA **Outcomes:** Self-report, and screening tools with low specificity **Retention:** Proportion of individuals with initial assessment who completed follow-up is not disclosed. Differences between those who complete follow-up and those who do not are not addressed.

NOTES: N/A—not available; PDHA—Post-Deployment Health Assessment (survey for all military personnel conducted immediately upon returning from any deployment); PDHRA—Post-Deployment Health Reassessment (survey for all military personnel conducted 3–6 months after returning from any deployment).

[a] PC-PTSD—Reporting 2 or more of 4 items on Primary Care–PTSD (PC-PTSD) Screen.

[b] PHQ-2—Positive response to question on depressed mood or anhedonia.

Table 3.15
Studies of Mental and Cognitive Conditions Among Servicemembers Returning from Afghanistan and Iraq: Rosenheck and Fontana, 2007

Rosenheck, R. A., and A. F. Fontana. Recent trends in VA treatment of post-traumatic stress disorder and other mental health disorders. *Health Affairs*, Vol. 26, No. 6, 2007, pp. 1720–1727.
Type of Report (e.g., peer-reviewed, gov't report): Peer-reviewed
N: >1 million
Design (e.g., prospective, cross-sectional, retrospective): Retrospective
Conditions Studied: PTSD, other mental health condition

Sample which Service (e.g., Army, Navy)	Assessment (e.g., survey, medical record)	Outcome Measures	Results	Correlates of Mental Health Conditions	Comparisons	Critique
Veterans receiving VA care in 1997, 1999, 2001, 2003, and 2005; OEF/OIF veterans were identified as being born after 1972 and having their first VA outpatient encounter after 1991	Medical-record review of users of the VA health care system	**PTSD:** ICD-9[a] PTSD diagnosis code **Other mental diagnosis:** ICD-9 code	**Average annualized percentage increase in PTSD diagnoses among approximated OEF/OIF sample:** 1997–2001: 31.2 2001–2003: 31.6 2003–2005: 232.1	N/A	Most of the increase in PTSD treatment between 1997 and 2005 in the VA represents increased use of services by veterans from earlier eras.	**Generalizability:** Sample restricted to only veterans who have sought treatment at VA **Misclassification:** Approximated sample of OEF/OIF veterans that is likely to exclude older veterans

NOTE: N/A—not available.

[a] ICD-9-CM (*International Classification of Diseases, Ninth Revision, Clinical Modification*)—Diagnostic code of PTSD from medical records.

Table 3.16
Studies of Mental and Cognitive Conditions Among Servicemembers Returning from Afghanistan and Iraq: Lapierre, Schwegler, and LaBauve, 2007

Lapierre, C. B., A. F. Schwegler, and B. J. LaBauve. Posttraumatic stress and depression symptoms in soldiers returning from combat operations in Iraq and Afghanistan. *Journal of Traumatic Stress*, Vol. 20, No. 6, 2007, pp. 933–943.
Type of Report (e.g., peer-reviewed, gov't report): Peer-reviewed
N: 4,089
Design (e.g., cross-sectional, longitudinal, medical-record review): Cross-sectional
Conditions Studied: PTSD, Depression

Sample which Service (e.g., Army, Navy)	Assessment (e.g., survey, medical record)	Outcome Measures	Results	Correlates of Mental Health Conditions	Comparisons	Critique
Army soldiers returning from Afghanistan and Iraq between February and July 2005	Survey administered to soldiers returning from Afghanistan (*n*=1,810) and Iraq (*n*=2,266) at an Army-sponsored reintegration training program	**PTSD:** SPTSS[a] **Depression:** Center for Epidemiologic Studies Depression Inventory, 20-item version (CES-D-20)[b]	**PTSD:** Afghanistan: 30% Iraq: 31% **Depression:** Afghanistan: 38% Iraq: 37%	**Junior enlisted** reported higher levels of post-traumatic distress and depression **Separated and divorced** reported higher levels of post-traumatic distress and depression **and divorced** reported higher levels of depression	Those deployed to OIF had higher PTSD scores than those deployed to OEF; depression scores were no different	**Outcomes:** Self-report, and not well-validated screening tool for PTSD (low specificity) **Generalizability:** Unknown

[a] SPTSS—An average total score of 4 or more (range: 0–10) on the Screen for Posttraumatic Stress Symptoms.

[b] CES-D-20—Averaged score across 20 depressive symptoms >16 (range: 0–20) on Center for Epidemiologic Studies Depression Inventory, 20-item version.

Table 3.17

Studies of Mental and Cognitive Conditions Among Servicemembers Returning from Afghanistan and Iraq: Smith et al., 2008

Smith, T. C., M. A. K. Ryan, D. L. Wingard, D. J. Slymen, J. F. Sallis, and D. Kritz-Silverstein, and Team for the Millennium Cohort Study. New onset and persistent symptoms of post-traumatic stress disorder self reported after deployment and combat exposures: Prospective population based US military cohort study. *British Medical Journal*, published online, January 15, 2008.

Type of Report (e.g., peer-reviewed, gov't report): Peer-reviewed

N: 50,184

Design (e.g., cross-sectional, longitudinal, medical-record review): Longitudinal

Conditions Studied: PTSD

Sample which Service (e.g., Army, Navy)	Assessment (e.g., survey, medical record)	Outcome Measures	Results	Correlates of Mental Health Conditions	Comparisons	Critique
U.S. armed forces deployed 1 or more days to Afghanistan and Iraq between July 2001 and June 2003 and between June 2004 and February 2006	Survey administered twice to cohort that included servicemembers who deployed (n=11,952) and those who did not deploy (n=38,176)	**PTSD:** PCL-DSM[a] PCL-DSM-50[b] or self-report of a doctor telling the respondent s/he had PTSD	**PTSD (DSM/DSM-50):** Among those without PTSD at baseline: Deployed with combat exposure: 8.7/7.3 Deployed without combat exposure: 2.1/1.4 Nondeployed:- 3.0/2.3 Among those with PTSD at baseline: Deployed with combat exposure: 47.9/43.5 Deployed without combat exposure: 22.4/26.2 Nondeployed:- 45.9/47.6	Across Service branches, **deployment** was strongly associated with onset PTSD status. After adjusting for deployment status, the following were linked with PTSD, by Service branch: Army: female, never married (less likely), enlisted Air Force: female, divorced, enlisted Navy/Coast Guard: female, divorced, Black non-Hispanic, enlisted Marine Corps: divorced	Members of the Air Force were less likely to develop onset PTSD than other Service branches	**Generalizability:** Overrepresented those least likely to experience combat (females, Air Force, and officers), with no adjustment to make results representative to deployed force. Excludes those deployed before baseline assessment, or who completed baseline or follow-up assessments while deployed **Outcomes:** Self-report **Attrition/Retention:** 36% response rate at baseline; 71% response rate at follow-up

[a] PCL-DSM—Reporting at least 1 intrusion symptom, 3 avoidance symptoms, and 2 hyperarousal symptoms at the moderate level on the PTSD Checklist.

[b] PCL-DSM-50—PCL-DSM = total score of at least 50 (range: 17–85) on the PTSD Checklist.

Table 3.18
Studies of Mental and Cognitive Conditions Among Servicemembers Returning from Afghanistan and Iraq: Hoge et al., 2008

Hoge, C. W., D. McGurk, J. L. Thomas, A. L. Cox, C. C. Engel, C. A. Castro. Mild traumatic brain injury in U.S. soldiers returning from Iraq. *New England Journal of Medicine*, Vol. 358, No. 5, 2008, pp. 453–463.
Type of Report (e.g., peer-reviewed, gov't report): Peer-reviewed
N: 2,714
Design (e.g., cross-sectional, longitudinal, medical-record review): Cross-sectional
Conditions Studied: mTBI

Sample which Service (e.g., Army, Navy)	Assessment (e.g., survey, medical record)	Outcome Measures	Results	Correlates of Mental Health Conditions	Comparisons	Critique
U.S. Army soldiers from two combat infantry brigades (one Active Component, one Reserve Component) 3–4 months after returning from OIF in 2006	Anonymous survey	**TBI:** Reporting having an injury that involved an injury to the head and at least one of the following: Losing consciousness (knocked out) Being dazed, confused, or seeing stars Not remembering the injury	mTBI: 15.2%	Relative to soldiers with injuries who did not experience mTBI symptoms, those with TBI symptoms were more likely to have reported **high combat intensity, a blast mechanism of injury, more than one exposure to an explosion, and hospitalization during deployment.** Also, those with TBI were **younger,** more likely to be junior in rank, and male.	Percentage of those meeting criteria for PTSD/Major Depression: Loss of consciousness: 43.9/22.9 Altered mental status: 27.3/8.4 Injury, no mTBI: 16.2/6.6 No injury: 9.1/3.3	**Generalizability:** Sample excludes severely wounded or those who may have been removed from units; not randomly selected **Outcomes:** Self-report

NOTE: mTBI—mild traumatic brain injury.

Table 3.19
Studies of Mental and Cognitive Conditions Among Servicemembers Returning from Afghanistan and Iraq: U.S. Department of the Army, Office of the Surgeon General (MHAT-I), 2003

U.S. Department of the Army, Office of the Surgeon General, Mental Health Advisory Team (MHAT). *Operation Iraqi Freedom (OIF), MHAT Report.*
U.S. Army Surgeon General and HDQA G-1, December 16, 2003.
Type of Report (e.g., peer-reviewed, gov't report): Gov't report
N: 756
Design (e.g., cross-sectional, longitudinal, medical-record review): Cross-sectional
Conditions Studied: PTSD, Depression

Sample which Service (e.g., Army, Navy.)	Assessment (e.g., survey, medical record)	Outcome Measures	Results	Correlates of Mental Health Conditions	Comparisons	Critique
Army soldiers in Iraq and Kuwait between August and October 2003	Anonymous surveys administered in base camps in Iraq (combat line companies from brigade combat teams, n=577) and Kuwait (areas thought to have high operational stress, n=179)	**Acute stress (PTSD):** Endorse "several items" as moderate on PCL[a] scale and mark that the problem caused functional impairment (if symptoms affect work) **Depression:** Endorse several items on PHQ[a] as occurring "more than half the days" and functional impairment (how difficult symptoms make it to do work or get along with people) at "very difficult" or "extremely difficult" level	**Acute stress:** 15% **Depression:** 7% **Depression, anxiety, or acute stress:** 19%	**Lower personal and unit morale** and **lower cohesion** were associated with reports of mental health symptoms	Relative to samples of pre-deployed troops preparing to deploy or just returning from Afghanistan, troops in Iraq had higher rates of mental health conditions, driven primarily by acute stress	**Quality control:** Not peer-reviewed **Generalizability:** Unknown

[a] No further information given on the scoring method used.

Table 3.20
Studies of Mental and Cognitive Conditions Among Servicemembers Returning from Afghanistan and Iraq: U.S. Department of the Army, Office of the Surgeon General (MHAT-II), 2005

U.S. Department of the Army, Office of the Surgeon General, Mental Health Advisory Team (MHAT-II). *Operation Iraqi Freedom (OIF-II), MHAT-II Report.* U.S. Army Surgeon general, January 30, 2005.
Type of Report (e.g., peer-reviewed, gov't report): Gov't report
N: 2,064
Design (e.g., cross-sectional, longitudinal, medical-record review): Cross-sectional
Conditions Studied: PTSD, Depression

Sample which Service (e.g., Army, Navy)	Assessment (e.g., survey, medical record)	Outcome Measures	Results	Correlates of Mental Health Conditions	Comparisons	Critique
Army soldiers in Iraq and Kuwait between August and October 2004	Anonymous survey administered in Iraq (line units from brigade combat teams, *n*=1,595) and Kuwait (battalion-level units more likely to experience combat or operational stress, *n*=469)	**Acute stress (PTSD):** PCL-DSM-50[a] **Depression:** PHQ-DSM-FI[b]	**Acute stress:** 10% **Depression:** 5% **Depression, anxiety, or acute stress:** 13%	Subjects in **Kuwait** had slightly lower levels of mental health problems than those in Iraq **Transportation and support personnel** had higher levels of screening positive for each mental health problem than soldiers in combat or other units	Lower levels of acute stress than in MHAT-I; no statistically significant difference for depression from MHAT-I	**Quality control:** Not peer-reviewed **Generalizability:** Unknown

[a] PCL-DSM-50—PCL-DSM + total score of at least 50 (range: 17–85) on the PTSD Checklist.
[b] PHQ-DSM-FI—PHQ-DSM on the PHQ-9 + self-reported functional impairment.

Table 3.21
Studies of Mental and Cognitive Conditions Among Servicemembers Returning from Afghanistan and Iraq: U.S. Department of the Army, Office of the Surgeon, Multinational Force–Iraq and Office of the Surgeon General, U.S. Army Medical Command (MHAT-III), 2006a

U.S. Department of the Army, Office of the Surgeon Multinational Force–Iraq and Office of the Surgeon General, U.S. Army Medical Command, Mental Health Advisory Team (MHAT-III). *Operation Iraqi Freedom 04-06, MHAT-III Report.* May 29, 2006a.
Type of Report (e.g., peer-reviewed, gov't report): Gov't report
N: 1,124
Design (e.g., cross-sectional, longitudinal, medical-record review): Cross-sectional
Conditions Studied: PTSD, Depression

Sample *which Service (e.g., Army, Navy)*	Assessment *(e.g., survey, medical record)*	Outcome Measures	Results	Correlates of Mental Health Conditions	Comparisons	Critique
Army soldiers in Iraq in October and November 2005	Anonymous survey delivered to sample of soldiers from 9 brigade combat teams located at 13 Forward Operating Bases and associated units throughout Iraq	**Acute stress (PTSD):** PCL-DSM-50[a] **Depression:** PHQ-DSM+FI[b]	**Acute stress symptoms:** 14% **Depression:** 8% **Depression, anxiety, or acute stress:** 17%	**Multiple deployment** (e.g., 1 or more prior deployments to Iraq) were associated with higher levels of acute stress (18.4%) relative to those on their first deployment (12.5%)	Relative to the MHAT-II Iraq-only samples, MHAT-III sample had significantly higher levels of depression and any psychological problem; no difference relative to MHAT-I Iraq-only sample	**Quality control:** Not peer-reviewed **Generalizability:** Unknown

[a] PCL-DSM-50—PCL-DSM + total score of at least 50 (range: 17–85) on the PTSD Checklist.
[b] PHQ-DSM+FI—PHQ-DSM on the PHQ-9 + self-reported functional impairment.

Table 3.22
Studies of Mental and Cognitive Conditions Among Servicemembers Returning from Afghanistan and Iraq: U.S. Department of the Army, Office of the Surgeon, Multinational Force–Iraq and Office of the Surgeon General, U.S. Army Medical Command, 2006b

U.S. Department of the Army, Office of the Surgeon, Multinational Force–Iraq and Office of the Surgeon General, U.S. Army Medical Command, Mental Health Advisory Team (MHAT–IV). *Operation Iraqi Freedom 05-07, MHAT-IV Report.* November 17, 2006b.
Type of Report (e.g., peer-reviewed, gov't report): Gov't report
N: 1,767
Design (e.g., cross-sectional, longitudinal, medical-record review): Cross-sectional
Conditions Studied: PTSD, Depression

Sample *which Service (e.g., Army, Navy)*	Assessment *(e.g., survey, medical record)*	Outcome Measures	Results	Correlates of Mental Health Conditions	Comparisons	Critique
Army soldiers and Marines in Iraq (May 2007)	Anonymous survey delivered to sample of soldiers and marine line companies, primarily from brigade combat teams (Army, n=1,320) and regimental combat teams (marines, n=447). Also included soldiers and marines in support units, and the corps and division levels from all Iraq regions where significant U.S. ground forces existed in May 2007	**Acute stress (PTSD):** PCL-DSM-50[a] **Depression:** PHQ-DSM+FI[b]	**Depression** (% Marines/ % Soldiers) 4/9% **Acute stress** (% Marines/% Soldiers) 14/17% **Depression, anxiety, or acute stress** (% Marines/ % Soldiers) 15/20%	**Level of combat** (low, medium, high) related to positive screen for anxiety, depression, or acute stress **Multiple deployment** (e.g., 1 or more prior deployments to Iraq) was associated with higher levels of acute stress, depression, anxiety, or any mental health problem **Deployment for more than 6 months** was positively associated with acute stress, depression, anxiety, and any mental health problem relative to deployment for less than 6 months	No differences among soldiers relative to MHAT-I and MHAT-III; Marines screening positive for depression had lower levels than Army soldiers in MHAT-I, MHAT-III, MHAT-IV.	**Quality control:** Not peer-reviewed **Generalizability:** Unknown

[a] PCL-DSM-50—PCL-DSM + total score of at least 50 (range: 17–85) on the PTSD Checklist.

[b] PHQ-DSM+FI—PHQ-DSM on the PHQ-9 + self-reported functional impairment.

Table 3.23
Studies of Mental and Cognitive Conditions Among Servicemembers Returning from Afghanistan and Iraq: Abt Associates Inc., 2006

Abt Associates Inc. *2003–2004 Active Duty Health Study: Final Report.* Falls Church, Va.: TRICARE Management Activity, Health Program Analysis and Evaluation Directorate, December 30, 2006.
Type of Report (e.g., peer-reviewed, gov't report): Gov't-sponsored report
N: 2,761
Design (e.g., cross-sectional, longitudinal, medical-record review): Cross-sectional
Conditions Studied: PTSD

Sample *which Service (e.g., Army, Navy)*	Assessment *(e.g., survey, medical record)*	Outcome Measures	Results	Correlates of Mental Health Conditions	Comparisons	Critique
Stratified, random sample of servicemembers from the Active Component who deployed to Iraq or Afghanistan on or after January 2003 and returned from theater by February 2004	Survey of deployed (n=1,419) and nondeployed (n=1,342) servicemembers from the Active Component	**PTSD:** PCL-DSM[a] **Other:** Quality of life, cognitive functioning, deployment, social support	**PTSD:** Deployed: 7.3% Nondeployed: 4.1%	**Unit cohesion** scores were negatively associated with PTSD scores Mean scores of all **quality-of-life** domains and **cognitive functioning** for deployed servicemembers with PTSD were much lower than for those deployed without PTSD	Deployed servicemembers were more likely to screen positive for PTSD than nondeployed servicemembers	**Generalizability:** Active Component only; no Reserve Component represented **Response rate:** 46%; may be less likely to capture those who are more severely impaired

[a] PCL-DSM—Reporting at least 1 intrusion symptom, 3 avoidance symptoms, and 2 hyperarousal symptoms at the moderate level on the PTSD Checklist.

References

Abt Associates Inc., *2003–2004 Active Duty Health Study: Final Report.* Falls Church, Va.: TRICARE Management Activity, Health Program Analysis and Evaluation Directorate, 2006.

American Psychiatric Association. *Diagnostic and Statistical Manual of Mental Disorders,* 4th ed., text revision. Washington, D.C., RC455.2.C4 D536 2000, 2000.

Andrykowski, M. A., M. J. Cordova, J. L. Studts, and T. W. Miller. Posttraumatic stress disorder after treatment for breast cancer: Prevalence of diagnosis and use of the PTSD Checklist–Civilian Version (PCL-C) as a screening instrument. *Journal of Consulting Clinical Psychology*, Vol. 66, No. 3, June 1998, pp. 586–590.

Blanchard, E. B., J. Jones-Alexander, T. C. Buckley, and C. A. Forneris. Psychometric properties of the PTSD Checklist (PCL). *Behavioral Research Therapist,* Vol. 34, No. 8, August 1996, pp. 669–673.

Brewin, C. R. Systematic review of screening instruments for adults at risk of PTSD. *Journal of Trauma and Stress*, Vol. 18, No. 1, February 2005, pp. 53–62.

Carlson, E. B. Psychometric study of a brief screen for PTSD: Assessing the impact of multiple traumatic events. *Assessment*, Vol. 8, No. 4, December 2001, pp. 431–441.

Coffey, S. F., B. Gudmundsdottir, J. G. Beck, S. A. Paylo, and L. Miller. Screening for PTSD in motor vehicle accident survivors using the PSS-SR and IES. *Journal of Trauma and Stress*, Vol. 19, No. 1, February 2006, pp. 119–128.

Colarusso, Laura M. Concerns grow about war veterans' misdiagnoses. *Boston Globe*, June 10, 2007.

Cuijpers, P., F. Smit, and A. van Straten. Psychological treatments of subthreshold depression: A meta-analytic review. *Acta Psychiatrica Scandinavia*, Vol. 115, No. 6, June 2007, pp. 434–441.

Dohrenwend, B. P., J. B. Turner, N. A. Turse, B. G. Adams, K. C. Koenen, and R. Marshall. The psychological risks of Vietnam for U.S. veterans: A revisit with new data and methods. *Science,* Vol. 313, No. 5789, August 18, 2006, pp. 979–982.

Engelhard, I. M., M. A. Van Den Hout, J. Weerts, A. Arntz, J. J. C. M. Hox, and R. J. McNally. Deployment-related stress and trauma in Dutch soldiers returning from Iraq. *British Journal of Psychiatry*, Vol. 191, August 2007, pp. 140–145.

Erbes, C., J. Westermeyer, B. Engdahl, and E. Johnsen. Post-traumatic stress disorder and service utilization in a sample of service members from Iraq and Afghanistan. *Military Medicine,* Vol. 172, No. 4, April 2007, pp. 359–363.

Fischer, H., and the Library of Congress. *United States Military Casualty Statistics: Operation Iraqi Freedom and Operation Enduring Freedom.* Washington, D.C.: Congressional Research Service, 2006.

Grieger, T. A., S. J. Cozza, R. J. Ursano, C. Hoge, P. E. Martinez, C. C. Engel, and H. J. Wain. Posttraumatic stress disorder and depression in battle-injured soldiers. *American Journal of Psychiatry,* Vol. 163, No. 10, October 2006, pp. 1777–1783.

Helmer, D. A., M. Rossignol, M. Blatt, R. Agarwal, R. Teichman, and G. Lange. Health and exposure concerns of veterans deployed to Iraq and Afghanistan. *Journal of Occupational and Environmental Medicine*, Vol. 49, No. 5, May 2007, pp. 475–480.

Hoge, C. W., J. L. Auchterlonie, and C. S. Milliken. Mental health problems, use of mental health services, and attrition from military service after returning from deployment to Iraq or Afghanistan. *Journal of the American Medical Association*, Vol. 295, No. 9, March 1, 2006, pp. 1023–1032.

Hoge, C. W., C. A. Castro, S. C. Messer, D. McGurk, D. I. Cotting, and R. L. Koffman. Combat duty in Iraq and Afghanistan, mental health problems, and barriers to care. *New England Journal of Medicine,* Vol. 351, No. 1, July 1, 2004, pp. 13–22.

Hoge, C. W., D. McGurk, J. L. Thomas, A. L. Cox, C. C. Engel, and C. A. Castro. Mild traumatic brain injury in U.S. soldiers returning from Iraq. *New England Journal of Medicine,* Vol. 358, No. 5, January 31, 2008, pp. 453–463.

Hoge, C. W., A. Terhakopian, C. A. Castro, S. C. Messer, and C. C. Engel. Association of posttraumatic stress disorder with somatic symptoms, health care visits, and absenteeism among Iraq war veterans. *American Journal of Psychiatry,* Vol. 164, No. 1, January 2007, pp. 150–153.

Hotopf, M., L. Hull, N. T. Fear, T. Browne, O. Horn, A. Iversen, M. Jones, D. Murphy, D. Bland, M. Earnshaw, N. Greenberg, J. H. Hughes, A. R. Tate, C. Dandeker, R. Rona, and S. Wessely. The health of UK military personnel who deployed to the 2003 Iraq war: A cohort study. *Lancet,* Vol. 367, No. 9524, May 27, 2006, pp. 1731–1741.

Jablensky, A. Research methods in psychiatric epidemiology: An overview. *Australia and New Zealand Journal of Psychiatry,* Vol. 36, No. 3, June 2002, pp. 297–310.

Jaycox, L. H., G. N. Marshall, and T. Schell. Use of mental health services by men injured through community violence. *Psychiatric Services,* Vol. 55, No. 4, April 2004, pp. 415–420.

Kendler, K. S., T. J. Gallagher, J. M. Abelson, and R. C. Kessler. Lifetime prevalence, demographic risk factors, and diagnostic validity of nonaffective psychosis as assessed in a US community sample. The National Comorbidity Survey. *Archives of General Psychiatry,* Vol. 53, No. 11, November 1996, pp. 1022–1031.

Kessler, R. C. Posttraumatic stress disorder: The burden to the individual and to society. *Journal of Clinical Psychiatry,* Vol. 61, Suppl. 5, 2000, pp. 4–14.

Kolkow, T. T., J. L. Spira, J. S. Morse, and T. A. Grieger. Post-traumatic stress disorder and depression in health care providers returning from deployment to Iraq and Afghanistan. *Military Medicine,* Vol. 172, No. 5, May 2007, pp. 451–455.

Kroenke, K., and R. L. Spitzer. The PHQ-9: A new depression diagnostic and severity measure. *Psychiatric Annals,* Vol. 32, No. 9, September 2002, pp. 1–7.

Kroenke, K., R. L. Spitzer, and J. B. Williams. The Patient Health Questionnaire–2: Validity of a two-item depression screener. *Medical Care,* Vol. 41, No. 11, November 2003, pp. 1284–1292.

Lapierre, C. B., A. F. Schwegler, and B. J. LaBauve. Posttraumatic stress and depression symptoms in soldiers returning from combat operations in Iraq and Afghanistan. *Journal of Trauma and Stress,* Vol. 20, No. 6, December 2007, pp. 933–943.

Manne, S. L., K. Du Hammel, K. Gallelli, K. Sorgen, and W. H. Redd. Posttraumatic stress disorder among mothers of pediatric cancer survivors: Diagnosis, comorbidity, and utility of the PTSD checklist as a screening instrument. *Journal of Pediatric Psychology,* Vol. 23, No. 6, December 1998, pp. 357–366.

Marshall R. D., M. Olfson, F. Hellman, C. Blanco, M. Guardino, E. L. Struening. Comorbidity, impairment, and suicidality in subthreshold PTSD. *American Journal of Psychiatry,* September 2001, Vol. 158, No. 9, pp. 1467–1473.

Martin, C. B. Routine screening and referrals for PTSD after returning from Operation Iraqi Freedom in 2005, U.S. Armed Forces. *MSMR: Medical Surveillance Monthly Report,* Vol. 14, No. 6, September/October 2007, pp. 2–7. As of February 6, 2008: http://amsa.army.mil/1msmr/2007/v14_n06.pdf#Cover

Milliken, C. S., J. L. Auchterlonie, and C. W. Hoge. Longitudinal assessment of mental health problems among Active and Reserve Component soldiers returning from the Iraq war. *Journal of the American Medical Association,* Vol. 298, No. 18, November 14, 2007, pp. 2141–2148.

Murray, C. K., J. C. Reynolds, J. M. Schroeder, M. B. Harrison, O. M. Evans, and D. R. Hospenthal. Spectrum of care provided at an Echelon II medical unit during Operation Iraqi Freedom. *Military Medicine,* Vol. 170, No. 6, June 2005, pp. 516–520.

O'Bryant, J., M. Waterhouse, and the Library of Congress. *U.S. Forces in Iraq.* Washington, D.C.: Congressional Research Service, 2006.

———. *U.S. Forces in Afghanistan.* Washington, D.C.: Congressional Research Service, 2007.

Prins, A., P. Ouimette, R. Kimerling, R. P. Cameron, D. S. Hugelshofer, J. Shaw-Hegwer, A. Thrailkill, F. D. Gusman, and J. I. Sheikh. The primary care PTSD screen (PC-PTSD): Development and operating characteristics. *Primary Care Psychiatry,* Vol. 9, No. 1, March 2004, pp. 9–14.

Rosenheck, R. A., and A. F. Fontana. Recent trends in VA treatment of post-traumatic stress disorder and other mental disorders. *Health Affairs (Millwood),* Vol. 26, No. 6, November–December 2007, pp. 1720–1727.

Ruo, B., J. S. Rumsfeld, M. A. Hlatky, H. Liu, W. S. Browner, and M. A. Whooley. Depressive symptoms and health-related quality of life. *Journal of the American Medical Association*, Vol. 290, No. 2, July 2003, pp. 215–221.

Santor, D. A., and J. C. Coyne. Shortening the CES-D to improve its ability to detect cases of depression. *Psychological Assessment,* Vol. 9, No. 3, September 1997, pp. 233–243.

Schwab, K. A., B. Ivins, G. Cramer, W. Johnson, M. Sluss-Tiller, K. Kiley, W. Lux, and D. Warden. Screening for traumatic brain injury in troops returning from deployment in Afghanistan and Iraq: Initial investigation of the usefulness of a short screening tool for traumatic brain injury. *Journal of Head Trauma Rehabilitation*, Vol. 22, No. 6, November–December 2007, pp. 377–389.

Seal, K. H., D. Bertenthal, C. R. Miner, S. Sen, and C. Marmar. Bringing the war back home: Mental health disorders among 103,788 US veterans returning from Iraq and Afghanistan seen at Department of Veterans Affairs facilities. *Archives of Internal Medicine,* Vol. 167, No. 5, March 12, 2007, pp. 476–482.

Smith, T. C., M. A. K. Ryan, D. L. Wingard, D. J. Slymen, J. F. Sallis, D. Kritz-Silverstein, and Team for the Millennium Cohort Study. New onset and persistent symptoms of post-traumatic stress disorder self reported after deployment and combat exposures: Prospective population based US military cohort study. *British Medical Journal*, January 15, 2008. As of January 28, 2008: http://www.bmj.com/cgi/content/abstract/bmj.39430.638241.AEv1

Spitzer, R. L., K. Kroenke, and J. B. Williams. Validation and utility of a self-report version of PRIME-MD: The PHQ primary care study. Primary Care Evaluation of Mental Disorders. Patient Health Questionnaire. *Journal of the American Medical Association,* Vol. 282, No. 18, November 10, 1999, pp. 1737–1744.

Stimpson, N. J., H. V. Thomas, A. L. Weighttman, F. Dunstan, and G. Lewis. Psychiatric disorders in veterans of the Persian Gulf War of 1991. Systematic review. *British Journal of Psychiatry*, Vol. 182, No. 5, May 2003, pp. 391–403.

The Traumatic Brain Injury Task Force. *Report to the Surgeon General,* Washington, D.C., 2007.

United States Department of Defense. "Post-Deployment Health Reassessment," 2006. As of January 28, 2008: http://www.pdhealth.mil/dcs/pdhra.asp

U.S. Department of the Army, Office of the Surgeon General, Mental Health Advisory Team (MHAT). *Operation Iraqi Freedom (OIF), MHAT Report.* U.S. Army Surgeon General and HQDA G-1, December 16, 2003.

U.S. Department of the Army, Office of the Surgeon General, Mental Health Advisory Team (MHAT-II). *Operation Iraqi Freedom (OIF-II), MHAT-II Report.* U.S. Army Surgeon General, January 30, 2005.

U.S. Department of the Army, Office of the Surgeon, Multinational Force–Iraq and Office of the Surgeon General, U.S. Army Medical Command, Mental Health Advisory Team (MHAT-III). *Operation Iraqi Freedom 04-06, MHAT-III Report.* 2006a.

U.S. Department of the Army, Office of the Surgeon, Multinational Force–Iraq and Office of the Surgeon General, U.S. Army Medical Command, Mental Health Advisory Team (MHAT-IV). *Operation Iraqi Freedom 05-07, MHAT-IV Report.* 2006b.

Vasterling, J. J., S. P. Proctor, P. Amoroso, R. Kane, T. Heeren, and R. F. White. Neuropsychological outcomes of army personnel following deployment to the Iraq war. *Journal of the American Medical Association,* Vol. 296, No. 5, August 2, 2006, pp. 519–529.

Walker, K. A., W. Katon, J. Russo, P. Ciechanowski, E. Newman, and A. W. Wagner. Health care costs associated with posttraumatic stress disorder in women. *Archives of General Psychiatry*, Vol. 60, No. 4, April 2003, pp. 369–374.

Warden, D. Military TBI during the Iraq and Afghanistan wars. *Journal of Head Trauma Rehabilitation,* Vol. 21, No. 5, September–October 2006, pp. 398–402.

Weathers, F. W., B. T. Litz, D. S. Herman, J. A. Huska, and T. M. Keane. The PTSD Checklist (PCL): Reliability, validity, and diagnostic utility. Abstract. San Antonio, Tex.: International Society of Traumatic Stress Studies, October 1993.

Zatzick, D. F., S. M. Kang, H. G. Muller, J. E. Russo, F. P. Rivara, W. Katon, G. J. Jurkovich, and P. R. Byrne. Predicting posttraumatic distress in hospitalized trauma survivors with acute injuries. *American Journal of Psychiatry*, Vol. 159, No. 6, June 2002, pp. 941–946.

Zoroya, G. Pentagon holds brain injury data. *USA Today,* June 8, 2006.

CHAPTER FOUR

Survey of Individuals Previously Deployed for OEF/OIF

Terry L. Schell and Grant N. Marshall

Introduction

RAND conducted a large population-based survey on individuals previously deployed as part of Operation Enduring Freedom or Operation Iraqi Freedom (OEF/OIF) to address several gaps in the existing literature concerning the prevalence and correlates of mental health conditions and traumatic brain injury (TBI) stemming from service in OEF/OIF. As reported in Chapter Three, research on the prevalence of post-traumatic stress disorder (PTSD) and major depression has typically focused on active duty Army personnel and has largely neglected several types of servicemembers deployed in OEF/OIF. For example, although Air Force and Navy personnel account for 38 percent of the deployed force, few studies have examined the prevalence of PTSD and major depression in these populations. Similarly, only minimal information concerning these conditions exists for marines. Moreover, little information is available regarding the mental health of previously deployed National Guard or Reserve personnel, despite evidence from post-deployment screening that servicemembers of the Army National Guard and Army Reserve are twice as likely as active duty personnel to suffer from mental health problems (Milliken, Auchterlonie, and Hoge, 2007). In addition, almost all research to date has focused on individuals who are within one year of their most recent deployment (e.g., Hoge, Auchterlonie, and Milliken, 2006). These omissions make it difficult to estimate the actual magnitude of combat-related mental disorders in this population.

Although research into the mental health of servicemembers who have served in OEF/OIF has focused on a narrow segment of the whole population, research into the prevalence and correlates of TBI is even less conclusive. With the exception of one recently published study of TBI in infantry soldiers from two brigades (Hoge et al., 2008), most information regarding TBI in previously deployed individuals is based on small samples of treatment-seeking individuals (Murray, Reynolds, Schroeder, et al., 2005) or on internal Department of Defense (DoD) research that has not been peer-reviewed or released publicly; results were available only through the news articles (e.g., TBI: Hidden wounds plague Iraq war veterans, 2007).

Another shortcoming of existing research is that most studies of previously deployed personnel have been conducted under the auspices of DoD, which raises the possibility that respondents may either underreport problems to avoid disclosing career-jeopardizing disorders or overreport to maintain disability or medical benefits. Finally, all publicly released results from DoD studies must be approved through DoD operational security and public-affairs offices. It is generally preferable that the design, analysis, and dissemination of research be controlled by organizations that do not have a direct interest in the outcome.

In this chapter, we describe the methods we employed and results of our large population-based survey of personnel previously deployed for OEF/OIF, designed to assess deployment experiences, current mental health symptoms, use of services, and barriers to care.

Methods

Eligibility and Sampling

To be eligible to participate in the survey, individuals must have been previously deployed as part of OEF/OIF and be reachable at a landline phone number within the United States during the study period. These requirements exclude currently deployed servicemembers, individuals who reside in households without a landline telephone, and those who are hospitalized or incarcerated.

The survey was designed to create a broadly representative sample of the population of individuals who have been deployed as part of OEF/OIF. The sampling strategy targeted 24 geographic areas of the United States that encompass the domestic military bases with the largest overall number of deployed personnel. The geographic sizes of the sampling areas varied according to the geographic distribution of numbers within the selected telephone exchanges and population density. Sizes ranged from approximately 35 square miles to more than 500 square miles. The sampling areas were large enough to encompass both on-base housing and the surrounding communities in which retired and separated servicemembers lived. As described below, screening calls were placed to identify eligible participants. The number of screening calls within each of the geographic areas was approximately proportional to the number of deployed personnel from that area. Table 4.1 lists military installations that are contained within or adjacent to the sampling areas. Because some areas include multiple military installations, the number of installations sampled is greater than 24.

We identified telephone exchanges that are common within the targeted geographic areas and dialed randomly selected numbers from those exchanges. This Random Digit Dialing (RDD) methodology ensures that a random sample of individuals who have telephone numbers in those exchanges were phoned. Randomly selected telephone numbers were dialed up to six times to reach any adult household member

Table 4.1
Major Military Installations in Sampled Areas

Service	Installation
Army	Fort Bragg, NC
	Fort Campbell, TN
	Fort Carson, CO
	Fort Hood, TX
	Fort Lewis, WA
	Fort Riley, KS
	Fort Stewart, GA
Navy	Coronado Naval Amphibious Base, CA
	Coronado North Island NAS, CA
	Little Creek Amphibious Base, VA
	Naval Medical Center Portsmouth, VA
	Naval Station Norfolk, VA
	Oceana NAS, VA
Air Force	Dover Air Force Base (AFB), DE
	Dyess AFB, TX
	Eglin AFB, FL
	Grand Forks AFB, ND
	Hurlburt Field, FL
	Moody AFB, GA
	Pope AFB, NC
	Warner Robbins AFB, GA
Marine Corps	Camp Lejeune, NC
	Camp Pendleton, CA
	Cherry Point Marine Corps Air Station, NC
	Marine Corps Base Hawaii, HI
	Miramar Marine Corps Air Station, CA
	Twentynine Palms Marine Corps Air-Ground Combat Center, CA

to screen for eligibility of all individuals within the household. Households were then screened to determine whether any member of the household had ever been deployed as part of OEF/OIF.

When a household was identified as containing an eligible individual, the telephone number was dialed up to 25 times to obtain either cooperation or a refusal to participate. A sampling flow diagram is included in Figure 4.1 to illustrate the

Figure 4.1
RDD-Sampling Flow Diagram

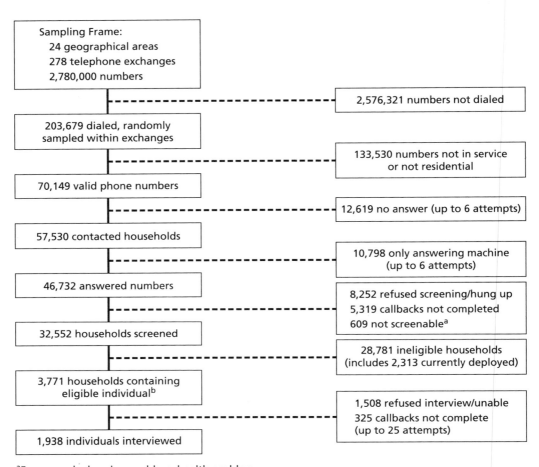

aFor example, hearing problem, health problem.
bPreviously deployed for OEF or OIF.

disposition of all randomly selected numbers. Following this sampling and recruitment procedure, we completed 1,938 interviews with an overall response rate of 0.44 ([28,781+1,938]/70,149; minimum response rate combined for screening interview and main interview). Interviews were conducted between August 2007 and January 2008. In addition to this RDD-based sample, the analytic sample includes 27 respondents who volunteered to participate in the research, through the Military Officers' Association of America and the Iraq and Afghanistan Veterans of America. In total, 1,965 respondents completed an interview.

Informed Consent

This study was approved and monitored by the RAND Institutional Review Board (IRB). We read a consent script to participants that was approved by the RAND IRB. This script read as follows:

> The purpose of this study is to learn about the physical, emotional and economic problems faced by people who have returned from a deployment to Iraq or Afghanistan. The research will help to document the medical and psychological needs of servicemembers returning from duty.

Respondents were also told about the risks of participating. The script stated that (1) the respondent could terminate the interview at any time, or skip any question, without penalty, (2) the survey responses themselves were confidential and cannot be revealed even under subpoena because the study has a National Institutes of Health (NIH) certificate of confidentiality, (3) any spontaneous mention of an intent to harm themselves or others would be reported to authorities, and (4) the survey would ask about mental health and traumatic experiences during deployment that may make some respondents uncomfortable. Interview completion was regarded as evidence of consent to participate. As a follow-up, participants were mailed an information sheet describing the study and giving information on how to contact the study investigators, the RAND IRB, and service providers for mental health problems.

Interviews

Trained interviewers used a computer-assisted telephone interview system to query participants. For the most part, we selected measures used in prior research efforts with veterans who had been deployed to Afghanistan and Iraq to maximize the ability to compare findings across studies. The survey, which covered the following topics, lasted 32 minutes on average. A copy of the instrument is available from the authors upon request.

Measures

Sociodemographics. Sociodemographic information, including branch of Service, current duty status, military rank, age, gender, marital status, race/ethnicity, and the nature, number and recency of deployments, was obtained by self-report. To determine duty status, respondents were asked if they were "still in the military" or had "separated from service." Those who were currently still in the military were also asked if they were currently in the "Guard or Reserve" or if they were "active duty."

Combat Trauma Exposure. Combat trauma exposure was measured using 11 items that form two indices: (1) a one-item measure that assesses whether the respondent had ever experienced an injury or wound that required hospitalization while deployed and (2) a scale derived by counting the number of ten specific trauma exposures that occurred during any of the respondents' OEF/OIF deployments. The list of traumatic combat experiences is adapted from Hoge et al. (2004) and includes both direct and vicarious trauma exposure (e.g., witnessing a traumatic event that occurred to others). The full instrument contained 24 traumatic exposures. However, many items were empirically redundant with one another. The subset of exposures used in the scale was chosen because the remaining items were not predictive of PTSD when controlling for these 11.

Probable PTSD. To assess post-traumatic stress symptoms, we used the Posttraumatic Symptom Checklist–Military Version (PCL-M; Weathers, Huska, and Keane, 1991), an instrument that contains 17 symptom items keyed directly to the *Diagnostic and Statistical Manual*, Fourth edition (DSM-IV; American Psychiatric Association, 1994) and answered with respect to combat-stress experiences on a 5-point scale reflecting extent of symptom severity. The symptoms are then scored according to the DSM-IV definition. Answers were provided for the period "in the last 30 days." The PCL-M has been used to study post-traumatic distress in various military samples (e.g., Grieger et al., 2006).

Probable diagnoses were derived following guidelines offered by Weathers et al. (1993). In particular, symptoms were counted as present if respondents indicated that they had been "moderately (3)" bothered by the symptom. This scoring has been shown to have high specificity and sensitivity, 0.92 and 0.99, respectively (see Brewin, 2005, for a review of different scoring methods). To examine barriers to care for persons who might have possible need for mental health treatment, we defined *subthreshold PTSD* by counting a symptom as present when it bothered the respondent at least "a little (2)."

Probable Major Depression. The Patient Health Questionnaire–8 was used to assess symptoms of major depression (PHQ-8; Kroenke, Spitzer, and Williams, 2001; Lowe, Kroenke, et al., 2004). The PHQ-8, a variant of the PHQ-9, consists of items assessing the actual criteria on which a DSM-IV diagnosis of major depression is based, with the exception of thoughts of suicide. Responses to the PHQ-8 are provided with respect to the frequency with which symptoms were experienced in the past two weeks, using a 4-point (0–3) scale. The PHQ-8 is well validated and widely used as a brief screening measure (e.g., Lowe, Spitzer, et al., 2004). Probable moderate or severe depression was indicated by a total score of 10 or above, following the recommended cutpoint (Kroenke, Spitzer, and Williams, 2001). This cutpoint yields a sensitivity of 0.99 and a specificity of 0.92, which is slightly more specific than the PHQ-9 (Kroenke, Spitzer, and Williams, 2001). For the purpose of examining barriers to care for persons who might have a possible need for mental health treatment, we also assessed mild depression as indicated by a total score of 5 or more.

Probable TBI. The Brief Traumatic Brain Injury Screen (BTBIS), which has been used by the military to assess personnel returning from OEF/OIF, was used to screen for the presence of probable TBI (Schwab et al., 2007). The BTBIS has demonstrated a positive value for predicting TBI in the OEF/OIF population (Schwab et al., 2007); however, no survey-based assessments of TBI have undergone a rigorous evaluation of diagnostic efficiency. Probable TBI is indicated by any injury during deployment that resulted in an alteration of consciousness immediately following the injury—e.g., being confused, experiencing memory loss, being unconscious. Meeting screening criteria for having experienced a probable TBI does not require current TBI-related morbidity. Thus, the instrument does not assess ongoing functional or cognitive impairment caused by a TBI. Most individuals who screen positive for having experienced a probable TBI are likely to have full cognitive functioning.

Barriers to Care. To assess barriers to seeking health care for mental health concerns, respondents were asked a single question: "If you wanted help for an emotional or personal problem, which of the following would make it difficult?" This question was followed by statements posed as potential barriers to treatment. Respondents endorsed each statement that they thought would make it difficult to get treatment by responding "yes." Potential barriers to care were drawn from three separate instruments: The National Comorbidity Survey Replication (NCS-R) (e.g., Kessler et al., 2005); the Hoge et al. (2004) study of barriers to care in the military; and our own instrument, which was developed for use among individuals with a range of traumatic experiences (e.g., Wong et al., 2006). From across these instruments, we selected distinct barriers, maintaining all of the factors found by Hoge et al. (2004) to be highly endorsed in a military sample. For heuristic purposes, we distinguished among three broad, classes of barriers to care: logistical barriers (e.g., "it would be difficult to schedule an appointment"), institutional and cultural barriers ("it could harm my career"), and beliefs and preference for treatment (e.g., "even good mental health care is not very effective").

Past-Year Service Utilization and Adequacy. To determine past-year utilization of services for mental health concerns, we posed several questions. A single question inquired whether respondents had seen any provider for mental health services in the past 12 months—i.e., "In the past 12 months have you visited any professional like a doctor, a psychologist, or a counselor to get help with issues such as stress, emotional, alcohol, drug, or family problem?" Psychotropic drug use was assessed with two questions—i.e., "Have you been prescribed any medication for a mental health or emotional problem in the past 12 months?" and "Did you take the medication for as long as your doctor wanted you to?" For each type of provider seen, additional questions inquired about the number of sessions and the length of the typical session.

Participants were judged to have had a *minimally adequate trial of a psychotropic drug* if they (1) had taken a prescribed medication as long as the doctor wanted, and (2) had at least four visits with a doctor or therapist in the past 12 months. *Minimally adequate exposure to psychotherapy* was defined as having had at least eight visits with a "mental health professional such as a psychiatrist, psychologist or counselor" in the past 12 months, with visits averaging at least 30 minutes. Criteria for minimally adequate courses of treatment were adapted from the NCS-R (Wang et al., 2005). These criteria for minimally adequate treatment of PTSD and major depression were developed by Wang et al. (2005) based on a comprehensive review of available guidelines for therapies that have demonstrated efficacy. The NCS-R requires that pharmacotherapy be supervised by a physician and be taken for at least eight weeks. We allowed that pharmacotherapy in the military may be supervised by medical personnel other than a physician; also, rather than require a specific treatment length, we asked respondents if they had completed their course of treatment. Whereas the NCS-R also requires that all eight psychotherapy sessions occur with the same provider, our definition did not require a single provider for all sessions.

To obtain information about services received for TBI, we included specific items that inquired whether participants had ever been screened by a doctor or health specialist for a TBI and whether screening was for an injury received during deployment.

Statistical Analysis

Sampling Weights. After we completed data collection, we developed post-stratification weights to improve the representativeness of the analytic sample relative to the target population—all OEF/OIF veterans—and to account for nonresponse in the sampling. The sampling strategy was designed to provide the lowest possible standard errors in our estimates of the overall rates of PTSD, depression, and TBI within the available resources. This strategy resulted in differential sampling probabilities across military groups. For example, we recruited fewer Navy and Air Force personnel than would be expected in a simple random sample (*N*'s = 1,073, 207, 235, and 450 for Army, Navy, Air Force, and Marines, respectively). The selection of 24 geographic areas with high total numbers of deployments resulted in a designed oversampling of active duty personnel (*N*'s =1,530, 360, and 75, for currently active duty, currently separated, and currently Reserve, respectively). In addition to these factors, which are built into the survey design, the study slightly underrepresented males, unmarried individuals, and younger individuals relative to their numbers in the population. These underrepresentations are similar to those found in most RDD studies and are likely related to differences in the use of cell phones and answering machines across these subpopulations. Therefore, our survey design requires weights to create an analytic sample that is broadly representative of the target population. Specifically, the sample was weighted to match the target population (all servicemembers previously deployed to OEF/OIF) on the marginal distribution of branch of Service, and within each branch of Service it is weighted to balance on median age, gender, marital status, officer rank, currently separated duty status, and Reserve Component. The resulting weights allowed us to create an analytic sample that closely matched the total deployed force on critical variables (Table 4.2). The characteristics of the population of previously deployed servicemembers were derived from the Contingency Tracking System Deployment File and the Work Experiences File from the Defense Manpower Data Center (DMDC).

Data Analysis. Using these sample weights, we conducted all analyses in SAS 9.1.3 with *proc genmod* and *proc surveyfreq*. Analyses account for the effects of the weights on both the parameter estimates and their standard errors. Throughout the text and

Table 4.2
Demographic Characteristics of Respondents (N=1,965)

Characteristic	Weighted Percentage	95% CI LL	95% CI UL
Branch			
Army	48.9	45.0	52.7
Navy	18.6	15.3	21.9
Air Force	19.8	16.6	23.1
Marine Corps	12.7	10.2	15.2
Current Duty Status			
Active	38.3	35.1	41.5
Reserve/Guard	14.7	11.1	18.3
Discharged/Retired	47.0	43.0	51.0
Rank			
Enlisted	85.9	83.6	88.2
Warrant Officer	1.8	1.0	2.5
Officer	12.3	10.1	14.6
Race			
White	65.7	61.8	69.5
Black	21.6	18.1	25.2
Hispanic	8.3	6.2	10.3
Other	4.4	2.8	6.0
Current Marital Status			
Not Married	31.8	27.4	36.2
Married	68.2	63.8	72.6
Sex			
Female	11.5	9.1	13.8
Male	88.5	86.2	90.9
Last Deployed			
OEF	21.9	18.4	25.4
OIF	78.1	74.6	81.6
Multiple Deployments			
Yes	46.5	42.6	50.3
No	53.5	49.7	57.4
Time Since Last Deployment (months)			
0–17	34.7	31.2	38.2
18–35	32.5	28.9	36.2
36+	32.8	28.9	36.7
Length of Last Deployment (months)			
<6	25.0	21.5	28.4
6–11	44.9	40.9	48.8
12+	30.2	26.8	33.5
Current Age (years)			
<30	49.9	46.0	53.8
30+	50.1	46.2	54.0

NOTES: CI = confidence interval; LL = lower limit; UL = upper limit.

tables, we report weighted proportions. Proportions and exact binomial 95-percent confidence intervals were calculated for dichotomous outcomes. After describing the rates of exposure to combat trauma, as well as the prevalence of probable PTSD, major depression, and TBI, we examined bivariate and multivariate predictors of the three health conditions. Relative risk ratios for both bivariate and multivariate models, as well as their confidence intervals, were calculated using the method outlined by Zou (2004). Relative risk ratios allow for a more straightforward interpretation than the odds ratios that are typically presented from logistic regressions.

We also estimated the extent to which the observed prevalence of these conditions was attributable to deployment experiences. Specifically, we estimated the prevalence of PTSD, major depression, and TBI for individuals with no reported combat trauma during deployment and compared those numbers to the prevalences in the full sample. We did so using predicted values from a linear model in which each disorder was predicted from the separate traumas. Predicted values and confidence intervals are generated for the case when no traumas occurred.

We then characterized past-12-month mental health service utilization of persons meeting screening criteria for probable PTSD, major depression, or TBI. Finally, we calculated rates of endorsement of barriers to service utilization for respondents who met relaxed criteria for possible need for mental health treatment (i.e., those with sub-threshold PTSD or mild depression).

Results

As shown in Table 4.3, rates of exposure to specific types of combat trauma ranged from 5 to 50 percent, with high reporting levels for many traumatic events. Vicariously experienced traumas (e.g., having a friend who was seriously wounded or killed) were the most frequently reported. Direct injuries were reported by between 10 and 20 percent of the sample.

A substantial percentage of previously deployed personnel are currently affected by probable PTSD and major depression, as displayed in Table 4.4. In particular, rates of PTSD and major depression were both 14 percent. Rates of probable TBI during deployment were also high, exceeding 19 percent. Approximately 19 percent of respondents met criteria for either PTSD or major depression, and 31 percent met criteria for TBI, PTSD, or major depression. Moreover, the three conditions tend to co-occur. Specifically, PTSD and major depression are highly correlated (Spearman's r=.60), and these mental health conditions are moderately associated with TBI (Spearman's r=.29 and .26 for PTSD and major depression, respectively). Approximately two-thirds of those with PTSD also have probable major depression, whereas only one-third of those with TBI also meet criteria for depression.

Table 4.3
Rates of Trauma Exposure in OEF/OIF (N=1,965)

Type of Combat Trauma	Weighted Percentage	95% CI LL	95% CI UL
Having a friend who was seriously wounded or killed	49.6	45.7	53.6
Seeing dead or seriously injured noncombatants	45.2	41.3	49.1
Witnessing an accident resulting in serious injury or death	45.0	41.1	48.9
Smelling decomposing bodies	37.0	33.3	40.7
Being physically moved or knocked over by an explosion	22.9	19.6	26.1
Being injured, not requiring hospitalization	22.8	19.2	26.3
Having a blow to the head from any accident or injury	18.1	15.1	21.1
Being injured, requiring hospitalization	10.7	8.2	13.1
Engaging in hand-to-hand combat	9.5	7.3	11.6
Witnessing brutality toward detainees/prisoners	5.3	3.3	7.3
Being responsible for the death of a civilian	5.2	3.0	7.4

NOTES: CI = confidence interval; LL = lower limit; UL = upper limit.

Table 4.4
Overall Rates of Probable PTSD, Major Depression, and TBI with Co-Morbidity (N=1,965)

Condition	Weighted Percentage	95% CI LL	95% CI UL	Population LL	Population UL
Probable PTSD	13.8	11.1	16.5	181,000	270,000
Probable major depression	13.7	11.0	16.4	181,000	270,000
Probable TBI	19.5	16.4	22.7	269,000	372,000
Co-morbidity					
No condition	69.3	65.7	73.0	1,079,000	1,198,000
PTSD only	3.6	2.0	5.2	32,000	86,000
Depression only	4.0	2.4	5.5	40,000	91,000
TBI only	12.2	9.6	14.8	157,000	243,000
PTSD and depression	3.6	2.3	4.8	38,000	79,000
PTSD and TBI	1.1	0.6	1.7	10,000	27,000
TBI and depression	0.7	0.1	1.4	1,000	22,000
PTSD, depression, and TBI	5.5	3.6	7.4	58,000	121,000

NOTES: Based on 1.64 million individuals deployed to OEF/OIF, assuming that the rate found in the sample is representative of the population. CI = confidence interval; LL = lower limit; UL = upper limit.

These percentages correspond to relatively large numbers of affected individuals. Using 1.64 million as the number of personnel deployed to OEF/OIF (through October 31, 2007) and assuming that the rates found in the current study are representative of the rates in the population, we found that there are 226,000 persons with PTSD, 225,000 individuals with major depression, and 303,000 having either disorder. In addition, our estimate of the prevalence of TBI implies that approximately 320,000 previously deployed persons have experienced a probable TBI.

To help interpret the observed rates of the three outcomes, we compared the prevalence from the full sample to the prevalence for servicemembers who had not experienced any traumatic events during deployment. The estimated rates of PTSD, major depression, and TBI for the unexposed group of deployed servicemembers was 1.5 percent (95-percent CI of 0.6–3.7 percent), 3.3 percent (95-percent CI of 1.5–6.8 percent), and 0.9 percent (95-percent CI of 0.3–2.6), respectively. This pattern suggests that the excess morbidity attributable to deployment-related trauma exposure is approximately 12 percentage points for PTSD, 10 percentage points for depression, and 19 percentage points for TBI.

As shown in Table 4.5, bivariate analyses indicate that several characteristics place individuals at risk for PTSD. Higher rates of PTSD are found for servicemembers of the Army and Marine Corps, and for servicemembers who are not on active duty—i.e., those in the National Guard or Reserve, as well as those who have left the military. Similarly, enlisted personnel, females, and Hispanics are more likely than their counterparts to meet screening criteria for PTSD. Finally, individuals with more-lengthy deployments and more-extensive exposure to combat trauma were at substantially greater risk of suffering from PTSD in the prior 30 days.

A very similar pattern of risk factors was found for major depression in the past two weeks, as shown in Table 4.6. On a bivariate basis, current duty status (i.e., discharged or retired) is associated with increased likelihood of major depression. Similarly, enlisted personnel, Hispanics, and females were more likely than their counterparts to experience current major depression. In contrast, airmen and sailors were less likely than soldiers and marines to meet screening criteria for probable major depression. As with PTSD, individuals with more-lengthy deployments and more-extensive exposure to combat trauma are at greater risk of meeting screening criteria for current major depression. Of particular note, the degree of exposure to combat trauma was the single-best predictor of both PTSD and major depression.

After controlling for differential trauma exposure and other factors in multivariate analyses, some characteristics continued to place individuals at increased risk for current PTSD and major depression. In particular, as shown in Tables 4.5 and 4.6, enlisted personnel, females, and Hispanics were more likely to suffer from both PTSD and major depression. Interestingly, age emerged as a significant multivariate predictor of major depression, with older individuals at greater risk of both conditions, when controlling for other predictors, such as traumatic exposures. Finally, as in the bivariate analyses,

Table 4.5
Correlates of Probable PTSD

Predictor	Bivariate RR	95% CI LL	95% CI UL	Adjusted RR	95% CI LL	95% CI UL
Branch						
Army	1			1		
Navy	0.365**	0.190	0.704	0.718	0.405	1.274
Air Force	0.088***	0.029	0.263	0.180*	0.049	0.668
Marine Corps	0.709	0.427	1.178	0.721	0.383	1.359
Current Duty Status						
Active	1			1		
Reserve/Guard	1.988*	1.033	3.826	1.652	0.885	3.084
Discharged/Retired	1.865***	1.354	2.570	1.487*	1.005	2.201
Rank						
Enlisted	1			1		
Officer/Warrant Officer	0.262**	0.117	0.588	0.396*	0.175	0.899
Gender						
Male	1			1		
Female	1.033	0.583	1.832	1.689*	1.048	2.723
Race						
White	1			1		
Black	1.314	0.778	2.219	1.334	0.795	2.238
Hispanic	3.332***	2.085	5.326	1.881***	1.308	2.705
Other	1.809	0.845	3.872	1.127	0.517	2.460
Current Marital Status						
Married	1			1		
Not Married	1.190	0.738	1.919	0.849	0.568	1.270
Other						
Age (per decade)	0.826	0.648	1.054	1.115	0.868	1.433
Months Since Last Return	1.001	0.991	1.010	1.003	0.991	1.015
Length of Last Deployment (months)	1.116***	1.073	1.161	1.011	0.964	1.061
Number of Traumas (0–10)	1.415***	1.334	1.501	1.341***	1.235	1.457
Seriously Injured	4.210***	2.911	6.087	1.305	0.868	1.964

NOTES: Adjusted relative risk ratios (RRs) control for all other variables included in the table. Relative risk associated with trauma exposure is the incremental risk associated with each additional trauma.
* $p<.05$; ** $p<.01$; *** $p<.001$. CI = confidence interval; LL = lower limit; UL = upper limit.

Table 4.6
Correlates of Probable Major Depression

Predictor	Bivariate RR	95% CI LL	95% CI UL	Adjusted RR	95% CI LL	95% CI UL
Branch						
Army	1			1		
Navy	0.376**	0.190	0.746	0.688	0.401	1.182
Air Force	0.415	0.184	0.935	0.932	0.399	2.176
Marine Corps	0.757	0.454	1.264	0.823	0.512	1.323
Current Duty Status						
Active	1			1		
Reserve/Guard	1.698	0.841	3.431	1.132	0.599	2.140
Discharged/Retired	1.863***	1.350	2.569	1.197	0.830	1.727
Rank						
Enlisted	1			1		
Officer/Warrant Officer	0.140***	0.055	0.357	0.155***	0.059	0.403
Gender						
Male	1			1		
Female	1.680*	1.038	2.718	2.390***	1.448	3.944
Race						
White	1			1		
Black	0.803	0.489	1.319	0.771	0.485	1.227
Hispanic	2.962***	1.827	4.803	1.830***	1.288	2.600
Other	1.878	0.923	3.821	1.583	0.754	3.323
Current Marital Status						
Married	1			1		
Not Married	1.464	0.947	2.264	1.204	0.795	1.825
Other						
Age (per decade)	0.915	0.745	1.125	1.355	1.108	1.657
Months Since Last Return	1.003	0.992	1.013	1.004	0.990	1.018
Length of Last Deployment (months)	1.084	1.037	1.134	1.019	0.968	1.072
Number of Traumas (0–10)	1.362	1.284	1.445	1.329	1.220	1.448
Seriously injured	4.093	2.826	5.930	1.404	0.912	2.160

NOTES: Adjusted risk ratios (RRs) control for all other variables included in the table. Relative risk associated with trauma exposure is the incremental risk associated with each additional trauma.

* $p<.05$; ** $p<.01$; *** $p<.001$. CI = confidence interval; LL = lower limit; UL = upper limit.

extent of exposure to trauma remained the most important multivariate predictor of both PTSD and major depression. For example, an individual who experienced five of the listed traumas is at more than 4 times the risk for both PTSD and depression relative to someone who experienced none of these traumas but who is otherwise similar in age, gender, rank, ethnicity, branch or Service, deployment length, etc.

As shown in Table 4.7, bivariate analyses indicate that several characteristics place individuals at risk for experiencing a probable TBI during deployment. Individuals who serve in the Army and the Marine Corps are more likely than others to have had a TBI. Similarly, males, enlisted personnel, and younger individuals are more likely to report experiencing a TBI during deployment. Finally, persons who experienced greater total deployment and more-extensive exposure to combat trauma were at greater risk of a probable TBI during deployment. After adjusting for covariates, however, we found that only the combat trauma exposures remained significant predictors of probable deployment-related TBI. In other words, differences between demographic groups were almost entirely attributable to differences in combat exposure among these groups.

Utilization of mental health services among persons with probable PTSD or major depression was similar to rates found in the general population of the United States (Wang et al., 2005). In particular, just over one-half of participants who met screening criteria reported having seen a physician or a mental health provider about a mental health problem in the previous 12 months (see Table 4.8). About one-third of those in need of assistance reported having been prescribed medication for a mental health problem. At the same time, the majority of individuals with a need for services had not received minimally adequate care. Specifically, only 30 percent had received any type of minimally adequate treatment; 18 percent had received minimally adequate psychotherapy and 22 percent had received a minimally adequate course of pharmacotherapy.

With respect to screening for TBI among persons who reported a probable TBI during deployment, the majority (57 percent) had never been evaluated by a physician or specialist for possible brain injury.

Self-assessed barriers to seeking care for mental health problems were examined among those who currently met screening criteria for either mild depression or subthreshold PTSD. Examination of the three broad classes of barriers revealed that institutional/cultural barriers were the most frequently endorsed class of obstacles (see Table 4.9). In particular, respondents were most likely to regard concerns about confidentiality and discrimination as presenting barriers to seeking treatment. For example, the belief that seeking care could harm one's career was endorsed by over 40 percent of persons. Concern about the possible inability to receive a security clearance in the future and the belief that medical records would not be kept confidential were also widely endorsed. Some beliefs about mental health treatment may also constitute significant barriers to service-seeking. Specific impediments include concerns about the

Table 4.7
Correlates of Probable TBI

Predictor	Bivariate RR	95% CI LL	95% CI UL	Adjusted RR	95% CI LL	95% CI UL
Branch						
Army	1			1		
Navy	0.465*	0.242	0.894	1.003	0.534	1.886
Air Force	0.209***	0.099	0.440	0.651	0.275	1.543
Marine Corps	1.188	0.815	1.732	1.053	0.705	1.572
Current Duty Status						
Active	1			1		
Reserve/Guard	0.921	0.496	1.710	0.884	0.519	1.507
Discharged/Retired	1.124	0.839	1.504	1.089	0.714	1.662
Rank						
Enlisted	1			1		
Officer/Warrant Officer	0.514*	0.300	0.882	0.843	0.501	1.418
Gender						
Male	1			1		
Female	0.414*	0.205	0.833	0.793	0.369	1.701
Race						
White	1			1		
Black	0.553*	0.356	0.859	0.714	0.464	1.100
Hispanic	1.288	0.762	2.177	0.904	0.625	1.307
Other	1.299	0.678	2.490	0.946	0.533	1.677
Current Marital Status						
Married	1			1		
Not Married	1.168	0.789	1.728	0.979	0.666	1.439
Other						
Age (per decade)	0.730**	0.600	0.889	1.020	0.839	1.239
Months Since Last Return	0.995	0.986	1.004	0.999	0.985	1.013
Length of Last Deployment (months)	1.077***	1.030	1.126	1.002	0.952	1.055
Number of Traumas (0–10)	1.525***	1.449	1.605	1.434***	1.340	1.535
Seriously Injured	5.058***	3.886	6.583	1.409*	0.989	2.009

NOTES: Adjusted relative risk ratios (RRs) control for all other variables included in the table. Relative risk associated with trauma exposure is the incremental risk associated with each additional trauma.

* $p<.05$; ** $p<.01$; *** $p<.001$. CI = confidence interval; LL = lower limit; UL = upper limit.

Table 4.8
Utilization of Mental Health Services in the Past 12 Months Among Those with a Need for Services (N=326)

	Weighted Percentage	95% CI LL	95% CI UL
Any mental health visit to doctor or mental health specialist	52.7	43.4	61.9
Any prescription for mental health	36.5	27.7	45.3
Any minimally adequate treatment	30.1	21.4	38.7
Minimally adequate talk treatment	18.4	11.6	25.2
Minimally adequate drug treatment	22.3	14.2	30.4

NOTES: *Need* defined by having probable major depression or probable PTSD.
CI = confidence interval; LL = lower limit; UL = upper limit.

side effects of medication, a preference for relying on friends and family rather than on mental health professionals, and reservations about the effectiveness or quality of available treatments. Logistical barriers (e.g., high cost of services) were generally endorsed at lower rates than is typical of the general population (Sareen et al., 2007). Yet, logistical barriers may still be important obstacles to care, particularly for individuals who are not on active duty.

Discussion

This study had two broad objectives concerning the mental health of military personnel deployed for OEF/OIF. The first objective was to determine the prevalence and correlates of PTSD, major depression, and deployment-related traumatic brain injury. The second was to assess mental health service utilization and self-assessed barriers to care for individuals with potential treatment needs.

With respect to the first objective, these results reveal that significant numbers of previously deployed personnel currently suffer from PTSD and major depression. In particular, 14 percent met screening criteria for probable PTSD and 14 percent met screening criteria for probable major depression. Moreover, the two conditions were frequently found to co-occur, with approximately two-thirds of those with PTSD also meeting criteria for major depression. The vast majority of both PTSD and major depression cases can be attributed to the traumatic experiences that occurred during OEF/OIF deployment. Assuming that the prevalence found in this study is representative of the population, these results suggest that as many as 300,000 previously deployed individuals suffer from one of these two disorders. Given the significant disability and functional impairment associated with PTSD and major depression (Kessler, 2000; Ustun and Kessler, 2002; see also Chapter Seven of this monograph), this

Table 4.9
Barriers to Care Among Those with a Possible Need for Services (*N*=752)

Type of Barrier	Weighted Percentage	95% CI LL	95% CI UL
Logistical			
It would be difficult to get childcare or time off of work	29.3	23.0	35.6
Mental health care would cost too much money	23.1	16.7	29.5
It would be difficult to schedule an appointment	15.9	11.8	20.1
I would not know where to get help or whom to see	15.9	10.6	21.2
It would be difficult to arrange transportation to treatment	6.6	2.6	10.5
Institutional and cultural			
It could harm my career	43.6	37.0	50.0
I could be denied a security clearance in the future	43.6	37.0	50.2
My coworkers would have less confidence in me if they found out	38.4	32.2	44.7
I do not think my treatment would be kept confidential	29.0	23.1	34.9
My commander or supervisor might respect me less	23.0	17.4	28.5
My friends and family would respect me less	11.5	7.6	15.5
I could lose contact or custody of my children	9.3	5.7	12.9
My commander or supervisor has asked us not to get treatment	7.8	3.4	12.2
My spouse or partner would not want me to get treatment	2.9	1.0	4.9
Beliefs and preferences for treatment			
The medications that might help have too many side effects	45.1	38.1	52.2
My family or friends would be more helpful than a mental health professional	39.4	32.7	46.1
I would think less of myself if I could not handle it on my own	29.1	23.3	35.0
Religious counseling would be more helpful than mental health treatment	28.8	22.9	34.7
Even good mental health care is not very effective	25.2	18.7	31.7
The mental health treatments available to me are not very good	24.6	18.3	30.8
I have received treatment before and it did not work	18.0	13.5	22.6

NOTES: *Possible need* is defined as having at least mild depression or subthreshold PTSD. CI = confidence interval; LL = lower limit; UL = upper limit.

estimate highlights the critical importance of providing appropriate mental health care to this population.

The rates of PTSD and major depression found in the current study are generally comparable to figures reported in other investigations of persons deployed for OEF/OIF, despite significant differences in the methods used and the samples studied (Hoge, Auchterlonie, and Milliken, 2006; Hoge et al., 2004; Erbes et al., 2007; Seal et al., 2007; Kolkow et al., 2007). Most of these studies focused on active duty, enlisted combat forces in the Army or Marine Cops. Thus, they typically underrepresented individuals at the highest risk (e.g., reservists and persons separated from service), as well as those at lowest risk (e.g., Air Force and officers). The major exception to this pattern involves a recent investigation of participants in a longitudinal study of military personnel (Smith et al., 2008). Although the overall prevalence of PTSD among previously deployed servicemembers was not included in the latter report, it can be calculated to be 6 percent based on data presented in their tables. The discrepancy in rates between Smith et al. (2008) and most other studies is likely due to a substantial overrepresentation in the Smith et al. study of those individuals at lowest risk for PTSD (e.g., officers and airmen). It may also be due to a focus on deployments that occurred primarily in 2002–2004, before the escalation of the Iraq insurgency.

For several methodological reasons, our estimates of the mental health problems suffered by deployed personnel are likely to constitute an undercount of servicemembers who will experience problems following deployment for OEF/OIF. First, many of the respondents who did not meet screening criteria for PTSD and major depression in the past 30 days will have met criteria at some time in the past or will meet it at some point in the future. This study is, essentially, a snapshot of mental health problems at one point in time, whereas the symptoms of those with PTSD or major depression tend to fluctuate over time. In addition, servicemembers who are currently deployed, and thus ineligible for study participation, are likely to have more total time deployed and greater trauma exposure than individuals who are in the United States. Stated differently, the servicemembers who have spent the most time in Iraq were more likely to be there during the study period. Finally, the total number of individuals who have been deployed continues to increase as combat continues, and trauma exposure is ongoing among those deployed.

This study also provides the best data available to date regarding the extent to which deployment is associated with probable TBI. Whereas Hoge et al. (2008) reported rates approaching 15 percent in a study of two brigades of infantry soldiers who had experienced significant combat, our research indicates that the overall deployed force is likely to have had similar exposure to TBI: 19 percent met screening criteria for having experienced a probable TBI. This rate is also similar to those reported in unpublished studies of persons previously deployed for OEF/OIF (e.g., TBI: Hidden wounds plague Iraq war veterans, 2007). Assuming the rate observed in this sample is representative of the full population, we suggest that there are approximately 300,000 injured persons.

From the available data in this population, it is not possible to estimate the overall level of impairment caused by these brain injuries. Traumatic brain injury varies in magnitude from mild to severe, and the extent of cognitive and functional impairment varies dramatically. In the civilian sector, at least 75 percent of head injuries is estimated to be mild in severity (National Center for Injury Prevention and Control, 2003), although we do not know if this distribution is similar to those injured in Afghanistan and Iraq. Historically used interchangeably with the term *concussion* (Bigler, 2008), mild brain injury is associated with full functional recovery in 85 to 95 percent of cases (e.g., Ruff, 2005; McCrea, 2007). In a systematic review of the civilian literature, Carroll et al. (2004) concluded that most persons with mild TBI recover within three to 12 months. Nonetheless, mild as well as moderate and severe brain injuries can all result in significant long-term impairment, including difficulty in returning to work.

These results should not be seen as direct evidence of a substantial TBI-related disability problem among those returning from deployment. Little is known about the long-term effects of this very common injury. Sequelae may be quite diverse and difficult to link to the injury. Moreover, most of those who reported experiencing this injury have not been evaluated or reassured that they are likely to have experienced a mild injury. Given this situation, the potential exists for ordinary post-deployment adjustment problems to be misattributed to TBI. For this reason, all persons with suspected TBI should be evaluated to document a disability, or the lack of a disability, and to ensure that necessary rehabilitation services are provided. Although military and Veterans Health Administration leaders have recently announced programs to expand TBI screening, future research will need to investigate the extent of progress on this issue. In addition, a great deal of research is needed to document the natural course of symptoms, to determine the association of TBI with other mental health symptoms, and to validate methods for identifying which injuries are likely to result in functional impairment.

The current research also determined that certain characteristics place individuals at risk for probable PTSD, major depression, and TBI. The same general pattern of findings was observed for both PTSD and major depression. In particular, after adjusting for a range of factors, we found that PTSD and major depression were more likely to be experienced by enlisted personnel, Hispanics, females, older persons, and those who had been injured or exposed to more extensive combat trauma.

These results are broadly consistent with findings that have emerged from studies of civilian populations. For example, relative to males, females are known to be at greater risk for depression (e.g., Kessler et al., 2005). Similarly, a growing body of data suggests that Hispanic Americans appear more likely than their non-Hispanic counterparts both to develop post-traumatic stress disorder and to experience more-extreme symptoms of PTSD in response to both combat-related and non-combat-related trauma exposure (Adams and Boscarino, 2006; Galea et al., 2002; Kulka et al., 1990; Pole et al., 2001). Moreover, our findings that servicemembers from the Reserve Component are at heightened risk for PTSD and major depression are in close agreement with other research indicating that Reserve personnel are approximately twice as likely as active duty personnel to meet screening criteria for needing mental health services following deployment for OEF/OIF (Milliken, Auchterlonie, and Hoge, 2007).

Many of these risk factors' effects were quite powerful. For example, very few cases of PTSD were found among Air Force personnel or officers, and almost no cases among those without combat trauma. These findings of subgroups with extremely low rates of PTSD are also helpful for evaluating the specificity of our PCL scoring. Such low rates are inconsistent with a scoring criterion that yields insufficient diagnostic specificity.

These findings support several broad conclusions relevant to the mental health of OEF/OIF veterans. First, this study highlights several risk factors for PTSD and major depression other than exposure to combat trauma. This knowledge could be used to target servicemembers of high-risk groups for possible preventive interventions, as well as to assist in outreach, identification, and treatment of persons in need of mental health treatment. These results also identify groups of individuals who are highly resilient (i.e., have low rates of mental health problems), even when controlling for exposure to trauma.

In particular, officers rarely develop mental health problems, even when exposed to trauma. However, it is possible that the low risk observed among officers and Air Force personnel is due to qualitatively different exposures to trauma. That is, these individuals' traumatic experiences may have been different from their counterparts' because of differences in scope of work or mission. Thus, officers and Air Force personnel may have experienced less severe forms of trauma, even when they had similar trauma scores. Further study of the origins, nature, and malleability of these risk factors is warranted. Such study might focus, in particular, on determining whether factors that confer resilience in officers might be amenable to modification in others at greater risk for mental health problems. In addition, although research has focused on PTSD as the most salient psychiatric sequelae of combat exposure, the results of this study, as well as those of other recent research (e.g., Grieger et al., 2006) reveal that major depression is also strongly associated with war trauma. This evidence suggests the need for additional research. Such research might examine, for example, whether treatments that are effective for major depression in the general population (e.g., pharmacotherapy) are also effective with major depression that occurs following combat trauma.

Finally, while controlling for combat trauma and demographic factors, we found no significant evidence that the length of time since deployment was associated with either PTSD or major depression. The latter finding may be important inasmuch as previous research has suggested that mental health problems associated with service for OEF/OIF may increase with the passage of time (Milliken, Auchterlonie, and Hoge, 2007). This difference across studies may be due to the different periods being studied.

The current sample includes a 0–5-year range of time since last deployment, whereas other studies (e.g., Milliken, Auchterlonie, and Hoge, 2007) have focused on a much narrower window. Longitudinal research is needed to rule out other explanations for these findings and to convincingly describe symptom trajectories.

These results also document a large—and largely unmet—need for psychological services in this population. More than half of those who had a need for treatment reported having visited a health professional for help with these problems in the previous 12 months. This rate of care-seeking is comparable with that reported for persons with PTSD or major depression in the general population (Wang et al., 2005). However, seeking help is not the same as getting treated, and a substantial majority of OEF/OIF veterans with a need for mental health services do not appear to be receiving adequate mental health care. Specifically, almost half of those who brought their problems to the attention of a health professional in the preceding 12 months did not receive minimally adequate treatment (i.e., they did not get at least eight sessions of psychotherapy or a minimal course of medication). Inasmuch as this study did not examine whether empirically supported therapies had been delivered, it is likely that the proportion of individuals who received care that has been demonstrated to be effective is necessarily even smaller. These findings suggest that there is considerable room for improvement in (1) referral into treatment, (2) retention in treatment, and (3) the adequacy of treatment provided for servicemembers in need of mental health treatment following deployment for OEF/OIF.

This study also suggests that nearly 60 percent of persons who experienced a probable brain injury during deployment for OEF/OIF have not been evaluated for this condition by a physician or other health specialist. Most brain injuries are mild in severity, and the injured individual is likely to recover fully within three to 12 months. Nonetheless, 5 to 15 percent of persons with mild brain injury suffer from protracted problems. Given the frequency with which OEF/OIF veterans meet screening criteria for probable brain injury, a substantial number of individuals are likely to suffer from the unrecognized and untreated consequences of TBI. At present, little empirical evidence exists to document the effectiveness of interventions for mild brain injury (Elgmark Andersson et al., 2007; Ghaffar et al., 2006; Paniak et al., 2000). The challenge of developing and conducting rigorous evaluation of treatments for mild brain injury presents an important opportunity to help OEF/OIF veterans.

Additionally, this research supports several conclusions regarding barriers to receiving care for mental health problems. Some of the most frequently reported obstacles are institutional or cultural. Respondents were particularly likely to report concerns that getting treatment would negatively affect their current or future occupational opportunities. In a similar vein, concerns about confidentiality were also paramount. Getting mental health treatment is perceived as restricting or foreclosing opportunities for promotions and future employment. Addressing these barriers will likely require some method for personnel to receive confidential services. Merely changing attitudes about mental health and cognitive conditions is, in itself, unlikely to lower these barriers to treatment, so long as treatment records could be used against an individual service-member in his or her assignments and promotions.

Given that efficacious treatments exist for both PTSD and major depression (e.g., Butler et al., 2006; Hollon et al., 2005; Institute of Medicine, 2007; Pampallona et al., 2004), most individuals who suffer from these conditions are likely to be able to return to normal levels of functioning with the provision of appropriate health care. Identification and implementation of strategies to facilitate confidential access to care for individuals in need is likely to raise overall levels of readiness of military personnel. To be clear, we are not suggesting that it is desirable to have absolute confidentiality in military mental health treatment; as in the civilian sector, treatment providers should have a legal obligation to report to authorities and commanders any patients who represent a threat to themselves or others. We are suggesting, however, that information about a servicemember's mental health services not be revealed to others unless he or she has been found to have a functional impairment that substantially affects assigned duties. The issue of facilitating utilization of available treatments will be discussed in more detail in Chapter Seven.

Other concerns of a substantial number of persons in need of mental health treatment include the potential side effects associated with medication use, as well as the belief that the mental health treatments available to them are unlikely to be helpful or are not of the highest quality. These concerns might best be addressed with multiple strategies, including education about mental health treatment and increasing the availability of a broader range of evidence-based psychotherapies. Given that many individuals wish to avoid the side effects of existing pharmacotherapies, and that psychotherapies are considered by many to be the best available treatment for PTSD (Institute of Medicine, 2007), the mental health care system servicing this population should seek both to expand the use of evidence-based psychotherapy for the treatment of PTSD and to address institutional factors that might hamper its use. In addition, it may be productive to further research the beliefs about the side effects of drugs used to treat PTSD and major depression. To the extent that these concerns are based on a misunderstanding of the actual side effects of these medications, education may diminish the prominence of this barrier to treatment.

Finally, this study found that a large number of individuals who might benefit from mental health services would prefer to seek help from friends, family, and clergy. To the degree that individuals with mental health problems are consulting with these nonprofessionals instead of seeking services from professional health care providers, programs designed to educate these lay-providers might help to facilitate ultimate referral to health care providers. In addition it may be possible to train such lay-providers to provide other helpful services and support to affected individuals that may improve recovery.

Strengths and Limitations

In considering these conclusions, it is important to recognize both the strengths and limitations of this study. RDD with post-stratification weights is the gold-standard method for sampling in telephone-based research, and it is used by almost every major public-opinion and public-health telephone survey that attempts to assess a broad population. This approach is used as the primary means of data collection for the best studies of mental health within the U.S. population, such as the National Comorbidity Survey Replication (e.g., Kessler et al., 2005).

The methodology used in this study has several significant advantages over other sampling methods that have been used to study mental health conditions and TBI in OEF/OIF veterans. The principal advantage, for our purpose, is that it enabled inclusion of a very wide range of individuals and experiences relative to samples that are collected within a single unit, base, or branch of Service. The approach allowed us to include personnel from each branch of Service and a broad spectrum of occupational specialties, as well as a range of deployment characteristics (e.g., length of deployments or elapsed time since previous deployment). A second advantage of this approach is that respondents were offered a level of confidentiality that is not always offered in the published studies conducted directly by the military or the VA. The participants' responses cannot be included in their personnel or medical records, the interviewer is not another servicemember or co-worker, and the data are protected from subpoena by virtue of an NIH certificate of confidentiality. This greater confidentiality may improve data quality by partially addressing servicemembers' concerns about disclosing mental health problems. In addition, this approach provides some measure of protection against overreporting biases associated with efforts to gain or maintain disability benefits (Smith et al., 1999). Although, these response biases are likely small, the research is a useful adjunct to the research conducted by DoD and the VA because it helps to corroborate findings using different methodologies.

In addition to these strengths, the methods used have several limitations. Several coverage limitations are inherent in telephone sampling. In particular, eligible individuals in the population can participate only if they have a land-based telephone number— i.e., calls cannot be placed to cell phones. Moreover, we do not have a good estimate of the number of eligible individuals excluded by the lack of a land-based telephone line. However, the omission of these individuals is a threat to the validity of the study only to the extent that having a landline is associated with outcomes of interest. Similarly, telephone-based samples often slightly underrepresent males and unmarried individuals relative to the population. The effects of these underrepresentations on population estimates have, however, been mitigated through application of post-stratification weights. We know the number of males and unmarried individuals in the eligible population and can create an analytic sample that reflects this composition.

RDD sampling is also limited in its ability to locate eligible individuals when the total pool of qualified participants is relatively rare. Whereas most active duty personnel live within geographic proximity to the military bases at which they are stationed, servicemembers of the National Guard and Reserve, as well as retired and discharged personnel, are more widely dispersed. Thus, these components are underrepresented in the sample. Although we were able to compensate partially for this underrepresentation using sampling weights, it is possible that National Guard/Reserve personnel living in proximity to domestic military installations are different in unmeasured ways from those who live elsewhere. Similarly, this study is missing individuals who were hospitalized, incarcerated, or currently deployed. To the extent that these groups of individuals constitute both a significant portion of the deployed personnel and have different rates of the three conditions, the overall results may be inaccurate.

In addition, this research relied on self-report as the sole method of data collection. The diagnostic measures used in this study have well-demonstrated sensitivity and specificity, and they are the standard measures used in epidemiological studies of the U.S. military. However, to the extent that additional sources of information might have yielded different findings, these results should be viewed with caution and additional research is warranted. Future research might, for example, document the presence of mental health problems using structured diagnostic interviews or other sources of data to assess the health care provided to OEF/OIF veterans. Specifically, our criteria for determining minimally adequate care are based solely on the number and duration of treatment, not on whether an individual was documented to have received an effective intervention. It would be helpful to determine whether the care received corresponds to documented evidence-based therapies. Moreover, many of the important predictors used in the current study (e.g., trauma exposure, rank), as well as the eligibility criteria (deployment for OEF/OIF), could be influenced by self-report biases and were not independently verified. For instance, it is possible that some Reserve Component servicemembers who were activated at the time of the study reported themselves as being on active duty, rather than in the Reserves. To the extent that the current results depend on the manner in which these constructs are assessed, additional research is required.

Finally, although the current study includes a relatively large number of respondents, samples of many subpopulations that may be of interest are relatively small (e.g., women, reservists, warrant officers, unmarried). Consequently, this study may not be able to detect as statistically significant some risk factors that are clinically meaningful. Because of the limited statistical power for estimates in these subpopulations, the reader is cautioned against inferring that a nonsignificant predictor in the current study indicates that this variable is not a clinically important risk factor.

Conclusions

A telephone study of 1,965 previously deployed individuals sampled from 24 geographic areas found substantial rates of mental health problems in the past 30 days, with 14 percent screening positive for PTSD and 14 percent, for major depression. Assuming that the prevalence found in this study is representative of the 1.64 million service-members who have been deployed for OEF/OIF, these findings suggest that approximately 300,000 servicemembers and veterans have combat-related mental health problems. A similar number, 19 percent, reported a probable TBI during deployment. More than two-thirds of the individuals with combat-related mental health problems did not receive minimally adequate mental heath treatment in the prior year. Similarly, most individuals who experienced a TBI have not been evaluated by a doctor to determine the extent of the injuries.

Respondents endorsed many barriers that inhibit getting treatment for mental health problems. In general, respondents were concerned that getting such treatment would not be kept confidential and would be used against them in future job assignments and career advancement. Respondents were also concerned that drug therapies for mental health problems may have unpleasant side effects. These barriers suggest the need for increased access to confidential, evidence-based psychotherapy to maintain high levels of readiness and functioning among previously deployed servicemembers and veterans.

References

Adams, R. E., and J. A. Boscarino. Predictors of PTSD and delayed PTSD after disaster: The impact of exposure and psychosocial resources. *Journal of Nervous and Mental Disease,* Vol. 194, No. 7, 2006, pp. 485–493.

American Psychiatric Association. *Diagnostic and Statistical Manual of Mental Disorders*, Fourth Edition. Washington, D.C.: American Psychiatric Association, 1994.

Bigler, E. D. Neuropsychology and clinical neuroscience of persistent post-concussive syndrome. *Journal of the International Neuropsychological Society*, Vol. 14, 2008, pp. 1–22.

Brewin C. R. Systematic review of screening instruments for adults at risk of PTSD. *Journal of Traumatic Stress*, Vol. 18, No. 1, 2005, pp. 53–62.

Butler, A. C., J. E. Chapman, E. M. Forman, and A. T. Beck. The empirical status of cognitive-behavioral therapy: A review of meta-analyses. *Clinical Psychology Review,* Vol. 26, 2006, pp. 17–31.

Carroll, L. J., J. D. Cassidy, L. Holm, J. Kraus, and V. G. Coronado. Methodological issues and research recommendations for mild traumatic brain injury: The WHO Collaborating Centre Task Force on Mild Traumatic Brain Injury. *Journal of Rehabilitative Medicine*, Vol. 43, Suppl., February 2004, pp. 113–125.

Elgmark Andersson, E., I. Emanuelson, R. Björklund, D. A. Stålhammar. Mild traumatic brain injuries: The impact of early intervention on late sequelae. A randomized controlled trial. *Acta Neurochirurgica*, Vol. 149, 2007, pp. 151–159.

Erbes, C., J. Westermeyer, B. Engdahl, and E. Johnsen. Post-traumatic stress disorder and service utilization in a sample of service members from Iraq and Afghanistan. *Military Medicine*, Vol. 172, 2007, pp. 359–363.

Galea, S., J. Ahern, H. Resnick, D. Kilpatrick, M. Bucuvalas, J. Gold, and D. Vlahov. Psychological sequelae of the September 11 terrorist attacks in New York City. *New England Journal of Medicine,* Vol. 346, No. 13, 2002, pp. 982–987.

Ghaffar, O., S. McCullagh, D. Ouchterlony, and A. Feinstein. Randomized treatment trial in mild traumatic brain injury. *Journal of Psychosomatic Research,* Vol. 61, 2006, pp. 153–160.

Grieger, T. A., S. J. Cozza, R. J. Ursano, C. Hoge, P. E. Martinez, C. C. Engel, and H. J. Wain. Posttraumatic stress disorder and depression in battle-injured soldiers. *American Journal of Psychiatry*, Vol. 163, No. 10, 2006, pp. 1777–1783.

Hoge, C. W., J. L. Auchterlonie, and C. S. Milliken. Mental health problems, use of mental health services, and attrition from military service after returning from deployment to Iraq or Afghanistan. *Journal of the American Medical Association,* Vol. 295, 2006, pp. 1023–1032.

Hoge, C. W., C. A. Castro, S. C. Messer, D. McGurk, D. I. Cotting, and R. L. Koffman. Combat duty in Iraq and Afghanistan, mental health problems, and barriers to care. *New England Journal of Medicine,* Vol. 351, No. 1, 2004, pp. 13–22.

Hoge, C. W., D. McGurk, J. L. Thomas, A. L. Cox, C. C. Engel, and C. A. Castro. Mild traumatic brain injury in US soldiers returning from Iraq. *New England Journal of Medicine*, Vol. 358, 2008, pp. 453–463.

Hollon, S. D., R. B. Jarrett, A. A. Nierenberg, M. E. Thase, M. Trivedi, and A. J. Rush. Psychotherapy and medication in the treatment of adult and geriatric depression: Which monotherapy or combined treatment? *Journal of Clinical Psychiatry*, Vol. 66, 2005, pp. 455–468.

Institute of Medicine, Committee on Treatment of Posttraumatic Stress Disorder. *Treatment of Posttraumatic Stress Disorder: An Assessment of the Evidence.* Washington, D.C.: The National

Academies Press, 2007. As of November 13, 2007:
http://www.nap.edu/catalog.php?record_id=11955#toc

Kessler, R. C. Posttraumatic stress disorder: The burden to the individual and to society. *Journal of Clinical Psychiatry*, Vol. 61, 2000, pp. 4–12.

Kessler, R. C., W. T. Chiu, O. Demler, et al. Prevalence, severity, and comorbidity of 12-month DSM-IV disorders in the National Comorbidity Survey Replication. *Archives of General Psychiatry*, Vol. 62, No. 6, 2005, pp. 617–627.

Kolkow, T. T., J. L. Spira, J. S. Morse, and T. A. Grieger. Post-traumatic stress disorder and depression in health care providers returning from deployment to Iraq and Afghanistan. *Military Medicine*, Vol. 172, 2007, pp. 451–455.

Kroenke, K., R. L. Spitzer, and J. B. Williams. The PHQ-9: Validity of a brief depression severity measure. *Journal of General Internal Medicine*, Vol. 16, 2001, pp. 606–613.

Kulka, R. A., J. A. Fairbank, B. K. Jordan, D. Weiss, and A. Cranston. *The National Vietnam Veterans Readjustment Study: Table of Findings and Appendices*. New York: Bruner/Mazel, 1990.

Lowe, B., K. Kroenke, W. Herzog, and K. Grafe. Measuring depression outcome with a brief self-report instrument: Sensitivity to change of the Patient Health Questionnaire (PHQ-9). *Journal of Affective Disorders*, Vol. 81, 2004, pp. 61–66.

Lowe, B., R. L. Spitzer, K. Grafe, et al. Comparative validity of three screening questionnaire for DSM-IV depressive disorders and physicians' diagnoses. *Journal of Affective Disorders*, Vol. 78, No. 2, 2004, pp. 131–140.

McCrea, M. *Mild Traumatic Brain Injury and Postconcussion Syndrome: The New Evidence Base for Diagnosis and Treatment*. New York: Oxford University Press, 2007.

Milliken, C. S., J. L. Auchterlonie, and C. W. Hoge. Longitudinal assessment of mental health problems among Active and Reserve Component soldiers returning from the Iraq war. *Journal of the American Medical Association*, Vol. 298, No. 18, 2007, pp. 2141–2148.

Murray, C. K., J. C. Reynolds, J. M. Schroeder, et al. Spectrum of care provided at an Echelon II medical unit during Operation Iraqi Freedom. *Military Medicine*, Vol. 170, 2005, pp. 516–520.

National Center for Injury Prevention and Control. *Report to Congress on Mild Traumatic Brain Injury in the United States: Steps to Prevent a Serious Public Health Problem*. Atlanta, Ga.: Centers for Disease Control and Prevention, 2003.

Pampallona, S., P. Bollini, G. Tibaldi, B. Kupelnick, and C. Munizza. Combined pharmacotherapy and psychological treatment for depression: A systematic review. *Archives of General Psychiatry*, Vol. 61, 2004, pp. 714–719.

Paniak, C., G. Toller-Lobe, S. Reynolds, A. Melnyk, and J. Nagy. A randomized trial of two treatments for mild traumatic brain injury: 1 year follow-up. *Brain Injury*, Vol. 14, 2000, pp. 219–226.

Pole, N., S. R. Best, D. S. Weiss, T. Metzler, A. M. Liberman, J. Fagan, and C. R. Marmar. Effects of gender and ethnicity on duty-related posttraumatic stress symptoms among urban police officers. *Journal of Nervous and Mental Disease*, Vol. 189, No. 7, 2001, pp. 442–448.

Ruff, R. Two decades of advances in understanding of mild traumatic brain injury. *Journal of Head Trauma Rehabilitation*, Vol. 20, 2005, pp. 5–18.

Sareen, J., A. Jagdeo, B. J. Cox, I. Clara, M. ten Have, S. L. Belik, R. de Graaf, and M. B. Stein. Perceived barriers to mental health service utilization in the United States, Ontario, and the Netherlands. *Psychiatric Services*, Vol. 58, No. 3, March 2007, pp. 357–364.

Schwab, K. A., B. Ivins, G. Cramer, W. Johnson, M. Sluss-Tiller, K. Kiley, W. Lux, and D. Warden. Screening for traumatic brain injury in troops returning from deployment in Afghanistan and Iraq: Initial investigation of the usefulness of a short screening tool for traumatic brain injury. *Journal of Head Trauma Rehabilitation*, Vol. 22, No. 6, 2007, pp. 377–389.

Seal, K. H., D. Bertenthal, C. R. Miner, S. Sen, and C. Marmar. Bringing the war back home: Mental health disorders among 103,788 US veterans returning from Iraq and Afghanistan seen at Department of Veterans Affairs facilities. *Archives of Internal Medicine*, Vol. 167, 2007, pp. 476–482.

Smith, D. W., B. C. Frueh, C. N. Sawchuck, and M. R. Johnson. Relationship between symptom over-reporting and pre- and post-combat trauma history in veterans evaluated for PTSD. *Depression and Anxiety*, Vol. 10, No. 3, 1999, pp. 119–124.

Smith, T. C., M. A. K. Ryan, D. L. Wingard, D. J. Slymen, J. F. Sallis, D. Kritz-Silverstein, and Team for the Millennium Cohort Study. New onset and persistent symptoms of post-traumatic stress disorder self reported after deployment and combat exposures: Prospective population based US military cohort study. *British Medical Journal*, January 15, 2008. As of January 28, 2008: http://www.bmj.com/cgi/content/abstract/bmj.39430.638241.AEv1

TBI: Hidden wounds plague Iraq war veterans. *Denver Post*, April 16, 2007. As of January 31, 2008: http://www.denverpost.com/ci_5675337

Ustun, T. B., and R. C. Kessler. Global burden of depressive disorders: The issue of duration. *British Journal of Psychiatry*, Vol. 181, 2002, pp. 181–183.

Wang, P. S., M. Lane, M. Olfson, H. A. Pincus, K. Wells, and K. C. Kessler. Twelve-month use of mental health services in the United States: Results from the National Comorbidity Survey Replication. *Archives of General Psychiatry*, Vol. 62, 2005, pp. 629–640.

Weathers, F., J. Huska, and T. Keane. *The PTSD Checklist Military Version (PCL-M)*. Boston, Mass.: National Center for PTSD, 1991.

Weathers, F. W., B. T. Litz, D. S. Herman, J. A. Huska, and T. M. Keane. The PTSD Checklist (PCL): Reliability, validity, and diagnostic utility. Paper presented at the International Society for Traumatic Stress Studies, San Antonio, Tex., 1993.

Wong, E. C., G. N. Marshall, T. L. Schell, M. N. Elliott, K. Hambarsoomians, C. Chun, and S. M. Berthold. Barriers to mental health care utilization for U.S. Cambodian refugees. *Journal of Consulting and Clinical Psychology*, Vol. 74, 2006, pp. 1116–1120.

Zou, G. A modified Poisson regression approach to prospective studies with binary data. *American Journal of Epidemiology*, Vol. 159, 2004, pp. 702–706.

Part III: Immediate and Long-Term Consequences of Post-Traumatic Stress Disorder, Depression, and Traumatic Brain Injury

In this part, we review the available literature on the short- and long-term consequences associated with psychological and cognitive injuries to inform predictions of the likely immediate and long-term consequences of mental health problems experienced by veterans of Afghanistan and Iraq. Our review is organized into three parts. First, we present *two theoretical perspectives* that can help to explain how specific symptoms arising from these conditions may give rise to broader short-term and long-term consequences, and we offer a *single integrated framework* that informs the remainder of our discussion. Second, we *summarize evidence from the scientific literature* documenting associations among post-traumatic stress disorder, major depression, and traumatic brain injury, as well as links between these conditions and specific domains, or areas, of functioning. This part is a brief version of a much longer review and analysis of existing literature, a RAND working paper titled *Invisible Wounds: Predicting the Immediate and Long-Term Consequences of Mental Health Problems in Veterans of Operation Enduring Freedom and Operation Iraqi Freedom* (available at http://veterans.rand.org). Finally, we *summarize common themes* emerging from the reviewed literature and offer *concrete recommendations* for future research to inform policies and interventions to mitigate the negative consequences of post-combat mental health and cognitive conditions.

CHAPTER FIVE

Predicting the Immediate and Long-Term Consequences of Post-Traumatic Stress Disorder, Depression, and Traumatic Brain Injury in Veterans of Operation Enduring Freedom and Operation Iraqi Freedom

Benjamin R. Karney, Rajeev Ramchand, Karen Chan Osilla, Leah Barnes Caldarone, and Rachel M. Burns

The Challenge of Predicting the Future

Although there is an emerging consensus that mental health and cognitive conditions stemming from service in Afghanistan and Iraq are likely to have severe and broad consequences if left untreated, allocating resources toward particular treatments and interventions requires a detailed understanding of what the consequences of these problems are likely to be. For example, if it can be reasonably assumed that servicemembers will manifest any mental health or cognitive conditions immediately upon return from deployment, then initial assessments will be sufficient to identify those who may require extra support. In contrast, if there are reasons to expect delayed reactions to deployments, then continued assessments of returning servicemembers would be warranted. Similarly, recommended treatment and policy options would differ according to the range of outcomes likely to be affected by veterans' and servicemembers' mental, emotional, and cognitive conditions.

But projecting the likely consequences of mental health and cognitive conditions suffered by returning servicemembers is complicated for several reasons. First, the mental health and cognitive problems of returning servicemembers may wax and wane over time. The short-term consequences of these problems may differ from consequences evolving over the long term. Moreover, even with treatment, symptoms may fluctuate for individuals, clouding attempts to predict future consequences. Second, there are limited data describing the mental health problems of individuals who have served in Afghanistan and Iraq. Not only are these problems yet to be studied extensively, but there has not yet been sufficient time to evaluate how veterans and servicemembers and their families may be affected in the long run.

Despite these complications, there are several legitimate bases for projecting the likely short-term and long-term consequences of the mental health and cognitive problems experienced by Operation Enduring Freedom (OEF) and Operation Iraqi Freedom (OIF) veterans. An extensive and rich body of research has examined the long-term consequences of traumatic experiences during prior military conflicts. To the extent that the results of these studies can be generalized to veterans of the current conflicts, they provide a reasonable foundation to guide projections. In addition, each of the conditions that are the focus of current concerns for returning servicemembers has been studied extensively in civilian populations. To the extent that the development and effects of these conditions in the civilian population generalize to the experiences of servicemembers, these literatures may also serve as a basis for projecting future needs of OEF/OIF veterans.

Goals and Scope of Our Discussion

In this part, we draw on the available literature to describe the likely immediate and emergent consequences of the invisible wounds of war—the mental, emotional, and cognitive injuries sustained during deployment to Afghanistan and Iraq. Our goal was to understand how these conditions would affect veterans and servicemembers, their families, and society, the duration of the consequences, and the range of services likely to be needed.

We focused our literature review on the correlates and consequences of three major mental health and cognitive conditions: post-traumatic stress disorder (PTSD), major depression and depressive symptoms, and traumatic brain injury (TBI). We focused on these disorders because they are the ones being assessed most extensively in servicemembers returning from combat. In addition, there are obvious mechanisms that might link each of these disorders to specific experiences in war—i.e., PTSD is a reaction to a traumatic experience, depression can be a reaction to loss, and TBI is a reaction to injury.

Theoretical Perspectives on the Consequences of Mental Health and Cognitive Conditions

PTSD, major depression, and TBI are conceptually distinct conditions, with different etiologies, symptoms, and recommended treatments. Nevertheless, from the perspective of understanding how these conditions affect the lives of those who suffer from them, developmental processes are likely to be common to all three. Here, we summarize prominent theoretical perspectives that suggest how mental, emotional, and cognitive impairments may give rise to additional problems and deficits over the life of an afflicted individual. We then draw on elements of these perspectives to create a general framework within which to view the empirical reviews.

The Stress-Diathesis Model

A common starting point for theories of illness and resilience is the stress-diathesis model, first articulated by Zubin and Spring (1977) as a framework for understanding the origins of schizophrenia. The stress-diathesis model is based on the premise that individuals vary in their levels of *diathesis*—i.e., those individual and environmental characteristics that increase their vulnerability to disease (Brewin, 1998; Hèanninen and Aro, 1996). Individual sources of vulnerability include pre-existing mental health problems, lack of education, experiences of criminal behavior or substance abuse, and a family history of mental disorders. Circumstantial sources of vulnerability include poverty, social isolation, lack of adequate employment, and physical distance from resources and potential avenues of support.

The central insight of the stress-diathesis model is that the presence of a diathesis, or vulnerability, is, by itself, insufficient to bring about a mental disorder. Vulnerable individuals will be most likely to experience the onset of problems when they are confronted by stress, and they may function normally in its absence (Kendler, Gardner, and Prescott, 2002).

Although the stress-diathesis model was designed and has mostly been applied toward understanding the origins of mental disorders, the principles of the model apply equally well to understanding the consequences of such disorders. From this perspective, the presence of a condition such as major depressive disorder (MDD), PTSD, or TBI may be considered a diathesis—i.e., a source of vulnerability. For any outcome or negative consequence of experiencing these conditions, an individual will be most at risk to the extent that (1) the individual has other vulnerabilities and (2) the individual encounters stressful or demanding events that tax resources and energy that are already limited by the condition and other vulnerabilities. Thus, for example, this model suggests that a servicemember returning from combat with a particular condition is most likely to experience negative consequences of that condition to the extent that the servicemember has other vulnerabilities and encounters stressful events and circumstances.

The stress-diathesis model has a number of important implications for minimizing negative consequences in servicemembers who suffer from mental health and cognitive conditions. *With respect to identifying those in greatest need:* Understanding individual vulnerability requires assessing not only the condition but also other possible sources of vulnerability, such as access to social support, the experience of other mental or physical illnesses, and the quality of family relationships. *With respect to protecting those in need:* Programs and policies that reduce vulnerability to further negative consequences (e.g., by ensuring extended health care coverage, promoting post-service employment) may be useful complements to treatments that directly address the symptoms of the condition.

Life-Span Developmental Perspectives

The stress-diathesis model offers a powerful framework for understanding who may be at risk for problems and when those problems are likely to occur. However, the model is silent regarding how mental disorders give rise to further difficulties throughout the life course. Theories of life-span development (e.g., Baltes, 1987; Ceci and Hembrooke, 1995; Zoccolillo et al., 1992) describe two distinct mechanisms to account for how mental disorders may give rise to future problems (e.g., Caspi, 1987; Elder, Pavalko, and Hastings, 1991).

The first mechanism is *interactional continuity*—the idea that enduring qualities of an individual affect the way that individual interacts with others, who generally respond in kind. Thus, aggressive individuals behave in ways that beget aggressive responses, and withdrawn individuals behave in ways that exacerbate their isolation. As a result of this form of continuity, the interpersonal relationships of both types of individuals tend to suffer and get worse over time (Caspi, Elder, and Bem, 1987, 1988). Interactional continuity highlights the ways that mental health and cognitive conditions, to the extent that they impair interpersonal functioning, can have lasting consequences for how individuals make their way in the world.

A second mechanism described by this perspective is *cumulative continuity*—the idea that behaviors and choices at each stage of life have consequences that accumulate to shape and constrain an individual's options at subsequent stages of life. Cumulative continuity highlights the ways that negative consequences can emerge over time. For example, servicemembers who are aggressive and uncontrolled upon return from deployment are likely to suffer professionally and socially. Especially after they separate from the structured environment of the military, the consequences of their behavior may accumulate, limiting their options for productive employment. Constrained economically, their options for maintaining and supporting successful family relationships are similarly limited (Caspi, Elder, and Bem, 1987). Thus, over time, the immediate symptoms of a condition may trigger a cascade of negative consequences that substantially affect later stages of life.

Applied specifically to servicemembers suffering from mental disorders, the life-span developmental perspective suggests that impairments observed immediately after a servicemember returns from combat may have consequences for a broad range of outcomes through two primary mechanisms. A condition alters the way the servicemember interacts with intimates, family members, and professional colleagues, impairing these relationships. A condition may also give rise to concrete outcomes (e.g., incarceration, substance abuse, unemployment) that significantly shape situations that the individual and family members will face later in life.

An Integrated Model of the Consequences of Post-Combat Mental Health and Cognitive Conditions

We have developed a general framework that incorporates elements from the stress-diathesis model and the life-span developmental perspective (see Figure 5.1). The logic of the model can be expressed as a series of propositions:

- Even individuals who share a common diagnosis may have symptoms that range from mild to severe.
- Impairments arising from post-combat mental health and cognitive conditions have direct, negative consequences for individual outcomes.

Figure 5.1
A Model of the Consequences of Post-Combat Mental Health and Cognitive Conditions

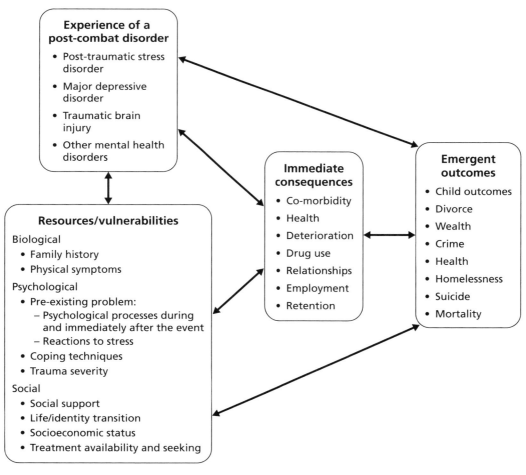

- A servicemember's resources and vulnerabilities can alter the immediate consequences of these conditions.
- Sufficient resources can act as a buffer, protecting individuals and minimizing the immediate consequences of these conditions, whereas significant vulnerabilities and other sources of stress can exacerbate the negative consequences of a condition.
- Over the life span, the immediate consequences of these disorders may themselves have long-term consequences for individuals and their family members.
- The immediate and emergent consequences of mental health and cognitive conditions feed back to affect the course of the condition.

This integrative model describes the consequences of post-combat mental health and cognitive conditions as a cascade of negative outcomes that, in the absence of intervention, can accumulate to affect a broad range of domains over the life span of the afflicted individual. Moreover, the model draws attention to events and circumstances external to the individual (e.g., the presence or absence of other sources of stress and support) that make a negative cascade more or less likely to occur. One implication of this perspective is that, to the extent that they prevent or ameliorate the short-term consequences of these conditions, early interventions may have significant indirect long-term benefits. A second implication is that interventions and policies that focus solely on ameliorating the specific symptoms of these conditions may be too narrow. On the contrary, the model suggests that programs that provide afflicted servicemembers with a supportive environment and the means by which to cope with their conditions may prove important complements to traditional interventions that treat each condition directly.

Empirical Research on the Consequences of Post-Combat Mental Health and Cognitive Conditions

To describe the range of personal, familial, and social outcomes likely to be affected by these disorders, we conducted a search of the scientific literature on the correlates and consequences of post-traumatic stress disorder, major depression and depressive symptoms, and traumatic brain injury. The full review is available as a RAND working paper titled *Invisible Wounds: Predicting the Immediate and Long-Term Consequences of Mental Health Problems in Veterans of Operation Enduring Freedom and Operation Iraqi Freedom* (available at http://veterans.rand.org), and we present here material that appears in expanded form in that paper. When possible, our review addressed research that examined these issues within military populations. When such research was unavailable, we reviewed and extrapolated from the extensive bodies of research that have examined the correlates and consequences of these conditions in civilian populations.

These literatures are massive and extend back decades; of necessity, we have been selective, drawing upon studies that used methods of sampling and assessment that experts consider the most reliable. When possible, we have favored *longitudinal research*, which follows individuals over time. Because the military recruits from the population over 18 years old, we have focused exclusively on research on adults.

Below we briefly summarize the key research findings for each of the following outcomes: other mental health problems; suicide; physical health and mortality; substance use and abuse; employment and productivity; homelessness; and marriage, parenting, and child outcomes.

Co-Morbidity and Other Mental Health Problems

Co-morbidity of conditions refers to two or more conditions co-occurring simultaneously. In civilian populations, individuals with co-occurring mental, medical, and substance use disorders have been shown to have more-severe symptoms, require more-specialized treatment, have poorer outcomes to treatment, and experience more disability in social and occupational functioning than individuals with one condition alone (Greenfield et al., 1998; Olfson et al., 1997; Ormel et al., 1994; Shalev et al., 1998). Co-occurring disorders among military personnel returning from Afghanistan and Iraq may be of particular concern because of the high estimates of co-morbidity found among individuals with PTSD. We know from research in the general population that about 88 percent of men and 79 percent of women with PTSD also experience one other disorder in their lifetime and that about half have three or more co-morbid diagnoses (Kessler, Sonnega, et al., 1995). These estimates are supported by other research showing that individuals with PTSD also have an average of 2.7 other diagnoses and that the number of co-morbid disorders increases with PTSD severity (Marshall et al., 2001). Although little research has examined rates of co-morbidity specifically within the current military cohort, rates of PTSD among returnees may offer preliminary insights into the co-morbidity rates we might anticipate.

PTSD and Depression. In civilian populations, PTSD and depression frequently co-occur. For example, among trauma survivors from a hospital emergency room, 78.4 percent of those with a diagnosis of PTSD experienced depression at some point in their lifetime following their PTSD diagnosis (Shalev et al., 1998). Within the current military cohort, a study of hospitalized soldiers assessed between March 2003 and September 2004 found that about 6.3 percent of the sample met criteria for both depression and PTSD up to seven months after injury (Grieger et al., 2006). In our own survey, we found that approximately two-thirds of those with PTSD also have probable major depression. Some evidence suggests that individuals with co-morbid PTSD and depression have more negative consequences than persons with either diagnosis alone. In one study, veterans in a VA setting with co-morbid depression and PTSD had more-severe depression, lower social support, more suicide ideation, and more-frequent primary care and mental health care visits than did individuals with depression only

(Campbell et al., 2007). Another study found that individuals with these dual diagnoses had more-severe symptom severity and lower levels of functioning (Shalev et al., 1998).

TBI and Depression. In civilian populations, co-morbidity between TBI and depression is common and can be experienced within months following the brain injury (Moldover, Goldberg, and Prout, 2004) and for many years after the injury (Busch and Alpern, 1998). The prevalence of depression among those with a brain injury varies between 15 and 61 percent (Deb et al., 1999; Kim et al., 2007). For example, among World War II veterans with penetrating head injury, 19 percent had a lifetime prevalence of depression compared with an estimated prevalence of depression of 13 percent among those without a head injury (Holsinger et al., 2002). One reason for the wide range in estimates is that symptoms of TBI overlap substantially with symptoms of depression, which makes it challenging to differentiate symptoms of depression from TBI (Babin, 2003; Kim et al., 2007). Our own survey found that one-third of those with TBI also meet criteria for depression. Depression may also develop indirectly years after an injury as a result of TBI-related consequences and maladaptive readjustment (Moldover, Goldberg, and Prout, 2004). In addition, individuals with co-morbid TBI and depression experience more functional impairment, more anxiety and aggressive behavior, and poorer social functioning, and they perceive their disabilities to be more severe than those with either condition alone (Fann et al., 1995; Jorge et al., 2005). Furthermore, individuals with TBI that develop MDD are at higher risk of cognitive disability, anxiety disorders, and poorer quality of life than are individuals who do not develop MDD (Levin et al., 2001). Among those with TBI, risk factors for developing depression include stress, social isolation, maladaptive coping, and lateral lesions (Kim et al., 2007).

TBI and PTSD. The co-morbidity between PTSD and TBI has been a controversial topic, because one symptom of TBI is the loss of consciousness or amnesia of the traumatic event, whereas an integral symptom of PTSD is a re-experiencing of the event. Experts in the literature have argued that, if individuals with TBI are unconscious at the time of the trauma, they therefore cannot retain the memories of the event to experience subsequent PTSD symptoms. Yet, recent research suggests that both diagnoses can co-occur either through a subconscious/implicit level or through social reconstruction (Joseph and Masterson, 1999). A study of U.S. Army infantry soldiers surveyed three or four months after return from Iraq showed that, among those reporting a TBI with loss of consciousness, 43.9 percent also reported symptoms consistent with PTSD. This percentage is greater than that for those reporting TBI with altered mental status, 27.3 percent; those reporting other injuries, 16.2 percent; and those with no injury, 9.1 percent (Hoge et al., 2008). Our survey (see Chapter Four) found that one-third of servicemembers with a probable TBI also met criteria for probable PTSD. Thus, it appears that there may be a strong association between TBI and PTSD, although there is very little supporting literature to date; research on this association is in its early stages.

Co-Morbidity with Other Psychiatric Disorders: PTSD. Among individuals with PTSD, the most common co-morbidities are with depression, substance use, and other anxiety disorders (Brady et al., 2000). For example, in the National Comorbidity Survey, PTSD was co-morbid with affective, anxiety, conduct, and alcohol/substance use disorders among men and women (Kessler, Sonnega, et al., 1995). Among patients in primary care with a diagnosis of PTSD, about 65 percent met criteria for another disorder, with the most common co-occurring diagnoses as phobia, major depression, and bipolar depression (Olfson et al., 1997). Rates of co-morbidity also increase as PTSD symptoms increase. Co-morbid anxiety disorders (e.g., panic disorder, social phobia, generalized anxiety, or obsessive-compulsive disorder) are associated with increasing PTSD symptoms (Marshall et al., 2001), suggesting that individuals are at increased risk for co-occurring disorders as PTSD symptoms worsen. These other psychiatric disorders also have adverse consequences. For instance, within the military, social phobia and current social anxiety have been associated with anxiety, reports of shame experienced pre-military, and homecoming adversity (Orsillo et al., 1996). Panic disorder is another anxiety disorder that overlaps with symptoms of PTSD (e.g., hypervigilance) and has been shown to be more common among veterans that were exposed to combat (Deering et al., 1996).

Co-Morbidity with Other Psychiatric Disorders: TBI. Rates of TBI have been associated with increased risk of psychiatric disorders—specifically, anxiety (Moore, Terryberry-Spohr, and Hope, 2006), depressive disorders, and substance use (Anstey et al., 2004; Hibbard et al., 1998; Silver et al., 2001). Rates of co-morbidity between TBI and other psychiatric disorders may be associated with more-complex and more-severe TBI than are milder forms of TBI. In a study of individuals with mild TBI, most patients recovered completely, but those who had poorer recovery outcomes were more likely to have depression and anxiety disorders (Mooney and Speed, 2001). TBI is also co-morbid with chronic pain, a condition that has a long and pervasive course after injury. Among patients in a brain injury rehabilitation center, 58 percent with mild TBI and 52 percent with moderate-to-severe TBI had chronic pain (Lahz and Bryant, 1996). Co-occurring TBI and chronic pain have been associated with longer treatment stays than has chronic pain alone (Andary et al., 1997).

Co-Morbidity with Other Psychiatric Disorders: Depression. About 45 percent of individuals with past-year depression diagnoses experience at least a second co-occurring diagnosis (Kessler, Chiu, et al., 2005), and depression is rarely the primary diagnosis (Kessler, Berglund, et al., 2003). As expected, slightly higher rates of co-morbidity are found with a treatment-seeking population in primary care and psychiatric outpatient settings; estimates of a co-morbid disorder among those with depression are about 65 percent (Olfson et al., 1997; Zimmerman, Chelminski, and McDermut, 2002). A recent general-population study using the National Epidemiologic Survey of Alcoholism and Related Conditions (NESARC) found that having major depression within the past year was most commonly associated with personality disorders (38 percent), anxiety disorders (36 percent), nicotine dependence (26 percent), alcohol use disorders (14 percent), and drug use disorders (5 percent). The most common personality disorders were obsessive-compulsive, paranoid, and schizoid disorders; the most common anxiety disorders included specific phobia, generalized anxiety, and social phobia. Depression severity is significantly and positively correlated with impaired functioning (Hasin et al., 2005).

Summary. Co-occurring disorders are common among individuals with TBI, depression, and PTSD, and they often result in more-negative outcomes than for individuals experiencing any of the disorders alone. Among other co-morbid diagnoses, anxiety and mood disorders seem to be most common for all diagnoses, plus chronic pain for TBI. Individuals with co-occurring disorders tend to have more-severe and more-complex symptoms, require specialized treatment, and often experience more distress associated with their disorders.

Suicide

Suicide is one of the leading causes of death among 10- to 44-year-olds in the United States, although it is still relatively rare, with a rate of around 10 per 100,000 persons (Heron and Smith, 2007). Among persons who have committed suicide, the majority have had one or more mental disorders, making psychiatric problems one of the strongest risk factors of this outcome (Harris and Barraclough, 1997). Accordingly, concerns about elevated rates of mental disorders among servicemembers returning from Afghanistan and Iraq lead to concerns about elevated rates of suicides as well.

Suicide in the Military. There is a long-standing concern about suicide among military personnel. According to the Department of Defense, in 2003 the rate of suicide across the armed forces was roughly 10 to 13 (depending on military branch) per 100,000 troops (Allen, Cross, and Swanner, 2005), an estimate that is comparable to the rate of suicide across all ages in the United States (Centers for Disease Control and Prevention, National Center for Injury Prevention and Control, 2007). However, while these figures and others (Lehmann, McCormick, and McCracken, 1995; Rothberg et al., 1990) may indicate that military personnel do not face a risk of suicide different from that of the general population, population-based studies have indicated that male veterans face roughly twice the risk of dying from suicide as their civilian counterparts (Kaplan et al., 2007). Analyses focused specifically on veterans of the Vietnam War indicate that these veterans were at increased risk of suicide-related mortality relative to veterans who did not serve in Vietnam; however, this increased risk occurred within five years from discharge from active duty, and the difference did not persist after this time (Boehmer et al., 2004). In 2006, there were 97 suicides among active duty Army soldiers (including members of the Reserve Component on active duty), and close to two-thirds of these had a history of at least one deployment to Afghanistan or Iraq (U.S. Department of the Army, Army Behavioral Health Technology Office, 2007)

Depression, PTSD, TBI, and Suicide. Depression, PTSD, and TBI all increase the risk for suicide. Psychological autopsy studies of civilians have consistently shown that a large number of suicides had a probable depressive disorder (Cavanagh et al., 2003; Henriksson et al., 1993; Isometsa, 2001). In a population-based study of civilians, 16 percent of those persons with a lifetime history of MDD had a lifetime history of one or more self-reported suicide attempts (Chen and Dilsaver, 1996). In the National Comorbidity Survey, persons with a lifetime history of a major depressive episode were 10 times more likely to report having thought about killing themselves and 11 times more likely to have made a nonfatal suicide attempt. The risk was even greater when the definitional criterion for depression was modified to exclude having thoughts of death, which could have potentially confounded the effect of depression on suicide outcomes (Kessler, Borges, and Walters, 1999). Among suicides over a one-year period across the VA medical center, 30 percent had an unspecified affective disorder, and 40 percent of patients who had attempted suicide had an affective disorder (Lehmann, McCormick, and McCracken, 1995).

Although not as strongly associated with suicide as depression, PTSD is more strongly associated with suicide ideation and attempts than any other anxiety disorder (Kessler, Borges, and Walters, 1999). In the National Comorbidity Survey, two different studies have indicated that persons with lifetime PTSD were significantly more likely to report having thought about killing themselves and to have made an attempt, even after accounting for a variety of potential sociodemographic and mental health confounding factors (Kessler, Borges, and Walters, 1999; Sareen et al., 2005). Among a sample of 100 Vietnam veterans with PTSD at a VA hospital, 19 had made a suicide attempt and 15 more had been "preoccupied" with thoughts of suicide since the war (Hendin and Haas, 1991). Psychological autopsies have also indicated that PTSD is linked to suicide deaths. In a study of Vietnam veterans, those who died from suicide were more likely to have symptoms of PTSD than a comparison group who died in motor vehicle crashes (Farberow, Kang, and Bullman, 1990).

Finally, research also has consistently shown that persons with TBI have a higher risk of suicide than persons without TBI. Among outpatients with TBI, 23 percent reported suicide ideation and 18 percent reported having made a suicide attempt post-injury (Simpson and Tate, 2002); in a similar sample, 26 percent of TBI outpatients had made a suicide attempt (Simpson and Tate, 2005). In a community-based sample, persons with a self-reported history of a "severe head trauma with loss of consciousness or confusion" had a higher lifetime risk of having attempted suicide (Hibbard et al., 1998). Using multiple years of population registry data, Teasdale and Engberg (2001) found that persons with concussions, cranial fractures, and cerebral contusions or traumatic intracranial hemorrhages each had at least a three-times-higher incidence rate of suicide mortality than the general population, after adjusting for sex and age.

Correlates and Modifiers of Suicide Risk. Research on suicide has identified a number of covariates, or factors, that are either correlated with suicide independent of depression, PTSD, and/or TBI or that modify the risk of these disorders on suicide outcomes. For example, in the civilian population, suicide rates differ by *gender*; men are at much higher risk of dying from suicide than females. The same is true in the armed forces, with men making up 95 percent of the Army suicide population but 85 percent of the total Army population (Allen, Cross, and Swanner, 2005). At the same time, depression, PTSD, and TBI have a greater effect on females' than on males' risk of suicide (Henriksson et al., 1993; Oquendo et al., 2003; Teasdale and Engberg, 2001). *Race* is another demographic correlate: Although Caucasians make up 59 percent of the total Army population, they account for 71 percent of all Army suicides (Allen, Cross, and Swanner, 2005). White veterans have a three-times-greater risk of dying from suicide than non-White veterans (Kaplan et al., 2007). Suicide rates have also been associated with specific *symptoms*. For example, a psychological autopsy study of suicides occurring during a major depressive episode found that suicides were less likely to express symptoms of fatigue, difficulties concentrating, or indecisiveness, and that only insomnia was an immediate indicator of risk (McGirr et al., 2007).

Different types of TBI have also been differentially linked with suicide; among persons with TBI, those with cerebral contusions or traumatic intracranial hemorrhage have higher rates than those with concussions or cranial fractures (Teasdale and Engberg, 2001). Symptom *severity* also matters. For example, higher levels of PTSD symptoms are associated with increased levels of suicide ideation (Marshall et al., 2001). For TBI, the length of an individual's hospital stay, a proxy for injury severity, increased the risk of a subsequent suicide (Teasdale and Engberg, 2001). *Nonfatal suicide attempts* are the strongest predictors of subsequent fatal suicides, even when controlling for past mood disorders, such as depression (Harris and Barraclough, 1997; Joiner et al., 2005). Among people with depression, PTSD, and TBI, suicide risk is also elevated among those with *substance use disorders* (Mills et al., 2006; Simpson and Tate, 2005; Waller, Lyons, and Costantini-Ferrando, 1999). In their empirical review, Wilcox, Conner, and Caine (2004) found that, with respect to suicide, the standardized mortality ratio for substance use disorders was 9 to 14 times higher than it was for those without these disorders, and variation was due to the specific substance under study (e.g., alcohol use disorders versus opioid drug use).

Among servicemembers specifically, *combat exposure* increases the risk of suicide. For example, Vietnam veterans face an increased risk of suicide mortality relative to non-Vietnam veterans, especially during the first five years after discharge from active duty (Boehmer et al., 2004). Additionally, mortality rates from external causes, which include suicide, were higher among Vietnam theater veterans with PTSD than among Vietnam theater veterans without PTSD (Boscarino, 2006a and 2006b). One study of veterans with PTSD found that it was not any particular PTSD symptom or cluster of symptoms, but rather combat-related guilt, that was the strongest predictor of suicidal behavior (Hendin and Haas, 1991).

Physical Health and Mortality

There are strong relationships between physical health and mental well-being. In some cases, physical symptoms are consequences of mental conditions. For example, insomnia may be a symptom of depression, or headaches may be symptoms of TBI. Alternatively, physical impairment may lead to mental impairment as a result of limitations in occupational or social functioning, which may foster increased reliance on others to perform basic tasks and compromised access to medical care. Mental health symptoms may also contribute to poor physical health through altered biological functions (e.g., decreased immune function) or by influencing individual health risk behavior (e.g., smoking, poor diet).

Mortality. Persons with depression face an increased risk of death relative to their similarly aged counterparts without depression (Wulsin, Vaillant, and Wells, 1999). In one study of Army veterans conducted 30 years after service, total mortality was higher among those with PTSD who served in theater than among those who served in theater but did not have PTSD (Boscarino, 2006b). The increased risk of death among persons with PTSD and depression appears to be driven by two primary causes: increases in the risk of death from unnatural causes (e.g., homicide, suicide, and unintentional injuries) and from cardiovascular disease. For the sample of Army veterans, combat veterans with PTSD had elevated risks of cardiovascular mortality, external-cause mortality, and cancer mortality relative to combat veterans without PTSD (Boscarino, 2006a). However, there is no evidence of an increased risk in cancer-related mortality among persons with depression.

The effect of TBI on mortality may be the most pronounced because these injuries can, in and of themselves, be life-threatening. In 1992, among military personnel with a medical discharge record indicating a TBI diagnosis, the reason for discharge from the military was more likely to be coded as "death" relative to the entire military discharged population without TBI. As would be expected, the likelihood of reason for discharge being death increased with injury severity: Persons with a mild TBI were 11.6 times more likely and servicemembers with a severe TBI diagnosis were close to 150 times more likely to have the reason for discharge coded as "death" (Ommaya et al., 1996b).

Morbidity. Cardiovascular diseases, particularly coronary heart disease (CHD), which includes myocardial infarctions (MIs), or heart attacks, are the most frequently studied morbidity outcome among persons with psychiatric disorders. In a meta-analysis, Rugulies (2002) found that persons who met probable diagnostic criteria for depression were nearly two times more likely to develop both fatal and non-fatal CHD than persons without depression. Research also documents a relationship between PTSD and CHD (Bankier and Littman, 2002; Boscarino and Chang, 1999;

Falger et al., 1992; Solter et al., 2002). In a prospective study of this relationship among men who had at one point served in the military, increasing levels of PTSD symptoms were associated with an increased risk of all CHD outcomes (i.e., nonfatal MI, fatal CHD, and angina), and specifically with nonfatal MI and fatal CHD (Kubzansky et al., 2007). Very little research has investigated cardiovascular outcomes after TBI.

With respect to physical non-heart-related morbidities, combat Vietnam veterans with PTSD had a greater number of unspecified physician-rated medical complaints than those without PTSD (Beckham et al., 1998). There is also evidence that depression directly affects conditions associated with aging, including osteoporosis, arthritis, Type 2 diabetes, certain cancers, periodontal disease, and frailty (Kiecolt-Glaser and Glaser, 2002). Finally, patients with TBI endure physical injuries that can include pulmonary dysfunction, cardiovascular dysfunction, gastrointestinal dysfunction, fluid and hormonal imbalances, and fractures, nerve injuries, blood clots, or infections (National Institute of Neurological Disorders and Stroke, 2002). As the severity of TBI increases, the rate and severity of physical health consequences do as well (National Institute of Neurological Disorders and Stroke, 2002). In the long-term, individuals with TBI may also be more likely to experience Alzheimer's disease, Parkinson's disease, and other disorders more specific to the cause of trauma (e.g., repetitive blows for boxers) or its severity (e.g., brain injury that results in coma) (National Institute of Neurological Disorders and Stroke, 2002).

Self-Reported Medical Symptoms. Deployed servicemembers report high levels of somatic complaints during deployment: In a survey of over 15,000 deployed military personnel, 77 percent of personnel deployed to Iraq and 54 percent of those deployed to Afghanistan experienced diarrhea (often associated with fevers and vomiting), 69 percent reported a respiratory illness, and 35 percent reported noncombat injuries (Sanders et al., 2005). When asked about their own health, persons with PTSD, depression, and TBI are consistently more likely to endorse physical problems than those without these disorders. Among servicemembers assessed one year after returning from Iraq, those who met probable diagnostic criteria for PTSD were more likely than soldiers who did not screen positive for PTSD to report being bothered by a variety of physical symptoms, including stomach pain, back pain, pain in the limbs, headaches, chest pain, dizziness, fainting spells, pounding or racing heart, shortness of breath, bowel symptoms, nausea, and pain or problems during sexual intercourse (Hoge et al., 2007). Soldiers in this study screening positive for PTSD were also more likely to rate their health as poor or fair and to report making sick calls or missing workdays. All of these associations remained even after controlling for suffering an injury during combat. Studies among both veteran and civilian populations have shown similar results (Beckham et al., 1998; Breslau and Davis, 1992; Dobie et al., 2004; Lauterbach, Vora, and Rakow, 2005). Soldiers with mild TBI, assessed three to four months after their return from Iraq, also reported significantly poorer general health and greater somatic symptoms than soldiers without TBI, but these associations were eliminated after controlling for concurrent PTSD and depression (Hoge et. al., 2008). This situation suggests that PTSD and depression may be important mediators of the effects of TBI on general physical health, although these results still await replication.

Quality of Life/Physical Functioning. Across studies, individuals with PTSD report lower quality of life and well-being than those without PTSD. For example, in clinical samples of veterans (Magruder et al., 2004; Schnurr et al., 2006) and community-based samples of Vietnam veterans (Zatzick et al., 1997), higher levels of PTSD symptoms are associated with lower levels of physical functioning. A recent study of 120 service-members who enrolled for health care after returning from OEF and OIF similarly found that self-reported health, emotional well-being, and energy were all significantly lower among those with PTSD than among those without the diagnosis (Erbes et al., 2007). Similar patterns of relationships exist for depression (Wells et al., 1989). The mechanism underlying cross-sectional relationships between these constructs remains unclear. In one of the few longitudinal studies of these relationships, there was evidence that self-rated overall health among older adults has a modest effect on depressive symptoms, but that depressive symptoms have very little effect on self-related health (Kosloski et al., 2005). The study of quality of life and physical functioning after TBI is relatively undeveloped. Most studies of functional outcomes after TBI occur during or after a rehabilitation program and indicate general improvement in these outcomes as the time from the injury increases; for example, among patients with severe TBI, there was general improvement across a variety of functional dimensions one year after the injury, signaling improvement (Lippert-Gruner et al., 2007).

Health-Compromising Behaviors. The link between negative physical health outcomes and PTSD, depression, and TBI may partially be explained by increases in other types of health-risk behaviors that are known to influence health outcomes as well. For example, there is a clear link between most psychiatric disorders, including PTSD and depression, and smoking. Cross-sectional analyses of the National Comorbidity Survey reveal that persons who met criteria for depression or PTSD at any point in their lives and in the past 30 days were more likely to be lifetime and current smokers than were persons without a mental disorder (Lasser et al., 2000). Samples of military veterans have found similar associations between smoking and PTSD (Buckley et al., 2004; Dobie et al., 2004). Studies also indicate unique smoking-related outcomes in PTSD and depression. For example, exposure to trauma and the development of PTSD increases smoking frequency (Feldner, Babson, and Zvolensky, 2007). In addition, some evidence suggests that persons with PTSD have harder times quitting smoking, although depressive symptoms do not appear to affect rates of cessation (Feldner, Babson, and Zvolensky, 2007; Kinnunen et al., 2006). In addition, mental health symptoms may also impact other health-compromising behaviors that increase the risk for adverse health outcomes. For example, symptoms of depression and PTSD increase sexual-risk-taking behaviors that, in turn, increase the risk of sexually transmitted infections, including HIV (Holmes, Foa, and Sammel, 2005). Among people with depression (Simon et al., 2006) and PTSD (Vieweg et al., 2006a, 2006b), epidemiological studies also reveal an elevated prevalence of obesity.

Substance Abuse

Substance use disorders often co-occur with other mental disorders. In the civilian population, about half of those with substance abuse also have a mental disorder, and about 15–40 percent of people with a mental disorder have substance abuse (Kessler, Nelson, et al., 1996; Regier et al., 1990). Individuals with substance use disorders that co-occur with other mental disorders have more-severe diagnostic symptoms, require more-specialized treatment, and have poorer treatment outcomes than individuals with a single disorder (Kessler, Nelson, et al., 1996; Watkins et al., 2001).

Alcohol and Drug Use. Alcohol and drug use disorders are highly prevalent among individuals with PTSD, MDD, and TBI. For PTSD, a study of Vietnam combat veterans showed that up to 75 percent of veterans with a history of PTSD in their lifetime met criteria for substance abuse or dependence (Kulka et al., 1990). Individuals in the general population with depression are 3.7 times more likely to meet alcohol-dependence criteria, 1.2 times more likely to meet alcohol-abuse criteria, 2.5 times more likely to meet drug-abuse criteria, and 9 times more likely to meet drug-dependence criteria (Grant et al., 2004). Finally, about 79 percent and 37 percent of individuals with traumatic brain injury met criteria for alcohol and drug use disorders, respectively (Taylor et al., 2003).

Several studies have attempted to discern the temporal relationship between mental disorders and alcohol and drug misuse, but to date the results have been mixed, depending on the specific disorder studied. For example, reviews of the literature on substance abuse and PTSD (Jacobsen, Southwick, and Kosten, 2001; Stewart, 1996) found most support for the *self-medication hypothesis*, which suggests that PTSD increases the risk of substance use disorders because individuals use substances to cope with their PTSD (Chilcoat and Breslau, 1998). According to Bremner and colleagues (1996), Vietnam combat veterans reported that alcohol, heroin, benzodiazepines, and marijuana "helped" their PTSD symptoms, although cocaine tended to worsen hyperarousal symptoms further, supporting the self-medication theory that substances may be used to relieve distressing PTSD symptoms. In contrast, models examining the relationship between depression and substance use suggest that depression and negative affect are a consequence of substance use rather than a cause (Swendsen and Merikangas, 2000). Even small amounts of alcohol use are associated with an increased prevalence of depression and poorer treatment outcomes, as well as increased morbidity, mortality, and disability (Rehm et al., 2003; Stinson et al., 1998; Sullivan, Fiellin, and O'Connor, 2005; Worthington et al., 1996).

Substance use and TBI co-morbidity has been specifically associated with military discharge. Compared with all those discharged from the military, persons with mild TBI were over two times more likely to be discharged for alcohol/drugs or criminal convictions, and persons with moderate TBI were about five times more likely to be discharged for alcohol/drug problems (Ommaya et al., 1996a). Additional consequences associated with TBI and substance use included lower likelihood of returning to work, decreased life satisfaction, greater risk of continued abuse post-injury, and that continued drinking post-injury perpetuated these consequences (Taylor et al., 2003).

To the extent that mental disorders related to military service predict subsequent drug use, there are likely to be wide-ranging implications for servicemembers, because even short-term drug use during military service has long-term consequences. One study examined the mortality of 1,227 Army male returnees 25 years after returning from Vietnam (Price et al., 2001). Compared with both civilian counterparts and non-drug-using Vietnam returnees, veterans who continued using opiates after the Vietnam War were more likely to experience premature death (Price et al., 2001). Short-term drug use has also been associated with alcohol abuse (Boscarino, 1981; O'Brien et al., 1980), depressive symptoms (Helzer, Robins, and Davis, 1976; Nace et al., 1977), and poor social adjustment (Mintz, O'Brien, and Pomerantz, 1979).

Tobacco Use. Despite public health efforts to reduce the prevalence of tobacco use, smoking is still the leading preventable cause of morbidity and mortality in the general population (United States Department of Health and Human Services, 1990) and is a considerable problem for the U.S. military, costing an estimated $952 million per year (Robbins et al., 2000). Research has shown that smoking is associated with disability, decreased productivity, increased absenteeism, and longer and more-frequent work breaks among Department of Defense personnel (Helyer, Brehm, and Perino, 1998). Klesges and colleagues (2001) found that Air Force recruits who smoke cost the U.S. military an additional $18 million per year in training costs; when applied to all branches of the military, the attitudes and behaviors associated with smoking status (which contribute to early discharge) cost the military an estimated $130 million per year in excess training costs (Klesges et al., 2001).

Recent research has indicated that tobacco use may also be associated with mental health behaviors and outcomes. For example, Shalev, Bleich, and Ursano (1990) found that Vietnam veterans with PTSD had a greater incidence of smoking than those without PTSD. Another study found similar rates of smoking among those with and without PTSD, but a higher prevalence of *heavy* smoking among those with PTSD than among those without (Beckham et al., 1997). For instance, McClernon and colleagues (2005) found that smokers with PTSD had higher puff volumes than smokers without PTSD. One study of civilians in southeast Michigan found a significantly increased risk of nicotine dependence in individuals exposed to trauma without the presence of PTSD; the risk was even greater among those with exposure to trauma and the presence of PTSD (Breslau, Davis, and Schultz, 2003). While the above studies do not provide causal evidence that PTSD leads to unhealthy smoking behaviors, they do suggest an association between the two.

Several studies have suggested that tobacco use may alleviate some symptoms of mental disorders, such as PTSD and depression. McFall, Mackay, and Donovan (1992) suggested that the association between PTSD and smoking may indicate the utilization of nicotine to alleviate PTSD symptoms of arousal, numbness, or detachment. Indeed, Beckham et al. (1997) found that heavy-smoking status was associated with hyperarousal and avoidance symptoms, as well as with general PTSD symptoms. Thorndike and colleagues (2006) found that severity of nicotine dependence was positively correlated with total PTSD symptoms, hyperarousal symptoms, and avoidance symptoms; this correlation remained after controlling for depression vulnerability.

Similar hypotheses have been generated with regard to major depression: In a prospective study, Breslau et al. (1998) found that those with a history of major depression were more likely to become daily smokers, suggesting possible self-medication of depressive symptoms. The researchers also found that a history of daily smoking at baseline increased the risk for major depression.

Correlates and Moderators. Men and women may experience stressors differently and may experience different vulnerabilities to substance use and co-occurring PTSD, MDD, and TBI. Men with PTSD are more likely to have alcohol abuse and dependence; women may be at greater risk for co-morbid depression rather than alcohol-abuse dependence (Jacobsen, Southwick, and Kosten, 2001). Additionally, the association between nicotine dependence and PTSD symptoms is stronger among men than women (Thorndike et al., 2006), although rates of substance abuse among women veterans with PTSD remain high (Dobie et al., 2004). Alcohol use is also greater and the consequences of alcohol use more severe among soldiers with less education, ethnic minority groups, males, those not in an intimate relationship, enlisted members, and those deployed in the United States (Gutierrez et al., 2006).

Summary. Co-occurring substance use disorders with PTSD, MDD, and TBI are common and are often associated with more-severe diagnostic symptoms and poorer treatment outcomes. These findings suggest that individuals with substance abuse co-morbidity may be more difficult to treat and may present more challenging and unique sequelae in treatment (Ouimette, Brown, and Najavits, 1998). It appears that substance use often results from PTSD and often precedes depression, and that this temporal understanding can help shape treatment programs to identify the risk factors associated with each of those conditions.

Labor-Market Outcomes: Employment and Productivity

The effect of mental health on employment outcomes in the military population requires an understanding of the structure of the military itself and of servicemembers' experiences in both the military and civilian labor force. Servicemembers from the Active Component perform full-time duty in a uniformed Service. Members of the Reserve Component, on the other hand, perform a minimum of 39 days of service per year and augment the active duty military, and may also hold jobs in the civilian labor force. There are active duty Reserve Component servicemembers who work full-time for their Service Reserve Component, yet who are considered reservists. However, these make up a small percentage of the total Reserve force. Upon redeployment from service, members of both the Active Component and Reserve Component may return to the same employment status they held prior to deployment. Alternatively, they may switch—i.e. members of the Reserve Component may transfer to the Active Component or vice versa—or they may separate from military service. If they separate, they may pursue employment opportunities in the civilian labor market or may be unemployed.

Employment. Studies of the effect of PTSD on current employment status have been conducted primarily on Vietnam veterans. Collectively, these studies indicate that veterans with PTSD are less likely to be currently employed than veterans without the disorder (McCarren et al., 1995; Savoca and Rosenheck, 2000; Smith, Schnurr, and Rosenheck, 2005; Zatzick et al., 1997). For example, Zatzick and colleagues (1997) found that veterans with a current probable PTSD diagnosis were over three times more likely to report currently not working relative to veterans without PTSD, even after adjustment for demographic characteristics and co-morbid conditions. Smith and colleagues (2005) extended these findings by showing that, among a sample of veterans receiving treatment for PTSD symptoms, as severity of these symptoms increased, the likelihood of both full-time and part-time work decreased.

Savoca and Rosenheck (2000) studied the effect of depression on employment among veterans, finding that a lifetime diagnosis of major depression was inversely associated with the probability of current employment. Similar findings have been shown in nationally representative studies of the civilian population. Both men and women with current depression are less likely to be employed than other civilian counterparts without the disorder (for men, 87 percent of those with major depression were employed as opposed to 93.3 percent of those without depression; for women, the prevalence of employment was 74 percent among those with depression and 82 percent for those without) (Ettner, Frank, and Kessler, 1997).

Whereas studies of employment outcomes for persons with PTSD and depression have generally relied on population-based samples, research on such outcomes after TBI have relied primarily on clinical samples of persons with brain injuries who may receive neurotrauma services and rehabilitation. A brain injury usually occurs in the context of an accident or injury at a discrete point in time, and research has thus generally investigated the proportion of employed persons who *return to work* after their injury. Data from one national database indicate that close to 60 percent of individuals with TBI are successfully rehabilitated and that of those, approximately 90 percent went on to be employed in the competitive labor market (Wehman et al., 2005). Among one sample of military personnel entering an eight-week clinical rehabilitation trial for moderate-to-severe closed head injury, over 90 percent were employed one year post-injury, and roughly three-quarters were deemed fit for duty (Salazar et al., 2000).

The probability of employment increases with less-severe injuries, shorter coma times, and shorter periods of rehabilitation (Wehman et al., 2005). In addition, the degree of impairment caused by the injury, pre-morbid employment factors (including educational level, occupational category, and job satisfaction), social and familial supports, and sociodemographic characteristics have all been associated with return-to-work outcomes (Wehman et al., 2005).

Productive Work: Absenteeism and Presenteeism. Poor mental health is associated with individuals' lower likelihood of employment, but it may also affect the performance of individuals who are or remain employed. Measures of productive work fall under two categories—absenteeism and presenteeism. *Absenteeism* reflects the number of lost workdays and has been measured by the number of sick days, missed workdays, or hours worked per week. *Presenteeism* generally refers to lost productivity at work and can be measured by individuals' reports of their level of focus on a task and productivity or performance while at work.

Studies of absenteeism in relation to mental health have focused overwhelmingly on depression. When workers are asked to recall the hours that they work, there is scant evidence of reduced work hours among those with depression compared with workers without these disorders, in either civilian or veteran populations (Ettner, Frank, and Kessler, 1997; Savoca and Rosenheck, 2000). However, studies that have used administrative data, which is less subject to self-report biases, find evidence of increased levels of absenteeism among individuals with depression. For instance, depressed workers in the civilian population have more short-term work-disability days than nondepressed workers (Kessler, Barber, et al., 1999). In another nationally representative sample (the American Productivity Audit/Depressive Disorders Study), workers with depression reported, on average, missing one hour per week due to absenteeism versus an expected loss of 0.4 hour per week in the absence of depression. The estimated costs of depression to the U.S. economy through lost productivity range in the billions of dollars (Greenberg et. al., 2003).

In comparison, there have been few studies of absenteeism among persons with PTSD and TBI, although we can glean some information from studies of military personnel. For instance, in a sample of active duty troops one year after returning from deployment to Iraq, those with PTSD were significantly more likely to report missing two or more workdays in the past month relative to redeployed soldiers without PTSD (Hoge et al., 2007). With respect to TBI, Ommaya et al. (1996b) examined one year of military hospital discharge data linked to military service discharge data and found that increases in the severity of head injuries corresponded with increases in total sick days. A recent survey of 2,525 soldiers collected three to four months after returning from Iraq similarly found that those reporting mild TBI also reported more missed workdays than those without TBI (Hoge et al., 2008).

Studies of presenteeism are rare; those that do exist tend to focus on depression. In a study that asked respondents to recall their work performance in the past two weeks across six work-related dimensions, those with depression lost on average 4.6 hours per week for presenteeism, which was significantly higher than the expected loss of 1.5 hours per week (Stewart et al., 2003). Although we found no observational studies relating PTSD or TBI to levels of work productivity, there is evidence to suggest that both PTSD and TBI are linked to lower levels of productivity. For instance, under experimental conditions, veterans with PTSD and patients with moderate-to-severe TBI are less attentive to common work tasks, particularly in the absence of distractions (Chemtob et al., 1999; Whyte et al., 2000). On the other hand, under experimental conditions, there was no indication that police recruits with PTSD performed worse during stressful situations than control recruits without PTSD (Leblanc et al., 2007). Thus, although evidence suggests that PTSD and TBI may impair work-related performance, the degree to which deficits in functioning are clinically relevant remains to be determined.

Wages and Income. There is evidence linking psychiatric disorders with decreased wages. For instance, among Vietnam veterans, both depression and PTSD had negative effects on hourly wages. More specifically, veterans suffering from PTSD had 16 percent lower hourly wages than veterans who do not, and those with depression had 45 percent lower hourly wages than veterans who do not (Savoca and Rosenheck, 2000). Wages are even lower for veterans with depression and a co-morbid substance-use disorder (Savoca and Rosenheck, 2000). However, a clinical study of veterans receiving treatment for PTSD found no evidence that severity of PTSD was related to monthly earnings (Smith et al., 2005). Results from the National Comorbidty Survey indicate that there may be a significant reduction in the earnings of men and women with any disorder, although not specifically for depression (Ettner, Frank, and Kessler, 1997). Among one sample of TBI rehabilitation patients, average mean income declined 48 percent per month one year after incurring the injury (Johnstone, Mount, and Schopp, 2003). Finally, using data from the American Community Survey, Gamboa and colleagues (2006) estimated the full economic consequences of having a cognitive disability lasting six months or more and found that those with such a disability earned, on average, $10,000 less than persons without such a disability. These differences, however, varied by highest level of education, with larger differences among those with higher levels of educational attainment.

Education. Although there are education requirements for entering the U.S. military service, many servicemembers may desire to continue their education by pursuing post-secondary schooling or graduate school. Previous studies indicate that achieving these educational goals has significant effects on a variety of outcomes, including occupational achievement, financial security, and health (Kessler, Foster, et al., 1995). Having PTSD, depression, or TBI is likely to affect how successful servicemembers will be at obtaining these future educational goals. Accounting only for mental disorders that occurred before terminating their schooling, beginning in high school, persons in the National Comorbidity Survey with one or more mental disorders were consistently more likely to terminate their education than those without a disorder. However, among persons who completed eighth grade, persons with mood disorders (which include depression) and anxiety disorders (which include PTSD) were less likely to complete high school; high school graduates were less likely to enter college, and college entrants were less likely to complete college (Kessler, Foster, et al., 1995).

Summary. PTSD, depression, and TBI all influence labor-market outcomes. Specifically, there is compelling evidence indicating that these conditions will affect servicemembers' return to employment, their productivity at work, and their future job prospects, as indicated by impeded educational attainment. However, these findings should be interpreted cautiously. The majority of those studies referenced above are cross-sectional; it is not yet clear that these mental conditions are underlying causes of the observed labor-market outcomes. In fact, working has many benefits in and of itself, ranging from enhancing social interactions to promoting self-esteem and expanding economic self-sufficiency (Wehman et al., 2005). Thus, poor performance in the workplace can influence the development of mental health symptoms or enhance symptoms that may already exist.

Homelessness

The Department of Veterans Affairs has identified over 1,000 veterans coming back from Afghanistan and Iraq as at risk for homelessness and has served about 3,000 in its homelessness programs (Perl, 2007). Psychiatric symptoms and substance use have been described as the primary risk factors for homelessness among veterans (Rosenheck et al., 1996). Studies of veterans indicate that psychiatric symptoms and substance use were stronger predictors of homelessness than combat exposure or any other military factor (Rosenheck and Fontana, 1994). Other veteran and civilian studies support the strong risk that mental health problems and substance use has for homelessness (Robertson, 1987; Roth, 1992). For instance, research from the National Vietnam Veterans Readjustment Study indicates that those who experienced stress in a war zone had more readjustment problems and that stress and readjustment problems were stronger predictors of homelessness than exposure to war zones alone (Kulka et al., 1990). Similarly, adverse effects of PTSD, including substance abuse, interpersonal difficulties, and unemployment, were associated with veterans' homelessness (Rosenheck, Leda, and Gallup, 1992). As for nonveteran populations, extreme poverty and social isolation are also risk factors for homelessness (Rosenheck, Kasprow, and Seibyl, 2004).

Mental Health and Homelessness. Few studies have examined the rates of homelessness among individuals with PTSD, MDD, or TBI. One study that has examined this relationship to some degree found that about 15 percent of individuals seeking mental health services in San Diego over one year were homeless; a severe mental disorder and poorer functioning were the greatest risk factors (Folsom et al., 2005). In a smaller New York study, rates of homelessness among a mental health treatment population were about 19 percent within three months of admission, 25 percent within three years, and 28 percent in their lifetime (Susser, Lin, and Conover, 1991).

Instead, the literature on homelessness has tended to focus on the reverse relationship—i.e., examining the prevalence of mental disorder among homeless populations. Compared with nonhomeless persons in the general population, homeless people have increased rates of mental disorder, including substance use (Breakey, 2004) and traumatic brain injury (Gonzalez et al., 2001). Homeless persons are also more likely to experience a severe mental disorder, such as schizophrenia, chronic depression, and bipolar depression (Susser et al., 1997). It is unclear whether mental disorders cause homelessness, or whether being homeless increases the risk of developing such conditions. Most research suggests the former, that mental disorders and dysfunction are risk factors for homelessness (Muñoz et al., 1998; Backer and Howard, 2007). In one study, about 75 percent of individuals with PTSD developed the diagnosis prior to becoming homeless (North and Smith, 1992), suggesting that a mental disorder may be a precursor to homelessness. Other risk factors that contribute to homelessness include poverty, disaffiliation, and personal vulnerability—each of which is overrepresented among persons with a severe mental disorder (Breakey, 2004).

The prevalence of mental disorders among homeless people may be overstated and may be the consequence of studies relying on poor sampling methods or research guided by the assumption that homelessness is caused by personal faults (e.g., inability of some persons to care for themselves) (Koegel, Burnam, and Baumohl, 1996). In fact, an integrated perspective on homelessness highlights that personal limitations (mental health, lack of support) interact with structural factors (low availability of low-cost housing, decreased resources for the vulnerably poor) to enhance the likelihood of homelessness (Koegel, 2004; Koegel, Burnam, and Baumohl, 1996).

Consequences of Mental Health and Homelessness. Compared with homeless people without mental disorders, homeless people with mental disorders have worse physical health; difficulty with subsistence needs, such as finding shelter, food, and clothing; victimization; and quality of life (Sullivan et al., 2000). Homeless veterans with depression are more than two times more likely to report fair or poor health than homeless veterans without depression (Nyamathi et al., 2004). Homeless men and women with depression or schizophrenia are at the greatest risk of victimization (physical and sexual assault); symptoms related to these disorders may decrease vigilance for danger or place those who have a disorder at greater observable risk to the community (Wenzel, Koegel, and Gelberg, 2000).

Marriage and Intimate Relationships

The effects of post-combat mental and cognitive conditions inevitably extend beyond the afflicted servicemember. As servicemembers go through life, their impairments cannot fail to wear on those with whom they interact, and those closest to the servicemember are likely to be the most severely affected (Galovski and Lyons, 2004). Indeed, a broad empirical literature has documented the range of negative consequences that post-combat mental disorders have had on the families of servicemembers returning from prior conflicts.

In general, research on the consequences of mental disorders for families has identified direct and indirect routes through which these consequences come about. In the direct route, the specific interpersonal deficits suffered by servicemembers have immediate effects on their loved ones and family members—e.g., difficulties with emotion regulation, which is a predictor of greater risk of physical violence in the home. In the indirect route, the other direct consequences of a servicemember's disorder (e.g., the inability to sustain employment) themselves have negative consequences for the servicemember's family (e.g., financial hardship, deprivation).

Consequences for Intimacy and Relationship Satisfaction. The cognitive and emotional deficits associated with PTSD, depression, and TBI inhibit activities crucial to maintaining intimacy in a relationship (Carroll et al., 1985). Successful intimacy requires that partners be capable of experiencing and expressing emotion, understanding and providing for each other's needs, and recognizing (and at times restraining) their own impulses. Mental disorders, whether psychological or neurological, interfere with all of these behaviors, leading to serious and negative consequences for intimate relationships. Within military populations, these sorts of effects have been documented most thoroughly with respect to PTSD. For example, MacDonald et al. (1999), in a study of Vietnam veterans living in New Zealand, asked 756 individuals about their combat experience, symptoms of PTSD, and intimate and family relationships. Those with higher levels of PTSD symptoms reported greater interpersonal problems (e.g., difficulties expressing intimacy, lack of sociability), and poorer marital and family relationships as well. Moreover, interpersonal problems were found to mediate the associations between PTSD and the quality of family relationships. That is, PTSD symptoms were directly associated with specific interpersonal deficits in these veterans, and those deficits appeared to account for the links between PTSD and impaired family relationships (see also Riggs et al., 1998). Studies such as these join an extensive literature that has linked PTSD with difficulties maintaining emotional intimacy (Jordan et al., 1992) and with greatly elevated risk of divorce (Kessler, Walters, and Forthofer, 1998; Kulka et al., 1990).

The effects of depression and TBI on emotional intimacy and relationship satisfaction have not been studied as extensively in military populations per se. However, the interplay between depression and marital relationships is one of the most thoroughly studied topics in marital research on civilian populations. Among other findings, this research has revealed that, compared with nondepressed individuals, depressed individuals are poorer at resolving marital conflicts (Du Rocher Schudlich, Papp, and Cummings, 2004; Hautzinger, Linden, and Hoffman, 1982), poorer at soliciting for and providing their partners with social support (Davila et al., 1997), more likely to blame their partners for negative behaviors (Fincham, Beach, and Bradbury, 1989), and more likely to seek excessive reassurance of their worth (Joiner and Metalsky, 1995). Perhaps as a consequence, after interacting with their depressed partners, intimates and spouses of these individuals are likely to experience negative emotions, such as anger and sadness (Kahn, Coyne, and Margolin, 1985). It is not surprising, then, that major depression and depressive symptoms are strongly linked to lower levels of marital satisfaction and higher rates of marital distress, both cross-sectionally (Whisman, 2001) and longitudinally (Davila et al., 2003), and higher risk for divorce as well (Kessler, Walters, and Forthofer, 1998).

The scant research on TBI in civilian populations paints a similar picture. For example, a study of 65 couples in which just over half of the husbands had experienced a brain injury found that, relative to men without a brain injury, the injured reported more difficulties resolving conflict in their marriages (Kravetz et al., 1995). There is no reason to believe that the processes through which depression and TBI damage these relationships should differ between military and civilian couples.

Consequences for the Well-Being of Spouses and Partners. In addition to the direct effect of PTSD, depression, and TBI on emotional intimacy, these impairments also represent a substantial, and usually unexpected, caregiving burden. Most often, it is the intimate partner or spouse who bears this burden. Figley (1993), writing specifically about the wives of Vietnam veterans with PTSD, suggested that the stress of caring for a loved one with a mental disorder can result in *secondary traumatization*—i.e., a situation in which the intimate partners of trauma survivors themselves begin to experience symptoms of trauma. Figley initially applied this term restrictively, referring only to spouses who develop stress reactions (e.g., nightmares, intrusive thoughts) to specific events that their partners had experienced. Later writers (Galovski and Lyons, 2004) expanded the use of this term to refer more broadly to any distress experienced by those close to a traumatized individual.

With respect to PTSD, there is extensive evidence that secondary traumatization, at least in its broader sense, occurs and has serious negative consequences for the emotional and psychological well-being of the spouses of veterans with PTSD (Dirkzwager et al., 2005; Verbosky and Ryan, 1988). An extensive program of research on the wives of Israeli soldiers traumatized during that country's 1982 war with Lebanon supports the idea that the more symptoms of PTSD reported by the veteran, the greater the caregiving burden reported by their wives, and the more likely that their wives also experienced anxiety and dysphoria (Solomon et al., 1992a, 1992b). It is worth noting that other family members are not equally at risk for secondary traumatization. A study of the wives and parents of Dutch peacekeepers found that higher levels of PTSD symptoms in peacekeepers were associated with higher levels of psychological symptoms in their wives, but had no relationship to symptoms in their parents (Dirkzwager et al., 2005). Thus, the brunt of the burden of servicemembers with PTSD appears to fall on the people who are most intimate with those individuals—their wives.

With respect to depression, the civilian literature that we reviewed shows that depression in one partner predicts declines in relationship quality and increased risk for divorce among married couples. The same literature has also shown that depression in one partner can lead to depressive moods in the other partner, increasing the risk of a depressive episode in that partner (Joiner and Coyne, 1999).

With respect to TBI, Ben Arzi, Solomon, and Dekel (2000) compared psychological symptoms in wives of veterans with post-concussion syndrome (similar to TBI), wives of veterans with PTSD, and wives of veterans without a diagnosis. Compared with the wives of the healthy veterans, wives of veterans with either of the disorders experienced significantly higher levels of distress and psychiatric symptoms. Thus, whether a servicemember experiences a trauma that is psychological or neurological, the trauma's negative effects appear to spread to the intimate partners.

Implications for Intimate-Partner Violence. In addition to their problems expressing positive emotions and experiencing intimacy, returning servicemembers suffering from mental disorders report problems restraining negative emotions, especially anger and aggression. After the Vietnam War, for example, veterans residing at the Northport Veterans Administration Medical Center in New York described managing anger as one of their most challenging issues (Blum et al., 1984). Chemtob et al. (1997) have suggested that deficits in regulating anger should be especially prevalent among veterans with PTSD. According to their conceptual framework, in veterans with PTSD the experience of traumatic events during combat leads to a chronic and excessive sensitivity to threats, even after returning from combat, and to a corresponding tendency to respond to perceived threats with hostility. Survey research on veterans with PTSD confirms that veterans with PTSD experience higher levels of anger than nonveterans with PTSD or veterans with other psychiatric diagnoses (Chemtob et al., 1994).

Among Vietnam veterans who have sought treatment for PTSD, rates of violence and abuse within their marriages are distressingly high. For example, Williams (1980) found that 50 percent of veteran couples seeking treatment reported physical aggression within their households. Studies that have compared veterans with PTSD with veterans seeking treatment for other reasons have further found that those with PTSD report higher rates of domestic violence than those with other diagnoses (Carroll et al., 1985). A more representative survey of 1,200 male Vietnam veterans reached similar conclusions: Those with higher levels of PTSD symptoms were more likely than other groups to engage in violent behavior within the home (Jordan et al., 1992).

As with the literature on PTSD, research on the implications of depression for intimate-partner violence has mostly addressed samples of couples seeking treatment, either for depression or for marital discord. For example, Boyle and Vivian (1996) examined nonviolent, moderately violent, and severely violent men seeking marital therapy with their wives and compared them with community males who were not seeking therapy. Controlling for other, related factors, such as relationship discord and problem-solving ability, levels of depressive symptoms were positively associated with degree of violent behavior toward the female partner, such that the most severely violent husbands reported the highest levels of depression. The most prominent study of depression and intimate-partner violence within military populations is a survey of 11,870 White males randomly sampled from Army bases between 1989 and 1992 (Pan, Neidig, and O'Leary, 1994). Controlling for demographic variables such as age and income, depressive symptoms were associated with rates of aggression against a female partner. The size of this association was substantial: Each 20-percent increase in depressive symptoms was associated with a 74-percent increase in the likelihood of being physically aggressive. A review by Schumacher et al. (2001) found depressive symptoms to be a consistent risk factor for intimate-partner violence across multiple studies.

Everything known about the implications of TBI for intimate-partner violence comes from research on civilian populations. Within that population, a loss of impulse control and an increase in aggressive behavior are known to be direct consequences of the neurological damage associated with TBI (Kim, 2002). In direct comparisons between individuals with TBI and individuals with other injuries (i.e., spinal-cord injuries), those with TBI are indeed more verbally aggressive and angry, as rated by themselves and by their peers; however, there are no differences in rates of physical aggression (Dyer et al., 2006). The research that has linked TBI specifically to intimate-partner violence and abuse has tended to sample from men receiving treatment for abusing their partners, among whom rates of TBI are higher than in the general population (Marsh and Martinovich, 2006).

Moderators of Effects on Relationship Outcomes. Although PTSD, depression, and TBI appear to have negative effects on families on average, the magnitude of these effects is not the same for all families. Faced with a family member afflicted with a mental disorder, some families are more resilient than others. Two potentially important moderators have been identified in multiple studies: pre-existing vulnerabilities and the quality of the marriage.

First, several studies indicate that individuals with *pre-existing vulnerabilities*—those with less education, less supportive extended families, or a history of adjustment problems—may experience worse family outcomes than individuals without these vulnerabilities. In one of the strongest studies of these issues to date, Gimbel and Booth (1994) examined associations between combat exposure and marital outcomes in 2,101 Vietnam veterans who varied in their levels of vulnerability before serving in that conflict. Results indicated that combat exposure predicted more antisocial behavior for veterans who had experienced more school problems in childhood, and that combat predicted more symptoms of PTSD for veterans who had experienced more emotional problems in childhood. In general, these researchers concluded, "for those who come into combat with problems, the outcomes of combat are likely to be more negative than if they did not have a history of problems" (Gimbel and Booth, 1994, p. 701).

Second, the way a marriage responds to one spouse's post-combat mental disorder may depend on *the quality of the marriage* before the onset of the disorder. Research on the wives of Israeli soldiers suffering from combat-stress reactions supports this idea (Mikulincer, Florian, and Solomon, 1995). Although, on average, the wives of injured soldiers fared worse than the wives of uninjured soldiers, greater intimacy between the spouses offered a measure of protection. In general, the way intimate relationships respond to post-combat mental disorders may be analogous to the way buildings respond to earthquakes: the stronger the structure initially, the greater its ability to weather a shock.

Parenting and Child Outcomes

As the ripple effects of servicemembers' post-combat mental disorders spread horizontally to affect their spouses, so too do they spread vertically to affect their children. In both directions, the mechanisms of the effects appear to be similar: The deficits that inhibit behaviors associated with effective intimacy also directly inhibit behaviors associated with effective parenting.

Consequences for Parenting. The largest survey to address associations between parenting behavior and PTSD in veterans is the National Survey of the Vietnam Generation (NSVG), the survey component of the National Vietnam Veterans Readjustment Study (NVVRS). One analysis of those data that focused specifically on the implications of post-combat PTSD for family outcomes examined responses from 1,200 male veterans (Jordan et al., 1992). Analyses revealed that men with PTSD reported significantly more problems and less satisfaction with parenting than did other veterans.

How does PTSD interfere with effective parenting? The few studies that have addressed this question highlight the fact that the heightened reactivity of veterans with PTSD can lead them to avoid intensely emotional experiences of any kind (Davidson and Mellor, 2001). Ruscio et al. (2002) directly examined the role of different clusters of PTSD symptoms in a study that conducted clinical interviews with 66 male Vietnam veterans associated with the Boston VA Medical Center. The emotional numbing and avoidance aspects of PTSD were associated with poorer parent-child relationships, even after controlling for a wide range of possible covariates, including substance abuse and degree of combat exposure. In contrast, other symptoms of PTSD (e.g., re-experiencing and hyperarousal) had no unique associations with parenting. The authors suggested that it is specifically "the disinterest, detachment, and emotional unavailability that characterize emotional numbing [that] may diminish a father's ability and willingness to seek out, engage in, and enjoy interactions with his children, leading to poor relationship quality" (Ruscio et al., 2002, p. 355).

Although no research has examined the implications of depression for parenting within military populations, an extensive literature has examined the effect of depression on parenting in civilian populations. Reviews of this literature consistently conclude that depression impairs parenting behaviors. For example, in an early review of this area, Downey and Coyne (1990) identified 15 studies that had observed depressed mothers interacting with their children in a controlled setting (i.e., semi-structured interactions, often observed in the home, ranging from 5 to 90 minutes long). In general, these studies found that depressed mothers' interactions with their children are characterized by reduced positive affect and energy, but at the same time increased levels of hostility and irritability, relative to nondepressed mothers' interactions. A later meta-analysis of this literature further revealed that even mothers who had recovered from depression still displayed impaired parenting behaviors relative to mothers who had never been depressed (Lovejoy et al., 2000).

Subsequent studies have found that depressed parents have particular difficulty with child management and discipline, vacillating between inconsistent and ineffective discipline on the one hand and rigid and controlling behavior on the other (Cummings and Davies, 1999; Oyserman et al., 2000). The consistency of the findings in this literature across several decades and multiple reviews offers some degree of confidence that depression in a parent is likely to be associated with less-effective parenting in military populations as well.

Given that TBI is a relatively recent concern for the military, no studies have examined the effect of TBI on parenting in military populations either. However, two studies have examined the implications of TBI for parenting in civilian populations. The earliest of these located 24 families in which one parent had experienced a brain injury some time after the birth of a first child (Pessar et al., 1993). Reports from the uninjured parent described negative changes in the parenting of the injured partner. A second study compared 16 families in which one parent had experienced a TBI with 16 families in which no parent was injured (Uysal et al., 1998). Interviews with family members indicated that, relative to uninjured parents, injured parents were less engaged, less encouraging, less consistent regarding discipline, and less emotionally expressive. Both of these studies addressed small, highly selective (i.e., may not represent the whole population with TBI more broadly) samples, and so their results cannot be taken as representative of the broader civilian population, let alone the military. Nevertheless, to the extent that parenting deficits continue to be observed in civilians with TBI, it is reasonable to expect that similar deficits will be observed among injured servicemembers as well.

Consequences for Child Outcomes. To the extent that servicemembers' post-combat mental disorders damage their intimate relationships, their spouses and partners, and their parenting practices, these disorders are likely to have long-term effects on the development of their children (e.g., Wamboldt and Reiss, 2006). Unlike many of the other effects described in this chapter, the effects of post-combat disorders on children's outcomes are likely to be indirect rather than direct consequences of servicemembers' symptoms (Cummings et al., 2001).

With respect to PTSD, in the NSVG survey described above, 376 spouses and romantic partners of Vietnam veterans were interviewed extensively about their family experiences, including detailed assessments of child-behavior problems (Jordan et al., 1992). Compared with the spouses of veterans without PTSD, the spouses of veterans with PTSD reported significantly greater and more-severe behavior problems in their children. Expanding the focus beyond behavior problems, Davidson, Smith, and Kudler (1989) asked 108 veterans of World War II, Korea, and Vietnam with PTSD to describe their own and their children's psychiatric experiences. Among the children of the PTSD veterans, rates of academic problems were higher, and 23 percent had received psychiatric treatment, whereas none of the children of the non-PTSD controls had received psychiatric treatment. Not surprisingly, outcomes for the children of abusive veterans are especially negative (Rosenheck and Fontana, 1998).

The implications of a parent's depression on children's outcomes has not been studied directly within military populations, but it has been studied extensively in civilian populations. The results of this research have been clear and consistent across numerous studies: The children of depressed parents are at several times greater risk for behavioral problems, psychiatric diagnoses, and academic disruptions than children of nondepressed parents (Beardslee et al., 1983; Beardslee, Versage, and Gladstone, 1998; Cummings and Davies, 1999). Although the negative associations between parental depression and children's well-being are beyond dispute, the explanations for these associations remain a topic of ongoing debate. At issue is the extent to which parental depression can be viewed as a cause of behavioral, emotional, and academic problems in children or merely a symptom of other factors that cause both depression in parents and maladjustment in children. Future research may reveal that genetically vulnerable servicemembers are the ones most likely to experience post-combat depression, and that processes in military families help to transmit problems to children.

Finally, the model described in this part strongly suggests that a TBI in a parent will have negative implications for child development. To date, however, the cross-generational effects of TBI have yet to be studied.

Summary. Populations suffering relatively high rates of PTSD, depression, or TBI are likely to demonstrate relatively high rates of family difficulties as well. Each of these disorders has been linked independently to difficulties maintaining intimate relationships, and these deficits account for a greatly increased risk of distressed relationships, intimate-partner violence, and divorce among those afflicted. In addition, the interpersonal deficits that interfere with emotional intimacy in the romantic relationships of servicemembers with these disorders appear likely to interfere with their interactions with their children as well. Thus, the effect of post-combat mental disorders may extend beyond the life span of the afflicted servicemember, stretching across generations. It may take decades to count the costs of these afflictions, and decades more to heal from them.

Summary and Recommendations

In general, the literature suggests that the three conditions we examined—PTSD, depression, and TBI—have wide-ranging and negative implications for those afflicted; moreover, the consequences of these conditions appear to have more notable similarities between conditions than differences. For example, the presence of any one of these conditions predicts a greater likelihood that an individual will experience other psychiatric diagnoses. All three conditions increase an individual's risk for attempting suicide. All three have been associated with higher rates of unhealthy behaviors (e.g., smoking, overeating, unsafe sex), higher rates of physical health problems, and higher rates of mortality.

In addition to the direct implications of these conditions for the afflicted individual, each of these conditions appears to affect the way that afflicted individuals interact with their social environments. Thus, individuals experiencing any one of these conditions, especially PTSD and depression, tend to miss more days of work, report being less productive while at work, and are more likely to be unemployed. Psychiatric illnesses appear to predict homelessness as well, although this literature suffers from serious methodological limitations. Finally, all three conditions have profound implications for interpersonal relationships—disrupting marriages, interfering with parenting, and ultimately giving rise to problems in children that extend the costs of combat experiences across generations.

The effects of a post-combat mental health conditions can be compared to ripples spreading outward on a pond. But whereas ripples diminish over time, the consequences of mental health and cognitive conditions may grow more severe, especially if left untreated.

The studies we summarized above offer consistent support for the integrative framework proposed here. That framework describes the consequences of mental health and cognitive conditions as a cascade of accumulating challenges and negative outcomes that, if allowed to continue, may expand to affect more and more domains in an individual's life. Prior research on military and civilian populations indicates that these cascades can and do occur. The direct results of a condition (i.e., impaired cognitive and emotional functioning) can have immediate consequences for the individual (e.g., additional psychiatric problems, poor health-maintenance behaviors), which themselves accumulate and contribute to additional problems (e.g., with physical health, work performance, and interpersonal relationships).

The model further suggests that the likelihood of experiencing a negative cascade is greater to the extent that (1) the initial symptoms of the condition are more severe and (2) the afflicted individual has other sources of vulnerability (e.g., unstable family relationships, low socioeconomic status, a prior history of psychopathology). Indeed, the research we reviewed consistently shows that individuals afflicted with one of these conditions experience worse consequences when they must simultaneously confront other sources of stress, whereas other sources of strength (e.g., supportive family relationships, high socioeconomic status, high education) may serve as buffers, even for those whose symptoms are relatively severe.

Given the estimated prevalence of PTSD, depression, and TBI in servicemembers returning from Afghanistan and Iraq, the picture that emerges from this review may appear bleak, but the accumulated results should be kept in perspective. Each of the studies reviewed here indicates only that servicemembers who return from their deployments with one of these conditions are *at increased risk for these negative outcomes*. Virtually none of the studies we reviewed were controlled trials, and thus may not be able to detect causal relationships between these disorders and subsequent adverse consequences such as homelessness, substance abuse, or relationship problems. However, these studies are important for understanding the range of co-moridities and behavioral outcomes likely to be associated with PTSD, depression, and TBI, as this information is relevant for determining the required resources for treating servicemembers and veterans with these conditions. Most servicemembers, however, are returning from combat free from any of these conditions. Moreover, even those afflicted with post-combat mental health and cognitive conditions may remit spontaneously and may, with adequate treatment and support, avoid negative outcomes altogether. Effective treatments for PTSD, depression, and TBI exist (see Chapter Seven for discussion of treatments) and can greatly improve functioning and outcomes. Even without treatment, however, some servicemembers and veterans with these conditions will recover. Therefore, although this research emphasizes probabilities, it should not be used to promote deterministic conclusions.

Recommendations for Future Research

The literature we reviewed offers helpful information about the potential short and long-term consequences of PTSD, depression, and TBI; however, more research would improve our understanding of how these conditions will affect servicemembers and veterans. Below, we outline some issues that require further investigation and research.

Address Causal Relationships. The integrative framework we presented suggests that a post-combat mental health condition or cognitive condition causes negative outcomes that the servicemember would not have experienced in the absence of the condition. The research we reviewed is consistent with this position, but it cannot rule out alternative interpretations. Most of the research on servicemembers returning from Afghanistan and Iraq has yet to be conducted, and those studies that have addressed servicemembers have relied primarily on cross-sectional and retrospective designs—i.e., research participants have been contacted on a single occasion and asked to report on their experience of psychiatric symptoms and their functioning in other life domains.

Supporting causal statements about the effect of mental health conditions for service-members will require longitudinal research assessing members of this population on multiple occasions to determine the temporal ordering of symptoms and outcomes. Longitudinal research that successfully follows servicemembers from pre-deployment, through post-deployment, and into post-service would provide crucial insights into the etiology and consequences of combat-related mental health conditions. In the absence of such data, the existing research supports conclusions about how these conditions are associated with subsequent negative outcomes for servicemembers, but not about whether the conditions may be considered causes of those outcomes.

Assessment and Diagnosis. Although research on the prevalence of PTSD, depression, and TBI in servicemembers has relied on only a small number of assessment tools, research on the consequences of these conditions in the general population has used a vast array of instruments and strategies. Some research has examined associations between each condition and outcomes shortly after combat, whereas other research, especially research on veterans of Vietnam, has examined these associations years or even decades after the veterans had their combat experiences. Understanding how these conditions affect the lives of afflicted veterans and servicemembers will require greater attention to how and when these conditions are assessed.

Generalizing Across Services and Components. Research on the implications of mental health conditions in veterans of Vietnam rarely specifies the component of the military (i.e., Active or Reserve Component) or the Service within which the veteran served. Because different segments of the military are likely to have different experiences and have access to different sources of support, careful attention to service and component will be important in future research to understand the mental health implications of deployment to Afghanistan and Iraq. To inform the future allocation of resources between reservists and active duty servicemembers, research is needed that directly compares the prevalence and consequences of mental health and cognitive conditions across the Services and across the components.

Gathering Population Data. Virtually all of the data on the implications of post-combat mental health and cognitive conditions come from treatment, clinical, and help-seeking samples. Because those who seek treatment are likely to differ from those who do not, these samples are an inadequate basis from which to draw conclusions about the military as a whole. Systematic assessments of the entire military population will provide a more accurate sense of the distribution of post-combat mental health and cognitive conditions and their consequences, and thus a more accurate view of the true costs of the current conflicts.

Conclusions

These three highly salient conditions in servicemembers returning from combat in Afghanistan and Iraq—PTSD, depression, and TBI—are not new. All three have been recognized for decades or more, and all three have been studied extensively for their associations with functioning in various domains of life. Although not without its limitations, this literature is nevertheless extensive and the results are consistent, providing a firm basis from which to project the likely consequences of these conditions for servicemembers returning from the current conflicts. In general, the review described here reveals those consequences to be severe, negative, and wide-ranging, affecting not only multiple domains of life for afflicted veterans and servicemembers, but their spouses, partners, and children as well. The predictions are not optimistic, but negative outcomes may be preventable with early and careful interventions. The research results assembled and summarized here may therefore serve as a call to action.

References

Allen, J. P., G. Cross, and J. Swanner. Suicide in the Army: A review of current information. *Military Medicine,* Vol. 170, No. 7, 2005, pp. 580–584.

Andary, M. T., N. Crewe, S. K. Ganzel, C. Haines-Pepi, M. R. Kulkarni, D. F. Stanton, et al. Traumatic brain injury/chronic pain syndrome: A case comparison study. *The Clinical Journal of Pain*, Vol. 13, No. 3, 1997, pp. 244–250.

Anstey, K. J., P. Butterworth, A. F. Jorm, H. Christensen, B. Rodgers, and T. D. Windsor. A population survey found an association between self-reports of traumatic brain injury and increased psychiatric symptoms. *Journal of Clinical Epidemiology,* Vol. 57, No. 11, 2004, pp. 1202–1209.

Babin, P. R. Diagnosing depression in persons with brain injuries: A look at theories, the DSM-IV and depression measures. *Brain Injury*, Vol. 17, No. 10, 2003, pp. 889–900.

Backer, T., and E. Howard. Cognitive impairments and the prevention of homelessness: Research and practice review. *Journal of Primary Prevention,* Vol. 28, Nos. 3–4, 2007, pp. 375–388.

Baltes, P. B. Theoretical propositions of life-span developmental psychology: On the dynamics between growth and decline. *Developmental Psychology*, Vol. 23, 1987, pp. 611–626.

Bankier, B., and A. B. Littman. Psychiatric disorders and coronary heart disease in women—a still neglected topic: Review of the literature from 1971 to 2000. *Psychotherapy and Psychosomatics*, Vol. 71, No. 3, 2002, pp. 133–140.

Beardslee, W. R., J. Bemporad, M. B. Keller, and G. L. Klerman. Children of parents with major affective disorder: A review. *American Journal of Psychiatry*, Vol. 140, No. 7, 1983, pp. 825–832.

Beardslee, W. R., E. M. Versage, and T. R. Gladstone. Children of affectively ill parents: A review of the past 10 years. *Journal of the American Academy of Child and Adolescent Psychiatry*, Vol. 37, 1998, pp. 1134–1141.

Beckham, J. C., A. C. Kirby, M. E. Feldman, M. A. Hertzberg, S. D. Moore, A. L. Crawford, et al. Prevalence and correlates of heavy smoking in Vietnam veterans with chronic posttraumatic stress disorder. *Addictive Behavior*, Vol. 22, No. 5, 1997, pp. 637–647.

Beckham, J. C., S. D. Moore, M. E. Feldman, M. A. Hertzberg, A. C. Kirby, and J. A. Fairbank. Health status, somatization, and severity of posttraumatic stress disorder in Vietnam combat veterans with posttraumatic stress disorder. *American Journal of Psychiatry*, Vol. 155, No. 11, 1998, pp. 1565–1569.

Ben Arzi, N., Z. Solomon, and R. Dekel. Secondary traumatization among wives of PTSD and post-concussion casualties: Distress, caregiver burden and psychological separation. *Brain Injury*, Vol. 14, No. 8, 2000, pp. 725–736.

Blum, M. D., E. M. Kelly, M. Meyer, C. R. Carlson, and W. L. Hodson. An assessment of the treatment needs of Vietnam-era veterans. *Hospital and Community Psychiatry*, Vol. 35, No. 7, 1984, pp. 691–696.

Boehmer, T. K., W. D. Flanders, M. A. McGeehin, C. Boyle, and D. H. Barrett. Postservice mortality in Vietnam veterans: 30-year follow-up. *Archives of Internal Medicine*, Vol. 164, No. 17, 2004, pp. 1908–1916.

Boscarino, J. Current excessive drinking among Vietnam veterans: A comparison with other veterans and non-veterans. *International Journal of Social Psychiatry*, Vol. 27, 1981, pp. 204–212.

Boscarino, J. A. External-cause mortality after psychologic trauma: The effects of stress exposure and predisposition. *Comprehensive Psychiatry*, Vol. 47, No. 6, 2006a, pp. 503–514.

————. Posttraumatic stress disorder and mortality among U.S. Army veterans 30 years after military service. *Annals of Epidemiology*, Vol. 16, No. 4, 2006b, p. 9.

Boscarino, J. A., and J. Chang. Electrocardiogram abnormalities among men with stress-related psychiatric disorders: Implications for coronary heart disease and clinical research. *Annals of Behavioral Medicine*, Vol. 21, No. 3, 1999, pp. 227–234.

Boyle, D. J., and D. Vivian. Generalized versus spouse-specific anger/hostility and men's violence against intimates. *Violence and Victims*, Vol. 11, No. 4, 1996, pp. 293–317.

Brady, K. T., T. K. Killeen, T. Brewerton, and S. Lucerini. Comorbidity of psychiatric disorders and posttraumatic stress disorder. *Journal of Clinical Psychiatry*, Vol. 61, Suppl. 7, 2000, pp. 22–32.

Breakey, W. R. Mental illness and health. In D. Levinson (Ed.), *Encyclopedia of Homelessness.* Thousand Oaks, Calif.: Sage Publications Ltd., 2004, Vol. 1, pp. 383–387.

Bremner, J. D., S. M. Southwick, A. Darnell, and D. S. Charney. Chronic PTSD in Vietnam combat veterans: Course of illness and substance abuse. *American Journal of Psychiatry*, Vol. 153, No. 3, 1996, pp. 369–375.

Breslau, N., and G. C. Davis. Posttraumatic stress disorder in an urban population of young adults: Risk factors for chronicity. *American Journal of Psychiatry,* Vol. 149, No. 5, 1992, pp. 671–675.

Breslau, N., G. C. Davis, and L. R. Schultz. Posttraumatic stress disorder and the incidence of nicotine, alcohol, and other drug disorders in persons who have experienced trauma. *Archives of General Psychiatry*, Vol. 60, No. 3, 2003, pp. 289–294.

Breslau, N., E. L. Peterson, L. R. Schultz, H. D. Chilcoat, and P. Andreski. Major depression and stages of smoking. A longitudinal investigation. *Archives of General Psychiatry*, Vol. 55, No. 2, 1998, pp. 161–166.

Brewin, C. R. Intrusive autobiographical memories in depression and post-traumatic stress disorder. *Applied Cognitive Psychology*, Vol. 12, No. 4, 1998, pp. 359–370.

Buckley, T. C., S. L. Mozley, M. A. Bedard, A.-C. Dewulf, and J. Greif. Preventive health behaviors, health-risk behaviors, physical morbidity, and health-related role functioning impairment in veterans with post-traumatic stress disorder. *Military Medicine,* Vol. 169, No. 7, 2004, pp. 536–540.

Busch, C. R., and H. P. Alpern. Depression after mild traumatic brain injury: A review of current research. *Neuropsychology Review*, Vol. 8, No. 2, 1998, pp. 95–108.

Campbell, D. G., B. L. Felker, C. F. Liu, E. M. Yano, J. E. Kirchner, D. Chan, et al. Prevalence of depression-PTSD comorbidity: Implications for clinical practice guidelines and primary care–based interventions. *Journal of General Internal Medicine,* Vol. 22, No. 6, 2007, pp. 711–718.

Carroll, E. M., D. B. Rueger, D. W. Foy, and C. P. Donahoe. Vietnam combat veterans with posttraumatic stress disorder: Analysis of marital and cohabitating adjustment. *Journal of Abnormal Psychology*, Vol. 94, No. 3, 1985, pp. 329–337.

Caspi, A. Personality in the life course. *Journal of Personality and Social Psychology*, Vol. 53, 1987, pp. 1203–1213.

Caspi, A., G. H. Elder, and D. J. Bem. Moving against the world: Life-course patterns of explosive children. *Developmental Psychology*, Vol. 23, 1987, pp. 308–313.

————. Moving away from the world: Life-course patterns of shy children. *Developmental Psychology*, Vol. 24, 1988, pp. 824–831.

Cavanagh, J. T., A. J. Carson, M. Sharpe, and S. M. Lawrie. Psychological autopsy studies of suicide: A systematic review. *Psychological Medicine*, Vol. 33, No. 3, 2003, pp. 395–405.

Ceci, S. J., and H. A. Hembrooke. A bioecological model of intellectual development. In P. Moen, G. H. Elder, and K. Lüscher (Eds.), *Examining Lives in Context: Perspectives on the Ecology of Human Development*. Washington, D.C.: American Psychological Association, 1995, pp. 303–345.

Centers for Disease Control and Prevention, National Center for Injury Prevention and Control. Web-based Injury Statistics Query and Reporting System (WISQARS), 2007 [online]. As of September 13, 2007:
http://www.cdc.gov/ncipc/wisqars

Chemtob, C. M., R. S. Hamada, H. L. Roitblat, and M. Y. Muraoka. Anger, impulsivity, and anger control in combat-related posttraumatic stress disorder. *Journal of Consulting and Clinical Psychology*, Vol. 62, No. 4, 1994, pp. 827–832.

Chemtob, C. M., R. W. Novaco, R. S. Hamada, D. M. Gross, and G. Smith. Anger regulation deficits in combat-related posttraumatic stress disorder. *Journal of Traumatic Stress*, Vol. 10, No. 1, 1997, pp. 17–36.

Chemtob, C. M., H. L. Roitblat, R. S. Hamada, M. Y. Muraoka, J. G. Carlson, and G. B. Bauer. Compelled attention: The effects of viewing trauma-related stimuli on concurrent task performance in posttraumatic stress disorder. *Journal of Trauma and Stress*, Vol. 12, No. 2, 1999, pp. 309–326.

Chen, Y. W., and S. C. Dilsaver. Lifetime rates of suicide attempts among subjects with bipolar and unipolar disorders relative to subjects with other Axis I disorders. *Biological Psychiatry*, Vol. 39, No. 10, 1996, pp. 896–899.

Chilcoat, H. D., and N. Breslau. Investigations of causal pathways between PTSD and drug use disorders. *Addictive Behavior*, Vol. 23, No. 6, 1998, pp. 827–840.

Cummings, E. M., and P. T. Davies. Depressed parents and family functioning: Interpersonal effects and children's functioning and development. In T. E. Joiner and J. C. Coyne (Eds.), *The Interactional Nature of Depression: Advances in Interpersonal Approaches*. Washington, D.C: American Psychological Association, 1999, pp. 299–327.

Cummings, E. M., G. DeArth-Pendley, T. Du Rocher Schudlich, and D. A. Smith. Parental depression and family functioning: Toward a process-oriented model of children's adjustment. In S. R. H. Beach (Ed.), *Marital and Family Processes in Depression: A Scientific Foundation for Clinical Practice*. Washington, D.C.: American Psychological Association, 2001.

Davidson, A. C., and D. J. Mellor. The adjustment of children of Australian Vietnam veterans: Is there evidence for the transgenerational transmission of the effects of war-related trauma? *Australian and New Zealand Journal of Psychiatry*, Vol. 35, No. 3, 2001, pp. 345–351.

Davidson, J. R., R. D. Smith, and H. S. Kudler. Familial psychiatric illness in chronic posttraumatic stress disorder. *Comprehensive Psychiatry*, Vol. 30, No. 4, 1989, pp. 339–345.

Davila, J., T. N. Bradbury, C. L. Cohan, and S. Tochluk. Marital functioning and depressive symptoms: Evidence for a stress generation model. *Journal of Personality and Social Psychology*, Vol. 73, 1997, pp. 849–861.

Davila, J., B. R. Karney, T. W. Hall, and T. N. Bradbury. Depressive symptoms and marital satisfaction: Within-subject associations and the moderating effects of gender and neuroticism. *Journal of Family Psychology*, Vol. 17, No. 4, 2003, pp. 557–570.

Deb, S., I. Lyons, C. Koutzoukis, I. Ali, and G. McCarthy. Rate of psychiatric illness 1 year after traumatic brain injury. *American Journal of Psychiatry*, Vol. 156, No. 3, 1999, pp. 374–378.

Deering, C. G., S. G. Glover, D. Ready, H. C. Eddleman, and R. D. Alarcon. Unique patterns of comorbidity in posttraumatic stress disorder from different sources of trauma. *Comprehensive Psychiatry*, Vol. 37, No. 5, 1996, pp. 336–346.

Dirkzwager, A. J. E., I. Bramsen, H. Adèr, and H. M. van der Ploeg. Secondary traumatization in partners and parents of Dutch peacekeeping soldiers. *Journal of Family Psychology*, Vol. 19, 2005, pp. 217–226.

Dobie, D. J., D. R. Kivlahan, C. Maynard, K. R. Bush, T. M. Davis, and K. A. Bradley. Posttraumatic stress disorder in female veterans: Association with self-reported health problems and functional impairment. *Archives of Internal Medicine*, Vol. 164, No. 4, 2004, pp. 394–400.

Downey, G., and J. C. Coyne. Children of depressed parents: An integrative review. *Psychological Bulletin*, Vol. 108, No. 1, 1990, pp. 50–76.

Du Rocher Schudlich, T. D., L. M. Papp, and E. M. Cummings. Relations of husbands' and wives' dysphoria to marital conflict resolution strategies. *Journal of Family Psychology*, Vol. 18, 2004, pp. 171–183.

Dyer, K. F. W., R. Bell, J. McCann, and R. Rauch. Aggression after traumatic brain injury: Analysing socially desirable responses and the nature of aggressive traits. *Brain Injury*, Vol. 20, No. 11, 2006, pp. 1163–1173.

Elder, G. H., E. K. Pavalko, and T. J. Hastings. Talent, history, and the fulfillment of promise. *Psychiatry*, Vol. 54, 1991, pp. 251–267.

Erbes, C., J. Westermeyer, B. Engdahl, and E. Johnsen. Post-traumatic stress disorder and service utilization in a sample of service members from Iraq and Afghanistan. *Military Medicine*, Vol. 172, 2007, pp. 359–363.

Ettner, S. L., R. G. Frank, and R. C. Kessler. The impact of psychiatric disorders on labor market outcomes. *Industrial and Labor Relations Review*, Vol. 51, No. 1, 1997, pp. 64–81.

Falger, P. R., W. Op den Velde, J. E. Hovens, E. G. Schouten, J. H. De Groen, and H. Van Duijn. Current posttraumatic stress disorder and cardiovascular disease risk factors in Dutch Resistance veterans from World War II. *Psychotherapy and Psychosomatics*, Vol. 57, No. 4, 1992, pp. 164–171.

Fann, J. R., W. J. Katon, J. M. Uomoto, and P. C. Esselman. Psychiatric disorders and functional disability in outpatients with traumatic brain injuries. *American Journal of Psychiatry*, Vol. 152, No. 10, 1995, pp. 1493–1499.

Farberow, N. L., H. K. Kang, and T. A. Bullman. Combat experience and postservice psychosocial status as predictors of suicide in Vietnam veterans. *Journal of Nervous and Mental Disorders*, Vol. 178, No. 1, 1990, pp. 32–37.

Feldner, M. T., K. A. Babson, and M. J. Zvolensky. Smoking, traumatic event exposure, and posttraumatic stress: A critical review of the empirical literature. *Clinical Psychology Review*, Vol. 27, No. 1, 2007, pp. 14–45.

Figley, C. R. Coping with stressors on the home front. *Journal of Social Issues*, Vol. 49, 1993, p. 51.

Fincham, F. D., S. R. H. Beach, and T. N. Bradbury. Marital distress, depression, and attributions: Is the marital distress-attribution association an artifact of depression? *Journal of Consulting and Clinical Psychology*, Vol. 57, 1989, pp. 768–771.

Folsom, D. P., W. Hawthorne, L. Lindamer, T. Gilmer, A. Bailey, S. Golshan, et al. Prevalence and risk factors for homelessness and utilization of mental health services among 10,340 patients with serious mental illness in a large public mental health system. *American Journal of Psychiatry*, Vol. 162, No. 2, 2005, pp. 370–376.

Galovski, T., and J. A. Lyons. Psychological sequelae of combat violence: A review of the impact of PTSD on the veteran's family and possible interventions. *Aggression and Violent Behavior*, Vol. 9, No. 5, 2004, pp. 477–501.

Gamboa, A. M., Jr., G. H. Holland, J. P. Tierney, and D. S. Gibson. American Community Survey: Earnings and employment for persons with traumatic brain injury. *NeuroRehabilitation*, Vol. 21, No. 4, 2006, pp. 327–333.

Gimbel, C., and A. Booth. Why does military combat experience adversely affect marital relations? *Journal of Marriage and the Family*, Vol. 56, 1994, pp. 691–703.

Gonzalez, E. A., J. N. Dieter, R. A. Natale, and S. L. Tanner. Neuropsychological evaluation of higher functioning homeless persons: A comparison of an abbreviated test battery to the mini-mental state exam. *Journal of Nervous and Mental Disease*, Vol. 189, No. 3, 2001, pp. 176–181.

Grant, B. F., F. S. Stinson, D. A. Dawson, P. Chou, M. C. Dufour, W. Compton, et al. Prevalence and co-occurrence of substance use disorders and independent mood and anxiety disorders: Results from the National Epidemiologic Survey on Alcohol and Related Conditions. *Archives of General Psychiatry*, Vol. 61, No. 8, 2004, pp. 807–816.

Greenberg, P. E., R. C. Kessler, H. G. Birnbaum, S. A. Leong, S. W. Lowe, P. A. Berglund, et al. The economic burden of depression in the United States: how did it change between 1990 and 2000? *Journal of Clinical Psychiatry*, Vol. 64, No. 12, 2003, pp. 1465–1475.

Greenfield, S. F., R. D. Weiss, L. R. Muenz, L. M. Vagge, J. F. Kelly, L. R. Bello, et al. The effect of depression on return to drinking: A prospective study. *Archives of General Psychiatry*, Vol. 55, No. 3, 1998, pp. 259–265.

Grieger, T. A., S. J. Cozza, R. J. Ursano, C. Hoge, P. E. Martinez, C. C.Engel, et al. Posttraumatic stress disorder and depression in battle-injured soldiers. *American Journal of Psychiatry*, Vol. 163, No. 10, 2006, pp. 1777–1783.

Gutierrez, C. A., A. W. Blume, K. B. Schmaling, C. J. Stoever, C. Fonseca, and M. L. Russell. Predictors of aversive alcohol consequences in a military sample. *Military Medicine*, Vol. 171, No. 9, 2006, pp. 870–874.

Harris, E. C., and B. Barraclough. Suicide as an outcome for mental disorders. A meta-analysis. *British Journal of Psychiatry*, Vol. 170, 1997, pp. 205–228.

Hasin, D. S., R. D. Goodwin, F. S. Stinson, and B. F. Grant. Epidemiology of major depressive disorder: Results from the National Epidemiologic Survey on Alcoholism and Related Conditions. *Archives of General Psychiatry*, Vol. 62, No. 10, 2005, pp. 1097–1106.

Hautzinger, M., M. Linden, and N. Hoffman. Distressed couples with and without a depressed partner: An analysis of their verbal interaction. *Journal of Behavior Therapy and Experimental Psychiatry*, Vol. 13, No. 4, 1982, pp. 307–314.

Hèanninen, V., and H. Aro. Sex differences in coping and depression among adults. *Social Science and Medicine*, Vol. 43, No. 10, 1996, pp. 1453–1460.

Helyer, A. J., W. T. Brehm, and L. Perino. Economic consequences of tobacco use for the Department of Defense, 1995. *Military Medicine*, Vol. 163, No. 4, 1998, p. 5.

Helzer, J. E., L. N. Robins, and D. H. Davis. Depressive disorders in Vietnam returnees. *Journal of Nervous and Mental Disorders*, Vol. 163, 1976, pp. 177–185.

Hendin, H., and A. P. Haas. Suicide and guilt as manifestations of PTSD in Vietnam combat veterans. *American Journal of Psychiatry*, Vol. 148, No. 5, 1991, pp. 586–591.

Henriksson, M. M., H. M. Aro, M. J. Marttunen, M. E. Heikkinen, E. T. Isometsa, K. I. Kuoppasalmi, et al. Mental disorders and comorbidity in suicide. *American Journal of Psychiatry*, Vol. 150, No. 6, 1993, pp. 935–940.

Heron, M. P., and B. L. Smith. Deaths: Leading causes for 2003. *National Vital Statistics Report,* Vol. 55, No. 10, 2007, pp. 1–92.

Hibbard, M. R., S. Uysal, K. Kepler, J. Bogdany, and J. Silver. Axis I psychopathology in individuals with traumatic brain injury. *Journal of Head Trauma Rehabilitation,* Vol. 13, No. 4, 1998, pp. 24–39.

Hoge, C. W, D. McGurk, J. L. Thomas, A. L. Cox, C. C. Engel, and C. A. Castro. A mild traumatic brain injury in U.S. soldiers returning from Iraq. *New England Journal of Medicine.* Vol. 358, No. 5, January 31, 2008, pp. 453–463.

Hoge, C. W., A. Terhakopian, C. A. Castro, S. C. Messer, and C. C. Engel. Association of posttraumatic stress disorder with somatic symptoms, health care visits, and absenteeism among Iraq war veterans. *American Journal of Psychiatry,* Vol. 164, No. 1, 2007, pp. 150–153.

Holmes, W. C., E. B. Foa, and M. D. Sammel. Men's pathways to risky sexual behavior: Role of co-occurring childhood sexual abuse, posttraumatic stress disorder, and depression histories. *Journal of Urban Health,* Vol. 82, No. 1, Suppl. 1, 2005, pp. i89–i99.

Holsinger, T., D. C. Steffens, C. Phillips, M. J. Helms, R. J. Havlik, J. C. Breitner, et al. Head injury in early adulthood and the lifetime risk of depression. *Archives of General Psychiatry,* Vol. 59, No. 1, 2002, pp. 17–22.

Isometsa, E. T. Psychological autopsy studies—a review. *European Psychiatry,* Vol. 16, No. 7, 2001, pp. 379–385.

Jacobsen, L. K., S. M. Southwick, and T. R. Kosten. Substance use disorders in patients with posttraumatic stress disorder: A review of the literature. *American Journal of Psychiatry,* Vol. 158, No. 8, 2001, pp. 1184–1190.

Johnstone, B., D. Mount, and L. H. Schopp. Financial and vocational outcomes 1 year after traumatic brain injury. *Archives of Physical Medicine and Rehabilitation,* Vol. 84, No. 2, 2003, pp. 238–241.

Joiner, T. E., and J. C. Coyne (Eds.). *The Interactional Nature of Depression: Advances in Interpersonal Approaches.* Washington, D.C.: American Psychological Association, 1999.

Joiner, T. E., Jr., Y. Conwell, K. K. Fitzpatrick, T. K. Witte, N. B. Schmidt, M. T. Berlim, et al. Four studies on how past and current suicidality relate even when "everything but the kitchen sink" is covaried. *Journal of Abnormal Psychology,* Vol. 114, No. 2, 2005, pp. 291–303.

Joiner, T. E., and G. I. Metalsky. A prospective test of an integrative interpersonal theory of depression: A naturalistic study of college roommates. *Journal of Personality and Social Psychology,* Vol. 69, 1995, pp. 778–788.

Jordan, B. K., C. R. Marmar, J. A. Fairbank, W. E. Schlenger, R. A. Kulka, R. L. Hough, et al. Problems in families of male Vietnam veterans with posttraumatic stress disorder. *Journal of Consulting and Clinical Psychology,* Vol. 60, No. 6, 1992, pp. 916–926.

Jorge, R. E., S. E. Starkstein, S. Arndt, D. Moser, B. Crespo-Facorro, and R. G. Robinson. Alcohol misuse and mood disorders following traumatic brain injury. *Archives of General Psychiatry,* Vol. 62, No. 7, 2005, pp. 742–749.

Joseph, S., and J. Masterson. Posttraumatic stress disorder and traumatic brain injury: Are they mutually exclusive? *Journal of Traumatic Stress,* Vol. 12, No. 3, 1999, pp. 437–453.

Kahn, J., J. C. Coyne, and G. Margolin. Depression and marital disagreement: The social construction of despair. *Journal of Social and Personal Relationships,* Vol. 2, 1985, pp. 449–461.

Kaplan, M. S., N. Huguet, B. H. McFarland, and J. T. Newsom. Suicide among male veterans: A prospective population-based study. *Journal of Epidemiological Community Health*, Vol. 61, No. 7, 2007, pp. 619–624.

Kendler, K. S., C. O. Gardner, and C. A. Prescott. Toward a comprehensive developmental model for major depression in women. *American Journal of Psychiatry,* Vol. 159, 2002, pp. 1133–1145.

Kessler, R. C., C. Barber, H. G. Birnbaum, R. G. Frank, P. E. Greenberg, R. M. Rose, et al. Depression in the workplace: Effects on short-term disability. *Health Affairs (Millwood)*, Vol. 18, No. 5, 1999, pp. 163–171.

Kessler, R. C., P. Berglund, O. Demler, R. Jin, D. Koretz, K. R. Merikangas, et al. The epidemiology of major depressive disorder: Results from the National Comorbidity Survey Replication (NCS-R). *Journal of the American Medical Association*, Vol. 289, No. 23, 2003, pp. 3095–3105.

Kessler, R. C., G. Borges, and E. E. Walters. Prevalence of and risk factors for lifetime suicide attempts in the National Comorbidity Survey. *Archives of General Psychiatry,* Vol. 56, No. 7, 1999, pp. 617–626.

Kessler, R. C., W. T. Chiu, O. Demler, and E. E. Walters. Prevalence, severity, and comorbidity of 12-month DSM-IV disorders in the National Comorbidity Survey Replication. *Archives of General Psychiatry*, Vol. 62, No. 6, 2005, pp. 617–627.

Kessler, R. C., C. L. Foster, W. B. Saunders, and P. E. Stang. Social consequences of psychiatric disorders, I: Educational attainment. *American Journal of Psychiatry*, Vol. 152, No. 7, 1995, pp. 1026–1032.

Kessler, R. C., C. B. Nelson, K. A. McGonagle, M. J. Edlund, R. G. Frank, and P. J. Leaf. The epidemiology of co-occurring addictive and mental disorders: Implications for prevention and service utilization. *American Journal of Orthopsychiatry*, Vol. 66, No. 1, 1996, pp. 17–31.

Kessler, R. C., A. Sonnega, E. Bromet, M. Hughes, et al. Posttraumatic stress disorder in the National Comorbidity Survey. *Archives of General Psychiatry*, Vol. 52, No. 12, 1995, pp. 1048–1060.

Kessler, R. C., E. E., Walters, and M. S. Forthofer. The social consequences of psychiatric disorders, III: Probability of marital stability. *American Journal of Psychiatry,* Vol. 155, No. 8, 1998, pp. 1092–1096.

Kiecolt-Glaser, J. K., and R. Glaser. Depression and immune function: Central pathways to morbidity and mortality. *Journal of Psychosomatic Research*, Vol. 53, No. 4, 2002, pp. 873–876.

Kim, E. Agitation, aggression, and disinhibition syndromes after traumatic brain injury. *NeuroRehabilitation*, Vol. 17, No. 4, 2002, pp. 297–310.

Kim, E., E. C. Lauterbach, A. Reeve, D. B. Arciniegas, K. L. Coburn, M. F. Mendez, et al. Neuropsychiatric complications of traumatic brain injury: A critical review of the literature (a report by the ANPA Committee on Research). *Journal of Neuropsychiatry and Clinical Neuroscience*, Vol. 19, No. 2, 2007, pp. 106–127.

Kinnunen, T., A. Haukkala, T. Korhonen, Z. N. Quiles, A. Spiro III, and A. J. Garvey. Depression and smoking across 25 years of the Normative Aging Study. *International Journal of Psychiatry in Medicine*, Vol. 36, No. 4, 2006, pp. 413–426.

Klesges, R. C., C. K. Haddock, C. F. Chang, G. W. Talcott, and H. A. Lando. The association of smoking and the cost of military training. *Tobacco Control*, Vol. 10, No. 1, 2001, pp. 43–47.

Koegel, P. Causes of homelessness: Overview. In D. Levinson (Ed.), *Encyclopedia of Homelessness.* Thousand Oaks, Calif.: Sage Publications Ltd., 2004, Vol. 1, pp. 50–58.

Koegel, P., and M. A. Burnam. Problems in the assessment of mental illness among the homeless: An empirical approach. In M. J. Robertson and M. Greenblatt (Eds.), *Homelessness: A National Perspective.* New York, NY: Plenum Press, 1992.

Koegel, P., M. A. Burnam, and J. Baumohl. The causes of homelessness. In J. Baumohl (Ed.), *Homelessness in America.* Phoenix, Ariz.: Oryx Press. 1996, pp. 24–33.

Kosloski, K., D. E. Stull, K. Kercher, and D. J. Van Dussen. Longitudinal analysis of the reciprocal effects of self-assessed global health and depressive symptoms. *Journal of Gerontology B: Psychological Science and Social Science,* Vol. 60, No. 6, 2005, pp. P296–P303.

Kravetz, S., Y. Gross, B. Weiler, M. Ben-Yakar, M. Tadir, and M. J. Stern. Self-concept, marital vulnerability and brain damage. *Brain Injury,* Vol. 9, No. 2, 1995, pp. 131–139.

Kubzansky, L. D., K. C. Koenen, A. Spiro III, P. S. Vokonas, and D. Sparrow. Prospective study of posttraumatic stress disorder symptoms and coronary heart disease in the Normative Aging Study. *Archives of General Psychiatry,* Vol. 64, No. 1, 2007, pp. 109–116.

Kulka, R. A., W. E. Schlenger, J. A. Fairbank, R. L. Hough, B. K. Jordan, C. R. Marmar, et al. *Trauma and the Vietnam War Generation: Report of Findings from the National Vietnam Veterans Readjustment Study.* Philadelphia, Pa.: Brunner/Mazel, 1990.

Lahz, S., and R. A. Bryant. Incidence of chronic pain following traumatic brain injury. *Archives of Physical Medicine and Rehabilitation,* Vol. 77, No. 9, 1996, pp. 889–891.

Lasser, K., J. W. Boyd, S. Woolhandler, D. U. Himmelstein, D. McCormick, and D. H. Bor. Smoking and mental illness: A population-based prevalence study. *Journal of the American Medical Association,* Vol. 284, No. 20, 2000, pp. 2606–2610.

Lauterbach, D., R. Vora, and M. Rakow. The relationship between posttraumatic stress disorder and self-reported health problems. *Psychosomatics Medicine,* Vol. 67, No. 6, 2005, pp. 939–947.

Leblanc, V. R., C. Regehr, R. B. Jelley, and I. Barath. Does Posttraumatic Stress Disorder (PTSD) affect performance? *Journal of Nervous and Mental Disorders,* Vol. 195, No. 8, 2007, pp. 701–704.

Lehmann, L., R. A. McCormick, and L. McCracken. Suicidal behavior among patients in the VA health care system. *Psychiatric Services,* Vol. 46, No. 10, 1995, pp. 1069–1071.

Levin, H. S., Brown, S. A., Song, J. X., McCauley, S. R., Boake, C., Contant, C. F., et al. Depression and posttraumatic stress disorder at three months after mild to moderate traumatic brain injury. *Journal of Clinical and Experimental Neuropsychology,* Vol. 23, No. 6, 2001, pp. 754–769.

Lippert-Gruner, M., M. Maegele, H. Haverkamp, N. Klug, and C. Wedekind. Health-related quality of life during the first year after severe brain trauma with and without polytrauma. *Brain Injury,* Vol. 21, No. 5, 2007, pp. 451–455.

Lovejoy, M. C., P. A. Graczyk, E. O'Hare, and G. Neuman. Maternal depression and parenting behavior: A meta-analytic review. *Clinical Psychology Review,* Vol. 20, No. 5, 2000, pp. 561–592.

MacDonald, C., K. Chamberlain, N. Long, and R. Flett Posttraumatic stress disorder and interpersonal functioning in Vietnam War veterans: A mediational model. *Journal of Traumatic Stress,* Vol. 12, No. 4, 1999, pp. 701–707.

Magruder, K. M., B. C. Frueh, R. G. Knapp, M. R. Johnson, J. A. Vaughan III, T. C. Carson, et al. PTSD symptoms, demographic characteristics, and functional status among veterans treated in VA primary care clinics. *Journal of Trauma and Stress,* Vol. 17, No. 4, 2004, pp. 293–301.

Marsh, N. V., and W. M. Martinovich. Executive dysfunction and domestic violence. *Brain Injury,* Vol. 20, No. 1, 2006, pp. 61–66.

Marshall, R. D., M. Olfson, F. Hellman, C. Blanco, M. Guardino, and E. L. Struening. Comorbidity, impairment, and suicidality in subthreshold PTSD. *American Journal of Psychiatry*, Vol. 158, No. 9, 2001, pp. 1467–1473.

McCarren, M., G. R. Janes, J. Goldberg, S. A. Eisen, W. R. True, and W. G. Henderson. A twin study of the association of post-traumatic stress disorder and combat exposure with long-term socioeconomic status in Vietnam veterans. *Journal of Trauma and Stress*, Vol. 8, No. 1, 1995, pp. 111–124.

McClernon, F. J., J. C. Beckham, S. L. Mozley, M. E. Feldman, S. R. Vrana, and J. E. Rose. The effects of trauma recall on smoking topography in posttraumatic stress disorder and non-posttraumatic stress disorder trauma survivors. *Addictive Behavior*, Vol. 30, No. 2, 2005, pp. 247–257.

McFall, M. E., P. W. Mackay, and D. M. Donovan. Combat-related posttraumatic stress disorder and severity of substance abuse in Vietnam veterans. *Journal of the Study of Alcohol*, Vol. 53, No. 4, 1992, pp. 357–363.

McGirr, A., J. Renaud, M. Seguin, M. Alda, C. Benkelfat, A. Lesage, et al. An examination of DSM-IV depressive symptoms and risk for suicide completion in major depressive disorder: A psychological autopsy study. *Journal of Affective Disorders*, Vol. 97, Nos. 1–3, 2007, pp. 203–209.

Mikulincer, M., V. Florian, and Z. Solomon. Marital intimacy, family support, and secondary traumatization: A study of wives of veterans with combat stress reaction. *Anxiety, Stress and Coping: An International Journal*, Vol. 8, No. 3, 1995, pp. 203–213.

Mills, K. L., M. Teesson, J. Ross, and L. Peters. Trauma, PTSD, and substance use disorders: Findings from the Australian National Survey of Mental Health and Well-Being. *American Journal of Psychiatry*, Vol. 163, No. 4, 2006, pp. 652–658.

Mintz, J., C. P. O'Brien, and B. Pomerantz. The impact of Vietnam service on heroin-addicted veterans. *American Journal of Drug and Alcohol Abuse*, Vol. 6, No. 1, 1979, pp. 39–52.

Moldover, J. E., K. B. Goldberg, and M. F. Prout. Depression after traumatic brain injury: A review of evidence for clinical heterogeneity. *Neuropsychology Review*, Vol. 14, No. 3, 2004, pp. 143–154.

Mooney, G., and J. Speed. The association between mild traumatic brain injury and psychiatric conditions. *Brain Injury*, Vol. 15, No. 10, 2001, pp. 865–877.

Moore, E. L., L. Terryberry-Spohr, and D. A. Hope. Mild traumatic brain injury and anxiety sequelae: A review of the literature. *Brain Injury*, Vol. 20, No. 2, 2006, pp. 117–132.

Muñoz, M., C. Vázquez, P. Koegel, J. Sanz, and M. A. Burnam. Differential patterns of mental disorders among the homeless in Madrid (Spain) and Los Angeles (USA). *Social Psychiatry and Psychiatric Epidemiology*, Vol. 33, No. 10, 1998, pp. 514–520.

Nace, E. P., A. L. Meyers, C. P. O'Brien, N. Ream, and J. Mintz. Depression in veterans two years after Viet Nam. *American Journal of Psychiatry*, Vol. 134, 1977, pp. 167–170.

National Institute of Neurological Disorders and Stroke. *Traumatic Brain Injury: Hope Through Research*. NIH Publication No. 02-158, 2002. As of January 30, 2008: http://www.ninds.nih.gov/disorders/tbi/detail%5Ftbi.htm

North, C. S., and E. M. Smith. Posttraumatic stress disorder among homeless men and women. *Hospital and Community Psychiatry*, Vol. 43, No. 10, 1992, pp. 1010–1016.

Nyamathi, A., H. Sands, A. Pattatucci-Aragâon, J. Berg, B. Leake, J. E. Hahn, et al. Perception of health status by homeless US veterans. *Family and Community Health*, Vol. 27, No. 1, 2004, pp. 65–74.

O'Brien, C. P., E. P. Nace, J. Mintz, A. L. Meyers, N. Ream. Follow-up of Vietnam veterans. I. Relapse to drug use after Vietnam service. *Drug and Alcohol Dependence*, Vol. 5, 1980, pp. 333–340.

Olfson, M., B. Fireman, M. M. Weissman, A. C. Leon, D. V. Sheehan, R. G. Kathol, et al. Mental disorders and disability among patients in a primary care group practice. *The American Journal of Psychiatry*, Vol. 154, No. 12, 1997, p. 7.

Ommaya, A. K., A. K. Ommaya, A. L. Dannenberg, and A. M. Salazar. Causation, incidence, and costs of traumatic brain injury in the U.S. military medical system. *Journal of Trauma*, Vol. 40, No. 2, 1996a, pp. 211–217.

Ommaya, A. K., A. M. Salazar, A. L. Dannenberg, A. K. Ommaya, A. B. Chervinsky, K. Schwab. Outcome after traumatic brain injury in the U.S. military medical system. *Journal of Trauma*, Vol. 41, No. 6, 1996b, pp. 972–975.

Oquendo, M. A., J. M. Friend, B. Halberstam, B. S. Brodsky, A. K. Burke, M. F. Grunebaum, et al. Association of comorbid posttraumatic stress disorder and major depression with greater risk for suicidal behavior. *American Journal of Psychiatry*, Vol. 160, No. 3, 2003, pp. 580–582.

Ormel, J., M. VonKorff, T. B. Ustun, S. Pini, et al. Common mental disorders and disability across cultures: Results from the WHO Collaborative Study on Psychological Problems in General Health Care. *Journal of the American Medical Association*, Vol. 272, No. 22, 1994, pp. 1741–1748.

Orsillo, S. M., R. G. Heimberg, H. R. Juster, and J. Garrett. Social phobia and PTSD in Vietnam veterans. *Journal of Traumatic Stress*, Vol. 9, No. 2, 1996, pp. 235–252.

Ouimette, P. C., P. J. Brown, and L. M. Najavits. Course and treatment of patients with both substance use and posttraumatic stress disorders. *Addictive Behavior*, Vol. 23, No. 6, 1998, pp. 785–795.

Oyserman, D., C. T. Mowbray, P. A. Meares, and K. B. Firminger. Parenting among mothers with a serious mental illness. *Journal of Orthopsychiatry*, Vol. 70, No. 3, 2000, pp. 296–315.

Pan, H. S., P. H. Neidig, and K. D. O'Leary. Predicting mild and severe husband-to-wife physical aggression. *Journal of Consulting and Clinical Psychology*, Vol. 62, No. 5, 1994, pp. 975–981.

Perl, L. *Veterans and Homelessness*. Washington, D.C.: Congressional Research Service, 2007.

Pessar, L. F., M. L. Coad, R. T. Linn, and B. S. Willer. The effects of parental traumatic brain injury on the behaviour of parents and children. *Brain Injury*, Vol. 7, No. 3, 1993, pp. 231–240.

Price, R. K., N. K. Risk, K. S. Murray, K. S. Virgo, and E. L. Spitznagel. Twenty-five year mortality of US servicemen deployed in Vietnam: Predictive utility of early drug use. *Drug and Alcohol Dependence*, Vol. 64, No. 3, 2001, pp. 309–318.

Regier, D. A., M. E. Farmer, D. S. Rae, B. Z. Locke, S. J. Keith, L. L. Judd, et al. Comorbidity of mental disorders with alcohol and other drug abuse. Results from the Epidemiologic Catchment Area (ECA) Study. *Journal of the American Medical Association*, Vol. 264, No. 19, 1990, pp. 2511–2518.

Rehm, J., R. Room, K. Graham, M. Monteiro, G. Gmel, and C. T. Sempos. The relationship of average volume of alcohol consumption and patterns of drinking to burden of disease: An overview. *Addiction*, Vol. 98, No. 9, 2003, pp. 1209–1228.

Riggs, D. S., C. A. Byrne, F. W. Weathers, and B. T. Litz. The quality of the intimate relationships of male Vietnam veterans: Problems associated with posttraumatic stress disorder. *Journal of Traumatic Stress*, Vol. 11, No. 1, 1998, pp. 87–101.

Robbins, A., S. Chao, G. Coil, and V. Fonseca, Costs of smoking among active duty U.S. Air Force personnel-United States, 1997. *Journal of the American Medical Association*, Vol. 283, 2000, pp. 3193–3195.

Robertson, M. J. Homeless veterans: An emerging problem? In R. D. Bingham, R. E. Green, and S. B. White (Eds.), *The Homeless in Contemporary Society* (Vol. 87). Thousand Oaks, Calif.: Sage Publications, 1987.

Rosenheck, R., and A. Fontana. A model of homelessness among male veterans of the Vietnam War generation. *American Journal of Psychiatry*, Vol. 151, No. 3, 1994, pp. 421–427.

———. Transgenerational effects of abusive violence on the children of Vietnam combat veterans. *Journal of Traumatic Stress*, Vol. 11, No. 4, 1998, pp. 731–742.

Rosenheck, R., C. Leda, L. K. Frishman, J. Lam, and A.-M. Chung. Homeless veterans. In J. Baumohl (Ed.), *Homelessness in America: A Reference Book*. Phoenix, Ariz.: Oryx Press, 1996, pp. 97–108.

Rosenheck, R. A., W. Kasprow, and C. Seibyl. Veterans. In D. Levinson (Ed.), *Encyclopedia of Homelessness*. Thousand Oaks, Calif.: Sage Publications Ltd., 2004, Vol. 2, pp. 587–591.

Rosenheck, R., C. Leda, and P. Gallup. Combat stress, psychosocial adjustment, and service use among homeless Vietnam veterans. *Hospital and Community Psychiatry*, Vol. 43, No. 2, 1992, pp. 145–149.

Roth, D. Homeless veterans: Comparisons with other homeless men. In M. J. Robertson and M. Greenblatt (Eds.), *Homelessness: A National Perspective*. New York, N.Y.: Plenum Press, 1992.

Rothberg, J. M., P. T. Bartone, H. C. Holloway, and D. H. Marlowe. Life and death in the US Army. In Corpore sano. *Journal of the American Medical Association*, Vol. 264, No. 17, 1990, pp. 2241–2244.

Rugulies, R. Depression as a predictor for coronary heart disease: A review and meta-analysis. *American Journal of Preventive Medicine*, Vol. 23, No. 1, 2002, pp. 51–61.

Ruscio, A. M., F. W. Weathers, L. A. King, and D. W. King. Male war-zone veterans' perceived relationships with their children: The importance of emotional numbing. *Journal of Traumatic Stress*, Vol. 15, No. 5, 2002, pp. 351–357.

Salazar, A. M., D. L. Warden, K. Schwab, J. Spector, S. Braverman, J. Walter, et al. Cognitive rehabilitation for traumatic brain injury: A randomized trial. Defense and Veterans Head Injury Program (DVHIP) Study Group. *Journal of the American Medical Association*, Vol. 283, No. 23, 2000, pp. 3075–3081.

Sanders, J. W., S. D. Putnam, C. Frankart, R. W. Frenck, M. R. Monteville, M. S. Riddle, et al. Impact of illness and non-combat injury during operations Iraqi Freedom and Enduring Freedom (Afghanistan). *American Journal of Tropical Medicine and Hygiene*, Vol. 73, No. 4, 2005, p. 713.

Sareen, J., T. Houlahan, B. J. Cox, and G. J. Asmundson. Anxiety disorders associated with suicidal ideation and suicide attempts in the National Comorbidity Survey. *Journal of Nervous and Mental Disorders*, Vol. 193, No. 7, 2005, pp. 450–454.

Savoca, E., and R. Rosenheck. The civilian labor market experiences of Vietnam-era veterans: The influence of psychiatric disorders. *Journal of Mental Health Policy and Economics*, Vol. 3, No. 4, 2000, pp. 199–207.

Schnurr, P. P., A. F. Hayes, C. A. Lunney, M. McFall, and M. Uddo. Longitudinal analysis of the relationship between symptoms and quality of life in veterans treated for posttraumatic stress disorder. *Journal of Consulting and Clinical Psychology*, Vol. 74, No. 4, 2006, pp. 707–713.

Schumacher, J. A., S. Feldbau-Kohn, A. M. S. Slep, and R. E. Heyman. Risk factors for male-to-female partner physical abuse. *Aggression and Violent Behavior*, Vol. 6, Nos. 2–3, 2001, pp. 281–352.

Shalev, A., A. Bleich, and R. J. Ursano. Posttraumatic stress disorder: Somatic comorbidity and effort tolerance. *Psychosomatics*, Vol. 31, No. 2, 1990, pp. 197–203.

Shalev, A. Y., S. Freedman, T. Peri, D. Brandes, T. Sahar, S. P. Orr, et al. Prospective study of posttraumatic stress disorder and depression following trauma. *American Journal of Psychiatry*, Vol. 155, No. 5, 1998, pp. 630–637.

Silver, J. M., R. Kramer, S. Greenwald, and M. A. Weissman. The association between head injuries and psychiatric disorders: Findings from the New Haven NIMH Epidemiologic Catchment Area Study. *Brain Injury*, Vol. 15, No. 11, 2001, pp. 935–945.

Simon, G. E., M. Von Korff, K. Saunders, D. L. Miglioretti, P. K. Crane, G. van Belle, et al. Association between obesity and psychiatric disorders in the US adult population. *Archives of General Psychiatry*, Vol. 63, No. 7, 2006, pp. 824–830.

Simpson, G., and R. Tate. Suicidality after traumatic brain injury: Demographic, injury and clinical correlates. *Psychological Medicine*, Vol. 32, No. 4, 2002, pp. 687–697.

———. Clinical features of suicide attempts after traumatic brain injury. *Journal of Nervous and Mental Disorders*, Vol. 193, No. 10, 2005, pp. 680–685.

Smith, M. W., P. P. Schnurr, and R. A. Rosenheck. Employment outcomes and PTSD symptom severity. *Mental Health Services Research*, Vol. 7, No. 2, 2005, pp. 89–101.

Solomon, Z., M. Waysman, R. Belkin, G. Levy, M. Mikulincer, and D. Enoch. Marital relations and combat stress reaction: The wives' perspective. *Journal of Marriage and the Family*, Vol. 54, 1992a, pp. 316–326.

Solomon, Z., M. Waysman, G. Levy, B. Fried, M. Mikulincer, R. Benbenishty, et al. From front line to home front: A study of secondary traumatization. *Family Process,* Vol. 31, No. 3, 1992b, pp. 289–302.

Solter, V., V. Thaller, D. Karlović, and D. Crnković. Elevated serum lipids in veterans with combat-related chronic posttraumatic stress disorder. *Croatian Medical Journal,* Vol. 43, No. 6, 2002, pp. 685–689.

Stewart, S. H. Alcohol abuse in individuals exposed to trauma: A critical review. *Psychological Bulletin*, Vol. 120, No. 1, 1996, pp. 83–112.

Stewart, W. F., J. A. Ricci, E. Chee, S. R. Hahn, and D. Morganstein. Cost of lost productive work time among US workers with depression. *Journal of the American Medical Association*, Vol. 289, No. 23, 2003, pp. 3135–3144.

Stinson, F. S., H. Yi, B.F. Grant, P. Chou, D. A. Dawson, and R. Pickering. *Drinking in the United States: Main Findings from the 1992 National Longitudinal Alcohol Epidemiologic Survey (NLAES) in U.S. Alcohol Epidemiologic Data Reference Manual, Vol 6*. Rockville, Md.: National Institute on Alcohol Abuse and Alcoholism, Division of Biometry and Epidemiology, 1998.

Sullivan, G., A. Burnam, P. Koegel, and J. Hollenberg. Quality of life of homeless persons with mental illness: Results from the course-of-homelessness study. *Psychiatric Services,* Vol. 51, No. 9, 2000, pp. 1135–1141.

Sullivan, L. E., D. A. Fiellin, and P. G. O'Connor. The prevalence and impact of alcohol problems in major depression: A systematic review. *American Journal of Medicine,* Vol. 118, No. 4, 2005, pp. 330–341.

Susser, E. S., S. P. Lin, and S. A. Conover. Risk factors for homelessness among patients admitted to a state mental hospital. *American Journal of Psychiatry*, Vol. 148, No. 12, 1991, pp. 1659–1664.

Susser, E., E. Valencia, S. Conover, A. Felix, W.-Y. Tsai, and R. J. Wyatt. Preventing recurrent homelessness among mentally ill men: A "critical time" intervention after discharge from a shelter. *American Journal of Public Health*, Vol. 87, No. 2, 1997, pp. 256–262.

Swendsen, J. D., and K. R. Merikangas. The comorbidity of depression and substance use disorders. *Clinical Psychology Review*, Vol. 20, No. 2, 2000, pp. 173–189.

Taylor, L. A., J. S. Kreutzer, S. R. Demm, and M. A. Meade. Traumatic brain injury and substance abuse: A review and analysis of the literature. *Neuropsychological Rehabilitation*, Vol. 13, Nos. 1-2, 2003, pp. 165–188.

Teasdale, T. W., and A. W. Engberg. Suicide after traumatic brain injury: A population study. *Journal of Neurological and Neurosurgical Psychiatry*, Vol. 71, No. 4, 2001, pp. 436–440.

Thorndike, F. P., R. Wernicke, M. Y. Pearlman, and D. A. Haaga. Nicotine dependence, PTSD symptoms, and depression proneness among male and female smokers. *Addictive Behavior*, Vol. 31, No. 2, 2006, pp. 223–231.

United States Department of Health and Human Services. *The Health Benefits of Smoking Cessation: A Report of the Surgeon General*. Washington, D.C.: Government Printing Office, 1990.

United States Department of the Army, Army Behavioral Health Technology Office. *Army Suicide Event Report (ASER): Calendar Year 2006*. Tacoma, Wash.: Army Behavioral Health Technology Office, 2007.

Uysal, S., M. R. Hibbard, D. Robillard, E. Pappadopulos, and M. Jaffe. The effect of parental traumatic brain injury on parenting and child behavior. *Journal of Head Trauma Rehabilitation*, Vol. 13, No. 6, 1998, pp. 57–71.

Verbosky, S. J., and D. A. Ryan. Female partners of Vietnam veterans: Stress by proximity. *Issues in Mental Health Nursing*, Vol. 9, No. 1, 1988, pp. 95–104.

Vieweg, W. V., A. Fernandez, D. A. Julius, L. Satterwhite, J. Benesek, S. J. Feuer, et al. Body mass index relates to males with posttraumatic stress disorder. *Journal of the National Medical Association*, Vol. 98, No. 4, 2006a, pp. 580–586.

Vieweg, W. V., D. A. Julius, J. Benesek, L. Satterwhite, A. Fernandez, S. J. Feuer, et al. Posttraumatic stress disorder and body mass index in military veterans. Preliminary findings. *Progress in Neuropsychopharmacological and Biolological Psychiatry*, Vol. 30, No. 6, 2006b, pp. 1150–1154.

Waller, S. J., J. S. Lyons, and M. F. Costantini-Ferrando. Impact of comorbid affective and alcohol use disorders on suicidal ideation and attempts. *Journal of Clinical Psychology*, Vol. 55, No. 5, 1999, pp. 585–595.

Wamboldt, M. Z., D. Reiss. Explorations of parenting environments in the evolution of psychiatric problems in children. *American Journal of Psychiatry*, Vol. 163, No. 6, 2006, pp. 951–953.

Wang, P. S., G. E. Simon, J. Avorn, F. Azocar, E. J. Ludman, J. McCulloch, et al. Telephone screening, outreach, and care management for depressed workers and impact on clinical and work productivity outcomes: A randomized controlled trial. *Journal of the American Medical Association*, Vol. 298, No. 12, 2007, pp. 1401–1411.

Watkins, K. E., A. Burnam, F.-Y. Kung, and S. Paddock. A national survey of care for persons with co-occurring mental and substance use disorders. *Psychiatric Services*, Vol. 52, 2001, pp. 1062–1068.

Wehman, P., P. Targett, M. West, and J. Kregel. Productive work and employment for persons with traumatic brain injury: What have we learned after 20 years? *Journal of Head Trauma Rehabilitation*, Vol. 20, No. 2, 2005, pp. 115–127.

Wells, K. B., Stewart, A., Hays, R. D., Burnam, M. A., Rogers, W., Daniels, M., et al. The functioning and well-being of depressed patients. Results from the Medical Outcomes Study. *Journal of the American Medical Association*, Vol. 262, No. 7, 1989, pp. 914–919.

Wenzel, S. L., P. Koegel, and L. Gelberg. Antecedents of physical and sexual victimization among homeless women: A comparison to homeless men. *American Journal of Community Psychology*, Vol. 28, No. 3, 2000, pp. 367–390.

Whisman, M. A. The association between depression and marital dissatisfaction. In S. R. H. Beach (Ed.), *Marital and Family Processes in Depression: A Scientific Foundation for Clinical Practice*. Washington, D.C.: American Psychological Association, 2001, pp. 3–24.

Whyte, J., K. Schuster, M. Polansky, J. Adams, and H. B. Coslett. Frequency and duration of inattentive behavior after traumatic brain injury: Effects of distraction, task, and practice. *Journal of the International Neuropsychology Society*, Vol. 6, No. 1, 2000, pp. 1–11.

Wilcox, H. C., K. R. Conner, and E. D. Caine. Association of alcohol and drug use disorders and completed suicide: An empirical review of cohort studies. *Drug and Alcohol Dependence*, Vol. 76 Suppl. 2004, pp. S11–19.

Williams, C. M. The "veteran system" with a focus on women partners: Theoretical considerations, problems, and treatment strategies. In T. Williams (Ed.), *Post-Traumatic Stress Disorders of the Vietnam Veteran: Observations and Recommendations for the Psychological Treatment of the Veteran and His Family*. Cincinnati, Ohio: Disabled American Veterans, 1980, pp. 73–122.

Worthington, J., M. Fava, C. Agustin, and J. Alpert. Consumption of alcohol, nicotine, and caffeine among depressed outpatients: Relationship with response to treatment. *Psychosomatics: Journal of Consultation Liaison Psychiatry*, Vol. 37, No. 6, 1996, pp. 518–522.

Wulsin, L. R., G. E. Vaillant, and V. E. Wells, A systematic review of the mortality of depression. *Psychosomatics Medicine*, Vol. 61, No. 1, 1999, pp. 6–17.

Zatzick, D. F., Marmar, C. R., Weiss, D. S., Browner, W. S., Metzler, T. J., Golding, J. M., et al. Posttraumatic stress disorder and functioning and quality of life outcomes in a nationally representative sample of male Vietnam veterans. *American Journal of Psychiatry*, Vol. 154, No. 12, 1997, pp. 1690–1695.

Zimmerman, M., I. Chelminski, and W. McDermut. Major depressive disorder and Axis I diagnostic comorbidity. *Journal of Clinical Psychiatry*, Vol. 63, No. 3, 2002, pp. 187–193.

Zoccolillo, M., A. Pickles, D. Quinton, and M. Rutter. The outcome of childhood conduct disorder: Implications for defining adult personality disorder and conduct disorder. *Psychological Medicine*, Vol. 22, No. 4, 1992, pp. 971–986.

Zubin, J., and B. Spring. Vulnerability—A new view of schizophrenia. *Journal of Abnormal Psychology*, Vol. 86, 1977, pp. 103–126.

Part IV: Economic Consequences

This part of the monograph discusses the consequences of post-deployment mental health and cognitive conditions in economic terms. It presents the approach to and results from a microsimulation model and cost-of-illness analysis.

CHAPTER SIX

The Cost of Post-Deployment Mental Health and Cognitive Conditions

Christine Eibner, Jeanne S. Ringel, Beau Kilmer, Rosalie Liccardo Pacula, and Claudia Diaz

Introduction

The previous part of this monograph (see Part III) described the consequences associated with deployment-related post-traumatic stress disorder (PTSD), major depression, and traumatic brain injury (TBI). In this chapter, we evaluate the costs associated with these conditions. Prior analyses of the costs associated with the conflicts in Afghanistan and Iraq have typically used standard accounting methodologies to project the costs that accrue to the government (Bilmes, 2007; Bilmes and Stiglitz, 2006; Goldberg, 2007), typically taking a per-person cost figure from existing data, multiplying by the projected population, and inflating over time with trend factors. These studies have focused on the total cost of the conflicts, with medical costs as one component (Bilmes and Stiglitz, 2006; Wallsten and Kosec, 2005), or specifically on the medical and disability costs (Goldberg, 2007; Bilmes, 2007). In our analysis, we focus on a narrower spectrum of conditions—costs related to TBI, PTSD, and major depression. However, we consider a wide array of consequences, including the costs related to mental health treatment, the costs of suicide, and costs stemming from reduced productivity. Moreover, we take a societal perspective and consider costs that accrue to all members of U.S. society, which potentially include not only government agencies (e.g., the Departments of Defense [DoD] and Veterans Affairs [VA]), but also servicemembers, their families, employers, private health insurers, taxpayers, and others.

Prior cost studies have considered three perspectives: the societal perspective, the government perspective, and the VA perspective. Gold (1996) recommends that all cost analyses consider the societal perspective, because this is the only approach that never counts a cost to one member of society as a benefit or savings to another (as would be the case, for example, if a charitable organization rather than the VA paid for mental health treatment for some returning veterans). However, at times, policymakers may be concerned only with costs that accrue to the government or to specific government agencies, such as the VA. In our analysis, we consider the U.S. societal perspective because we believe that the cost of treating servicemembers injured in Afghanistan or

Iraq is a national responsibility and that we as a society should be committed to minimizing all costs, regardless of whether they accrue to government agencies, military servicemembers, their families, taxpayers, or others.

We use several approaches to estimate costs related to mental health and cognitive injuries. For PTSD and major depression, we use a microsimulation model to project current-year costs as well as costs incurred in the future. Unlike standard accounting methods, a microsimulation model takes a hypothetical group of simulated individuals and predicts future cost-related events, allowing the simulated population to experience mental conditions, mental health treatment, and secondary outcomes, such as employment. An advantage of the microsimulation approach is that it treats mental disorders as chronic conditions, allowing for both remission and relapse over time. In addition, the microsimulation model can be useful for evaluating different policy scenarios. In our case, we are particularly interested in asking the policy question: "If we increase the use of evidence-based treatment, will we save money in the long run?" This type of question would be difficult to evaluate in a standard accounting framework, because standard accounting models are based on average expenditures for a population and do not allow different individuals to experience different treatments, subsequent outcomes, and costs.

A challenge for building a microsimulation model is the availability of information to estimate key parameters, such as the probability of developing a mental health condition, the probability of getting treatment depending on having a condition, and the probability of experiencing secondary outcomes, such as unemployment. Because these parameters must come from either published literature or secondary data analysis, the literature and available data must be relatively well developed to ensure that the probabilities used in the model are credible. In our literature review to examine the consequences of a mental health condition (see Chapter Five), we found that, while the literature on PTSD and major depression is reasonably well developed (although, at points, it is thin), the literature on TBI is much less comprehensive. As a result, we could not include TBI in our microsimulation model, and we instead calculated the costs of TBI using a prevalence-based cost-of-illness approach. While the cost-of-illness approach enables us to predict costs associated with TBI in a particular year (in this case, 2005), we could not use this methodology to evaluate policy changes, such as an increase in evidence-based treatment. Moreover, because of differences in time frame and methodology, the estimates from the cost-of-illness approach for TBI are not directly comparable with those for PTSD and major depression. However, in the absence of more-complete data, we believe that the cost-of-illness approach provided useful information about the total and per-case cost of deployment-related TBI in a given year.

The main cost outcomes that we consider in our analysis include treatment costs, the costs of lives lost to suicide, costs related to lost productivity (including reduced employment and lower earnings), and costs associated with TBI-related death. Many other secondary costs are likely to be related to PTSD, major depression, and TBI, such as costs stemming from family stress, caregiver burden, homelessness, and substance abuse co-morbidity. We do not incorporate these effects into our cost estimates for several reasons, including sparse literature, uncertainty about whether a mental health condition causes the problem (as opposed to simply being correlated with the problem), and difficulty assigning a dollar figure to intangible outcomes, such as family well-being. To the extent that these omitted costs are caused by psychological and cognitive injuries, our cost figures should be considered lower-bound estimates of the true costs. While a limitation of our study is that we cannot address all costs associated with mental health and cognitive conditions, we nevertheless think this analysis provides valuable information in that it presents what can be thought of as a lower-bound estimate of societal costs.

Our microsimulation model predicts that two-year costs resulting from PTSD and major depression for the approximately 1.6 million individuals who have deployed since 2001 could range from $4.0 to $6.2 billion, depending on how we account for the costs of lives lost to suicide. Because this calculation includes costs for servicemembers who returned from deployment starting as early as 2001, many of these two-year costs have already been incurred. However, if servicemembers continue to be deployed in the future, expected costs will increase beyond the range discussed in this chapter. Providing evidence-based treatment to everyone in need could reduce these costs by as much as 27 percent. The cost savings associated with evidence-based treatment are clear for major depression and less robust for PTSD or co-morbid PTSD and major depression. The instability of the results for PTSD stems from the fact that the research base on effective treatments is still growing (Institute of Medicine, 2007; discussed in Chapter Seven), as well as from limited information on potential reductions in productivity stemming from PTSD. Our cost-of-illness estimates indicate that the cost of deployment-related TBI ranged from $90.6 to $135.4 million in 2005 ($96.6 to $144.4 million at 2007 price levels). When applying the per-case cost in 2005 to the total number of TBI cases identified (2,726),[1] we estimated the total cost of deployment-related TBI to be between $591 and $910 million (2007 dollars). Again, many of these costs have already been incurred, given that the figures account for all cases of TBI identified since September 2001. For all three conditions, costs related to reduced productivity accounted for a large share of total costs.

The remainder of this chapter is organized into four sections. First, we provide an overview of the previous literature on medical costs related to deployment. Second, we discuss the PTSD and major depression simulation model and ask whether society could save money by investing more in evidence-based treatment for these conditions. Third, we present the cost analysis for traumatic brain injury. Finally, we offer overall

---

[1]   The total number of cases is taken from *Serve, Support, Simplify* (President's Commission on Care for America's Returning Wounded Warriors, 2007, p. 2).

conclusions about the societal costs of deployment-related mental health and cognitive conditions.

Prior Cost Estimates

Several prior studies have projected the medical costs associated with the wars in Afghanistan and Iraq (Bilmes, 2007; Goldberg, 2007; Bilmes and Stiglitz, 2006; Wallsten and Kosec, 2005). While some studies estimate the overall cost of the war, with medical care as one component (Bilmes and Stiglitz, 2006; Wallsten and Kosec, 2005), others have focused specifically on the medical costs associated with deployment to Operation Enduring Freedom (OEF) and Operation Iraqi Freedom (OIF) (Bilmes, 2007; Goldberg, 2007). In general, these studies have used a standard accounting framework to project these costs. This methodology typically involves taking an average cost per veteran for each cost component (e.g., injuries, fatalities), multiplying this cost by the expected number of veterans, and applying trend factors to inflate these costs over time. While some studies have estimated separate costs for TBI, other medical costs in these studies have been measured at a very aggregate level, such as average cost per patient regardless of condition, and cannot easily be disaggregated to estimate costs for particular illnesses.

Although the studies use similar methods, they differ in important ways. For example, some have focused on the costs that accrue to the federal government (Bilmes, 2007; Goldberg, 2007), while others have taken a societal perspective and included costs such as the loss in future productivity from injury-related disability (Bilmes and Stiglitz, 2006; Wallsten and Kosec, 2005). In addition, some include costs from Afghanistan and Iraq (Bilmes, 2007), while others focus solely on Iraq (Wallsten and Kosec, 2005; Bilmes and Stiglitz, 2006; Goldberg, 2007). While most studies have focused specifically on costs accruing to either the U.S. government or U.S. society at large, Wallston and Kosec (2005) consider costs to other countries as well. Moreover, each study includes a somewhat different set of costs. Given these differences, the estimates from these studies can be difficult to compare. Table 6.1 summarizes the perspectives and cost components included in several recent studies.

The first estimate of the medical costs of the war in Iraq was generated by Wallsten and Kosec (2005). This study took a societal perspective and estimated the lifetime costs associated with lives lost ($14 billion) and injuries incurred ($18.2 billion) between March 20, 2003, and August 25, 2005, to be $32.2 billion. A primary limitation of this estimate is that it does not include any costs associated with deployment-related mental health problems and thus may understate the true medical costs.

Bilmes and Stiglitz (2006) generate an estimate of the governmental costs of the war in Iraq through 2015 of between $700 billion and $1.2 trillion. In their conservative estimate (i.e., $700 billion), VA costs are estimated to be $40 billion, the cost of brain injuries $14 billion, and the cost of veterans disability payments $37 billion. Unfortunately, the VA cost estimate is at a very aggregate level; therefore, we are unable

Table 6.1
Studies of the Cost of the Wars in Afghanistan and Iraq

Study	Perspective(s) Considered	Goal of Study	Cost Categories Included
Our report	Societal (within the United States)	To project 2-year post-deployment costs associated with PTSD and depression; to calculate total costs associated with TBI in 2005	Treatment and rehabilitation costs for PTSD, depression, and TBI Medical costs associated with suicide attempts and completions Value of lives lost to suicide Value of lives lost to TBI Lost productivity stemming from PTSD, TBI, and depression

Bilmes and Stiglitz (2006)	Governmental and societal (within the United States)	To project total governmental and societal costs of the Iraq war through 2015	Governmental costs
			  Money spent to date
			  Future spending on operations
			  VA costs
			  Cost for brain injuries
			  Veterans disability payments
			  Demobilization costs
			  Increased defense spending
			  Interest on the debt
			Societal costs
			  Governmental costs minus veterans disability pay
			  Cost of Reserve personnel
			  Cost of fatalities
			  Loss due to brain injuries
			  Loss due to other injuries
			  Depreciation of military hardware

Bilmes (2007)	VA	To project long-term costs to the VA	Disability compensation Medical costs
Goldberg (2007)	VA	To project 10-year costs to the VA	Medical costs Disability compensation Dependency and indemnity compensation
Wallsten and Kosec (2005)	Societal, including non-U.S. societies	To project costs and benefits of the war in Iraq through 2015	Military and government expenditures Fatalities Injuries, including TBI Lost wages of Reserve personnel Avoided costs, such as avoided murders by Saddam Hussein

to separate from the total the costs associated with treating deployment-related mental health conditions. To provide another perspective, Bilmes and Stiglitz (2006) make several adjustments to the estimate of governmental costs to provide an estimate of the societal costs of the war. Their societal estimate accounts for additional costs that accrue to parties other than the federal government, such as the loss in productivity associated with injury-related disabilities or premature death. Including such costs adds another $105 to $167 billion to the total cost estimates.

In a recent study, Bilmes (2007) expands on her prior work (Bilmes and Stiglitz, 2006) to generate a more detailed estimate of the lifetime costs of veterans' medical care and disability payments. She estimates projected VA medical costs to be between $208 and $600 billion. Again, the medical cost estimate is at an aggregate level and does not allow us to separate out the costs of specific conditions, such as PTSD, major depression, or TBI. Disability payments are projected to be between $68 and $127 billion.

In recent testimony before the U.S. House of Representatives Committee on Veterans' Affairs, the Deputy Assistant Director for National Security at the Congressional Budget Office (CBO), Matthew S. Goldberg, presented projections on the VA costs of care for OEF/OIF veterans (Goldberg, 2007). The CBO estimates that VA medical costs associated with OEF/OIF veterans are between $7 and $9 billion over the period 2008 through 2017. Disability and survivor benefits are estimated to contribute an additional $3 to $4 billion over the same time period. In the testimony, the CBO argues that the medical cost estimates generated by Wallsten and Kosec (2005) and Bilmes and Stiglitz (2006) are too high, largely stemming from the assumptions they make regarding the number and severity of TBI cases and overall service utilization among OEF/OIF veterans.

There are a number of similarities and differences between the methodology used in this report and those employed in prior studies. For example, like Wallsten and Kosec (2005), we take a societal perspective and consider costs that accrue to all potential payers, including the government, individuals, employers, and private health insurers. However, unlike Wallsten and Kosec, we focus our examination of societal costs on those costs incurred by the United States and its citizens and consider costs over a much shorter time frame. The basic method we use to generate the estimated cost of TBI is quite similar to that used in prior studies; however, for PTSD and major depression, we use a microsimulation model to generate our cost estimates. With the microsimulation model, we follow each modeled individual over time, accounting for the effects of a mental health condition and treatment trajectories on productivity and suicide. We can then model alternative policy scenarios, such as an increase in the fraction of veterans receiving evidence-based treatment, and reevaluate costs after accounting for such changes. Standard accounting methodologies, in contrast, typically project future costs in a relatively stable policy environment.

The prior estimates have focused on a comprehensive or nearly comprehensive array of medical care cost components; we limit our analysis to costs stemming specifically from TBI, PTSD, and major depression. We include costs related to treatment, mortality, productivity, and suicide. These are appropriately considered societal costs because they represent new expenditures or losses that would not have been incurred, or that could have been used for other purposes, in the absence of combat-related mental health injuries. None of the prior studies has accounted for the costs associated with suicide. At the same time, we omit some costs that have been included in prior studies. For example, we do not include disability payments in our calculations because they are intended to replace lost wages, which are already included in our model.

Finally, the time frame for our analyses is different from that of prior studies. Our microsimulation model for PTSD and major depression focuses on a two-year time horizon, and our TBI estimate is for a single year, whereas previous estimates have projected costs over a much longer time frame—ten years (Goldberg, 2007; Bilmes and Stiglitz, 2006) or a lifetime (Bilmes, 2007; Wallsten and Kosec, 2005). We limit our model time horizon to two years because we do not have enough information to break down costs by type of service or to parameterize the course of remission and relapse from mental health conditions over a longer time frame. Although several studies (Angst, 1986; Judd et al., 1998; Judd et al., 2000; Kennedy, Abbott, and Paykel, 2004) have traced the course of depression for ten years or more, these publications do not report sufficient information to model the timing of transitions between relapse and remission. To our knowledge, no studies analyze long-term relapse and remission rates for PTSD. Other studies of the medical costs of the conflicts in Afghanistan and Iraq have been able to analyze a longer time frame because they have explored average costs per patient across a wide range of conditions and projected this number over time, adjusting for expected number of patients, inflation, and other factors. While some of these studies have generated long-term costs for TBI, they have used an aggregate estimate (i.e., total costs not broken down across different types of services or levels of injury severity) of the lifetime treatment costs of TBI (Wallsten and Kosec, 2005). Because the focus of these studies is broad and the costs of TBI are only one component of the total, the lack of detail in the lifetime cost estimate is not a concern. However, for this monograph, we focus specifically on the costs of major depression, PTSD, and TBI, and we consider the costs associated with different types of treatment and different degrees of severity and co-morbidity, allowing—in the simulation model—remission and relapse rates to be influenced by treatment type.

The Cost of PTSD and Major Depression and the Benefits of Evidence-Based Care

Background

Many veterans return from deployment with a mental health condition or the likelihood of developing a mental health condition. Chapter Three concludes that probable rates of PTSD in returning veterans range from 5 to 15 percent and that probable rates of major depression range from 2 to 10 percent. Our survey of returning servicemembers and veterans (Chapter Four) found similar results, with 13.8 percent of all previously deployed troops meeting screening criteria for PTSD and 13.7 percent meeting screening criteria for major depression. Hoge et al., (2004) found that less than half of returning soldiers and marines with a probable mental health condition received any care within three to four months after returning from Iraq or Afghanistan; an even smaller number received evidence-based care. The evidence suggests that increasing the percentage of veterans who receive care would improve health outcomes and that increasing the percentage of veterans who receive evidence-based care would lead to even greater improvements.

Although the treatment costs could be substantial in the short term, providing evidence-based care to all returning veterans with a mental health condition may in fact be a cost-saving strategy when viewed over the longer term. The societal costs of forgone care or inadequate care can also be substantial: They include treatment costs for relapses and lost productivity. Conversely, positive outcomes associated with effective treatment can lead to improved productivity, health, and quality of life. Thus, any calculation of post-deployment mental health treatment costs needs to include potentially offsetting savings that follow from improving mental health outcomes among veterans. In this section, we present the results of a microsimulation model to estimate these costs. Our model predicts two-year costs associated with three care alternatives for veterans returning to the states with post-traumatic stress disorder or major depression: usual care, evidence-based care, or no care.

Motivation for the Microsimulation Approach

Both major depression and PTSD are likely to be costly to society, not only because treatments are expensive but also because these illnesses are associated with significant reductions in productivity. Studies of the civilian population have found that lost productivity associated with a mental health condition represents a significant cost to society and to employers (Ettner, Frank, and Kessler, 1997; Kessler, Borges, and Walters, 1999; Druss, Rosenheck, and Sledge, 2000), with one study reporting that workers with depression cost employers as much as $44 billion a year (Stewart et al., 2003). Studies of veterans with PTSD have similarly found that these individuals have a lower probability of working (Zatzick et al., 1997; Smith, Schnurr, and Rosenheck, 2005), higher missed days at work conditional on working (Hoge et al., 2007), reduced productivity—known as "presenteesim"—while at work (Stewart et al., 2003), and lower earnings (Savoca and Rosenheck, 2000) than peers without a mental health condition. In addition, there may be significant costs stemming from the downstream consequences of these illnesses, including increased non–mental health related medical costs, caregiver burden, strain on family relationships, domestic violence, substance abuse, crime, and homelessness (Dekel and Solomon, 2006; Brooks, 1991; Liss and Willer, 1990; Kozloff, 1987; Solomon et al., 1992; Calhoun and Beckham, 2002; Kulka et al., 1990; Ommaya et al., 1996; Rosenheck and Fontana, 1994).

We used a microsimulation model to estimate the costs and benefits associated with three courses of treatment that may be provided to military servicemembers returning home with major depression, PTSD, or both conditions. Our model took a representative cohort of individuals returning from OEF and OIF and mapped their trajectories over a period of two years, taking into account treatments received and events that may occur as a result of a mental health condition.[2] The treatment pathways that we considered in our model are

- usual care
- evidence-based care
- no care.

We estimated the costs associated with PTSD and major depression among post-deployed servicemembers from prevalence rates found in prior literature. However, it is not clear that all of these costs are causally attributable to the conflicts in Afghanistan and Iraq. While deployment likely increases the chance that a servicemember develops PTSD or major depression, some servicemembers would have developed these conditions even without deployment. As a result, our analysis focused on the full costs associated with mental health conditions among the post-deployed population, rather than the incremental costs attributable to deployment in Afghanistan or Iraq. Nevertheless, understanding the costs of these conditions, and the potential reduction in costs associated with evidence-based care, is valuable because the nation has obligated itself to providing health care for all returning servicemembers, regardless of where their injuries were sustained.

Events addressed in the model include labor market outcomes (retention within DoD, career progression within the military conditional on retention, employment in the civilian sector, and civilian earnings), suicide attempts, and suicide completions. Although we do not currently model other cost categories, such as costs related to domestic violence, homelessness, or substance abuse, the model could be expanded to incorporate these costs if adequate data were available. The model estimates both the total costs of illness and the societal costs associated with forgone or inadequate care.

Note that the estimates presented here are necessarily imprecise. The data on which to base model parameters are thin, and thus there are often a number of assumptions that must be made to generate important model parameters. Because of this uncertainty, we developed three cost projections: a baseline scenario, a low-cost scenario, and a high-cost scenario.

Overview of the Microsimulation Framework

The simulation model develops a two-year life-course projection for a group of 25-year-old military servicemembers returning from OEF/OIF at a rank of E-5 with 5 to 7 years of service, the modal rank for an individual returning from OIF.[3] Costs for E-5s

---

[2] We considered estimating these costs over a longer period, which is possible using this framework. However, we could not gain access to appropriate data that would enable us to reliably parameterize the model over a longer time for the military population.

[3] Because we did not have access to data describing the joint distribution of age, rank, and years of service among returning veterans, we made the simplifying assumption that everyone in our synthetic cohort is a 25-year-

may differ from costs for other servicemembers because E-5s are relatively young and therefore have lower wages and a higher risk of suicide than other servicemembers. Average wages for E-5s are also lower than average wages for officers of comparable age. In general, it is not clear whether mental health–related costs for E-5s should be higher or lower than mental health–related costs for other servicemembers. To the extent that wages for E-5s are lower than wages for other personnel, the costs for E-5s will also be lower. However, to the extent that the risk of suicide for E-5s is relatively high, costs will be higher. In sensitivity tests, we considered alternative combinations of age, rank, and years of service. To develop total cost estimates, we then took a weighted average of costs for each rank considered (E-4, E-5, E-7, and O-2) to estimate an approximate average cost per returning servicemember.

Modeled individuals are randomly assigned a gender, race/ethnicity, education, military branch, rank, and age using distributions reported in published studies (*Medical Surveillance Monthly Report*, 2007; DoD Office of the Under Secretary of Defense for Personnel and Readiness [OUSDPR], 2005; Congressional Budget Office, 2004; Defense Manpower Data Center, 2000). While assigned demographic characteristics are specific to rank, we were unable to model the joint distribution of these variables because of lack of data. Each individual has a probability of experiencing major depression, PTSD, or co-morbid major depression and PTSD based on prevalence rates found in published literature specific to OEF/OIF veterans (Hoge et al., 2004; Grieger et al., 2006; Milliken, Auchterlonie, and Hoge, 2007); for PTSD, these probabilities can increase over time to reflect delayed or gradual onset (Wolfe et al., 1999). Specifically, 5 percent of modeled individuals have PTSD immediately after returning from deployment, increasing to 15 percent over two years. Half of all individuals with PTSD are assigned co-morbid major depression. Another 7.2 percent of individuals are assigned major depression alone.

Figure 6.1 illustrates the model dynamics, with arrows showing possible transitions across states. Each state is defined by an individual's mental health status, treatment status, and employment status. For ease of presentation, this figure focuses on a single mental health condition, but our model incorporates three possible mental health conditions (PTSD, major depression, and co-morbid PTSD and major depression). As a simplifying assumption, we constrain individuals from switching across conditions. This assumption implies that, while some individuals in our model have a single mental health condition and some have co-morbid mental health conditions, no one with a single condition will ever develop a co-morbid condition, and no one with co-morbid conditions will ever recover from one condition but not the other. Appendix 6.A provides a "model map" that walks through the model dynamics in more detail.

---

old E-5 returning to the states with 5 to 7 years of service. E-5 is approximately the modal rank of individuals returning from OIF, based on statistics reported in the *Medical Surveillance Monthly Report* (September–October 2007). Data reported by Hoge, Auchterlonie, and Milliken (2006) suggest that the median age of returning servicemembers who complete a post-deployment health assessment is approximately 25.

Figure 6.1
Model Dynamics

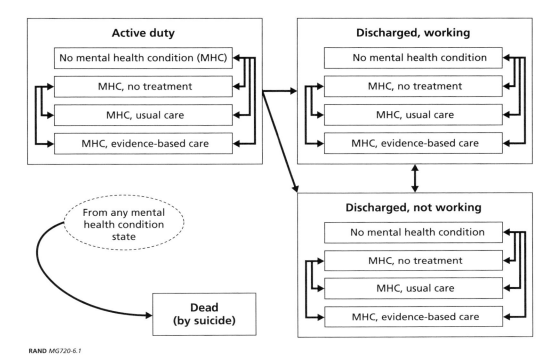

Modeled individuals with a mental health condition have a probability of receiving evidence-based treatment or usual care, and these treatments influence the course of illness. Studies of the civilian population find that it is relatively common for individuals with a probable mental health condition to receive no treatment for these conditions. In a sample of adults with likely major depression or anxiety disorder interviewed in 1997 and 1998, 17 percent received no treatment at all during a one-year period (Young et al., 2001). A more recent study (Wang et al., 2005) found that about 43 percent of individuals with PTSD or major depression received no treatment during the past year. Among returning veterans, rates of care may be even lower. Hoge et al. (2004) found that only 23 to 40 percent of veterans returning from OEF and OIF who screened positive for a probable mental health condition, including major depression and post-traumatic stress disorder, sought care within three to four months of returning from deployment. Our survey (discussed in Chapter Four) found that approximately 50 percent of post-deployed servicemembers with mental health conditions received any treatment. Using figures reported in Hoge et al. (2004), Young et al. (2001), and Wang et al. (2005), we model a "status quo" scenario in which 30 percent of individuals in need get any care and 30 percent of the care that the individuals receive is evidence-based. We then consider alternative situations in which (1) 50 percent of individuals in need get treatment and 30 percent of treatment is evidence-based, (2) 50 percent of individuals in need get treatment and all treatment is evidence-based, and (3) 100 percent of individuals in need get evidence-based treatment.

Details on the dosages of medication, psychotherapy, and maintenance medication provided for evidence-based and usual care for each of the three conditions are discussed in Appendix 6.B (see Tables 6.B.1 and 6.B.2). We assigned treatment success probabilities based on remission rates reported in existing literature (Schnurr et al., 2007; Kessler et al., 1995; Keller et al., 2000; Dimidjian et al., 2006; Ludman et al., 2007; Wells et al., 1992; Kocsis et al., 1988). Table 6.2 shows the probability of remission after three months in each treatment assignment.

On average, individuals receiving evidence-based treatment have a higher probability of remission than individuals receiving usual care, who in turn have a higher probability of remission than those receiving no care. Once in remission, labor-market outcomes will, on average, improve. Individuals in remission have a probability of relapsing, based on figures reported in published studies (Perconte, Griger, and Bellucci, 1989; Melfi et al., 1998; Vittengl et al., 2007). The evidence on the probability of relapse conditional on successful treatment for PTSD is relatively thin, and estimates of the probability of relapse conditional on successful treatment for major depression have ranged considerably across studies (Vittengl et al., 2007). As a result, we explore alternative assumptions regarding relapse in our high- and low-cost scenarios.

Based on their mental health state and demographic characteristics, individuals are assigned labor-market outcomes and labor-market transitions for each quarterly period included in our model. For example, each person currently on active duty has a military wage (based on rank and years of service) and a quarterly probability of leaving military service based on rates reported in Hoge, Auchterlonie, and Milliken (2006), measured from the date of return from deployment. Military wages are calculated using pay tables reported by DoD,[4] and promotion probabilities are derived from the 2007 *Defense Manpower Requirements Report* (DoD OUSDPR, 2006). A mental health condition influences DoD career trajectories by increasing the probabil-

Table 6.2
Remission Probabilities Following Three Months of Illness

Condition(s)	Treatment Assignment			Sources
	Evidence-Based Treatment	Usual Care	No Care	
PTSD or co-morbid PTSD and major depression	39%	30%	~5%[a]	Schnurr et al. (2007) Kessler et al. (1995) Wolfe et al. (1999)
Major depression alone	48%	40%	12%	Keller et al. (2000) Dimidjian et al. (2006) Ludman et al. (2007) Wells et al. (1992) Kocsis et al. (1988)

[a] Remission rates are derived from Wolfe et al. (1999)

---

[4]   See DoD's "Military Pay and Benefits" Web page (2008b).

ity of leaving the military (Hoge, Auchterlonie, and Milliken, 2006). We do not allow mental health treatment to affect promotions within DoD because we do not have data on how this treatment would affect career outcomes, and—intuitively—we are not sure of the expected direction of this effect. To the extent that mental health treatment improves productivity, it might lead to quicker promotion. However, if mental health treatment can affect performance reviews, it could potentially have adverse consequences for career progression.

Individuals who have left active duty are assigned a probability of working in the civilian sector and a civilian wage—these outcomes are influenced by mental health status as well as other factors, such as age and sex. We calculated wages and employment probabilities using data on veterans in the March 2007 Current Population Survey (CPS). For those with a mental health condition, we reduced the probability of working and wages conditional on working based on a study of mental health condition and productivity in a group of Vietnam veterans (Savoca and Rosenheck, 2000); these estimates imply a 15.75-percent wage reduction for PTSD and a 45.23-percent wage reduction for major depression. Individuals with co-morbid PTSD and major depression were assigned the same wage reduction as individuals with major depression alone. Because the reduction in wages associated with major depression in this study is high relative to similar studies of the civilian population (Ettner, Frank, and Kessler, 1997), we used a more conservative figure in our low-cost scenario.

Few studies besides Savoca and Rosenheck (2000) have examined wage reductions associated with PTSD or co-morbid PTSD and major depression, so it is difficult to compare the assumptions used in our model with other literature. However, a recent report by CNA Corporation (Christensen et al., 2007) finds that—for recently discharged veterans in their twenties and thirties with Service-connected disabilities—the probability of working is 5 percent lower than the probability for comparable veterans with no disability, and wage rates are approximately 14 percent lower. Although these rates are slightly lower than the rates reported by Savoca and Rosenheck (2000), they combine physical and mental disabilities. Additional analyses in the CNA report confirm that wage differentials are higher for individuals with mental health conditions.[5]

Individuals who have left active duty also have a probability of joining the Reserves, but—in the absence of any data on how a mental health condition influences the chance of joining the Reserves—the probability of joining the Reserves does not vary with mental health status.

Military compensation policies imply that wages for active duty personnel are almost completely determined by rank and years of service. Kilburn, Louie, and Goldman (2001) analyzed this issue empirically. They found that there were statistically significant differences in total compensation, including benefits, across enlisted per-

---

[5] For example, the annual earned-income loss for an individual with a 10-percent mental health disability rating is $7,676, compared with $2,543 for an individual with a 10-percent physical disability rating.

sonnel, but that these differences were small and driven by years of service and number of dependents.[6] As a result, a mental health condition will not influence DoD salaries through a direct reduction in wage. However, given the civilian literature summarized in Part III (see Chapter Five) finding an association between mental health conditions and reduced wages (Ettner, Frank, and Kessler, 1997; Savoca and Rosenheck, 2000), higher missed days at work (Druss, Rosenheck, and Sledge, 2000; Kessler, Borges, and Walters, 1999), and poorer work performance (Wang et al., 2004; LeBlanc et al., 2007), we think it is likely that a mental health condition would indirectly reduce DoD salaries through a decreased likelihood of promotion and through increased "presenteeism." Hosek and Mattock (2003) find evidence to substantiate the hypothesis that DoD personnel of lower "quality" (where quality is measured using educational attainment and Armed Forces Qualification Test scores) have a greater length of time until promotion. Stewart et al. (2003) find that depressed individuals lose approximately 4.6 hours per workweek because of "presenteeism," or reduced performance during work hours. For civilian workers, we anticipate that lower productivity (e.g., presenteesim) among individuals with mental disorders would be accounted for in wage differences; thus, the cost of reduced productivity is borne by the worker, who is paid less. However, since military wages cannot adjust as easily, the cost of presenteeism among active duty servicemembers may be disproportionately borne by DoD, which pays workers a fixed salary for lower-quality work. Because we have no data that would enable us to quantify the combined effect of reduced promotion probabilities and increased presenteeism for active duty servicemembers, our baseline scenario assumes that productivity within DoD is reduced by half of the civilian productivity-reduction factor found in Savoca and Rosenheck (2000). Thus, for a servicemember with PTSD, DoD wages are reduced by a factor of 7.88 percent; for a servicemember with major depression or co-morbid PTSD and major depression, DoD wages are reduced by a factor of 22.62 percent. In our low-cost scenario, we assumed that mental health conditions have no effect on wages within DoD; in our high-cost scenario, we assumed that mental health conditions have the same effect for active duty and non–active duty workers.

At each quarter, individuals with a mental health condition have a probability of death from suicide.[7] Because our model time frame is only two years and our population is relatively young, we did not allow for other causes of death. We assigned the probability of a suicide attempt using the age-specific probability of a suicide attempt prior to treatment for major depression in a population of veterans (Gibbons et al.,

---

[6]   We accounted for dependents in our model by assuming that 50 percent of personnel are married.

[7]   It is the tradition in cost-of-illness studies, whether estimated for a year or over a period of time, to include the full lifetime loss associated with early death at the time the death occurs (Hodgson and Meiners, 1979; Hodgson and Meiners, 1982; Rice, Kelman, and Miller, 1991; Harwood, Fountain, and Fountain, 1998). Given that suicide is our only method for dying, this cost category is large relative to the other cost categories, because the present value of the individual's life is assigned fully to the period when the death occurs. Other cost categories consider only actual costs incurred during that period, consistent with the cost-of-illness approach.

2007). The probability of dying conditional on a suicide attempt is derived from the *2006 Army Suicide Event Report* (U.S. Army, 2007). Because both the rate of attempted suicide and the rate of suicide conditional on attempt used in our analysis are based on suicide attempts that led to contact with the health care system, these estimates likely understate the true costs of suicide. Specifically, we were unable to capture either "minor" suicide attempts that required no medical treatment or serious attempts and completions that might have been recorded as accidents (e.g., single-car crashes). To address this issue, we increased the probability of a suicide attempt by 25 percent in our high-cost model estimate. In our low-cost estimate, we decreased the probability of a suicide attempt for individuals with PTSD and co-morbid PTSD and depression, based on a recent study suggesting that depressed veterans have a higher rate of suicide attempt than veterans with co-morbid PTSD and depression (Zivin et al., 2007).

Consistent with research showing a high rate of attrition among active duty personnel hospitalized for mental disorders (Hoge et al., 2002) and conversations with servicemembers suggesting a limited tolerance within DoD for maintaining personnel who have had a suicide attempt, we assumed that 80 percent of individuals attempting suicide will leave DoD within three months. In all model scenarios, we assumed that individuals without mental health conditions and individuals in remission from mental health conditions have a zero probability of suicide.

Costs in our model came from treatment expenditures, lost productivity, and costs associated with suicide. Because the medical costs of evidence-based treatment (pharmaceutical costs and psychotherapy visits) are higher than the medical costs associated with usual care and no care, any cost savings associated with evidence-based care compared with usual care stem from secondary effects. Such savings include better productivity outcomes, lower risk of suicide, and fewer treatment episodes over the modeled time frame (because of both a higher probability of treatment success and, in the case of major depression, a lower probability of relapse). Table 6.3 describes the source of data for our cost estimates.

We assumed that all active duty personnel receive mental health treatment through the TRICARE system. In theory, individuals who have been discharged from DoD can get care either through the VA or through private health insurance offered by an employer, a spouse's employer, or an alternative source. Because pharmaceutical costs can vary substantially depending on whether care is provided through the VA or through alternative sources, we tested the sensitivity of our estimates to various assumptions about prescription drug costs for discharged personnel in our high- and low-cost scenarios. In our baseline scenario, we assumed that 35 percent of discharged veterans get prescription drugs through the VA, based on VA utilization among OEF/OIF veterans reported by the Veterans Health Administration Office of Public Health and Environmental Hazards (Veterans Health Administration, 2007).

We assumed that medical care costs related to suicide, which come from Corso et al. (2007), are equivalent for active duty and discharged personnel. The cost of lives lost

Table 6.3
Data Sources for Cost Information

Cost Component	Active Duty Personnel	Discharged Personnel and Reservists
Psychotherapy, primary, and specialty care costs	TRICARE Reimbursement Rates[a]	Medicare Reimbursement Rates[b]
Pharmaceutical costs	DoD Pharmacoeconomic Center (2004)	Fleming (2007b); Dobscha, Winterbottom, and Snodgrass, (2007)
Wage rates	Pay Tables, Office of the Secretary of Defense[c]	Calculated using veterans from the March 2007 Current Population Survey
Value of lives lost to suicide	Viscusi and Aldy (2003)	Viscusi and Aldy (2003)
Medical care costs associated with suicide	Corso et al. (2007)	Corso et al. (2007)

[a] TRICARE, "Allowable Charges," Web page, no date.

[b] Department of Health and Human Services, Centers for Medicare and Medicaid Services, "Physician Fee Schedule Search," Web page, no date.

[c] Department of Defense, "Pay and Allowances," Web page, no date-a.

to suicide comes from a review by Viscusi and Aldy (2003), who found that most studies of the value of a statistical life yield estimates in the range of $4 million to $9 million in 2000 dollars. Wallsten and Kosec (2005) used the midpoint of this range ($6.5 million) as their estimate of the value of a life in 2000 and inflated it for the year in which they were evaluating costs. We used the same approach and inflated the $6.5-million estimate to 2007 price levels, giving us a value of a statistical life of $7.5 million. The studies used to derive this estimate are based on wage-risk trade-offs, whereby researchers use differences across occupations in wage and risk of dying to estimate an approximate value of life for a statistical individual.[8] In theory, these estimates should capture all costs associated with death that would conceivably be valued by a worker, including lost quality of life, grief and loss to family members, and pain and suffering.

There is substantial uncertainty in our estimates owing to uncertain parameters, uncertainty about the prevalence of mental health conditions, uncertainty about which costs are causally attributable to PTSD and major depression, and other factors. We attempted to convey this uncertainty in our results in several ways. In our analysis of E-5s, we calculated high, low, and "baseline" cost estimates that allow key parameters to vary, using ranges of parameters found in the literature. Rather than allowing each model parameter to vary across the three scenarios, we only varied model parameters for which there was a great deal of uncertainty and that were likely to have a large

---

[8]   The literature draws a distinction between a statistical life and an identified life. A *statistical life* represents a hypothetical individual who might be saved by a particular intervention or policy change. An *identified life*, in contrast, is an actual person. The value of an identified life would far exceed the value of a statistical life and cannot be appropriately valued using economic techniques.

bearing on costs (e.g., parameters related to suicide and productivity). Table 6.4 shows the assumptions that varied across the three cost scenarios that we model. Because of the high degree of uncertainty regarding the number of completed suicides that might occur as a result of PTSD or major depression,[9] we consistently present results with and without costs associated with lives lost to suicide. Because prevalence rates for mental health conditions in this population are uncertain, and because there is uncertainty regarding how many people receive evidence-based care, usual care, and no care, we show costs per case for each possible treatment regimen. We also present costs for four alternative personnel types (E-4, E-5, E-7, and O-2) to demonstrate the potential difference in outcomes stemming from evaluating individuals with different

Table 6.4
Assumptions That Vary Across Model Scenarios

Assumption	Baseline	Low-Cost	High-Cost
DoD earnings for those on active duty	PTSD reduces wage by 7.88%, major depression or co-morbid PTSD and major depression reduce the wage by 22.6%	DoD wages are unrelated to a mental health condition	PTSD reduces wage by 15.75%, major depression or co-morbid PTSD and major depression reduce the wage by 45.23%
Medication costs for discharged personnel	35% of discharged personnel get prescriptions at the VA-negotiated price	All discharged personnel get prescriptions at the VA-negotiated price	All discharged personnel get prescriptions through private health insurance
Wage adjustment for discharged personnel with major depression, or co-morbid major depression and PTSD	45.23% lower than CPS estimate	15.75% lower than CPS estimate	45.23% lower than CPS estimate
Relapse rates for major depression	54% relapse over 2 years	26% of those with evidence-based treatment relapse over 2 years; 36% of those with usual care or no care relapse over 2 years	54% of those with evidence-based treatment relapse over 2 years; 75% of those with usual care or no care relapse over 2 years
Relapse rates for PTSD	55% relapse over 2 years	25% relapse over 2 years	55% relapse over 2 years
Rate of attempted suicide	Use age-specific rates reported in Gibbons et al. (2007)	Use age-specific rates reported in Gibbons et al. (2007), but reduce by 25% for individuals with PTSD or co-morbid PTSD and major depression	Use age-specific rates reported in Gibbons et al. (2007), but increase by 25% to account for attempts and completions that were missed or not recorded as suicide

[9] The *2006 Army Suicide Event Report* (U.S. Army, 2007) did not find a direct relationship between increased deployment and suicide, and it noted that most soldiers who completed suicide did not have a prior psychiatric condition. Further, suicide rates found in the ASER were lower than gender-matched suicide rates for the U.S. population.

wage profiles. In addition, we estimated total costs using several alternative assumptions about the fraction of servicemembers who receive any treatment and who receive evidence-based treatment.

Finally, an important advantage of the microsimulation framework is that it allows us to capture uncertainty that exists in event probabilities and outcomes, because individuals in our model experience events and outcomes with chance rather than with certainty. For example, a modeled individual with PTSD has a 39-percent chance of recovery following an episode of evidence-based treatment. But, in each model run, some individuals recover and some individuals remain sick. Because our model population is relatively large (a minimum of 20,000 observations in each run), the law of large numbers usually implies that separate model runs will produce similar results. But, for outcomes that are very rare or very uncertain, alternative model runs can produce markedly different outcomes. By being run several times and analyzing differences in outcomes across runs, our model can shed light on which cost components are relatively stable and which cost components can vary depending on the population, circumstances, and random chance. A more detailed discussion of the model parameters, assumptions, and architecture—including a comparison of several alternative model runs—can be found in the technical appendixes to this chapter (Appendixes 6.A and 6.B).

Model Limitations

All models, including both microsimulation and standard accounting models, are abstractions from reality and rely on simplifications and assumptions in order to be tractable and computationally feasible. A disadvantage of microsimulation models is that, because the methodology is complex, it can be difficult to effectively convey these omitted details and the underlying assumptions. Another challenge that is particularly relevant to microsimulation models is that model results can be highly dependent on the parameters used to assign event probabilities—such as the probability of developing a mental health condition, the probability of working conditional on having a mental health condition, and expected salary conditional on working. If these parameters are incorrect, model results will be misleading.

The challenge of assigning appropriate model parameters is nontrivial in the case of mental health conditions stemming from the conflicts in Afghanistan and Iraq. The population that we are trying to model—previously deployed veterans—is very unique, and relatively few studies focus specifically on these individuals. While data on prevalence of illness, attrition conditional on mental health conditions, and the probability of receiving treatment come from studies of servicemembers returning from OEF and OIF, most other parameters are drawn from data on veterans of prior conflicts (e.g., the Gulf War and the Vietnam War) or from the civilian population. Parameters related to DoD career transitions were particularly difficult to estimate with available data. In particular, we had no information on how a mental health condition affects DoD promotion probabilities among those who continue to serve—a particularly important parameter, given that DoD wages are determined almost entirely by promotion. Further, with the exception of a recent CNA report (Christensen et al., 2007), there is limited information on discharged personnel's labor-market experiences immediately following separation from DoD or on how a mental health condition affects the probability of joining the Reserves. There is also limited literature on the relationship between PTSD and productivity.

Model limitations that we view as particularly important are listed below. In general, these limitations are due either to data constraints or to simplifications that we made in order to develop this model within a limited time horizon. Many of these limitations could be at least partially addressed with additional time, data, and resources:

- There was a lack of data on how mental health conditions affect DoD wages and career outcomes.
- Employment status was assumed to have no effect on mental health.
- We did not allow mental health treatment to directly influence DoD career outcomes (although treatment can indirectly influence career outcomes if it causes mental health status to improve).
- Model time horizon was limited to two years.
- Characteristics assigned to individuals (e.g., age, race, sex, education) were generally based on univariate rather than joint distributions of these characteristics.
- Mental health prevalence used in the model was based on population averages and was not specific to age, rank, gender, race, or other characteristics.
- We made simplifying assumptions about career transitions within the Reserves (apart from those attempting suicide, mental health has no influence on the probability of joining the Reserves; we did not model promotion among reservists).
- The probability of mental health treatment success was independent of previous treatment outcomes.
- Modeled suicides and suicide attempts captured only suicides that would have led to contact with the health care system.
- Data on remission from PTSD following evidence-based treatment were limited, and estimates used in the model came from a sample of female veterans.
- We assumed that no servicemembers redeploy within the model time horizon.

Qualitatively, we think the most important limitations stem from (1) the fact that we are not certain of the full number of suicides and suicide attempts that may be causally related to PTSD and depression and (2) the fact that wage reductions for active duty servicemembers with mental health conditions are unclear. Because we were missing suicide attempts and completions that do not lead to contact with the health care system (or lead to contact with the system but are recorded as accidents), we think that we were likely underestimating the costs resulting from suicide. However, we were less certain of the direction of bias inherent in our assumptions about productivity. As a result, our low-cost, "baseline," and high-cost estimates allow for substantial difference in the wage reductions associated with mental disorders, particularly for active duty personnel.

In addition to these limitations, at least two additional costs are associated with evidence-based treatment that were not considered in our model. First, there could be costs associated with implementing programs that exceed the costs captured in our model. Such costs would include training providers in evidence-based practices and providing outreach to servicemembers to encourage them to seek care. Yet, while we did not address these costs in our model, prior studies have found that vigorous outreach aimed at moving depressed workers into evidence-based care leads to cost savings from the employer's perspective (Wang et al., 2007). Second, there could be spillover costs associated with bringing veterans into the health care system—for example, individuals who seek treatment at the VA for PTSD might be prompted to seek care for unrelated health concerns. These spillover costs are particularly difficult to evaluate, both because it is hard to know whether the additional utilization would have occurred without the mental health visit and because the additional utilization could either create new costs (e.g., costs for unnecessary care) or save costs downstream (e.g., early detection of illness). More generally, the model is only able to consider anticipated costs—in some cases, there may be additional costs that are completely unanticipated.

Finally, our model was designed to analyze the effects of guideline-concordant treatment. There are two reasons that treatment as practiced might differ from suggested guidelines. First, patients may not adhere to treatments with perfect fidelity. Because figures from the randomized control studies used to parameterize the model (Schnurr et al., 2007; Ludman et al., 2007; Keller et al., 2000; Casacalenda, Perry, and Looper, 2002) were based on the intent-to-treat methodology, our estimates incorporate lack of patient fidelity. Second, provider fidelity may be imperfect, leading care as implemented to be less successful than care provided in a controlled setting. Our analysis assumed that care is implemented as intended, in part because our intent was to analyze the potential costs and benefits associated with appropriately implemented care. Our cost estimates for usual care can be viewed as a lower bound of the potential effect of poorly implemented evidence-based care. However, we did not attempt to model evidence-based care *as-implemented* separately from evidence-based care *as-intended*.[10]

Despite these limitations, we have done our best to produce what we believe will be a conservative estimate of the total cost. When uncertain about the actual cost of particular services or outcomes, we used low estimates of these costs. In addition, we excluded a range of additional outcomes that are believed to be associated with each of

---

[10] Previous literature has found that quality-of-care improvements for depression implemented in local, "naturalistic" care settings have produced cost savings (Schoenbaum et al., 2001).

these conditions and focused instead on outcomes for which we have reasonably good data: treatment, productivity, and suicide.

Model Results

Table 6.5 shows the predicted costs over two years associated with PTSD and major depression for a cohort of 50,000 E-5s (this is approximately the number of E-5s that returned from OIF in 2005, based on data reported in the *Medical Surveillance Monthly Report*, September–October 2007). The baseline, low-, and high-cost scenarios incorporate different assumptions about wage reductions for individuals with mental health conditions, relapse probabilities, and rates of suicide attempt. A full description of the differences across scenarios is provided in Table 6.4. We assumed that 30 percent of individuals with mental health conditions get treatment and that—of this 30 percent—30 percent get evidence-based treatment. Throughout this monograph, we refer to these rates of treatment receipt (30 percent in need get treatment and 30 percent of treatment is evidence-based) as the "status quo." We think that these proportions approximate the likelihood of receiving any care and evidence-based care, given figures reported in prior studies (Hoge, 2004; Wang et al., 2005; Young et al., 2001).

Our baseline results indicate that, for 50,000 E-5s returning from OEF and OIF, two-year costs associated with PTSD and major depression range from $119.8 million to $204.7 million (at 2007 price levels), depending on whether or not we included the value of lives lost to suicide in our estimates. We present results with and without costs stemming from suicide deaths because the cost of a completed suicide is extremely high and—even among those with a mental disorder—the probability of committing suicide is very low. As a result, model estimates can vary widely depending on the number of suicides occurring in a particular model run. In a series of ten alternative model runs (shown in Appendix Table 6.B.5), the number of suicides ranged from 4 to 11, and, as a consequence, total cost figures ranged from $147.3 million to $204.7 million when we included the value of lives lost to suicide in our estimates. Because of uncertainty regarding the suicide rate and potential volatility in cost estimates that include the

Table 6.5
Status Quo Cost Projections for 50,000 E-5s

	Baseline	Low-Cost	High-Cost
Total cost, including lives lost to suicide	$204,691,652	$120,736,359	$231,455,009
Total cost, excluding lives lost to suicide	$119,829,381	$51,184,350	$149,009,345
Total number of suicides	11	9	11

NOTE: Status quo assumes that 30 percent of individuals with mental health conditions receive treatment and that 30 percent of individuals receiving treatment get evidence-based care.

value of lives lost to suicide, we present results with and without suicide mortality costs in all subsequent tables.

Table 6.5 also shows that there is a wide range between our low- and high-cost estimates. This range primarily reflects our uncertainty about how much a mental health condition affects the productivity of DoD personnel. In the low-cost scenario, we assumed that a mental health condition has no effect on productivity for active duty personnel, and—when we separate productivity costs out of the figures reported in Table 6.5 (not shown)—estimated productivity losses account for $46.5 million. In our high-cost scenario, in which we assumed that a mental health condition has the same effect on productivity for active duty personnel as it does for civilian veterans, productivity losses (not shown in Table 6.5) account for $141.6 million. Figures 6.2 and 6.3 show the distribution of costs for our baseline model, with and without the cost of lives lost to suicide, under our status quo treatment assumptions. In both cases, lost productivity accounts for the majority of costs—making up 55.3 percent of total costs when we include suicide mortality and 94.5 percent of total costs when we exclude suicide mortality.

One of our primary questions is: How much money could be saved by investing in evidence-based treatment? Tables 6.6a and 6.6b show the expected costs, and total savings, associated with increasing the share of E-5s with PTSD or major depression that get mental health treatment. Relative to the status quo, in which 30 percent get treatment and 30 percent of treatment is evidence-based, we considered scenarios in which 50 percent of those in need get treatment and 30 percent of treatment is evidence-based; in which 50 percent of those in need get treatment and all treatment is evidence-based; and in which 100 percent of those in need get evidence-based treatment.

Using our baseline model and including the costs of lives lost to suicide (Table 6.6b, Panel A), we predicted that society could save money by increasing the share of individuals who received any treatment from 30 to 50 percent and that even more could be saved if all treatment were evidence-based. We predicted that society could save approximately $86.2 million over two years if all of the 50,000 E-5s in our model with PTSD or major depression received evidence-based treatment. If we exclude the value of lives lost to suicide, the results are not as straightforward (Table 6.6b, Panel B). Although we predicted that society could save money by increasing the share of individuals who receive treatment from 30 to 50 percent, there is a net loss associated with ensuring that 50 percent of individuals in need receive evidence-based treatment. This result stems from the fact that evidence-based treatment is expensive and that the marginal benefit of evidence-based treatment over usual care is small when we do not account for lives lost to suicide. Put differently, if we exclude the cost of lives lost to suicide, our model predicts that cost savings come primarily from providing treatment to individuals who are currently untreated, rather than from moving those in usual care to evidence-based care.

Figure 6.2
Status Quo Distribution of Costs,
Including Suicide Mortality

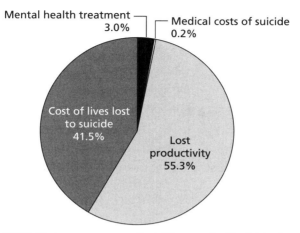

NOTE: *Status quo* assumes that 30 percent of individuals
with mental health conditions receive treatment and that
30 percent of individuals receiving treatment get
evidence-based care.

RAND *MG720-6.2*

Figure 6.3
Status Quo Distribution of Costs,
Excluding Suicide Mortality

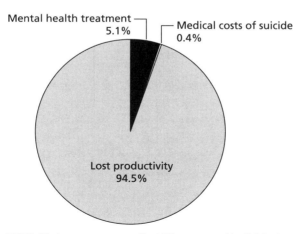

NOTE: *Status quo* assumes that 30 percent of individuals
with mental health conditions receive treatment and that
30 percent of individuals receiving treatment get
evidence-based care.

RAND *MG720-6.3*

Table 6.6a
Cost Projections with Alternative Treatment Assumptions, Cohort of 50,000 E-5s

Treatment Scenario	Baseline	Low-Cost	High-Cost
A. Cost for 50,000 E-5s, including lives lost to suicide			
50% receive treatment; 30% of treatment is evidence-based	$190,754,753	$107,221,965	$212,216,948
50% receive treatment; all treatment is evidence-based	$172,023,750	$110,606,850	$210,119,625
100% receive evidence-based treatment	$118,450,500[a]	$80,205,750	$159,927,150
B. Cost for 50,000 E-5s, excluding lives lost to suicide			
50% receive treatment; 30% of treatment is evidence-based	$115,582,035	$51,063,450	$143,660,408
50% receive treatment; all treatment is evidence-based	$122,325,450	$57,978,225	$150,906,825
100% receive evidence-based treatment	$118,450,500[a]	$64,590,750	$144,780,900

[a] Costs associated with evidence-based treatment are the same with and without the value of lives lost to suicide because there were no suicides in our evidence-based care group. Although the model allows for suicides among those with evidence-based care, suicides rarely occur in this group because the probability of suicide is low and individuals with evidence-based care are, on average, affected by the condition for a shorter period of time than individuals with usual care or no care.

Table 6.6b
Projected Savings Relative to Status Quo with Increased Treatment, Cohort of 50,000 E-5s

Treatment Scenario	Baseline	Low-Cost	High-Cost
A. Savings relative to status quo, including cost of lives lost to suicide			
50% receive treatment; 30% of treatment is evidence-based	$13,936,899	$13,514,394	$19,238,061
50% receive treatment; all treatment is evidence-based	$32,667,902	$10,129,509	$21,335,384
100% receive evidence-based treatment	$86,241,152	$40,530,609	$71,527,859
B. Savings relative to status quo, excluding cost of lives lost to suicide			
50% receive treatment; 30% of treatment is evidence-based	$4,247,346	$120,900	$5,348,937
50% receive treatment; all treatment is evidence-based	−$2,496,069	−$6,793,875	−$1,897,481
100% receive evidence-based treatment	$1,378,881	−$13,406,400	$4,228,445

NOTES: *Status quo* assumes that 30 percent of those in need get treatment and that 30 percent of treatment is evidence-based. Positive entries in the table indicate cost savings, whereas negative entries represent cost increases.

Because there is uncertainty regarding the total number of cases of PTSD and major depression, and because our cohort of 50,000 E-5s does not encompass the total spectrum of returning veterans, it is informative to consider costs per case in addition to total costs. Table 6.7 shows the predicted two-year costs per case for each modeled condition and type of treatment.

For E-5s, evidence-based treatment for major depression saves money relative to no care and—in most cases—relative to usual care (an exception is that evidence-based care is slightly more expensive than usual care in the low-cost scenario when we exclude the cost of suicide mortality). However, results are not as clear when we consider PTSD and co-morbid PTSD and major depression. In our baseline scenario, when we included the cost of suicide mortality, evidence-based care for PTSD or co-morbid PTSD and depression saves money relative to no care, but not relative to usual

Table 6.7
Predicted Two-Year Costs per Case, E-5

Condition, Type of Treatment	Baseline	Low-Cost	High-Cost
A. Cost per case, including suicide mortality			
PTSD, no care	$11,986	$7,671	$13,007
PTSD, usual care	$13,935	$4,246	$10,661
PTSD, evidence-based care	$7,933	$10,264	$12,914
Co-morbid PTSD/major depression, no care	$17,746	$6,846	$14,759
Co-morbid PTSD/major depression, usual care	$14,356	$3,529	$12,469
Co-morbid PTSD/major depression, evidence-based care	$13,641	$6,761	$16,923
Major depression, no care	$31,695	$24,047	$43,386
Major depression, usual care	$18,299	$11,494	$21,995
Major depression, evidence-based care	$10,430	$4,545	$13,344
B. Cost per case, excluding suicide mortality			
PTSD, no care	$5,635	$4,495	$6,750
PTSD, usual care	$5,664	$4,246	$6,462
PTSD, evidence-based care	$7,933	$6,100	$8,875
Co-morbid PTSD/major depression, no care	$11,781	$3,863	$14,759
Co-morbid PTSD/major depression, usual care	$10,176	$3,529	$12,469
Co-morbid PTSD/major depression, evidence-based care	$13,641	$6,761	$16,923
Major depression, no care	$16,914	$5,562	$21,215
Major depression, usual care	$11,051	$4,355	$14,746
Major depression, evidence-based care	$10,430	$4,545	$13,344

care. Without accounting for the costs associated with lives lost to suicide, evidence-based care for PTSD or co-morbid PTSD and depression is more costly even than no treatment. The less robust results for PTSD reflect the relatively high cost of treatment for this disorder, the limited evidence on the benefits of treatment for PTSD (Institute of Medicine, 2007), and a relatively small wage reduction associated with PTSD (Savoca and Rosenheck, 2000).

Table 6.7 shows that, occasionally, per-case costs estimated in the high-cost scenario are *lower* than per-case costs found in the baseline scenario (e.g., for PTSD with usual care). This finding stems from the fact that there is volatility in suicide outcomes, and an additional suicide in the baseline group can increase costs substantially.[11] Figures 6.4 and 6.5 show the predicted cost per case associated with treatment for PTSD alone, PTSD and co-morbid major depression, and major depression averaged over ten model runs. By averaging across several runs, we reduced the volatility in suicide outcomes and increased the probability that the high-cost, baseline, and low-cost estimates will align in the expected order. These figures report the expected per-case costs for each mental health condition under the "status quo," in which 30 percent of individuals receive treatment and 30 percent of treatment is evidence-based.

Figures 6.4 and 6.5 show that depression is the most costly outcome within two years post-deployment, followed by co-morbid depression and PTSD, and PTSD alone. Two-year costs are lower for co-morbid PTSD and major depression than they are for major depression alone because individuals in our model can develop late-onset PTSD with co-morbid major depression. As a result, individuals with co-morbid PTSD and major depression tend to be sick for a shorter period of time over two years, since some of these individuals develop illness near the end of the model time frame. A larger discussion of the model runs used to derive Figures 6.4 and 6.5 can be found in Appendix 6.B.

A drawback of our model is that it is specific to 25-year-old E-5s returning from deployment with 5 to 7 years of service. We restricted our cohort to this group because, when developing the model, we did not have access to data on the joint distribution of age, rank, and years of service among all returning veterans. Because rank and years of service jointly determine DoD salaries, and because productivity is the largest driver of costs, incorrect assumptions about the distribution of these variables could lead to erroneous cost projections. To get a sense of how cost projections might vary for alternative personnel types, we show in Table 6.8 results from the baseline cost scenario for three different combinations of rank, years of service (YOS), and age.

Cost estimates are different across personnel types because of age-specific differences in the probability of suicide and wide differences in salary, and because the model has a two-year duration. We estimated that annual earnings for a healthy service-

---

[11] Recall that suicides occur with an expected probability based on published studies, but the realized number of suicides in each model run varies.

Figure 6.4
Average Two-Year Cost per Case for the Status Quo, Including Value of Lives Lost to Suicide

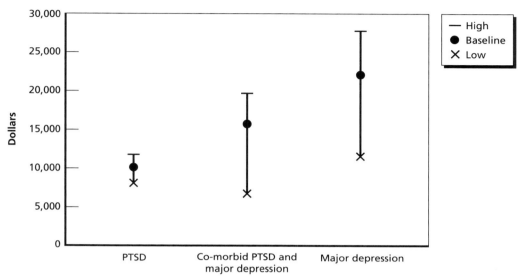

NOTE: *Status quo* assumes that 30 percent of individuals with mental health conditions receive treatment and that 30 percent of individuals receiving treatment get evidence-based care.
RAND *MG720-6.4*

Figure 6.5
Average Two-Year Cost per Case for the Status Quo, Excluding Value of Lives Lost to Suicide

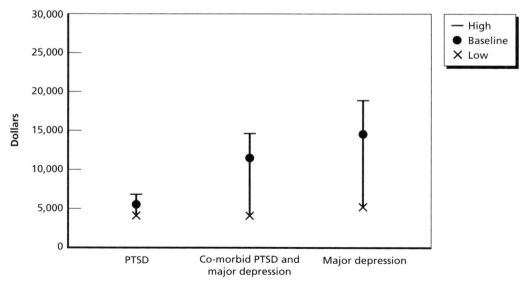

NOTE: *Status quo* assumes that 30 percent of individuals with mental health conditions receive treatment and that 30 percent of individuals receiving treatment get evidence-based care.
RAND *MG720-6.5*

Table 6.8
Predicted Two-Year Cost per Case, Alternative Personnel Types

Condition, Type of Treatment	E-4, 20 Years Old, 2 YOS	E-7, 31 Years Old, 13 YOS	O-2, 24 Years Old, 1 YOS
A. Cost per case, including suicide mortality			
PTSD, no care	$8,205	$11,986	$14,768
PTSD, usual care	$4,717	$13,935	$12,431
PTSD, evidence-based care	$7,718	$7,933	$9,594
Co-morbid PTSD/major depression, no care	$17,645	$17,746	$25,591
Co-morbid PTSD/major depression, usual care	$8,606	$14,356	$15,887
Co-morbid PTSD/major depression, evidence-based care	$12,499	$13,641	$17,967
Major depression, no care	$28,674	$31,695	$34,005
Major depression, usual care	$13,033	$18,299	$17,495
Major depression, evidence-based care	$22,166	$10,430	$15,745
B. Cost per case, excluding suicide mortality			
PTSD, no care	$5,098	$5,635	$8,536
PTSD, usual care	$4,717	$5,664	$8,433
PTSD, evidence-based care	$7,718	$7,933	$9,594
Co-morbid PTSD/major depression, no care	$11,293	$11,781	$19,282
Co-morbid PTSD/major depression, usual care	$8,606	$10,176	$15,887
Co-morbid PTSD/major depression, evidence-based care	$12,499	$13,641	$17,967
Major depression, no care	$14,008	$16,914	$26,596
Major depression, usual care	$9,373	$11,051	$17,495
Major depression, evidence-based care	$10,429	$10,430	$15,745

NOTE: YOS = years of service.

member returning from Iraq or Afghanistan as an O-2 with one year of service would be $58,090, compared with $50,741 for an E-7 with 13 years of service, $40,119 for an E-5 with 5 to 7 years of service, and $34,174 for an E-4 with 2 years of service. As a result of these productivity differentials, costs are generally higher for O-2s and E-7s, particularly when we exclude costs from suicide mortality (E-7s have a lower suicide-attempt rate because they are older). However, despite the differences in magnitudes, the same patterns hold in terms of the benefits of evidence-based treatment. Specifically, evidence-based treatment clearly saves money relative to no care for major depression, but the evidence is less robust for PTSD.

Although we lacked detailed information on the joint distribution of age, rank, and years of service, the *Medical Surveillance Monthly Report* (September–October 2007) reports that 42 percent of servicemembers returning from Iraq in 2005 were between the ranks of E-1 and E-4, 36 percent were ranks E-5 or E-6, 8.9 percent were between ranks E-7 and E-9, and 13.1 percent were officers. If we use our baseline cohort and the alternative personnel types shown in Table 6.8 to proxy for the four grades reported in the *Medical Surveillance Monthly Report*, we can get an approximate cost per case for an "average" returning veteran. Table 6.9 shows average costs, assuming our status quo, in which 30 percent of all veterans with a mental health condition get treatment and 30 percent of treated individuals receive evidence-based care.

Depending on whether or not we include suicide-related mortality, approximate average costs per case over two years for *all returning servicemembers* range from $5,904 to $10,298 for PTSD, $12,427 to $16,884 for co-morbid PTSD and major depression, and $15,461 to $25,757 for major depression alone. Using the same approach, we could determine the DoD-wide cost savings that would accrue over two years if we increased the share of individuals receiving treatment or the share of individuals receiving evidence-based care (Table 6.10).

As with the earlier results, when we include the cost of lives lost to suicide, increasing the share of individuals receiving any treatment saves money. For co-morbid PTSD and major depression, and for major depression alone, the cost savings associated with increasing the share of people who receive any care exceed the cost savings associated with ensuring that all individuals receive evidence-based treatment. For example, for major depression, the cost savings relative to the status quo associated with moving

Table 6.9
Status Quo Cost per Case

Condition	E-4	E-5	E-7	O-2	Approximate DoD Average
A. Including cost of lives lost to suicide					
PTSD	$7,429	$12,031	$11,661	$13,812	$10,298
Co-morbid PTSD and major depression	$15,284	$16,665	$16,512	$22,867	$16,884
Major depression	$24,804	$26,968	$20,740	$28,895	$25,757
B. Excluding cost of lives lost to suicide					
PTSD	$5,254	$5,848	$5,214	$8,610	$5,904
Co-morbid PTSD and major depression	$10,837	$11,611	$14,366	$18,451	$12,427
Major depression	$12,713	$15,099	$17,758	$23,708	$15,461
Approximate share	0.42	0.36	0.089	0.131	

NOTE: *Status quo* assumes that 30 percent of individuals with mental health conditions receive treatment and that 30 percent of individuals receiving treatment get evidence-based care.

Table 6.10
Potential per-Case Cost Savings Relative to the Status Quo Associated with Increasing Treatment

Condition(s)	50% Get Treatment, 30% of Treatment Is Evidence-Based	50% Get Treatment, All Treatment Is Evidence-Based	100% Get Evidence-Based Treatment
A. Including cost of lives lost to suicide			
PTSD	$445	$819	$2,306
Co-morbid PTSD and major depression	$1,264	$551	$2,997
Major depression	$5,327	$2,483	$9,240
B. Excluding cost of lives lost to suicide			
PTSD	–$110	–$961	–$2,088
Co-morbid PTSD and major depression	$291	–$948	–$1,459
Major depression	$1,189	$1,214	$4,212

NOTES: *Status quo* assumes that 30 percent of individuals with mental health conditions receive treatment and that 30 percent of individuals receiving treatment get evidence-based care. Positive entries in the table indicate cost savings, whereas negative entries represent cost increases.

50 percent of people into treatment are $5,327 per case, compared with a cost savings of $2,483 per case associated with ensuring that 50 percent of those in need get evidence-based care. As a result, it looks as though the main margin on which society saves money is by moving individuals from no care to any care, as opposed to moving them from usual care to evidence-based care. However, we do not intend to suggest that usual care is preferable to evidence-based care, for two reasons. First, usual care is less effective than evidence-based care, so people with usual care are more likely to remain sick. Had we been able to account for all costs associated with PTSD and major depression, including lost quality of life, relationship strain, substance abuse, and violence, evidence-based care may well have saved money relative to usual care. Second, we model usual care as an average of different types of suboptimal care. In reality, some individuals who receive usual care might get treatments that are very similar to evidence-based care, while others get treatments that are very different. Without a more thorough model of the many different types of usual care, we cannot conclude that all usual care would produce cost savings.

When we exclude the cost of lives lost to suicide, expanding access to evidence-based care only saves money for major depression. For PTSD or co-morbid PTSD and depression, cost savings are small or negative when we increase the share of individuals who receive any treatment, and increased utilization of evidence-based treatment appears to increase costs. This finding reflects the relatively high cost of treatment for PTSD and the limited evidence on the benefits of treatment for PTSD.

Discussion

For a typical service person returning from Iraq or Afghanistan (an E-5 with 5 to 7 years of service), our baseline scenario predicts that two-year post-deployment costs range from $5,635 to $13,935 for PTSD, $10,176 to $17,746 for co-morbid PTSD and major depression, and $10,430 to $31,695 for major depression alone. Costs vary depending on the type of treatment received and on whether or not we include the value of lives lost to suicide in our estimates. Based on the *Medical Surveillance Monthly Report* (September–October 2007), approximately 50,000 E-5s returned from OIF in 2005, suggesting a total cost for E-5s of approximately $119.8 million over two years if we exclude suicide mortality, or $204.7 million if we include the value of lives lost to suicide. Our results also suggest that productivity is the largest driver of costs, accounting for between 55.3 and 94.5 percent of all costs attributable to PTSD and major depression.

Because productivity is specific to rank, age, and years of service, it is not clear that these cost figures can be generalized to the entire post-deployed population. In our sensitivity analyses (Table 6.8), we showed that the cost per case varied substantially depending on the years of service and rank of the individual considered. Nevertheless, we can develop an approximate average cost for all returning personnel if we take a weighted average of the four combinations of rank and years of service evaluated in our model. In Table 6.11, we apply the approximate cost per case to a population of 1.6 million—the approximate total number of servicemembers who have been deployed since 2001.

Using prevalence rates discussed earlier in this chapter, we can calculate approximate total two-year PTSD and major depression costs for all servicemembers who ever deployed. There are several caveats associated with this approach. First, these estimates represent costs incurred within the first two years after returning home from deployment, so they accrue at different times for different personnel. For servicemembers who returned more than two years ago and have not redeployed, these costs have already been incurred. However, this calculation omits costs for servicemembers who may deploy in the future, and it does not include costs associated with chronic or recurring cases that linger beyond two years. Costs presented in Table 6.11 are shown at 2007 price levels. Second, our cost figures assume that individuals who develop PTSD or major depression will never redeploy—an assumption that is almost surely violated in reality. Third, we are assuming that the total number of individuals who have ever deployed is a good estimate of the total number of individuals who return to the States. As of December 2007, there had been 3,439 hostile deaths in OEF and OIF,[12] a relatively small fraction of the total number of servicemembers deployed since 2001. Finally, we do not know how long the current conflicts will continue, and we cannot predict the total number of people who will deploy to Iraq or Afghanistan in the future.

---

[12] See Department of Defense, "Military Casualty Information," Web page, 2008b.

With these caveats in mind, results in Table 6.11 suggest that total PTSD and major depression–related costs incurred for 1.6 million troops within the first two years after returning home could range from $4.0 billion to $6.2 billion, depending on whether we include the value of lives lost to suicide mortality in our figures (Panel A). These estimates are unavoidably imprecise because of uncertainty in estimates of prevalence rates, individuals' willingness to seek care, treatment efficacy, the effect of mental health conditions on productivity, and other estimates used to parameterize our model. Nevertheless, all of the parameters used in our model are grounded on prior literature, and we have done our best to be conservative in generating the cost predictions. Although our exact estimates may be imprecise, we think it is clear from this analysis that the costs are extremely high and that the majority of costs stem from lost productivity. By ensuring

Table 6.11
Approximate Societal Costs for All Servicemembers Returning in 2005

Condition(s)	Prevalence[a]	Including Suicide Mortality		Excluding Suicide Mortality	
		Cost per Case	Total Cost	Cost per Case	Total Cost
A. Costs for 1.6 million returning servicemembers, status quo (30% of those with need receive treatment, 30% of treatment is evidence-based)					
PTSD alone	120,000	$10,298	$1,235,779,451	$5,904	$708,454,129
Co-morbid PTSD and major depression	120,000	$16,884	$2,026,022,762	$12,427	$1,491,283,466
Major depression alone	115,200	$25,757	$2,967,212,796	$15,461	$1,781,137,099
Total cost			$6,229,015,009		$3,980,874,695

Condition(s)	Prevalence[a]	Savings per Case	Total Savings	Savings per Case	Total Savings
B. Savings for 1.6 million returning servicemembers, assuming that all individuals with need receive evidence-based treatment[b]					
PTSD alone	120,000	$2,306	$276,768,131	–$2,088	–$250,557,191
Co-morbid PTSD and major depression	120,000	$2,997	$359,655,122	–$1,459	–$175,084,174
Major depression alone	115,200	$9,240	$1,064,471,676	$4,212	$485,219,121
Total savings			$1,700,894,929		$59,577,757
% savings			27.3%		1.5%

[a] Prevalence estimates are derived by assuming that 15 percent of individuals got PTSD within two years and that half of these cases were co-morbid with major depression; 7.2 percent of individuals had major depression alone.

[b] Positive entries indicate cost savings, whereas negative entries represent cost increases.

that all individuals in need receive evidence-based treatment (Panel B), we could reduce two-year post-deployment costs from 1.5 to 27.3 percent.

Our model suggests that, within two years, evidence-based treatment would more than pay for itself *from a societal perspective*, largely through increased productivity. However, the benefits of evidence-based treatment are more pronounced for major depression than they are for PTSD and co-morbid PTSD and major depression. These results reflect uncertainty regarding appropriate treatment for individuals with PTSD, as well as a lower reduction in productivity associated with PTSD (which may—in part—stem from the limited literature on PTSD and productivity). These results should be interpreted carefully because of the dimensions of costs that we were unable to capture in our model. On the one hand, because we do not consider costs related to homelessness, domestic violence, family strain, and several other consequences of mental health conditions, the true benefit of providing evidence-based treatment may be even larger than predicted.

However, it is also likely that there are additional costs of evidence-based treatment that we have ignored in this model. One potential cost is that associated with implementation, such as training staff and expanding capacity to accommodate increased utilization. Costs associated with implementation could include one-time start-up costs, as well as ongoing costs associated with ensuring program performance. A second cost could include the cost of increased service utilization among veterans who access the health care system for mental health–related conditions (e.g., if visiting a provider to receive mental health care prompts an individual to seek care for unrelated problems). A broader issue is that—as with all models—we are only capturing costs that can be anticipated ahead of time. In reality, outcomes may be more complex than anticipated, which would lead to differential results. Despite these caveats, we think there is strong reason to believe that increased provision of evidence-based treatment could be a cost-saving strategy, particularly if DoD is able to provide evidence-based treatment to individuals who previously received no care.

The Cost of Deployment-Related Traumatic Brain Injury in 2005

TBI is an injury to the brain that may range in severity from relatively mild (e.g., concussion from exposure to a blast) to severe (e.g., penetrating head wound). We use a standard cost-of-illness approach to assess the costs associated with deployment-related TBI for the single year of 2005 because data are insufficient to build a microsimulation model. The costs examined include treatment and rehabilitation, TBI-caused death, suicide (both attempts and completions), and productivity losses.

Although the cost-of-illness approach requires fewer data to implement than the microsimulation approach, it is still data-intensive. Generating the cost of deployment-related TBI in 2005 requires estimates of the number of TBI cases, the utilization of treatment, the prevalence of the related outcomes (e.g., suicide, unemployment), and the associated costs. Because there are substantial differences in the outcomes and associated costs between mild and more severe cases of TBI, throughout this section we provide separate prevalence and cost estimates by severity (i.e., for mild and moderate/severe). In addition, because there is a high level of uncertainty around many of the needed estimates, we develop different assumptions and generate estimates for both a high- and a low-cost scenario. In the following sections we (1) discuss the previous literature estimating the cost of TBI, (2) outline the data used and the assumptions made to generate the cost estimate, (3) present our findings, and (4) discuss the policy implications.

Previous Estimates of the Cost of TBI

Because we are adopting a similar methodology to that which has been applied in the past, it is important to provide a more detailed discussion of the relatively small literature that has examined the cost of TBI. Most of this work has focused on civilian populations. An early study by Max, MacKenzie, and Rice (1991) estimates the lifetime cost of brain injuries sustained in 1985 at $37.8 billion, or $115,305 per injury. The cost components included in the estimate are medical services (12 percent of total), productivity losses (54 percent of total), and mortality (34 percent of total). The study includes only the costs for those injuries for which people were hospitalized or died. Because it does not include mild cases of TBI that do not require hospitalization, the Max MacKenzie, and Rice (1991) estimate should be viewed as conservative. More recent studies have updated the Max, MacKenzie, and Rice (1991) estimate with new data on the incidence of TBI and have adjusted costs to reflect medical inflation (Lewin-ICF, 1992; Thurman, 2001).

Miller et al. (1994) analyze fatalities, hospital admissions, and emergency department visits in national data collected between 1979 and 1989 to estimate the annual costs of TBI. While the estimate for the annual costs of medical care for TBI, $5.8 billion in 1992 dollars, is in line with estimates from Max, MacKenzie, and Rice (1991) when converted to constant dollars, the total cost estimate, $274.5 billion in 1992 dollars, is much higher because they include costs associated with a reduced quality of life. Miller et al. (1994) report that quality-of-life costs account for two-thirds of the cost of nonfatal injuries.

We identified one prior study that estimates the cost of deployment-related TBI. Wallsten and Kosec (2005) estimate the societal costs associated with the conflict in Iraq. Their comprehensive estimate includes the lifetime cost of treating TBI and the associated loss in quality of life. They estimate that 20 percent of all injured troops have sustained a severe head injury. Based on information from the National Association of State Head Injury Administrators, Wallsten and Kosec assume that the lifetime cost of treating a single case of TBI ranges from between $600,000 and $4 million. They calculate the loss in quality of life as the value of a statistical injury. That is, they infer the loss in quality of life by measuring what people are actually willing to pay to reduce the risk of certain types of injuries. In total, they estimate that the lifetime cost of TBI is $16 billion in 2005 dollars. It has been argued that the Wallsten and Kosec (2005) estimate is too high, largely due to their assumptions regarding the number of TBI cases and their level of severity. For example, CBO Director Peter Orszag, in congressional testimony before the House Committee on the Budget on October 24, 2007 (House of Representatives, 2007), stated that assuming that 20 percent of all injured troops experience severe brain injuries is grossly overstating the problem. He argues that, based on data from a DoD medical census, there had been 1,950 traumatic brain injuries through December 2006 and that about two-thirds of the diagnoses were for mild TBI as opposed to moderate or severe TBI.

None of the studies described here provided estimates that are directly comparable to those generated for this report. While the methodology that we employ is similar to that used by Max, MacKenzie, and Rice (1991), we focus on the costs incurred within a single year rather than the lifetime costs associated with those same injuries, which would cause our estimates to be smaller. We should also note that older studies, such as Max, MacKenzie, and Rice (1991), are less useful as a point of comparison because of the possible changes in medical technology and practice patterns. Moreover, Max, MacKenzie, and Rice (1991) describe the costs for a civilian population. The types of injuries observed may vary substantially from those observed in a military population. In that regard, Wallsten and Kosec (2005) provide the most comparable estimate because their estimate is based on TBI that occurred in combat in Iraq. However, there are some important differences in methods that should be noted. For example, they present lifetime costs as opposed to single-year costs. In addition, they use a different method to account for productivity losses that is based on people's willingness to pay to avoid an injury. Moreover, the willingness-to-pay methodology incorporates additional costs that we do not capture, such as quality of life. While their comprehensive estimate includes lives lost, it is not broken out by type of injury, and thus the TBI-related mortality costs cannot be broken out.

Data and Assumptions Regarding Deployment-Related TBI and Costs

In this section, we lay out the data and assumptions we have made to generate our estimate of the number of cases. However, given the uncertainty surrounding the prevalence of TBI, particularly the breakdown between mild and more severe cases, in the results section we present both a total cost and a per-case cost of TBI. The per-case cost can then be used to generate different total cost estimates for different assumptions regarding the number of TBI cases and level of severity (i.e., mild versus moderate/severe) among veterans returning from OEF and OIF.

The Number of TBI Cases in 2005. The estimate of the number of deployment-related TBI cases in 2005 is taken from the *Medical Surveillance Monthly Report* (MSMR) (2007, p. 30). The MSMR identifies TBI cases using diagnosis codes (ICD-9s) from inpatient and outpatient records. As such, people who are experiencing symptoms of TBI but who have not been formally diagnosed are not reflected in this count. Therefore, the prevalence estimates used for this analysis are substantially lower than those generated in the survey discussed in Chapter Four, which used self-reported symptoms to screen for probable TBI. The report does not distinguish between mild and moderate/severe cases. To generate separate estimates for mild and moderate/severe cases of TBI, we assume, based on the statement of CBO Director Orszag (House of Representatives, 2007), that two-thirds of cases are mild and the remaining one-third are moderate/severe. In addition, to reflect the fact that some moderate/severe cases of TBI that occurred prior to 2005 will still require treatment and potentially have negative outcomes associated with their injury in 2005, we use data from the MSMR (2007) to include one-third of TBI cases for 2004 (the moderate/severe cases) and one-ninth of TBI cases from 2003. Using one-ninth of the cases from 2003 assumes that one-third of the moderate/severe cases that occurred in 2003 still require treatment in 2005. We expect that this is a very conservative estimate, because many moderate/severe cases of TBI require rehabilitative treatment and incur productivity losses for longer than three years. However, we were unable to obtain any additional data on this issue and thus only made use of the MSMR data that went back to 2003.

Using this approach, we estimated a total of 609 TBI cases in 2005, with 279 being new mild cases, 139 being new moderate/severe cases, and 191 being remaining moderate/severe cases from 2003 and 2004 (Table 6.12).

The Cost of Treatment for TBI and TBI-Related Outcomes. We were unable to obtain any data on the cost of treating TBI in the military or the VA; therefore, all treatment cost estimates are based on civilian populations. Similarly, information on standard treatments used for deployment-related TBI and the duration of use of these treatments and/or rehabilitation are not available. Thus, when developing our estimates of rehabilitation costs and productivity losses, we rely on information available on civilian TBI patients. Specific information used for generating these costs estimates is discussed below.

Treatment for TBI. We estimated the cost of TBI for three categories of treatment: acute hospital care, inpatient rehabilitation, and outpatient rehabilitation. We know from

Table 6.12
Number of Deployment-Related TBI Cases

Type of TBI Case	Number of Cases[a]
Mild cases in 2005	279
Moderate/severe cases in 2005	139
Moderate/severe cases from 2003–2004 remaining in 2005	191
Total	609

[a] Calculations based on data from MSMR (2007).

the MSMR the number of TBI cases seen in a hospital setting versus seen on an out-patient basis. Using this information, combined with the assumption that one-third of all new TBI cases are moderate/severe, we can allocate injuries as shown in Table 6.13.

The MSMR (2007) reported that 332 known TBI cases presented in military hospitals in 2005. Given that there were only 418 new TBI cases in 2005 in total, the number of hospitalizations for TBI exceeds our estimate of the number of moderate/severe TBI cases (which we assumed is one-third of the 418 cases, which equals 139). Thus, to determine the number of mild and moderate/severe cases that require acute hospital care, we assumed that all moderate/severe cases were hospitalized and that any remaining hospitalizations come from the mild-TBI category.

The average cost of acute hospital care for TBI is obtained on HCUPNet, which tabulates data from the National Inpatient Sample (NIS) of the Healthcare Cost and Utilization Project (HCUP). The HCUP NIS is an inpatient care database that contains all discharge data from a sample of community hospitals. In 2005, the NIS included data from 1,054 hospitals located in 37 states. The NIS contains clinical and resource use information and can be weighted to produce national estimates. To estimate the average cost of acute hospital treatment for mild and moderate/severe cases of TBI, we tabulated average charges for various Diagnosis-Related Groups (DRGs). DRGs are used to classify hospital patients into groups expected to have similar resource use.

Table 6.13
Treatment for TBI and Associated per-Case Costs

	Number of Cases	Average Cost per Case	
		High	Low
Acute Hospital Care[a]			
Mild cases	193	$21,346	$15,144
Moderate/severe cases	139	$73,443	$28,747
Inpatient Rehabilitation[b]			
Mild cases	0	N/A	N/A
Moderate/severe cases	139	$14,007	$14,007
Outpatient Rehabilitation[c]			
Mild cases	279	$1,487	$618
Moderate/severe cases	139	$1,487	$618
Remaining moderate/severe cases from 2003–2004	191	$1,487	$618

NOTE: N/A = Not applicable.

[a] SOURCE: Average cost per case calculated from the National Inpatient Sample of the Healthcare Cost and Utilization Project 2005 data.

[b] SOURCE: Buntin et al. (2006).

[c] SOURCE: GAO (2004).

Using the DRGs allowed us to generate different hospital costs for moderate/severe and mild TBI cases. To represent moderate/severe cases, we tabulated the average charge for the DRG titled "Craniotomy with Complications and Comorbidities" in the high-cost scenario and the DRG titled "Traumatic Stupor and Coma >1 hour" for the low-cost scenario. For mild cases, the high-cost estimate was tabulated for the DRG titled "Concussion with Complications and Comorbidities" and the low-cost scenario is based on "Concussion without Complications and Comorbidities."

We were unable to find data on the proportion of TBI cases that require inpatient rehabilitation. We found a study conducted on a civilian population, however, that used the Colorado TBI Registry and Follow-up System and determined that 35 percent of patients hospitalized with TBI injuries are still functionally disabled one year post-injury (Brooks et al., 1997). In the absence of similar data specific to military personnel, we made the conservative assumption that only moderate/severe cases of TBI will require inpatient rehabilitation. The cost of inpatient rehabilitation was taken from a technical report produced by RAND titled *Inpatient Rehabilitation Facility [IRF] Care Use Before and After Implementation of the IRF Prospective Payment System* (Buntin et al., 2006). From this report, it was possible to generate an average episode reimbursement rate cost for TBI-specific injuries, although the report did not allow us to distinguish mild injuries from severe injuries. In other words, we could generate only an average episode cost across all TBI cases requiring inpatient rehabilitation services. We recognize that Medicare reimbursement rates may not be reflective of the actual value of resources used in the treatment of TBI, particularly among military patients.[13] However, in the absence of accurate information on rehabilitation services used by the military, the Medicare reimbursement rate represents a reasonable approximation of what these services could cost if treated in the civilian sector.

The data on the utilization of outpatient rehabilitation services were very thin. In fact, we were unable to find any information on the typical pattern of use, that is, the number and type of visits a TBI patient would be expected to receive. In the absence of solid data, we assumed that all identified TBI patients receive some outpatient rehabilitative services. The estimated cost per case is taken from a GAO report on comprehensive outpatient rehabilitation facilities (GAO, 2004) that compares the average Medicare payment for outpatient therapy across different provider types in Florida. We used the average per-patient cost for Rehabilitation Agencies for the high-cost scenario and for Hospital Outpatient Departments for the low-cost scenario. While there may

---

[13]   Under the Inpatient Rehabilitation Facility Prospective Payment System, Medicare pays facilities a predetermined rate per episode that varies by case mix group and geographic factors, such as local area costs and poverty rate. The case mix group is determined by the patient's age, impairment, functional status (motor and cognitive) at admission, and additional co-morbidities of the population served in these facilities. Hence, the mix of injuries may differ from those observed among military personnel, leading to a difference in average cost of rehabilitation services. Given that military injuries are likely to be even more severe than civilian injuries, we expect that this Medicare reimbursement rate will underestimate the true cost per episode.

be differences in the average cost of care across geographic regions that treat military personnel, we could not identify another source containing rate information. Thus, we relied on the Florida-specific Medicare estimates and recognize this as another limitation of the current study.

Mortality and Associated Costs. To estimate the number of TBI-related deaths in 2005 (excluding deaths by suicide), we used data from Ivins et al. (2006) that examined trends in hospital admissions associated with TBI and related deaths in the U.S. Army as well as information from HCUP NIS on the percentage of TBI cases (defined by ICD-9 diagnosis codes 800-804, 850-854, 959.01) that resulted in death in the hospital. Ivins et al. (2006) report that in 1990 the TBI death rate per 100,000 active duty personnel was 4.7 and declined to 2.5 by 1999, a 42.3-percent reduction. These are peacetime data, however, and may not reflect the death rate during the OEF and OIF conflicts if the severity of injury is higher. Using the rate of 2.5 deaths per 100,000 active duty personnel, we calculated that 9 percent of moderate/severe cases result in death. We used this as the high-cost scenario, but realize that it is likely still rather conservative. For the low-cost scenario, we used an estimate of the percentage of TBI hospitalizations that result in death from the HCUP NIS, 6.8 percent of hospital cases (HCUPnet, no date). Table 6.14 shows the total number of deaths included in our estimates.

As in the earlier model of PTSD and major depression, we used an estimate of the value of a statistical life employed by Wallsten and Kosec (2005). We inflated their estimate to 2005 dollars, yielding a value of $7,057,700.

Suicide and Associated Costs. As reported in Part III of this monograph, research also has consistently shown that persons with TBI have a higher risk of suicide than persons without TBI (e.g., Simpson and Tate, 2002, 2005; Hibbard et al., 1998; Teasdale and Engberg, 2001). However, none of these studies was able to conclusively show a causal relationship. Therefore, to estimate the number of suicide attempts and completions attributable to TBI in the high-cost scenario, we used estimates from Simpson and Tate (2002) showing that, among outpatients with TBI, 23 percent reported suicide ideation and 18 percent reported having had a suicide attempt post-injury. That is, we assumed that 18 percent of the moderate/severe TBI cases resulted in attempted

Table 6.14
Mortality from Deployment-Related TBI and the Value of a Statistical Life

| | Number of Deaths | | Value of Statistical Life[a] |
	High	Low	
Mild cases	0	0	$7,057,700
Moderate/severe cases	13[b]	9[c]	$7,057,700

[a] SOURCE: Wallsten and Kosec (2005).

[b] SOURCE: Calculations based on Ivins et al. (2006).

[c] SOURCE: Calculations based on HCUP NIS (2005) data.

suicide. To determine the number of associated deaths, we used information from the *2006 Army Suicide Event Report* (U.S. Army, 2007) indicating that 8 percent of suicide attempts in the Army are successful. This calculation assumes that all post-TBI suicide attempts are caused by TBI, thus providing an upper bound. For the low-cost scenario, we assumed that none of the post-TBI suicide attempts is caused by TBI and therefore that the cost is not attributable to the condition.

To estimate the costs associated with suicide, we included the average medical cost for each attempt and the value of a statistical life when death occurs, as was done in the microsimulation model. The estimated cost of medical treatment for suicide attempts was taken from a recent article by Corso et al. (2007) showing the medical cost in 2000 dollars for a fatal suicide attempt ($2,596), a nonfatal hospitalized suicide attempt ($7,234), and a nonfatal, nonhospitalized suicide attempt ($1,139). We inflated the medical costs to 2005 dollars and used a weighted average cost of nonfatal attempts that are hospitalized (53 percent of cases) and nonhospitalized (47 percent of cases).[14] Assumptions regarding the number of suicide attempts, deaths, and associated costs are shown in Table 6.15.

Productivity Reductions and Associated Costs. TBI can influence productivity in two distinct ways. First, it can reduce employment, as patients deal with treatment and rehabilitation or adjust to new limitations caused by the injury. Second, it can reduce the amount of work that can be done while on the job, because of limitations caused by the injury. Our estimate of lost productivity attempts to measure productivity losses

Table 6.15
Suicide Attempts, Fatal Attempts, Associated Medical Costs, and the Value of a Statistical Life

Suicide Attempts	Number of Attempts[a]		Medical Costs per Attempt[b]	Value of Statistical Life[c]
	High	Low		
Nonfatal Attempts				
Mild cases	0	0	$4,937	N/A
Moderate/severe cases	25	0	$4,937	N/A
Fatal attempts				
Mild cases	0	0	$2,933	$7,057,700
Moderate/severe cases	2	0	$2,933	$7,057,700

NOTE: N/A = Not applicable.
[a] SOURCE: Calculations based on Simpson and Tate (2002).
[b] SOURCE: Corso et al. (2007).
[c] SOURCE: Wallsten and Kosec (2005).

---

[14] The weights are based on a personal communication with Ted Miller and unpublished data provided by Eduard Zaloshnja, Pacific Institute for Research and Evaluation, supporting Finkelstein, Corso, and Miller (2006).

associated with time unable to work and lower production when on the job. First, to capture reduced employment, we used information from a study by Boake et al. (2005) comparing the rate at which civilians return to work after experiencing a mild or moderate TBI with that of civilians experiencing a trauma not involving a head injury. Thus, the study attempts to isolate the effects of head trauma independent of other elements of trauma. The study follows patients treated with both injuries and assesses the number of people who are able to return to work at one month, three months, and six months post-injury. The results are presented by TBI severity and, in the case of mild TBI, those admitted to a hospital versus those treated in an emergency department and discharged. From these, the fraction of patients suffering from TBI who remain unable to work can be easily calculated. We used linear interpolation to construct rates of not working at months two, four, and five. We then combined information from this study with that reported by Salazar et al. (2000), who find that 90 percent of military personnel with moderate to severe closed head injury were employed one year post-injury. Using linear interpolation between this one-year mark and Boake et al.'s six-month estimate, we were able to fill in the rate of TBI-caused unemployment for each month in between. Table 6.16 shows the unemployment rates associated with TBI injury.

As noted above, the second way productivity might be affected by TBI is through reduced production by those who return to work with TBI. Wages are typically used as a measure of a worker's marginal productivity (or incremental production) on the job, because they represent what the firm is willing to pay the individual to work. To generate an estimate of reduced productivity on the job, we need information on the number of people who return to work with a serious disability caused by TBI and the extent to which this impacts their productivity. Very little evidence is available on which to base such an estimate. Johnstone, Mount, and Schopp (2003) found in one civilian population that average income among individuals with TBI was 48 percent lower one year after injury. And Brooks et al. (1997) suggest that 34 percent of hospitalized survivors of TBI injuries were still disabled one year after the injury.

Given the scarcity of information, particularly for the military population, we assumed that only individuals with a moderate/severe TBI injury were likely to expe-

Table 6.16
Unemployment Rates Associated with TBI Injury

	Percentage Unemployed at 1 Month[a]	Percentage Unemployed at 3 Months[a]	Percentage Unemployed at 6 Months[a]	Percentage Unemployed at 1 Year[b]
Mild TBI ED only	0.54	0.34	0.32	0.1
Mild TBI (hospitalized)	0.61	0.38	0.29	0.1
Moderate TBI (hospitalized)	0.85	0.65	0.6	0.1

[a] SOURCE: Boake et al. (2005)
[b] SOURCE: Salazar et al. (2000)

rience long-term disability severe enough to affect their income. Furthermore, we assumed that only those people who were unable to return to work after being off work for six months or longer would experience a reduction in pay, equivalent to a 48-percent annualized reduction.

Information on annual income converted to monthly income (by dividing by 12) was used to estimate the cost associated with lost productivity when considering both time spent not working and reduced productivity on the job. Because average income varies depending on the individual's military status, we obtained separate average-income figures for those in active duty and Reserve, and those who have left the military. The average income for reservists, $33,465, was taken from Wallsten and Kosec (2005), who calculate the average wage of reservists based on a weighted average of wages earned in civilian occupations by reservists in 2005. We took this average reservist income and added in Reserve personnel pay received from DoD, where Reserve personnel pay was calculated for an E-5 with 5 to 7 years of service. Based on these calculations, the average income for Reserve personnel was estimated to be $36,977. For active duty personnel, the average income, $61,460, was taken from the GAO Military Compensation Report (GAO, 2005) for 2004 and inflated to 2005 dollars. This compensation reflects cash compensation in the form of basic pay, housing allowances, and special incentives. For those who left the military in 2005 after returning from deployment, we used information on average income generated from full-time workers who are part of the 2005 National Compensation Survey (NCS), conducted by the Bureau of Labor Statistics (Department of Labor, 2006). According to the NCS, average annual income for 2005 was $39,629.

Estimates of the Cost of Deployment-Related TBI in 2005

Using the data and methods described above, we estimated the cost of deployment-related TBI to be between $90.6 and $135.4 million in 2005.

Table 6.17 presents the total and per-case cost estimates for 2005 overall and by injury severity for each cost category. As can be seen within and across cost categories, costs vary substantially by severity of injury. For mild TBI, the per-case cost for 2005 was estimated to be between $25,571 and $30,730. Because this estimate was built from diagnosed mild TBI, it likely reflects the cost of the more serious mild cases. Some cases of mild TBI go undiagnosed and untreated. These cases may incur some costs, but the costs will likely not be as high as those reported here. Since individuals who screen positively for probable TBI but who have not accessed the health care system or received a formal diagnosis may incur fewer costs, it would be inappropriate to apply these cost-per-case figures to the prevalence estimates for probable TBI discussed in Chapter Four. For moderate/severe cases, we estimated a range of $252,251 to $383,221.

In addition, we saw differences in the key cost drivers between mild and moderate/severe cases. For mild cases, Figure 6.6 shows that productivity losses account for 47

Table 6.17
Total and per-Case Costs of Deployment-Related TBI in 2005

	Overall		Mild		Moderate/Severe	
	High	Low	High	Low	High	Low
Treatment Costs						
Hospital acute care	$14,328,355	$6,918,625	$4,119,778	$2,922,792	$10,208,577	$3,995,833
Inpatient rehabilitation	$1,952,535	$1,952,535	0	0	$1,952,535	$1,952,535
Outpatient rehabilitation	$906,734	$376,941	$414,836	$172,453	$491,898	$204,489
Mortality Costs						
TBI-related deaths	$88,715,289	$66,709,380	0	0	$88,715,289	$66,709,380
Suicide Costs						
Deaths from suicide	$14,721,421	0	0	0	$14,721,421	0
Suicide attempts	$123,533	0	0	0	$123,533	0
Productivity Costs						
Unemployment (lost productivity)	$13,465,192	$13,465,192	$4,039,099	$4,039,099	$9,426,092	$9,426,092
Reduced wages for those working	$1,206,715	$1,206,715	0	0	$1,206,715	$1,206,715
Total cost of TBI	$135,419,773	$90,629,389	$8,573,713	$7,134,344	$126,846,060	$83,495,045
Total cost per case of TBI	$222,000	$148,573	$30,730	$25,571	$383,221	$252,251

percent to 57 percent and treatment accounts for 43 percent to 53 percent of total costs. Mortality and suicide costs are assumed to be zero for mild-TBI cases. For moderate/severe cases (Figure 6.7), mortality is the largest cost component, accounting for 70 percent to 80 percent of costs, while productivity losses account for 8 percent to 13 percent, treatment accounts for 7 percent to 10 percent, and suicide accounts for up to 12 percent of total costs.

The estimates presented thus far represent the costs of deployment-related TBI cases in 2005. We used an adjusted per-case cost estimate for 2005 to generate a total cost of all deployment-related TBI cases identified since September 2001 (2,726) as reported in *Serve, Support, Simplify*, the report of the President's Commission on Care for America's Returning Wounded Warriors (2007, p. 2). We adjusted the 2005 per-case cost estimate by eliminating the residual moderate/severe TBI cases from prior years, so that the per-case cost just reflects the costs incurred in the first year post-injury. This is done primarily because we did not have good information on the timing of the 2,726 TBI cases or on the pattern of treatment and productivity losses beyond one year. From the testimony of CBO Director Orszag, we assumed that one-third of

Figure 6.6
Total Cost of Mild TBI, by Cost Component and High/Low Scenario

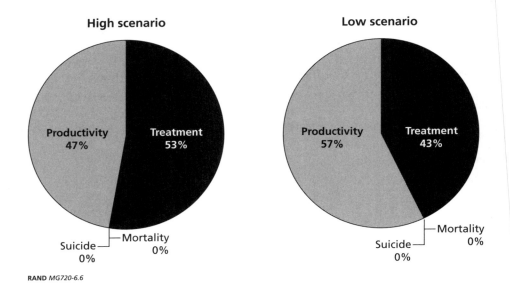

Figure 6.7
Total Cost of Moderate/Severe TBI, by Cost Component and High/Low Scenario

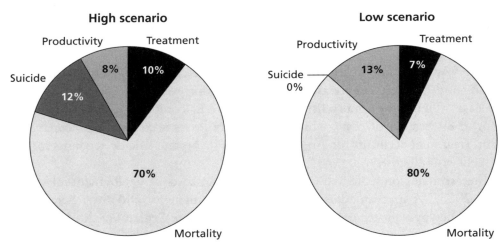

the total cases are moderate/severe and the remaining two-thirds are mild (House of Representatives, 2007). The estimates, shown in Table 6.18, indicate that total costs for TBI range between $554 million and $854 million, with moderate/severe cases accounting for approximately 92 percent of the total.

Several caveats regarding the total cost estimates must be considered. First, as noted above, the per-case cost includes only the costs incurred during the first year post-injury. For mild cases, this is probably reasonable. For moderate/severe cases, however, this is likely to understate the costs because it does not include the cost of treatment or any reduction in productivity that extends beyond the first year. Second, this estimate assumes that the per-case costs are constant over time; in reality, it is possible that medical technologies used to treat TBI changed over time, which would have an effect on costs. However, because we are considering a relatively short time frame (2001 through 2007), the effect of this assumption on the overall estimate is mitigated.

Limitations

A number of important caveats are associated with our general estimation strategy that should be noted. First and foremost, the estimates are imprecise because we did not have access to high-quality data on which to formulate many of the inputs in this calculation. Most findings were drawn from studies or cost information related to civilian patients, who likely experience very different types of TBI that could require very different treatment resources. Furthermore, the cost of those resources might differ for civilian versus military populations. Given the scarcity of reliable information related to the prevalence, treatment, and costs of TBI in the military, such assumptions are necessary. They clearly, however, introduce a conservative bias into the overall estimate that needs to be kept in mind when discussing the final cost estimates.

A second limitation is that the estimate is not comprehensive because we were unable to include a number of important cost categories, such as caregiver burden, substance abuse co-morbidity, TBI-related health problems, violence, and family functioning owing to a lack of data. Finally, our estimates include only costs incurred in a given year. Many of the effects and associated costs of TBI, particularly for those with moderate/severe injuries, will continue in the long term. We attempted to address this to

Table 6.18
Total Cost of Deployment-Related TBI

	Mild		Moderate/Severe		Total	
	High	Low	High	Low	High	Low
Number of cases	1,800	1,800	926	926	2,726	2,726
Per-case cost	$30,730	$25,571	$862,621	$549,183	$313,317	$203,438
Total	$55,314,277	$46,028,025	$798,786,794	$508,543,345	$854,101,071	$554,571,370

some extent by including a fraction of moderate/severe cases that occurred in 2003 and 2004 in the 2005 estimate. However, we expect that this is insufficient to capture the full costs of TBI in 2005. There are probably people who experienced a TBI between 2001 and 2003 who are still receiving treatment and who are incurring productivity losses. Therefore, our estimate, even the high scenario, is likely conservative.

Discussion

Despite these limitations, we believe that the estimates presented here provide useful information to policymakers regarding the costs associated with deployment-related TBI. The estimates show that the costs are substantial and are driven primarily by the loss of life and loss of productivity associated with TBI, rather than the treatment costs. The productivity losses could be mitigated by improving access to high-quality treatment for TBI. Rehabilitative services designed to help individuals increase functionality and return to work could increase employment and income among those employed.

A particularly striking result of this analysis is the fact that costs associated with mild TBI are an order of magnitude lower that costs associated with moderate or severe TBI. Based on our review of the evidence, we have little reason to believe that mild TBI would be associated with mortality—a large driver of costs for severe and moderate TBI. Moreover, mild TBI may not require inpatient rehabilitation. Given these very large differences in both costs and mortality outcomes, this analysis raises the question of whether it makes sense to group mild TBI with moderate and severe TBI when making policy decisions about how to care for injured servicemembers.

Conclusion

The costs associated with mental and cognitive conditions stemming from the conflicts in Afghanistan and Iraq are substantial. On a per-case basis, two-year post-deployment costs associated with PTSD are approximately $5,904 to $10,298, two-year post-deployment costs associated with major depression are approximately $15,461 to $25,757, and two-year post-deployment costs associated with co-morbid PTSD and major depression are approximately $12,427 to $16,884 (at 2007 price levels). These costs vary depending on whether or not we include the value of lives lost to suicide in our estimates; because suicide is a rare and uncertain event, cost estimates that exclude suicide-related mortality costs are more precise.

Annual costs associated with traumatic brain injury are even higher, ranging from $25,571 to $30,730 per case for mild cases in 2005 (or $27,259 to $32,759 at 2007 price levels[15]) and from $252,251 to $383,221 for moderate/severe cases in 2005 ($268,903

---

[15] We converted 2005 costs to 2007 levels using the July Consumer Price Index (CPI; the annual CPI for 2007 was not available as of this writing). The specific conversion ratio that we used is: 208.3/195.4 = 1.07.

to $408,519 at 2007 price levels). These estimates include treatment costs and costs associated with suicide, lost productivity, and death. However, our cost figures omit downstream costs stemming from substance abuse, domestic violence, homelessness, family strain, and several other factors. We also did not consider costs associated with implementing evidence-based treatment on a large scale (e.g., outreach, provider training) or spillover costs that might stem from increased contact with the health care system among veterans in need of mental health care.

Translating these cost estimates into a total dollar figure is challenging because there is uncertainty about the total number of cases in a given year, as well as the severity of those cases and the extent of co-morbidity among the three conditions. Despite these caveats, we estimated that the total cost of TBI in 2005 ranged from $90.6 to $135.4 million in 2005, which is equivalent to $96.6 to $144.4 million at 2007 prices. We applied an adjusted per-case cost to the total number of deployment-related TBI cases to generate an estimate of the total one-year post-deployment costs, which range between $591 and $910 million (2007 dollars). Within the first two years after returning from deployment, we estimate that costs associated with PTSD and major depression for 1.6 million servicemembers could range from $4.0 to $6.2 billion, depending on whether we include the costs of lives lost to suicide. These costs are for the number of servicemembers deployed since 2001 and the total number of TBI cases identified as of June 2007. Because total cost estimates are based on historical deployments and identified TBIs, most of the costs included in these estimates have already been incurred. However, since the conflicts in Afghanistan and Iraq are ongoing and the consequences of psychological and cognitive injuries may last for many years post-deployment, these figures are an underestimate of the total costs that will be incurred in the future.

Our results also suggest that lost productivity can be a large driver of costs. For PTSD and major depression, 55.3 to 94.5 percent of total costs can be attributed to reduced productivity; for mild TBI, productivity losses may account for between 47 and 57 percent of total costs. VA disability payments are intended to compensate veterans with Service-connected disabilities for reduced wages; as a result, these high productivity losses could potentially become the responsibility of the VA. Because severe TBI can lead to death, mortality is the largest component of cost for moderate to severe TBI, accounting for 70 to 80 percent of total costs.

The microsimulation model that we developed for PTSD and major depression suggested that there are potential cost savings associated with evidence-based treatment within the first two years after a servicemember returns to the United States, even without accounting for downstream costs stemming from substance abuse, homelessness, and other factors. In our estimates that include the cost of lives lost to suicide, we predict that evidence-based treatment for PTSD and major depression could save as much as $1.7 billion within two years post-deployment, or $1,063 per returning veteran. These cost savings come from increases in productivity, as well as reductions in the expected number of suicides. The benefits of evidence-based treatment are most pronounced for major depression; the benefits of evidence-based treatment for PTSD and co-morbid PTSD and major depression are sensitive to whether or not we include the value of lives lost to suicide in our cost estimates.

These findings lead to several recommendations regarding caring for veterans, as well as for understanding the costs associated with war-related psychological and cognitive injuries. First, cost studies that do not account for reduced productivity may significantly understate the true costs of the conflicts in Afghanistan and Iraq. Currently, there is limited information on how mental health conditions affect career outcomes within DoD. Given the large association between mental health status and productivity found in civilian studies, research that explores how active duty personnel's mental health status affects career outcomes would be valuable. Ideally, studies would consider how mental health conditions influence job performance, promotion within DoD, and transitions from DoD into the civilian labor force. In this chapter, we used data from civilian studies to estimate the relationship between a mental health condition and productivity among active duty personnel—in the absence of other information, these estimates are valuable. However, they could be improved upon with better data.

If our estimates of productivity loss are appropriate for the active duty population, our findings suggest that—from a societal perspective—evidence-based treatment for PTSD and major depression would pay for itself within two years. Given these results, investments in evidence-based treatment might make sense from DoD's standpoint not only because of higher remission and recovery rates but also because it would increase productivity of servicemembers. Hoge, Auchterlonie, and Milliken (2006) show that retention within DoD is higher among those without a deployment-related mental health condition. More generally, to the extent that DoD and the VA demonstrate a commitment to providing injured servicemembers the most effective care, as well as minimizing costs that accrue to disabled servicemembers, retention and recruitment might be improved. Increased productivity among servicemembers who have separated from DoD might also be a policy goal because higher productivity reduces the need for disability payments, which are intended to offset lower earnings among servicemembers who have a reduced ability to work because of a Service-connected disability. Finally, as a society, we may benefit by investing in evidence-based treatment for returning servicemembers, not only because it is our responsibility to provide these individuals with effective treatment but also because doing so may reduce downstream costs stemming from unemployment, need for disability payments, and public assistance. Had we been able to account for omitted cost components—such as substance abuse, domestic violence, and homelessness—the savings to society would likely be even greater.

Appendix 6.A: Model Map

NOTE: r^* denotes a random number that is drawn separately for each bullet. *Day 1* refers to the first day home following deployment.

1. Create synthetic cohort.

- Determine the number of individuals returning from OIF/OEF.
- Assign age, gender, race, education, branch, reserve status, rank, and civilian labor force status (if individuals leave full-time active duty; based on March 2007 Current Population Survey).
- Reservists immediately transition to nonmilitary civilian status on Day 1.

2. Assign mental health status at return.

- To reduce computing time, we ran a simulation with a relatively high number of individuals with mental health conditions and then weighted costs to reflect prevalence estimates derived from the literature (15 percent of all individuals get PTSD within two years, 50 percent of all PTSD is co-morbid with depression, and 7.2 percent of individuals get depression alone).
- Randomly assign 60 percent of the sample to PTSD; 20 percent will have PTSD on Day 1 and 40 percent will have PTSD onset during the simulation (the quarter for delayed-onset PTSD is determined randomly).
- 50 percent of those with PTSD will also have co-morbid depression (if it is delayed-onset PTSD/depression, the depression will be delayed, too).
- Randomly assign depression alone to 75 percent of the sample that will not have PTSD during the simulation.

3. Allow instantaneous attrition for full-time active duty.

- If $r^* \leq A^*$, individual leaves military on Day 1.
- A^* is based on Hoge, Auchterlonie, and Milliken (2006) and depends on mental health status.
- Individuals who leave the military at this point do not enter the Reserves.

The remaining sections of this model map describe what happens in every quarter (Q). The simulation used for this monograph is based on two years ($Q_1 - Q_8$).

4. Did the individual attempt suicide in Q_t?

- If individual has a mental health condition and $r^* \leq S^*$, he or she attempts suicide.
- S^* is based on Gibbons et al. (2007) and varies by age.

- Because attempt probabilities are annual and the model is updated quarterly, we randomly chose the quarter when a suicide attempt can occur.

5. Did the individual complete suicide in Q_t?

- If individual attempts suicide and $r^* \leq F^*$, the suicide attempt is fatal.
- F^* varies by military status. (F^* equals 8.6 percent for active duty personnel and 4 percent for non–active duty or discharged personnel; various sources.)
- Suicide is the only way someone can die in the model.

6. What was the individual's civilian labor force status (CLFS) during Q_t?

- Irrelevant if full-time military, because we assume no moonlighting.
- Initial CLFS (full, part, or unemployed) is based on distribution of veterans in the 2007 CPS.
- CLFS can change only when an individual experiences a change in mental health status. These probabilities are based on Savoca and Rosenheck (2000).

7. How much did the individual earn in Q_t?

- Military pay for active duty servicemembers and reservists is taken from official military pay tables (depends on rank and years of service).
- Full-time military personnel also receive a subsistence allowance (depends on rank) and a housing allowance (depends on number of dependents; we use a weighted average).
- Civilian wages for non–active duty and discharged servicemembers come from wage regressions based on veterans in the 2006 CPS. Predictors include age, gender, race/ethnicity, education, and marital status (this last variable is not tracked in the simulation, and we impute the sample average).
- We ran separate regressions for full- and part-time workers.
- Those who are unemployed were assigned a wage = 0.
- For individuals with a mental health condition, wages were decremented based on rates reported in Savoca and Rosenheck (2000).
- Wages in quarter of fatal suicide (and in subsequent quarters) = 0.

8. Did the individual enter mental health treatment in Q_t?

- To reduce computing time, we ran a simulation with a relatively high number of individuals entering treatment and then weighted costs to reflect estimates derived from the literature.
- If individual has a mental health condition and $r1^* \leq 0.66$, the individual receives treatment.

- If individual receives treatment and $r2^* \leq 0.50$, the individual receives evidence-based treatment instead of usual care.
- In our status quo estimates, we re-weighted so that 30 percent of individuals with mental health conditions receive treatment and 30 percent of treatment is evidence-based.
- If treatment in Q_t has an effect, we assumed that we would not see that effect until the beginning of Q_{t+1}.
- If treatment in Q_t is unsuccessful, the individual has an 80 percent chance of continuing the same course of treatment in Q_{t+1}.
- Individuals cannot switch between evidence-based treatment and usual care.

9. Did the individual leave full-time active duty at the end of Q_t?

- If $r1^* \geq A^*$, individual leaves DoD.
- A^* is based on data reported by Hoge, Auchterlonie, and Milliken (2006), and it varies depending on mental health status and length of time since returning home.
- Attrition only occurs at the end of a quarter.
- If individual has a nonfatal suicide attempt and $r2^* \leq 0.80$, the individual leaves military.

10. Did the individual leave full-time active duty and enter the Reserves at the end of Q_t?

- If individual leaves DoD and $r^* \leq R^*$, individual joins the Reserves.
- R^* varies depending on rank and branch.
- Individuals leaving because of suicide attempt do not enter the Reserves.

11. Was individual promoted to a higher rank at the beginning of Q_{t+1}?

- This is not a function of mental health.
- Everyone in the military is eligible for a promotion.
- If $r^* \leq P^*$, individual is promoted.
- P^* is based on the *Defense Manpower Requirements Report* (Department of Defense, OUSD, 2007) and varies depending on rank and branch.
- Because promotion probabilities are annual and model is updated quarterly, the quarter of promotion consideration is randomly assigned across the year.
- Individuals can be promoted only once during the simulation.

12. What was the individual's mental health status at the beginning of Q_{t+1}?

- Depends on whether treatment was received in Q_t, the effectiveness of that treatment, and the natural course of the disorder (remission, delayed-onset, and relapse).
- If $r1^* \leq T^*$, person remits.
- T^* varies with treatment and type of mental health condition.
- If $r2^* \leq E^*$, then person relapses.
- E^* varies with illness, and in some specifications, with treatment.
- Because relapse probabilities are biennial and model is updated quarterly, the quarter of relapse consideration is randomly assigned across a two-year period after the illness remits. In some cases, the quarter of relapse consideration is greater than eight; thus, the individual does not relapse during the simulations.
- If quarter of delayed-onset PTSD or PTSD/depression = t, illness begins at the beginning of Q_{t+1}.

Appendix 6.B: Model Architecture, Assumptions, and Parameters

Model Dynamics

Our model has a two-year time horizon, and the information in the model is updated quarterly. At the beginning of the model, each individual is assigned a mental health status and probability of getting evidence-based or usual care conditional on mental health. Modeled individuals are then assigned an employment status (active duty, employed full-time or part-time in the civilian sector, or not employed), a wage rate conditional on employment, a probability of having a suicide attempt, and a probability of death conditional on a suicide attempt. We assumed that all servicemembers of the Reserve Component immediately return to civilian status when they return from OEF or OIF (this is the entry point into the model). Mental health status affects employment, treatment entry (only individuals with mental health conditions may enter treatment), and suicide-related outcomes. Mental health treatment affects the probability of recovering from a mental health condition, and—in some scenarios—the probability of relapse.

At each quarter, individuals make transitions across mental health status, treatment status, and employment status. Lower employment probabilities, wage reductions, suicide risks, and an increased probability of military attrition were assigned to individuals who suffer from a mental health condition.

Modeled Individuals

We populated our model using a cohort of "synthetic" individuals who have returned from deployment to Iraq or Afghanistan at the rank of E-5.[1] These individuals were assigned race/ethnicity, gender, educational attainment, component status (Reserve/Guard or active duty), and military branch (Army, Navy, Air Force, or Marine Corps). Gender, component, and branch assignments were based on data on servicemembers completing OIF deployments in 2005 (*Medical Surveillance Monthly Report*, 2007). Education levels for E-5s were based on data reported by the Congressional Budget Office (2004) and the Defense Manpower Data Center (2000); race/ethnicity assignments were based on the racial and ethnic distribution of all enlistees in 2005 (DoD, OUSDPR, 2005). Because we did not have access to data describing the joint distribution of age, rank, and years of service among returning veterans, we made the simplifying assumption that everyone in our synthetic cohort is a 25-year-old enlistee with 5 to 7 years of service, returning from

---

[1]   This is likely an underestimate of the number of E-5s returning from OIF or OEF in 2005. If we assume that 50 percent of the E-5s or E-6s completing OIF deployments in 2005 were E-5s, we get over 52,000 troops from all four branches for OIF alone (*Medical Surveillance Monthly Report*, 2007).

the conflict at a rank of E-5.[2] In sensitivity analyses, we considered alternative combinations of age, rank, and years of service, including officer-level ranks.

States. The model contains 31 states defined by employment status, mental health status, mental health treatment status, and suicide-related death. Figure 6.B.1 illustrates the states in the model, with arrows indicating possible transitions across states.[3] A *mental health condition* can be any one of three conditions: PTSD, major depression, or co-morbid PTSD/major depression. As a simplifying assumption, we constrained individuals from switching across conditions. This implies that, while some individuals in our model have a single mental health condition and some have co-morbid mental health conditions, no one with a single condition will ever develop co-morbid conditions, and no one with co-morbid conditions will ever recover from one co-morbidity but not the other.

Mental Health Status Assignments. An individual's initial assignment into a mental health state is based on prevalence data reported in Hoge et al. (2004) and Grieger et al. (2006). We assumed that, immediately after returning from OEF/OIF, 5 percent of the sample has PTSD and 7 percent of the sample has major depression alone. Delayed-onset PTSD can develop at any time during our two-year time horizon, such that an additional 10 percent of the sample will develop PTSD during the two-year period considered in the model. This rate of growth in PTSD over time corresponds to growth rates reported in Wolfe et al. (1999) in an 18-to-24-month analysis of PTSD among veterans of the first Gulf War. In addition, the rate is roughly consistent with Milliken, Auchterlonie, and Hoge (2006), who report that 6 percent of Army soldiers meeting screening criteria for PTSD immediately after return from OIF, with an additional 8 percent meeting screening criteria at a median of six months later. Our model assumptions also imply that 50 percent of individuals with PTSD develop the condition after six months, a figure that is consistent with rates of delayed-onset PTSD among military populations reported by Andrews et al. (2007).[4]

From figures reported in Grieger et al. (2006), we assumed that 50 percent of individuals with PTSD also have co-morbid major depression. Because mental health outcomes in our model are assigned stochastically, realized rates of mental health conditions will be variable. However, the model is designed so that, on average, 7 percent

---

2   Age, rank, and years of service are highly interrelated, and all three of these characteristics have a large bearing on wage outcomes—a key element of cost in our model. Given the lack of available data, we felt that it would be inappropriate to use assumptions to jointly impute these characteristics, since inaccuracies in our imputation process could have a large effect on projected costs.

3   For ease of presentation, Figure 6.B.1 illustrates only a single, generic mental health condition. The states in the full model consist of 3 employment states times 1 non-illness state (=3), plus 3 employment states times 3 mental health condition states times 3 mental health conditions (=27), plus death, for a total of 31 states.

4   Andrews et al. (2007) report that, in a sample of six studies of military populations, the weighted average proportion of PTSD cases with delayed onset of six months was 38 percent. Three of the six studies reported delayed-onset rates of 50 percent or higher (and a fourth reported a delayed onset rate of 49 percent).

Figure 6.B.1
Model Dynamics

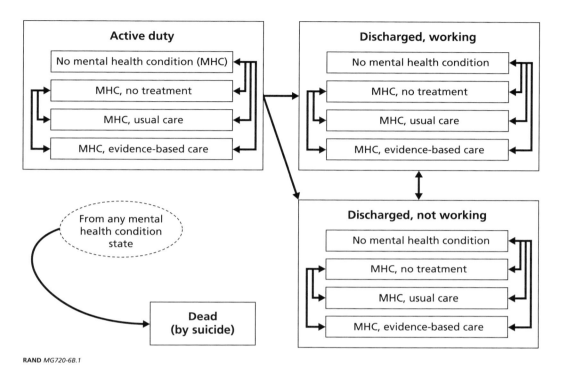

RAND *MG720-6B.1*

of the sample will experience at least one bout of major depression, 7.5 percent of the sample will experience at least one bout of PTSD, and 7.5 percent of the sample will experience at least one bout of co-morbid PTSD and major depression during the two-year projection interval.

Mental Health Treatment and Treatment Assignments. Evidence-based therapies, described in Table 6.B.1, are based on published guidance, recent randomized controlled trials showing effectiveness, and the 2007 Institute of Medicine report on evidence-based treatment for PTSD. Because guidance for major depression varies depending on the severity of the illness and the patient's response to therapies, we allowed three potential treatment regimes among those getting evidence-based care for major depression. Specifically, 37.5 of individuals receiving evidence-based care for major depression will get regime 1 (drugs only), 37.5 will get regime 2 (psychotherapy only), and 25 percent will get regime 3 (combined therapy). We assumed that individuals receiving combined therapy, as well as individuals receiving evidence-based treatment for co-morbid PTSD/major depression, will take maintenance medication for a one-year period should their symptoms remit following an episode of treatment.

Usual care for PTSD and major depression, shown in Table 6.B.2, reflects the fact that it is common for individuals with mental health conditions to receive suboptimal

Table 6.B.1
Evidence-Based Treatment for PTSD and Major Depression

Condition	Medication over 12 Weeks	Psychotherapy over 12 Weeks	Maintenance Medication Required?	Source(s)
PTSD only	Daily SSRI	Ten 75–80-minute sessions of psychotherapy	No	Foa, Davidson, and Frances (1999), Institute of Medicine (2007); Schnurr et al. (2007)
Major depression only				
Regime 1	Daily SSRI	None	No	Keller et al. (2000), Friedman and Detweiler-Bedell (2004), De Maat et al. (2006), Pampallona and Bollini (2004), Ludman et al. (2007), Whooley and Simon (2000)
Regime 2	None	Ten 45–50-minute sessions of psychotherapy	No	
Regime 3	Daily SSRI	Ten 45–50-minute sessions of psychotherapy	Yes	
Co-morbid PTSD/ major depression	Daily SSRI	Ten 75–80-minute sessions of psychotherapy	Yes	Foa, Davidson, and Frances (1999)

NOTE: SSRI = selective serotonin reuptake inhibitor

Table 6.B.2
Usual Care for PTSD and Major Depression

Condition	Medication over 12 Weeks	Psychotherapy over 12 Weeks	Maintenance Medication Required?	Source(s)
PTSD, co-morbid PTSD/ major depression	32% get daily SSRI, 48% get daily SSRI for 1 month	3.2 50-minute sessions	No	Rosenheck and Fontana (2007), Simon et al. (2004)
Major depression only	26% get an SSRI; of these, 60% get the recommended dose and 40% discontinue after 1 month	100% get 1 visit with a PCP; 15% get a visit with a mental health specialist; 38% get 2 30-minute sessions of counseling	No	Young et al. (2001), Simon et al. (2004)

NOTE: SSRI = selective serotonin reuptake inhibitor; PCP = primary care provider

levels of medication and psychotherapy. In the absence of comprehensive information on usual care for veterans with co-morbid PTSD and major depression, we assume that these individuals get the same treatment as individuals with PTSD only.

Employment Assignments. We assumed that individuals in the Reserve Component convert immediately to civilian status on returning from OEF/OIF, and that those in the Active Component remain active for at least three months following their return home (unless they commit suicide). Those who return to civilian status are assigned employment probabilities (working full-time, working part-time, or not working) based on employment probabilities observed among veterans of a similar age range in the 2007 Current Population Survey. Conceivably, individuals who leave DoD may be unemployed for several months before finding a job in the civilian sector. Because we did not have data on employment during this transitional period, we made the assumption that employment probabilities are similar to the employment outcomes found in the CPS veteran population.

Cohort Used for Model Runs. Based on figures reported in the *Medical Surveillance Monthly Report* (2007), we determined that there were approximately 50,000 E-5s who returned from OIF in 2005. We initially populated our model with a cohort of 50,000 individuals to represent the actual number of E-5s returning from deployment. However, it took several hours for our model to run, and we still had a very small number of individuals receiving evidence-based treatment, causing model results to be volatile. To address this problem, we reduced the model cohort to 20,000 but allowed an equal number of people to experience each possible mental health and treatment combination. We then estimated costs for a cohort of 50,000 people by re-weighting the costs in each model cell to reflect the expected number of people in each group.

State Transitions. Individuals in the model can move across states, as described by the arrows in Figure 6.B.1. State transitions in the model include transitions out of the military, transitions into and out of the civilian labor force, remission and relapse following a mental health condition, transitions into and out of mental health treatment, and death via suicide. Each of these is described in more detail below.

Transitions out of the Military. Attrition from the military is based on rates reported by Hoge, Auchterlonie, and Milliken (2006), who found that soldiers and marines returning from OEF/OIF who meet screening criteria for mental health risk have greater attrition from DoD than those without mental health risk.[5] Specifically, within one year of return, 21 percent of those with a mental health condition had left the Service, versus 16 percent of those without. Because the study does not report separate attrition rates by type of mental health condition, we assumed that attrition is the same regardless of condition.

Among those who leave the Active Component, we assumed that a certain percentage will join the Reserves. Given the statistics provided by the Army Human Resources Policy Directorate (also known as the Army G-1), we assumed that 21 percent of enlisted soldiers and 15 percent of Army officers join the Reserves immediately after leaving the active duty force. Although we could not find data to validate Reserve transition rates for the other branches of the Services, we communicated with several DoD researchers who believed that transition rates were substantially lower for the Navy, Air Force, and Marine Corps. We therefore assumed that, among servicemembers leaving the Active Component of the Navy, Air Force, or Marine Corps, 11 percent of enlisted personnel and 5 percent of officers directly transition into the Reserves.

---

[5] *Mental health risk* in Hoge, Auchterlonie, and Milliken (2006) is based on a positive response to any of the mental health items included in the Post-Deployment Health Assessment (PDHA), including a modified version of the two-item Patient Health Questionnaire (PHQ-2) and a four-item PTSD screener.

In addition to their civilian wages, reservists are assigned a drill pay to reflect compensation for military service.[6] Since we did not have any data on the relationship between a mental health condition and the probability of joining the Reserves, we assumed that a mental health condition has no influence on the probability of joining the Reserves. This assumption is likely to be conservative, given that the civilian studies have found that a mental health condition can substantially reduce the probability of employment (Ettner, Frank, and Kessler, 1997; Stewart et al., 2003; Wang et al., 2007).

Transitions into and out of the Civilian Labor Force. Those who have left the military have a probability of joining the civilian labor force as either a full-time or a part-time worker, based on probabilities observed among veterans in the 2007 CPS. When a person has an active mental health condition, we reduced the probability of employment using figures reported by Savoca and Rosenheck (2000).[7] Specifically, relative to baseline probabilities reported in the CPS, those with PTSD are 8.6 percentage points less likely to be currently working, and those with major depression or co-morbid PTSD and major depression are 7.0 percentage points less likely to be currently working. We did not allow labor force participation to have an influence on mental health status.

Remission and Relapse Following a Mental Health Condition. All individuals in our model have a probability of experiencing remission following the onset of the mental health condition. Individuals receiving treatment have a higher probability of remission than those not receiving treatment, and individuals with evidence-based care have a higher probability of remission than those with usual care. Table 6.B.3 shows the probability of remission following an episode of treatment for each illness and type of care.

Conditional on recovery, individuals in our model also have a probability of relapse. Among those with PTSD or co-morbid major depression and PTSD, 55 percent of those receiving any treatment will relapse within two years, based on rates reported in Perconte, Griger, and Bellucci (1989). Because few studies have examined relapse among veterans who have recovered from PTSD, and because the sample in Perconte, Griger, and Bellucci (1989) may have had unusually severe symptoms, our lower-bound cost estimate reduces this relapse rate to 25 percent over two years. Although it is plausible that individuals who received evidence-based treatment might have lower rates of relapse than individuals who received usual care or no care, we did not have any data to confirm this hypothesis or to quantify the magnitude of the dif-

---

[6]   Drill pay information came from Department of Defense, "Reserve Drill Pay," Web page, no date-b.

[7]   Dohrenwend et al. (2006) argue that the data set that Savoca and Rosenheck use (the National Survey of the Vietnam Generation) overestimates PTSD. If anything, we expected this would bias downward the relationship between PTSD and labor force outcomes, since respondents flagged as having PTSD will include some individuals without a mental health condition.

Table 6.B.3
Remission Probabilities Following Three Months of Illness

	Treatment Assignment			
Condition(s)	Evidence-Based Treatment	Usual Care	No Care	Sources
PTSD, co-morbid PTSD and major depression	39%	30%	~5%[a]	Schnurr et al. (2007) Kessler et al. (1995) Wolfe et al. (1999)
Major depression alone	48%	40%	12%	Keller et al. (2000) Dimidjian et al. (2006) Ludman et al. (2007) Wells et al. (1992) Kocsis et al. (1988)

[a] Remission rates were derived from Wolfe et al. (1999).

ferential. As a result, we assumed that the probability of relapse is constant, regardless of treatment condition.

The baseline relapse rate for major depression is 54 percent over two years, based on a meta-analysis of 28 studies of relapse following major depression treated successfully with cognitive-behavioral therapy (Vittengl et al., 2007). While the average two-year relapse rate found in this analysis was 54 percent, the range varied between 15 and 85 percent. Moreover, the 54-percent figure does not include relapse rates for usual care or no care. Melfi et al. (1998) found that patients treated for major depression with at least four prescriptions of an antidepressant had lower relapse rates over 18 months than patients who discontinued treatment early. However, the proportion of patients experiencing relapse in this study (approximately 26 percent in the continuous-treatment group and 36 percent in the discontinued-treatment group) was far lower than the average rate reported in Vittengl et al. (2007). As a result, we used the Melfi et al. (1998) figures for our lower-bound cost estimate. For our upper-bound relapse estimate, we inflated the 54-percent baseline figure by 38 percent to get a predicted two-year relapse rate of 75 percent for individuals with usual care or no care. The 38-percent inflation rate comes from the relative increase in relapse for those who discontinued care in Melfi et al. (1998) (i.e., (36/26) = 1.38).

Transitions into and out of Mental Health Treatment. The probability of receiving treatment conditional on having a mental health condition is a key policy parameter in our model. As discussed in Chapter Five, rates of evidence-based care are relatively low in the civilian population, and rates may be even lower among veterans returning from OEF and OIF. In our "status quo" scenario, we assumed that 30 percent of veterans with a mental health condition receive any care and that 30 percent of these individuals (9 percent of those who are sick) receive usual care. We then altered these probabilities to evaluate the potential for cost savings if a larger share of individuals received any treatment and if a larger share of individuals received evidence-based treatment.

We assumed that those who have an unsuccessful treatment episode (i.e., they are still sick after 90 days of treatment) have an 80-percent chance of continuing treatment in the next quarter, regardless of whether they received evidence-based or usual care.

Suicide Attempts, Suicide Completions, and Death. The probability of a suicide attempt comes from Gibbons et al. (2007), who report attempted suicide rates for depressed veterans by age group.[8] A recent study (Zivin et al., 2007) finds that depressed veterans with PTSD have a lower probability of suicide than depressed veterans without PTSD. Our baseline estimates use the age-specific attempted suicide rates reported by Gibbons et al. (2007) for all three mental health conditions—for veterans between the ages of 18 and 25 with a mental disorder, the annual probability of a suicide is 1.1 percent. In our lower-bound scenario, we discounted this rate by a factor of 0.75 for individuals with PTSD or co-morbid PTSD and major depression, based on the relative differences in suicide probabilities found in Zivin et al. (2007).[9]

Conditional on attempting suicide, the probability of death is 8.6 percent, the rate reported in the *2006 Army Suicide Event Report* (U.S. Army, 2007). For individuals who have been discharged from DoD, we assumed that the success rate conditional on an attempt is 4.0 percent (Goldsmith et al., 2002).

We assumed that 80 percent of active duty personnel who have a suicide attempt will leave the military within 90 days. This assumption stems from conversations with DoD personnel suggesting a low command tolerance for retaining individuals who have attempted suicide, as well as a study (Hoge et al., 2002) finding high rates of attrition for servicemembers hospitalized for mental health conditions. We further assumed that individuals discharged for attempting suicide will not join the Reserves.

DoD Promotion Probabilities. Individuals on active duty have a probability of being promoted in each quarter, based on promotion rates observed in the 2007 *Defense Manpower Requirements Report* (DoD OUSDPR, 2006). Tracking promotions within DoD is important because wage is almost completely determined by an individual's rank. Because the transitions in the *Defense Manpower Requirements Report* are reported on an annual basis, we randomly assigned a quarter when eligibility for promotion and promotion completions will be considered.

---

[8]   We used "before treatment" attempted suicide rates reported in Gibbons et al. (2007, Table 5). Veterans in this study were observed for an average of 297 days prior to treatment. We assumed that the suicide attempt rate represents an annual probability; this is likely to be a conservative estimate, given that the mean observation period was slightly less than one year.

[9]   Zivin et al. (2007) found 90.6 suicides per 100,000 person-years among depressed veterans, compared with 68.2 suicides per 100,000 person-years among veterans with co-morbid PTSD and depression. The ratio of these two figures, which we used to deflate our age-specific suicide attempt rates for PTSD, is 0.75.

Costs.

Treatment Costs. The cost of psychotherapy, visits with primary care physicians, and visits with psychiatrists come from TRICARE and Medicare reimbursement rates.[10] Because TRICARE reimbursement rates reported by DoD are state-specific, we took a weighted average, using counts of the number of deployed troops from each state (DoD, 2007). TRICARE reimbursement rates were assigned to active duty personnel, and Medicare reimbursement rates were assigned to those who have left DoD.

Drug costs for DoD personnel come from the Department of Defense Pharmacoeconomic Center (2004), and drug costs for non–active duty or discharged servicemembers come from the 2007 *Red Book* (Fleming, 2006) and Dobscha et al. (2007). Drug costs vary substantially depending on where an individual seeks treatment. According to the 2007 *Red Book* (Fleming, 2006), the price of a 30- to 40-milligram dose of fluoxetine is approximately $5.34 in the civilian health care sector; this compares with a price of $0.05 for a 40-milligram dose faced by DoD and the VA (Dobscha, Winterbottom, and Snodgrass, 2007; DoD Pharmacoeconomic Center, 2004). While we assumed that all active duty personnel get care through DoD, discharged veterans can seek care either through the VA health care system or through private health insurance plans provided by an employer, a spouse's employer, or an alternative source. In our baseline projections, we assumed that 35 percent of discharged veterans seek mental health care through the VA; this assumption is based on a Veterans Health Administration briefing stating that 35 percent of OEF/OIF veterans have accessed the VA health system (Veterans Health Administration, 2007). In our upper-bound cost scenario, we assumed that all discharged veterans get prescriptions through the private sector; in our lower-bound scenario, we assumed that all discharged veterans get care through the VA. In all model scenarios, we assumed that everyone who receives an anti-depressant prescription gets generic Prozac (fluoxetine), one of the least expensive selective serotonin reuptake inhibitors available on the market. This assumption is conservative, because some individuals will likely receive more expensive, brand-name drugs. Table 6.B.4 shows the costs for a three-month course of treatment that we estimate for each condition and treatment combination.

Wages. Civilian wages were estimated using a regression framework that draws on data from the 2006 Current Population Survey. The regression sample is limited to veterans who are currently working and who report positive earnings. For individuals with a mental health condition, predicted wages were reduced using rates reported by Savoca and Rosenheck (2000). Specifically, wages were reduced by 15.75 percent for individuals with PTSD and by 45.23 percent for individuals with major depression or co-morbid PTSD and major depression. Savoca and Rosenheck (2000) analyze the

---

[10] TRICARE reimbursement rates were found at TRICARE, "Allowable Charges," Web page, no date. Medicare reimbursement rates were found at Department of Health and Human Services, Centers for Medicare and Medicaid Services, "Physician Fee Schedule Search," Web page, no date.

Table 6.B.4
Treatment Cost Estimates Used in Model

Condition(s)	DoD	Civilian, Baseline	Civilian, Lower-Bound	Civilian, Upper-Bound
Evidence-Based Treatment				
PTSD	$1,374.48	$1,658.34	$1,334.70	$1,810.80
Major depression	$585.56	$1,099.16	$568.75	$1,349.03
Co-morbid PTSD/ major depression	$1,392.73	$2,989.13	$1,352.95	$3,759.90
Usual Care				
PTSD	$298.19	$444.93	$289.58	$518.11
Major depression	$239.57	$294.09	$232.38	$323.16
Co-morbid PTSD/ major depression	$298.19	$444.93	$289.58	$518.11

NOTE: The civilian baseline estimate assumes that 35 percent of discharged personnel get care through the VA; the lower-bound estimate assumes that all discharged personnel get care through the VA; and the upper-bound assumes that no discharged personnel get care through the VA.

relationship between wages and a mental health condition in a population of Vietnam veterans; however, for major depression, Savoca and Rosenheck's wage effect is high relative to similar studies of the civilian population. For example, Ettner, Frank, and Kessler (1997) find that employed men with a mental health condition have wage rates that are 9 to 20 percent lower than their counterparts without a mental health condition. Because Savoca and Rosenheck's major depression figure may be high, we reduced the wage penalty for major depression in our lower-bound cost estimate. Instead of a 45-percent wage reduction, our lower-bound estimate assumes a 15.75-percent wage reduction—this is equivalent to the wage reduction for PTSD and is approximately the midpoint of the wage reduction found in Ettner, Frank, and Kessler (1997).

Wages for active duty personnel were calculated by adding an individual's basic pay, housing allowance, and subsistence allowance as reported by the Office of the Secretary of Defense.[11] Because housing allowance varies depending on whether the individual has dependents, we took a weighted average, assuming that half of all returning servicemembers have dependents.[12] DoD basic pay is almost completely determined by rank and years of service. As a result, a mental health condition will not influence DoD salaries through a direct reduction in wage. However, given the civilian literature summarized in Part III/Chapter Five finding a strong association between a mental health

---

[11] DoD, "Military Pay and Benefits" Web page (DoD, 2008b).

[12] This is consistent with Hoge, Auchterlonie, and Milliken (2006), who report that approximately 50 percent of returning servicemembers are married.

condition and reduced wages (Ettner, Frank, and Kessler, 1997; Savoca and Rosenheck, 2000), higher missed days at work (Druss, Rosenheck, and Sledge, 2000; Kessler, Borges, and Walters, 1999), and poorer work performance (Wang et al., 2004; LeBlanc et al., 2007), we thought it was likely that a mental health condition would indirectly reduce DoD salaries through a decreased likelihood of promotion. Because we had no data that would enable us to quantify this effect, our baseline scenario assumes that productivity within DoD is reduced by half of the civilian productivity-reduction factor found in Savoca and Rosenheck (2000). Thus, for a servicemember with PTSD, DoD wages were reduced by a factor of 7.88 percent; for a servicemember with major depression or co-morbid PTSD and major depression, DoD wages were reduced by a factor of 22.62 percent. In our low-cost scenario, we assumed that a mental health condition has no effect on wages within DoD.

Suicide Costs. Health care costs attributable to suicide are based on Corso et al. (2007), who report medical costs associated with suicide attempts and completions by age and gender. We assumed that medical costs associated with suicide are equivalent for those in DoD and those in the civilian sector. We assessed the cost of lives lost to suicide using published estimates of the value of a statistical life. Viscusi and Aldy (2003) review this literature and find that estimates of the value of a statistical life based on wage-risk trade-offs have ranged from $4 million to $9 million. In an analysis of the costs of TBI, Wallsten and Kosec (2005) use the midpoint of this range ($6.5 million), but inflate it to represent 2005 dollars using the CPI. We used the same approach, but we further inflated this value to represent 2007 dollars, leading to a final estimate of $7,523,602.

Predicted Costs, Ten Model Runs. Table 6.B.5 shows the predicted costs generated in ten alternate model runs using the baseline assumptions. The first row of the table (Alternate 1) shows the model results that we report in the main text of this chapter (we report results from this scenario in the main text only because this was the first run that we generated). A key result stemming from this analysis is that the predicted number of suicides varies from run to run and that the volatility in suicides can have a large influence on costs. When we accounted for suicide mortality, total two-year costs for a cohort of 50,000 E-5s range from $147.3 million to $204.7 million, a difference of 39.0 percent. In contrast, when we exclude costs related to suicide mortality, our cost estimates range from $111.0 million to $121.9 million, a difference of 9.8 percent. As a result of the increased volatility stemming from suicide, we report model results with and without suicide mortality costs throughout this chapter.

Table 6.B.6 reports means and standard deviations of cost estimates in the high, low, and baseline scenarios for E-5s, averaged across ten model runs. When calculating totals and average costs per case, we used the status quo assumptions—30 percent get treatment and 30 percent of treatment is evidence-based. These estimates are used to derive Figures 6.4 and 6.5 in the main text. The findings in Table 6.B.6 show that, even when averaging over a relatively small number of model runs, the model estimates are

Table 6.B.5
Ten Alternate Model Runs Using Baseline Parameter Assumptions and Status Quo Treatment Assumptions, Cohort of 50,000 E-5s

Run	Total Costs, Without Suicide Mortality	Total Costs, with Suicide Mortality	Number of Suicides	Savings from Evidence-Based Treatment, Not Including Suicide Mortality	Savings from Evidence-Based Treatment, Including Suicide Mortality
Alternate 1	$119,829,381	$204,691,652	11	$1,378,881	$86,241,152
Alternate 2	$120,302,270	$183,180,920	8	$1,441,220	$7,406,270
Alternate 3	$114,214,326	$185,743,140	10	–$2,311,974	$69,216,840
Alternate 4	$111,785,505	$147,268,571	4	–$4,864,545	–$56,480
Alternate 5	$113,985,461	$150,395,996	5	–$5,249,990	$15,988,046
Alternate 6	$116,318,535	$157,390,425	6	$2,722,335	–$2,315,775
Alternate 7	$121,951,614	$158,831,390	5	$6,439,314	$29,498,690
Alternate 8	$120,699,597	$192,432,462	10	–$3,434,403	$37,705,962
Alternate 9	$111,664,698	$197,001,200	11	–$5,352,102	$36,747,050
Alternate 10	$111,021,318	$188,043,261	10	–$3,280,032	$43,724,961

NOTE: The status quo treatment assumptions are that 30 percent of individuals with mental health conditions receive treatment and that 30 percent of individuals receiving treatment get evidence-based care. Baseline parameter assumptions are reported in Table 6.4.

Table 6.B.6
Average Status Quo Costs Found in Ten Alternate Model Runs, Cohort of 50,000 E-5s

	Baseline	Low	High
A. Includes Value of Lives Lost to Suicide			
Total costs	$176,497,901 ($20,937,686)	$49,886,346 ($5,675,280)	$217,512,552 ($16,975,703)
Per-case cost, PTSD	$10,151 ($3,359)	$8,127 ($2,597)	$11,838 ($2,422)
Per-case cost, co-morbid PTSD and major depression	$15,748 ($2,741)	$6,688 ($3,555)	$19,673 ($2,948)
Per-case cost, major depression	$22,044 ($3,934)	$11,512 ($3,809)	$27,727 ($5,879)
B. Excludes Value of Lives Lost to Suicide			
Total costs	$116,177,270 ($4,203,965)	$96,789,689 ($24,325,303)	$147,947,486 ($3,355,368)
Per-case cost, PTSD	$5,534 ($416)	$4,145 ($520)	$6,736 ($424)
Per-case cost, co-morbid PTSD and major depression	$11,486 ($416)	$4,106 ($801)	$14,606 ($388)
Per-case cost, major depression	$14,537 ($408)	$5,251 ($495)	$18,856 ($540)

NOTE: *Status quo* assumes that 30 percent of individuals with mental health conditions receive treatment and that 30 percent of individuals receiving treatment get evidence-based care. Baseline, high-cost, and low-cost parameter assumptions are reported in Table 6.4.

very stable when we exclude the cost of lives lost to suicide. In the baseline scenario, the coefficient of variation (i.e., the standard deviation divided by the mean) is 0.036, indicating that the variation in model outcomes is small relative to the estimated mean. However, the coefficient of variation in the baseline scenario is 0.119 when we include the value of lives lost to suicide. These findings further emphasize the fact that, while suicide mortality is a large and important component of costs, figures that incorporate mortality costs associated with suicide are uncertain.

References

Andrews, B., C. R. Brewin, R. Philpott, L. Stewart. Delayed-onset posttraumatic stress disorder: A systematic review of the evidence. *American Journal of Psychiatry*, Vol. 164, No. 9, 2007, pp. 1319–1326.

Angst, J. "The course of major depression, atypical bipolar disorder, and bipolar disorder," in H. Hippius et al., ed., *New Results in Depression Research*. Berlin/Heidelberg: Springer-Verlag, 1986, pp. 26–35.

Bilmes, L. *Soldiers Returning from Iraq and Afghanistan: The Long-Term Costs of Providing Veterans Medical Care and Disability Benefits*. Cambridge, Mass.: Harvard University John F. Kennedy School of Government, 2007.

Bilmes, L. and J. Stiglitz. *The Economic Costs of the Iraq War: An Appraisal Three Years After the Beginning of the Conflict*. Cambridge, Mass.: National Bureau of Economic Research, 2006.

Boake, C., S. R. McCauley, C. Pedroza, H. S. Levin, S. A. Brown, and S. I. Brundage. Lost productive work time after mild to moderate traumatic brain injury with and without hospitalization. *Neurosurgery*, Vol. 56, No. 5, 2005, pp. 994–1003.

Brooks, C. A., B. Gabella, R. Hoffman, D. Sosin, and G. Whiteneck. Traumatic brain injury: Designing and implementing a population-based follow-up system. *Archives of Physical Medicine and Rehabilitation*, Vol. 78, No. 8, Suppl. 4, 1997, pp. S26–S30.

Brooks, D. N. The head-injured family. *Journal of Clinical and Experimental Neuropsychology*, Vol. 13, 1991, pp. 155–188.

Buntin, M. B., G. M. Carter, O. Hayden, C. Hoverman, S. M. Paddock, and B. O. Wynn. *Inpatient Rehabilitation Facility Care Use Before and After Implementation of the IRF Prospective Payment System*. Santa Monica, Calif.: RAND Corporation, TR-257-CMS, 2006. As of March 2, 2008: http://www.rand.org/pubs/technical_reports/TR257/

Calhoun, P. S., and J. C. Beckham. Caregiver burden and psychological distress in partners of veterans with chronic posttraumatic stress disorder. *Journal of Traumatic Stress*, Vol. 15, No. 3, 2002, pp. 205–212.

Casacalenda, N., J. C. Perry, and K. Looper. Remission in major depressive disorder; a comparison of pharmacotherapy, pschotherapy and control conditions. *American Journal of Psychiatry*, Vol. 159, No. 8, 2002.

Casbon, T. S., J. J. Curtin, A. R. Lang, and C. J. Patrick. Deleterious effects of alcohol intoxication: Diminished cognitive control and its behavioral consequences. *Journal of Abnormal Psychology*, Vol. 112, No. 3, 2003, pp. 476–487.

Christensen, E., J. McMahon, E. S. Schaefer, T. Jaditz, and D. Harris. *Final Report for the Veterans' Disability Benefits Commission: Compensation, Survey Results, and Selected Topics*. Washington, D.C.: The CNA Corporation, 2007.

Congressional Budget Office. *Educational Attainment and Compensation of Enlisted Personnel*. Washington, D.C., February 2004. As of March 2, 2008: http://www.cbo.gov/ftpdoc.cfm?index=5108&type=0&sequence=1

Corso, P. S., J. A. Mercy, T. R. Simon, E. A. Finkelstein, and T. R. Miller. Medical costs and productivity losses due to interpersonal and self-directed violence in the United States. *American Journal of Preventive Medicine*, Vol. 32, No. 6, 2007, pp. 474–482.

De Maat, S., J. Dekker, R. Schoevers, and F. De Jonghe. Relative efficacy of psychotherapy and pharmacotherapy in the treatment of depression: A meta-analysis. *Psychotherapy Research*, Vol. 16, No. 5, pp. 566–578.

Defense Manpower Data Center. *Tabulations of Responses from the 1999 Survey of Active Duty Personnel: Volume 2*. Washington, D.C., DMDC Report No. 2000-007, September 2000. As of March 2, 2008:
http://www.dmdc.osd.mil/surveys/act_tab/pdfs/2000-007.pdf

Dekel, R., and Z. Solomon. Marital relations among former prisoners of war: Contribution of posttraumatic stress disorder, aggression, and sexual satisfaction. *Journal of Family Psychology*, Vol. 20, No. 4, 2006, pp. 709–712.

Department of Defense. "Pay and Allowances," Web page, no date-a. As of March 2, 2008:
http://www.defenselink.mil/militarypay/pay/index.html

——— "Reserve Drill Pay," Web page, no date-b. As of March 2, 2008:
http://www.defenselink.mil/militarypay/pay/bp/02_reservedrill.html

———. "U.S. Troops Deployed: Operation Enduring Freedom and Operation Iraqi Freedom, Primarily Iraq and Afghanistan," January 31, 2007. As of March 2, 2008:
http://majorityleader.house.gov/docUploads/DeployedJan312007.pdf

———. "Military Casualty Information," Web page, 2008a. As of March 2, 2008:
http://siadapp.dmdc.osd.mil/personnel/CASUALTY/castop.htm

———. "Military Pay and Benefits," Web page, January 24, 2008b. As of March 2, 2008:
http://www.defenselink.mil/militarypay/

Department of Defense, Office of the Under Secretary of Defense for Personnel and Readiness. *Population Representation in the Military Services, 2005*, 2005. As of March 2, 2008:
http://www.defenselink.mil/prhome/poprep2005

———. *Defense Manpower Requirements Report (DMRR): Fiscal Year 2007*, Washington, D.C., 2006.

Department of Defense Pharmacoeconomic Center. Selective Serotonin reuptake inhibitors. *PEC Update*, Vol. 4, No. 2, 2004. As of March 2, 2008:
http://www.pec.ha.osd.mil/Updates/0402web/Mar_04_Update_Page_7.htm

Department of Health and Human Services, Centers for Medicare and Medicaid Services. "Physician Fee Schedule Search." Web page, no date. As of March 2, 2008:
http://www.cms.hhs.gov/pfslookup/02_PFSsearch.asp

Department of Labor. National Compensation Survey: Occupational Wages in the United States, Supplementary Tables, July 2006.

Dimidjian, S., S. D. Hollon, K. Dobson, K. B. Schmaling, R. J. Kohlenberg, M. E. Addis, R. Gallop, J. B. McGlinchey, D. K. Markley, J. K. Gollan, D. C. Atkins, D. L. Dunner, and N. S. Jacobson. Randomized trial of behavioral activation, cognitive therapy, and antidepressant medication in the acute treatment of adults with major depression. *Journal of Consulting and Clinical Psychology*, Vol. 74, No. 4, 2006, pp. 658–670.

Dobscha, S. K., L. M. Winterbottom, and L. S. Snodgrass. Reducing drug costs at a veterans affairs hospital by increasing market-share of generic fluoxetine. *Community Mental Health Journal*, Vol. 43, No. 1, 2007.

Dohrenwend, B. P., J. B. Turner, N. A. Turse, et al. The psychological risks of Vietnam for U.S. veterans: A revisit with new data and methods. *Science*, Vol. 313, No. 5789, 2006, pp. 979–982.

Druss, B. G., R. Rosenheck, and W. H. Sledge. Health and disability costs of depressive illness in a major US corporation. *American Journal of Psychiatry,* Vol. 157, No. 8, 2000, pp. 1274–1278.

Du Rocher Schudlich, T. D., L. M. Papp, and E. M. Cummings. Relations of husbands and wives' dysphoria to marital conflict resolution strategies. *Journal of Family Psychology,* Vol. 18, No. 1, 2004, pp. 171–183.

Ettner, S. L., R. G. Frank, and R. C. Kessler. The impact of psychiatric disorders on labor market outcomes. *Industrial and Labor Relations Review,* Vol. 51, No. 1, 1997, pp. 64–81.

Finkelstein, E. A., P. S. Corso, and T. R. Miller. *The Incidence and Economic Burden of Injuries in the United States.* Cambridge, UK: Oxford University Press, 2006.

Fleming, T. *Redbook: Pharmacy's Fundamental Reference.* Montvale, N.J.: Thompson Healthcare, 2006.

Foa, E. B., J. R. T. Davidson, and A. Frances. Treatment of posttraumatic stress disorder. *Journal of Clinical Psychiatry,* Vol. 60, 1999.

Friedman, M. A., and J. B. Detweiler-Bedell. Combined psychotherapy and pharmacotherapy for the treatment of major depressive disorder. *Clinical Psychology: Science and Practice*, Vol. 11, 2004, pp. 47–68.

Gibbons, R. D., C. H. Brown, K. Hur, S. M. Marcus, et al. Relationship between antidepressants and suicide attempts: An analysis of the Veterans Health Administration data sets. *American Journal of Psychiatry,* Vol. 164, No. 7, 2007.

Gold, M. R., J. E. Siegel, L. B. Russell, and M. C. Weinstein. Cost-effectiveness in health and medicine. *Oxford University Press*, New York, NY, 1996.

Goldberg, M.S. *Projecting the Costs to Care for Veterans of U.S. Military Operations in Iraq and Afghanistan.* Testimony before the Committee on Veterans' Affairs, U.S. House of Representatives, Washington, D.C.: Congressional Budget Office, October 17, 2007.

Goldsmith, S., T. C. Pellmar, A. M. Kleinman, W. E. Bunney, eds. *Reducing Suicide: A National Imperative.* Washington, D.C.: National Academies Press, 2002.

Government Accountability Office. *Comprehensive Outpatient Rehabilitation Facilities: High Medicare Payments in Florida Raise Program Integrity Concerns.* Washington, D.C., GAO-04-709, 2004.

———. *Military Personnel: DoD Needs to Improve the Transparency and Reassess the Reasonableness, Appropriateness, Affordability, and Sustainability of Its Military Compensation System.* Washington, D.C., GAO-05-798, 2005.

Grieger, T. A., S. J. Cozza, R. J. Ursano, C. Hoge, P. E. Martinez, C. C. Engel, and H. J. Wain. Posttraumatic stress disorder and depression in battle-injured soldiers. *American Journal of Psychiatry,* Vol. 163, No. 10, 2006.

Harwood, H. J., D. Fountain, and G. Fountain. *The Economic Cost of Alcohol and Drug Abuse in the United States, 1992.* Bethesda, Md.: National Institute on Drug Abuse, 1998.

HCUPnet. Web site, no date. As of March 2, 2008:
http://hcupnet.ahrq.gov/

Hibbard, M. R., S. Uysal, K. Kepler, J. Bogdany, and J. Silver. Axis I psychopathology in individuals with traumatic brain injury. *Journal of Head Trauma Rehabilitation,* Vol. 13, No. 4, 1998, pp. 24–39.

Hirsch, B. T., and S. L. Mehay. Evaluating the labor market performance of veterans using a matched comparison group design. *Journal of Human Resources,* Vol. 38, No. 3, 2003, pp. 673–700.

Hodgson, T. Z., and Meiners, M. R. *Guidelines for Cost of Illness Studies in the Public Health Service: Task Force on Cost of Illness Studies.* Washington, D.C.: U.S. Public Health Services, 1979.

———. Cost-of-illness methodology: A guide to current practices and procedures. *Milbank Memorial Fund Quarterly,* Vol. 60, 1982, pp. 429–462.

Hoge, C. W., J. L. Auchterlonie, and C. S. Milliken. Mental health problems, use of mental health services, and attrition from military service after returning from deployment to Iraq or Afghanistan. *Journal of the American Medical Association,* Vol. 295, No. 9, 2006.

Hoge, C. W., C. A. Castro, S. C. Messer, D. McGurk, D. I. Cotting, and R. L. Koffman. Combat duty in Iraq and Afghanistan, mental health problems, and barriers to care. *New England Journal of Medicine,* Vol. 351, No. 1, 2004, pp. 13–22.

Hoge, C. W., S. E. Lesikar, R. Guevara, J. Lange, J. F. Brundage, C. C. Engel, S. C. Messer, and D. T. Orman. Mental disorders among U.S. military personnel in the 1990s: Association with high levels of health care utilization and early military attrition. *American Journal of Psychiatry,* Vol. 159, No. 9, 2002, pp. 1576–1583.

Hoge, C. W., A. Terhakopian, C. A. Castro, S. C. Messer, and C. C. Engel. Association of posttraumatic stress disorder with somatic symptoms, health care visits, and absenteeism among Iraq war veterans. *American Journal of Psychiatry,* Vol. 164, No. 1, 2007, pp. 150–153.

Horvitz-Lennon, M., S. T. Normand, R. G. Frank, and H. H. Goldman. "Usual Care" for major depression in the 1990s: Characteristics and expert-estimated outcomes. *American Journal of Psychiatry,* Vol. 160, No. 4, 2003.

Hosek, J., and M. Mattock. *Learning About Quality: How the Quality of Military Personnel Is Revealed over Time,* Santa Monica, Calif.: RAND Corporation, MR-1593-OSD, 2003. As of March 2, 2008: http://www.rand.org/pubs/monograph_reports/MR1593/

House of Representatives. *Estimated Cost of U.S. Operations in Iraq and Afghanistan and of Other Activities Related to the War on Terrorism.* Hearing before the Committee on the Budget, October 24, 2007.

Institute of Medicine. *Treatment of PTSD: An Assessment of the Evidence.* Washington, D.C.: National Academies Press, 2007.

Ivins, B. J., K. A. Schwab, G. Baker, and D. L. Warden. Hospital admissions associated with traumatic brain injury in the US Army during peacetime: 1990s trends. *Neuroepidemiology,* Vol. 27, No. 3, 2006, pp. 154–163.

Johnstone, B., D. Mount, and L. H. Schopp. Financial and vocational outcomes 1 year after traumatic brain injury. *Archives of Phyical Medicine and Rehabilitation,* Vol. 84, No. 2, 2003, pp. 238–241.

Judd, L. L., H. S. Akiskal, J. D. Maser, P. J. Zeller, J. Endicott, W. Coryell, M. Paulus, J. L. Kunovac, A. C. Leon, C. W. Mueller, J. A. Rice, and M. B. Keller. Telephone psychotherapy and telephone care management for primary care patients starting antidepressant treatment: A randomized controlled trial. *Archives of General Psychiatry,* Vol. 55, 1998, pp. 694–700.

Judd, L. L., M. J. Paulus, P. J. Schettler, H. S. Akiskal, J. Endicott, A. C. Leon, J. D. Maser, T. Mueller, D. A. Solomon, and M. B. Keller. Does incomplete recovery from first lifetime major depressive episode herald a chronic course of illness? *American Journal of Psychiatry,* Vol. 157, No. 9, 2000, pp. 1501–1504.

Keller, M. B., J. P. McCullough, D. N. Klein, and B. Arnow. A comparison of Nefazodone, the cognitive behavioral-analysis system of psychotherapy, and their combination for the treatment of chronic depression. *New England Journal of Medicine,* Vol. 342, No. 20, 2000, pp. 1462–1471.

Kennedy, N., R. Abbott, and E. S. Paykel. Longitudinal syndromal and sub-syndromal symptoms after severe depression: 10-year follow-up story. *British Journal of Psychiatry*, Vol. 184, 2004, pp. 330–336.

Kessler, R. C., G. Borges, and E. E. Walters. Prevalence of and risk factors for lifetime suicide attempts in the National Comorbidity Survey. *Archives of General Psychiatry*, Vol. 56, 1999, pp. 617–626.

Kessler, R. C., A. Sonnega, E. Bromet, M. Huges, and C. Nelson. Posttraumatic stress disorder in the National Comorbidity Survey. *Archives of General Psychiatry*, Vol. 52, 1995, pp. 1048–1060.

Kilburn, M. R., R. Louie, and D. Goldman. *Patterns of Enlisted Compensation*, Santa Monica, Calif.: RAND Corporation, MR-807-OSD, 2001. As of March 2, 2008: http://www.rand.org/pubs/monograph_reports/MR807/

Kocsis, J. H., A. J. Frances, C. Voss, J. J. Mann, B. J. Mason, and J. Sweeney. Imipramine treatment for chronic depression. *Archives of General Psychiatry*, Vol. 45, 1988, pp. 253–257.

Kozloff, R. Networks of social support and the outcome for severe head injury. *Journal of Head Trauma Rehabilitation*, Vol. 2, 1987, pp. 14–23.

Kulka, R. A., W. E. Schlenger, J. A. Fairbank, R. L. Hough, B. K. Jordan, C. R. Marmar, et al. *Trauma and the Vietnam War Generation: Report of Findings from the National Vietnam Veterans Readjustment Study*. Philadelphia, Penn.: Brunner/Mazel, 1990.

LeBlanc V. R., C. Regehr, R. B. Jelley, and I. Barath. Does posttraumatic stress disorder affect performance? *Journal of Nervous and Mental Disease*, Vol. 195, No. 8, 2007, pp. 701–704.

Lewin-ICF. *The Cost of Disorders of the Brain*. Washington, D.C.: The National Foundation for Brain Research, 1992.

Liss, M., and B. Willer. Traumatic brain injury and marital relationships: A literature review. *International Journal of Rehabilitation Research*, Vol. 13, No. 4, 1990, pp. 309–320.

Ludman, E. J., G. E. Simon, S. Tutty, and M. Von Korff. A randomized trial of telephone psychotherapy and pharmacotherapy for depression: Continuation and durability of effects. *Journal of Consulting and Clinical Psychology*, Vol. 75, No. 2, 2007, pp. 257–266.

Max, W., E. J. MacKenzie, and D. P. Rice. Head injuries: Costs and consequences. *Journal of Head Trauma Rehabilitation*, Vol. 6, 1991, pp. 76–91.

Medical Surveillance Monthly Report (MSMR): A Publication of the Armed Forces Health Surveillance Center, Vol. 14, No. 6, September–October, 2007.

Melfi, C. A., A. J. Chawla, T. W. Croghan, M. P. Hanna, S. Kennedy, and K. Sredl. Reducing relapse and recurrence in unipolar depression: A comparative meta-analysis of cognitive-behavioral therapy's effects. *Archives of General Psychiatry*, Vol. 55, 1998, pp. 1128–1132.

Miller, T. R., J. B. Douglass, M. S. Galbraith, D. C. Lestina, and N. M. Pindus. "Costs of head and neck injury and a benefit-cost analysis of bicycle helmets," in *Head and Neck Injury*. Warrendale, Penn.: Society of Automotive Engineers, Inc., 1994, pp. 211–240.

Milliken, C. S., J. L. Auchterlonie, and C. W. Hoge. Longitudinal assessment of mental health problems among Active and Reserve Component soldiers returning from the Iraq war. *Journal of the American Medical Association*, Vol. 298, No.18, 2007, pp. 2141–2148.

Ommaya, A. K., A. M. Salazar, A. L. Dannenberg, A. K. Ommaya, A. B. Chervinsky, and K. Schwab. Outcome after traumatic brain injury in the U.S. military medical system. *Journal of Trauma*, Vol. 41, No. 6, 1996, pp. 972–975.

Pampallona, S., and P. Bollini. Combined pharmacotherapy and psychological treatment for depression. *Archives of General Psychiatry*, Vol. 61, 2004, pp. 714–719.

Perconte, S. T., M. L. Griger, and G. Bellucci. Relapse and rehospitalization of veterans two years after treatment for PTSD. *Hospital and Community Psychiatry,* Vol. 40, No. 10, 1989.

President's Commission on Care for America's Returning Wounded Warriors. *Serve, Support, Simplify: Report of the President's Commission on Care for America's Returning Wounded Warriros.* July 2007.

Rice, D. P., S. Kelman, and L. S. Miller. Estimates of economic costs of alcohol and drug abuse and mental illness, 1985 and 1988. *Public Health Reports,* Vol. 106, No. 3, 1991, pp. 281–292.

Rosenheck, R., and A. Fontana. A model of homelessness among male veterans of the Vietnam War generation. *American Journal of Psychiatry,* Vol. 151, No. 3, 1994, pp. 421–427.

———. Recent trends in VA treatment of post-traumatic stress disorder and other mental disorders. *Health Affairs,* Vol. 26, No. 6, 2007.

Salazar, A. M., D. L. Warden, K. Schwab, J. Spector, S. Braverman, J. Walter, R. Cole, M. M. Rosner, E. M. Martin, J. Ecklund, and R. G. Ellenbogen. Cognitive rehabilitation for traumatic brain injury: A randomized trial. Defense and Veterans Head Injury Program (DVHIP) Study Group. *Journal of the American Medical Association,* Vol. 283, No. 23, 2000, pp. 3075–3081.

Savoca, E., and R. Rosenheck. The civilian labor market experiences of Vietnam-era veterans: The influence of psychiatric disorders. *Journal of Mental Health Policy and Economics,* Vol. 3, 2000, pp. 199–207.

Schnurr, P. P., M. J. Friedman, C. C. Engel, E. B. Foa, M. T. Shea, B. K. Chow, P. A. Resick, V. Thurston, S. M. Orsillo, R. Haug, C. Turner, and N. Bernardy. Cognitive behavioral therapy for posttraumatic stress disorder in women: A randomized controlled trial. *Journal of the American Medical Association*, Vol. 297, No. 8, 2007, pp. 820–830.

Schoenbaum, M., J. Unutzer, C. D. Sherbourne, N. Duan, L. V. Rubenstein, J. Miranda, L. S. Meredith, M. F. Carney, and K. Wells. Cost-effectiveness of practiced-initiated quality improvement for depression: Results of a randomized controlled trial. *Journal of the American Medical Association,* Vol. 286, No. 11, 2001, pp. 1325–1330.

Simon, G. E., E. J. Ludman, S. Tutty, B. Operskalski, and M. Von Korff. Telephone psychotherapy and telephone care management for primary care patients starting antidepressant treatment: A randomized controlled trial. *Journal of the American Medical Association*, Vol. 292, No. 8, 2004, pp. 935–942.

Simpson, G., and R. Tate. Suicidality after traumatic brain injury: Demographic, injury and clinical correlates. *Psychological Medicine,* Vol. 32, No. 4, 2002, pp. 687–697.

———. Clinical features of suicide attempts after traumatic brain injury. *Journal of Nervous and Mental Disease,* Vol. 193, No. 10, 2005, pp. 680–685.

Smith, M. W., P. P. Schnurr, and R. A. Rosenheck. "Employment outcomes and PTSD symptom severity. *Mental Health Services Research,* Vol. 7, No. 2, 2005, pp. 89–101.

Solomon, Z., M. Waysman, G. Levy, B. Fried, M. Mikulincer, R. Benbenishty, V. Florian, and A. Bleich. From front line to home front: A study of secondary traumatization. *Family Process Journal,* Vol. 31, No. 3, 1992, pp. 289–302.

Stewart, W. F., J. A. Ricci, E. Chee, S. R. Hahn, and D. Morganstein. Cost of lost productive work time among US workers with depression. *Journal of the American Medical Association,* Vol. 289, No. 23, 2003.

Teasdale, T. W., and A. W. Engberg. Suicide after traumatic brain injury: A population study. *Journal of Neurology, Neurosurgery, and Psychiatry,* Vol. 71, No. 4, 2001, pp. 436–440.

Thurman, D. J., "The epidemiology and economics of head trauma," in L. P. Miller and R. L. Hayes, eds., *Head Trauma: Basic, Preclinical, and Clinical Directions,* New York: John Wiley and Sons, Inc., 2001.

TRICARE. "Allowable Charges." Web page, undated. As of March 2, 2008: http://www.tricare.mil/allowablecharges/default.aspx

U.S. Army, Suicide Risk Management and Surveillance Office, Army Behavioral Health Technology Office. *2006 Army Suicide Event Report.* Tacoma, Wa.: Madigan Army Medical Center, August 2007.

Veterans Health Administration, Office of Public Health and Environmental Hazards. "Analysis of VHA Healthcare Utilization Among US Global War on Terrorism Veterans: Operation Iraqi Freedom and Operation Enduring Freedom." Power Point Presentation, October 2007.

Viscusi, W. K., and J. E. Aldy. The value of a statistical life: A critical review of market estimates throughout the world. *Journal of Risk and Uncertainty,* Vol. 27, No. 1, 2003, pp. 5–76.

Vittengl, J. R., L. A. Clark, T. W. Dunn, and R. B. Jarrett. Reducing relapse and recurrence in unipolar depression: A comparative meta-analysis of cognitive-behavioral therapy's effects. *Journal of Consulting and Clinical Psychology,* Vol. 75, No. 3, 2007, pp. 475–488.

Wells, K. B., M. A. Burnam, W. Rodgers, R. Hays, and P. Camp. The course of depression in adult outpatients: Results from the Medical Outcomes Study. *Archives of General Psychiatry*, Vol. 49, 1992, pp. 788–794.

Wallsten, S., and K. Kosec. *The Economic Costs of the War in Iraq.* AEI-Brookings Joint Center for Regulatory Studies Working Paper 05-19, 2005.

Wang, J. L. A longitudinal population-based study of treated and untreated major depression. *Medical Care*, Vol. 42, No. 6, 2004, pp. 543–550.

Wang, P. S., A. L. Beck, P. Berglund, D. K. McKenas, N. P. Pronk, G. E. Simon, and R. C. Kessler. Effects of major depression on moment-in-time work performance. *American Journal of Psychiatry*, Vol. 161, No. 10, 2004, pp. 1885–1891.

Wang, P. S., G. E. Simon, J. Avorn, F. Azocar, E. J. Ludman, J. McCulloch, M. Z. Petukhova, and R. C. Kessler. Telephone screening, outreach, and care management for depressed workers and impact on clinical and work productivity outcomes. *Journal of the American Medical Association,* Vol. 298, No. 12, 2007, pp. 1401–1411.

Wang, P., M. L. Olfson, H. A. Pincus, K. B. Wells, and R. C. Kessler. Twelve-month use of mental health services in the United States: Results from the National Comorbidity Survey Replication. *Archives of General Psychiatry*, Vol. 62, 2005 pp. 629–640.

Whooley, M. A., and G. Simon. Managing depression in medical outpatients. *New England Journal of Medicine*, Vol. 343, No. 26, 2000, pp. 1942–1950.

Wolfe, J. W., D. J. Erickson, E. J. Sharkansky, D. W. King, and L. A. King. Course and predictors of posttraumatic stress disorder among Gulf War veterans: A prospective analysis. *Journal of Consulting and Clinical Psychology,* Vol. 67, No. 4, 1999, pp. 520–528.

Young, A. S., K. Kapur, and D. Murata. The time course of treatment costs among patients with severe mental illness. *Psychiatric Services*, Vol. 52, No. 1, 2001.

Young, A. S., R. Klap, C. D. Sherbourne, and K. Wells. The quality of care for depressive and anxiety disorders in the United States. *Archives of General Psychiatry,* Vol. 58, 2001.

Zatzick, D. F., C. R. Marmar, D. S. Weiss, W. S. Browner, T. J. Metzler, J. M. Golding, A. Stewart, W. E. Schlenger, and K. B. Wells. Posttraumatic stress disorder and functioning and quality of life outcomes in a nationally representative sample of male Vietnam veterans. *American Journal of Psychiatry,* Vol. 154, No. 12, 1997, pp. 1690–1695.

Zivin, K., H. M. Kim, J. F. McCarthy, K. L. Austin, K. J. Hoggatt, H. Walters, and M. Valenstein. Suicide mortality among individuals receiving treatment for depression in the Veterans Affairs Health System: Associations with patient and treatment setting characteristics. *American Journal of Public Health*, Vol. 97, No. 12, 2007, pp. 2193–2198.

Part V: Caring for the Invisible Wounds

How can we best provide services for military personnel who are suffering from mental health and cognitive problems? The answer to that question is the focus of Chapter Seven. This part of the monograph provides an overview and analysis of our review of the services and systems of care designed to address PTSD, major depression, and TBI among servicemembers and veterans who returned from Operations Enduring Freedom and Iraqi Freedom (OEF/OIF).

Systems of Care: Challenges and Opportunities to Improve Access to High-Quality Care

M. Audrey Burnam, Lisa S. Meredith, Todd C. Helmus, Rachel M. Burns,
Robert A. Cox, Elizabeth D'Amico, Laurie T. Martin, Mary E. Vaiana,
Kayla M. Williams, and Michael R. Yochelson

Introduction

How can we best provide services for military personnel who are suffering from mental health and cognitive problems? The answer to that question is the focus of Chapter Seven.

We examine the health care services available to military servicemembers who have returned from Afghanistan and Iraq with post-traumatic stress disorder or depression, or who have suffered a traumatic brain injury during their deployment.

We also examine gaps in these services, with the goal of supporting efforts to meet the mental health and cognitive needs of returning OEF/OIF servicemembers and veterans. We consider two kinds of service gaps: *gaps in access to care* and *gaps in quality of care*.

A *gap in access* exists when many individuals who need services are not using them. Many factors can contribute to underuse of services. Following a conceptual model commonly used in health services research (Institute of Medicine, 1993), we organize the contributing factors into two broad domains: (1) structural and financial aspects of the health service systems (e.g., eligibility rules, financial incentives, availability of services) and (2) personal and social factors (e.g., individual values and beliefs, military culture) (see Figure 7.1).

These factors can be either *barriers*, reducing the probability of service use, or *facilitators*, increasing use. Eliminating gaps in access to care will increase use of services among those who might benefit from the services.

Figure 7.1
Health Care Systems Improve Health Outcomes by Facilitating Access to Services That Provide High-Quality Care

RAND *MG720-7.1*

A gap in quality exists when the services that individuals typically receive are not consistent with high-quality care. Following the Institute of Medicine's Quality Chasm reports (Institute of Medicine, 2001, 2006), we define *high-quality care* as care that is

- based on the best available evidence and expert consensus about what is most effective
- safe (the expected health benefit is higher than the expected health risk)
- patient-centered, meaning that the values and preferences of individuals are respected in clinical decisionmaking and that patients are fully informed participants in decisions about their treatment
- timely (delays that might be harmful to health are avoided)
- efficient (waste of resources is avoided)
- equitable (care does not vary by gender, ethnicity, geographic location, etc.).

Eliminating gaps between high-quality care and usually practiced care will improve health outcomes among those who use services.

Figure 7.1 highlights that health outcomes are a function of *access to care* that results in use of services and *receipt of high-quality care* in the course of using those services. Thus, maximizing the benefits of health care services requires simultaneously facilitating access to services and ensuring that the services received are of high quality. Providing access to services that are not effective or that have unknown effectiveness may have little or no positive effect on outcomes, and they may incur costs to both the systems and the individuals who use services. Similarly, high-quality clinical care will have limited effect on outcomes if access to this care is poor for the broader population of those who would be expected to benefit from it.

There are many challenges to facilitating good access to services and ensuring high quality of care for mental and cognitive health. These challenges exist across the U.S. health care system and thus are not unique to the systems of care designed to serve military servicemembers and veterans.

Access and Quality Challenges

Epidemiologic studies of the general U.S. adult population show that, among individuals likely to have experienced a mental disorder in the past year, six in ten do not use any health care services for their mental health problems. Of the four in ten who do use services, only about half of these receive care from a mental health specialist (Wang, Lane, et al., 2005).

Good access to mental health care in the United States has long been hampered by limited mental health benefits in employer-sponsored health insurance and by cost-constrained publicly funded services that provide access to the most severely disabled but have limited resources for serving a broader array of problems and populations. Other long-standing barriers to access include poor availability of specialty mental health services in rural areas and the difficulties of developing capacities to provide language and culturally appropriate services for the diversity of Americans.

Thanks to advocacy, education, and growing public awareness, social and personal barriers to access—including the stigma associated with being viewed as having a mental disorder and public attitudes and misunderstandings about mental health conditions and their treatments—have lessened over time. However, these attitudes still significantly affect the willingness of individuals to consider and seek care for mental health problems.

Studies that have examined the discrepancy between typical health care received by Americans and high-quality, evidence-based care inevitably find a striking gap, not only for care of mental disorders but for care of many other medical conditions. In a large study of adult populations of 12 metropolitan areas of the country, researchers found that, among those with major depression, about six in ten who used any health services received recommended care—that is, care meeting standards of professionally accepted practice guidelines (McGlynn et al., 2003). Similar findings were reported for stroke, coronary artery disease, and asthma. So large and pervasive is this gap that it is often termed the "Quality Chasm" by health policy and services researchers, after the title of a seminal report published by the Institute of Medicine in 2001.

The failure to provide high-quality care is, by and large, not a problem of health professionals being uncaring or incompetent; rather, poor quality often stems from multiple and complex failures involving the policy and regulatory environment, coordination among multiple and complex systems of care, the organization of the health care facility and its staff, information systems, interactions between professionals and patients, and financial incentives that have perverse effects on quality at all levels—from patient to system (Berwick, 2002).

Barriers to access and failures to provide high-quality care are challenges that confront health care and mental health care systems generally. However, American leaders, the Department of Defense (DoD), the Department of Veterans Affairs (VA), and the public concur that military servicemembers who have served in Afghanistan and Iraq should receive care of the highest quality. Americans want the nation's servicemembers and their families to have good access to appropriate and high-quality health care for service-related mental health and cognitive problems—both during their active duty service and after they have returned to civilian life.

With political will galvanized to improve care for mental health conditions and traumatic brain injury for American servicemembers, there is an historic opportunity for transformation that can facilitate access to and improve quality of care. But the magnitude of the challenges should not be underestimated. Mandates that assume quick, simple solutions to these complex problems are unlikely to significantly affect the bottom line—more servicemembers getting care that helps them recover from their mental health and cognitive conditions—even when there is some satisfaction to seeing things happen quickly.

Lessons from the broader health services field suggest that a sustained systems approach will be required to make significant advances in care. Such an approach would encompass a broad perspective—from policy environment, to organization of the delivery of care, to patient-therapist interaction—concerning the policy levers that can drive change. This broad perspective would also point toward sustained investment in an information infrastructure that can support continuous assessment and evaluation and would engender an organizational environment and culture that can learn from experience and strive toward improvements.

Study Approach

We aimed to address the following questions regarding gaps in care for military servicemembers and veterans who have been deployed in OEF or OIF:

Access-to-Care Questions

1. What is the gap in access to care?
2. What structural factors impede or facilitate access?
3. What social, cultural, and personal factors impede or facilitate access?

Quality-of-Care Questions

1. What is high-quality, evidence-based care for the key mental and cognitive injuries of war?
2. What organizational models are needed to support high-quality care?
3. To what extent are quality standards and processes supported in systems of care serving servicemembers and veterans of OEF/OIF?

Our study focused on post-deployment services in the United States for active duty military servicemembers, including deployed members of the Reserve Components (reservists and National Guardsmen), and for veterans of OEF/OIF. We examined both the Military Health System (MHS) and VA health services. In addition, we considered the broader array of community services that may be available to military servicemembers and veterans. We did not focus on services provided in theater during deployments. We recognize that in-theater care, including early intervention and acute treatment, is very important, but an examination of these approaches and services was beyond the scope of our effort.

To address the study questions, we reviewed existing published literature and special reports that focus on services available to military servicemembers and veterans. Our review was intended to provide a broad picture of the systems of care and services available for care of mental health conditions and TBI, as these systems are currently organized. We recognize, however, that much change is under way to implement numerous recent recommendations calling for changes and expansion of services, through efforts led by the President, Congress, the Department of Defense, and the Department of Veterans Affairs. Although it was not possible to describe the nature and extent of change that is being undertaken at present, when relevant, we refer to published plans to implement recommendations.

To enrich our understanding of these systems of care, we conducted semi-structured interviews with selected policy administrators and health service system managers within the MHS and Veterans Health Administration (VHA). Interviews elicited these leaders' perspectives on how care is structured and on issues related to access and quality of care. See Appendix 7.A for details about how we identified interview participants, as well as the content and analysis of those interviews.

We also conducted focus groups with soldiers, marines, reservists, and guardsmen who had returned from deployments, and with some of their spouses, to understand their perspective as consumers of military and veteran health services. We asked participants about the signs and symptoms of stress that servicemembers experience when returning from deployment, where they would seek care for these types of signs and symptoms, and about the types of barriers they might experience in obtaining services. Appendix 7.B provides additional details about the focus-group methods. We use selected quotes from the focus-group participants to illustrate points that are consistent with existing literature and government reports, rather than relying on them as stand-alone evidence.

Finally, we drew lessons from the broader general health and mental health services research field to provide a framework for understanding and illuminating both gaps in care and promising approaches for improving access and quality. This included a review of the scientific evidence for specific treatments for PTSD, major depression, and TBI, the details of which are provided in Appendix 7.C.

We endeavored to review and synthesize information in a way that would shed light on key gaps in access to and quality of care across the multiple and complex systems of health care that are available for returning OEF and OIF servicemembers and veterans. While our review broadly encompassed relevant systems of care from a national perspective, it did not include a detailed examination of specific treatment programs, facilities, regions, or installations. We recognize that this broad approach does not provide insight into the large variation that exists across locales and organizations, and that there is much to be learned from examining localized examples of innovation, excellence, and gaps in care. This more-detailed level of examination, however, was beyond the scope of our effort. Our examination focuses on larger, overarching issues that need to be addressed within and across the systems to facilitate improvements.

The first part of this chapter is focused on mental health services for PTSD and major depression; it addresses questions regarding gaps in access to and quality of services for these conditions. Because services for TBI primarily fall outside of mental health specialty care, instead involving acute medical care, neurology, and rehabilitative care specialties, we consider separately gaps in access to and quality of care for TBI, as a second part of the chapter.

Access to Mental Health Care for PTSD and Major Depression

Barriers that limit access to post-deployment mental health services are addressed in this section. First, we review the evidence suggesting an unmet need for mental health treatment services. We then consider structural factors that underpin problems with treatment access, which include the organization of the DoD and VA health care systems, limitations in staffing, and challenges to continuity of care. Finally, we discuss social, cultural, and personal factors influencing attitudes toward seeking mental health care.

What Is the Gap in Access to Care?

Increasing numbers of U.S. servicemembers serving in Afghanistan and Iraq develop mental disorders and cognitive injuries while deployed. PTSD is the most prevalent mental health condition, affecting between 5 and 15 percent of servicemembers, depending on who is assessed and when and how they are assessed (see Chapters Three and Four). Depression also affects a substantial number of servicemembers, with 2 to 14 percent meeting diagnostic criteria for major depression (see Chapters Three and Four).

Despite the relatively high prevalence of mental health conditions among deployed servicemembers, information about their access to mental health services, both in-theater and post-deployment, is limited. However, available data point to substantial unmet need for services (see Figure 7.2). The research findings on mental health service utilization referred to in this chapter are listed in Appendix 7.D.

Mental Health Needs During Deployment. Only about one-third of OIF soldiers and marines who screened positive for a mental health condition reported receiving mental health care while deployed (U.S. Department of the Army, Office of the Surgeon General, 2003, 2005; U.S. Department of the Army, Office of the Surgeon General, Office of the Surgeon, Multinational Force–Iraq and Office of the Surgeon General, U.S. Army Medical Command, 2006a, 2006b). Not all servicemembers who screen positive for mental disorders may welcome mental health services, particularly if there are negative attitudes toward or consequences associated with receiving care. However, one study found that a similarly low proportion of solders (32 percent) who were interested in receiving mental health services actually received treatment (Grieger et al., 2007).

Mental Health Service Needs After Deployment. The need for mental health treatment does not end when the servicemember returns from deployment. In fact, the need is likely to increase because conditions such as PTSD may appear months or even years after exposure to the traumatic event. Only about one-third (23–40 percent) of military personnel who met screening criteria post-deployment received any professional help; 13 to 27 percent received care from mental health professionals (Hoge et

Figure 7.2
Profile of Gaps in Mental Health Care

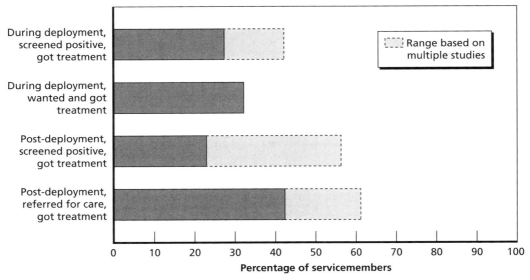

SOURCES: U. S. Department of the Army, Office of the Surgeon General, 2003, 2005; U. S. Department of the Army, Office of the Surgeon, Multinational Force–Iraq and Office of the Surgeon General, United States Army Medical Command, 2006a, 2006b; Hoge, Castro, et al., 2004; Hoge, Auchterlonie, and Milliken, 2006; Milliken, Auchterlonie, and Hoge, 2007.
RAND *MG720-7.2*

al., 2004). These rates are comparable to those found in the general population (Wang, Berglund, et al., 2005; Wang, Lane, et al., 2005). In our survey (see Chapter Four), we found that only half of those who met criteria for PTSD or major depression in the past 30 days had seen a physician or mental health provider at least once about a mental health condition in the past year.

An additional concern is the large proportion of individuals with a post-deployment health-assessment referral for mental health services who do not receive treatment. The *assessment*, which is designed to identify post-deployment health concerns early, entails completing an online health screening, then having an interview with a medical provider, wherein the servicemember's responses are discussed and, if necessary, a referral for mental health services is provided. (A revised version of this form in September 2007 added questions related to traumatic brain injury.)

Only about half of OEF or OIF veterans with a referral for a mental health problem listed on the post-deployment health assessment used mental health services (Hoge, Auchterlonie, and Milliken, 2006; Milliken, Auchterlonie, and Hoge, 2007). Rates of mental health problems were higher among the Reserve Component than among the Active Component (Milliken, Auchterlonie, and Hoge, 2007). Most mental health services were delivered through mental health clinics; a few were delivered in a primary care setting (Hoge, Auchterlonie, and Milliken, 2006).

The number of servicemembers receiving a mental health referral following the post-deployment health screening may be artificially low. Servicemembers say they do not always report mental health concerns because they fear that doing so might delay their return home (finding from the focus group). GAO (2006b) also identified that only one in five of those who met screening criteria for PTSD on the assessment were referred for follow-up evaluation, indicating that a substantially smaller percentage of servicemembers who need services upon returning home might actually receive them. At the same time, others who do not receive referrals still seek care; approximately 15 to 18 percent of individuals who did not receive a referral for mental health services did, in fact, access services once home (Milliken, Auchterlonie, and Hoge, 2007).

The limited data available suggest substantial gaps between the need and the desire for mental health services and access to care. Reasons for these gaps include structural issues, such as the organization of the DoD and VA health care systems; eligibility requirements for using care; staffing; and information flows. However, negative attitudes about mental health care or the consequences associated with receiving care are key access issues for military servicemembers and are the most challenging to overcome.

To understand access to mental health care for military servicemembers and veterans, we must understand the organization of the health service systems that provide services to these individuals. Below, we provide a brief overview of health systems that serve military servicemembers and veterans. In the remainder of the section, we review structural and personal factors that affect access to mental health care.

Overview of Health Service Systems

The Department of Defense and Department of Veterans Affairs provide extensive health care services, ranging from preventive services to the care of multiple combat-related injuries (polytrauma). DoD's military health system has two primary missions: to enhance DoD's and our nation's security by providing health support for the full range of military operations, and to sustain the health of all those entrusted to its care. This system serves members of the Active Component and their family members, military retirees and their families, as well as some Reserve Component personnel. In FY2006, the MHS spent about $41.6 billion on health care (TRICARE, 2007).

The component of the Department of Veterans Affairs that deals with veterans' health care is the VHA, whose mission is to honor America's veterans by providing exceptional health care to improve their health and well-being. As such, the VHA is designed to provide health care services to eligible veterans of military service. In FY2006, Congress appropriated $31 billion for health care to the VHA for its 7.9 million enrolled veterans and active duty and retired military personnel and their beneficiaries (Department of Veterans Affairs, 2007e).

In addition to DoD and VA health service systems, servicemembers and veterans may access mental health services that are generally available in the community. Key service systems available to servicemembers and veterans are summarized in Table 7.1.

The Department of Defense. The Office of the Assistant Secretary of Defense for Health Affairs establishes policies, procedures, and standards that govern DoD health care programs, manages DoD health and medical resources, oversees TRICARE (the health plan of the MHS), directs deployment medicine policies, and ensures consistent, effective implementation of DoD policy throughout the MHS. The individual Services (Army, Navy, Air Force) are responsible for managing and delivering the health care services in garrison and health care support during military operations.

The MHS provides *direct care* to its beneficiaries through Military Treatment Facilities and clinics, supplemented by *purchased care* through civilian health professionals, hospitals, and pharmacies, which are financed through managed care contracts and fee-for-service (FFS) reimbursements (TRICARE, 2007).

TRICARE. Roughly 9 million active duty servicemembers, active duty family members, retirees,[1] and families of retirees are eligible to receive medical care through TRICARE (TRICARE, 2007). Beneficiaries have two primary TRICARE options: an HMO-like plan called *TRICARE Prime*, which delivers care through military hospitals and clinics, and contracted civilian network providers; and a fee-for-service plan called *TRICARE Standard*. Within Standard, beneficiaries can exercise a preferred provider option (PPO), *TRICARE Extra*, which requires that an individual use in-network providers, but lowers the out-of-pocket co-payment costs to 15 to 20 percent of standard

---

[1]   *Retirees* refers to those servicemembers who retire after a required number of years of service and qualify for military retirement benefits, including TRICARE.

Table 7.1
Summary of Systems Providing Mental Health Services

System	Services Offered Through (or by)	Population
In-Theater: DoD	Embedded MH providers/support (chaplains) Treatment facilities in theater	Active duty forces in theater
Stateside: DoD	Embedded MH providers/support (chaplains) Military Treatment Facility (TRICARE) Military OneSource Community providers in TRICARE network	Active duty Reserve/Guard[a] Retired military Dependents of active duty, military retirees, and Reserve/Guard[a]
VA	VA health facilities and clinics VA polytrauma centers[b] Vet Centers	Combat veterans Individuals with Service-connected disability[c]
Community	Private physicians or clinics Other community support programs Public health clinics or providers	Access may require employer-sponsored health insurance[d]

SOURCES: TRICARE, 2007; Department of Veterans Affairs Web site.

[a] Based on duty status and TRICARE eligibility.

[b] Active duty servicemembers with multiple combat-related injuries may receive initial care through the VA polytrauma centers and may transfer back to DoD upon recovery.

[c] Access is based on priority rating system and enrollment; for those without rating, depends on time since separation from service.

[d] Services may be paid out of pocket or through other insurance.

costs (TRICARE, 2003, 2007). Individuals eligible for TRICARE Standard/Extra may also receive care at an MTF at no charge on a space-available basis. All active duty servicemembers, including reservists and guardsmen who are called to active duty for more than 30 days, are automatically enrolled in TRICARE Prime at no charge. Active Component servicemembers and activated Reserve Component personnel who do not live close to an MTF are enrolled in *TRICARE Prime Remote*, which provides comparable benefits to TRICARE Prime. Table 7.2 describes these options and their eligibility requirements for active duty and retired servicemembers.

In FY2006, the MHS direct-care system included 83,800 primary care providers, 77,300 specialists, 65 inpatient hospitals and medical centers, 412 ambulatory medical clinics, and 414 ambulatory dental clinics within the United States (TRICARE, 2007). However, despite the large number of MHS providers and facilities, many beneficiaries, particularly retirees and members of the Reserve Component, and their families, rely more heavily on purchased care because they reside outside of MTF Catchment and Prism areas (TRICARE, 2007).

Table 7.2
TRICARE Plans for Active Duty Servicemembers and Retired Servicemembers

Plan	Description	Eligibility

Prime	HMO
	  No charge for active duty personnel.
	  Retired veterans pay to enroll and have applicable co-pays.
	  Must receive care through primary care provider unless referred out.
		All active duty automatically enrolled. Reserve and Guard eligible if called to active duty for 30+ days.
		Retired veterans not eligible for Medicare are eligible, at beneficiary level.

Standard/Extra	Standard: Fee for service
	  20–25% co-pay; may see any authorized provider.
	Extra: PPO
	  15–20% co-pay.
	  Must see TRICARE network provider.
		Retired veteran not eligible for Medicare.

Prime Remote	HMO No charge for active duty personnel.	Active duty and activated Guard and Reserve who do not live close to an MTF.
Reserve Select	Similar to Standard/Extra and requires monthly premium.	Members of the Selected Reserve. Must commit to 1 year of service.

What Structural Factors Impede or Facilitate Access to DoD Mental Health Services?

Various Sources of Mental Health Care Are Available. U.S. military personnel have several options when seeking help for mental health problems: talking with U.S. military chaplains or mental health practitioners embedded in operational units, seeking counseling offered in community service programs, obtaining mental health services provided by MTFs within both specialty mental health and primary care settings, getting information and counseling available through Military OneSource, and pursuing a range of health and specialty mental health services available from TRICARE civilian network providers. Other treatment options are also available and often vary from one military installation to another. The review below is intended to provide a broad but not exhaustive overview of DoD mental health services available to servicemembers.

Chaplains. Multifaith chaplains are available to every military unit and may be uniquely suited as a first point of entry for mental health care. They train and deploy with units, get to know unit needs, and provide what is called a "ministry of presence." Military chaplains offer *nonclinical counseling*, which means that it does not rely on formal psychotherapeutic approaches. Since discussions with chaplains are confidential, they may serve as "safe havens" for troubled servicemembers who feel they have nowhere else to turn. Chaplains routinely refer servicemembers to other sources of care and assistance, including formal mental health resources; help implement the Army and Marine Corps' return and reunion educational program; and assist in suicide-prevention programs (Force Health Protection and Readiness Military Mental Health, 2007).

Unit-Embedded Mental Health Providers. Each of the Services is actively embedding mental health professionals into operational line units. For example, a Marine Corps program called the Operational Stress Control and Readiness Program, or OSCAR, integrates mental health teams at the regimental level.[2] It has been implemented in all three active divisions and will eventually expand to the entire force (Gaskin, 2007). In addition, the Army is embedding a behavioral health officer and an enlisted mental health specialist into the new Brigade Combat Team structure to augment division mental health assets, which include a division psychiatrist and a senior noncommissioned officer (NCO).

Embedded programs increase access to providers in garrison for servicemembers. But they may also offer other strengths. According to a stakeholder interview, because military practitioners learn about the culture in which they are embedded, they are likely to better understand the challenges, barriers to care, and obstacles that servicemembers face. More important, mental health professionals may become trusted members of the operations community. Surveys conducted by the Mental Health Advisory Team have shown that Army soldiers experiencing significant distress while deployed in Iraq were three times more likely to turn to a fellow soldier for help than to mental health personnel (U.S. Department of the Army, Office of the Surgeon General, 2003).

Counseling Within Community Service Programs. Each branch of the military has community service programs at the local-installation level, including short-term individual and group counseling, generally provided by civilian masters-level counselors or social workers. The programs offer assistance on issues ranging from combat stress, anxiety, and sadness to marital and parenting problems and financial difficulties. Servicemembers who present to these programs with a major mental health condition, such as PTSD or major depression, are supposed to be referred to the MTF. However, many program counselors may provide treatment for less-serious cases of PTSD or depression. Counseling services offered through these service programs are confidential: Counseling visits are not recorded or linked to the medical facility; thus, the encounter is not recorded in the servicemember's medical record. Mental health conditions and other problems are reported to command, mainly in cases of suspected abuse or intention to inflict harm on oneself or others. The availability of such counseling services varies from base to base, as do the background, skills and training of counseling staff.

Specialty Mental Health Care Within Medical Treatment Facilities. A more formal avenue for mental health treatment, Medical Treatment Facilities are the primary source of specialty mental health care for military personnel. Services are traditionally provided by mental health clinics that are either stand-alone entities or located in base hospitals. Staff include military and civilian psychiatrists, psychologists, social workers, and enlisted mental health technicians. Services include diagnostic evalua-

---

[2]   A regiment in the Marine Corps is composed of approximately 4,800 marines.

tions, medication management, and psychotherapeutic treatments for mental health conditions, such as PTSD and major depression. Treatment sessions are supposed to be unlimited, and program descriptions found on the Internet frequently assert that walk-in consultations are available. Treatment slots are primarily reserved for active duty servicemembers; within MTFs, treatment for retired personnel and families of active duty personnel depends on availability.

Most MTF-based mental health treatment is conducted on an outpatient basis; specialized PTSD programs are available only at select installations, such as the National Naval Medical Center. The Department of Defense also runs a three-week program of customized PTSD treatment at Walter Reed Army Medical Center. Inpatient psychiatric care is available at several MTF locations across the military system.

Mental Health Services in Primary Health Care. A growing trend in both civilian and military sectors is integration of mental health professionals into primary care medical practices. Integration has several potential benefits, including increased recognition of mental disorders, improved clinical outcomes and satisfaction with care, and reduction in health care costs (Beardsley et al., 1998; Smit et al., 2006; Katon, Von Korff, et al., 1995; Katon, Robinson, et al., 1996). Mental health practitioners provide unique services in primary care settings, including "short, focused assessments; brief interventions in support of the primary care treatment plan; skill training through psycho-education and patient education strategies; training in self-management skills and behavioral change plans; and on-the-spot consultation" (Department of Defense Task Force on Mental Health, 2007a, p. 18). These responsibilities differ significantly from the longer-term, more focused services provided by staff in traditional military mental health clinics.

In response to the findings of the Mental Health Task Force (Department of Defense Task Force on Mental Health, 2007a), DoD plans to focus on greater adoption of primary care–mental health integration. The Army has implemented the RESPECT-Mil program in several MTFs. Based on a civilian version of the program, this intervention integrates efforts of a primary care clinician, a care manager, and a mental health professional, working in conjunction to manage a patient's depression. This program is described in more detail in the Quality of Mental Health Care section. In addition, the Navy is instituting Deployment Health Clinics at installations throughout the Department of the Navy and Marine Corps. Staff will include primary care providers, psychologists, psychiatrists, social workers, and certified medical assistants. Care for mental health problems, including PTSD, will be a key focus (Koffman, 2007). Because sailors and marines have reason to visit these clinics for purposes other than mental health issues—e.g., for their annual preventive health assessments and Post Deployment Health Assessments and Reassessments—the clinics can serve as a "non-stigmatizing portal of care" (Koffman, 2007, p. 25). Thirteen clinics were opened in FY2007, and another five clinics were brought online early in FY2008 (Koffman, 2007).

Military OneSource. Military OneSource is an information and consultation service offered by the Department of Defense (through the Military, Family, and Community Policy directorate within the Under Secretary of Defense for Personnel and Readiness) to servicemembers in the Active and Reserve Components (regardless of activation status) and their families. Retired or separated servicemembers and their family members are eligible to receive services at no cost for up to six months after separation. When a military member has an emotional, family, or adjustment problem, he or she may call a Military OneSource consultant for assistance. According to a stakeholder interview, OneSource services are not intended to provide medical treatment for PTSD, major depression, or other major mental health conditions. The consultants triage calls, referring the caller either to a counselor for six prepaid counseling sessions or, for those identified with a major mental disorder (including PTSD and major depression), to the appropriate medical care provider, which may be a Military Treatment Facility, VA hospital, or TRICARE civilian provider. However, triage is not perfect, and, according to a stakeholder interview, some individuals with these health conditions may be receiving treatment via the six free counseling sessions.

The majority of Military OneSource consultants have master's-level training and a license to provide counseling or an employee assistance professional (EAP) certification. After the initial contact, the OneSource consultant remains in contact with the military or family member to ensure that the recommended provider connection was made and that the service was perceived to be satisfactory. The six free counseling sessions are provided by a network of community specialty mental health providers, usually via office visits, but individuals who live in remote locations, lack transportation or adequate childcare, or work overseas may receive telephonic counseling sessions. Use of OneSource resources is confidential; use is not disclosed to the military, unless there is evidence that an individual may be a threat to him-/herself or others.

Civilian TRICARE Providers. Civilian TRICARE networks are another important source of mental health care for the military community. Active duty servicemembers must obtain a referral from the local MTF or service point of contact in remote locations to receive care from a civilian provider. However, TRICARE civilian networks do provide an increasing level of services for families, retirees, and active duty servicemembers stationed far from installations. In addition, several different TRICARE benefits programs also help fill potential gaps in health insurance coverage for Reserve Component servicemembers.

TRICARE does not offer specialized PTSD or depression treatment programs. Instead, beneficiaries can identify locally based providers for treatment through a central referral process that can be accessed by Web or by phone. TRICARE will reimburse for a maximum of two psychotherapy sessions per week in any combination of individual, family, or group sessions. Eight sessions are provided without the need for referral from a primary care provider.[3] TRICARE Prime involves no deductible or co-pay for active duty personnel and their dependents.

Service Availability Is Variable, and Some Gaps Are Reported. With the burgeoning patient population, the availability of mental health care at MTFs has come into question. Several recently published reports attest that servicemembers interested in accessing mental health care often face long wait lists (Johnson et al., 2007; Department of Defense Task Force on Mental Health, 2007a). Although these wait times can vary considerably from one behavioral health clinic to another; the DoD Mental Health Task Force noted that delays of 30 days for an initial mental health appointment are not uncommon. The problem with delays is not just a matter of inconvenience. Timely enrollment in treatment following a decision to seek treatment is critical to ensuring proper compliance with treatment protocols and successful treatment outcomes. Delays in treatment may "result in people not obtaining treatment at all" (Johnson et al., 2007, p. 46).

In some cases, the treatment provided is not available to everyone who needs it. The three-week program of intensive PTSD care by the Deployment Health Clinical Center at Walter Reed has the capacity to treat only a limited number of patients a year (Hull and Priest, 2007), likely far less than the number of people who would benefit from the program.

These challenges in providing services are distributed unevenly across the United States. "Some communities have adequate numbers of providers who are well-qualified to care for military personnel and their families. Unfortunately, shortages of qualified providers in other communities raise significant barriers to the provision of needed care" (Johnson et al., 2007, p. 43). The Department of Defense Mental Health Task Force (2007a, p. 44) notes that "too often, the psychological health services available to servicemembers and their families depend on their location rather than their psychological health needs."

Providing mental health services for the Reserve Component constitutes a special challenge. When reservists are deactivated, they return to their homes across the country. This geographic dispersion can create a significant distance between those needing care and the MTFs or VA facilities that can provide it. Distance from a facility may also affect Active Component dependents, because many spouses and their children move away from installations during deployment and may lose easy access to MTF or civilian network services.

Unfortunately, DoD's provider-allocation system cannot systematically assess where shortages occur. The system is based on services that clinics render. It does not track suppressed demand (i.e., those who need care but are unable to access it). Indeed,

---

[3]   Where necessary, 30 days of hospitalization are permitted per fiscal year for beneficiaries 19 and over, and up to 45 days are allowed for those age 18 or under. Children and adolescents receive coverage for residential treatment care for 150 days per fiscal year, and partial hospitalizations are covered for up to 60 days.

one interview contact noted, "Access cannot be measured without first knowing the need, and we don't know what the need is."

Responding to recommendations from the Mental Health Task Force, DoD is implementing a population-based risk-adjusted model that may more accurately gauge installation-specific mental health staffing needs. The Center for Naval Analyses will evaluate and refine the model (Department of Defense Task Force on Mental Health, 2007a).

Challenges in Meeting the Mental Health Demands of Servicemembers. There are a number of reasons that the military services may have a difficult time providing servicemembers with full access to mental health care. First, outpatient care in DoD behavioral health clinics is usually available during standard working hours (i.e., 0730–1630 or 0800–1700). When units return from deployment, they immediately begin a new training cycle to prepare for their next rotation in-theater. To obtain a mental health evaluation or participate in weekly treatment sessions, servicemembers must take time away from what is already a robust deployment-training tempo. Many are hesitant to take time away from such training, much less identify the reasons for their absence. Of surveyed soldiers, 55 percent cited the inability to take time off of work as a major impediment to seeking mental health care (Hoge et al., 2004). Our own study also shows concerns about getting time off of work (see Chapter Four).

Second, there are not enough military mental health providers on staff: "The DoD currently lacks the resources—both funding and personnel—to adequately support the psychological health of servicemembers and their families" (Department of Defense Task Force on Mental Health, 2007a, p. 41). The Mental Health Task Force Report cautions that, absent increased congressional funding, few Task Force recommendations can be implemented.

Third, it is often suggested that uniformed mental health providers offer a service that cannot easily be replaced by their civilian counterparts. Military providers understand the military culture and the social context in which mental health problems are manifested, diagnosed, and treated. They are best able to make judgments about fitness for duty, and they have the requisite credibility to educate commanders and form an alliance of trust with their uniformed patients.

Unfortunately, it is with these uniformed providers that manpower shortages are most acutely felt. Available data suggest significant vacancies in prewar mental health personnel slots for social workers, psychologists, and psychiatrists for the Navy, Air Force, and the Army (Russell, 2007). The number of active duty mental health professionals dropped by 20 percent for the Air Force from FY2003 through FY2007, 15 percent for the Navy from FY2003 through FY2006, and 8 percent for the Army from FY2003 through FY2005. Data from FY2006 and FY2007 may reveal even larger declines (Department of Defense Mental Health Task Force, 2007a).

The U.S. military acquires its licensed psychologists and psychiatrists through internship training programs and Graduate Medical Education residency programs, respectively. The psychology internship program is a coveted training slot, and more highly qualified candidates routinely apply than can otherwise be accepted. However, this trend is reversing. For the 2007/2008 training year, the Navy filled all ten of its training vacancies, but the Army filled 13 of 36 slots, and the Air Force, 13 of 24 slots (Department of Defense Task Force on Mental Health, 2007a). Anecdotal evidence suggests that psychiatry-residency positions are similarly becoming difficult to fill. If the new trend continues, its ramifications for providing military mental health care will be felt for years (Department of Defense Task Force on Mental Health, 2007a).

A related challenge is effective utilization of social workers. Social workers represent the largest group of mental health practitioners in the nation; in the Army and Air Force, they are 33 and 38 percent, respectively, of the mental health provider workforce (Defense Manpower Data Center, 2006). However, in the Navy, social workers constitute only 11 percent of the mental health provider workforce, and they are encumbered by significant practice limitations. In addition, the Navy is civilianizing all 32 social-work slots as part of its strategy to decrease end-strength by 30,000 (Arthur, 2007).

Challenges with Recruiting and Retaining Uniformed Providers. Several factors contribute to problems with acquiring and retaining uniformed providers. To reduce costs, DoD has cut the number of active duty personnel slots for mental health staff and has relied more heavily on civilian contract providers. But with the high deployment tempo, uniformed providers are required to deploy overseas at an increasing rate, leaving fewer to provide for in-garrison psychological health needs. The result is high work-related stress for both deployed providers and those remaining behind. *MHAT-II Report* (U.S. Department of the Army, Office of the Surgeon General, 2005) documented that 33 percent of Army behavioral health personnel suffer from high levels of burnout. "That's something that we didn't anticipate five years ago," observed one mental health provider.

Comparability of pay and opportunities for promotion are other issues. Medical officers are eligible for a variety of retention bonuses or special pays. For example, an anesthesiologist who signs a three-year contract is eligible for a $38,000 bonus. Psychiatrists are eligible for a $19,000 bonus. The U.S. Navy just recently authorized a retention bonus for psychologists. However, no such bonuses for psychologists are scheduled for the U.S. Army (Medical Service Corps, 2002; Military.com, 2007b). As military officers, psychologists and social workers must also perform well as leaders and managers to successfully compete for promotion. In addition to being a capable provider, each must be a capable officer. In the opinion of one commentator, "Being an outstanding or 'expert' clinician in military medicine is not an advantage for promotion . . . ," particularly for master's-level clinicians, such as social workers and psychologists (Russell, 2007, p. 16). This situation may be due, in part, to the difficulty of objectively measuring how well clinicians are practicing.

Hiring civilian mental health practitioners to provide care within MTFs may offer a short-term, albeit imperfect, solution to the shortfall in uniformed providers, but there are challenges with this option as well. DoD salaries for civilian psychologists and social workers are not competitive with rates provided in the civilian market or the VA system, which increases the "likelihood that DoD will lose civilian providers to the VA system as they learn that they can earn substantially higher salaries for performing essentially the same job" (Department of Defense Task Force on Mental Health, 2007a, p. 48). MTF commanders do not have the authority to fill critical gaps by offering competitive recruitment packages to civilians.

Variations in Availability of Services Among Civilian TRICARE Providers. As with the MTFs, access to mental health services varies within the network of civilian TRICARE providers. Many TRICARE providers are no longer accepting new patients. In one instance, a mental health professional reportedly called over 100 mental health providers within the TRICARE network and found only three who would accept new TRICARE referrals (Department of Defense Task Force on Mental Health, 2007a).

Two recent GAO reports bear directly on access to care from TRICARE civilian providers.

The first, published in 2003, concluded that DoD's ability to oversee the civilian-provider network was hindered by using measures that likely underestimate the number of providers needed in geographical areas. In addition, DoD does not systematically collect and analyze beneficiary complaints that might identify inadequacies in the civilian provider network (GAO, 2003).

The second, more recent, GAO report (GAO, 2007a) surveyed reservists about their overall satisfaction with TRICARE compared with private-sector insurance coverage. Only 12 percent of reservists reported that the availability of providers and specialists was superior in TRICARE, and 50 percent stated that availability was greater in the private sector (GAO, 2007a).

Factors Limiting Availability of Civilian Mental Health Providers. Several factors likely account for limited availability of TRICARE civilian network and nonnetwork providers. About 20 percent of surveyed providers who would not accept TRICARE patients cited concerns about the adequacy of TRICARE's reimbursement rates, which are tied to Medicare rates (GAO, 2006a). The TRICARE Management Activity (TMA) has the authority to adjust reimbursement amounts in locales in which reimbursement rates appear to negatively affect beneficiary access to care. However, as of August 2006, TMA had approved only 15 waivers, and the waivers have not been used to increase the availability of any mental health services (GAO, 2006a).

In addition, 15 percent of network providers cited perceived administrative hassles as the reason they were not accepting new TRICARE patients (GAO, 2006a). Although TRICARE has improved its claims processing, early problems with the system may have left a lasting negative impression on some providers. Also, the application process for becoming a TRICARE network provider is reportedly cumbersome. Outreach efforts are under way to educate health care personnel about the system improvements (GAO, 2006a).

Other factors limiting access to providers cannot be attributed to TRICARE. For example, some providers' practices cannot accommodate additional patients, regardless of health insurance payments. Problems in provider capacity are most pronounced in geographically remote areas. TRICARE has designated two bonus payment systems to motivate providers to practice in such areas.[4] However, more-robust efforts may be necessary to ensure that military personnel, their families, and veterans receive appropriate and timely care.

The Department of Veterans Affairs. The mission of the Department of Veterans Affairs is to serve America's veterans and their families by promoting the health, welfare, and dignity of all veterans in recognition of their service to this nation. The VA is the principal agency charged to provide veterans with medical care, benefits, social support, and lasting memorials.

The VA is made up of a central office and three major organizations: the Veterans Health Administration (VHA), the Veterans Benefits Administration (VBA), and the National Cemetery Administration (NCA). The Veterans Health Administration administers and operates the VA's health care system.

VA Health Care System. The VA operates the largest integrated health care system in the United States. In 2006, the VA health care system had 7.9 million enrollees (Department of Veterans Affairs, 2007e). The VA health care system is organized into 21 Veterans Integrated Service Networks (VISNs), which provide a full spectrum of comprehensive health services, including primary and specialty care, as well as a comprehensive pharmaceutical benefits program and other ancillary services. These semi-autonomous Service Networks are charged with developing cost-effective health care programs that are responsive to both the national mission of the VA and to local circumstances and trends in health care service delivery.

There are currently 877 VA in-patient medical centers and outpatient clinics (Department of Veterans Affairs, 2007e). The VA also maintains partnerships with numerous academic institutions so that it can enhance quality of care and promote education, training, and research. The majority of services provided by the VA are delivered in facilities owned and maintained by the VA and staffed by VA and contract employees. The balance, referred to as *purchased services*, is paid for on a fee-for-service basis.

What Structural Factors Impede or Facilitate Access to Mental Health Services Within the VA?

Eligibility and Priorities for VA Health Services Guide Access. The Veterans' Health Care Eligibility Reform Act of 1996 expanded the types of services available to

---

[4] The Department of Health and Human Services designates both the Health Professional Shortage Areas and the Physician Scarcity Areas. The former are deemed to have a shortage of primary care, dental, or mental health providers. Physician Scarcity Area designations are based on calculations of ratios of active providers of primary and specialty care to Medicare beneficiaries in every county in the United States.

VA patients and extended coverage, through a priority-based enrollment system, to veterans with at least 24 months of continuous active duty military service and an "other-than-dishonorable" discharge (Department of Veterans Affairs, 2007l). Although the option of coverage is extended to all veterans, veterans are not entitled to VA health benefits by statute. Instead, the VA system relies on a discretionary budget.

Effective in FY1999, veterans were prioritized for enrollment according to eight tiers: those with Service-connected disabilities (priority levels 1 to 3); prisoners of war and recipients of the Purple Heart (priority 3); veterans with catastrophic disabilities unrelated to service (priority 4); low-income veterans (priority 5); veterans who meet specific criteria, such as having served in the first Gulf War (priority 6); and higher-income veterans who do not qualify for other priority groups (priorities 7 and 8). Enrollment is currently suspended for priority group 8 to ensure that the VA can meet the needs of its higher-priority enrollees (Department of Veterans Affairs, 2007k). Co-payments vary by the veteran's priority level; veterans in priority levels 1 through 6 receive care without co-payments. The financial threshold for *low income* increases slightly each year and varies by the number of dependents. Co-payment rates for inpatient and ambulatory care services for veterans in higher-income priority levels 7 and 8 are comparable to those required by Medicare.

The Veterans' Health Care Eligibility Reform Act of 1996 broadened the VA's contracting authority to enable the department to enter into contracts with non-VA health care providers. This new flexibility allowed the VA to open hundreds of Community-Based Outpatient Clinics located in areas that are far from a medical center and have a high concentration of veterans. These Outpatient Clinics may improve veterans' access to care, including preventive care that can potentially alleviate conditions before they require more-specialized and more-expensive treatment. The VA also provides specialized services to address the unique needs of military veterans, including treatment for blindness, spinal-cord injury, traumatic brain injury, post-traumatic stress disorder, and other mental disorders.

Access to VA Care for Combat Veterans of OEF/OIF. All veterans with combat service after November 11, 1998, and who were discharged under other-than-dishonorable conditions, are eligible to receive cost-free health care through the VA for five years after separation from active military service, regardless of whether they have sustained Service-connected injuries or illness. During this five-year eligibility period, veterans have a level 6 priority rating, unless they meet criteria that qualify them for a higher priority (Department of Veterans Affairs, 2007k).

Servicemembers are not required to enroll with the VA to receive services during the initial five-year period. However, veterans who enroll with the VA during this time retain eligibility for VA health services after the five years have elapsed. At that time, veterans who have not received a disability rating will switch to level 7 or 8, depending on income (Department of Veterans Affairs, 2007l). These veterans will be required to make applicable co-payments for medical care services received through the VA.

The current conflicts in Afghanistan and Iraq have increased tremendously the demand for mental health services across the VA. According to recent estimates, approximately 18 percent of OEF/OIF veterans seeking care through the VA were receiving care for PTSD (Department of Veterans Affairs, 2007e). In one study, about 184,500 sought care from a VA Medical Center between October 2001 (the start of OEF) and May 2006 (Department of Veterans Affairs, 2006b). Of these, about 29,000 had a probable diagnosis of PTSD.

Specialized Mental Health Services Are Available Within the VA for Post-Traumatic Stress Disorder (PTSD). Historically, the VA has adapted its programs and treatment approaches to meet the changing mental health needs of returning troops. Currently, the VA offers a mix of onsite and offsite programs for evaluating and treating PTSD. The VA's approach promotes early recognition of individuals who meet formal criteria for diagnosis, as well as those with subthreshold symptoms. The goal is to make evidence-based treatments available early to prevent chronic symptoms and lasting impairment (Department of Veterans Affairs, 2007c). According to the Veterans Affairs' National Center for PTSD Web site (Department of Veterans Affairs, 2007d), each VA Medical Center offers some type of specialized expertise with PTSD, resulting in a network of more than 200 specialized treatment programs and trauma centers. In addition, many VA Medical Centers offer walk-in clinics to provide immediate care (Cross, 2006). Tables 7.3 and 7.4 provide an overview of the specialized PTSD outpatient and inpatient programs within the VA, respectively.

In addition to the national inpatient and outpatient treatment programs, some VA Medical Centers run their own local specialized PTSD programs.

Table 7.3
VA Outpatient PTSD Treatment Programs

Outpatient Treatment Programs (Number of Programs)	Description of Service
PTSD Clinical Team (152)	Group and one-on-one evaluation, education, counseling, and psychotherapy.
Substance Use and PTSD Team (10)	Education, evaluation, and counseling, with a focus on veterans with both substance abuse and PTSD.
Women's Stress Disorder Treatment Team/Military Sexual Trauma Team (17)	Individual evaluation, counseling, and psychotherapy for women. Group counseling and psychotherapy for women. Mostly women; may include a small number of men separate from women.
PTSD Day Hospital (11)	Organized in an outpatient setting. Provides individual treatment. Patient comes in daily or several times a week for 4 to 8 hours each visit. Social, recreational, and vocational activities and counseling.

SOURCE: GAO, *Posttraumatic Stress Disorder: DoD Needs to Identify the Factors Its Providers Use to Make Mental Health Evaluation Referrals for Service Members,* Washington, D.C.: GAO-06-397, 2006b.

Table 7.4
VA Inpatient PTSD Treatment Programs

Inpatient Treatment Programs (Number of Programs)	Description of Service
Evaluation and Brief Treatment PTSD Unit (4)	Provides inpatient evaluation, education, and psychotherapy for PTSD. Duration of service: 14 to 28 days.
PTSD Domiciliary (8)	Residential program providing integrated rehabilitative and restorative care with the goal of helping veterans with PTSD achieve and maintain the highest level of functioning and independence possible. Aim is to facilitate transition to outpatient mental health care. Duration of service: about 85 days.
PTSD Residential Rehabilitation Program (14)	Residential service providing evaluation, education, counseling, and case management that focuses on helping the survivor resume a productive involvement in community life. Duration of service: 28 to 90 days.
Specialized Inpatient PTSD Unit (5)	Provide trauma-focused evaluation, education, and counseling for substance use and PTSD psychotherapy. Duration of service: 28 to 90 days.
Women's Trauma Recovery Program (2)	Residential service with an emphasis on interpersonal skills for veterans with PTSD and a focus on war-zone-related stress, as well as military sexual trauma. Duration of service: up to 60 days.

SOURCE: GAO, *Posttraumatic Stress Disorder: DoD Needs to Identify the Factors Its Providers Use to Make Mental Health Evaluation Referrals for Service Members,* Washington, D.C.: GAO-06-397, 2006b.

The VA's National Center for PTSD was created in 1989 to address the needs of veterans with military-related post-traumatic stress disorder. The Center's mission is to advance the clinical care and social welfare of America's veterans through research, education, and training in the science, diagnosis, and treatment of PTSD and stress-related disorders (Department of Veterans Affairs, 2007c). The Center, which is head-quartered in White River Junction, VT, currently consists of seven VA academic centers of excellence across the United States.

The National Center is not a clinical program. It is organized with the goal of facilitating rapid translation of science into practice, ensuring that the latest research findings inform clinical care, and with translating of practice into science, ensuring that questions raised by clinical challenges are addressed using rigorous experimental protocols (Department of Veterans Affairs, 2007c).

Availability of Services for Major Depression Is Predominantly Integrated into Primary Care. Major depression is the second most prevalent illness in the Veterans Administration. Approximately 7 percent of VA patients meet criteria for major depression (Yu et al., 2003), a level of prevalence consistent with that found in the general

U.S. population. Primary care is an attractive environment for treating depressed VA patients (Katon and Schulberg, 1992). Most veterans treated for depression in the VA are treated in primary care settings (Department of Veterans Affairs, 2007g), with only a quarter (26.4 percent) who are seen in primary care needing referral to a specialty mental health setting (Kilbourne et al., 2006). In addition, offering depression services for veterans in a primary care setting may help alleviate the negative attitudes about seeking care in a designated mental heath environment. With these considerations in mind, we focus our discussion on treating depression in the primary care setting.

Appropriate treatment for depression begins with effective screening. Depression may go unrecognized in one-third to one-half of primary care patients (Kirklady and Tynes, 2006). Acknowledging this gap, the VA mandated annual depression screening in all VA primary care clinics in 1998. From 1997 to 2001, the frequency with which depression was diagnosed, as well as the percentage of the primary care population who received a diagnosis of depression, increased. However, the average number of primary care visits for depression treatment did not increase, falling below recommended guidelines for depression (Kirchner, Curran, and Aikens, 2004). This pattern may in part reflect increased demand in recent years from veterans serving both before and during the Gulf War era, potentially straining capacity and, in turn, reducing service intensity (Rosenheck and Fontana, 2007).

Despite these challenges, the VA has been working on innovative ways to improve depression treatment for veterans in primary care. One such strategy is the development of the Behavioral Health Laboratory to help assess patients potentially in need of mental health care (Oslin et al., 2006). The Behavioral Health Laboratory, which has been implemented in many VA primary care clinics, performs specific tests when ordered by primary care providers, interprets the results, and assists in clinical decisionmaking. Another recent advance in depression treatment is the depression prognosis index, which demonstrated notable success in predicting outcomes at a six-month interval, helping clinicians and researchers better understand various factors that affect depression-treatment outcomes (Oslin et al., 2006).

The collaborative care (or chronic care) model has also recently emerged as a potentially effective approach to providing care for depression in primary care. The model involves integrating a number of quality-improvement strategies and tools, including patient self-management support; clinician education and decision support; care management; and interactions between primary care and mental health specialists (Wagner, Austin, and Von Korff, 1996). Treatment options may include medication therapy, cognitive-behavioral therapy; patient education; patient support; and intervention of a mental health specialist. The collaborative care model is well documented as a cost-effective approach to improving depression-treatment outcomes in a primary care setting; however, the model has not yet been implemented nationally across any large health care system, including the VA (Fortney et al., 2007).

The VA, however, has launched a program that builds on the collaborative care model. "Translating Initiatives for Depression into Effective Solutions" is an evidence-based program for improving depression care, implemented in seven VA primary care clinics in five states. The program involves collaboration between primary care providers and mental health specialists, with support from a depression care manager. In interviews, VA administrators and providers have mentioned several other experimental programs aimed at integrating mental health services into primary care.

While the VA is working to improve mental health services in the promising environment of primary care clinics, differences in the organization of VA treatment facilities may present challenges for implementing systemwide approaches to improvement (Kilbourne et al., 2006). Additionally, primary care clinics within the VA may need to customize their respective treatment models according to available resources and the needs of the veterans they serve.

Challenges Related to VA Health Care Access. In September 2004, the Government Accountability Office issued a report assessing whether the VA is prepared to meet increased demand for PTSD treatment services among servicemembers who have served in Afghanistan and Iraq (Bascetta, 2004). The GAO concluded that the VA could not assess capacity for expanded treatment services because it did not know how many veterans were currently receiving PTSD services.

Competing Service Eras. The increased demand for mental health and PTSD services is not limited to veterans who have served (or are serving) in current conflicts. It also reflects the needs of veterans from previous wars (George, 2006).

The increase in use of VA mental health services among veterans of earlier wars has been 5 times greater than that observed among Gulf-era veterans, especially among Vietnam-era veterans diagnosed with PTSD (Rosenheck and Fontana, 2007). The exact reasons for this disparity remain unclear. One possibility may be related to changes in VA policy that allowed disability for diabetes among Vietnam veterans, resulting in a substantial increase in the number of veterans eligible for VA care, many of whom may also have mental health issues (Rosenheck and Fontana, 2007). Other reasons could be related to mental stress factors associated with aging and retirement, and decreased access to mental health services in the general population (Rosenheck and Fontana, 2007). Although the patient load has been increasing, the number of clinic visits per veteran is decreasing, dropping by about 38 percent from 1997 to 2005. Fewer visits may mean poorer continuity of care and increased risk of veterans' prematurely dropping out of treatment. Reduction in visits may also reduce the likelihood that evidence-based psychotherapies are delivered, because evidence-based therapy requires a certain frequency and length of treatment.

To explore access issues in greater detail, the VA reportedly is in the process of instituting a system redesign collaborative in which mental health providers throughout the system are going to work together to evaluate, among other issues, access and continuity of care—a large-scale initiative that will take place over the next year, with a conference planned for early in 2008, according to a stakeholder interview.

Vet Center Services Available to All Combat Veterans in Many Communities. Vet Centers play a critical role in providing mental health services for those whose injuries do not qualify them for high-priority access to VA care. Any veteran who has served in a war zone is eligible for care at a Vet Center. The Centers, often located in storefront settings, offer individual and group counseling; marital and family counseling; bereavement counseling for family members; medical referrals; assistance in applying for VA benefits; employment counseling; military sexual-trauma counseling; alcohol and drug abuse assessments; outreach; and community education. Services are offered at no cost to eligible veterans and their families, and there is no limit on the duration or frequency of services.

There are currently 209 Vet Centers located in all 50 states, the District of Columbia, Guam, Puerto Rico, and the U.S. Virgin Islands; the VA plans to expand the number of Vet Centers to 232 by 2009. Veterans may contact Vet Center staff during regular business hours at a toll-free phone number, and some Vet Centers have extended hours to facilitate counseling for those who work during the day.

Vet Center staff typically consist of four or five members, including a team leader who supervises an interdisciplinary team of social workers, psychologists, nurses, and/ or paraprofessional counselors. Of Vet Center counselors and team leaders, 73 percent are veterans themselves and have experienced readjustment issues firsthand. According to a stakeholder interview, each counselor receives standardized training in cognitive-behavioral therapy and exposure therapy (for a description of the therapies, see Appendix 7.C), suicide prevention, and TBI recognition and assessment. Counselors do not offer inpatient care or provide medical prescriptions (Democratic staff of the House Committee on Veterans Affairs, 2006). If a counselor detects a serious mental or physical health problem, the veteran will be referred to a VA hospital for more intensive treatment.

A veteran seeking care at a Vet Center goes through an intensive assessment protocol that may take place over three to five sessions. Following assessment, the counselor develops a treatment plan, which may include some combination of group, individual, marital, or family therapy. The treatment plan is periodically revised as treatment progresses. According to a stakeholder interview, to protect a veteran's confidentiality, Vet Center records are separate from VA administrative benefits and medical records.

About 250,600 OEF/OIF veterans have received some form of assistance from Vet Center staff through May 2007; 51,734 of these received care within the Centers, and 198,878 were contacted by outreach specialists (Frame, 2007).

VA data also indicate that 5,339 OEF/OIF veterans who have been diagnosed as having PTSD have been treated exclusively through Vet Centers (Democratic staff of the House Committee on Veterans Affairs, 2006; Kang, 2006). An additional 3,764 OEF/OIF veterans with a diagnostic code for PTSD were seen at both a VA medical facility and a Vet Center (Democratic staff of the House Committee on Veterans Affairs, 2006). Vet Centers also provided care to 2,290 OEF/OIF veterans who had PTSD symptoms that did not warrant a clinical diagnosis of PTSD; these individuals' conditions were identified by Vet Center staff as subthreshold PTSD (Kang, 2006).

In 2006, the House Committee on Veterans' Affairs surveyed 60 of the 207 Vet Centers from all 50 states, Puerto Rico, the Virgin Islands, the District of Columbia, and Guam to review their capacity for meeting the mental health needs of OEF/OIF veterans (Democratic staff of the House Committee on Veterans Affairs, 2006). All of the Vet Centers reported an increase in outreach and services to these veterans in the past year (Democratic staff of the House Committee on Veterans Affairs, 2006). Half of the Centers reported that the increase had resulted in higher demand for their services and had potentially hampered their ability to treat the existing patrons; 30 percent explicitly stated that they need more staff. One in four Centers reported that they were taking actions to manage the increasing workload (e.g., shifting veterans to group therapy when individual therapy is more appropriate, limiting access to family therapy, establishing wait lists). However, some Centers stated that they were adequately staffed and running efficiently.

Transitions and Coordination Across Systems Pose Challenges to Access and Continuity of Care

For American service men and women, frequent changes in duty stations necessitate changes in health care providers. In addition, when individuals separate from military service or when reservists deactivate, they often experience a change in health-insurance coverage and providers. These transitions pose significant challenges to the continuity of mental health care, particularly care initiated within one facility or system but to be continued by another. Below, we describe the systems in place for sharing medical records and helping patients to transition between providers.

Continuity of Care Between Military Treatment Facilities. Military servicemembers change service stations frequently. As the DoD Mental Health Task Force notes, these changes can occur as frequently as once every year or two. Servicemembers receiving treatment for mental health problems should continue their care at their new service station.

Transfer of Medical Records. The Armed Forces Health Longitudinal Technology Application (AHLTA) is DoD's electronic health record system. The system is intended to provide "seamless visibility" of health care information across the DoD medical system (McKaughan, 2007). However, although ambulatory visits to Military Treatment Facilities are captured in the system, the system lacks a specific electronic module for mental health treatment that could record psychiatric evaluations, histories, or detailed treatment notes (Department of Defense Task Force on Mental Health, 2007a). Consequently, a new mental health provider cannot electronically access specific information on a patient's diagnostic and treatment history. New providers may need to rely on paper records, or they may need to repeat psychiatric evaluations and retake patient histories. Depending on the availability and quality of paper records, they also risk beginning treatments that have already proven ineffective for the patient. DoD has committed to developing an AHLTA mental health module by May 2008 (Department of Defense Task Force on Mental Health, 2007b).

Patient Handoffs. With exception of the Air Force, none of the services provides written instructions that guide the transfer of patients across installations (DoD Task Force on Mental Health, 2007a). Consequently, many relocating servicemembers must navigate the new installation's patient care system on their own. Some will fail to reinitiate treatment. For those who do begin treatment, clinicians at the new installation may lack access to complete historical mental health treatment records. The Mental Health Task Force recommended that each military Service issue policies outlining the responsibilities of mental health professionals at the losing and gaining installations so that care can be properly handed off from one mental health provider to another. DoD has said that such policies will be reviewed and clarified (Department of Defense Task Force on Mental Health, 2007b).

Continuity of Care Between Military Treatment Facilities and Other DoD-Sponsored Counseling Programs. Some servicemembers will first seek mental health care from other DoD-sponsored counseling programs, which include OneSource-referred counselors and Service branch counseling programs, such as Marine Corps Community Services. As noted earlier, they do so in part because these programs offer increased confidentiality. However, servicemembers may need to transfer treatment from one provider to another for a number of reasons—for example, a severity of illness that warrants care in an MTF or, as with OneSource, the capitation of treatment to only six free sessions. It is important that continuity of care be maintained across these transitions.

Community-based providers to whom OneSource may refer military servicemembers pose special challenges for continuity. They have no formal communication pathways or shared medical-record systems with the MTF or with base counseling programs. However, they must be sufficiently familiar with MTFs and base counseling programs to make appropriate referrals. OneSource offers training to address this need, including information on military culture and on PTSD and TBI, so that counselors can refer servicemembers as needed to the local MTF, to the TRICARE civilian network, or to other civilian providers. Provider-to-provider handoff is one way to ensure continuity of care under these conditions. However, there is no publicly available information on how often or in what fashion those handoffs take place.

Base Counseling Services. As noted above, base counseling records are confidential. In addition, DoD's medical departments and counseling centers have distinct and separate standard operating procedures and use separate forms and databases to track workload. The base programs certainly have the capability to refer patients to the MTF.

However, the extent to which the MTFs and counseling centers otherwise interact or coordinate care reportedly varies from extensive to highly infrequent (Russell, 2007).

Continuity of Care Between Military Treatment Facilities and the VA. Whether temporary or permanent, separation from military service presents another challenge to continuity of care. Individuals who separate from military service will ideally continue Service-connected mental health care with the VA. Reserve Component members who return to their communities may also require continued care. Some servicemembers receive simultaneous care from both the VA and DoD. DoD and the VA both use electronic medical record systems, but the VA system—the Veterans' Health Information Systems and Technology Architecture—and the DoD system (AHLTA) are not compatible for sharing electronic records.

Efforts are under way to address the compatibility and electronic transmission of patient health information between these systems; however, sharing of patient records across the systems still presents a challenge for continuity of care. This is a two-way challenge, from DoD to the VA and from the VA to DoD. For example, when a reservist receiving treatment through the VA is called back to active duty, the treating VA clinician has limited communication tools to enable a handoff for evaluating deployability or continued care in DoD.

Patient Handoffs. Transition to post-military, civilian life requires navigating a new health care system, an experience that leaves many individuals resigned to not seeking care. The failure to continue mental health care in the VA was confirmed by the only study that examined the flow of mental health patients from DoD to VA systems of care. The study found that only 52 percent of discharged veterans with schizophrenia, bipolar, or major affective disorders made contact with the VA health care system (Mojtabi et al., 2003). The Mental Health Task Force recommended provider-to-provider handoffs to guide transition to civilian care (Department of Defense Task Force on Mental Health, 2007b). May 2008 is the target date for DoD to draft guidelines for transferring mental health patients to VA, TRICARE, and other post-DoD providers.

The VA has undertaken a number of community-outreach efforts to ensure that servicemembers with mental health problems or other Service-connected ailments resume or initiate treatment in the VA health care system. From October 1, 2000, through May 31, 2006, the VA provided approximately 36,000 briefings on available health care services to nearly 1.4 million active duty and Reserve Component servicemembers and their families. A VA-sponsored Web site (Department of Veterans Affairs, 2007l) provides information on VA health services aimed specifically at OEF/OIF veterans. Other promotional programs include wallet-sized cards with VA telephone numbers and a monthly video magazine called the *American Veteran* (GAO, 2006c).

Confidentiality. The confidentiality of mental health care within the VA presents a special challenge for exchanging medical records with DoD. Currently, the

VA requires the consent of Reserve Component servicemembers before their medical records can be transferred to DoD. The Mental Health Task Force recommended that DoD and the VA establish formal agreements for medical records–sharing, but the VA is concerned about maintaining confidentiality (Department of Defense Task Force on Mental Health, 2007a). The VA and DoD are currently discussing how to resolve this issue (Cross, 2007).

Continuity of Care Between Community Treatment Centers and VA/DoD. Some veterans, and Reserve Component servicemembers seek care from non-VA or non-DoD facilities, such as community mental health centers or other private-practice providers, perhaps because they do not live near a VA facility, are unfamiliar or uncomfortable with VA services, or value the confidentiality that using community and private resources provides. Some military servicemembers pay for community-provided treatment out of pocket to avoid the stigma associated with receiving mental health care on base. Active outreach from DoD and the VA could help military servicemembers become more familiar with their own systems and services. However, the negative attitudes within the military culture associated with having and treating a mental disorder are a major barrier to care that must be addressed systemwide (Department of Defense Task Force on Mental Health, 2007a).

Seamless Transitions: DoD to the VA. A major challenge faced by wounded servicemembers is transitioning their health care from DoD's Military Treatment Facilities to the VA's health care system. The VA has made some administrative changes to smooth the transition. To reduce the time between separation from the military and access to VA benefits, servicemembers may now enroll for VA health care and file for benefits before leaving active duty. OEF/OIF servicemembers who are not seriously injured may begin the disability-compensation application process 180 days before separation, through the Benefits Delivery at Discharge Program (Department of Veterans Affairs, 2007f). Other changes include creation of a special office (Seamless Transition Office) to help patients transition between military and VA health care facilities (U.S. Department of the Army, Office of the Surgeon General, *MHAT-II Report*, 2005).

More-comprehensive and more-coordinated care and services can also be achieved through case management. Recognizing this need, the VA Task Force on Returning Global War on Terror Heroes recommended a system of co-management and case management for active duty servicemembers who receive care in both DoD and VA facilities by suggesting that each of these patients be assigned to a primary case manager and that formal agreements on how these patients will be co-managed be instituted (Department of Veterans Affairs, 2007i).

As of December 2007, full-time benefit counselors and social workers were stationed at seven major MTFs. These case managers work with servicemembers and their families to facilitate health care coordination and discharge planning as servicemembers transition from military to VA care (Brown, 2005). In addition, the four VA Level I Polytrauma Centers assign one social worker to every six patients to serve as their case manager. On October 31, 2007, following the recommendation of the President's Commission on the Care of America's Returning Wounded Warriors (referred to here-inafter as PCCWW) and the Wounded, Ill, and Injured Senior Oversight Committee (referred to hereinafter as the Senior Oversight Committee), DoD and the VA agreed to establish a joint Recovery Coordinator Program (GAO, 2007b). These federal recovery coordinators are intended to be the patient's and family's single point of contact for all care (Bascetta, 2007).

A final transition issue concerns timeliness and consistency of disability decisions. DoD's evaluation is used to determine medical fitness for duty and DoD disability compensation, and the VA's evaluation is used to award VA disability compensation and access to VA health care. In November 2007, based on the recommendation of the PCCWW and the Senior Oversight Committee, DoD and the VA agreed to develop and pilot a joint disability-evaluation system, which will enable individuals to know their eligibility for VA compensation before they return home (Bascetta, 2007). The joint evaluation system is likely to include a single, comprehensive medical examina-tion, a single disability rating established by the VA, and a DoD-level evaluation board for adjudicating servicemembers' fitness for duty.

State and Local Community Initiatives Aim to Fill Gaps in Access

In addition to mental health services and programs offered through DoD and VA sys-tems, returning military servicemembers may receive mental health services through local state or community-based resources. Above, we note the challenges in coordinat-ing across these services and DoD or the VA; however, these initiatives may offer an additional resource for servicemembers and veterans who either are not eligible or do not have access to government-sponsored programs. The availability and characteris-tics of these local initiatives are varied, and many may offer innovative approaches for increasing access to mental health care for returning servicemembers and veterans. For example, through some programs, servicemembers may access online lists of provid-ers offering counseling services to returning military servicemembers and receive free counseling and psychotherapy from licensed mental health care providers. A few states have developed programs that integrate all the state's mental health resources so that military servicemembers can easily determine which services are available and appro-priate. University counseling centers offer free services for student veterans. Faith-based organizations provide counseling and retreat programs to returning servicemembers to facilitate the post-deployment transition. We note that many of these programs lack rigorous evaluation or information on whether they offer evidence-based treatment ser-vices. Concerns about quality of mental health care, including the care provided within these programs, are discussed in the next section, Quality of Mental Health Care.

These initiatives may increase access to mental health care for servicemembers and their families. But before these individuals can access these services, they must be aware of them. Thus, outreach is essential. State-based programs that integrate services and provide comprehensive lists of available resources may help servicemembers and their families locate appropriate services.

Some of the state and local programs are described in Appendix 7.E. Program availability depends on geographical region.

In the following subsection, we describe other personal, social, and cultural factors that may impede use of the array of services described above.

What Social, Cultural, and Personal Factors Impede or Facilitate Servicemembers' and Veterans' Access to Mental Health Care?

In this subsection, we examine social, cultural, and personal factors that impede or facilitate access to mental health care for servicemembers. The Department of Defense Task Force on Mental Health (2007) identified the stigma of mental illness as a significant issue preventing servicemembers from seeking help for mental health problems and made recommendations to dispel stigma. Below, we discuss the variety of potential influences and meanings of the term *stigma*, then we review specific attitudinal barriers to mental health use for military servicemembers.

Definitional Issues Related to the Term *Stigma*. The term *stigma* is referred to in multiple places as it relates to care seeking behaviors in mental health, and in fact it is referenced and discussed in the DoD Task Force on Mental Health. To more fully appreciate these issues, we first discuss the definition of this term in order to draw distinctions among the various subtypes of stigma. *Stigma* is a term that can refer to various types of social, cultural, and personal factors affecting access to mental health care. In the social science literature, it is defined as a "negative and erroneous attitude about a person, a prejudice, or negative stereotype" (Corrigan and Penn, 1999, p. 765). When negative attitudes about those who experience mental health conditions or who receive mental health care are widely held by military servicemembers, these pose a significant hurdle to effective mental health assessment and treatment. In the discussion below, we consider the general consequences of negative attitudes associated with mental health conditions, the profound presence of negative attitudes associated with mental health problems in military culture, specific types of attitudes and concerns that serve as barriers to mental health care, and DoD recommendations to mitigate the effects of stigma.

General Consequences of Negative Attitudes. Negative attitudes associated with mental health conditions appear at societal, individual, and institutional levels. *Societal* or *public stigma* refers to public misperceptions and reactions toward individuals with emotional or psychological problems (Corrigan and Watson, 2002; Sammons, 2005). *Individual stigma* occurs when individuals internalize the general public's negative perception of those with mental disorders (Corrigan and Watson, 2002). *Institutional-level stigma* occurs when institutional policies or practices regarding mental health issues unreasonably limit an individual's opportunities (Sammons, 2005). Efforts to mitigate stigma need to address all three types.

The public's negative perceptions of those with mental disorders include the belief that these individuals are more likely to be violent. Perceptions such as this often translate into social isolation for those suffering mental health problems (Link et al., 1999). People say they would be less willing to socialize or work closely with someone who is "depressed" rather than simply "troubled" (Link et al., 1999). Perhaps in part to avoid this kind of "mental illness" labeling, individuals subject to public stigma are less likely to seek treatment for a mental health condition (Corrigan, 2004) and also less likely to adhere to a treatment plan (Kessler et al., 2001).

When individuals internalize these negative attitudes, their perception of self-worth is diminished and confidence in their future prospects declines (Corrigan, 2004). These individuals often consider themselves to be less-valuable members of society (Link, 1982; Link and Phelan, 2001); the resulting shame degrades their quality of life (Corrigan, 2004) and makes them less likely to seek treatment (Sirey et al., 2001).

Institutional stigma includes public and private policies that restrict opportunities for those with mental health conditions, such as laws that restrict their right to vote or to participate in juries (Corrigan, 2004). However, institutional stigma also includes policies that do not deliberately discriminate but still have negative consequences for those with mental disorders (Corrigan, Markowitz, and Watson, 2004)—for example, less-generous insurance benefits for treatment of mental health conditions, and the small amount of funds allocated for research on treatment for psychiatric disorders relative to other conditions, such as heart disease or cancer (Link and Phelan, 2001).

Military Culture and Attitudes That Inhibit Access to Mental Health Care. To develop and maintain an effective fighting force, military culture must promote individual strength and selfless devotion to both nation and fellow comrades in arms. This culture can at times prove detrimental to the mental and physical health needs of individual service men and women. In particular, there are three aspects of this culture that pose significant barriers to seeking mental health care: attitudes and beliefs about mental health and treatment-seeking, unit cohesion, and unit dynamics.

Attitudes and Beliefs. Throughout their military careers, servicemembers develop a set of values and attitudes that are essential for maintaining force readiness and strength:

- Every war fighter has a culture of toughness, independence, not needing help, not being weak, and expecting to be able to master any and every stress without problems. There is a huge barrier to acknowledge even to themselves that there is a problem (stakeholder interview).
- Soldiers, sailors, airmen, and marines are encouraged to develop inner strength and self-reliance. They take pride in their toughness and ability to "shake off" ailments or injuries. One former battalion surgeon noted that his marines did not

want to seek help for any medical problems and took pride in their never having stepped foot into a battalion aid station.

Concerns about mental health problems are discordant with these attitudes and values. Many military servicemembers will attempt to "suck it up" or "tough it out," fearing that admitting a mental health problem or seeking treatment is a sign of weakness (PCCWW, 2007a). When asked how military servicemembers cope with mental health problems, one marine stated, "You don't want people to think you're weird, so you bury it" (Marine Corps enlisted focus groups).

A survey from the Office of the Surgeon General's Mental Health Advisory Team asked soldiers and marines about barriers to receiving mental health care services while in theater (U.S. Department of the Army, Office of the Surgeon General, 2003, 2005; U.S. Department of the Army, Office of the Surgeon General, Office of the Surgeon, Multinational Force–Iraq and Office of the Surgeon General, U.S. Army Medical Command, 2006a, 2006b). Figure 7.3 highlights some of their responses. Approximately half of the servicemembers who screened positive for mental disorders cited concerns about appearing weak, being treated differently by leadership, and losing the confidence of members of the unit as barriers to receiving behavioral health care. More than a third of respondents stated that mental health treatment-seeking would have a harmful effect on his or her career.

Figure 7.3
Perceived Barriers of Deployed Servicemembers

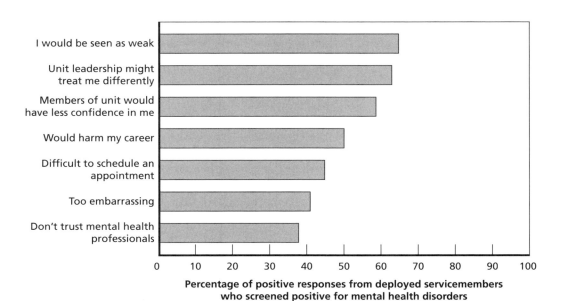

SOURCE: Hoge et al., 2004.
RAND *MG720-7.3*

The perceived benefit of mental health services may also influence the decision to seek treatment upon returning from deployment. One-quarter of military servicemembers who screened positive for a mental disorder said that they did not believe mental health treatments were effective and cited this belief as a reason not to seek services (Hoge et al., 2004). Some focus-group participants expressed concerns that mental health care providers push medications when counseling might be the more appropriate, desirable, or effective treatment. One marine suggested that, "If people knew that someone was going to listen to their problems and not just push medication, more people would go [get treatment]" (Marine Corps enlisted focus groups). This attitude is not unique to the military culture. Among a sample of primary care patients with depressive symptoms, the majority of those who wanted treatment preferred counseling over medication (Dwight-Johnson et al., 2000).

Unit Cohesion. Military servicemembers develop a close bond with their comrades. This bond is referred to as *unit cohesion* (National Defense Research Institute, 1993). Through arduous and stressful training, military servicemembers learn to rely on each other for support and encouragement. During deployment, they live and fight together and confront life and death scenarios as a team. They build a culture of interdependence.

Unit cohesion affects morale and psychological resilience. During combat, support and encouragement from other members of the unit provide strength and motivation. Most consider unit cohesion to be the most important protective factor in preventing psychiatric breakdown (Helmus and Glenn, 2005). After the Lebanon War, researchers found that social isolation was the best predictor of combat-stress reactions in Israeli soldiers (Solomon, Mikulincer, and Hobfoll, 1986). Others have argued that, "When morale is high, stress casualties are low, and vice versa" (Labuc, 1991).

Military servicemembers frequently resist being separated from their unit and their buddies. Many wounded during combat operations experience a sense of shame over having left their comrades. News reports of the 379th Expeditionary Medical Group stationed in Iraq quote the unit's Master Sergeant Paul Martin: "The patients that come through here are true warriors. More than ninety-nine percent of them feel guilty about being here—they just want to get better and get back to their units despite facing the horrors of war" (Foster, 2007).

This reluctance to leave the unit may apply equally to garrison training activities. Units that return from deployment often begin preparing immediately for their next deployment. Such preparations involve a very demanding training tempo. Outpatient services in DoD behavioral health clinics are available only during standard working hours (i.e., 0730–1630 or 0800–1700) (Johnson et al., 2007); thus, to receive treatment, servicemembers must take time away from training. Many are reluctant to do so. Consequently, the cohesion that protects military servicemembers from psychological injury may also keep them from seeking mental health services and treatment when injuries do occur. As previously noted, more than half of returning soldiers and marines identified in screening as having mental health problems cited "members of my unit might have less confidence in me" as a reason for not seeking mental health care. Fifty percent or more also said it was difficult to take time off from work (Hoge et al., 2004).

The unit command climate probably also contributes to the stigma associated with mental health problems. Several focus-group participants said that while some commanders support soldiers who seek mental health services, many do not take mental health problems seriously (RAND focus groups with servicemembers and spouses). Command support is also essential for adherence: Individuals who were referred to mental health treatment by the command were much more likely to complete a treatment regimen than those who were self-referred (Rowan and Campise, 2006).

Trust between a military servicemember and his or her mental health care provider is essential. However, recent surveys suggest that such trust is lacking. Thirty-eight percent of servicemembers who met screening criteria for mental disorders report that they did not trust mental health providers (Hoge et al., 2004). Similar results emerged from the most recent Surgeon General's Mental Health Advisory Team survey (Hoge et al., 2004).

The separation of mental health providers from line and support units may account for this distrust. For example, the Marine Corps has historically relied on division psychiatrists to provide most evaluation and treatment services for marines. The division psychiatrist's practice model was similar to civilian office-based consultation. Marines were consequently evaluated without an in-depth understanding of the unit and operational context. Line leaders were dissatisfied with mental health services, which were consequently underused, and a perception of weakness was associated with seeking treatment. Many marines evaluated by the division psychiatrist received recommendations for separation from service. This earned some mental health providers the nickname of "wizard" because marines sent to them would "mysteriously disappear" (Sammons, 2005). Soldiers experiencing significant distress were three times more likely to turn to a fellow soldier in their unit for help than to formal mental health assets (U.S. Department of the Army, Office of the Surgeon General, 2003).

Unit Dynamics. Specific dynamics of military units may also affect a military member's decision to seek mental health care. One issue is accountability. Focus-group participants stated that noncommissioned officers (NCOs) are required to know the whereabouts of their soldiers and marines at all times. Observes one marine, "there is no way to keep mental health treatment confidential. The facilities are only open during the hours when you're supposed to be at work, so you need to tell someone where you're going" (RAND focus group of enlisted marines).

Another factor contributing to lack of confidentiality is the escorting of soldiers to mental health evaluations. Individuals with command referrals for evaluation are escorted to their clinic by another soldier. Perceptions also exist at Fort Hood that such escorts are required for even self-referred evaluations. Requiring an escort undoubtedly increases the concerns associated with disclosing a mental health problem and proves a significant manpower drain for commanders and NCOs (Army focus group).

Receiving a mental health diagnosis may also have significant career implications, particularly in some career tracks that require higher fitness standards (e.g., Air Force pilots). Evidence of a mental health problem may also result in questioning of a military servicemember's security clearance and hinder promotion. The fitness-for-duty profiles of servicemembers receiving mental health treatment may limit their ability to carry weapons or perform other duties. Thus, the profile creates individual embarrassment and a burden to commanders, who must assign unfulfilled responsibilities to other soldiers in the unit.

Perceptions regarding malingering further dissuade individuals with true signs and symptoms of PTSD from seeking treatment. The view that many soldiers with PTSD are faking their symptoms was common in focus groups conducted with senior NCOs. One participant believed that as many as 75 percent of all individuals who said they had PTSD were faking (Army focus group).

Addressing Negative Attitudes Associated with Mental Health Conditions Within DoD. The Department of Defense recognizes that the stigma associated with mental health conditions and its consequences have an implication for access to mental health care, and it is working to reduce many of the stigma-related barriers to access. Approaches to reduce the perception of harmful consequences associated with seeking mental health treatments are summarized below.

Approaches to Combating Public Stigma: Public Education Campaigns. The DoD Task Force on Mental Health asserted that an anti-stigma public-education campaign could use evidence-based techniques to effectively disseminate factual information about mental health conditions (Department of Defense Task Force on Mental Health, 2007a). Scholars argue that the campaign should include realistic descriptions of mental health problems and emphasize the success of proven treatments (Britt, Greene-Shortridge, and Castro, 2007). For example, stigmatizing attitudes about PTSD might shift if the military community and the general public accept the notion that PTSD results from exposure to extremely stressful experiences rather than weakness of character (Britt, Greene-Shortridge, and Castro, 2007). Focusing on the effectiveness of treatments and demonstrating treatment efficacy through further research will also help to reduce public stigma (Sammons, 2005). Efforts to convey the effectiveness of treatment should further motivate individuals to seek mental health treatment.

There is some limited evidence that public-education campaigns can influence attitudes toward mental health conditions in nonmilitary populations. Two National Institute of Mental Health public-education campaigns to reduce mental health stigma provide examples of success. The Depression Awareness, Recognition, and Treatment Program (Regier et al., 1988; O'Hara, Gorman, and Wright, 1996; Rix et al., 1999) found that, at six months following the two-day training programs, participants (physicians, nurses, and mental health professionals) had increases in levels of knowledge of depression and were satisfied with the program. Preliminary data from a qualitative evaluation of the educational brochures used in the "Real Men. Real Depression" program (Rochlen, Whilde, and Hoyer, 2005) suggest that, overall, men evaluated the material positively and indicated that these materials show promise for improving help-seeking attitudes and facilitating treatment decisions (Rochlen, McKelley, and Pituch, 2006). Additionally, national depression education and anti-stigma programs have also been shown to increase public acceptance of antidepressant medication, as reflected in public-opinion polls (Olfson et al., 2002).

Approaches to Reducing Negative Personal Attitudes. Scholars suggest that the military could reduce the feelings of shame and negative self-perceptions associated with receiving mental health care by treating individuals with the appropriate level of care and in the appropriate setting, based on the severity of the problem (Sammons, 2005). For example, individuals with minor mental health issues will be less likely to avoid seeking help if they understand that they will receive quick and effective treatment within their unit, without evacuation and separation from their buddies.

Many military health professionals argue that such programs as OSCAR, which embed mental health care providers within units, allow marines and their commanders to build rapport and trust with the mental health care providers (Britt, Greene-Shortridge, and Castro, 2007). Because military servicemembers can more comfortably disclose information to those with an understanding of military life and culture, advocates believe that embedding mental health providers within the unit is an effective strategy.

Placing mental health providers in primary care clinics may also help reduce apprehension associated with seeking mental health treatment. Advocates argue that military servicemembers have fewer apprehensions about seeing a primary care physician for psychological as well as physical problems, and the availability of mental health professionals in the primary care setting would facilitate referrals and initiation of mental health treatment. They also argue that receiving mental health care in a primary care setting does not trigger as much concern about negative consequences as receiving care in a mental health clinic.

However, others suggest that clandestinely providing treatment in primary care clinics and medicalizing normal combat-stress reactions reinforce the perceptions of shame and weakness associated with receiving mental health services (Sammons, 2005). One interviewee suggested that access options that are intended to be nonstigmatizing actually reinforce stigma because they provide alternative avenues to treatment that do not include military mental health clinicians. He believes that these programs essentially attempt to evade stigma rather than address it directly.

To reduce the perceived negative attitudes about seeking mental health treatment, the DoD Mental Health Task Force recommended establishment of training programs and further development and dissemination of clinical treatment guidelines, suggesting that DoD collaborate with both public- and private-sector experts to establish a set of best practices and ensure that providers are adhering to them (Department of Defense Task Force on Mental Health, 2007a). If military servicemembers realize that use of mental health services is encouraged by military and civilian-sector experts, they may be less inclined to believe that mental health treatments are ineffective; consequently, they may seek services more readily.

Emphasizing treatment as a way to "return to normal" and countering perceptions that soldiers should be able to handle problems on their own have also been suggested as ways to combat the attitudes that inhibit mental health treatment-seeking (Stecker et al., 2007). Conducting unit-level interventions may be a good venue for this form of education. During these interventions, soldiers with PTSD who were successfully treated could effectively dispel myths about seeking mental health care services (Britt, Greene-Shortridge, and Castro, 2007).

Approaches to Reducing Institutional or Structural Stigma. There is a pervasive view that seeking mental health services is detrimental to one's military career, and thus many servicemembers may avoid seeking mental health care to prevent such information from impinging on their military records or coming to the attention of military command. Such fears of negative career consequences could be alleviated by allowing servicemembers with less-severe mental health issues to easily and confidentially receive mental health services. Making such services available and openly encouraging their use would likely lessen the perceived negative consequences associated with seeking mental health care, and they could result in broader and earlier treatment-seeking that could reduce the probability of mental health problems becoming prolonged or severe.

The DoD Mental Health Task Force did not include recommendations for approaches that would alleviate concerns about negative career consequences associated with use of mental health services. Encouraging use of confidential mental health services runs counter to prevailing views that command should have access to information about all mental health service use to evaluate individual readiness.

Quality of Mental Health Care

In this section, we turn our attention to the quality of care provided to military servicemembers suffering from post-traumatic stress disorder or major depression. We describe treatments for these conditions and summarize the scientific evidence about the treatments' effectiveness. We provide some perspective on quality of care by putting the current VA and DoD treatment guidelines for these conditions in the context of the evidence. We review some successful strategies for improving care. We conclude by briefly reviewing efforts to measure and improve the quality of mental health care provided for military servicemembers and veterans.

What Is High-Quality Evidence-Based Treatment for PTSD and Major Depression?

PTSD is an anxiety disorder that occurs after a traumatic event in which there was a threat of serious injury or death and to which the individual's response involved intense fear, helplessness, or horror. We conducted a literature review to establish the evidence base for current PTSD treatments, using the relevant online databases. A detailed discussion of our review process and findings appears in Appendix 7.C.

There are four basic kinds of treatment for PTSD:

- *Cognitive-behavioral treatments* (e.g., exposure therapy, cognitive processing therapy)
- *Pharmacotherapy* (e.g., tricyclic antidepressants, monoamine oxidase inhibitors, and selective serotonin reuptake inhibitors [SSRIs])
- *Psychological debriefing*, including critical-incident stress debriefing
- *Other treatments* (e.g., eye-movement desensitization and reprocessing [EMDR], imagery rehearsal therapy, psychodynamic therapy, hypnosis).

These therapies are described in more detail in Appendix 7.C. Each is usually delivered by an individual provider to an individual patient. Other delivery modes include group therapy, marital therapy, and inpatient treatment. Inpatient programs are usually designed for individuals who have had multiple traumatic episodes and suffer from chronic and prolonged PTSD or for those who are considered to be a danger to themselves or others.

Several meta-analyses compare the effectiveness of specific treatments. One of the most comprehensive is Van Etten and Taylor (1998). They found that psychological therapies had significantly lower dropout rates (14 percent) than drug therapies (32 percent); they were also more effective than drug therapies in reducing symptoms. Behavior therapy and EMDR were the most effective psychological therapies. Among the drug therapies, the SSRIs and carbamazepine (an anticonvulsant and mood-stabilizing drug) had the largest treatment improvement effects. SSRIs had some advantage over psychosocial therapies in treating major depression. However, the (British) National Institute for Health and Clinical Excellence practice guidelines (2005) discussed several studies of SSRIs, suggesting inconclusive evidence that these drugs were effective for PTSD symptoms. Similarly, the Institute of Medicine (2007) summary of available treatments for PTSD concluded that exposure-based cognitive-behavioral treatments have the most evidence to support them, whereas the evidence for medications is still weak. Evidence does not support psychological debriefing as an effective treatment.

The scientific literature supports the VA/DoD guidelines for PTSD treatment, which include various forms of cognitive-behavioral therapy, as well as medication. However, neither the literature nor the guidelines address the issue of how much training is required to deliver these therapies effectively.

Major depression is a serious mental disorder. Its symptoms, including feeling hopeless or sad most of the time, loss of interest in activities previously enjoyed, energy loss, and thoughts of suicide, interfere with daily functioning. Major depression can also have long-term chronic effects on physical health and other outcomes (see Chapter Five). As we did for PTSD, we conducted a literature review to establish the evidence base for current treatments for major depression, using the relevant online databases. Details appear in Appendix 7.C.

Recognizing major depression can be difficult. Many studies have shown that primary care providers fail to detect depression 35 to 50 percent of the time (Gerber et al., 1989; Simon and Von Korff, 1995); military providers appear to have similar difficulties (Hunter et al., 2002).

There are four basic types of major depression treatments:

- *Psychotherapy,* including cognitive-behavioral therapy, cognitive therapy, and interpersonal therapy
- *Pharmacotherapy,* using many different kinds of medications
- *Shocks or stimulation to the brain,* including electroconvulsive therapy and transcranial magnetic stimulation
- *Complementary treatments*, such as relaxation and herbal remedies.

These types of treatments are described in greater detail in Appendix 7.C. As with PTSD treatments, depression treatment is usually delivered by an individual clinician to an individual patient. However, these therapies can also be delivered in group therapy, marital therapy, or inpatient treatment modes. Inpatient treatment is designed for people with severe depression, including those who have made suicide attempts or are a threat to others.

The scientific literature supports use of psychotherapies as effective treatment for major depression. There is also evidence that medication is efficacious, especially SSRIs. Severe major depression is effectively treated with electroconvulsive therapy and transcranial magnetic stimulation. There is less definitive evidence that some complementary therapies, such as St.-John's-wort or exercise, are effective.

The scientific literature provides a firm basis for VA/DoD's depression practice guidelines. As with PTSD, neither literature nor guidelines provide information about how much training is required to deliver these therapies effectively.

What Organizational Models Support High-Quality Mental Health Care?

Organizational strategies and models are needed to translate knowledge about effective treatments into the day-to-day operations of health care systems and services. The broad definition of *quality* presented in Figure 7.1 must be kept in mind when we consider the kinds of organizational approaches that have been most successful in improving quality. Beyond delivering treatments supported by scientific evidence, organizational models that support high-quality care must attend to safety, efficiency, timeliness of care, as well as informing and involving patients in decisionmaking.

Many of the most obvious strategies aimed at closing the gap between high-quality care and usual practice simply do not translate into actual improvement. In fact, the literature on health care provider behavior suggests that many quality-improvement (QI) interventions do not change provider behavior (Berwick, 1989; Davis et al., 1995; Lomas and Haynes, 1988) especially over the long term (Lin et al., 1997).

One potential explanation is that providers' attitudes, beliefs, and motivations are rarely considered in the design of interventions. Decades of behavioral science theory and research have shown that these factors are key determinants of behavior change (see, for example, Ajzen and Fishbein, 1980; Bandura, 1986; Rubenstein et al., 2000). An intervention is unlikely to succeed unless physician leadership and organizational buy-in are achieved in advance. Studies have found that provider participation in QI can be limited without strong support from leadership (Parker et al., 2007) and that care management teams believe support from leadership to be a critical factor in implementing successful QI for depression care (Rubenstein et al., 2002).

Many of the models that have been developed for improving the care of chronic illness in medical settings, including care for depression, are potential models for addressing post-deployment mental health problems. Extending these models to improve the care of both major depression and PTSD has potential utility for military servicemembers because the two diseases are common, often co-occurring, and the medical setting is associated with less stigma than a mental health setting.

These models include collaborative care, which promotes coordination between mental health specialists and primary care providers. Other team-based models of QI also have the potential to improve care for military mental health problems. Central features of these approaches include patient self-management, which addresses the goal of *patient-centeredness* from the IOM framework (defined in the beginning of this chapter) and the use of a care manager to coordinate disease-management activities. In the remaining subsections, we discuss findings related to different approaches to improving care. These are grouped by the characteristics of the interventions and include multicomponent interventions (those interventions that involve mixing modalities or treatment components), collaborative care approaches, multicomponent quality-improvement techniques, and telephone screening, outreach, and care-management approaches.

Multicomponent Interventions. Interventions that use a single approach (such as education alone or reminders alone) do not improve care (Rollman et al., 2002; Thompson et al., 2000); interventions that include multiple components in a comprehensive program do. For example, systematic reviews of randomized trials have shown that such multimodal interventions, which are based on standardized approaches for primary care management of depression, can improve depression outcomes (Gerrity et al., 2001; Gilbody et al., 2003; Gilbody et al., 2006; Rubenstein et al., 2006).

The Institute for Healthcare Improvement's Chronic Illness Model is a widely accepted approach to improving care that incorporates six key components for targeting change (The Chronic Care Model, undated; Wagner et al., 2001): (1) *delivery system redesign*, which incorporates the care-management role, a practice team to facilitate coordination and communication, the care delivery process, proactive follow-up, and planned visits; (2) *self-management strategies*, which include patient education and activation, needs and readiness assessment, self-management support, and collaborative decisionmaking with patients; (3) *decision support*, which includes institutionalizing guidelines and protocols, provider education, and consultation support; (4) *clinical information systems*, which include use of a patient registry system or electronic medical record (EMR), care planning and management information, and performance data or feedback; (5) *community linkages* for patients and the community; and (6) *health system support*, which includes support from leadership, provider participation, and a coherent approach to system improvement.

Data from the Improving Chronic Illness Care Evaluation (ICICE Web site) suggest that nearly all of the sites that used the model to improve depression care were able to sustain practice changes over an 18-month period, including enhanced clinical protocols; improved systems for identifying, treating, and following patients with depression; and better linkages with mental health services (Meredith et al., 2006).

Collaborative Care Models. Important lessons can be learned from collaborative care experiences about how to support quality improvement. *Collaborative care* is a disease-management approach that highlights optimal care-management roles for primary care, mental health specialty, and allied health professionals to improve the delivery of services for patients with chronic medical conditions and psychiatric disorders (Katon et al., 2001; Von Korff et al., 1997). These models of care have the potential to improve clinical outcomes for patients with mental disorders (Katon et al., 1999; Katon et al., 1996; Roy-Byrne et al., 2001; Zatzick et al., 2004; Zatzick et al., 2001). These interventions have also been shown to be cost-effective (Katon et al., 2002).

As noted earlier in this chapter, the VA's national depression collaborative care program (Department of Veterans Affairs, 2007g) to enhance screening, case management, outcomes monitoring, and referral for patients with persistent symptoms of depression (Rubenstein et al., 2004) is an example of success. Other successful quality-improvement programs include the Bureau of Primary Health Care effort to integrate mental health professionals into primary care for low-income patients (Mauksch et al., 2001) and a program in Maine that targets patients identified as depressed by primary care providers and starts them on antidepressants with telephone follow-up by case managers (Korsen et al., 2003).

Collaborative models have also been successful in treating anxiety disorders, including panic and PTSD. For example, a collaborative care intervention significantly improved the quality of care and clinical and functioning outcomes for patients with panic disorder in primary care (Roy-Byrne et al., 2001). This same intervention produced significantly more anxiety-free days and equivalent total outpatient costs compared with usual care (Katon et al., 2002). An assessment by Rollman and colleagues (2005) showed that telephone-based collaborative care for panic and generalized anxiety disorders improved clinical (anxiety symptoms) and functional outcomes (health-related quality of life and work productivity) more than usual care. Another study found that collaborative care was significantly more effective than usual care in treating older adults with and without co-occurring panic disorder and PTSD (Hegel et al., 2005). Other applications to PTSD are being developed but as yet are untested.

Multicomponent Quality-Improvement Programs. Quality-improvement programs that emphasize the role of a care manager are also worthy of consideration for military mental health. Partners in Care (Rubenstein et al., 1999; Wells, 1999) compared two types of enhanced-care programs with usual care in 46 diverse primary care clinics. In one type of enhanced care, nurse specialists were trained to provide follow-up assessments and support patients' adherence to treatment through monthly contacts for 6 or 12 months. In another type of enhanced care, local psychotherapists were trained to deliver a manualized form of individual and group cognitive-behavioral therapy for 12 to 16 sessions. To increase access to therapy, the organizations reduced the therapy co-payment to the level of the co-payment for a primary care visit.

Both enhanced-care programs increased the proportion of patients who received appropriate care at 6 and 12 months, as well as improving outcomes, including work productivity (Wells et al., 2000). The programs also improved primary care clinician knowledge and practices regarding depression care over 18 months (Meredith et al., 2000) and long-term (two-year and nine-year) patient outcomes (Sherbourne et al., 2001; Wells et al., 2007), and they were found to be cost-effective (Schoenbaum et al., 2001).

Team-based care also has been shown to improve care for depressed older adults (Katon et al., 2006; Schoenbaum et al., 2001; Sherbourne et al., 2001; Ünützer et al., 2005; Wells et al., 2000).

The MacArthur Initiative on Depression and Primary Care developed the Re-Engineering Systems for Primary Care Treatment of Depression Project (RESPECT), another highly successful systematic QI program for depression in primary care (Dietrich et al., 2004). This intervention integrates efforts of a primary care clinician, a care manager, and a mental health professional, working in conjunction to manage a patient's depression. Care managers provide telephone support weekly after the initial visit and monthly thereafter and help patients overcome barriers to adherence. Psychiatrists supervise care managers through weekly telephone contact, and clinicians may also contact psychiatrists for informal telephone advice. The evaluation found that patients treated for depression in those primary care settings showed significant improvement and increased satisfaction with care relative to the care-as-usual control.

Even quality-improvement interventions that do not involve a predesigned program have proven successful in lowering rates of major depression, improving functioning, and increasing satisfaction. The Mental Health Awareness Project compared two alternative approaches to structuring quality-improvement teams and designing evidence-based interventions in three VA and six managed care clinics (Rubenstein et al., 2006). One approach was decentralized; it emphasized meetings in the local primary care practice involving a multidisciplinary team and a quality-improvement facilitator, with some expert input. The other approach emphasized delegation of planning to regional experts, with some input from local leaders. Both types of teams were responsible for implementing locally the interventions they designed. Patients treated in both programs received more-appropriate care for depression and had improved social functioning after one year.

Telephone-Screening, Outreach, and Care-Management Approaches. A recent randomized controlled trial investigated how a depression outreach-treatment program affected work productivity (Wang et al., 2007). The intervention used telephonic outreach and care management to encourage workers who met positive screening criteria for depression to begin outpatient treatment (e.g., psychotherapy and/or antidepressant medication), monitored treatment quality continuity, and tried to improve treatment by making recommendations to providers. The intervention also offered telephone cognitive-behavioral therapy for workers reluctant to enter treatment. The program significantly improved both clinical outcomes and workplace outcomes. These findings underscore employers' return on investments for such programs in increased productivity. Extending such a program to the military or VA settings could potentially improve care for military personnel without compromising workplace productivity.

To What Extent Are Quality Standards and Processes for Mental Health Care Supported in Systems of Care for Veterans and Military Servicemembers?

In this section, we discuss findings with respect to how the systems of care for veterans and military servicemembers are using quality standards and processes for mental health care.

Veterans Health Administration. To counter a growing reputation for inefficient and mediocre health care, the Veterans Health Administration (VHA) underwent a major strategic transformation beginning in 1995. The VHA sought to develop an integrated health system defined by patient-centered, high-quality, and high-value health care (Kizer, 1995). This transformation shifted services from inpatient settings to outpatient clinics and home care, helping to increase access to services while cutting costs. As discussed above, the VA also organized itself into geographically defined networks, called Veterans Integrated Service Networks, to enhance the coordination of services and resources at the network level and to move from a facility-centric model to a population- and patient-centric one.

The VHA began an extensive program of national performance measurement that systematically assessed a number of performance indicators using administrative data, as well as patient satisfaction. To promote a culture of accountability, the VHA provided detailed and publicly available information on the performance of each network and medical center.

Quality Management. The VA has established a robust infrastructure to actively manage quality. In the clinical area, the VA is affiliated with 107 academic health systems and the DoD MHS, which helps drive implementation of evidence-based practices (Perlin, Kolodner, and Roswell, 2005).

The VHA's Health Services Research and Development Service is an intramural research program. Its goal is to identify and evaluate innovative strategies that lead to accessible, high-quality, cost-effective care for veterans and the nation (Department of Veterans Affairs, 2007a). Its 13 Centers of Excellence[5] are affiliated with VA Medical Centers, and each Center develops its own research agenda and collaborates with local schools of public health to carry out its mission (Department of Veterans Affairs, 2007b).

Most research projects are distinct, relatively short-term efforts to study and support specific aspects of the VHA transformation. However, these individual efforts are complemented by the Quality Enhancement Research Initiative (QUERI) (McQueen, Mittman, and Demakis, 2004), a larger sustained effort to systematically study and enhance VHA clinical programs, including their quality, processes, and outcomes. QUERI's mission is to facilitate and support ongoing improvement in outcomes and in clinical care delivery. QUERI centers currently exist for colorectal cancer, diabetes mellitus, HIV/AIDS, ischemic heart disease, mental health, spinal-cord injury and disorder, stroke, and substance-use disorders (McQueen, Mittman, and Demakis, 2004). See the subsection Quality Management of Mental Health below for specific QI efforts related to mental health.

Another key component of the VA's system design that supports high quality of care is its health information technology system. The VA's computerized patient record system (CPRS) was developed to provide a single interface for health care providers to review and update a patient's medical record and to place orders. CPRS is integrated throughout the VA system and can be used across the spectrum of health care settings. The VA patient record system organizes and presents all relevant patient data in a

---

[5]   Ann Arbor, MI: Center for Practice Management & Outcomes Research; Bedford, MA: Center for Health Quality, Outcomes, and Economic Research; Boston, MA: Center for Organization, Leadership and Management Research; Durham, NC: Center for Health Services Research in Primary Care; Hines, IL: Center for Management of Complex Chronic Care; Houston, TX: Houston Center for Quality of Care and Utilization Studies; Indianapolis, IN: Center of Excellence on Implementing Evidence-Based Practice; Iowa City, IA: Center for Research in the Implementation of Innovative Strategies in Practice; Minneapolis, MN: Center for Chronic Disease Outcomes Research; Palo Alto, CA: Center for Health Care Evaluation; Pittsburgh/Philadelphia, PA: Center for Health Equity Research and Promotion; Seattle, WA: Northwest Center for Outcomes Research in Older Adults; Sepulveda, CA: Center for the Study of Healthcare Provider Behavior.

manner that supports clinical decisionmaking. For example, the system's comprehensive cover sheet displays timely, patient-centric information including active problems, allergies, current medications, recent laboratory results, vital signs, hospitalization, and outpatient clinic history. Moreover, this information is displayed immediately when a patient record is selected and provides an accurate overview of the patient's current status before any clinical interventions are ordered (Perlin, Kolodner, and Roswell, 2005). The VA is planning to make further enhancements to CPRS to allow for greater customization, expanded functionality, and easier integration with commercial software (Department of Veterans Affairs, 2007i). Specifically, recommendations from the Task Force on Returning Global War on Terror Heroes have given impetus to a series of seven information-technology initiatives, which include the development of a veterans' tracking application, a TBI database, a DoD/VA theater interface, the creation of a polytrauma marker, the creation of an OEF/OIF combat-veteran identifier, an electronic patient handoff information system, and a DoD scanning interface with CPRS (Department of Veterans Affairs, 2007i).

There is also evidence suggesting that these VA efforts have resulted in documented improvements in the quality of care the VA provides: in standard indicators, reflecting, among other things, the delivery of preventive primary care, care of chronic disease, and palliative care (Jha et al., 2003).

For example, one study compared the quality of VA care with quality of care in a national sample of patients and found that VA patients with specific medical conditions, including major depression, received higher-quality care. The differences were greatest in areas in which the VA has established and actively monitored performance measures (Asch et al., 2004), including quality of care for depression. No similar evaluation of the quality of care for PTSD is available. Another study found that the quality of diabetes care was better for VA patients than for patients enrolled in commercial managed care organizations (Kerr et al., 2004).

These changes in the VA health system have also been met with increases in veterans' satisfaction. On the American Customer Satisfaction Index (University of Michigan School of Business, 2004), satisfaction had improved for both inpatients and outpatients of VA Medical Centers.

Quality Management of Mental Health. The VHA transformation of 1995 mandated the development of a National Mental Health Program Performance Monitoring System to be developed by the Northeast Program Evaluation Center (Kizer, 1995). This organization focuses on inpatient and outpatient mental health service delivery, including reports on special programs. Performance measures evaluating mental health services are reported for seven areas (Rosenheck, 2006):

1. Health Care for Homeless Veterans, and Domiciliary Care for Homeless Veterans Programs

2. Compensated Work Therapy, and Compensated Work Therapy/Transitional Residence Programs
3. PTSD Performance Monitors and Outcome Measures
4. Mental Health Intensive Case Management
5. Performance Measures from the National Mental Health Program Performance Monitoring System
6. Adherence to Pharmacotherapy Guidelines for Patients with Schizophrenia
7. Outcomes on the Global Assessment of Functioning Scale.

In addition, the Mental Health Quality Enhancement Research Initiative (MH-QUERI) helps improve the quality of care and health outcomes of veterans with schizophrenia and major depression (Department of Veterans Affairs, 2007h). MH-QUERI utilizes the following process to identify gaps in performance and implement strategies to address these areas (Department of Veterans Affairs, 2007h):

- Identify high-volume/high-risk diseases
- Identify best practices
- Identify existing practice patterns and outcomes across the VA and current variation from best practices
- Implement strategies to promote best practices
- Document that best practices improve outcomes
- Document that outcomes are associated with improved health-related quality of life.

One of MH-QUERI's primary efforts is to focus on implementing the collaborative care model for major depression. Researchers adapted a depression collaborative care model for use in VA settings, including planning for implementation and evaluation of these programs (Department of Veterans Affairs, 2007g). A key feature of this treatment model is collaboration between primary care providers and mental health specialists, supported by a depression care manager. The care manager, under supervision of a mental health specialist, works with a primary care provider to assess and manage patients suffering from depression (Department of Veterans Affairs, 2007g).

A study conducted in 2000 found that, although the VA treats a more psychiatrically troubled population, the VA appeared to have made greater improvements in quality of treatment over time than had the private sector, possibly demonstrating the return on investment for its various quality activities (Leslie and Rosenheck, 2000).

The VHA's long-standing focus on mental-health performance assessment and quality improvement makes it a leading model of an integrated health systems approach to quality. Nonetheless, significant challenges remain, including maintaining the quality of care with the increasing demand for services resulting from benefit enhancements and with the influx of veterans who have served in OEF/OIF (Rosenheck,

2006). For example, a recent report (Rosenheck and Fontana, 2007) showed that the number of veterans using specialty mental health services in the VA increased by 56 percent between 1997 and 2005. Most of this increase is due to an increased demand by Vietnam-era veterans, but the number of young Gulf conflict veterans receiving VA mental health services grew rapidly after 2001. In 2005, this group accounted for up to 3 percent of users of VA mental health services. This expansion of mental health services to a larger number of veterans was associated with a reduction in the average number of mental health visits received by users per year. Veterans with PTSD, for example, received an average of 25 mental health visits in 1997, compared with 14 visits in 2005.

DoD Health Care System. DoD undertakes significant efforts to monitor quality of care and consumer satisfaction through surveys and other methods. However, it currently lacks a programmatic and synchronized focus on performance measurement or quality-of-care indices.[6] In this regard, the VA's model of performance monitoring and quality management may provide a template for the U.S. military health system. Just as the VA's quality infrastructure has led to significant advances in health care and metrics by which that health care can be judged, so too would the U.S. military health system benefit from a rigorous and scientifically based quality-assurance process.

One critical element of quality relates to the delivery of evidence-based therapies for PTSD or major depression. As previously noted in this chapter, the Departments of Defense and Veterans Affairs published clinical-practice guidelines for the treatment of PTSD in 2004. The guidelines advocate the use of four PTSD psychotherapies: cognitive therapy, eye-movement desensitization and reprocessing, exposure therapy, and stress inoculation. Unfortunately little is known regarding the extent to which DoD clinicians actually deliver these therapies during routine therapeutic contacts. Only one study is known to address this issue (Russell and Silver, 2007). However, it used a convenience sample and so should not be taken as authoritative on DoD clinical practice. That said, the report found that only 10 percent ($n = 14$) of 137 DoD mental health professionals surveyed (consisting mostly of psychologists and social workers) use any of the four recommended psychotherapeutic modalities. Of these 14 clinicians, only four reported that DoD funded their training.

These results are consistent with other study findings suggesting that passive dissemination of clinical-practice guidelines has only a nominal effect on implementation (Grol and Grimshaw, 1999). As Parry, Cape, and Pilling (2003, p. 45) observe, "Even well-resourced, national guidelines, published in multiple media, can fail to reach, let alone impact, their target audience."

DoD has consequently developed several programs designed to train clinicians in the therapeutic guidelines. One such program is run by the Center for Deployment

---

[6]   This is of course not to argue that DoD health care is of poor quality. It is simply that processes and systems are not in place to systematically measure and report quality of care.

Psychology, which provides a two-week psychotherapy training course for military and civilian psychologists and psychology interns (Russell, 2007). The program has already trained 120 DoD clinicians (Department of Defense Task Force on Mental Health, 2007b). Other efforts include a joint DoD-VA regional training initiative and training programs developed by the individual Service branches. According to a stakeholder interview, all of these programs utilize the contracted help of nationally recognized experts in PTSD therapies.

DoD recently created the Defense Center of Excellence for Psychological Health and Traumatic Brain Injury, in part based on a recommendation from the DoD Mental Health Task Force and from the Army Task Force on TBI (discussed in the section on TBI below). As part of its mission, the Defense Center of Excellence will establish a core curriculum to train all DoD mental health personnel on current and emerging clinical-practice guidelines. The Center would further develop mechanisms to ensure widespread dissemination of this curriculum. The program will apply the model initiated by the Center for Deployment Psychology by contracting with clinical-practice experts to provide intensive training and will use ongoing supervision to ensure the application of knowledge to clinical practice (Department of Defense Task Force on Mental Health, 2007b).

A well-planned and active approach to training clinicians in evidence-based treatments is a key first step in ensuring the delivery of evidence-based care. However, training seminars, in and of themselves, may not be sufficient. As previously noted, multifaceted approaches to disseminating clinical-practice guidelines are important. These approaches ensure clinician training while providing clinical reminders to follow practice guidelines and audit compliance (Parry, Cape, and Pilling, 2003).

This multifaceted strategy may be missing from the Department of Defense's plans to ensure implementation of clinical-practice guidelines. The Mental Health Task Force was unable to identify any mechanism within the medical community that ensures widespread use of evidence-based treatments. For example, at present there is no monitoring system in place that systematically documents the specific treatments provided to military mental health patients (Russell, 2007). There is likewise no system in place for auditing patient charts. Without such a system, even training that is broadly and fully implemented may fail to change the individualized habits of mental health clinicians.

Multifaceted strategies are not simple to implement and often require additional staffing, along with organizational changes to the clinical practice (Parry, Cape, and Pilling, 2003). The Mental Health Task Force was correct to assert that "assuring these practices and guidelines are actually implemented throughout the system is a daunting challenge that requires significant attention by mental health providers" (Department of Defense Task Force on Mental Health, 2007a, p. 33).

One example of implementation of a multifaceted model in a military health setting is the RESPECT-Mil program. RESPECT-Mil, based on the RESPECT program described above, is designed to decrease stigma and improve access to care by providing behavioral health care within the primary care setting. The intervention provides primary care–based screening, assessment, treatment, and referral of soldiers with depression and PTSD through a RESPECT-Mil facilitator, who provides continuity of care for mental health problems. The program preserves soldier choice by motivating patients to work with their provider to choose counseling or medication; it also allows soldiers to work with the facilitator to learn about the range of available resources, such as Military OneSource, chaplains, and the Army Community Services.

The study was first piloted at Fort Bragg. The pilot was successful, based on feasibility testing with 30 primary care providers in one troop medical clinic. Those providers received training on the RESPECT-Mil model and on care for depression and PTSD (Engel et al., in press). Over 4,000 patients were screened; 10 percent met screening criteria for depression, PTSD, or both. Sixty-nine patients participated in collaborative care for at least six weeks, and most made clinically significant improvements. Currently, the program is being expanded to 14 other Army locations representing 40 primary clinics.

Community-Based Mental Health Specialists. Active-duty military service-members, veterans, and reservists who are unable to or choose not to receive care through Military Treatment Facilities or the VA may access a broad array of mental health service providers in the community. Care from these providers may be covered and reimbursed by TRICARE insurance or another health insurance plan (e.g., an employer-sponsored plan), or may be paid for out of pocket by the individual receiving care.

These civilian mental health specialty practitioners are licensed and accredited providers. However, they operate as independent solo or group practitioners, and they are affiliated with a broad range of hospitals, clinics, or specialty facilities. They typically accept reimbursement from a broad range of health insurance plans, and participate in preferred-provider networks across multiple health plans. Unlike VA facilities or Military Treatment Facilities, these providers do not work within an integrated staff model, so there is much less opportunity for DoD or the VA to directly assess and influence clinical-practice patterns.

Health plans, to distinguish their health care services in the marketplace and often to meet requirements of large purchasers (e.g., employers, government entities), play a central role in quality assessment and assurance. An important trend in the commercial health-insurance industry over the past 20 years has been to "carve out" mental health and substance abuse benefits from other medical benefits; these benefits are then managed by behavioral health plans that assume responsibility for providing health-plan members with access to mental health specialty care networks, reimbursing those clinical providers, and managing aspects of the costs and quality of care (Burnam, 2003; Feldman, 2003).

Measuring Quality of Community-Based Services. Behavioral health plans manage quality by ensuring that providers are appropriately licensed and credentialed; maintain systems that monitor utilization of services and performance; and meet quality standards promulgated by independent accrediting organizations, including the National Committee for Quality Assurance (NCQA) and the Joint Commission for the Accreditation of Healthcare Organizations (JCAHO). Performance measures used by health plans are based on routinely collected administrative data (claims, or encounter data) that are generated by outpatient visits, hospital stays, medical procedures/tests, and the filling of prescriptions. Many plans report a standardized set of performance measures, known as HEDIS (Healthcare Effectiveness Data and Information Set) to NCQA, which in turn generates reports comparing plans and reporting national statistics (NCQA, 2007).

Health plans and purchasers face significant challenges in measuring and influencing the quality of care delivered by a vast network of providers whom they do not directly employ. However, some approaches are promising. Behavioral health plans have taken a leading role in efforts to improve measures of the quality of mental health care delivered to their beneficiaries, to disseminate information about evidence-based practices and guidelines to clinical providers, and to participate in demonstrations of state-of-the-art quality-improvement strategies. Particularly promising are approaches that measure satisfaction with mental health care using such instruments as the Experiences of Care and Health Outcomes survey (Eisen et al., 2001) and routine assessment of mental health symptoms/outcomes using self-report surveys (G. S. Brown et al., 2001).

A particularly challenging problem is developing performance indicators that provide information about the type of psychotherapeutic techniques used in treatment, since administrative data are not detailed enough to capture this information (Institute of Medicine. Committee on Crossing the Quality Chasm: Adaptation to Mental Health and Addictive Disorders, 2006). As a result, we know little from descriptive studies or reports from health care systems about the extent to which appropriate, evidence-based therapies are being received by patients who see those providers for therapy. Nonetheless, there are some innovative models of ways that behavioral health plans can influence care to improve psychotherapy, including the facilitation of goal-focused psychotherapy (Goldman, McCulloch, and Cuffel, 2003), and using trained clinical staff to provide care management at the level of the behavioral health care organization (Wang et al., 2007). By contrast, simply distributing guideline information to clinical providers has no demonstrable effect (Azocar et al., 2003).

Measuring Quality of TRICARE Community-Based Services. TRICARE health benefits used outside the Military Treatment Facilities are managed through contracts with commercial health plans for each of the three TRICARE regions. In two of these regions, management of treatment benefits for mental health and substance abuse is carved out to behavioral health plans. All of these plans report HEDIS measures to

NCQA; these measures include some indicators of quality of care for major depression, but no indicators for PTSD or other anxiety disorders. They also collect information on patient satisfaction with general health services, using self-report surveys. Regional TRICARE staff work with health-plan managers to review HEDIS and other performance indicators and patient-satisfaction reports.

It is our understanding that, to date, there has been relatively little focus on examining performance indicators and no measurement of patient satisfaction for the mental health services beneficiaries receive (stakeholder interviews). DoD could focus efforts on these areas and, in collaboration with regional health and behavioral health plans, develop better information for evaluating the quality of mental health services delivered by community-based providers.

Summary of Critical Gaps

We began this chapter by describing a conceptual model commonly used in health services research, and we used the model's components—barriers and facilitators to care, service use, quality of care, and outcomes—to organize our review of services available to military servicemembers returning from deployment with mental disorders. We identified two kinds of service gaps—gaps in access and gaps in quality, and we use these categories to summarize our discussion below.

However, our overarching conclusion from our review is that efforts to fill service gaps will not be successful unless they take into account the other components of the system. For example, expanding the number of mental health providers will not make care more accessible if the concerns about negative consequences associated with getting care are not addressed. Evidence-based care cannot be implemented effectively unless there is a way to continuously measure and improve it. Our specific recommendations should be interpreted in the context of this broader systems framework.

Gaps in Access to Care and Care Quality for Active Duty Military Servicemembers

Access. Available literature documents a large gap between need for mental health services and use of such services by active duty servicemembers. Structural aspects of services, as well as personal and cultural factors, are important to understanding and narrowing this gap.

Evaluating and Expanding Access to Mental Health Services Will Require a Broad Approach That Allows Coordination of Resources and Services Across DoD Organizational Silos. A broad array of mental health services is available to active duty military servicemembers: intensive inpatient services in a few select military hospital sites, outpatient medical services available in the Military Treatment Facilities of most installations, mental health specialists and chaplains attached to units, installation-based community service counseling, counseling from community-based providers through Military OneSource, and TRICARE-covered services delivered by community providers and facilities for the small but increasing number of servicemembers (including those in the Reserve Component) who are not in proximity to a Military Treatment Facility.

Much attention has been focused on barriers to accessing services within one of these organizational silos—the Military Treatment Facilities—including the shortage of uniformed mental health specialty providers, long waiting times, and unfilled training slots. DoD has plans to expand MTF capacity to provide mental health services by hiring additional providers. Part of the solution is likely to be increasing incentives of various kinds to recruit and retain more uniformed mental health specialty providers. However, these changes will not bear fruit for several years.

A broader and more integrative view of available mental health specialty and counseling resources could help to close gaps in the nearer term by making more-efficient use of existing resources to better meet mental health needs of military servicemembers. For example, DoD could revise policies that limit military community service counselors to behaviorally or environmentally defined problems, such as work stress and anger management. These counseling resources might be more efficiently and effectively used if the scope of practice were expanded to include evidence-based counseling, such as cognitive-behavioral therapy, for military servicemembers with PTSD and major depression, with referrals to an MTF if disorders are severe, complex, or unremitting. Reconsidering the roles for Military OneSource and TRICARE network providers could also expand access to care.

Military Institutional and Cultural Barriers to Access Are Considerable and Not Easily Surmounted. The stigma associated with having a mental disorder is a broad national concern, not solely a concern within the military. However, military training, culture, institutional structures, and policies foster stigma and prevent individuals from seeking care because they fear that using services will limit their military-career prospects or cause them to be viewed as weak or unreliable. These cultural and institutional influences are pervasive and powerful, and thus not easily overcome.

In response to recommendations from the DoD Mental Health Task Force, DoD has developed a plan to achieve the vision embodied in the recommendations. One of six key objectives of the plan is to "build psychological fitness and resilience, while dispelling stigma" (Department of Defense Task Force on Mental Health, 2007b, p. 41). To achieve this objective, DoD plans educational efforts (anti-stigma campaign, psychological-health education) and the implementation of a program to embed operational "psychological health professionals" into line units—similarly to the Marine Corps OSCAR program.

Educational efforts to increase knowledge about psychological and mental health might convince military servicemembers that treatment is beneficial, or they might help them manage problems on their own. However, education is unlikely to significantly affect servicemembers' willingness to seek treatment for mental health problems, because it does not address what servicemembers see as the negative consequences of doing so. In making a decision to seek mental health care, an individual weighs the benefits of using services (might help relieve my symptoms, my family would benefit if I felt better) against the costs (might affect my promotion, have to take time off work, medications have bad side effects). These fears are based on perceptions of institutional policies and practices that are, in fact, associated with some risk of negative career consequences.

Bringing about cultural change that reduces resistance to use of services and promotes psychological health for active duty personnel will require confronting institutional barriers. One recent change, which modified the inquiry about previous mental health care on the application form for a security clearance, is an important step in this direction. It is clear, however, that many servicemembers will be reluctant to use services unless they are convinced that there will be no negative work repercussions.

DoD Could Reduce Barriers to Using Mental Health Services by Making Confidential Counseling Available to Military Personnel During Off-Duty Hours. A "safe" counseling services program in garrison could support and supplement psychological health providers embedded in units. Programs could offer evidence-based psychotherapies for PTSD and depression, as well as counseling for a broader range of emotional and situational problems, with the overarching goal of early intervention to promote effective coping and resilience among those who have experienced the stresses of combat. If counseling is to be perceived as safe, confidentiality would have to be explicitly ensured and clearly communicated. As with mental health counseling available to the general civilian population, confidentiality would be broken only if the counselor determines that the individual is a threat to him- or herself or to others. Counseling services that could be broadened in this way already exist within the array of available community support programs, but they have not been explicitly tasked to address the mental health needs of those returning from deployment.

We recognize the challenges to providing "safe" counseling services to active duty military servicemembers. One challenge is that command would not necessarily be notified when a servicemember uses such services. Commanders value information that a servicemember is receiving mental health services to help determine fitness for duty and individual readiness, and to evaluate whether an individual's mental status limits his or her proper handling of weapons and other ordnance. Second, treatments provided by "safe" counseling programs cannot be continued during deployments, and this temporary termination of treatment could theoretically cause complications in mental health status. Furthermore, formal availability and recognition of "safe" counseling programs will inevitably result in the development of guidelines for cases that require referral to command or traditional Military Treatment Facility mental health services; these guidelines may diminish perceptions about the program's confidentiality.

These challenges understood, "safe" counseling programs can address a key barrier to mental health treatment and result in more servicemembers receiving mental health treatment that they would not have otherwise accessed. Guidelines for command notification may be required, but benefits may still accrue if those guidelines were less conservative than they are currently, and transparent to servicemembers. It is true that treatment would be temporarily put on hold during deployment; however, such a hiatus seems a superior alternative to not receiving treatment at all. If these counseling programs treated less-severe forms of mental disorders, as would be the case, then the risks of terminating counseling would be extremely minimal. Regular contact with a counselor may also provide an opportunity to motivate servicemembers to disclose their condition to command and arrange for referral to a Military Treatment Facility and the deployment-related treatment that would ensue.

"Safe" counseling would not replace mental health services within the Military Treatment Facilities, nor the usual channels of command referral to these services. Those whose mental health problems are severe, who require medications, who are command-referred because their ability to function is in question, or who prefer medical evaluation and treatment would still have access to the broad range of specialty mental health services available within the MTFs.

Unit Cohesion Can Help to Stem or Even Reverse Development of Mental Health Problems, and NCO Programs May Provide an Approach That Strengthens the Supportive Capacity of Unit Peers. Previous research has documented that high unit cohesion protects soldiers and marines from combat-stress reactions. The social support that cohesive units provide to individual servicemembers no doubt plays a critical role in this protection.

Several initiatives have sought to further harness the supportive role of unit peers. The original, but not currently implemented, version of the Marine Corps's OSCAR program requires one or two mid-level NCOs per company to be trained as peer mentors. Referrals from commanders for mental health care would go directly to these NCOs, who would interview the marine and, if evaluations or treatment were necessary, serve as case managers and coordinate care from disparate health providers. The NCOs would also help units cope with deployment-related stressors. A similar program was developed by the British Royal Marines.

NCO programs would fill a critical gap. Unlike typical mental health practitioners, NCOs are recruited from or serve in the line community and would be known and trusted by line personnel and command alike. With a basic level of mental health training, they could greatly expand the military's ability to detect budding mental health problems. Importantly, they may also serve as peer counselors and consequently act as an initial and knowledgeable go-to source for troubled soldiers. Given the promise of these NCO programs for improving the health and resilience of the force, such programs merit serious consideration by both the Marine Corps and Army (Helmus and Glenn, 2005).

Battlemind training is one example of how the military is harnessing unit-level social support. *Battlemind* is a system of U.S. Army trainings (presented in group settings using PowerPoint presentations and other educational materials) designed to help soldiers cope with the stressors of the deployment cycle. Specially tailored pre- and post-deployment briefs inform soldiers on what they are likely to see and experience, describe common and normative mental health reactions, and give guidance for seeking mental health support. The briefings convey a key message: that soldiers are responsible for each other's emotional well-being. This responsibility includes speaking to each other about troublesome experiences and being on the look out for budding mental health problems. Battlemind has not yet been subjected to rigorous scientific evaluation, so its effectiveness is not yet known. However, unit peers and small-unit leadership continue to be the first line of defense in ensuring a psychologically fit military force.

Quality. Relatively little information is available about the quality of mental health care provided in military settings, in large part because DoD has not developed the infrastructure to routinely measure processes or outcomes of care. There have been some efforts to train providers in evidence-based practices, but these efforts have not been broadly disseminated and supported with system redesign.

The newly created DoD Center of Excellence for Psychological Health and Traumatic Brain Injury is envisioned to furnish an organizational structure that will provide leadership and institutionalize excellence in care for psychological health and traumatic brain injury. The Center represents an exciting and historic opportunity to plan and implement a cross-service, system-level focus on monitoring and improving quality of care. Many lessons can be learned from the VA, which has focused on performance measurement and quality-of-care improvement for over a decade. A well-planned approach to train clinicians in evidence-based practices is a necessary but not sufficient first step to improving quality.

Successful quality-improvement efforts in health care in the VA and elsewhere have been multifaceted, including systems to support provider-patient communication and proactive follow-up, patient-centered self-management strategies, clinical information systems that assist delivery of care and provide performance feedback, linkages to community support services, and a coherent approach to system improvement. In the military context, special attention to communication with leadership and issues related to determination of fitness will add further complexities to system redesign, but these communication and decision processes could also be improved and better documented if incorporated into system redesign.

Psychotherapy is one area in which routine performance measurement has been notably lacking, beyond simply counting the number of psychotherapy visits that an individual receives. Because there are numerous psychotherapy approaches and clinicians tend to have preferred approaches, it is particularly difficult to know whether military personnel are receiving therapies that have been demonstrated to be effective. For this reason, training in evidence-based psychotherapy techniques has been most successful if it includes a period of supervised practice and if techniques are monitored on an occasional but ongoing basis (e.g., review of taped sessions) to evaluate fidelity to the practice.

Counseling resources outside the MTF, such as specialists embedded in units and counselors in community service programs, may have licensing and the capacity to provide evidence-based psychotherapies for PTSD and major depression (for example, cognitive-behavioral therapies) or to provide advice (e.g., chaplains) that is consistent with and supports these approaches. As noted above, these nonmedical and more-informal sources of care could be essential components of an institutional approach that reduces stigma and promotes resilience and positive mental health. But attention must also be given to training, supervising, and providing feedback to support these staff and services so that appropriate, high-quality counseling will be provided.

Gaps in Access to Care and Care Quality for OEF/OIF Veterans

Access. All OEF/OIF veterans, including deactivated reservists, are eligible to receive services from the VA. Because the VA operates under a fixed budget, access to its health care services is limited by design and guided by a priority system, with non-disabled veterans lower in priority than those with designations of disability.

Recent congressional budget allocations to the VA have increased funding to expand capacity and improve services for OEF/OIF veterans. New resources will help the VA reduce gaps in access to health services for such veterans, but it will take time to plan where expansion is most critical, to fill new positions with qualified personnel, and to develop and provide appropriate training and supervision for these staff. Rushed expansion could have deleterious effects on quality, so the VA must plan and implement carefully, even though political pressures to expand access quickly are intense.

Successfully Improving Access to Mental Health Services for OEF/OIF Veterans Will Require Attention to Two Major Challenges: Expanding Service Capacity and Appealing to Younger Veterans. Expanding the capacity of services, such as PTSD clinics, does not ensure increased availability for OEF/IEF veterans. The VA has documented a surprisingly large increase in the number of Vietnam-era veterans using mental health services, greatly exceeding the increase in the number of OEF/OIF veterans. Increased demand for services from older veterans likely reflects recurrence of mental health problems and legitimate need. However, this dynamic may result in lowered access for lower-priority OEF/OIF veterans.

Young veterans are reporting that they feel uncomfortable and out of place in VA facilities, where they see that most patients are much older and receiving care for chronic mental and physical illnesses. Such perceptions can undermine younger veterans confidence in receiving the kinds of services they need. Changing this image to become a highly regarded source of care for the country's current generation of veterans will require new approaches that are likely to involve both marketing and system redesign.

It Is Important to Improve Access to Mental Health Services Beyond the VA System. We cannot expect that the VA will meet the mental health needs of all OEF/OIF veterans, both because the VA operates within a fixed budget and thus must focus on higher-priority disabled veterans and because many veterans do not live close to a VA facility. For example, traveling long distances to get a typical course of cognitive-behavioral therapy for problems with PTSD or major depression, which requires 15 to 20 weekly outpatient visits, would be a significant obstacle for most people.

Other options for mental health services are often available to veterans, including Vet Centers and care from community-based providers. Ability to pay for services from community providers depends on veterans' insurance; many have private employer-sponsored health insurance or TRICARE (i.e., if eligible). Veterans living in rural and frontier regions of the country, remote from Vet Centers and community-based specialty mental health providers, may have particularly poor access to mental health care.

Vet Centers Can Play a Critical Role in Providing Access to Mental Health Services for Those Whose Injuries Do Not Qualify Them for High-Priority Access to VA Care. Although community-based mental health specialists are unlikely to have much experience with military life or military clients, Vet Centers are uniquely designed to understand and meet the needs of military clients. Peer counselors and clinical staff who have experience with the military environment help to overcome stigma and provide social support, as well as treatment and assistance in linking to other needed services. The Centers' original focus on Vietnam-era veterans was a drawback for younger veterans, but the Centers have been changing their image and appear to be successful in adapting to better serve younger OEF/OIF veterans.

The number of Centers is growing rapidly, but further expansion could be a particularly effective way of broadening access. A needs assessment of the OEF/OIF veteran populations should guide decisions about how best to expand this capacity and reach out to veterans in underserved areas. Because Vet Centers are small, storefront operations, they may be relatively easy to expand (and later cut back) in response to changing needs.

Access to Community-Based Mental Health Specialists Through Private Employer-Based Insurance or TRICARE Is an Alternative for OEF/OIF Veterans, but Availability of These Specialists Is Highly Variable. The mental health providers participating in health plan networks are qualified, licensed professionals encompassing a range of independent-practice specialists (e.g., psychiatrists, psychologists, and social workers) and specialty facilities. However, network participation of these providers varies highly by region, and among participating providers, availability to see new clients is also highly variable. TRICARE reimbursement rates (linked by statute to Medicare reimbursement rates) may also be too low in some markets, restricting the accessibility of mental health care available to TRICARE beneficiaries. Although the MHS plans to expand capacity for mental health services by adding civilian providers to MTFs and expanding the TRICARE network (see Department of Defense, Military Health System Web site for testimony of the Assistant Secretary of Defense for Health Affairs), analyses of the geographic distribution of these providers may prove informative for future planning. At the same time, consideration of the adequacy of reimbursement rates to retain these providers will be important.

State Governments and Community Groups Have Generated Innovative and Promising Approaches to Increasing Access to Community-Based Care for OEF/OIF Veterans. We are not aware of any current efforts to examine the effect of these access initiatives. It would be very useful if these approaches—and lessons learned from their implementation—were documented, synthesized, updated, and shared via a national clearinghouse. A potential strength of these initiatives is that they can draw on a community's intrinsic understanding of its own needs and resources to meet those needs and can flexibly build collaborations across governmental agencies, private organizations, mental health professionals, and community leaders to respond to these needs. A potential weakness of these initiatives is that they may lack capacities to mobilize needed resources or to monitor the impact of their efforts and use this feedback to guide improvements in access and quality of care. In some cases, the initiatives might benefit from additional resources or technical assistance to help them develop key capacities that will close gaps in care for OEF/OIF veterans.

Quality. The VA is at the forefront of quality assessment and improvement in health care, including care for PTSD and major depression, and is continuing to push forward. A congressionally mandated and independent study of the VA's mental health care will soon be released, providing a national, comprehensive assessment of its quality. The evaluation is likely to highlight areas in which the VA can serve as a model of quality improvement for DoD and the nation, as well as areas to target for future improvement efforts.

Vet Centers have been embracing opportunities to train their counselors in evidence-based therapies for PTSD. It is important that such training be broadly available on an ongoing basis and supported with a level of supervision that will result in high-quality care. Developing the capability to provide cognitive-behavioral therapy, an effective treatment for both PTSD and major depression, seems an obvious priority. The Centers could also benefit from systems that support delivery of quality care: information systems that track planned care and assist in follow-up, and performance-feedback systems that monitor the fidelity of therapeutic approaches and customer satisfaction.

It is extremely difficult to obtain information about the quality of care provided by the broad array of community-based independent mental health specialty practitioners, at either a group or individual level. However, commercial managed health care plans, such as those holding the regional TRICARE contracts, have both leverage and tools to assess and influence the performance of these providers. Currently, DoD staff work with regional health-plan contractors to monitor the performance of network providers by examining administrative and claims data and conducting consumer-satisfaction surveys; however, to date, TRICARE has not focused on mental health services. DoD and its TRICARE commercial contractors trail the state of the art in assessing performance and consumer satisfaction in mental health care. These are areas in which the broader mental health services field could offer approaches and measures.

State, local, and grassroots efforts to reach out to veterans and provide access to community services are admirable. However, there may be no information about or oversight of the quality of those services. Increasing access to mental health services that are not beneficial is ultimately of little value to our country's veterans. It is important that such efforts include some attention to the quality of care that is provided.

An approach to quality improvement that merits attention is developing tools that can provide consumers with more information to evaluate the quality of community providers. One relatively easy approach would be to give veterans and their families information resources (e.g., Web-based educational resources, pamphlets, media campaigns) to learn about mental health problems and treatment and to help them select and access community providers who will provide effective treatments. A second, longer-range strategy to explore would involve designating certain network providers as being especially qualified to treat military servicemembers and families affected by combat stress–related mental and emotional problems. It could be accomplished in a variety of ways that involve different cost-benefit trade-offs: for example, from a formal training and certification program administered by DoD to an evaluation process that reviews existing documentation of experience and performance and results in TRICARE's designating certain providers as having special expertise.

Special Issues for Traumatic Brain Injury

We now turn our attention to the special issues associated with addressing traumatic brain injuries. We explore the differences in access and services available to servicemembers and veterans with traumatic brain injuries according to how their injury is detected (whether in-theater or post-deployment) and the level of injury severity. These two factors determine how the servicemember accesses the care systems available. We then discuss the barriers to receiving proper care, including documentation issues, common co-occurring problems of TBI, the need for qualified care managers, and the frequency of co-occurring emotional and behavioral problems. We describe treatments for traumatic brain injuries and summarize the scientific evidence about their effectiveness; we provide some perspective on quality of care by putting the current VA and DoD treatment guidelines for these conditions in the context of the evidence. We end with a review of some successful strategies for improving care.

Note that several other recent reports (besides this one) have addressed the identification and treatment of TBI among servicemembers. For example, the VA Office of the Inspector General released a Healthcare Inspection on the Health Status of and Services for Operation Enduring Freedom/Operation Iraqi Freedom Veterans After Traumatic Brain Injury Rehabilitation in July 2006 (Department of Veterans Affairs, 2006a). The Department of the Army created a Traumatic Brain Injury Task Force, which released its report to the Surgeon General in May 2007 and released a final report including updates on the status of recommendation implementation in January 2008. Additionally, the President's Commission on Care for America's Returning Wounded Warriors released a report in July 2007 that gave significant attention to TBI (PCCWW, 2007a and 2007b). We draw heavily on these existing reports with the goal of describing the services available, access, and barriers to care, while highlighting areas that need further research or attention—particularly gaps in access to and in quality of care (again drawing upon the model presented in Figure 7.1). It is important to note that many changes in the care systems for TBI are being planned, are in progress, or have already been implemented as a result of these earlier reports. We attempt to note this progress where possible. Further research and oversight will be necessary to accurately determine the extent and success of those changes over time.

Traumatic brain injury is an injury to the brain that may range in severity from mild (e.g., a concussion from exposure to a blast) to severe (e.g., a penetrating head wound). Often referred to as a signature wound of OEF/OIF, TBI poses special challenges for the military medical system.

Although accurate figures for the total number of servicemembers who have suffered a TBI are difficult to estimate, the Defense and Veterans Brain Injury Center (DVBIC) reported that, as of March 2007, 2,726 servicemembers had been reported to the DVBIC with a diagnosis of traumatic brain injury. Of these, 2,094 were classified as mild and 255 as moderate. Another 192 had severe traumatic brain injuries, and 171 had penetrating brain injuries (PCCWW, 2007b). Other reports indicate potentially higher rates of probable mild TBI: Of 35,000 otherwise-healthy servicemembers who were screened for TBI after deployment, 10 to 20 percent met screening criteria for mild TBI (PCCWW, 2007b). In our survey (see Chapter Four), 19 percent reported a probable TBI. These data suggest that, out of 1.64 million deployed, the number of servicemembers with mild TBI could be as high as 160,000 to 320,000 soldiers.

Issues regarding TBI identification, access to care, availability and quality of services, and barriers to care vary by severity of TBI and the method of returning home from deployment. Moreover, these two variables are related. Soldiers with milder cases of TBI typically redeploy home with their units. Those with moderate to severe cases (including penetrating head wounds) are more likely to be medically evacuated from theater to a military care setting. This latter group may also include individuals with mild TBI that co-occurs with other serious physical injuries.

The discussion below reflects this bifurcation. The first section relates to mild TBI—specifically, that among those individuals who redeploy with their units. The second section relates to moderate and severe TBI.

Mild TBI

Identification. DoD has been criticized for lacking a systemwide approach to the proper identification, management, and surveillance of individuals who sustain a mild TBI (U.S. Department of the Army, 2008). Until September 2007, there was no DoD-wide post-deployment screening for TBI. However, at that time, the Post-Deployment Health Assessment (PDHA) (DD Form 2796) and Post-Deployment Health Reassessment (DD Form 2900) were revised to include several questions related to TBI, including exposure to blasts, loss of consciousness, and symptoms of a probable TBI. Screening for TBI is now also included in revised versions of the Army's yearly physical health assessment. Although the addition of these questions will facilitate the identification of individuals with a probable TBI, the questions do not capture sufficient information on the injury itself (e.g., whether from blast exposure) or about the associated impairments to provide for adequate categorization of possible ongoing problems. DoD is attempting to improve in-theater documentation of exposure to TBI, however.

Currently available prevalence estimates of TBI among those who served in Afghanistan or Iraq come from those bases and medical facilities that have begun systematic screening of servicemembers. Landstuhl Regional Medical Center (a large Army medical facility through which virtually all medically evacuated servicemembers transit from Afghanistan and Iraq) screens everyone with a new injury, and Walter Reed Army Medical Center (a large Army trauma center that receives the majority of those medically evacuated from Landstuhl) screens everyone who may have been exposed. In addition, in April 2007 the VA began screening all OEF/OIF veterans who seek care within their system for a possible TBI (U.S. Department of the Army, 2008). Fort Carson (an Army base located in Colorado) has also instituted TBI-specific post-deployment screening in collaboration with the DVBIC; it screens 100 percent of soldiers returning from combat, as well as soldiers arriving from other posts (Pach, 2007). In addition to the standard questions asked on the Post-Deployment Health Assessments, Fort Carson also uses a TBI-specific screening form, which captures detailed information about events that may have caused a TBI during deployment. Soldiers who screen positive for TBI then have access to a wide range of specialty services. As of November 2007, Fort Carson was the only base with this level of universal screening in place.

The above estimate of 10 to 20 percent screening positive for probable TBI (PCCWW, 2007b) does not predict the number of servicemembers who need care, since the majority of mild TBIs do not require medical treatment. One challenge to identifying those who need follow-up may result from poor reporting of symptoms upon redeployment. For example, Fort Carson's routine TBI screening of returning servicemembers found that a higher proportion of individuals reported symptoms of TBI after being home for several months than reported symptoms immediately after redeployment. This increase over time is likely attributable to three issues. First, soldiers may not be willing to disclose TBI symptoms at the time of the PDHA for fear of delaying their return home (Maugh II, 2007). Second, symptoms may be masked by the euphoria of returning home (Lorge, 2007). Third, TBI symptoms may be more apparent to soldiers or their loved ones after they have been out of the combat zone for several months (Pach, 2007). For these reasons, the inclusion of the TBI screening questions on the Post-Deployment Health Reassessment, which is typically implemented three to six months after returning from deployment, may help to ensure that the majority of individuals in need of follow-up for a possible TBI are identified.

An additional challenge in identifying and treating TBI among returning servicemembers is that many symptoms, such as anger, difficulty concentrating, and diminished interest, are characteristic of both TBI and certain mental health conditions, such as PTSD and major depression. Patients who have sustained a mild TBI may also have a mental health condition, and when they seek care for symptoms such as headache, irritability, sleep disturbance, and memory difficulty, those symptoms may be misattributed (U.S. Department of the Army, 2008; Hoge et al., 2008). Thus, the possibility of a misdiagnosis or an incomplete diagnosis is a concern because those who have not been identified as having a probable TBI may not receive appropriate treatment and rehabilitation services (Arlinghaus, 2007).

What Is the Gap in Access to Care? Screening positive for mild TBI does not necessarily indicate a need for treatment services. Of those who screen positive for mild TBI, between 60 and 80 percent will resolve without medical attention and are best served by receiving educational materials (Department of Veterans Affairs, 2004; Hoge et al., 2008). However, the remaining 20 to 40 percent may have significant long-term residual neurological symptoms and will require some form of medical or rehabilitative services.

How individuals with long-term symptoms access care depends in part on whether they are still on active duty or have separated from the military. If an individual is still on active duty, care would be received through the MTF, and appropriate referrals to specialty services would be given as necessary.

Regardless of severity, if a TBI-related disability is serious enough that a servicemember is no longer fit for duty, the individual may be separated or retired from the military. All servicemembers serving in OEF/OIF are eligible for five years of free care through the VA after separation from the military; however, without a disability rating, their priority for care will be low, potentially posing difficulty for accessing health services in a timely manner. Receiving a disability rating enables these separated servicemembers access to VA services well beyond the five-year period after military discharge, although conditions may apply depending on their resulting priority level (see the section earlier in this chapter titled "Eligibility and Priorities for VA Health Services Guide Access"). A key challenge for individuals who may suffer from mild TBI to obtaining a disability evaluation and rating, however, may be documentation of exposure in theater and recognition of potential symptoms.

What Structural Factors Impede or Facilitate Access to Care for TBI? Many programs provide acute care for individuals with moderate and severe TBIs. However, the care and services for those with mild TBI rely more heavily on shorter-term outpatient care and rehabilitation. Returning servicemembers may receive care through the MTF (if continuing on active duty) and the VA (if separated military or deactivated Reserve Component), but seeking care for blast-related TBI may be more challenging for Reserve Component servicemembers who live far from a military or veterans' medical facility. To address this disparity, the military established Community Based Health Care Organizations (CBHCOs), which coordinate ongoing general medical care for Reserve Component servicemembers. These organizations include a network of 18 sites that provide shorter-term care for TBI-related issues. They do not, however, focus on longer-term rehabilitation (Schraa et al., 2007).

In addition to medical facilities, there are over 1,000 local and national nonprofit organizations that assist injured servicemembers and their families with all levels of care, education, and support. Anecdotal evidence suggests that coordination between DoD or the VA and these organizations is limited at best (see Coordination of TBI care subsection for further details). It is unknown how many veterans or servicemembers are taking advantage of these services instead of or in addition to DoD or VA services to supplement gaps in coverage.

Another challenge is that quality[7] can vary widely between these programs. Patients and/or their families noted minimal interdisciplinary communication; a lack of understanding of military-specific issues; and that, although many nonmilitary medical centers delivered high-quality care, they lacked understanding of issues unique to this population and did not have strong systems for supporting servicemembers (U.S. Department of the Army, 2008).

Given that these resources are used not only by individuals with mild TBI but by soldiers with moderate and severe TBI who have been discharged from VA facilities, coordination with other resources, whether community, state, or other federal systems, may be an important step in ensuring that all individuals with TBI receive needed services.

Barriers to Care. Although many barriers to care are shared by servicemembers with mild, moderate, and severe TBI, individuals with mild TBI also face a unique set of barriers to care. Below we highlight some of these issues.

---

[7]   *Quality of care for TBI* is defined as care that is concordant with TBI guidelines and practice standards that are based on the available evidence for effectiveness. However, there is limited evidence for quality of care for TBI relative to the evidence base for mental disorders. See Appendix 7.C, Table 7.C.12.

Medical Documentation. Currently, medical documentation is not standardized, making it impossible to reliably retrieve and update information related to an injured servicemember's treatment and prognosis over time and across systems of care (U.S. Department of the Army, 2008). Early and thorough documentation of the injury and immediate symptoms is particularly crucial in ensuring proper care for servicemembers, especially given the high turnover in many military units: Witnesses to the precipitating event may not be available at a later date to provide corroborating information. Without documentation, servicemembers who show subsequent behavioral changes or present with TBI symptoms at a later date may not have those changes attributed to their TBI, particularly if the servicemember has encountered legal problems or become involved in drug or alcohol abuse, according to a stakeholder interview. As a result of these secondary problems, personnel actions could result in the denial of access to DoD and/or VA services.

Co-Morbidity. Given that individuals with TBI are also likely to have mental health conditions (Trudel, 2007a), overlapping symptoms may make it more difficult to guide injured servicemembers to appropriate rehabilitative services. In addition, a common symptom of PTSD—lack of sleep—can also significantly affect TBI symptoms, such as memory problems, according to a stakeholder interview. According to the VA's mental health experts, "mild TBI can produce behavioral manifestations that mimic PTSD or other mental health symptoms and the veteran's denial of problems that accompany damage to certain areas of the brain often leads to difficulties receiving services" (Atizado, 2007, p. 3).

TRICARE Coverage of TBI Services. One barrier faced by servicemembers regardless of TBI severity is that TRICARE does not fully cover many TBI services. Former servicemembers with TBI who live far from a VA facility and cannot access the VA treatment and rehabilitation services may rely on TRICARE Prime or TRICARE Standard/Extra for medical coverage. However, TRICARE currently does not have a protocol for treating TBI, and most services are considered specialist services, subject to referral requirements.

Regional Variation and Lack of Community Providers. Another barrier faced by all servicemembers with TBI is regional variation in care. The VA's study on OEF/OIF veterans with TBI found that 48 percent of the patients believed that there were very few resources in the community to address the needs of individuals with a brain injury (Department of Veterans Affairs, 2006a). This belief may be due, in part, to the compensation structure for community providers. Some providers within the community feel that the government is not compensating them at a reasonable rate; as a result, they are not accepting or treating injured servicemembers, according to a stakeholder interview.

Moderate and Severe TBI

We now turn to issues related to TBI identification, access to services, TBI program quality, and barriers to care for individuals with moderate and severe TBI. As noted above, this section may also be relevant for those with mild TBI who were medically evacuated home due to another severe injury. We do not address issues of the most severely injured servicemembers requiring 24-hour care and support. Rather, our focus is on outpatient treatment and rehabilitative services; describing acute inpatient hospital care for severe TBI is beyond the scope of this study.

What Is the Gap in Access to Care? TBI occurs when the brain hits the inside of the skull. It can be caused by improvised explosive devices (IEDs), mortars, vehicle accidents, grenades, bullets, mines, and falls. As noted earlier, TBI can be difficult to diagnose. Symptoms can range from headaches, irritability, and sleep disorders to memory problems and depression (Department of Veterans Affairs, 2004).

Individuals with moderate and severe TBIs often require immediate medical care. According to a stakeholder interview, increasing concerns about TBI have resulted in new policies requiring that all those medically evacuated to Landstuhl or Walter Reed Army Medical Center be assessed for TBI. This assessment may include a neurological examination, brief cognitive assessment, and, if needed, additional assessments, such as neuroimaging. This assessment also helps to identify mild-TBI cases when TBI may not be the primary injury or reason for being medically evacuated.

Given the almost-universal screening for TBI among this population, the identification of individuals with TBI is more comprehensive and straightforward than for individuals with mild TBI who redeployed with their unit. At Walter Reed, approximately 29 percent of returning casualties are diagnosed with a TBI; about half of these are diagnosed with mild TBI and the others with TBI characterized as moderate, severe, or penetrating (U.S. Department of the Army, 2008).

What Structural Factors Impede or Facilitate Access to Care? Since the majority of individuals experiencing a moderate or severe TBI receive immediate medical care, their injury is readily documented in the medical record as service-related. Therefore, unlike servicemembers with a mild TBI, those who were medically evacuated home do not have the challenge of proving that their medical or rehabilitative needs are connected to a TBI incurred while in service. This documentation facilitates access to long-term and rehabilitative care from DoD and the VA (U.S. Department of the Army, 2008).

A Wide Range of TBI Services Is Available to Servicemembers. Many programs provide treatment, rehabilitative care, and case coordination within DoD, the VA, and the larger community. Individuals with moderate and severe TBI are eligible for and typically receive the most intensive services, which allow for gradual, extended treatment and the possibility of long-term support. This type of care targets cognitive functions, psychosocial elements, life skills, and social/vocational roles (Trudel, 2007b).

Below, we describe several specialty services or programs that may facilitate access to health care for servicemembers and veterans with moderate to severe TBI.

Polytrauma System of Care. Polytrauma is a term that includes TBI and other injuries that blast victims typically sustain, such as amputations, burns, hearing and vision problems, and psychological trauma. The VA's integrated Polytrauma System of Care provides medical, rehabilitation, and support services for injured veterans and active duty servicemembers. The system, which includes four Polytrauma Rehabilitation Centers and 21 Polytrauma Network Sites located across the country, is designed to provide access to life-long rehabilitation care for veterans and active duty servicemembers recovering from polytrauma and TBI (Feeley, 2007).

The VA's four Polytrauma Rehabilitation Centers are located in Palo Alto CA, Richmond VA, Tampa FL, and Minneapolis MN. Staff include multidisciplinary teams of specialists in psychiatry, rehabilitation nursing, neuropsychology, psychology, speech-language pathology, occupational therapy, physical therapy, social work, therapeutic recreation, prosthetics, and blindness rehabilitation (Department of Veterans Affairs, 2007m). Specialized services include comprehensive acute rehabilitation care for complex and severe polytraumatic injuries, emerging consciousness programs, outpatient programs, and residential transitional rehabilitation programs (Feeley, 2007). In 2007, staffing for the Polytrauma Rehabilitation Centers was increased to respond to patient demand and to enhance coordination of care and support for family caregivers.

The 21 Polytrauma/TBI Network Sites, designated in December 2005, are the second level in the Polytrauma System of Care. Each Polytrauma Rehabilitation Center houses a Polytrauma Network Site, and there are 17 additional Network Sites (Department of Veterans Affairs, 2007m). Overall, there is one Network Site within each of the VA's 21 service areas (Feeley, 2007).

The TBI Network Sites provide specialized, post-acute rehabilitation in consultation with the Rehabilitation Centers. They also provide proactive case management for existing and emerging conditions and identify local resources for VA and non-VA care. In March 2007, the Polytrauma System of Care network was expanded to include two new components of care: Polytrauma Support Clinic Teams and Polytrauma Points of Contact. Geographically distributed across the VA, 75 Polytrauma Support Clinic Teams facilitate access to specialized rehabilitation services for veterans and active duty servicemembers at locations closer to their home communities (Feeley, 2007). These interdisciplinary teams manage the care of patients with stable treatment plans, providing regular follow-up visits, responding to emerging medical and psychosocial problems, and consulting with their affiliated Polytrauma Network Site or Polytrauma Rehabilitation Center when more-specialized services are required (Feeley, 2007).

The remaining 54 VA Medical Centers have an identified Polytrauma Point of Contact. The Point of Contact is responsible for managing consultations for patients with polytrauma and TBI and for assisting with referrals of these patients to programs capable of providing the appropriate level of services (Feeley, 2007).

Patient management is a key component to ensuring coordination of patient services in the Polytrauma System. The VA assigns every patient a care manager, who maintains scheduled contacts with veterans and their families to coordinate services and to address emerging needs. VA social worker or nurse liaisons are located at ten Military Treatment Facilities. The VA also has benefit liaisons located at the commonly referring MTFs to give patients and families an early briefing on the full array of VA services and benefits (Feeley, 2007). "Case management is also a critical function in the polytrauma system of care and it's designed to ensure lifelong coordination of services for patients with polytrauma and TBI" (Sigford, 2007).

Defense Veterans Brain Injury Center. Since 1992, DoD has partnered with the VA and the civilian sector to operate the DVBIC. One of the DVBIC goals is to ensure expert case management and individualized, evidence-based treatment to each patient in order to maximize function and decrease or eliminate TBI-related disability. Working across agencies, the DVBIC provides outreach, educational resources, and treatment services to help each TBI patient return to duty, work, and the community. The DVBIC has recently been reorganized within the newly established Defense Center of Excellence for Psychological Health and Traumatic Brain Injury. Through the DVBIC, DoD and VA treatment sites have access to similar educational resources for servicemembers and veterans with TBI, as well as training materials for those providing their care.

Servicemembers Can Receive Care in Multiple Systems, Depending on Their Level of Need. Individuals suffering more-severe TBI often require more-intensive rehabilitation. Such individuals generally receive acute care through DoD (for example, at the National Naval Medical Center). DoD and the VA have agreed that patients with moderate to severe TBI, or mild TBI with co-occurring mental disorder or severe injuries, may access care though VA polytrauma centers while remaining on active duty (Veterans Health Administration, 2006). They may also be sent to specialized civilian inpatient treatment facilities. The VA has a long history of providing specialized rehabilitation services, and its facilities have traditionally been equipped to address long-term rehabilitation needs. In 2007, DoD also began equipping its facilities and providers for long-term rehabilitation needs. Since servicemembers with severe TBI may receive care for their injury across all three sectors—DoD, the VA, a civilian facility, or a combination of these—more-intensive case management and care coordination is required, particularly if the soldier transitions back and forth between systems (especially if he or she remains on active duty during the rehabilitation period).

In addition to receiving medical care through MTFs and the VA, servicemembers with moderate to severe TBI are also eligible for a range of DoD-wide and service-specific programs and support services (detailed below). Eligibility for most programs requires that the injury be incurred after September 10, 2001, *and* that the injury was sustained in combat or training for combat. Many further restrictions may be placed on the timing and duration of program support relative to either the nature of injury or time since separation from service.

   Other Programs and Services Also Offer Support. Other, more-specialized programs and services have also been developed for servicemembers with TBI or other severe injuries. Each is described briefly below.

- *Center for the Intrepid.* A privately funded state-of-the-art rehabilitation center located next to the Brooke Army Medical Center in Texas. Built to provide care for servicemembers who sustained injuries in OEF and OIF, it also serves other injured veterans. The Center emphasizes multidisciplinary treatment teams (Wilson, 2007).
- *Wounded Warrior Program* (Army). Provides personal recovery services for severely wounded soldiers and assists and advocates for wounded soldiers and their families through counseling and support (U.S. Department of the Army, 2007).
- *Marine for Life Injured Support* (Marine Corps). Helps marines, sailors, and their families with case assistance and coordination and provides advocacy and education on issues of TBI and related benefits (U.S. Marine Corps, 2005).
- *Safe Harbor* (Navy). Provides personalized support and assistance to severely injured sailors and their families (U.S. Navy, 2007b).
- *Palace HART (Helping Airmen Recover Together)* (Air Force). Provides individualized personal support to airmen with combat-related illnesses or injuries resulting from Operations Enduring Freedom and Iraqi Freedom (Military.com, 2007a).
- *Military Severely Injured Center.* This specialty service under the Military OneSource contract provides support and augmentation of the severely injured programs of the various services. In addition, it supports families and serves as a safety net for injured servicemembers by providing Counselor Advocates.
- *Community Based Health Care Organizations.* CBHCOs arrange ongoing general medical care for Army Reserve Component servicemembers. They also include a TBI network of 18 sites that provide shorter-term care for TBI-related issues, but they do not focus on longer-term rehabilitation (Schraa et al., 2007).

   Whereas the military TBI programs highlighted above emphasize treatment, case coordination, and support for more severely injured servicemembers, a number of community-based facilities focus on treatment, rehabilitation, and long-term support for patients with TBI and their families. Although the federal system has no quality control over these civilian facilities, some have established histories of working with DoD and the VA. Two examples include the Scripps Rehabilitation Center and Lakeview:

- *Scripps Rehabilitation Center.* An accredited Brain Injury Day Treatment Program that has had experience providing rehabilitative care to non-combat-injured servicemembers for over ten years. In 2006, the program expanded to include specialized rehabilitation for combat brain-injured military personnel with mild TBI. Over 70 percent of Scripps' treated patients return to their units (Lobatz, Martinez, and Romito, 2007).
- *Lakeview.* With 14 residential and community-integrated programs across five states, Lakeview's specialized neurobehavioral and community-integrated rehabilitation programs focus predominantly on the care of adults with neurobehavioral diagnoses (typically brain injury–related) who have not succeeded as outpatients or with in-home supports and who require treatment, supervision, and support related to their significant cognitive and/or behavioral challenges. Physical-disability issues also are addressed.

The services described above focus primarily on more-intensive treatment and rehabilitation needs, but individuals may recover to the point that they no longer need such services. If so, their care and needs are similar to those described above for mild TBI and, when there are concerns regarding variation in quality, cost, and lack of long-term coordination with DoD or the VA, they may rely on a combination of military and civilian providers. In particular, active duty patients who recover sufficiently to return to their duty stations may have trouble finding rehabilitation (Department of Veterans Affairs, 2006a).

Coordination of TBI Care. The coordination of care for individuals with TBI can present a serious challenge. As noted, many with moderate to severe TBI have other injuries as well. Further, many soldiers who receive TBI care at VA Polytrauma Centers remain on active duty, which means that they must simultaneously navigate both DoD and the VA health systems. A final, often-overlooked, challenge is that, without care coordination and case management, injured servicemembers and their families are left to navigate these systems alone. Doing so may be particularly challenging, given that the servicemembers may be cognitively or emotionally impaired and their families may have a limited understanding of the systems. Each of these issues suggests an increased need for effective care coordination and case management (George, 2007).

Care Managers. TBI patients with moderate to severe TBI often have long-term cognitive and behavioral sequelae, such as memory loss and disruptive behavior, requiring long-term care management to coordinate their care (Department of Veterans Affairs, 2006a). Without specific guidelines for care managers, variation across facilities and across levels of care remains (U.S. Department of the Army, 2008). Injured veterans can have multiple care managers concurrently (see Barriers to Care subsection below). It can be difficult for TBI patients to know whom to contact, when, and about what issue. The DVBIC has a TBI-specific care-coordination system in place for those who have been medically evacuated more recently; however, servicemembers who were discharged before this program was initiated may still lack care coordination, according to a stakeholder interview.

Within the VA health care system, every patient now seen in one of the Polytrauma Rehabilitation programs is assigned a care manager who is responsible for coordination of all VA services and benefits and maintains contact with the patient and the families (Sigford, 2007). However, of the patients interviewed by the VA in their health care inspection for OEF/OIF veterans with TBI, only 65 percent said that they were in contact with someone in the VA who was coordinating their care; of those, 68 percent "were able to name that person or to specifically describe that person's position" (Department of Veterans Affairs, 2006a, p. 22).

Patients and families told VA inspectors that "the effectiveness of individual case managers ranged from outstanding to poor," and gave examples of excellent, invaluable assistance from case managers, as well as problems navigating the system, such as getting reimbursed, discharge planning, making appointments, and getting accurate information (Department of Veterans Affairs, 2006a, p. 26). The VA inspection also found that "case managers do not consistently coordinate the care of active duty patients following discharge from Lead Centers," and that "long-term case management for patients already retired from the military is inconsistent" (Department of Veterans Affairs, 2006a, p. 35). In fact, case managers at two of the Lead Centers reported using no tracking system for following patients after discharge (Department of Veterans Affairs, 2006a). Obstacles that the case managers themselves reported included limited ability to follow patients after discharge to a military facility or a remote living environment; difficulty in securing long-term placements of TBI patients with extreme behavioral problems; lack of adequate transportation and other resources, such as dental care, support groups, and interim housing; and inconsistency in long-term case management (Department of Veterans Affairs, 2006a).

According to at least one source, public attention and increased funding have led the system from inadequate care management to the other extreme, with multiple care managers and an excess of services that are poorly integrated. Some patients have multiple care managers at a time. Another challenge is a lack of qualified candidates from which to fill open care-management positions. In particular, there is a severe shortage of Certified Rehabilitation Registered Nurses, who are often used as highly skilled care managers for complex polytrauma cases, according to a stakeholder interview. As a result, there is often considerable variation in the qualifications of and quality of care from managers.

Severely wounded patients and their families need a single point of contact who is able to help coordinate all aspects of the recovery process: benefits, the disability-rating process, linking up with community programs, financial aid, transition between services and off of active duty, transportation issues, psychological support for the family, and so on (PCCWW, 2007b). Many services are available, but families and patients are often unaware of either the range of available services or how to access the necessary assistance. Both DoD and the VA are aware of these challenges, and they have responded with a number of intraservice and interservice initiatives (see above under Other programs and services also offer support subsection). However, problems of duplication of services and challenges navigating the road to recovery may remain (George, 2007). To address case management, the PCCWW has recommended that patient care be managed by Recovery Coordinators employed within the U.S. Public Health Service's Commissioned Corps (PCCWW, 2007b). The Recovery Coordinator program is now being implemented for severely injured servicemembers; it will serve most new moderate to severe cases of TBI.

Coordination with Other Resources. Many individuals recover to the point that they no longer need intensive treatment and rehabilitation services. However, they will likely need continued support, ranging from a few weeks of cognitive therapy to transitional community reentry services (U.S. Department of the Army, 2008). Through the DVBIC, DoD has established a working relationship with Virginia Neuro Care (a nonprofit organization that provides rehabilitation to individuals with brain injury) and Lakeview Brain Injury Programs. However, the partnership has yet to expand to a larger network of providers that could complement the existing acute rehabilitation services offered by the DoD and VA health care systems (George, 2007).

Barriers to Care. Despite a range of treatment and rehabilitative services for TBI, not all injured servicemembers are receiving appropriate services (Department of Veterans Affairs, 2006a; U.S. Department of the Army, 2008; PCCWW, 2007b). Below, we highlight access barriers most relevant to moderate and severe TBI.

Regional Variations. Inpatient care for TBI is available within the VA polytrauma systems of care; however, access to outpatient care shows more variation. One challenge pertains to regional variation in the availability of services and financing of those services. For example, while private neurobehavioral programs and private Community Integrated Rehabilitation programs may be available to supplement the care that the VA provides, they are not available in all locations. Further, these services may not be covered by TRICARE, Medicare, or Medicaid, although many states have instituted Medicaid waiver programs to address these needs within the civilian population (Trudel, 2007b). Therefore, where servicemembers live may significantly affect whether they can access covered services. According to a stakeholder interview, efforts are being made to better integrate civilian facilities into the TRICARE system to address the needs of those requiring specialized rehabilitation.

Delays in Receiving TBI Rehabilitation Services. There are also concerns about the amount of time it can take to get an appointment through the VA. For example, VA patients have a substantially longer median length of time from injury to initiation of comprehensive TBI rehabilitation than a similar group of patients in Model Systems, a community health care provider (6.1 weeks for the injured veterans tracked in the VA study versus 2.7 weeks for Model Systems) (Department of Veterans Affairs, 2006a). This disparity is particularly important because delaying comprehensive rehabilitation may negatively affect long-term outcomes. It is not clear whether the longer time from injury to beginning of rehabilitation reflects more-severe injuries, which require extended acute care, or the necessity of transferring between the DoD and VA health care systems.

What Cultural and Personal Factors Impede or Facilitate Access? While issues related to identification, access, services, and barriers were separated above by TBI severity, most cultural and personal factors—including stigma, knowledge and attitudes, and peer and family influences—affect all servicemembers with TBI regardless of severity level. Therefore, below, we discuss these issues for all TBI patients, noting variations by severity when applicable.

Military Culture and Negative Attitudes About Seeking Care. How military culture and personal attitudes and beliefs about care function may be different for those with mild TBI from those with moderate or severe TBI. As we have noted earlier, symptoms of mild TBI are often "invisible," and there is a great deal of overlap between the symptoms of mild TBI and PTSD. Thus, the perceived consequences associated with having a mental health condition (e.g., revocation of security clearances, inability to receive promotions or hold certain positions, accusations of malingering, and fears of being viewed as "weak-minded" or incompetent) may also be applicable to those with mild TBI.

In addition, according to a stakeholder interview, the military culture emphasizes toughness and unit cohesion and discourages soldiers from admitting to injuries. Regardless of symptom severity, military servicemembers may be concerned about the effect of traumatic brain injury on their military careers. Since soldiers with symptoms of brain injury will be sent home from Iraq or Afghanistan, the desire to stay with their peer group may encourage them to cheat on tests designed to detect brain injuries.

Many military servicemembers believe that mild TBIs, or concussions, can be easily "shaken off," as is done often with sports injuries, according to a stakeholder interview. This view is supported in part by the fact that many mild-TBI symptoms resolve themselves in a short time without treatment. However, some individuals may experience persistent and disabling symptoms that will not resolve on their own, so that personal attitudes about seeking help and military culture may inhibit individuals from receiving the benefits of treatment. At a town hall meeting on TBI, for example, soldiers mentioned that they fear ridicule from their peers and do not want to admit that they have a problem that could end their careers (Pach, 2007).

A related issue is that other individuals equate "traumatic brain injury" with brain damage or with being in a vegetative state, according to a stakeholder interview. This perception of traumatic brain injury is equally problematic, because it has implications for whether an individual will recognize that he or she needs treatment or believes that the treatment will be beneficial. Despite the importance of identifying and diagnosing individuals with mild TBI, one stakeholder interview suggested that there is a danger of pathologizing a condition that may heal without medical intervention because individuals' strongly held negative beliefs about their prospects of recovery may play a part in maintaining their TBI symptoms and reduced functioning (Jones, Fear, and Wessely, 2007).

Knowledge and Attitudes About TBI. A poorly understood fact is that TBI is typically classified by the severity of the initial injury and is not usually reclassified as the patient improves. This can be confusing to patients, families, and commanders, who may see one servicemember with mild TBI who has persistent debilitating symptoms, while another servicemember with severe TBI has recovered to a higher level of functioning than the counterpart with mild TBI (U.S. Department of the Army, 2008).

Another issue is the vast amount of official and nongovernmental information about TBI prevention, treatment, rehabilitation, and family assistance available for soldiers, their families, units, and care teams. However, that vastness may be overwhelming or inaccessible to soldiers suffering from TBI and their families. Furthermore, not all of the information is appropriate; literature needs to be targeted to the level of disability and the phase of recovery. Materials about severe TBI should not be given to those with a mild concussion, and long-term care/family-burnout materials should not be given to people at the beginning of a program (according to a stakeholder interview). Additionally, media outlets often misinterpret TBI data, and successful recoveries from TBI are not widely publicized (U.S. Department of the Army, 2008).

Cognitive Impairment. The most common cognitive consequences following moderate to severe TBI are problems with attention and concentration and deficits in new learning and memory (Department of Veterans Affairs, 2004)—problems that can make it more difficult to understand what types of rehabilitation are needed and then to schedule and keep appointments. Additionally, servicemembers with severe levels of brain injury "are compromised in their ability to navigate their environments and the systems needed to make forward progress along the recovery continuum" (George, 2007, p. 4). These cognitive problems emphasize the need for competent, engaged case managers who can assist veterans and their families in navigating those systems and ensuring that they seek and receive all needed care.

Emotional Problems. Emotional difficulties following a brain injury include increased anger, lowered frustration tolerance, increased anxiety, depression, and low self-esteem (Department of Veterans Affairs, 2004). All of these emotional issues can make it more difficult to schedule appointments, travel to those appointments, navigate check-in procedures, sit in waiting rooms, and participate fully and actively in rehabilitation activities. For some patients, going to facilities being used by people of varying levels of disability can increase anxiety, either by increasing fears that they are destined to be more disabled or adding to the frustration that they have not progressed further.

Disciplinary Actions That Inhibit Eligibility for VA Services. Some symptoms of TBI, such as irritability, outbursts, difficulty concentrating, memory deficits, and sleep problems, can also lead to disciplinary actions when soldiers have not been properly diagnosed (according to a stakeholder interview). Therefore, it is essential that exposure to a TBI be properly documented as soon as possible after the event, should symptoms not become apparent until a later time. Behavioral problems manifesting upon return from deployment may indicate the need to screen for TBI. Accurate diagnosis is crucial because, if disciplinary problems are severe enough, servicemembers can be dishonorably discharged from the military, which causes veterans to be ineligible for many military and VA benefits.

Family. Families of those who have suffered a TBI will likely need psychosocial support, as well as resource and logistical support to ensure that they can facilitate their loved one's gaining access to quality services. Family members are often heavily involved in caregiving and provide advocacy, supervision, direct care, and behavior management, which can be emotionally draining, particularly when the recovery process is variable and unpredictable. In addition, they may have to move to be closer to their loved one. Families may also have difficulty accessing expert resources in rural areas of the country, and they may have to quit their jobs to care for a loved one, which may curtail not only the financial resources of the family but also their employer-sponsored health care benefits (U.S. Department of the Army, 2008). In response to these and other issues, the VA has recently announced that it will provide nearly $4.7 million for "caregiver assistance pilot programs" to improve resources and education available to those who assist disabled veterans in their homes (Department of Veterans Affairs, 2007j).

The TBI Task Force has recommended reviewing the benefits packages provided by TRICARE, the VA, and other state-level organizations and advocacy groups providing medical assistance to determine an optimal uniform package (U.S. Department of the Army, 2008). Additionally, family members provide approximately 80 percent of all long-term services and support for family members in their homes (Seaton, 2007). There is a great need for more financial and other support for family members, and the Task Force has recommended that additional resources be provided for family members who have chosen to leave their jobs to care for a servicemember, including considering providing health insurance to family members who provide full-time care to an injured service member or veteran (U.S. Department of the Army, 2008). Both the VA Healthcare Inspection (Department of Veteran Affairs, 2006a) and the PCCWW (2007a and 2007b) also recommend improving financial and other support for family members of injured servicemembers. However, to date most of these recommendations have not been implemented.

Also of note, there are significant regional differences in the average disability compensation from the VA (GAO, 2007c). These differences, such as the varying disability ratings and payments within DoD, can significantly govern whether injured servicemembers and their families have available financial resources to actively pursue the best care.

What Is High-Quality Care for TBI?

Delivering quality care to TBI patients remains a major challenge. There is limited research about the effectiveness of treatments for patients with TBI. At present, the only TBI treatment recommendation with strong support in the research literature is that steroids should not be used to manage increased intracranial pressure in this population.[8] Table 7.5 briefly summarizes the guidelines that are elaborated upon in Appendix 7.C. Because relevant research is so limited, much of currently practiced TBI rehabilitation and medical management is not evidence-based practice but rather is based primarily on expert opinion. The current VA/DoD guidelines for TBI incorporate the limited evidence from the literature with expert opinion. More research is urgently needed to establish evidence-based practice guidelines, particularly in the area of rehabilitation.

For several reasons, implementing quality-improvement initiatives for the treatment of TBI is more difficult than implementing such initiatives for PTSD or major depression. First, TBI requires both traditional medical treatment and mental health care. Second, as noted earlier in the chapter, TBI symptoms include symptoms of PTSD or other mental health conditions. Thus, providing care to address the full spectrum of symptoms requires a number of different professionals from physical medicine and rehabilitation to mental health. In addition, addressing TBI requires both acute care for the injury and long-term or chronic care for any associated impairments. A

Table 7.5
Summary of TBI Guidelines

Guideline	Source	Evidence Base
TBI Treatment	Panel of 22 experts assembled by the Brain Trauma Foundation et al. (2007)	Comprehensive electronic database searches of the neurotrauma literature; each study independently reviewed by two experts for level of evidence/confidence
TBI Rehabilitation	Turner-Stokes and Wade (2004); Cochrane review (Turner-Stokes et al., 2007)	Review of the scientific literature
Clinical Practice Guidelines and Recommendations	Defense and Veterans Brain Injury Center, Working Group on the Acute Management of Mild Traumatic Brain Injury in Military Operational Settings (2006)	Expert opinion and some randomized outcome studies
Training Guidelines	None available	Not applicable

[8]   We conducted a literature review to establish the evidence base for current TBI treatments, using the relevant online databases. A detailed discussion of our review process and findings appears in Appendix 7.C.

third unique aspect is the need for close coordination across the VA/DoD with other community services and agencies.

Because addressing TBI requires a variety of professional disciplines, across specialty areas and sectors of care, another challenge to ensuring quality of care comes from structural and system factors that may inhibit coordination and integration. Druss (2007) noted that poor quality in mental health care originates from a complicated array of system factors. These system factors include four causes of separation between mental and medical health services. The first is geography, because specialists may not all be collocated in the same facility. The second is financing: Different systems are funded through independent streams. A third factor is organization: Information and expertise are not shared across the different systems. Fourth, the culture of the care paradigm can be a cause of poor care. For example, a focus on particular symptoms of the biological disorder rather than using a patient-centered approach that elicits patient needs and preferences as part of the treatment plan can potentially erode the quality of services. These problems are likely to be similar for TBI, and they can perhaps be compounded by the complexity of medical and rehabilitative needs and the necessity of accessing multiple systems of care to address those needs.

Despite these challenges, several quality-improvement initiatives for TBI are under way. However, to date, few of these efforts have been evaluated. Some of the efforts under way or planned take advantage of approaches that have been used for improving chronic illness care, including that for mental health problems. One model that is particularly promising for TBI is the use of integrated team-based care. In fact, the GAO report (PCCWW, 2007a) recommended integrated care management as an improvement over the fragmented case-management system that is generally used to help servicemembers navigate the different systems of care. The advantages of integrated care management are its comprehensive, patient-centered approach to evaluation by a multidisciplinary team of physicians, nurses, mental health professionals, rehabilitation and vocational rehabilitation specialists, social workers, and other allied health professionals, depending on need.

The TBI experts whom we interviewed also suggested that TBI patients would have better treatment outcomes with comprehensive treatment from a multidisciplinary team. In fact, preliminary work is finding that patients who received more-intensive rehabilitation have better outcomes than those who receive less-intensive services, and there is no evidence that there can be too much rehabilitation (Trudel, Nidiffer, and Barth, 2007; stakeholder interviews).

Multidisciplinary teams are efficacious in maintaining patients in post-acute rehabilitation (Sander et al., 2001). This treatment approach (Malec and Basford, 1996) is guided by four general principles: (1) educating patients about strategies to compensate for residual cognitive deficits, (2) providing environmental support (e.g., housing at treatment locations, transportation, family involvement) to maximize patient functioning, (3) offering counseling and education to address personal and family adjustment, and to improve accurate self-awareness, and (4) focusing initially on simulated activities in the clinic with a transition to productive community-based activities.

A UK study of outreach by multidisciplinary teams (Powell, Heslin, and Greenwood, 2002) was successful in yielding improvement in self-organization, psychological well-being, personal care, and cognitive functioning. That intervention, which used multidisciplinary teams made up of occupational therapists, a physiotherapist, a speech and language therapist, a clinical psychologist, and a half-time social worker, provided individualized care through community visits for two to six hours per week.

The Presidential Commission on Care of America's Returning Wounded Warriors (PCCWW, 2007a, p. 5) made several recommendations relevant to quality improvement. One recommendation was for creating "comprehensive recovery plans to provide the right care and support at the right time in the right place." One way to do this is to install "Recovery Coordinators" to work with existing case managers. These coordinators manage different aspects of care, including engaging family members, arranging for support programs, and serving as advocates for servicemembers across systems of care, including getting them timely services. This role would require coordination across different departments, benefits programs, and across sectors of care (public and private). The Commission also recommended that DoD should establish a network of public and private-sector expertise in TBI and partner with the VA to expand the network for TBI treatment in order to address the problem of poorly coordinated community services.

Although implementing such a program for military personnel may encounter many practical challenges, similar programs have succeeded in the civilian sector. However, civilian successes have been based on smaller-scale implementation, largely within a health system. Given the scope of services provided in DoD, implementing such a program in the military would present additional organizational challenges. Nevertheless, as summarized earlier in this chapter, models of improving care for chronic illness, such as the Improving Chronic Illness Care approach (ICIC Web site), which incorporates the role of a care manager in a collaborative approach to coordinating care, to improve the quality of care for diabetes, depression, and heart failure, are worthy of consideration.

More recently, there is evidence that models of care based on this chronic-illness model can also improve outcomes for people with serious mental disorders (Simon et al., 2005). These studies suggest that, with appropriate adaptation to the military culture, a collaborative model of recovery (Lester and Gask, 2006) may also succeed in improving care for servicemembers with TBI. However, many individuals with TBI do not view their illness as chronic. Rather, a social model of illness that emphasizes aspects of recovery and quality of life (e.g., returning to work and regaining family relationships) is more consistent with the nature of the injury and associated consequences (Lester, Tritter, and Sorohan, 2005).

Integrated teams are already in use at some military medical facilities. For example, the Center for the Intrepid at Brooke Army Medical Center in San Antonio is developing a unique program for TBI that uses integrated teams of specialists (e.g., occupational therapists, physiatrists) to treat TBI. These different specialists do not see patients sequentially but together as a team. Although there is no evidence yet for its effectiveness, such a program has the potential to improve TBI care, and future evaluation data will be important for understanding any challenges faced in implementing team-based care, if any, and, it is hoped, to what extent such teams can be successful (Ian Coulter, personal communication).

Fort Carson is currently implementing a "One Stop Health Shop" program that draws upon many of the lessons from other areas, as well as from the various committee recommendations (Terrio, Prowell, and Brenner, 2007). The objectives of the program are to improve customer service, provide comprehensive care using a multi-disciplinary approach, enhance communication, and centrally track TBI. The program increases access for patients, who can schedule an appointment or walk in without an appointment. Much like the patient-registry component of the chronic illness care model, all patients are screened for TBI and their information is collected in a database and updated regularly. The interdisciplinary provider team works together to perform the screening and implement a treatment plan. All patients who screen positive for TBI are given an educational handout that explains symptoms and access to care. Those with current symptoms are seen "on the spot" in the TBI clinic and assessed. They are followed up within two weeks and, if clinically indicated, are given a more immediate referral. The provider team also meets regularly to discuss cases. The TBI Task Force Report notes that this project is being expanded to other installations and that population needs may lead to enhanced or reduced versions of that model (U.S. Department of the Army, 2008).

Summary of Gaps and Recommendations for TBI Services

Key gaps and recommendations differ for those with mild TBI and those with more moderate to severe TBI or TBI associated with other severe injuries. Regardless of severity level, almost all treatments and services for TBI lack a strong evidence base. Thus, continued research on what treatment and rehabilitation are most effective is needed.

Mild TBI. For mild TBI, key gaps in access to services arise from failures to identify individuals with probable TBI and poor documentation of blast exposure. Factors that contribute to this gap include inconsistent screening practices, personal and military cultural factors (reluctance to admit weakness or shirk responsibilities to the unit and mission, fear of negative career consequences), the similarity of mild TBI symptoms to acute stress reactions and mental health conditions, and possible delayed emergence of symptoms. DoD and the VA are attempting to improve both screening for and documentation of probable TBI. The program at Fort Carson may function as an example of a comprehensive program that provides both screening and follow-up diagnostic and treatment services.

There are potential negative consequences of under-identification for both affected individuals and for the military. These individuals may lack sufficient recovery time and be at higher risk for cumulative effects of repeat exposure to blasts. They may also experience TBI-related problems in their work performance or social behavior. Military servicemembers may not recognize or understand the nature of their cognitive problem, and others, including family, friends, and supervisors, may misinterpret problems. If TBI-related impairments emerge later or persist over time, it can be difficult to establish the relationship of the impairment to a service-related injury, which may in turn delay or limit access to appropriate rehabilitation services.

To address these issues, DoD has focused on improving cognitive assessment both pre- and post-deployment and improving documentation of exposure to blasts. Additionally, the VA has instituted systemwide screening for all OEF/OIF veterans who seek care for any health issue at a VA facility. Illinois has also developed a state initiative to offer screenings for all veterans and provide mandatory screening for Illinois Army National Guard servicemembers.

Another area for improvement is the development of appropriate strategies and materials to educate the military community, service providers, and families about mild TBI. Materials developed for more-severe brain injury can misguide or unnecessarily alarm those suffering from only mild TBI. Military leadership, medical providers, servicemembers, and families need to understand signs and symptoms of mild TBI and the importance of documentation, general guidelines in the management of mild TBI, and the expected course of TBI-related impairments and recovery. The Defense Veterans Brain Injury Center has been increasing its outreach and training to meet this need.

Moderate and Severe TBI, or Mild TBI with Other Severe Injuries. Those with moderate to severe TBI face different gaps in care. Their injuries typically involve complex needs for treatment and supportive and rehabilitative services that change over time. Particularly problematic are transitions from the DoD Military Health System (where acute inpatient care is delivered), to the VA health care system, in which the highly specialized and comprehensive polytrauma services are located. A number of problems have been identified and are the focus of joint DoD-VA improvement efforts, including failures in the transfer of medical information and other relevant documentation from DoD to the VA; duplicative, discrepant, and unreliable processes for determining disability ratings; inadequate coordination of care across the two systems; and perceptions that active duty personnel can languish in the system while they wait on the decision for a return to duty or medical discharge (Department of Veterans Affairs, 2006a; Independent Review Group, 2007; PCCWW, 2007a; U.S. Department of the Army, 2008).

The types of services needed by those with TBI and co-morbid physical injuries are complex. Treatment planning must be individually tailored and requires that patients and/or their family caregivers understand the plan and follow through with appointments and recommendations, which can be particularly challenging for patients with TBI, especially those with severe cognitive impairments. Accordingly, the principles of patient-centered care that have been applied within the primary care civilian sector may be particularly relevant for TBI. These models suggest that, to improve quality of care, it will be important for TBI services to orient care around each specific patient's preferences and needs.

Care coordination is also important to ensure access to needed services, and lack of it has been a key gap in the provision of quality care. As described above, DoD has begun implementing a number of initiatives to improve TBI care through care coordination. The VA has also announced plans to quickly hire and expand capacity to provide care coordination. It will be important to assess whether these efforts are successful in assisting veterans with TBI and their families with access to needed services.

The vision put forth in the PCCWW Report to train professionals for managing support program services and to serve as patient advocates through recovery coordinators would likely be an effective way to restructure care for TBI. This program is now being implemented. However, to properly implement such system change, the training of these Recovery Coordinators will be critical. Coordinators will need to understand not only DoD and VA guidelines for the effective treatment of TBI but also have a clear comprehension of eligibility for services and programs in both systems of care and how to access them. Finally, coordinators will need automated tools and databases, ongoing supervision, continuing-education support, and the authority to be effective in this role (e.g., "authority to tap all resources necessary to implement each patient's Recovery Plan" [PCCWW, 2007b, p. 22]).

Another important gap is VA and DoD coordination with community-based services outside the MTF and the VA. For many veterans, access to community-based services is desirable, because they live distant from a VA or MTF. Traveling long distances to a VA hospital for frequent rehabilitation visits, for example, may not be feasible for many veterans who need these services. Theoretically, VA care coordinators could assist veterans in identifying and accessing appropriate community services, but it is not clear whether care coordinators will have available to them the necessary information about community-based services that would enable them to provide assistance. State initiatives, like that in Rhode Island, may fill this key gap through local planning efforts that provide coordination across DoD, the VA, and local community service providers to meet the needs of local servicemembers, veterans, and their families.

A key challenge to expanding DoD and VA capacity to meet the needs of those with TBI is hiring qualified staff and providing appropriate training, supervision, and oversight. No systematic study of this issue is available, but a number of our informants representing health provider organizations noted the difficulty of identifying

and attracting qualified staff to open positions in TBI specialty areas, including rehabilitation (according to stakeholder interviews). It may be necessary to increase incentives to attract qualified applicants to VA or DoD positions, and/or to increase incentives for community-based providers to provide specialty care targeted to OEF/OIF
veterans.

Appendix 7.A: Approach to Interviews with Administrators and Providers

Overview

The RAND study team conducted 30 telephone interviews with health policy leaders and direct-care providers of health services for OEF and OIF veterans suffering from PTSD, major depression, and TBI. The interviews were conducted from October to December 2007. The objective of these interviews was to better understand the availability, accessibility, and capacity of existing programs and services to address these needs in servicemembers with mental health and cognitive conditions.

Design and Procedure

Interviews were voluntary and lasted up to 45 minutes. A team of two researchers participated in each interview; one member of the interview team led the conversation, and the other documented the respondents' answers on a laptop computer in real-time to increase the accuracy of the interview record. The research team debriefed immediately following each interview while the information was fresh, to achieve consensus regarding what was conveyed during the interview; they modified the notes accordingly.

Sample and Participants

Our objective was to talk with a broad range of high-level individuals who set mental health policies and direct mental health care at national and local levels within the Departments of Defense and Veterans Affairs. To capture perspectives from a range of policymakers and providers, we used a two-pronged strategy to obtain the interviews Recognizing that service delivery will depend on the structure of services, we identified key policymakers from each system of care (military, TRICARE, and VA). Once we identified key mental health leaders, we asked them to identify potential providers to interview. We interviewed 20 program managers/policymakers and seven direct-care service providers across the DoD and VA. We also interviewed three additional leaders of community-based organizations (one nonclinical counseling provider, one private organization director, and one community organization leader). The 30 completed interviews represent a participation rate of 58 percent of the 52 individuals contacted.

Interview Content

We used the interviews to expand our knowledge of the mental health treatment and services that are available and the extent to which they are consistent with best practices in caring for PTSD, major depression, and TBI. The interview included questions about the extent to which clients suffering from the targeted problems are seen and what is done to help them. We also asked about what educational materials are available and given to clients.

Analysis

Once all interviews were completed and documented, the qualitative team reviewed them to identify both *common themes* that prevailed across systems of care and also *unique themes* that pertained only to a particular system. Findings from these interviews are integrated into the relevant sections of Chapter Seven.

Appendix 7.B: Summary of Focus Groups with Military Servicemembers and Spouses

The RAND study team conducted a series of focus groups with military veterans from OEF and OIF and their spouses during November 2007. Groups were conducted with participants in three U.S. cities, each with a strong military presence (Oceanside, CA; San Antonio, TX; and Washington, DC). The objective of these groups was to elicit feedback about challenges faced and health care service needs for the psychological and cognitive injuries resulting from deployment to the conflicts in Afghanistan and Iraq.

Focus Group Methods

Participant Recruitment

We recruited participants from the communities surrounding one Army base and one Marine base. We also identified family members, guardsmen, reservists, and veterans through local chapters of national member associations. Our main source for recruiting was through contact information that was obtained from military servicemembers who agreed to be recontacted by the study team to participate in other aspects of the study, at the close of the telephone interviews conducted for our survey (described in Chapter Four). We supplemented this list of potential participants with names of those who responded to flyers distributed by military and military family-member organizations in the areas surrounding Camp Pendleton (CA) and Fort Hood (TX). Groups of military servicemembers may have included both active duty and retired servicemembers, as long as they did not mix component or branch of Service (for Active Component only) and rank. We did not seek volunteers with mental health conditions or TBI, nor did we ask about these conditions specifically.

Design

To maximize homogeneity and, in turn, comfort with discussing the sensitive topic, groups were stratified by three characteristics: (1) component and branch of Service (Active or Reserve Component; Army or Marine Corps), (2) rank (noncommissioned officer [NCO] and officer or junior enlisted), and (3) role (military member or spouse). We recognize the importance of eliciting feedback from all possible groups; however, circumstances precluded our studying them all. Therefore, we emphasized obtaining data from those populations most affected by the current deployments, because soldiers and marines are far more likely to be deployed for combat duty in Afghanistan and Iraq. We conducted a total of nine groups: four Marine Corps groups (by rank and type of participant), four Army groups (also by rank and type), and one group of Army Reserve Component members (Reserve and Guard personnel). We also convened a tenth discussion/feedback group made up of military fellows currently at RAND.

The last group included a multi-Service mix of officers from the Army, Air Force, and Marine Corps. Although not all members of this group are OEF/OIF veterans, these officers provided a valuable exchange, given their analytic expertise and insights into military culture.

Group Process

Each of the ten groups lasted up to two hours and had between three and eight participants. Groups were co-moderated by two members of the research team, with one person taking detailed notes. After obtaining verbal informed consent, we audiotaped the group discussion, with permission from all group members, to ensure accurate note-taking. Tapes were destroyed after the discussion was documented and vetted by the research team. At the end of the discussion groups, participants were compensated for their time and for incidentals, such as transportation and childcare.

Discussion Content

The focus group discussions were structured in three sections. First, we explained the study objectives and focus group procedures, including oral consent and rules, after which we allowed for brief introductions so that people would feel more comfortable. Second, we elicited and then summarized the different signs and symptoms associated with each of the key disorders we were targeting (PTSD, TBI, and major depression) to familiarize participants with the subject matter. Third, we asked participants about where they would typically go to seek care if they were experiencing these signs and symptoms of stress (or where they would recommend that someone go for help). We probed for where they would go for information (e.g., the Internet, the VA), whether they would seek direct services on base or within the civilian sector, and how they would pay for such services. We asked them about the types of health care and mental health services that would be helpful to them and what types of barriers, if any, they might face in obtaining services. We also asked about the materials they received post-deployment and whether those materials included anything about mental health services. Finally, we showed participants drafts of educational materials designed to provide information about PTSD, major depression, and TBI for servicemembers and their family members (Meredith et al., 2008a, 2008b) and asked for their feedback. In particular, we asked them whether the materials were helpful, whether they would keep/use them, and whether they liked the content and format.

Analysis

Following each group, the note-taker listened to the audiotape to supplement notes. The moderator then reviewed the notes and added further information to produce final documentation of the discussion. Once all groups were completed and documented, the qualitative team reviewed the notes to identify both common themes that prevailed regardless of group characteristics and also unique themes that pertained only to particular groups. This information was used to inform our review study by providing the military-member and family perspectives regarding available services and satisfaction with mental health care.

Results

Participant Characteristics

Of the 71 recruited, 46 servicemembers and spouses of personnel (65 percent, not including military fellows) participated in the nine focus groups, in addition to the five RAND military fellows, for a total of 51 participants. Table 7B.1 shows the characteristics of each group. Because of the greater difficulty in recruiting military spouses than servicemembers, groups with servicemembers were larger.

Signs and Symptoms

Some of the most common types of reactions that participants talked about were difficulty readjusting to family life, hyperalertness, sleep problems, and anger. All the groups discussed family readjustment as a challenge, regardless of branch, rank, or type (personnel, spouse, or RAND military fellow). One marine in the higher-rank group characterized this sentiment as, "it's hard to come back and be thrown into a family situation." Returning personnel had difficulty being around children. For example, a spouse of a junior enlisted marine told us that, "He was so used to being surrounded by all military people; he started treating everyone around him like marines, including our small children. . . ." Another spouse (Army NCO/officer) said that she "needed to

Table 7.B.1
Size and Gender Mix of Focus Groups

Group Description	Number of Participants	Gender Mix
Junior Enlisted (E-1–E-6)		
Marines	8	All male
Marine Spouses	5	All female
Army Personnel	7	All male
Army Spouses	3	All female
Senior Enlisted (E-7–E-9)/Officers		
Marines	6	All male
Marine Spouses	3	All female
Army Personnel	7	All male
Army Spouses	3	All female
Army Reservists/ Guardsmen	4	1 female, 3 male
RAND Military Fellows	5	1 female, 4 male
Total	51	16 female, 35 male

buffer the kids from her husband for the first 30–40 days." An Army officer noted that, "My wife was tired and ready for me to take over, but I wasn't."

Hyperalertness was explained as being part of the job when in Iraq or Afghanistan. One marine (NCO/officer) participant found himself outside patrolling his yard in the middle of the night in pajamas with his weapon. Others spoke of needing their weapon by them when they sleep. The adrenaline is so high for returning military that they avoid situations that drive it up. For example, we were told by several marines that situations such as amusement parks and driving are difficult for the first few months. Symptoms of anxiety also make loud noises (including those from small children) difficult to take. One marine summed it up: "4th of July will never be the same again."

Related to hyperalertness is problems with sleep. All personnel groups and several spouse groups talked about difficulty getting to sleep and staying asleep. One Army spouse (NCO/officer rank) said, "My husband didn't sleep for six months."

Some participants also mentioned a number of symptoms commonly associated with depression and anxiety.

Anger issues were also prevalent among these focus group participants. Soldiers and marines mentioned the problem of aggressive driving, lack of patience, and becoming frustrated easily. When asked about when counseling for anger problems might be helpful, one soldier replied:

If I had to take an anger class right after returning, that would piss me off.

Spouses reported their soldiers and marines "snapping" at the kids and noted that

. . . they know how to interact with [family], but for everyone else, it's hard for them. They go off at the simplest things.

Uniquely, members of the Reserve Component spoke less of symptoms and changes and focused more on issues of being isolated upon return from deployment. For example, they all noted that they had little support from their civilian employer. They also mentioned that many are not deployed in units so do not have the cohesion of a group to identify with or have access to a buddy system when they return home.

Coping

Participants reported both avoidant and active forms of coping. Some of the commonly reported strategies that involved avoidant coping were to postpone dealing with their emotional and behavioral problems. For example, all of the Marine Corps groups and several of the Army groups said that they initially covered up any problems so that they could get back to their lives at home. One marine said, "I lied on my post-deployment forms. Whatever got me back to my family quicker . . . ." Another common theme in most of the personnel groups that was echoed was to keep busy as a method of coping. Although this form of coping can be seen as negative in terms of postponing or avoiding dealing with problems, it also can be seen as positive in that keeping busy means spending more time with family, in traveling, physical activity, or faith-based activities. One servicemember said that, "If you don't stay busy, you can fall into a trap." Some military personnel further identified self-medication with alcohol as a means of coping with the anxiety and sleep symptoms described above. All of the military-personnel groups mentioned drinking heavily initially upon returning. The military fellows echoed this perception, noting that binge-drinking is the norm for about a week, "and if they live through that, they come back."

Some of the other active ways that people coped were to "talk to your buddies" and to seek professional help, either through a counselor or chaplain. However, all groups across the board tended to be more reluctant to talk to professionals for fear of negative consequences, including being perceived as weak and losing career opportunities. As described by one junior enlisted soldier:

> In my battalion, if you go to see mental health, you're the weak guy, the weak gal. I took leave to see a counselor based on everything I went through over there. My unit doesn't have knowledge, but my commander said I have PTSD . . . there's a stigma. A brand new guy goes over at 18, comes back feeling 40. He worries about promotion. They still view it negatively, going to see a mental health care provider.

Communication

The key communication themes observed through the focus group discussions were that marines and soldiers prefer to talk to other marines and soldiers who have had similar experiences. In addition, while military personnel also relied heavily on communication and interaction with immediate family members (wife and kids), especially for the first few weeks, they did not think that it was as helpful as talking with "war buddies":

> You could talk to mom or wife or force someone else to talk to me but they haven't shared the same experiences that his buddies have.

Participants, particularly the junior enlisted and therefore younger marines and soldiers, also talked about using the Internet to chat and blog about their experiences. This seemed to be a good outlet because of its anonymity. In fact, one person in the Reserve Component group characterized technological communication as a means of avoiding stigma in the chain of command:

> [Stigma] would vary by chain of command. It's totally different people now so wouldn't feel comfortable.

> Using blogging—blogging helps a lot of people. There's a lot of blog sites/bulletin boards of people who have been through the VA/military system.

Even military spouses preferred to talk with other military wives to whom they can relate. Several spouses of marines mentioned that the "key volunteers" (military wives designated to support other military wives) available for informal support can be helpful, although more so if those wives have had their spouses deployed. Accordingly, they are less comfortable talking with health professionals.

Mental Health Services and Barriers

In terms of access and quality of mental health services, participants had a mixture of experiences. Some had experience with using community counselors through TRI-CARE. Both Marine Corps and Army spouses said that they had sought care from community providers because they were told that the military hospitals were overbooked.

Many participants knew about and had accessed services from Military One-Source. While Military OneSource was seen as a definite option, one Army enlisted participant thought that its utility was not well understood: "Everyone knows that OneSource exists, but no one knows how to use it or what it does."

There was little discussion about receiving mental health services from the military health system, only about the potential for perceived stigma and negative consequences on careers (including loss of a security clearance) if they did seek care from that source. Some of the concerns related to stigma are illustrated by quotes from these three servicemembers:

> [Soldier, NCO/Officer] Anything to do with mental health in the military, the chain of command is going to know. If you're on certain medications, it will kick the clearance back.

> [Soldier, Enlisted] If you want to get confidential care, you need to go off post. Otherwise, they will find out.

> [Marine, Enlisted] It's supposed to be confidential, but that never works. It goes up the rank.

The VA came up infrequently during the discussions. However, one Army spouse mentioned the VA outreach center, which "is a great thing."

Several military personnel and also military spouses talked about getting help from chaplains, but the extent to which chaplains were helpful was perceived as mixed. Some of the problems with chaplains include their being in short supply, their lack of support across religious preferences, and their limited knowledge about mental health issues.

Finally, while some participants found counseling to be helpful, several had negative experiences.

More-detailed information and results are available from the authors.

Appendix 7.C: Evidence-Based Practices

This appendix provides information about the evidence-based practices currently available for the treatment of post-traumatic stress disorder, depression, and traumatic brain injury. We review the evidence base for treatment of each condition in turn, including a definition of the problem, a description of available treatments, evidence for each type, and an evaluation of the evidence underlying existing treatment guidelines.

Post-Traumatic Stress Disorder

Definition. *Post-traumatic stress disorder* (PTSD) is an anxiety disorder that occurs after a traumatic event in which a threat of serious injury or death is experienced or witnessed and to which the individual's response involved intense fear, helplessness, or horror. A further distinction is sometimes made between PTSD and Acute Stress Reaction (ASR) and Combat or [Ongoing Military] Operational Stress Reaction (COSR). *ASR* is a severe but transient disorder that develops in an individual in response to exceptional physical or mental stress. Symptoms are usually minimal after about three days. *COSR*, also known as battle fatigue or battle shock, is any response to battle stress that renders a solder unable to remain on duty.

Literature Review. We conducted a literature review to find studies focusing on the treatment of PTSD, ASR, and COSR. We used PubMED (MEDLINE), PsychINFO, and GoogleScholar and limited our searches to English-language articles from 1998 to the present. We also found additional references within the papers and included some of those references that we thought would provide additional background information, regardless of the year of publication.

We used the following search terms: "treatment"; "early intervention"; "prevention"; "services"; "adult"; "symptoms"; "post traumatic stress disorder"; "combat stress reaction"; "combat stress"; "combat anxiety"; "anxiety"; "ptsd"; "partial post traumatic stress disorder"; "partial ptsd"; "battle fatigue"; "stress exposure training"; "stress training"; "anxiety"; "combat stress control units". Our searches also included combinations of terms.

When possible, we selected articles that focused on treatments among a military population; however, we also reviewed the literature focusing on civilian populations. Overall, we reviewed 22 treatment-outcome studies, 14 meta-analyses[9] and reviews, and three sets of treatment guidelines.

Treating PTSD

Prevention and Management. Many different therapies have been used to treat veterans diagnosed with PTSD. But few treatments are available *before* symptoms may

---

[9] A *meta-analysis* is a study that reviews outcome studies in a particular area and assesses how small or large the effect size of each outcome is. *Effect size* provides information about how much change is evident across all studies and for subsets of studies.

arise, and little research has been done on primary prevention—in the case of soldiers, *before they are deployed.* Some work has shown that cognitive-behavioral therapy can be used to target PTSD early on for people who may have experienced discrete events (e.g., an accident) (Bryant et al., 1998; Ehlers and Clark, 2003). There is also recent evidence that propranolol can help decrease the likelihood of a physiological response when thinking about trauma if it is administered fairly early after the trauma has taken place. Thus, propranolol could be used as a pharmacological preventive effort to potentially attenuate the psychophysiological response to trauma (Pitman et al., 2002). However, further research is needed with larger samples and longer-term follow-up of patients.

Battlemind is a program developed by the Walter Reed Army Institute of Research that is currently being provided for all soldiers when they return from deployment and again three to six months later. The goal of Battlemind is to help solders identify whether they are experiencing symptoms that may require additional help. The Institute is currently preparing a pre-deployment version of Battlemind. The evidence-based treatments that are discussed in this monograph (e.g., cognitive-behavioral therapy, pharmacotherapy) are treatments that could be provided either during deployment or post-deployment.

Types of Treatment. To organize our discussion of PTSD treatment, we use the treatment types described by Foa, Keane, and Friedman (2000b), who also assessed the level of evidence in the literature for each type of treatment.

Foa, Keane, and Friedman (2000b) wrote the article "Guidelines for the treatment of PTSD," in which different therapies were rated from Level A to Level F according to a literature review of studies that conducted trials to examine the efficacy of these different therapies:

- *Level A:* Evidence is based on randomized, well-controlled clinical trials for individuals with PTSD.
- *Level B:* Evidence is based on well-designed clinical studies, without randomization or placebo comparison for individuals with PTSD.
- *Level C:* Evidence is based on service and naturalistic (non-experimental) clinical studies, combined with clinical observations that are sufficiently compelling to warrant use of the treatment technique or to follow the specific recommendation.
- *Level D:* Evidence is based on long-standing and widespread clinical practice that has not been subjected to empirical tests on PTSD.
- *Level E:* Evidence is based on long-standing practice by circumscribed groups of clinicians that has not been subjected to empirical tests on PTSD.
- *Level F:* Evidence is based on recently developed treatment that has not been subjected to clinical or empirical tests on PTSD.

Table 7.C.1 provides information from this review.

Table 7.C.1
Level of Evidence for the Different PTSD Treatments

Type of Therapy	Evidence Base
Exposure therapy	Level A, based on 12 studies as of 2000. Overall, effective in treating PTSD. 5 of 6 studies conducted with Vietnam veterans found positive effects, and four of these were well-controlled studies.
Systematic desensitization	Level B and Level C, based on 6 studies as of 2000. Most studies have methodological problems. Some found that SD was effective, whereas other studies did not. 4 of 5 studies were conducted with Vietnam veterans, but these were not well-controlled studies, and many used a large number of sessions over a long period of time.
Stress inoculation training	Level A, based on 2 well-controlled and 2 less well-controlled studies as of 2000. SIT was effective in all 4 studies; however, SIT has been conducted only with female sexual-assault survivors. Efficacy with other trauma populations is not established.
Cognitive therapy	Level A, based on 2 well-controlled studies as of 2000. CT was effective. Studies were conducted with civilian trauma survivors. CT has not been tested with veterans.
Cognitive processing therapy	Level B, based on 1 published study as of 2000. CPT effective, but conducted only with female sexual-assault survivors. A recent study by Monson and colleagues (2006) conducted CPT with veterans and compared them to a wait-list control group. CPT decreased PTSD symptoms and co-morbid symptoms in relation to the wait-list control group.
Assertiveness training	Level B, based on 1 less well-controlled study as of 2000. Conducted with female sexual-assault survivors, and no differences were found between AT and comparison treatments. Has not been tested with veterans.
Biofeedback and relaxation training	Not rated. As of 2000, only one study examined BIO in a controlled design. BIO was not supported because the comparison was more effective. Relaxation is generally utilized as a control treatment and has been found to be less effective than comparison treatments in 4 studies. Thus, BIO and relaxation training are not rated.
Combo treatments	There is no evidence that combination treatments are more effective than their single components.

Table 7.C.1—Continued

Type of Therapy	Evidence Base
Pharmacotherapy	Level A and Level B for SSRIs [fluoxetine (A); paroxetine, fluvoxamine (A/B)]. Level A and Level B for MAOIs [phenelzine (A/B); moclobemide (B)]. Level A for TCAs (imipramine; amitriptyline, desipramine). Level C for antiadrenergic agents (clonidine, guanfacine, propranolol). Level B for anticonvulsants (carbamazepine, valproate). Level B and Level C for benzodiazepines [alprazolam (B); clonazepam (C)]. Levels B–F for other serotonergic agents [nefazodone (B); trazodone (C); cyproheptadine, buspirone (F)]. Level F for antipsychotics [thioridazine, clozapine, risperidone (F)]. There are multiple studies in this area, making it difficult to provide general conclusions for each drug. Some evidence suggests that efficacy for SSRIs is stronger for civilians than for Vietnam-veteran cohorts and that TCAs may be more effective with Vietnam-veteran cohorts than with civilian cohorts.
Psychological debriefing	Neither one-time nor individual PD can be advocated as being able to prevent the subsequent development of PTSD following a traumatic event.
Eye-movement desensitization and reprocessing	Levels A and B, based upon 12 studies as of 2000. There is stronger evidence for EMDR among people with single-event civilian trauma than on war veterans who have endured multiple traumas. Support for EMDR does not imply support for the role of eye movements. Randomized dismantling studies (which assess the components of a treatment individually) provide little support that eye movements are critical to the effects of EMDR.[a]
Psychodynamic therapy	Level A to Level D based on 3 empirical studies and numerous clinical studies as of 2000. There are few empirical investigations of psychodynamic therapy. Single or small-series case reports make up most of the evidence for this treatment. There was only one Level A investigation with people with PTSD. Results indicated greater improvement among those who received PT than hypnosis and desensitization. A Level B study of 37 combat veterans indicated positive results for those who participated in PT compared with a volunteer sample of veterans who received no treatment.
Hypnosis	Level C, based on one study as of 2000. Only one study from 1989 showed that hypnosis decreased intrusion and avoidance symptoms. It was conducted with 112 people who were diagnosed with PTSD based on DSM-III. The majority of patients had experienced the loss of a loved one. Two recent studies found that a CBT-hypnosis group did not report greater clinical gains overall than a CBT group (Bryant et al., 2005; Bryant et al., 2006).
Psychosocial rehabilitation	Level C as of 2000 (based on naturalistic and clinical observations). There was little Level A or B research as of 2000; however, techniques used in PR, such as education and skills training, have been supported by Level C studies (e.g., naturalistic studies and clinical observations). Currently, PR techniques are suggested to be an adjunct to other forms of treatment for PTSD. These techniques have been used with people who have PTSD and could have included veteran populations.

Table 7.C.1—Continued

Type of Therapy	Evidence Base
Group therapy	Levels A, B, and C, based on 14 studies as of 2000. Studies ranged from Level A—randomized control (2), Level B—nonrandomized control design (5), and Level C—single-group designs in which pre and post differences were examined (7). Positive treatment outcomes were reported in most studies, lending general support to the use of group therapy with trauma survivors. Treatment outcomes do not at present favor a particular type of group therapy. Most studies have been conducted with female sexual-assault survivors. One study conducted with 11 male Vietnam veterans found positive results.
Marital and family therapy	Level D, based on clinical practice as of 2000. There are few empirical investigations of MFT for PTSD. There is one Level B dissertation study with a very small sample of veterans. Improvements were seen for both veterans and spouses, and MFT is recommended as a technique to be utilized in conjunction with other techniques designed to address PTSD more directly.
Inpatient treatment	Levels B through F as of 2000. Inpatient treatment typically incorporates many different interventions and utilizes longer stays (2–12 weeks) rather than crisis admissions. There is limited research in this area. 13 Level B studies have been conducted with small convenience samples of veterans, and only 3 had comparison groups. Overall, findings suggested that moderate-length specialized programs, ranging from 2 to 12 weeks, and general psychiatric units are more effective than long-term specialized programs. However, these findings could be due in part to shorter-term stays being associated with crisis admissions and crisis resolving, whereas longer-term stays involved planned admissions with fewer initial symptoms.

NOTES: MAOI = monamine oxidase inhibitor; SSRI = selective serotonin reuptake inhibitor; TCA = tricyclic antidepressant.

[a] There is some controversy in the literature regarding the efficacy of EMDR and the use of the saccadic eye movements. The Institute of Medicine committee reviewed several studies of EMDR and concluded that the evidence did not adequately support its efficacy (Institute of Medicine, 2007). A review by Perkins and Rouanzoin (2002) emphasizes that the treatment effects of EMDR are larger and longer-lasting than placebo effects in PTSD. The efficacy of EMDR has also been supported in two large meta-analyses in this area (Sherman, 1998; van Etten and Taylor, 1998). What is not conclusive, however, is the role of eye movement; further empirical validation is needed (Perkins and Rouanzoin, 2002). There is also mixed opinion about whether EMDR is a unique form of therapy or a derivative of CBT (Hamblen et al., 2006).

The four basic kinds of treatment for PTSD, ASR, and COSR are as follows:

1. Cognitive-behavioral treatments (e.g., exposure therapy, cognitive processing therapy)
2. Pharmacotherapy
3. Psychological debriefing
4. Other treatments (e.g., imagery rehearsal therapy, psychodynamic therapy, hypnosis).

Below, we briefly describe each type of treatment and summarize available evidence about its effectiveness.

Cognitive-Behavioral Therapy (CBT). CBT combines elements of cognitive and behavioral approaches, and it emphasizes changing biased patterns of beliefs and modifying harmful behavior. CBT is the treatment approach with the most research supporting both its immediate and long-term effectiveness. It relieves symptoms during an acute episode, and over time it can help to prevent future episodes. CBT treatment for PTSD is structured (the therapist usually has an agenda for each session) and time-limited.

There are eight different kinds of CBT-related therapies for PTSD. They are typically used as separate treatments (e.g., 15 sessions of exposure therapy), although some studies have examined combinations of treatments (see number 8 below).

1. *Exposure therapy (EX):* Exposure therapy is a type of behavior therapy in which the patient confronts the feared situation, object, thought, or memory; the exposure is continued until the anxiety is reduced (Rothbaum et al., 2000). This therapy has been used with Vietnam veterans and female sexual-assault survivors, and for a mixed variety of traumas. There is a great deal of evidence from well-controlled trials that supports the use of exposure-based therapy (Foa, Keane, and Friedman, 2000b; Institute of Medicine, 2007).
2. *Systematic desensitization (SD):* SD is a form of exposure therapy that teaches relaxation skills in order to control fear and anxiety. The patient is exposed gradually to objects or situations that are typically fear-producing. The goal is to reduce or eliminate fears that people may find distressing or that impair their ability to manage daily life. Few well-controlled trials of SD have been conducted. Thus, SD has not received strong support and "has largely been abandoned in favor of exposure without relaxation" (Courtois and Bloom, 2000; Foa, Keane, and Friedman, 2000b, p. 559).
3. *Stress inoculation training (SIT):* SIT is a form of cognitive-behavioral therapy tailored to the needs of an individual patient. Its goal is to help patients add to their repertoire of coping skills and to use existing skills more effectively. Four studies found SIT to be effective when used with female sexual-assault survi-

vors; the efficacy of SIT with other trauma populations has not yet been established (Foa, Keane, and Friedman, 2000b).

4. *Cognitive therapy (CT):* Cognitive therapy postulates that dysfunctional thinking patterns produce pathologic emotions that can lead to psychiatric disorders. These thinking patterns can lead the person to feel anxious or depressed in situations in which these emotions are unwarranted (Foa, Keane, and Friedman, 2000a). Cognitive therapy is focused on the present. Skills involve identifying distorted thinking, modifying beliefs, relating to others in different ways, and changing behaviors (Beck Institute Web site). CT is typically used for depression. Two controlled studies of CT found that it was effective in reducing post-trauma symptoms (Foa, Keane, and Friedman, 2000b).

5. *Cognitive processing therapy (CPT):* CPT incorporates cognitive therapy and exposure therapy (Rothbaum et al., 2000). It is usually conducted in 12 sessions, which systematically build the client's skills to deal first with the traumatic event itself and then with its effects in other areas of life. CPT is designed specifically for female sexual-assault survivors; however, a recent study by Monson and colleagues (2006) used CPT with veterans and found that veterans who received CPT had fewer PTSD symptoms and related symptoms compared with a wait-list control group.

6. *Assertiveness training (AT):* AT is a method of psychotherapy that reinforces people for stating negative and positive feelings directly. People are helped to be assertive rather than passive or aggressive in talking to others about their assaults, in asking for social support, or in correcting misinformation (Rothbaum et al., 2000). One poorly controlled study tested AT with female sexual-assault survivors and found no difference between AT and comparison treatments. Thus, more support is needed for this treatment (Foa, Keane, and Friedman, 2000b).

7. *Biofeedback (BIO) and Relaxation training (RT):* BIO is a complementary- and alternative-medicine approach that measures a subject's bodily processes, such as blood pressure, heart rate, skin temperature, galvanic skin response (sweating), and muscle tension, and conveys that information to the individual in real-time to increase awareness and control of the related physiological activities. Biofeedback allows users to gain control over physical processes previously considered automatic (Foa, Keane, and Friedman, 2000b). *RT* involves training individuals in deep breathing and progressive muscle relaxation to remove tension and negative emotions (Thompson, 2004). There is little evidence that either BIO or RT is effective in treating PTSD (Foa, Keane, and Friedman, 2000b).

8. *Combined SIT/EX, combined EX/Relax/CT, and combined CT/EX.* Combination approaches have received support; however, the combination treatments do not appear to be more effective than their single-component treatments (Foa, Keane, and Friedman, 2000b).

Pharmacotherapy. A variety of drug treatments has been used for PTSD, including tricyclic antidepressants (TCAs), monoamine oxidase inhibitors (MAOIs), and selective serotonin reuptake inhibitors (SSRIs). The strongest evidence to date is for antidepressant medications, particularly SSRIs (Davis et al., 2006; van Etten and Taylor, 1998); however, overall effects for SSRIs, even in the largest clinical trials, are modest (Keane, Marshall, and Taft, 2006). The (British) National Institute for Health and Clinical Excellence (2005) report on several trials of SSRIs (e.g., paroxetine, fluoxetine) indicated inconclusive evidence that these drugs reduce severity of PTSD symptoms. Recent research suggests that serotonin-noradrenaline reuptake inhibitors (SNRI; venlafaxine, milnacipran, and duloxetine) are at least as effective as SSRIs across the range of anxiety disorders, including PTSD. Further research is needed in this area (Baldwin, 2006).

Benzodiazepines do not appear to have any advantages over other drugs in treating PTSD. Antipsychotic agents are also not recommended (Davis et al., 2006). Overall, SSRIs tend to be more effective in treating the intrusive symptoms of PTSD (nightmares, flashbacks, etc.) than avoidance symptoms according to self-report, but not observer-rated measures (van Etten and Taylor, 1998). In addition, there is a problem with attrition in many of the pharmacotherapy studies; approximately 32 percent of participants drop out by post-test (van Etten and Taylor, 1998). Table 7.C.2 contains data from Seedat and colleagues (2006) summarizing pharmacotherapy trials for different drugs and the overall effect of these medications on the participants' quality of life (QOL). Table 7.C.3 from Davis and colleagues (2006) summarizes effects of long-term (>14 weeks) pharmacological treatment for PTSD. Two recent studies have shown that Prazosin, a brain-active alpha-1 adrenergic receptor antagonist, is effective in reducing nighttime PTSD symptoms and sleep disturbance in both civilian (Taylor et al., 2007) and veteran (Raskind et al., 2007) samples.

The results of this review of the pharmacotherapy literature pertaining to PTSD treatment are in accordance with those found by the Institute of Medicine committee, which reviewed 37 pharmacotherapy studies and determined that treatment efficacy cannot be determined from the current study findings (Institute of Medicine, 2007).

A few studies have examined the effect of combining psychotherapy and drug treatments (Humphreys et al., 1999; Mark et al., 1996; Marshall et al., 2003). Overall, findings suggest that combining these two types of treatment can help patients reduce their depression, anxiety, and PTSD symptoms (Humphreys et al., 1999); however, further study is needed.

Psychological Debriefing (PD). Most researchers consider PD to be a single-session semi-structured crisis intervention designed to reduce and prevent continued anxiety and distress following traumatic events. PD focuses on helping people process their emotions by normalizing emotional reactions to trauma.

The quality of the studies of PD is poor, including the randomized controlled trials. The studies provide little evidence that early PD prevents psychopathology fol-

Table 7.C.2
Overview of 12-Week Acute Randomized, Controlled Treatment Studies in Patients with Post-Traumatic Stress Disorder Reporting Positive Effects on Quality of Life (QOL) and Functional Measures

Study (no. of patients)	Treatment	QOL/Functional Measure	Mean-Change Score		p-value for Change; Difference Between Groups
			Active Drug	Placebo/ Active Comparator	
Malik et al. (16)	Fluoxetine vs PL	SF-36 mental subscale score	44	20	<0.01
		SF-36 vitality subscale score	35	10	<0.05
		SF-36 social-functioning subscale score	38	12	< 0.05
Brady et al. (187)	Sertraline vs PL	Q-LES-Q	11.7	3.3	0.004
Rapaport et al.[a]	Sertraline vs PL	Q-LES-Q	12.0 ($n = 64$)	5.2 ($n = 67$)	0.010
		SF-36 emotional role functioning subscale score	25.9	3.7	0.002
		SF-36 mental health subscale score[b]	14.5	3.4	0.032
Tucker et al. (307)	Paroxetine[c] vs PL	SDS	7.2	4.6	0.007
Marshall et al. (551)	Paroxetine vs PL	SDS	7.0 (20 mg/day) 6.4 (40 mg/day)	4.5	< 0.02 (for both dosages)
McRae et al. (26)	Sertraline vs nefazodone	SDS	Sertraline 7.2	Nefazodone 7.5	0.0007[d]

SOURCE: S. Seedat, C. Lochner, B. Vythilingum, and D. Stein. Disability and quality of life in post-traumatic stress disorder: Impact of drug treatment. *PharmacoEconomics*, Vol. 24, No. 10, 2006, Table 1, p. 994. Used with permission.

NOTES: PL = placebo; Q-LES-Q = Quality of Life Enjoyment and Satisfaction Questionnaire; SDS = Sheehan Disability Scale; SF-36 = Medical Outcomes Study Short Form 36-item.

[a] Data from two pooled studies. There were 285 and 131 patients in the Q-LES-Q and SF-36 analyses, respectively.

[b] Patients without co-occurring depression (there were no significant treatment differences in these domains in patients with co-occurring depression).

[c] Flexible dose.

[d] Time factor (no significant differences between the two treatment groups on any of the eight outcome measures employed in the study; however, significant effect for time in both groups on all eight outcome measures, including QOL.

Table 7.C.3
Long-Term Studies of Pharmacotherapy for Post-Traumatic Stress Disorder (PTSD)

Drug	Design and Duration	Objective	No. of Patients	Patient Disposition	Results/Outcome	Reference
SSRIs						
Sertraline	Open-label; 24wk (36wk cumulative)	Rate of sustained responder status or conversion to responder status during long-term treatment	128	Participants on sertraline in a 12wk double-blind, placebo-controlled, randomized trial	Significant improvement in PTSD; response rate = 74%. 92% acute-phase responders maintained response; 8% lost response. 54% acute-phase nonresponders converted to responder status; 46% did not convert.	Londborg et al., 2001
Sertraline	Double-blind, placebo-controlled, randomized; 28wk	Relapse rate and time to relapse with long-term treatment vs. discontinuation	96	Responders from a 24wk open-label maintenance trial	Sertraline group reported significantly lower rates of relapse, discontinuation due to lack of clinical response, and acute exacerbation compared with placebo.	Davidson, et al., 2001
Sertraline	Pooled analysis; 64wk	Effects of long-term treatment vs. discontinuation on QOL and overall function	369	Participants from three previous studies; 12wk double-blind placebo-controlled, randomized trial, 24wk open-label trial, and 28wk double-blind, placebo-controlled randomized trial	Marked improvement in QOL and overall functional impairment. 58% of the sertraline responders achieved QOL within 10% of community norms. Recurrence in PTSD and decrease in QOL with treatment discontinuation.	Rapaport et al., 2002
Paroxetine	Open-label; 9mo.	Effects of long-term treatment on PTSD, memory, and hippocampal volume	28	Outpatients: 11 from a 12wk double-blind, placebo-controlled, randomized trial	Mean 54% reduction in CAPS score. Significant improvement in declarative memory deficits; 4.6% increase in hippocampal volume.	Vermettea et al., 2003

Table 7.C.3—Continued

Drug	Objective	Design and Duration	No. of Patients	Patient Disposition	Results/Outcome	Reference
Fluoxetine	Relapse rate and time to relapse with long-term treatment vs. discontinuation	Double-blind, placebo-controlled, randomized; 24wk	131	Patients responding to 12wk acute-phase trial	Fluoxetine associated with significantly lower likelihood of relapse, and greater improvement in TOP-8 and CGI-S score. Relapse seen in 16% and 5.8% of placebo and fluoxetine recipients, respectively.	Martenyi et al., 2002
Atypical antipsychotics						
Risperidone	Effects of long-term treatment	Double-blind, placebo-controlled, randomized; 16wk	65	Combat veterans in 5wk VA residential program	Greater improvements in CAPS, CAPS-D, HAM-A, and PANSS-P at 16wk in risperidone compared with placebo recipients. Most cases, risperidone was given as an adjunctive treatment.	Bartzokis et al., 2004
Clozapine	Effects of long-term treatment	Retrospective chart review; 6mo	6	Adolescents with history of abuse in residential care	Descriptive improvement, and indication that cloazapine is effective in treating psychosis and hallucinatory behavior.	Wheatley et al., 2004
Other medications						
Valproate	Effects of long-term treatment	Open-label, adjunct; 10.6mo	14	Combat-related PTSD	Quality and duration of sleep improved in 9 of 14 subjects, hyperarousal improved in 11 of 14 subjects, and avoidance improved in 9 of 14 subjects.	Fesler et al., 1991
Nefazodone	Effects of long-term treatment	Open-label; 3–4 years	10	Combat-related PTSD, previously in a 12wk open-label trial	Significant improvement in PTSD, sleep, and depression. Well tolerated.	Herzberg et al., 2002

SOURCE: L. L. Davis, E. C. Frazier, R. B. Williford, and J. M. Newell. Long-term pharmacotherapy for post-traumatic stress disorder. *CNS Drugs*, Vol. 20, No. 6, 2006, pp. 465–476. Used with permission.

NOTES: CAPS = Clinician-Administered PTSD Scale; CAPS-D = CAPS Criterion D (hyperarousal); CGI-S = Clinical Global Impression Scale–Severity; HAM-A = Hamilton Rating Scale for Anxiety; PANSS-P = Positive and Negative Syndrome Scale–Positive Subscale; QOL = quality of life; TOP-8 = Treatment Outcome for PTSD–8 item; VA = Veterans Affairs.

lowing trauma. Neither one-time group nor individual PD can be recommended to prevent subsequent development of PTSD following a traumatic event. Some studies of individual PD suggest that the intense re-exposure involved in PD can retraumatize some individuals (Foa, Keane, and Friedman, 2000b).

One form of psychological debriefing is critical-incident stress debriefing (CISD). A recent meta-analysis conducted by van Emmerik and colleagues (2002) found that CISD interventions did not improve severity of symptoms. They state that "claims that a single session of psychological debriefing can prevent development of chronic negative psychological sequelae are empirically unwarranted" (p. 770).

Another term for CISD is critical-incident stress management (CISM). A recent review by Bledsoe (2003) also concluded that there is a limited amount of quality data on CISD/CISM/PD. In addition, Bledsoe also notes that the higher-quality studies that have been conducted raise doubts about these types of procedures in treating PTSD symptoms, because findings indicate that in some cases CISD/CISM/PD can be harmful.

Other Psychological Treatments.

Eye-Movement Desensitization and Reprocessing (EMDR). EMDR is an integrative treatment during which people are asked to hold in mind a disturbing image, an associated negative cognition, and bodily sensations associated with a traumatic memory, while tracking the clinician's moving finger in front of his/her visual field. Variations of this procedure are repeated until distressing aspects of the traumatic memory are reduced (Foa, Keane, and Friedman, 2000b). EMDR treatment includes aspects of cognitive-behavioral therapy, such as desensitization and installation of positive cognitions (Foa, Keane, and Friedman, 2000b). The largest effects have been found for EMDR versus no treatment or EMDR versus nonspecific treatment (Davidson and Parker, 2001). Evidence is also stronger for persons with single-event civilian trauma than on multiply traumatized chronically ill veterans (Foa, Keane, and Friedman, 2000b).

Imagery Rehearsal Therapy (IRT). IRT uses a combination of exposure to images, CT, and instruction in sleep habits. It is intended to help the patient gain control of the content of nightmares so that the meaning, importance, and orientation to the nightmare are altered. The key to a successful approach is the use of imagery. IRT avoids discussion of trauma or the traumatic content of nightmares (Forbes et al., 2003; Krakow et al., 2001).

Psychodynamic therapy (PT). PT seeks to address what is unconscious by making it conscious. It does so by exploring the psychological meaning of the traumatic event. There are different types of PT. Formal psychoanalysis involves four to five 45–50-minute sessions each week over the course of two to seven years. PT can also involve one or two meetings a week and can be short-term (a few months) or open-ended (lasting years). Brief PT involves meeting once or twice a week for 12 to 20 sessions (Kudler, Blank, and Krupnick, 2000). There are few empirical investigations of

PT (Foa, Keane, and Friedman, 2000b); thus, there is little empirical evidence for its effectiveness in treating PTSD.

Hypnosis. Typically used as an adjunct to other therapies and shown to increase their effectiveness (Kirsch et al., 1998), hypnosis is used to suggest changes in behavior and mental processes. There is little empirical evidence for the effectiveness of hypnosis in treating PTSD. Foa, Keane, and Friedman (2000b) found only one relevant study; that study showed that hypnosis improved PTSD symptoms. A more recent study compared six sessions of cognitive-behavioral therapy with hypnosis, and supportive counseling with civilian trauma survivors (Bryant et al., 2005). Findings indicated that fewer participants in the CBT and the CBT-hypnosis group met criteria for PTSD at the six-month follow-up than did the supportive counseling group. The CBT-hypnosis group did not report greater clinical gains overall than the CBT group (Bryant et al., 2005). A three-year follow-up of these groups showed that both the CBT and CBT-hypnosis group were less likely to re-experience the traumatic event and to avoid situations than patients who received supportive counseling. There were no clinical differences between the CBT group and the CBT-hypnosis group (Bryant et al., 2006).

Psychosocial Rehabilitation (PR). PR involves several techniques, including (1) education, (2) training in independent-living skills, (3) supported housing, (4) family skills training, (5) social-skills training, (6) vocational rehabilitation, and (7) case management. These techniques are suggested as an adjunct to other forms of PTSD treatment. The techniques are considered to be effective; however, none has been tested with persons with PTSD in well-controlled trials (Penk and Flannery, 2000).

Modes of Treatment. The therapies described above are usually delivered by a clinician to an individual patient. Other modes include group therapy, marital therapy, and inpatient treatment.

Group Therapy (GT). GT for PTSD focuses on offering cohesion, encouragement, and support from other group members. GT is typically offered in two formats. One avoids focusing on the details of the trauma; instead, it helps servicemembers cope. The other focuses on the trauma directly, using prolonged exposure and other techniques to help servicemembers gain control over their symptoms. Despite some limitations, GT studies report favorable effects; however, there is no evidence that one type of group therapy outperforms another (Foy et al., 2000). Based on a review of four studies, the Institute of Medicine committee decided that there was insufficient evidence to determine the efficacy of group therapy as a treatment for PTSD (Institute of Medicine, 2007).

Marital and Family Therapy (MFT). MFT has been recommended for treating traumatized adults. Typically used as an adjunct to other PTSD treatments (Riggs, 2000), MFT comprises two categories: approaches that address family disruption and supportive approaches designed to help family members provide support for the individual being treated for PTSD. Only one randomized controlled study was found for

MFT. Information about the effectiveness of MFT is usually anecdotal and includes clinical descriptions (Riggs, 2000).

Inpatient Treatment. Inpatient programs are designed for people who have had multiple traumatic episodes and who suffer from chronic and prolonged PTSD. Inpatient treatment may also be indicated for patients who have complex needs (e.g., multiple problems that might require observation to assess and evaluate their response to treatment) and for those who may be considered a threat to themselves or others. Inpatient treatment is available on general psychiatric units and in specialty units and treatment tracks. Inpatient treatment typically uses many different interventions and involves longer stays (2–12 weeks) rather than crisis admissions. To date, specialty programs have been organized for combat veterans and adult survivors of childhood trauma. There is limited research on the efficacy of specialized inpatient PTSD treatment (Courtois and Bloom, 2000).

Comparing the Effectiveness of Treatments. Several meta-analyses make it possible to compare the effectiveness of specific treatments. Van Etten and Taylor (1998) conducted one of the most comprehensive meta-analyses on treatment for PTSD, reviewing 61 treatment-outcome trials for PTSD, which included the following treatments: drug therapies (TCAs, carbamazepine, MAOIs, SSRIs, and benzodiazepines [BDZs]), psychological therapies (behavior therapy, EMDR, relaxation training, hypnotherapy, and dynamic therapy), and control conditions (pill placebo, wait-list controls, supportive psychotherapies, and nonsaccade EMDR control).

Van Etten and Taylor found that psychological therapies had significantly lower dropout rates than pharmacotherapies (14 percent versus 32 percent). Psychological therapies were also more effective in reducing symptoms than drug therapies. Both psychological therapies and drug therapies were more effective than controls. Among the drug therapies, the SSRIs and carbamazepine had the largest effects. Behavior therapy and EMDR were the most effective psychological therapies. SSRIs had some advantage over psychosocial therapies in treating depression. Tables 7.C.4 through 7.C.7 provide effect sizes for all these different therapies on both self-reported and observer-reported symptoms of intrusion, avoidance, overall PTSD symptoms, and overall anxiety and depression at immediate post-test.

Follow-up results were not available for most of the therapies; however, the available data suggest that the positive treatment effects of behavior therapy and EMDR were maintained at 15-week follow-up. Table 7.C.4 provides effect sizes for the different PTSD symptoms at post-test. Table 7.C.5 provides effect sizes for these same therapies at post-test on overall anxiety and depression. Tables 7.C.6 and 7.C.7 provide effect sizes for behavior therapy and EMDR on intrusion, avoidance, PTSD symptoms, and overall anxiety and depression at 15-week follow-up.

The most recent meta-analysis, by Bisson and colleagues (2007), focused only on psychological treatments, which included such therapies as trauma-focused cognitive-behavioral therapy, EMDR, stress management, and group CBT. They included

Table 7.C.4
Pre-Post Effect Sizes for Measures of PTSD Symptoms

Condition	No. of Trials	Intrusions Self-Report M	90% CI	Observer-Related M	90% CI	Avoidance Self-Report M	90% CI	Observer-Related M	90% CI	Total Severity of PTSD Symptoms Self-Report M	90% CI	Observer-Related M	90% CI
TCA	6	0.64	0.30–0.98	0.46	—	0.35	0.22–0.48	0.55	—	0.54	0.34–0.74	0.86	0.75–0.97
Carbmz	1	1.53	—	—	—	0.52	—	—	—	0.93	—	1.45	—
MAOI	7	0.64	0.27–1.01	—	—	0.40	−0.21–1.01	—	—	0.61	0.38–0.84	0.92	0.73–1.11
SSRI	4	1.71	1.08–2.34	1.28	0.90–1.66	0.92	0.73–1.11	1.37	1.05–1.69	1.38	1.02–1.74	1.43	1.19–1.67
BDZ	1	0.51	—	0.66	—	0.16	—	0.32	—	0.49	—	0.54	—
Drug Txs (overall)	19	0.86	0.63–1.09	1.01	0.71–1.31	0.45	0.31–0.59	1.00	0.64–1.36	0.69	0.55–0.83	1.05	0.91–1.19
Behav Tx	13	1.12	0.49–1.75	1.76	−0.05–3.57	1.12	0.61–1.63	1.45	−0.10–3.00	1.27	0.80–1.74	1.89	1.66–2.12
EMDR	11	1.12	0.72–1.52	1.39	0.99–1.79	1.27	0.74–1.80	2.01	1.25–2.77	1.24	0.99–1.49	0.69	−0.06–1.44
Relaxation	1	0.54	—	—	—	0.46	—	—	—	0.45	—	—	—
Hypnosis	1	1.06	—	—	—	0.80	—	—	—	0.94	—	—	—
Dynamic	1	0.70	—	—	—	0.64	—	—	—	0.90	—	—	—
Psych Tx (overall)	27	1.02	0.80–1.24	1.57	1.12–2.02	1.03	0.77–1.29	1.74	1.23–2.25	1.17	0.99–1.35	1.51	1.17–1.85
Pill Placebo	4	0.48	−0.17–1.13	—	—	0.07	0.05–0.09	—	—	0.51	0.29–0.73	0.77	0.63–0.91
WLC	5	0.32	0.28–0.36	0.74	0.72–0.76	0.21	0.14–0.28	0.22	−0.65–1.09	0.44	0.28–0.60	0.75	0.67–0.83
Sup Psych	5	0.95	—	0.53	—	0.77	—	0.09	—	0.34	0.01–0.67	0.92	—
No Sacc	1	—	—	—	—	—	—	—	—	—	—	—	—
Controls (overall)	15	0.49	0.29–0.69	0.66	0.54–0.78	0.23	0.06–0.46	0.17	−0.18–0.52	0.43	0.33–0.53	0.77	0.71–0.83

SOURCE: M. L. van Etten and S. Taylor. Meta-analysis of PTSD treaments. *Clinical Psychology and Psychotherapy*, Vol. 5, No. 3, September 1998, Table 2, p. 135. Copyright© 1998 John Wiley & Sons Limited. Used with permission.

NOTES: Effect size = $(M_{pre} - M_{post})/SD_{pooled}$, where $SD_{pooled} = \sqrt{[(SD^2_{pre} + SD^2_{post})/2]}$. All means are weighted by sample size. 90%CI = 90th percentile confidence interval around weighted mean. Note that "—" refers to data missing or not reported. For the 90%CIs, "—" appears when there was only one effect size. Within each row, the total number of trials may differ across outcome domains (intrusions, avoidance, and global severity) because some trials did not assess all domains. BDZ = benzodiazepines; Behav Tx = behaviour therapy; Carbmz = carbamazepine; Dynamic = psychodynamic psychotherapy; EMDR = eye-movement desensitization and reprocessing; MAOI = monoamine oxidase inhibitors; No Sacc = no saccade control (control for EMDR); SSRI = selective serotonin reuptake inhibitors; Sup Psych = supportive psychotherapy; TCA = tricyclic antidepressants; WLC = wait-list control.

Table 7.C.5
Pre-Post Effect Sizes for Measures of Anxiety and Depression

	Anxiety				Depression			
	Self-Report		Observer-Related		Self-Report		Observer-Related	
Condition	M	90% CI	M	90% CI	M	90% CI	M	90% CI
TCA	0.44	−0.08–0.96	0.54	0.13–0.95	0.44	0.09–0.79	0.85	0.53–1.17
Carbmz	0.47	—	1.73	—	0.48	—	1.25	—
MAOI	0.65	—	0.92	0.44–1.40	0.98	—	0.43	0.28–0.58
SSRI	1.24	—	1.20	—	1.41	—	1.38	—
BDZ	—	—	0.72	—	—	—	0.11	—
Drug Txs (overall)	0.61	0.39–0.83	0.64	0.61–1.09	0.65	0.39–0.91	0.72	0.55–0.89
Behav Tx	1.12	0.84–1.40	1.47	—	0.97	0.80–1.14	—	—
EMDR	0.95	0.69–1.21	—	—	1.05	0.81–1.29	—	—
Relaxation	0.83	—	—	—	0.67	—	—	—
Hypnosis	0.95	—	—	—	—	—	—	—
Dynamic	1.07	—	—	—	—	—	—	—
Psych Tx (overall)	1.04	0.89–1.19	1.47	—	1.00	0.87–1.13	—	—
Pill Plac	0.03	—	0.38	—	0.24	—	0.36	0.19–0.53
WLC	0.25	0.14–0.36	—	—	0.25	0.12–0.42	—	—
Sup Psych	0.25	0.04–0.46	—	—	0.25	0.12–0.42	—	—
No Sacc	0.06	—	—	—	0.14	—	—	—
Controls (overall)	0.17	0.06–0.28	0.38	—	0.23	0.16–0.30	0.36	0.19–0.53

SOURCE: M. L. van Etten and S. Taylor. Meta-analysis of PTSD treatments. *Clinical Psychology and Psychotherapy*, Vol. 5, No. 3, September 1998, Table 4, p. 138. Copyright© 1998 John Wiley & Sons Limited. Used with permission.

NOTE: See the note to Table 7.C.4 for definitions of statistics and acronyms.

38 randomized controlled trials. The meta-analysis showed that trauma-focused CBT and EMDR were more effective than wait-list/control groups on most outcome measures. There was limited evidence that these treatments were superior to supportive/nondirective treatments that did not provide exposure. The meta-analysis also found that studies conducted with Vietnam veterans showed less evidence of these treatments' effectiveness than wait-list groups.

Guidelines for Treating PTSD. We now draw on the results of our literature review to compare the guidelines provided by the VA/DoD for treatment of PTSD with the evidence base. Table 7.C.8 displays these comparisons. The first and second columns list the practice guideline and the corresponding recommended treatment. The third column mentions the evidence from the research literature supporting the recom-

Table 7.C.6
Effect Sizes at Follow-Up (i.e., Symptom Reductions from Pre-Treatment to 15-Week Follow-Up) for PTSD Symptoms

Condition	No. of Trials	Intrusions				Avoidance				Total Severity of PTSD Symptoms			
		Self-Report		Observer-Rated		Self-Report		Observer-Rated		Self-Report		Observer-Rated	
		M	90% CI	M	90% CI	M	90% CI	M	90% CI	M	90% CI	M	90% CI
Behav Tx	5	1.56	0.81–2.29	1.47	0.60–2.34	1.44	0.47–2.41	1.32	0.71–1.93	1.63	1.10–2.16	1.93	1.67–2.19
EMDR	6	1.75	1.46–2.04	2.07	1.77–2.37	1.89	1.08–2.70	2.34	1.76–2.92	1.33	0.89–1.77	2.27	1.78–2.76

SOURCE: M. L. van Etten and S. Taylor. Meta-analysis of PTSD treatments. *Clinical Psychology and Psychotherapy*, Vol. 5, No. 3, September 1998, Table 5, p. 138. Copyright© 1998 John Wiley & Sons Limited. Used with permission.

NOTE: See the note to Table 7.C.4 for definitions of statistics and acronyms.

Table 7.C.7
Effect Sizes at Follow-Up for Measures of Anxiety and Depression

Condition	No. Trials	Anxiety		Depression	
		Self-Report		Self-Report	
		M	90% CI	M	90% CI
Behav Tx	9	0.99	0.66–1.32	0.93	0.76–1.10
EMDR	5	0.90	0.64–1.16	0.91	0.46–1.36

SOURCE: M. L. van Etten and S. Taylor. Meta-analysis of PTSD treatments. *Clinical Psychology and Psychotherapy*, Vol. 5, No. 3, September 1998, Table 5, p. 138. Copyright© 1998 John Wiley & Sons Limited. Used with permission.

NOTE: See the note to Table 7.C.4 for definitions of statistics and acronyms.

Table 7.C.8
VA Guidelines Compared with the Literature on Evidence-Based Treatments for PTSD, ASR, and COPR

VA/DoD Clinical Practice Guidelines	VA/DoD Interventions	Evidence from the Literature[a]	Level of Evidence
Are trauma related symptoms present?	Provide:		
Acute Stress Reaction	Acute symptom management	Meet basic needs (e.g., sleep, nutrition), re-establish routine, consider short course of medication, provide positive social supports.	Expert opinion
	Education and normalization	Educate survivors and families about symptoms.	Expert opinion
	Social & spiritual support	No direct evidence that religious/spiritual practices are effective in treating PTSD.	Expert opinion
	Consider medication	Strongest evidence of effectiveness is for antidepressant medications, particularly SSRIs (Davis et al., 2006; Seedat et al., 2006; van Etten and Taylor, 1998).	Randomized outcome studies (for PTSD)
	Avoid: Psychological debriefing Individual debriefing Compulsory group debriefing	Psychological debriefing does not prevent subsequent development of PTSD after a traumatic event and may retraumatize patients (van Emmerik et al., 2002).	Randomized outcome studies (for PTSD)

Table 7.C.8—Continued

VA/DoD Clinical Practice Guidelines	VA/DoD Interventions	Evidence from the Literature[a]	Level of Evidence
Combat or ongoing military operation stress reaction (COSR):	Provide the following as needed:		
	Reunion or contact with primary group	Based on assumption that soldiers seek to maintain their identities as warfighters in their group (Helmus and Glenn, 2005; Noy, 1987; Solomon, Mikulincer, and Benbenishty, 1989).	Expert opinion
	Respite from intense stress	Experience suggests that soldiers need to be rotated in and out of combat.	Expert opinion
	Sleep Thermal comfort Oral hydration Oral food Hygiene	Evidence for how loss of sleep affects mental performance is based mostly on anecdotal evidence from the battlefield (Belenky, 1997).	Expert opinion
	Assign appropriate duty tasks and recreational activities that will restore focus and confidence. Avoid further traumatic events until recovered for full duty.	Harsh environmental conditions and lack of nutritious food precipitate stress reactions (Mericle, 1946).	Expert opinion
	Encourage individual to discuss event with others. Reserve group debriefing for members of existing groups.	Military personnel with low confidence in military skills are more prone to disease and nonbattle injury (Stouffer and Lumsdaine, 1965). Psychological debriefing is not recommended as a treatment. Discussion of the event can be helpful as part of a comprehensive treatment plan (Foa, Keane, and Friedman, 2000a).	Expert opinion
	Consider medication	Discussed above	Randomized outcome studies

Table 7.C.8—Continued

VA/DoD Clinical Practice Guidelines	VA/DoD Interventions	Evidence from the Literature[a]	Level of Evidence
Acute and Chronic PTSD	Stabilize and/or arrange treatment for: Medical condition Psychosocial services Acute psychiatric symptoms.	See respite from intense stress, social and spiritual support, and acute symptom management above.	
	Educate patient and family about PTSD.	See above.	Expert opinion
	Develop collaborative interdisciplinary treatment plan.	Patient may benefit from range of assistance from a range of disciplines.	
	Initiate therapy for PTSD: Educate about medication Initiate pharmacotherapy to willing patients	See above.	Randomized outcome studies
	Initiate psychotherapy: Cognitive therapy	Most evidence of effectiveness comes from studies of female assault survivors (Resick et al., 2002). One recent study found it effective with veterans (Monson et al., 2006).	Randomized outcome studies
	Exposure therapy	Strong evidence of effectiveness (Foa, Keane, and Friedman, 2000a; Sherman, 1998; van Etten and Taylor, 1998).	Randomized outcome studies
	Stress inoculation training	Effective for treating PTSD in female assault survivors. Effectiveness with other populations unknown (Foa, Keane, and Friedman, 2000b).	Randomized outcome studies
	EMDR	Strong evidence of effectiveness (Davidson and Parker, 2001; van Etten and Taylor, 1998). Role of eye movement unclear (Perkins and Rouanzoin, 2002).	Randomized outcome studies
	Imagery rehearsal therapy	Effective in treating nightmares and sleep disruption (Krakow et al., 2001; Krakow et al., 1995).	Randomized outcome studies
	Psychodynamic therapy	Few empirical investigations of psychodynamic therapy. (Foa, Keane, and Friedman, 2000a).	Expert opinion
	Patient education	See above.	

Table 7.C.8—Continued

VA/DoD Clinical Practice Guidelines	VA/DoD Interventions	Evidence from the Literature[a]	Level of Evidence
	Group therapy	Some evidence that GT is effective; no evidence that one type of GT outperforms others (Foa, Keane, and Friedman, 2000b; Schnurr et al., 2003).	Randomized outcome studies Quasi-experimental studies
	Dialectical behavior therapy for patients with borderline personality disorder (BPD) BPD is a serious mental illness characterized by pervasive instability in moods, interpersonal relationships, self-image, and behavior.	No trials for use of DBT with PTSD patients.	Expert opinion
	Hypnosis	A recent study found that a CBT-hypnosis group was not more effective than a CBT group (Bryant et al., 2005).	Expert opinion One randomized outcome study

[a] Almost all available literature focuses on outcomes for PTSD treatment; thus, guidelines for treating ASR and COSR are based on expert opinion.

mended treatment. The final column indicates whether this evidence is based on randomized-outcomes studies, quasi-experimental studies, or expert opinion.

Almost all the available literature focuses on outcomes for PTSD treatment; thus, guidelines for treating ASR and COSR are based on expert opinion. However, because VA/DoD guidelines include ASR and COPR, we include them in the table.

Training of Practitioners. There is very little explicit documentation in the literature of "how much" training is enough training. However, the literature has indicated that "the treatment of PTSD is to be applied by skilled clinicians only . . . and . . . diagnosis and careful evaluation must precede treatment" (Shalev et al., 2000, p. 361). Foa, Keane, and Friedman (2000a, p. 14) state that "typical training would include a graduate-level degree, a clinical internship or equivalent, and past supervision in the specific technique or approach employed." In their meta-analysis paper, van Etten and Taylor (1998) found that, for the psychological therapies, 75 percent of the studies reviewed reported the level of therapist training. They coded studies as having adequate training if the study specifically reported "adequate years of therapist experience (e.g., over five years) or formal training with a senior colleague experienced in the treatment modality" (van Etten and Taylor, 1998, p. 133).

In response to a need for more trained clinicians, the DoD recently provided a training program in EMDR to 175 DoD/VA clinicians providing trauma services (Russell et al., 2007). Participants responded positively to the workshop. In addition, the patients of these clinicians showed reduced symptoms of depression and PTSD (Russell et al., 2007). The authors suggest that short-term training can provide clinicians with additional skills that appear to transfer to the clinical setting and help patients improve their symptoms.

Depression

Literature Review. We conducted a literature review to find studies focusing on the treatment of depression. We used PubMED (MEDLINE), PsychINFO, and GoogleScholar and limited our searches to English-language articles from 1998 to the present. We also found additional references within the papers and included some of those sources that we thought would provide additional background information, regardless of the year of publication.

We used the following search terms: "treatment," "early intervention," "prevention," "services," "adult"; "symptoms," "depression," "major depressive disorder," "major depressive episode"; "major depression"; "dysthymia" and "depressive symptoms." We also used combinations of terms, such as "depression and treatment," and "major depressive disorder and early intervention." We focused on recent meta-analyses[10] that

---

[10] A *meta-analysis* is a study that reviews outcome studies in a particular area and assesses how small or large the effect size of each outcome is. *Effect size* provides information about how much change is evident across all studies and for subsets of studies.

examined outcomes of a range of evidence-based treatments for depression. Overall, we reviewed 80 studies.

Studies are usually assigned to one of three levels of evidence, suggesting the level of confidence with which study findings can be viewed:

1. Randomized clinical trial (RCT). RCTs are considered the gold standard for scientific evidence in health care because they eliminate spurious causality and bias. In an RCT, subjects are randomly allocated to different treatments to ensure that confounding factors are evenly distributed between treatment groups. As a result, outcomes can be linked to treatment with substantial reliability.
2. Nonrandomized controlled trials, cohort or case analysis, or multiple time series. These are studies that utilize various quasi-experimental designs and statistical methods to control for spurious causality and bias, but they do not control for these confounding sources as completely as RCTs.
3. Textbooks, opinions, or descriptive studies. Many recommendations are based on best practices conducted in the field, but rigorous empirical evaluation is lacking.

We refer to these categories in our discussion of VA/DoD guidelines.

Treating Depression.

Diagnosis. Recognizing depressive disorders is often difficult. Studies have shown that primary care providers fail to diagnose depression 35 to 50 percent of the time (Gerber et al., 1989; Katon et al., 1995). The literature suggests that military providers have similar difficulties. In 2002, Hunter and colleagues assessed the detection of depressive disorders in a military primary care setting. The sample comprised 337 patients who made a primary care visit during a five-day period in October 1999. Patients completed several questionnaires, including the depression module of the Patient Health Questionnaire (PHQ). Of the 337 patients, 19 were identified on the PHQ as having symptoms consistent with major depression. Providers identified four of these 19 individuals.

Early diagnosis of depression is important: Recent research suggests that treating subthreshold depression may decrease subsequent symptoms and prevent the onset of major depression (Cuijpers, Smit, and van Straten, 2007). Cuijpers, Smit, and van Straten (2007) conducted a meta-analysis of seven randomized controlled trials examining the effects of psychological treatments for subthreshold depression. Results indicated that treatment was associated with a reduction in depressive symptoms in the short term. Over time, the effects were smaller, but they still suggested the superiority of psychological treatment compared with usual care. Although the number of studies examining psychological treatment for subthreshold depression is small, the research is promising.

Types of Depression Treatment. The four types of depression treatments are as follows:

1. *Psychotherapy,* including cognitive-behavioral therapy, cognitive therapy, and interpersonal therapy
2. *Pharmacotherapy,* using many different kinds of medications
3. *Shocks or stimulation to the brain,* including electroconvulsive therapy and transcranial magnetic stimulation
4. *Complementary treatments,* such as relaxation and herbal remedies.

Below, we describe each type of treatment and summarize available evidence about its effectiveness.

Cognitive Behavioral Therapy (CBT). CBT is a psychotherapy based on modifying patient assumptions, evaluations, and beliefs that might be unhelpful or unrealistic, and on helping the patient to try new ways of behaving and reacting. CBT is a collaborative effort. The therapist's role is to listen, teach, and encourage; the client's role is to express concerns, learn, and implement that learning (NACBT [National Association of Cognitive-Behavioral Therapists] Online Headquarters Web site). CBT is a very structured treatment, and the therapist typically has a specific agenda for each session, in which specific techniques and concepts are taught. CBT is brief and time-limited; for example, an average course of CBT is 15 sessions.

There is strong evidence that CBT improves depressive symptoms (Hollon, Thase, and Markowitz, 2002). CBT has more research than any other psychotherapy supporting its effectiveness for both short-term and long-term improvement in patient outcomes.

A recent meta-analysis (Vittengl et al., 2007) examined 28 studies of CBT involving 1,880 adults. They estimated the proportion of patients who had depressive symptoms after treatment during the acute phase and during the *continuation phase* (e.g., treatment given to prevent symptoms from recurring). Focusing on relapse and recurrence of depression, Vittengl et al. found that, compared with pharmacotherapy, CBT during the acute phase significantly reduced relapse. Adding pharmacotherapy to CBT also significantly reduced relapse compared with pharmacotherapy alone. Relapse-recurrence rates for CBT were comparable to those of other depression-specific psychotherapies, such as interpersonal therapy. In the continuation phase, Vittengl et al. (2007) found that CBT reduced relapse-recurrence compared with non-active controls (e.g., assessment only); however, CBT did not reduce relapse-recurrence rates compared with active controls (e.g., supportive therapy).

Butler and colleagues (2006) reviewed meta-analyses of CBT conducted between 1967 and July 2004 and found 16 that met their criteria of being both extensive and rigorous. These meta-analyses analyzed outcomes from CBT for many different disorders, including depression, generalized anxiety disorder, panic disorder, and obsessive-compulsive disorder. Several meta-analyses showed that CBT was typically superior to wait-list or placebo controls. Butler et al. suggest the need for future meta-analyses that directly compare CBT with specific alternative therapies versus comparing CBT with a heterogeneous collection of therapies.

Cognitive Therapy. Cognitive therapy postulates that dysfunctional thinking patterns generate pathologic emotions that can lead to psychiatric disorders. For example, these thinking patterns can lead a person to feel anxious or depressed in situations in which these emotions are unwarranted (Foa, 2000). Cognitive therapy is focused on the present and helps the patient identify and correct his or her inaccurate beliefs. Skills involve identifying distorted thinking, modifying beliefs, relating to others in different ways, and changing behaviors (Beck Institute Web site). The ultimate aim of CT is to modify patients' cognitions, behavior, emotions, and, sometimes, physiological reactions (Beck, 2001). There is extensive evidence that cognitive therapy is efficacious in treating depression (Hollon, Thase, and Markowitz, 2002). However, results from a large National Institute of Mental Health (NIMH) study raised questions about the effectiveness of CT compared with medication (Elkin et al., 1989) or pill placebo (Elkin et al., 1995). Hollon, Thase, and Markowitz (2002) hypothesize that differing results for CT are due to quality of implementation and suggest that not all therapists implement CT adequately, particularly in patients with more severe depression. Thus, it is not that CT is ineffective but that the therapist's expertise makes a difference when the patient's depression is more severe and difficult to treat. CT has also been shown to have an enduring effect that extends beyond treatment: Patients who receive CT are half as likely to relapse after treatment is completed as are patients who receive medication (Blackburn, Eunson, and Bishop, 1986; M. D. Evans et al., 1992).

Other studies since the NIMH study have shown that cognitive therapy is as effective as MAOIs and that it is also superior to a pill-placebo control (Jarrett et al., 1999).

Recent evidence has shown that the behavioral activation (BA) component of CBT is comparable to antidepressant medication in improving depressive symptoms (Dimidjian et al., 2006). BA emphasizes the relationship between activity and mood, focusing on patterns of avoidance and withdrawal. It promotes involvement with activities and contexts that are reinforcing and consistent with a person's long-term goals. Dimidjian et al. (2006) compared cognitive therapy with behavioral activation and pharmacotherapy at an 8- and 16-week follow-up period. They found that participants in the BA condition improved more per treatment-week than participants in the CT condition. Similarly, participants receiving medication improved more than participants receiving CT; however, they found no differences between BA and medication. Cuijpers and colleagues (Cuijpers, van Straten, and Warmerdam, 2007a), who conducted a recent meta-analysis on BA treatments for depression, focusing on activity-scheduling (e.g., having patients schedule daily activities that are pleasurable to them), found 16 studies with 780 participants and a nonsignificant effect size (.13) that favored activity-scheduling when they compared it with other psychological treatments (e.g., CT, medication).

DeRubeis and colleagues (2005) conducted a study in which participants were randomly assigned to 16 weeks of medications (n=120), 16 weeks of cognitive therapy (n=60), or 8 weeks of pill placebo (n=60). At 8 weeks, response rates in the medications (50 percent) and cognitive therapy (43 percent) groups were both superior to the placebo (25 percent) group. At 16 weeks, response rates were 58 percent in the medication and CT groups; remission rates were 46 percent for medication, 40 percent for cognitive therapy, and did not differ between medication and CT. In later follow-up assessments, the authors found that, at one site, symptoms improved more for those who received medication than for CT. Similar to other studies, they hypothesized that site differences in patient characteristics and in experience levels of the cognitive therapists may have contributed to this result (DeRubeis et al., 2005).

Interpersonal Therapy (IPT). Interpersonal therapy (IPT) is a short-term supportive psychotherapy that focuses on the link between the development of a person's psychiatric symptoms and his or her interactions with other people. IPT focuses on current problems and people who are important in the patient's life, and helps patients assess how these problems may be related to relationships with others. IPT also helps the patient master problems by recognizing emotional responses to situations and providing education and correcting misinformation about depression. The efficacy of IPT has been tested in numerous controlled clinical trials; but it has only been implemented in clinical practice in the past decade (Weissman and Markowitz, 1994).

A systematic review of IPT on depressive disorders was conducted in 2005 to update the prior reviews, to assess whether IPT was superior to other brief psychotherapies, and to determine whether combining IPT with antidepressant medications increases improvements in depressive symptoms (Feijo de Mello et al., 2005). Databases were searched from 1974 to 2002 for randomized controlled trials. Thirteen trials met inclusion criteria. Overall, recent studies have shown that IPT is effective in treating depressive disorders and also appears to prevent relapse. IPT was more effective than placebo. Nine studies compared IPT alone with medication. Five of these studies reported remission during treatment in the acute stage; remission was more likely to occur in the medication group than in the IPT group. Remission after six months or more was reported in three studies; again, remission was more likely to occur with patients receiving medication, but this result was not statistically different (Feijo de Mello et al., 2005). In studies with IPT plus medication compared with medication alone, remission was more likely in the combination group after four months or less of therapy. IPT was also compared with CBT. When depressive symptoms were compared at the endpoint, there was a statistically significant difference favoring IPT.

General Predictors of Effectiveness of Psychotherapy. Certain factors seem to be associated with better outcomes regardless of the kind of psychotherapy provided (e.g., CBT or IPT). A recent meta-analysis examined studies of therapy designed for the general population (*universal programs*), for subgroups at risk (*selective programs*), and for those who have been treated but are at high risk for relapse (*indicated programs*) to determine what factors were associated with improvement in depressive symptoms (Jane-Llopis et al., 2003). They found no differences in effect sizes among children, adolescents, and adults or between universal, selective, and indicated programs. Longer programs (e.g., with eight or more sessions) were better than programs with fewer than eight sessions. In addition, programs that used a combination of health care professionals and lay personnel had the largest effect sizes. Programs provided by health care professionals had larger effect sizes than programs run by lay personnel for selective and indicated programs. Thus, more-severe depression may require trained personnel who are skilled in delivering treatment. Finally, programs that had well-defined interventions performed better than those that did not have a well-defined intervention.

Problem-Solving Therapy. Problem-solving therapy (PST) involves having the patient systematically identify his or her problems, generate solutions for these problems, create and implement a plan, and evaluate whether or not this process has solved the problem (D'Zurilla and Nezu, 1982; Mynors-Wallis et al., 1995). Overall, PST has been shown to be effective in treating depression, although further research is needed to clarify the conditions and participants for which it may have more-positive effects (Cuijpers, van Straten, and Warmerdam, 2007b).

There have been many randomized controlled studies of PST for depression; however, until 2007, there has been no effort to integrate these findings. Cuijpers, van Straten, and Warmerdam (2007b), who conducted a meta-analysis using papers from 1966 to March 2005, studies in which the effects of PST were examined for adults and were compared with a control or other treatment in a randomized controlled trial. They identified 13 studies with a total of 1,133 participants. Overall, the effects varied among the different studies, with some effect sizes below zero (indicating that the control treatment was superior) to very large effect sizes. Cuijpers and colleagues concluded that more research is needed to clarify the conditions and participants in which the positive effects are found.

Self-Help Therapy. *Self-help treatments*, or *self-administered treatments*, are typically defined as treatments without therapist contact. They usually encompass media-based treatments, such as books, manuals, audiotapes, or some combination (Gellatly et al., 2007; Menchola, Arkowitz, and Burke, 2007). However, there is no agreed-upon definition of *self-help* and there is no consensus concerning the appropriate amount of therapist contact for a treatment to be described as "self-help" (Gellatly et al., 2007). Findings have shown that self-help treatments can be effective in treating depression (Gellatly et al., 2007); however, effectiveness can depend, in part, on how serious the patient's depressive symptoms are, because these treatments may be insufficient for patients with more-severe depressive symptoms (Menchola, Arkowitz, and Burke, 2007).

Two recent meta-analyses examined the effect of self-help treatments on depression. Gellatly and colleagues (2007) identified 34 studies between 2002 and 2005 and examined factors that might determine effectiveness, such as patient populations or intervention content. Overall, they found a medium effect size of self-help interventions. Studies involving patients recruited in nonclinical settings and studies using a guided self-help approach (versus a "pure" self-help approach) had higher effect sizes (Gellatly et al., 2007).

Menchola, Arkowitz, and Burke (2007) conducted their review of self-administered treatments because they wanted to control for several confounding factors that were present in previous meta-analyses. They included 11 studies on depression. Overall, self-administered treatments were more effective than the no-treatment control; the level of improvement was significantly lower than therapist-administered treatment. For milder disorders, reviews have suggested that self-administered treatments may be helpful; for more-serious disorders, self-administered treatments may be insufficient without additional contact from a therapist.

Pharmacotherapy. Antidepressant medications can be used for depressive disorders at all levels of severity (Hollon, Thase, and Markowitz, 2002). Specific medication choice is based on the medication's side effect, safety in overdose, the patient's history of prior response to medication, the patient's other medical conditions, family history of response, and type of depression. Medications include monoamine oxidase inhibitors; tricyclic antidepressants; selective serotonin reuptake inhibitors; dual-mechanism antidepressants (e.g., bupropion, nefazodone, venlafaxine, mirtazapine); and other antidepressants, such as amoxapine, maprotiline, and trazodone.

MAOIs were the first antidepressants to be identified. They work by inhibiting the action of monoamine oxidase, a liver and brain enzyme that burns up the brain's neurotransmitters serotonin, norepinephrine, and dopamine. (Low levels of the neurotransmitters are associated with depression.) MAOIs are no longer used frequently to treat depression because of their side effects; however, they are still used as an alternative treatment for patients who may not respond to other medications (Hollon, Thase, and Markowitz, 2002).

TCAs work by inhibiting reuptake of either norepinephrine or both norepinephrine and serotonin. The major drawback of using TCAs is the high potential for overdose. There are also multiple side effects, including fainting, and an effect on the heart that may contraindicate use for people with irregular heartbeats (Hollon, Thase, and Markowitz, 2002). One study found that, on average, 30 percent of patients in controlled trials stopped taking TCAs because of the side effects (Depression Guideline Panel, 1993).

SSRIs are currently the medication most frequently prescribed for treating depression. SSRIs work by blocking the reuptake of serotonin. Their side effects include diminished libido, nervousness, and insomnia.

Some studies have suggested that the side effects of nervousness and insomnia may help explain the link that has been shown between SSRI use and an increase in suicidal thoughts (Teicher, Glod, and Cole, 1990). Gunnell, Saperia, and Ashby (2005) recently examined whether adults prescribed SSRIs have an increased risk of suicide, nonfatal self-harm, or suicidal thoughts. Pooling data from several hundred randomized controlled trials involving more than 40,000 patients, they found no increased risk of suicidal thoughts, but there was a possible increased risk of nonfatal self-harm in the early weeks of treatment (Gunnell, Saperia, and Ashby, 2005). The researchers did not have access to individual patient data, and they pooled results across several SSRIs. Such findings highlight the importance of further research in this area to clarify appropriate use of these medications and to better understand how to identify people at risk for increased suicidal behavior (Gunnell, Saperia, and Ashby, 2005).

Several dual-mechanism antidepressants have multiple direct effects on neuronal systems, which may give them an advantage over conventional SSRIs (Hollon, Thase, and Markowitz, 2002). For example, at high doses, venlafaxine potentially inhibits reuptake of serotonin and norepinephrine. Side effects include tremor, headache, sexual dysfunction, and insomnia and are comparable to those of the SSRIs; however, it may have an advantage over SSRIs in treating relatively severe depression (Thase, Entsuah, and Rudolph, 2001).

Nefazodone works by blocking a specific serotonin receptor (D. P. Taylor et al., 1995). It has a low risk of sexual side effects (Ferguson et al., 2001) and improves sleep (Rush et al., 1998).

Mirtazapine works by blocking serotonin receptors as well as selected norepineph-rine and other receptors (Hollon, Thase, and Markowitz, 2002). It tends to be more sedating than other antidepressants, but studies have shown that it decreases symptoms more quickly than the SSRIs (Quitkin, Taylor, and Kremer, 2001).

In the past two decades, many meta-analyses have been conducted to assess the effects of various medications on depressive symptoms. We describe some of the more recent studies. Table 7.C.9 provides the classification and dosage range for antidepressants.

In 2000, Anderson conducted a meta-analysis of the efficacy and tolerability of TCAs and SSRIs. He examined data on nearly 11,000 patients from 102 randomized controlled trials. He found no overall differences in efficacy between SSRIs and TCAs; however, TCAs appeared to be more effective than SSRIs for inpatient populations. SSRIs appeared to be better tolerated than the TCAs, and there were lower side effect–related rates of dropout for SSRIs (Anderson, 2000).

Arroll and colleagues (2005) conducted a similar meta-analysis of the efficacy and tolerability of TCAs and SSRIs compared with a placebo in the primary care setting. They included 17 studies. Similar to Anderson (2000), they found that TCAs and SSRIs were more effective than placebo for both major depressive disorder and *heterogeneous depression* (e.g., patients thought by their general practitioner to be depressed, which may or may not include patients with major depression), which is more commonly seen in primary care settings. They also found a lower dropout rate for SSRIs

Table 7.C.9
Classification and Dosages for Antidepressants[a]

Class	Mechanism of Action	Generic Name (U.S. Trade Name)[b]	Recommended Dosage (mg/day)
Selected newer antidepressants			
Selective serotonin reuptake inhibitors	Selectively inhibit the reuptake of 5-HT at the presynaptic neuronal membrane	Fluoxetine (Prozac) Fluvoxamine (Luvox) Paroxetine (Paxil) Sertraline (Zoloft) Citalopram (Celexa)	20–60 100–300 20–50 50–200 20–80
Serotonin and noradrenaline reuptake inhibitors	Potent inhibitors of 5-HT and norepinephrine uptake; weak inhibitors of dopamine reuptake	Venlafaxine (Effexor) Mirtazapine (Remeron) Milnacipran	75–350 15–45 Undetermined
Norepinephrine reuptake inhibitor	Inhibits norepinephrine reuptake without inhibiting serotonin reuptake	Viloxazine[c] Reboxetine[c]	100–400 Undetermined
Reversible inhibitors of monoamine oxidase A	Selective, reversible inhibitors of monoamine oxidase A, resulting in increased concentrations of norepinephrine, 5-HT, and dopamine	Moclobernide[c] Brofaromine[c]	300–600 75–150
5-HT2 receptor antagonists	Mixed serotonin effects	Nefazodone (Serzone) Ritanserin[c]	300–600 Undetermined
5-HT1a receptor agonists	Partial agonist of serotonin 5-HT1a	Gepirone,[c] ipsapirone,[c] tandospirone,[c] felsinoxan[c]	Undetermined
GABAmimetics	GABAA and GABAB receptor agonists	Fengabine[c]	900–1,800
Dopamine reuptake inhibitor	Increases activity of norepinephrine and dopamine only; does not significantly affect serotonin	Buproprion (Wellbutrin, Zyban)	200–450
Herbal remedy	Unclear	Hypericum (also known as St.-John's-wort)	300–900
Mixed serotonin and norepinephrine reuptake inhibitors	Potentiate serotonin and norepinephrine activity; potency and selectivity differ by agent		
Selected older antidepressants			
First-generation tricyclic antidepressants		Amitriptyline (Elavil, Endep)[d] Clomipramine (Anafranil) Doxepin (Adapin, Sinequan)[d] Imipramine (Tofranil)[d] Trimipramine (Surmontil)	100–300 100–250 100–300 100–300 100–300
Second-generation tricyclic antidepressants		Despramine (Norpramin)[d] Nortriptyline (Pamelor)[d]	100–300 50–150

Table 7.C.9—Continued

Class	Mechanism of Action	Generic Name (U.S. Trade Name)[b]	Recommended Dosage (mg/day)
Tetracyclic antidepressant		Maprotiline (Ludiomil)[d]	100–200
Triazolopyridines	Mixed serotonin effects	Trazondone (Desyrel)	150–400
Monoamine oxidase inhibitors	Nonselective inhibitor of monoamine oxidase A and B	Phenelzine (Nardil) Tranylcypromine (Parnate)	60–90 20–60

SOURCE: J. W. Williams, Jr., C. D. Mulrow, E. Chiquette, P. H. Noël, C. Aguilar, and J. Cornell, A systematic review of newer pharmacotherapies for depression in adults: Evidence report summary. *Annals of Internal Medicine*, Vol. 132, No. 9, 2000, pp. 2–11. Used with permission.

[a] GABA 5 g-aminobutyric acid; HT 5 hydroxy-tryptophan.

[b] Brand-name drugs are produced by the following manufacturers: Adapin, Fisons Pharmaceuticals, Rochester, New York; Anafranil and Tofranil, Novartis, East Hanover, New Jersey; Celexa, Forest Pharmaceuticals, Inc., St. Louis, Missouri; Desyrel and Serzone, Bristol-Myers Squibb, Princeton, New Jersey; Effexor and Surmontil, Wyeth-Ayerst, Philadelphia, Pennsylvania; Elavil, Zeneca Pharmaceuticals, Wilmington, Delaware; Endep, Hoffman-LaRoche, Nutley, New Jersey; Luvox, Solvay Pharmaceuticals, Inc., Marietta, Georgia; Nardil, Parke-Davis, Morris Plains, New Jersey; Norpramin, Aventis Pharmaceuticals, Parsippany, New Jersey; Pamelor and Ludiomil, Novartis, East Hanover, New Jersey; Paxil and Parnate, SmithKline Beecham Pharmaceuticals, Philadelphia, Pennsylvania; Prozac, Eli Lilly and Co., Indianapolis, Indiana; Remeron, Organon, Inc., West Orange, New Jersey; Wellbutrin and Zyban, Glaxo Wellcome, Research Triangle Park, North Carolina; Zoloft and Sinequan, Pfizer, New York, New York.

[c] Not available in the United States.

[d] Generic form available.

than for TCAs (Arroll et al., 2005). These results are consistent with other individual trials of these medications (e.g., Bech et al., 2000).

Williams and colleagues (2000) compared new antidepressants, such as SSRIs, to older antidepressants, such as TCAs and MAOIs. They found no difference in effects between the two types of antidepressants; about half of the patients randomly assigned to each type reported improvement in depressive symptoms. Dropout rates were higher for older antidepressants.

In 2006, Kennedy, Anderson, and Lam reviewed studies of escitalopram, the most selective of the SSRI antidepressants. They found ten studies, which included about 2,700 patients. Conducting a comparison of escitalopram with active controls (e.g., citalopram, fluoxetine, paroxentine, sertraline, and venlafaxine XR), they found that escitalopram was superior in efficacy to other SSRIs and comparable to venlafaxine. In addition, the superiority of escitalopram over other agents increased with the severity of depression (Kennedy, Anderson, and Lam, 2006).

Pharmacotherapy and Psychotherapy. Research has shown that pharmacotherapy and psychological treatment (primarily CBT and IPT) can be equally effective in treating depression (Casacalenda, Perry, and Looper, 2002; Hollon, Thase, and Markowitz, 2002). Some studies have found that combining pharmacotherapy and psychotherapy can be more effective than a single treatment (Friedman et al., 2004; De Maat et al., 2006; Pampallona et al., 2007). For example, in a systematic review of 16 trials from 1980 to 2002, Pampallona et al. (2004) found that psychotherapy in addition to antidepressant medication was associated with greater improvement than pharmacotherapy treatment alone.

Friedman and colleagues (2004) also examined studies that randomized patients to a combined-treatment condition or at least one other treatment, such as psychotherapy or pharmacotherapy. They found that combined treatments had small benefits compared with medication alone. There were fewer studies that compared combined treatment to psychotherapy alone; however, results from these studies indicated that there was no benefit of combined treatment versus psychotherapy. Similarly, De Maat and colleagues (2006) found that combined therapy only outperformed psychotherapy alone for moderate chronic depression. No differences were found for mild and moderate nonchronic depression. Thus, combined treatment may be more effective than a single treatment for treating chronic depression (De Maat et al., 2006; Friedman et al., 2004), and adding CBT to medication may also be helpful in preventing relapse (Friedman et al., 2004).

Electroconvulsive Therapy (ECT). *Electroconvulsive therapy* uses electricity to induce seizures. ECT is the most effective and most rapidly acting treatment available for severe major depression (American Psychiatric Association, 2007; American Psychiatric Association Web site, Electroconvulsive Therapy [ECT] page). ECT typically begins during an inpatient stay and involves a course of six to 12 electrically induced grand-mal seizures that are spaced several days apart (Hollon, Thase, and Markowitz, 2002). Its cost and potential side effects mean that ECT is typically used for treatment of only severe mood disorders that have not responded to other treatment (Hollon, Thase, and Markowitz, 2002). Overall, ECT has been shown to be efficacious in treating severe depression (Fink and Taylor, 2007). Many studies have documented that, for patients with severe depressive illness, ECT is effective and superior to sham ECT and to medications (Abrams, 2002). Two large studies were conducted to evaluate the efficacy of ECT and examine relapse prevention among patients with unipolar depression (Kellner et al., 2006; Sackeim et al., 2001). Remission rates for patients who were given ECT were 55 percent in the Columbia University Consortium study (Abrams, 2002) and 86 percent in the Consortium for Research in ECT (Kellner et al., 2006). These results compare favorably with remission rates of antidepressants (e.g., 21 percent for sertraline and 25 percent for venlafaxine) found in another large trial of outpatients with nonpsychotic major depression (Rush et al., 2006). Remissions are earlier for patients who do not have psychosis (Petrides et al., 2001). One concern with ECT is memory loss. Previous research has shown that the memory loss is mostly transient and circumscribed (Abrams, 2002).

Transcranial Magnetic Stimulation (TMS). *TMS* is a technique for gently stimulating the brain. It uses a specialized electromagnet placed on the patient's scalp that generates short magnetic pulses, roughly the strength of a magnetic resonance imaging (MRI) scanner's magnetic field, but much more focused. The magnetic pulses pass easily through the skull, just as the MRI scanner fields do, but because they are short pulses and not a static field, they can stimulate the underlying cerebral cortex (brain). Low-frequency (once per second) TMS has been shown to reduce brain activation, whereas stimulation at higher frequencies (>5 pulses per second) has been shown to increase brain activation. These changes can last for periods of time after stimulation is stopped.

TMS was first developed in 1985 and has been studied since 1995. TMS is currently being investigated as a potential treatment for patients with major depression. For patients with major depression, many studies have shown clinical improvement following TMS (National Alliance on Mental Illness Web site, Transcranial Magnetic Stimulation page).

Gershon, Dannon, and Grunhaus (2003) reviewed the effect of TMS on the treatment of depression. Several studies have shown that fast, repetitive TMS (rTMS) to the left prefrontal cortex and slow rTMS to the right prefrontal cortex are associated with improvements in depressive symptoms. Studies comparing long courses for high-frequency rTMS to ECT have found similar remission rates between these two treatments (Gershon, Dannon, and Grunhaus, 2003).

Across all of these studies, the effectiveness of rTMS differed. Gershon, Dannon, and Grunhaus (2003) believe this difference to be due to several factors, including whether or not the patient has psychosis (i.e., absence of psychosis may be a predictor of success), age (i.e., older patients respond less well to rTMS [Figiel et al., 1998; Kozel et al., 2000]), and underlying brain physiology (Gershon, Dannon, and Grunhaus, 2003). In addition, the frequency at which the magnetic field oscillates during the magnetic stimulation and other aspects of the simulation, including the duration, pulse intensity, and quantity, all vary among these studies, which could affect findings (Gershon, Dannon, and Grunhaus, 2003).

Complementary Therapies. These therapies include popular alternatives to the above-discussed treatments, such as exercise, relaxation, and herbal remedies (Ernst, 2007). For example, *acupuncture therapy* involves sticking needles into certain points along the body to restore the body's flow of energy. *Aromatherapy* combines gentle massage techniques with essential oils from plants. *Relaxation therapy* is a term that encompasses many techniques whose objective is to decrease physical and mental tension (e.g., yoga).

St.-John's-wort (*Hypericum perforatum*) is one of the few herbal remedies that has been extensively tested in randomized controlled trials (Williams et al., 2000). Overall, evidence suggests that St.-John's-wort and exercise are two complementary therapies that can effectively treat mild to moderate depression. Few rigorous studies have been conducted on the other complementary therapies, although some findings were promising for acupuncture, massage, and relaxation (Ernst, Rand, and Stevenson, 1998).

Modes of Treatment. The therapies described above are usually delivered by a clinician to an individual patient. Other modalities include group therapy, marital therapy, and inpatient treatment.

Group Therapy. Group therapy is typically provided as a cognitive and/or behavioral treatment.

A meta-analysis of 48 studies on group therapy for depression found that group therapy is effective in treating depression (McDermut, Miller, and Brown, 2001). The types of group therapy that were examined included behavioral treatments (23 studies), cognitive therapy (18), cognitive-behavioral therapy (11), psychodynamic and interpersonal therapies (8 studies), social support (3 studies), nondirective/attention control (5 studies), and other therapies (4 studies). Of the 46 studies (two of the 48 did not report statistics), 43 found that group therapy significantly improved symptoms. Fifteen of these studies compared group treatment to a control group; findings suggest that the average treated participant improved significantly and was better off than 85 percent of the untreated participants (McDermut, Miller, and Brown, 2001).

Marital Therapy. Much research has shown a strong relationship between marital distress and depression (e.g., Fincham et al., 1997). Marital therapy has been shown to help couples improve their communication, problem solving, and interpersonal relationship skills (Jacobson and Christensen, 1996).

Mead (2002) reviewed the treatments used for marital therapy. The treatments are similar to the treatments provided in individual settings (e.g., CT and CBT); however, they are provided to the couple. Studies have shown that conjoint interpersonal marital therapy, cognitive marital therapy, and behavior-focused marital therapy are all effective in treating marital distress and depression. To date, the most evidence exists for behavior marital therapy, and this treatment is also the most widely utilized (Mead, 2002).

Inpatient Treatment. Inpatient treatment is available in general psychiatric units and in specialty units and treatment tracks. It typically incorporates many different interventions and involves longer stays (2–12 weeks) rather than crisis admissions. Inpatient programs are designed for people who have severe depression and who may have made suicide attempts and/or who are a danger to themselves until some of their depressive symptoms are alleviated.

Guidelines for Treating Depression. Table 7.C.10 lists the guidelines provided by the VA/DoD for the treatment of depression. The column next to the intervention column reports on the evidence from the research literature that supports these guidelines; and the next column indicates whether this evidence from the literature is based on randomized outcome studies, quasi-experimental studies, or expert opinion.

Overall, the therapies proposed for use by the VA/DoD have a strong evidence base in the literature. The VA/DoD guidelines do not discuss Transcranial Magnetic Stimulation, a more recent treatment that has been shown to be effective in treating

Table 7.C.10
VA Guidelines Compared with the Literature on Evidence-Based Treatments for Depression

VA/DoD Clinical Practice Guidelines	VA/DoD Interventions	Evidence from the Literature	Level of Evidence
Major Depressive Disorder	Discuss treatment options and patient's preferences		Expert opinion
	Provide patient/family education		Expert opinion
	Psychotherapy:		
	Cognitive therapy	Effective in treating depression (Hollon, Thase, and Markowitz, 2002). Patients who receive CT are half as likely to relapse as patients who receive medication (Blackburn, Eunson, and Bishop, 1986; M. D. Evans et al., 1992).	Randomized outcomes studies
	Behavior therapy	Behavioral-activation component of CBT is as effective as antidepressant medication in improving depressive symptoms (Dimidjian et al., 2006).	Randomized outcomes studies
	Interpersonal therapy	Effective in treating depression (Feijo de Mello et al., 2005).	Randomized outcomes studies
	Brief dynamic therapy	Effective in treating psychiatric disorders when compared with wait-list controls; otherwise, does not differ from other forms of psychotherapy (Leichsenring, Rabung, and Leibing, 2004).	Randomized outcome studies
	Marital psychotherapy	Behavioral marital therapy is effective for treating co-occurring marital distress and depression (Beach, 2001; Cordova, Warren, and Gee, 2001; Prince and Jacobsen, 1995).	Randomized outcome studies
	Clinical evaluation of one to three visits	For patients who do meet criteria for complexity, an extended two or three visits can help identify those whose depressive symptoms may be transient.	Expert opinion

Table 7.C.10—Continued

VA/DoD Clinical Practice Guidelines	VA/DoD Interventions	Evidence from the Literature	Level of Evidence

	Psychosocial interventions described as beneficial, although not established empirically as treatments for major depressive disorder:
	    Spiritual counseling
	    Family therapy
	    Grief therapy
	    Ancillary services
	    Vocational therapy
	    Financial/money management or socioeconomic assistance
			Expert opinion

	Avoid:
	    Long-term therapy (psychodynamic treatment)
	    Brief supportive counseling
		There is no evidence that long-term psychodynamic treatment and brief supportive counseling are effective treatments of depression.	None

	Pharmacotherapy	Improves symptoms for many patients. Few differences between SSRIs and TCAs, but TCAs are more effective than SSRIs in inpatient populations (Anderson, 2000; Arroll et al., 2005; Bech et al., 2000).	Randomized outcome studies
	Electroconvulsive therapy	Effective for patients with severe depression (Abrams, 2002).	Randomized outcome studies
	Combined psychotherapy and pharmacotherapy	Combined treatment may be more effective than a single treatment for treating chronic depression (Friedman et al., 2004; De Maat et al., 2006), and adding CBT to medication may help prevent relapse (Friedman et al., 2004).	Randomized outcome studies
	Continuation and maintenance treatment	Continuation and maintenance-phase treatments are discussed in the context of all treatments for MDD to prevent relapse and recurrence of symptoms.	Randomized outcome studies

Table 7.C.10—Continued

VA/DoD Clinical Practice Guidelines	VA/DoD Interventions	Evidence from the Literature	Level of Evidence

	Continuation-phase treatment:
	  Sustaining the dose of medication resulting in acute-phase symptom remission
	  Preventing relapse or recurrence of depressive symptoms
	  Monitoring depressive symptoms and functional status
	  Building a constructive therapeutic alliance
	  Maintenance plan should be developed during the course of therapy:
	    •Summary of learning that occurred during therapy
	    •Ways patient will continue to use lessons from the therapy
	  Prediction of times of high recurrence
	  Coping approaches for such crisis periods
	  Use of booster sessions, occasional reassessment of depressive symptoms
	
	Maintenance-phase treatment:
	  For those with 3 or more MDD episodes or 2 or more with another risk factor for recurrence should remain on prophylactic antidepressant medication for one or more years following remission of acute episodes at continuation-phase dosage		

	For an inpatient mental health setting, guidelines suggest
	  Developing an Interdisciplinary Treatment Plan
	    Psychiatry
	    PCP
	    Medical specialists (for co-occurring illness)
	    Psychology
	    Social work
	    Nursing
	    Pharmacist
	    Dietary
	    Occupational therapy
	    Recreational therapy
	    Vocational rehabilitation
	    Chaplaincy
		It is preferable to have one provider coordinate the patient's care and consult with the team. Collaborative management of MDD improves symptoms of depression and treatment adherence (Fann et al., 1995).	Randomized outcome studies

Table 7.C.10—Continued

VA/DoD Clinical Practice Guidelines	VA/DoD Interventions	Evidence from the Literature	Level of Evidence
Acute suicide risk, acute violence risk due to mental illness, grave disablement due to mental illness	Inpatient hospitalization: Specialized treatments only available or best provided in a hospital include: electro-convulsive therapy (ECT) close monitoring and daily titration of medication with disabling side effects or toxicity constant staff observation as part of an intensive behavior-modification program close monitoring of behavior in an episodic disorder close monitoring of vital signs or need for multiple daily laboratory or electrophysiological testing		Expert opinion, randomized outcome studies

depression and is as effective as ECT in reducing depressive symptoms. Table 7.C.10 compares the guidelines to the evidence base.

Training. Many studies have measured patient adherence to treatment and the competence with which treatment is delivered (DeRubeis et al., 2005; Dimidjian et al., 2006). Some studies have found that the therapist's expertise can make a difference in the patient's improvement, particularly when the patient's depression is more severe and difficult to treat (DeRubeis et al., 2005; Hollon, Thase, and Markowitz, 2002; Jane-Llopis et al., 2003). For example, for CT, the quality of the treatment is important and it may be difficult to provide high-quality CT, even in clinical trials. Hollon, Thase, and Markowitz (2002) report that therapists at different sites did less well because they had less experience; however, they "caught up" with other, more-experienced therapists as they received additional training and experience. These authors do not provide details on the amount of training and experience required to increase the quality of implementation of the psychotherapy (in this case, CT).

Other research has also shown that training can affect remission. A large meta-analysis found that patients with severe depression had better outcomes when they were treated by trained personnel instead of by lay personnel (Jane-Llopis et al., 2003). The VA/DoD guidelines mention training briefly when they discuss psychotherapy, indicating that "referral should be made to a therapist experienced in the use of at least one of these [evidence-based] psychotherapies for the treatment of depression" (Veterans Health Administration, 2004, p. 135).

Traumatic Brain Injury (TBI)

Literature Review. To find studies that focused on treatment of TBI, we conducted a literature review, using PubMED (MEDLINE), PsychINFO, and GoogleScholar and limiting our searches to English-language articles from 1998 to the present. We also found additional references within the papers and used sources from the papers that we thought would provide further background, regardless of the year of publication. We used the following search terms: "traumatic brain injury"; "brain injury"; "head injury"; "TBI"; "post concussion syndrome"; "post concussional disorder."

When possible, we selected articles that focused on treatments among a military population; however, we also reviewed the literature focusing on civilian populations. Ultimately, we reviewed 25 treatment-outcome studies, 14 meta-analyses and reviews, and seven sets of treatment guidelines. Below, we summarize the evidence of effectiveness for each treatment, based on our review findings.

Description of TBI. Traumatic brain injury (TBI) is the most common cause of death and chronic disability for people under the age of 35 (Ministry of Health [Singapore], no date). In the United States, the estimated annual incidence of hospitalizations for TBI is approximately 200 per 100,000 persons (Chua et al., 2007).

Severity of TBI is an important determinant of outcome (*Veterans Health Initiative*, 2004). *Severity* (e.g., mild, moderate, severe) is defined by using one of three indexes: score on the Glasgow Coma Scale (GCS), which reflects the patient's eye-opening, motor, and verbal responses; length of loss of consciousness (LOC); and length of post-traumatic amnesia (PTA). The *GCS* is a 15-point scale based on ratings of the patient's best eye-opening, motor, and verbal responses. Lower scores indicate worse functioning. A score of GCS 13 to 15 is considered mild injury, a score of 9 to 12 denotes moderate injury, and a score of 3 to 8 denotes severe injury. *Loss of consciousness* is assessed as the length of time the patient is nonresponsive, with longer nonresponsive times associated with more severe TBI. *Post-traumatic amnesia* is the interval from when the person regains consciousness until he/she is able to form memories for ongoing events. A PTA of more than 24 hours is deemed severe TBI, and PTA duration of more than four weeks is indicative of a very severe brain injury (Lewin, Marshall, and Roberts, 1979).

Mild TBI. Approximately 80 percent of patients with TBIs have mild TBI (Alexander, 1995). Diagnostic criteria for mild TBI include loss of consciousness (for less than 30 minutes), memory loss (for less than 24 hours), and no persistent neurological deficits (Kay et al., 1993).

For the majority of individuals, symptoms of mild TBI have usually resolved by three months after injury (Levin, Mattis, and Ruff, 1987; Rutherford, 1989); however, there is a substantial literature indicating that symptoms may last for six to 12 months or longer in some cases (R. W. Evans, 1992; J. H. Jones et al., 1992; Leininger et al., 1990). Such individuals may need ongoing medical treatment (Jay, Goka, and Arakaki, 1996). The most common physical problems following mild TBI include the following:

1. headache and musculoskeletal pain
2. disturbance of the vestibular system, which controls eye movements and equilibrium
3. visual disturbance
4. fatigue.

Common cognitive, emotional, and behavioral signs and symptoms include the following (Jay, Goka, and Arakaki, 1996):

- memory impairment
- depression/ irritability/anxiety
- loss of self-esteem
- job loss/disruption
- denial
- difficulties with social interactions
- strained family relationships
- lack of initiative
- problems findings words
- decreased ability to concentrate
- poor impulse control
- slowed information processing
- behavioral/personality changes
- uncontrolled repetition of a response despite absence of the stimulus (perserveration).

Moderate to Severe TBI. Recovery after moderate to severe TBI is variable and depends on a variety of factors, including the extent and degree of the initial injury (*Veterans Health Initiative*, 2004). The Rancho Los Amigos Levels of Cognitive Functioning Scale (Hagan et al., 1979) is typically used to characterize the level of functioning and the level of cognitive and behavioral impairment after moderate to severe TBI (see Table 7.C.11). The scale can be used as a tool to make recommendations about where a patient should receive care and to demonstrate to family the different stages of recovery.

Acute and chronic symptoms associated with TBI include physical, emotional, and cognitive complaints, which are referred to as *post-concussion syndrome* (*Veterans Health Initiative*, 2004). Defining symptoms for this syndrome include the following:

- head injury with concussion (see definition below)
- attention or memory difficulties on formal testing
- three or more of the following symptoms: fatigue, sleep disorders, headache, dizziness, irritability, anxiety/depression, personality changes, poor social or occupational functioning.

Table 7.C.11
Rancho Los Amigos Levels of Cognitive Functioning Scale

Level	Description[a]	Care at This Level[b]
I	No response	Unresponsive to sound, light, touch, or pain. The individual appears to be in a deep sleep.	Care is focused on preventing complications.
II	Generalized Response	Individual reacts inconsistently in a nonspecific manner to stimulation. May be gross body movements, unintelligible vocalizations, etc. Earliest response is frequently to severe pain. Responses to stimuli often are delayed.	Increase level of responsiveness, initiation of responses, localization of specificity of responses. Sensory stimulation is used.
III	Localized Response	Reacts to specific stimuli (e.g., eye blink to strong light, turns toward sound). Responses are often inconsistent. May inconsistently follow simple, direct commands (e.g., close your eyes, squeeze my fingers).	Begin to work on simple activities of daily living (ADLs), such as face washing. Work on mobility and truncal stability. Establish voice and stimulate swallowing.
IV	Confused—Agitated	Alert and active but has severely limited ability to process information. Disoriented and responds primarily to internal stimuli. Behavior is bizarre or not purposeful, and the ability to focus and sustain attention is extremely limited. Does not differentiate among people or objects. Speech may be incoherent or bizarre. Short-term memory is impaired: Patient may fill memory gaps with fabrications.	Reduce agitation and increase consistency and functionality of responses. Work on functional activities, such as activities of daily living, mobility, and establishing a consistent yes/no response.
V	Confused—Inappropriate	Alert and active and can respond consistently to simple commands. Disoriented and requires redirection but is not responding primarily to internal stimuli. Short-term memory is impaired; patient may fill memory gaps with fabrications. May be able to perform basic activities of daily living with assistance and supervision.	Work on attention, memory, and *executive functions* (i.e., brain processes that guide behavior). Work on functional activities and assist with dressing and grooming.
VI	Confused—Appropriate	Alert and inconsistently oriented. Follows simple directions consistently and begins to show carryover of new learning. Recognizes staff and has increased awareness of self, family, and others.	Decrease confusion; improve independence, cognition, and information-processing speed. May require cues or checklists to complete activities of daily living.
VII	Automatic—Appropriate	Alert and oriented to person, place, and time but shows a shallow awareness of medical condition. Performs self-care and daily routines with supervision but in a robotlike manner. Performance may deteriorate in unfamiliar circumstances. Can remember and use new information but at a reduced rate. Judgment and problem-solving remain impaired.	Appropriate in highly structured environment, but still shows impaired judgment and limited insight into deficits.

Table 7.C.11—Continued

Level		Description[a]	Care at This Level[b]
VIII	Purposeful—Appropriate	Alert and oriented. Can recall and integrate past and current events. Shows carryover of new learning and is independent, within physical limitations, at home and in the community. Cognitive abilities may still be lower than premorbid levels.	Able to better function without supervision. Treatment at this level could be provided in an outpatient setting. Focus on ADLs, education for safe participation in leisure activities. Provide references for community resources. Provide continued exposure to community activities, increasing the individual's responsibility for planning and carrying out the activities.

[a] Adapted from C. D. Hagan, D. Malkus, P. Durham, and K. Bowman, Levels of cognitive functioning, in *Rehabilitation of the Head-Injured Adult: Comprehensive Physical Management.* Downey, Calif.: Professional Staff Association, Rancho Los Amigos Hospital, 1979.

[b] Adapted from *Veterans Health Initiative, Traumatic Brain Injury—Independent Study Course,* Washington, D.C.: Department of Veterans Affairs, 2004.

Additional Symptoms. Other symptoms of TBI include nausea/vomiting; hearing loss, tinnitus; visual changes (blurry vision, diplopia, difficulty focusing, visual-field cuts); focal neurological changes (e.g., weakness, sensory changes, reflex changes); imbalance/problems with coordination; and a variety of cognitive and language disorders.

None of these additional symptoms is unique to mild, moderate, or severe TBI. However, severity of cognitive dysfunction tends to increase with the severity of the TBI. In addition, focal neurological problems (e.g. hemiparesis, visual-field cuts, neglect, language problems [aphasia]) tend to occur in patients who have more focal lesions, which are more consistent with more severe TBI.

Concussion. *Concussion* is a complex pathophysiological process affecting the brain, caused by a direct blow to the head, face or neck, or elsewhere on the body, with force transmitted to the head. Defining features of concussion include the following:

- Rapid onset of short-lived impairment of neurological function that resolves spontaneously
- Neurological changes, but symptoms largely reflect a functional disturbance rather than structural injury
- May or may not involve loss of consciousness
- Normal neuroimaging studies.

TBI in the Afghanistan and Iraq Conflicts. Compared with soldiers in previous wars, a greater percentage of soldiers in the Afghanistan and Iraq conflicts who are wounded in combat have TBI. The Joint Theater Trauma Registry, which is compiled by the U.S. Army Institute of Surgical Research, reported that 22 percent of wounded soldiers from the conflicts in Afghanistan and Iraq have had injuries to the head, face, or neck (Okie, 2005). However, prevalence of TBI is probably higher because some cases of closed brain injury, caused by hard blows to the head, are not diagnosed properly (Okie, 2005).

There are three basic reasons for the higher proportion of TBIs among soldiers wounded in the current conflicts. First, the Kevlar body armor and helmets protect soldiers from bullets and shrapnel, improving overall survival rates; however, the helmets cannot prevent closed brain injuries or completely protect the face, head, and neck (Okie, 2005). Second, both medical and lay communities are more knowledgeable about brain injuries, and more-extensive literature is available on concussion and mild TBI (Warden, 2006), making diagnosis more likely. Third, explosive devices are used more extensively in the current conflicts, leading to blast injuries (Army Medical Department [AMEDD] evacuation statistics, OEF/OIF).

All of these factors contribute to the increased number of TBIs in the current conflicts—more than 2,000 documented cases since the conflicts began (Grady, 2006; PCCWW, 2007). A recent analysis of 433 individuals with TBI who were treated at the Walter Reed Army Medical Center indicated that mild TBI accounted for less than half the sample, and 56 percent of the group had moderate and severe TBI. Closed brain TBI accounted for 88 percent of the total group (Warden, 2006). These numbers may reflect selection bias, because the people being screened at Walter Reed had more severe injuries overall (not just TBI), which is why they were at that facility. Thus, even this high rate of moderate and severe TBI may not accurately reflect the rate overall (personal communication with Michael Yochelson, M.D., Director, Head Injury Program, National Rehabilitation Hospital, November 2007).

Guidelines for Treatment of TBI. *Cardiopulmonary resuscitation* is the first priority in initial care of the brain-injured patient. Next is *control of intracranial pressure* to maintain oxygen flow to the brain (Chua et al., 2007). A panel of 22 experts, assembled by the Brain Trauma Foundation (2007), developed TBI treatment guidelines. The panel conducted comprehensive electronic database searches of the neurotrauma literature up to April 2006. Two experts independently reviewed each study and classified it according to the level of evidence available, which in turn suggests the level of confidence with which study findings can be viewed.

The levels of recommendations defined by the panel reflect these levels of confidence:

- Level I recommendations represent principles of patient management that reflect a high degree of clinician certainty.
- Level II recommendations reflect a moderate degree of clinical certainty.
- For Level III recommendations, the degree of clinical certainty is not established.

There is only one Level I recommendation: Steroids should not be used to manage increased intracranial pressure. Details of the panel's clinical recommendations and the evidence to support them are described in Table 7.C.12.

Guidelines and Practice Standards for TBI Rehabilitation. We now focus on rehabilitation for TBI patients, describing the types of rehabilitative services often used, including visual-spatial, cognitive, linguistic, and emotional and behavioral.

Rehabilitation involves several domains, including physical, communication and language, vocational, sexual, and cognitive domains (National Guideline Clearinghouse, 2007). For example, individuals can experience physical complications, such as seizures, neuroendocrine dysfunction, and gastrointestinal complications. They may also have cognitive difficulties, such as problems with attention and concentration, reasoning and problem-solving, and/or memory.

Various assessment instruments can help track improvements in overall responsiveness. It is also important to conduct a neuropsychological evaluation, which includes measures of general intelligence, attention and concentration, learning and memory, language, visual-spatial abilities, and *executive functions* (e.g., brain processes

Table 7.C.12
TBI Treatment Recommendations and Supporting Evidence

Treatment Guideline and Level	Summary of Supporting Evidence
Blood-pressure regulation and oxygenation *Level I:* There are insufficient data to support a Level I recommendation. *Level II:* Blood pressure should be monitored and hypotension avoided. *Level III:* Oxygenation should be monitored and hypoxia avoided.	In TBI patients, secondary brain injury may result from systemic hypotension and hypoxemia (Cooke, McNicholl, and Byrnes, 1995; Stochetti, Furlan, and Volta, 1996), which can increase morbidity and mortality (Brain Trauma Foundation, American Association of Neurological Surgeons, and Congress of Neurological Surgeons, 2007). Clinical intuition indicates that correcting hypotension and hypoxemia improves outcomes; however, clinical studies have not provided supporting data (Brain Trauma Foundation et al., 2007).
Hyperosmolar therapy *Level I:* There are insufficient data to support a Level I recommendation. *Level II:* Mannitol is effective for controlling raised intracranial pressure (ICP) at doses of 0.25 gm/kg to 1 g/kg body weight. Arterial hypotension should be avoided. *Level III:* Restrict mannitol use prior to ICP monitoring to patients with signs of transtentorial herniation or progressive neurological deterioration not attributable to extracranial causes.	Mannitol is widely used to control raised ICP following TBI. Its use is advocated in two circumstances: A single short-term administration can have short-term benefits, during which further diagnostic procedures (e.g., computerized tomography [CT] scan) and interventions (e.g., evacuation of intracranial mass lesions) can be accomplished. Mannitol has also been used as a prolonged therapy for raised ICP. There is no evidence to recommend repeated, regular administration of mannitol over several days (Brain Trauma Foundation et al., 2007). Current evidence is not sufficient to make recommendations on use, concentration, and method of administration of hypertonic saline for the treatment of traumatic intracranial hypertension.
Infection prophylaxis *Level I:* There are insufficient data to support a Level I recommendation. *Level II:* Periprocedural antibiotics for intubation should be administered to reduce the incidence of pneumonia. However, they do not change length of stay or mortality. *Level III:* Routine ventricular catheter exchange or prophylactic antibiotic use for ventricular catheter placement is not recommended to reduce infection. Early extubation in qualified patients can be done without increased risk of pneumonia.	There is no support for use of prolonged antibiotics for systemic prophylaxis in intubated TBI patients, given the risk of selecting for resistant organisms. A single study supports the use of a short course of antibiotics at the time of intubation to reduce the incidence of pneumonia (Brain Trauma Foundation et al., 2007).

Table 7.C.12—Continued

Treatment Guideline and Level	Summary of Supporting Evidence
Deep-vein thrombosis (DVT) prophylaxis *Level I*: There are insufficient data to support a Level I recommendation. *Level II*: There are insufficient data to support a Level II recommendation. *Level III*: Graduated compression stockings or intermittent pneumatic compression stockings are recommended, unless lower-extremity injuries prevent their use. Use should be continued until patients are ambulatory. Low molecular weight heparin or low-dose unfractionated heparin should be used in combination with mechanical prophylaxis. However, there is an increased risk for expansion of intracranial hemorrhage. There is insufficient evidence to support recommendations regarding the preferred agent, dose, or timing of pharmacologic prophylaxis for DVT.	
Indications for intracranial monitoring *Level I*: There are insufficient data to support a Level I recommendation. *Level II*: Intracranial pressure should be monitored in all salvageable patients with a severe TBI and an abnormal CT. An *abnormal CT scan* of the head is one that reveals hematomas, contusions, swelling, herniation, or compressed basal cisterns. *Level III*: ICP monitoring is indicated in patients with severe TBI with a normal CT scan if two or more of the following features are noted at admission: age over 40 years, unilateral or bilateral motor posturing, or systolic blood pressure <90 mm Hg.	There is evidence to support the use of ICP monitoring in severe TBI patients at risk for intracranial hypotension.
Intracranial pressure thresholds *Level I*: There are insufficient data to support a Level I recommendation. *Level II*: Treatment should be initiated with ICP thresholds >20 mm Hg. *Level III*: A combination of ICP values and clinical and brain CT findings should be used to determine the need for treatment.	

Table 7.C.12—Continued

Treatment Guideline and Level	Summary of Supporting Evidence
Cerebral perfusion thresholds *Level I:* There are insufficient data to support a Level I recommendation. *Level II:* Aggressive attempts to maintain cerebral perfusion pressure (CPP) >70 mm Hg with fluids and pressors should be avoided because of the risk of adult respiratory distress. *Level III:* CPP of <50 mm Hg should be avoided. The CPP value to target lies within the range of 50–70 mm Hg. Patients with intact pressure autoregulation tolerate higher CPP values. Ancillary monitoring of cerebral parameters that include blood flow, oxygenation, or metabolism facilitates CPP management.	At this time, it is not possible to posit an optimal level of CPP to target to improve outcome in terms of avoiding clinical episodes of ischemia and minimizing the cerebral vascular contributions to ICP instability (Brain Trauma Foundation et al., 2007).
Brain oxygen monitoring and thresholds *Level I:* There are insufficient data to support a Level I recommendation. *Level II:* There are insufficient data to support a Level II recommendation. *Level III:* Jugular venous saturation (<50%) or brain tissue oxygen tension (<15 mm Hg) are treatment thresholds. Jugular venous saturation or brain tissue oxygen monitoring measures cerebral oxygenation.	
Anesthetics, analgesics, and sedatives *Level I:* There are insufficient data to support a Level I recommendation. *Level II:* Prophylactic administration of barbiturates to induce burst suppression electroencephalogram (EEG) is not recommended. High-dose barbiturate administration is recommended to control elevated ICP refractory to maximum standard medical and surgical treatment. Hemodynamic stability is essential before and during barbiturate therapy. Propofol is recommended for the control of ICP, but not for improvement in mortality or 6-month outcome. High-dose Propofol can produce significant morbidity.	Analgesics and sedatives are a common management strategy for ICP control, although there is no evidence to support their efficacy in this regard and they have not been shown to positively affect outcomes (Brain Trauma Foundation et al., 2007).
Nutrition *Level I:* There are insufficient data to support a Level I recommendation. *Level II:* Patients should be fed to attain full caloric replacement by day 7 post-injury.	Data indicate that feeding should occur by the end of the first week. There is no established documentation that one method of feeding is better than another or that early feeding prior to 7 days improves outcomes (Brain Trauma Foundation et al., 2007).

Table 7.C.12—Continued

Treatment Guideline and Level	Summary of Supporting Evidence
Antiseizure prophylaxis *Level I*: There are insufficient data to support a Level I recommendation. *Level II*: Prophylactic use of phenytoin or valproate is not recommended for preventing late post-traumatic seizures (PTS). Anticonvulsants are indicated to decrease the incidence of early PTS (within 7 days of injury). However, early PTS is not associated with worse outcomes.	The rationale for use of seizure prophylaxis is that TBI patients experience a relatively high incidence of PTS and there are benefits to preventing seizures following TBI (Temkin, Dikmen, and Winn, 1991; Yablon, 1993). Although treatment with anticonvulsants can reduce incidence of early post-injury seizures, there is no support for the use of anticonvulsants for the prevention of late PTS; therefore, it is not currently recommended (Brain Trauma Foundation et al., 2007; Bullock et al., 1996; Schierhout and Roberts, 2001).
Hyperventilation *Level I*: There are insufficient data to support a Level I recommendation. *Level II*: Prophylactic hyperventilation (PaCO2 of ≤25 mm Hg) is not recommended. *Level III*: Hyperventilation is recommended as a temporizing measure for the reduction of elevated ICP. Hyperventilation should be avoided during the first 24 hours after injury, when cerebral blood flow is often critically reduced. If hyperventilation is used, jugular venous oxygen saturation or brain tissue oxygen tension measurements are recommended to monitor oxygen delivery.	Hyperventilation is *not* recommended in the first 24 hours after severe brain injury, because it causes cerebral vasoconstriction and reduces CPP (Chua et al., 2007).
Steroids *Level I*: The use of steroids is not recommended for improving or reducing intracranial pressure. In patients with moderate or severe TBI, high-dose methlyprednisolone is associated with increased mortality and is contraindicated.	Routine use of steroids is *not* recommended (Roberts, 2000; Whyte et al., 2005).

SOURCE: Adapted from Brain Trauma Foundation, American Association of Neurological Surgeons, and Congress of Neurological Surgeons. Guidelines for the management of severe and traumatic brain injury, 3rd edition. *Journal of Neurotrauama*, Vol. 24, 2007.

NOTE: Level I recommendations present principles of patient management that reflect a high degree of clinical certainty; Level II recommendations reflect a moderate degree of clinical certainty. For Level III recommendations, the degree of clinical certainty is not established.

that guide behavior). Sometimes, cognitive deficits can be managed by medication. The most commonly used medications are neurostimulants, antidepressants, SSRIs, dopaminergic agents, and cholinesterase inhibitors. However, the scientific literature shows no pharmacological intervention to improve post-TBI cognitive deficits (*Veterans Health Initiative*, 2004).

Emotional and behavioral problems are also common after TBI. Therapies for addressing these problems include cognitive-behavioral interventions, such as self-monitoring, relaxation techniques, and anger management; supportive therapies that address issues of poor self-esteem; family or marital therapy; spiritual guidance; and education (*Veterans Health Initiative*, 2004). Obtaining collateral information from family members is important, because many individuals with TBI are not aware of their impairments.

Turner-Stokes and Wade (2004) provide summary guidelines for assessment, treatment, and referral to rehabilitation (see Figure 7.C.1).

Rehabilitation for Mild TBI. Treatment of mild TBI includes education, a period of rest and observation, and treatment of persistent or disabling symptoms, such as headache (*Veterans Health Initiative*, 2004).

Pharmacologic interventions can be used to treat specific symptoms, such as headache and sleep disorder. Typically, post-traumatic headache is treated with nonsteroidal anti-inflammatory drugs (e.g., aspirin, ibuprofen, sodium naproxen), Midrin, and triptans. Individuals who experience headaches and problems with depression, anger, irritability etc., may benefit from valproate acid. Selective serotonin reuptake inhibitors may help to alleviate depression and irritability following TBI (Fann, Uomoto, and Katon, 2001).

Nonpharmacologic interventions include providing individuals with educational materials regarding such symptoms as fatigue, irritability, and mood swings. It is also important to provide referrals for additional assessment (e.g., audiologist, speech and language pathologist, psychiatrist).

Rehabilitation for Moderate to Severe TBI. Following acute emergency care and medical stabilization, individuals with moderate to severe TBI usually require a period of inpatient rehabilitation. Such services are best provided in an established interdisciplinary brain-injury program. The goal in the early rehabilitation phase is to help the individual restore maximal functional independence. Comprehensive, integrated post-acute programs are designed to serve clients with impaired awareness and other cognitive and behavioral difficulties (Sander et al., 2001). Patients who participate in these types of programs tend to show positive changes and improved functioning in independent living, productivity, and social functioning at both discharge (Prigatano et al., 1994) and over the longer term (Sander et al., 2001). As length of stay in inpatient rehabilitation after TBI has decreased, post-acute rehabilitation programs have become increasingly important in helping patients return to their homes and communities

Figure 7.C.1
Overview of Assessment, Treatment, and Rehabilitation Referral for TBI Patients

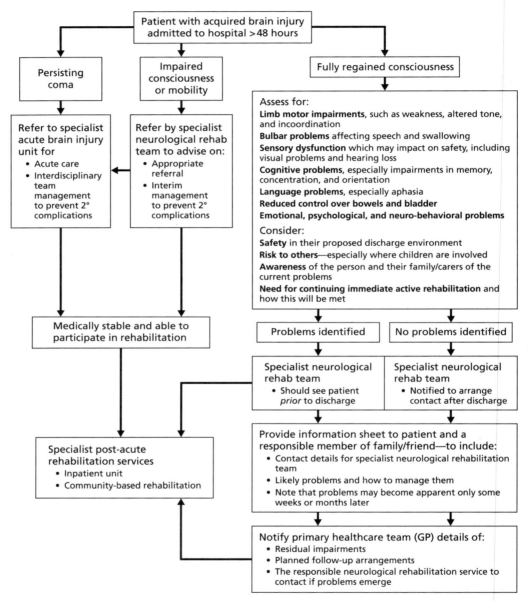

SOURCE: L. Turner-Stokes and D. Wade. Rehabilitation following acquired brain injury: Concise guidance. *Clinical Medicine*, Vol. 4, No. 5, January 2004, Figure 1, p. 65. Copyright © 2004 Royal College of Physicians. Reproduced with permission.
RAND *MG720-7C.1*

(Sander et al., 2001). In addition, long-term services may help prevent decline in individual cases (Sander et al., 2001).

When patients are in pain, the drug of choice is the one that controls the pain most effectively with the fewest central nervous system effects and drug-drug interactions. Acetaminophen is often used because it is safe, inexpensive, and has very little central nervous system interaction. Many hospitals automatically order it to be given on an as-needed basis so that nurses do not have to call doctors; at home, people can buy it over the counter. Acetaminophen is administered using a dosing schedule rather than on-demand dosing (*Veterans Health Initiative*, 2004).

Early rehabilitation for moderate to severe TBI includes

1. getting patients out of bed and into street clothes (i.e., not hospital gowns)
2. avoiding over- or understimulation
3. avoiding cognitively impairing medications; using cognitively stimulating ones
4. using behavior-modifying therapies and medications
5. assessing and managing pain regularly
6. removing the catheter early and helping to use the bathroom as often as needed.

Inpatient interdisciplinary programs generally provide three hours or more of formal therapy (physical, occupational, speech, recreational, neuropsychological) per day. Such programs include therapists and nurses, along with the patient, the patient's family, and the doctor all working together to reach common goals (*Veterans Health Initiative*, 2004).

Because co-occurring problems may impede the rehabilitation process, they should be assessed and managed. Common co-occurring problems include, but are not limited to, wound care; pressure sores; spasticity; post-traumatic epilepsy; associated orthopedic injuries (e.g., fractures); heterotopic ossification (bone formation around a joint); deep venous thrombosis; and such infections as of the urinary tract or pneumonia.

Approaches to Community Integrated Rehabilitation. Trudel, Nidiffer, and Barth (2007) provide a framework for community integrated rehabilitation that is based on work by Malec and Basford (1996). *Community rehabilitation* should include neurobehavioral programs, residential programs, comprehensive holistic day-treatment programs, and home-based programs. Briefly, *neurobehavioral programs* focus on treating mood, behavior, and executive functions in a safe residential, nonhospital setting. These programs, which typically have interdisciplinary teams, emphasize development of functional skills (Wood et al., 1999). Residential programs were initially developed for individuals who required extended rehabilitation and 24-hour supervision but did not have access to adequate outpatient services. More recently, the lines have been blurred between neurobehavioral and community programs (Trudel, Nidiffer, and

Barth, 2007). Comprehensive holistic day-treatment programs target awareness, cognitive functions, social skills, and vocational preparation through individual, group, and family interventions delivered by an interdisciplinary team (Ben-Yishay et al., 1987). Finally, home-based programs involve a variety of services and supports so that the individual can live at home. There is usually no identified treatment team, although a number of health- and social-service systems may be collaborating to provide treatment (Vander Laan et al., 2001).

Levels of Evidence Supporting Treatment. In the following discussion, we describe the evidence for the effectiveness of specific TBI treatments.

Patient Education. Comper et al. (2005) reviewed seven studies in which patients were given an information intervention. The interventions included reassurance, information on the recovery process, or strategies for managing mild-TBI symptoms. Comper and associates found sufficient evidence to conclude that interacting with patients in a supportive way and providing information about symptoms were effective in helping individuals recover from mild TBI

Cognitive Rehabilitation. *Cognitive rehabilitation* is "a systematic functionally oriented service of therapeutic activities that is based on assessment and understanding of the patient's brain-behavioral deficits" (Cicerone et al., 2000, pp. 1596–1597). Personality and behavioral change are fairly common after TBI (Ommaya et al., 1996).

Cicerone and colleagues (2000) reviewed 655 articles on standards, guidelines, and options for cognitive rehabilitation. Of the 29 randomized controlled studies they found, 20 provided clear evidence that cognitive rehabilitation is effective. Of 64 controlled studies that were reviewed, only two studies failed to show improved functioning among participants who received cognitive rehabilitation (Cicerone et al., 2000).

A 2003 report from the members of the Task Force on Cognitive Rehabilitation (Cappa et al., 2003) reviewed the available evidence on the effectiveness of cognitive rehabilitation. They noted that there are few studies in this area and that the studies are often of poor quality. However, the task-force report concluded that there is evidence, of varying levels, for some forms of cognitive rehabilitation in patients with TBI. These forms include aphasia therapy, rehabilitation of unilateral spatial neglect, attentional training in the post-acute stage after TBI, the use of electronic memory aids in memory disorders, and the treatment of apraxia with compensatory strategies (Cappa et al., 2003).

Turner-Stokes and Wade (2004) suggest that there is good evidence for the effectiveness (Chesnut et al., 1999; High, Boake, and Lehmkuhl, 1995; Turner-Stokes, 1999) and cost benefits (Cardenas et al., 2001) of rehabilitation. For example, studies have shown that cognitive-behavioral psychotherapy and cognitive remediation therapy can diminish psychological distress and improve functioning among mild and moderate TBI patients (Tiersky et al., 2005). In addition, studies have shown the importance of beginning post-acute rehabilitation as early as possible, because receiving treatment early can substantially improve outcomes (High et al., 2006). Studies have also shown that increasing the intensity of rehabilitation therapy can accelerate recovery of personal independence, enhance functional recovery, and shorten hospital stays (Shiel et al., 2001). Furthermore, patients who receive intensive cognitive rehabilitation show clinically significant improvement in their community functioning compared with patients who receive standard neurorehabilitation (Cicerone et al., 2004).

A 2007 Cochrane review (Turner-Stokes et al., 2007) assessed the effects of multidisciplinary rehabilitation following brain injury in adults ages 16 to 65. They found ten trials of good methodological quality. Overall, for mild TBI, providing information and advice was usually more appropriate than having the person undergo intensive rehabilitation. For the groups with moderate to severe TBI, there was strong evidence that more intensive programs produced earlier functional gains. There was moderate evidence that continued outpatient therapy could help sustain the gains made in early post-acute rehabilitation.

Rehabilitation appears to be most effective when the relevant health- and social-care practitioners work as a coordinated interdisciplinary team toward a common set of goals (Langhorne and Duncan, 2001). More research is needed on effective approaches to rehabilitation, in part because rehabilitation is an individual and long-term process, which makes it difficult to draw general conclusions (Turner-Stokes et al., 2007). The small numbers and heterogeneity of brain-injured patients pose additional challenges (Turner-Stokes and Wade, 2004).

Pharmacotherapy. Comper and colleagues (2005) conducted one of the most recent reviews of treatments for mild traumatic brain injury. The results for pharmacotherapy were based on eight studies that evaluated use of a wide range of drugs, including the antidepressant amitriptyline as a treatment for both depression and headaches; sertraline; dihydroergotamine, which is a migraine-abortive preparation; and the antidiuretic medication desmopressin acetate to improve mental performance. They concluded that there is no solid evidence that any specific drug treatment is effective for one or more symptoms of mild TBI.

Chang and Lowenstein (2003) reviewed studies on antiepileptic drug prophylaxis in severe traumatic brain injury. They found that, for adult patients with severe TBI, prophylaxis with phenytoin was effective in decreasing the risk of early post-traumatic seizures, but it was not effective in preventing late post-traumatic seizures. They suggest that further studies are needed for mild TBI and the use of newer antiepileptic drugs.

Progesterone. A recent pilot clinical trial assessed the potential safety and benefit of administering progesterone to patients with acute TBI: Laboratory evidence suggests that progesterone has neuroprotective effects (Wright et al., 2007). The trial established that progesterone caused no discernable harm and appeared to have some potential benefit.

Corticosteroids. Alderson and Roberts (1997) reviewed studies of corticosteroids to treat acute TBI using randomized trials available by March 1996. It is known that in the acute period of TBI, corticosteroids are not recommended for improving or reducing increased intracranial pressure (Roberts, 2000; Whyte et al., 2005). Alderson and Roberts confirmed that, despite 25 years of randomized controlled trials in this area, the effectiveness of using corticosteroids to treat TBI patients after this acute period is still unclear.

Excitatory Amino Acid Inhibitors. Willis, Lybrand, and Bellamy (2007) conducted a review to assess the efficacy of excitatory amino acid inhibitors on improving patient outcomes following brain injury. Of the 12 trials they found that fit the criteria of being randomized, double-blind controlled trials, data were available for two of these trials. They did not find any differences in mortality between those patients who received excitatory amino acid inhibitors and those who received placebo; therefore, they conclude that efficacy for excitatory amino acid inhibitors remains unproven.

Hypothermia. Harris and colleagues (2002) conducted a meta-analysis of the role of hypothermia in the management of severe brain injury. Their review of studies in this area indicated that hypothermia is not beneficial in the management of severe head injury.

VA/DoD Guidelines for TBI. Table 7.C.13 describes the current VA/DoD practice guidelines for TBI treatment. The guidelines are very broad and do not directly address specific cognitive and behavioral interventions that are reported in the rehabilitation literature.

Training. There are currently no guidelines that specifically address training. Expert opinion suggests that training should include the following (personal communication with Michael Yochelson, M.D., November 2007):

1. Medical Directors for an inpatient or outpatient TBI program should have completed a residency in Physical Medicine and Rehabilitation (PM&R) or neurology and either (a) a fellowship in either neurorehabilitation or brain-injury rehabilitation or (b) have at least one year's experience in the field.

2. Physicians practicing inpatient or outpatient TBI rehabilitation should have completed a residency in PM&R or neurology that included TBI rehabilitation training or have worked with a physician with experience in the field for at least three months. Physicians in other fields with an interest in TBI should either take continuing medical education (CME) courses in the field or work closely for at least six months with a physician who has experience in the field.

3. Psychologists or neuropsychologists who work in an inpatient or outpatient TBI program should have significant experience in evaluating and managing patients with TBI. They should also be experienced at performing and accurately interpreting neuropsychological examinations.

4. Physical and Occupational Therapists who work in an inpatient or outpatient TBI program should have at least six months' experience working with a therapist experienced in the rehabilitation of TBI patients.

Table 7.C.13
VA/DoD Guidelines for TBI Treatment

VA Clinical Practice Guidelines for TBI[a]	VA Interventions	Level of Evidence
Neurocognitive assessment	Use the Military Acute Concussion Evaluation tool	Expert opinion [evidence further suggests that formal neuropsychological testing by a *neuropsychologist or neurologist* is indicated when the assessment identifies abnormalities consistent with cognitive impairment]
Headache management	Use acetaminophen; avoid tramadol, narcotics, NSAIDs, ASA, or other platelet inhibitors until CT confirmed negative	Expert opinion [management of other symptoms (fatigue, inattention, agitation, depression, etc.) is also important]
Educational information	Provide educational information sheet to all positive mild-TBI patients	Expert opinion Some randomized outcome studies
Trauma care	Emergency Room /Trauma Center/ICU	Expert opinion
Specialized acute inpatient rehabilitation	High-intensity rehabilitation (3–5 hr/day in which patient actively participates)	Some randomized outcome studies
Sub-acute rehabilitation	Lower-intensity rehabilitation (<3 hr/day in which patient actively participates) Ventilator care Coma care	Some randomized outcome studies
Post-acute rehabilitation	Outpatient day treatment Home care	Some randomized outcome studies
Community re-entry	Transitional living Independent living Vocational rehabilitation Supportive employment	Some randomized outcome studies
Extended care	Skilled Nursing Facility Neurobehavioral management Assisted living Adult day care Respite care	Expert opinion

NOTE: NSAIDS = non-steroidal anti-inflammatory drugs; ASA = acetylsalicyclic acid (or aspirin).

[a] From *Veterans Health Initiative: Traumatic Brain Injury–Independent Study Course*, Washington, D.C.: Department of Veterans Affairs, 2004 (http:www1.va.gov/vhi/docs/TBI.pdf) and Defense and Veterans Brain Injury Center, Working Group on the Acute Management of Mild Traumatic Brain Injury in Military Operational Settings. *Clinical Practice Guidelines and Recommendations*, December 22, 2006.

5. Speech Language Pathologists who work in an inpatient or outpatient TBI program should have extensive experience in assessing cognitive function and in providing therapy aimed at improving cognitive function as well as language. They should have at least three months' experience working with a therapist experienced in the rehabilitation of TBI patients.

6. Nurses working in an inpatient TBI rehabilitation unit should have either a certificate in rehabilitation nursing or be supervised by a certified rehabilitation nurse for one year. Inpatient and outpatient nurses working with TBI patients should be trained to manage complications associated with TBI, including wound care management, spasticity management, and neurogenic bowel and bladder management, and to understand the general concepts of rehabilitation nursing.

All of the above-mentioned practitioners should receive annual training (e.g., continuing education) specifically related to TBI.

Training should be made available on an annual basis to non-TBI specialists (particularly to primary care providers: family practitioners, pediatricians, internists, physician's assistants, and nurse practitioners) who are practicing in the military or VA health care system. It is critical that these providers be able to recognize signs and symptoms of TBI, as well as late sequelae, and be able to manage the symptoms or refer the patient to the appropriate providers.

A recent report to the Surgeon General on TBI (Bradshaw et al., 2007) indicated that providers who are screening for or treating TBI have varying levels of experience with and knowledge about TBI. In addition, there are currently no policies related to education of providers in TBI treatment. This Surgeon General's task force recommended that a systemwide policy be developed to institute best practices for patients with TBI (Bradshaw et al., 2007). Once these best practices are developed, it will be easier to develop a training program for providers so that they can effectively recognize and treat TBI.

Appendix 7.D: Studies of Mental Health Services Utilization Among Servicemembers

Table 7.D.1
Studies of Mental Health Services Utilization Among Servicemembers

Type of Report	Sample (*n*)	Design	Disorders Studied	Utilization of Service	Other Utilization Information
Hoge C. W., C. A. Castro, S. C. Messer, D. McGurk, D. I. Cotting, and R. L. Koffman. Combat duty in Iraq and Afghanistan, mental health problems, and barriers to care. *New England Journal of Medicine*, Vol. 351, No. 1, July 2004, pp. 13–22.					
Peer-reviewed	Convenience sample of 3 Army units and 1 Marine Corps unit (6,201)	Cross-Sectional	Depression PTSD	Among those meeting screening criteria: Received Professional Help (% any professional/ % mental health professional) In past year: Pre-OIF Army: 28/15 Post-OEF Army: 23/13 Post-OIF Army: 40/27 Post-OIF Marine Corps: 29/21 In past month: Pre-OIF Army: 18/11 Post-OEF Army: 17/13 Post-OIF Army: 32/21 Post-OIF Marine Corps: 21/14	NA

Table 7.D.1—Continued

Type of Report	Sample (n)	Design	Disorders Studied	Utilization of Services	Other Utilization Info
				Hoge C. W., J. L. Auchterlonie, and C. S. Milliken. Mental health problems, use of mental health services, and attrition from military service after returning from deployment to Iraq or Afghanistan. *Journal of the American Medical Association*, Vol. 295, No. 9, 2006, pp. 1023–1032.	
Peer-reviewed	Army and Marine Corps (303,905)	Prospective	Depression PTSD	% with a mental health referral who utilized mental health treatment: •OIF 56.3% •OEF 48.2% •Other deployments 51.4% Among OIF veterans: 9,611 had a mental health referral indicated on the PDHA •5,216 (54.3%) of these were seen in a mental health clinic during follow-up. •2,978 (57.1% of those seen in a mental health clinic) received a mental health condition diagnosis. •192 (2%) of veterans with PDHA referrals were seen in a primary care setting and received a mental health diagnosis. Incidence rate of utilization of mental health services among OIF veterans: 346.2/1,000 persons/year (35%). •118.9/1,000 persons/year received mental health services •84.1/1,000 persons/year were given an ICD-9 code (290–219) •34.8/1,000 persons/year were given a v code for a mental health problem •227.3/1,000 persons/year visited a mental health clinic but did not receive a mental health condition diagnosis (general health exam or ill-defined condition code)	Significant increase in mental health service utilization (number of visits/1,000 individuals/year) over time: 145.3/1,000/year in 2000 175.3/1,000/year in 2001 199.8/1,000/year in 2002 218.8/1,000/year in 2003 222.3/1,000/year in 2004 The total number of mental health–related visits also increased annually: 687.1 in 2000 783.3 in 2001 858.4 in 2002 853.3 in 2003 887.5 in 2004

Table 7.D.1—Continued

Type of Report	Sample (n)	Design	Disorders Studied	Utilization of Services	Other Utilization Info
Kolkow, T. T., J. L. Spira, J. S. Morse, and T. A. Grieger. Post-traumatic stress disorder and depression in health care providers returning from deployment to Iraq and Afghanistan. *Military Medicine*, Vol. 172, No. 5, May 2007, pp. 451–455.					
Peer-reviewed	US Military Health Care Providers—Naval (previously deployed to Iraq or Afghanistan) (102)	Cross-Sectional	Depression PTSD	Mental Health Visits 10%—before enlistment 14%—1 year before deployment 16%—during deployment 32%—since returning from deployment Ongoing treatment 5%—before enlistment 3%—1 year before deployment 0%—during deployment 13%—since returning from deployment	NA
U.S. Department of the Army, Office of the Surgeon General. *Operation Iraqi Freedom (OIF-II) Mental Health Advisory Team (MHAT-I) Report*, Washington, D.C.: U.S. Army Surgeon General, D104.2:M 52/2, December 16, 2003.					
Government Report	Army (OIF 1) (756)		Depression PTSD	During deployment: 27% of those meeting screening criteria for mental health condition reported receiving help 32% of those interested in getting help actually received some form of help	NA
U.S. Department of the Army, Office of the Surgeon General. *Operation Iraqi Freedom (OIF-II) Mental Health Advisory Team (MHAT-II) Report*. Washington, D.C.: U.S. Army Surgeon General, D104.2:M 52/2, January 30, 2005.					
Government Report	Army (OIF II) (2,064)		Depression PTSD	During deployment: 40% of those meeting screening criteria for mental health condition reported receiving help	NA
U.S. Department of the Army, Office of the Surgeon, Multinational Force–Iraq and Office of the Surgeon General. *Mental Health Advisory Team (MHAT-III) Operation Iraqi Freedom 04–06 Report*. Washington, D.C., May 29, 2006a.					
Government Report	Army (OIF 04–06) (1,124)		Depression PTSD	During deployment: 30% reported receiving care	NA

Table 7.D.1—Continued

Type of Report	Sample (n)	Design	Disorders Studied	Utilization of Services	Other Utilization Info
U.S. Department of the Army, Office of the Surgeon, Multinational Force–Iraq and Office of the Surgeon General, U.S. Army Medical Command. *Mental Health Advisory Team (MHAT-IV) Operation Iraqi Freedom 05-07 Report*, Washington, D.C., November 17, 2006b.					
Government Report	Army, Marine Corps (OIF 05–07) (1,767)		Depression PTSD	During deployment: Among those meeting screening criteria for a mental health problem: 42% of soldiers sought mental health care 38% of marines sought mental health care	NA
Seal, K. H., D. Bertenthal, C. R. Miner, S. Sen, and C. Marmar. Bringing the war back home: Mental health disorders among 103,788 US veterans returning from Iraq and Afghanistan seen at Department of Veterans Affairs facilities. *Archives of Internal Medicine.* Vol. 167, No. 5, 2007, pp. 476–482.					
Peer-reviewed	OEF/OIF veterans (103,788)	Retrospective	PTSD	25% had an outpatient mental health visit 5% were seen in mental health clinics but did not receive a diagnosis 43% of those with an inpatient visit had a primary diagnosis of a mental disorder	Median time from first VA visit to mental health diagnosis was 13 days (interquartile range, 0–118 days)
Department of Defense Task Force on Mental Health. *An Achievable Vision: Report of the Department of Defense Task Force on Mental Health.* Falls Church, Va.: Defense Health Board, 2007.					
Government Report	NA			Mental health task force visits to providers revealed that patients followed up on referrals to mental health providers 90–100% of the time when that provider was located in a primary care setting. This rate dropped to 20–25% when the referral was made to a separate mental health clinic. Self-reported rates of substance use and treatment-seeking: According to anonymous Defense Survey of Health-Related Behaviors (Department of Defense, 2005), 23% of respondents acknowledged a significant alcohol problem; while Bray et al. (2005) found that only 15% actually seek treatment for a mental health issue.	NA

Table 7.D.1—Continued

Erbes, C., J. Westermeyer, B. Engdahl, and E. Johnsen. Post-traumatic stress disorder and service utilization in a sample of service members from Iraq and Afghanistan. *Military Medicine*, Vol. 172, No. 4, 2007, pp. 359–363.

Type of Report	Sample (n)	Design	Disorders Studied	Utilization of Services	Other Utilization Info
Peer-reviewed	Convenience sample of OEF/OIF vets enrolling for care during the deactivation or discharge process (still awaiting completion of surveys; this is a preliminary analysis) (120)	Cross-sectional	Depression, PTSD, Hazardous Alcohol Use	In the sample as a whole, some form of mental health care since returning home was reported by 62%. This included: Medication (11% of sample) Individual therapy (13%) Group therapy (12%) Marital or family therapy (10%) Chemical-dependency treatment (2%) Briefings/debriefings (51%, likely an underestimate, because follow-up contacts with many returnees suggest that they did not realize that certain outprocessing sessions they underwent upon return [which in fact were debriefings] would be described by that label) Among those meeting screening criteria for PTSD, 56% reported receiving individual therapy, group therapy, and/or psychiatric medication since their return. Service utilization rates for risky drinkers were much lower, with only 18% reporting receipt of any mental health services and only 3% reporting receiving chemical-dependency treatment. Many reported receiving more than one type of service.	A positive PTSD status was significantly associated with use of psychiatric medications and individual therapy, and there was a trend ($p < 0.10$) for higher group therapy participation. Hazardous drinking was not associated with greater mental health service use, including chemical-dependency treatment. The higher service utilization rates may be due to the sampling strategies, but could also reflect the longer time that these returnees have been home. The logistic regression analysis indicated that it is the general distress and negative affect expressed through depressive symptoms, rather than PTSD per se, that independently led to seeking services. This suggests that those suffering from PTSD symptoms without the negative affect and accompanying symptoms of depression may be less likely to seek services.

Table 7.D.1—Continued

Type of Report	Sample (n)	Design	Disorders Studied	Utilization of Services	Other Utilization Info

Milliken C. S., J. L. Auchterlonie, and C. W. Hoge. Longitudinal assessment of mental health problems among Active and Reserve Component soldiers returning from the Iraq war. *Journal of the American Medical Association*, Vol. 298, No. 18, 2007, pp. 2141–2148.

| Peer-reviewed | Active Duty and Army National Guard and Reserve Soldiers returning from OIF (88,235) | Prospective | Depression PTSD | Of those with referral for a mental health problem on the PDHA: 41.8% accessed mental health care services. Of those with referral for a mental health problem on the PDHRA: 61.0% accessed mental health care services. Of those without a referral for a mental health problem on the PDHA: 14.6% accessed mental health care services. Of those without referral for a mental health problem on the PDHRA: 17.8% accessed mental health care services. Of those with a referral for substance abuse on the PDHRA: 21.6% accessed mental health care services. Of those without a referral for substance abuse on the PDHRA: 2.9% accessed mental health care services. | For Active Component soldiers with high PTSD symptoms reported on the PDHA, there was an inverse relationship between receiving mental health services and improvement in symptoms by the time of the PDHRA. |

Rosenheck, R. A., and A. F. Fontana. Recent trends in VA treatment of post-traumatic stress disorder and other mental disorders. *Health Affairs*, Vol. 26, No. 6, 2007, pp. 1720–1727.

| Peer-reviewed | All veterans who received services for any mental disorder from inpatient or outpatient specialty mental health care programs in FY 1997, 1999, 2001, 2003, 2005 | Retro-spective | PTSD | Number of patients born after 1972 treated for PTSD in a VA specialty mental health care clinic: 1997: 430 1999: 636 2001: 967 2003: 1,578 2005: 8,904 | NA |

Table 7.D.1—Continued

Type of Report	Sample (n)	Design	Disorders Studied	Utilization of Services	Other Utilization Info
Okie, S. Traumatic brain injury in the war zone. *New England Journal of Medicine*, Vol. 352, No. 20, 2005, pp. 2043–2047.					
Journalistic	NA	NA	TBI	More than 450 patients with TBI were treated between January 2003 and February 2005 at Walter Reed	NA

NOTES: NA = not available. V code = part of the DSM-IV coding system for mental health disorders; relational problems and problems related to abuse and neglect are included in this designation.

Appendix 7.E: State and Local Mental Health Resources

Many mental health professionals, organizations, and community members have made a significant effort to provide services to returning servicemembers and assist them with reintegration. Although the quality of these programs is still unknown (the programs have not been formally evaluated), we postulate that they may increase accessibility of mental health treatment in several ways. Those that offer services to veterans with less than honorable discharges, or to friends or unmarried partners of servicemembers, expand access to care to individuals who may not be eligible for military or VA mental health services. Programs offering free counseling expand access to those who would be unable to afford it otherwise. Those programs that are offered in a confidential setting away from the military installation may be appealing to military servicemembers concerned with the stigma of seeking mental health services and those who worry that receiving mental health treatment may adversely affect their military careers. To help provide models for improving access that also deliver care that is most likely to be beneficial, we must emphasize that evaluations of the quality of such programs will be extremely important. This appendix summarizes some of the mental health programs that have been developed by individuals and organizations on the state or local level. This list is illustrative and not meant to be comprehensive.

Pro Bono Counseling and Psychoeducation

In response to the perceived need for psychotherapy and psychoeducational programs among returning OEF/OIF veterans and their families, many civilian mental health professionals and professional organizations developed programs to provide free counseling and psychotherapy to servicemembers and their families. Some examples follow.

The Coming Home Project. The Coming Home Project is made up of veterans, family members, psychotherapists (licensed psychologists, psychiatrists, social workers, and marriage and family therapists), and interfaith leaders in the greater San Francisco Bay area. The psychotherapists offer free counseling services to address the mental, emotional, spiritual, and relationship problems that servicemembers face upon return from deployment to Afghanistan or Iraq. The Coming Home Project emphasizes the confidentiality of its services. There is no limit on the frequency or duration of sessions. Regardless of reason for discharge or relationship to the veteran, veterans and family members are eligible for services through the Coming Home Project. Servicemembers and veterans outside of the San Francisco Bay area may contact the Coming Home Project for information or referrals and are also invited and encouraged to share their experiences in "therapeutic, but not psychotherapy" workshops and retreats. Travel and lodging scholarships are available for these free services. Additionally, the Coming Home Project offers training to health care providers and family members who provide care to returning servicemembers.

Give an Hour. Give an Hour is a national network of licensed mental health professionals who are willing to volunteer one hour of their time to provide free counseling to servicemembers and families. These providers are recruited through professional mental health organizations, professional publications, conferences and workshops, personal contacts, and Web sites. Counseling is offered away from the military installation in a confidential setting. To advertise and promote its services, Give an Hour plans to coordinate with the Department of Defense, the Veterans Administration, the National Military Family Association, and religious communities. It also plans to link with other Web-based groups that provide support services to the military. It hopes to collaborate with the Department of Defense, developing relationships and trust with officers so that they are willing to refer those in need of mental health services to Give an Hour counselors. Give an Hour volunteers from the community will check provider licenses, conduct community outreach, and coordinate volunteer opportunities for those servicemembers and families interested in giving an hour back to the community. In addition to identifying sources of free counseling services, the Give an Hour Web site provides informational materials to servicemembers and families, as well as to community members and care providers.

ONE Freedom. ONE Freedom is a Colorado-based nonprofit organization that offers tailored education and training on the neurophysiology of stress, its effect on daily life and relationships, and coping strategies to returning military servicemembers, their families, community leaders, family readiness groups (military-organized and command-supported groups that serve to help families), Reserve and Guard drill leaders, veterans' service organizations, and care providers. The program emphasizes the normalness of stress reactions and identifies resiliency and strength after service as tools for stress management. ONE Freedom utilizes both military and civilian instructors and provides information through several venues, including hour-long seminars and weekend retreats. On its Web site, ONE Freedom indicates that each skill taught has been validated by scientific research in university or hospital settings.

Operation Comfort. The mission of Operation Comfort is to create a nationwide network of licensed mental health care providers who are willing to offer free mental health services to family members of those soldiers deployed to Afghanistan or Iraq. Originating in California, the network has expanded to include other states. Family members interested in receiving services through Operation Comfort can visit its Web site, click on their state, and see a list of providers by city. Providers are not listed for every state, but there is a forum for providers interested in joining the program to sign up.

Returning Veterans Resources Project NW. The Returning Veterans Resources Project NW is an Oregon-based nonprofit organization comprising politically unaffiliated, independently licensed mental health professionals offering free and confidential counseling to veterans and their families. The program focuses on problems associated with reintegration, including employment concerns, anger, depression, relationship problems, and other stressors. In addition to providing pro bono counseling services, the organization also plans to educate the community and raise awareness about the problems that returning veterans and their families face, as well as providing training for therapists and other caregivers working with returning veterans.

The Soldiers Project. The Trauma Center of the Los Angeles Institute and Society for Psychoanalytic Studies has established the Soldiers Project in the Southern California region. The Soldiers Project consists of a group of licensed psychiatrists, psychologists, social workers, and marriage and family therapists voluntarily providing free counseling to those servicemembers serving in Afghanistan or Iraq, family members of servicemembers, and family members of servicemembers who died in Afghanistan or Iraq. The Soldiers Project provides services for problems relating to the deployment, regardless of whether they occur before, during, or after the deployment. It discloses that the volunteer providers may not be able to give the necessary level of care but are willing to assist individuals in identifying more appropriate resources. If the therapist and individual receiving therapy decide to add medication to the treatment plan, The Soldiers Project will coordinate medication management with the VA health care system. The services offered through The Soldiers Project are confidential unless the servicemember or family member gives consent to pass information to another provider.

Strategic Outreach to Families of All Reservists (SOFAR). Initiated by the Psychoanalytic Couple and Family Institute of New England and other psychoanalytic groups in the New England region, Strategic Outreach to Families of All Reservists (SOFAR) coordinates free psychotherapy and psychoeducational sessions for families of Reserve and Guard servicemembers, to assist them in learning to cope with the stressors associated with periods of mobilization, activation, deployment, and reunion/reintegration. When a family member requests assistance through SOFAR, a clinician conducts an assessment and formulates a treatment plan. If SOFAR does not have adequate resources to provide necessary services to a family, he or she will assist them with locating the appropriate services within the community. The New England branch of SOFAR serves as a pilot project; after further development and modification of the program, SOFAR plans to replicate itself nationally through 27 local chapters of the Division of Psychoanalysis of the American Psychological Association and the 31 institutes of the American Psychoanalytic Association.

Support Our Family in Arms (SOFA). Psychotherapists affiliated with the Colorado Psychological Association have established Support Our Family in Arms (SOFA), a program that provides pro bono individual, group, couples, family, and child therapies; support group leadership; psychological assessments and evaluations; psychoeducational presentations and workshops; and other mental health services to returning Colorado National Guard and Reserve servicemembers and their families. Therapists not affiliated with the Colorado Psychological Association are also welcome to volunteer their time with SOFA. SOFA receives referrals from the Family Readiness and

Support Group at Buckley Air Force Base and other organizations, including Military OneSource, the National Vet Center Program, the National Gulf War Resource Center, Operation Just One, the National Military Family Association, Give an Hour, and the Strategic Outreach to Families of All Reservists. SOFA provides services in conjunction with, but not in place of, mental health services offered through the Department of Defense or the U.S. Department of Veterans Affairs. Military servicemembers are encouraged to determine what mental health services are already available from DoD and the VA when they seek assistance from SOFA.

Swords to Plowshares. The Swords to Plowshares program in San Francisco was developed in 1974 for Vietnam veterans who had other than honorable discharges, were struggling to reintegrate, and were encountering the criminal justice system. The program initially provided assistance with finding employment and advocated access to government benefits for these veterans. The advocacy program also raised awareness of post-traumatic stress disorder and exposure to Agent Orange in Vietnam veterans. The program's mission has evolved. It now offers services to those who have deployed to Afghanistan or Iraq. The drop-in counseling center offers services for drug and alcohol abuse and post-traumatic stress disorder, as well as referrals and case-management services.

State-Based Programs

Several states have developed programs to aid returning servicemembers with their mental health care needs. We describe the programs in Illinois, Ohio, Rhode Island, Vermont, and Washington.

Illinois. Illinois recently launched Veteran's Care, a program that offers access to affordable, comprehensive health care to all veterans across Illinois. It is the first state in the nation to create such a program. Veterans pay a monthly premium of $40 or $70 and receive medical coverage and limited dental and vision coverage.

Illinois is also the first state to establish a statewide traumatic brain injury program. The program has two parts: a TBI portion and a PTSD portion. The TBI portion will mandate screening for all Illinois National Guard servicemembers returning from deployment and offer free screening to all Illinois veterans, especially those returning from Operation Enduring Freedom and Operation Iraqi Freedom. Staffed by trained clinicians and nurses, with at least one psychiatrist on call at all times, the PTSD component of this program will offer 24-hour, toll-free psychological assistance. Due to the unique experiences of combat veterans, call-center staff will be trained in combat-related PTSD and other psychological issues facing veterans.

Ohio. The Ohio National Guard developed the OHIOCares program to assist returning National Guard servicemembers in connecting with the appropriate mental health resources according to the severity of their mental health issues. The program organized the state's mental health resources so that military servicemembers can more easily discern which services would be appropriate for their problems. The online Reintegration Action Plan provides advice for the common problems that military service-members and their families face upon the military member's return. Military service-members and their families may call a toll-free number or access the OHIOCares Web site to learn about the available services.

Rhode Island. To address the needs of veterans, military servicemembers, and their families during pre- and post-deployment, the Veterans Task Force of Rhode Island was developed by a group of individuals, organizations, and local, state, and federal agencies interested in sharing expertise and experiences. Six committees formed to independently research addictive disorders, peer support, community outreach, public awareness, family networks, and women veterans. From the committees' find-ings, the task force created a handbook entitled *The Rhode Island Blueprint.* to serve as a resource guide for all military servicemembers, families, and civilian partners and agencies. The handbook contains information on common post-deployment challenges among returning veterans and lists available resources for each topic.

Vermont. In response to the lack of a comprehensive support network for return-ing National Guard troops, Vermont developed the Vermont Military, Family and Community Network. The network's mission is to develop and maintain a multigroup community network among community, government, and private sectors in order to raise awareness regarding the needs of servicemembers and to provide services to all returning servicemembers and their families. The network includes a state-level steer-ing committee and local task forces. It also educated non-VA practitioners about the needs of servicemembers, as well as the need for integrated school counselors to assist the children of deployed and recently deployed soldiers. Several states across the coun-try have started similar efforts.

Washington. The state of Washington has implemented a free post-traumatic stress disorder program, which creates community-based avenues to counseling ser-vices that are less formal in nature than many mental health services. Services provided through the program include individual, couples, family, and veteran group counsel-ing. Some contractors offer group services to women veterans and spouses of veterans. This program is also linked with national programs for veterans, so that veterans with more serious need may be referred to specialized inpatient or outpatient treatment offered by the U.S. Department of Veterans Affairs Medical Centers or Vet Centers within Washington State.

In addition to working with veterans, this PTSD program provides free counsel-ing and consulting resources to educate teachers and school counselors of the potential needs of school-aged children of parents who have been exposed to war. Parents' war and trauma experiences can affect their children in a variety of ways (see Chapter Five), and early identification and referral of children and families who are in need of sup-portive mental health services are a high priority of this program.

University-Based Counseling

Veterans returning to college after deploying to Afghanistan or Iraq may receive mental health counseling services through university counseling programs. California State University, San Bernardino, and the University of Texas advertise psychological services targeted specifically at the veteran student population. The University of Texas counseling center offers face-to-face as well as telephonic counseling for those who may not be comfortable going to the student services office for counseling.

References

Abrams, R. *Electroconvulsive Therapy*. New York: Oxford University Press, 2002.

Ajizen, I., and M. Fishbein. *Understanding Attitudes and Predicting Social Behavior*. Englewood Cliffs, N.J.: Prentice-Hall, 1980.

Alderson, P., and I. Roberts. Corticosteroids in acute traumatic brain injury: Systematic review of randomised controlled trials. *British Medical Journal*, Vol. 314, 1997, pp. 1855–1859.

Alexander, M. P. Mild traumatic brain injury: Pathophysiology, natural history, and clincial management. *Neurology*, Vol. 45, 1995, pp. 1253–1260.

American Psychiatric Association Web site, Electroconvulsive Therapy (ECT) page. As of March 10, 2008:
http://www.psych.org/Departments/APIREandResearch/ResearchTraining/clin_res/index.aspx

Anderson, I. M. Selective serotonin reuptake inhibitors versus tricyclic antidepressants: A meta-analysis of efficacy and tolerability. *Journal of Affective Disorders*, Vol. 58, 2000, pp. 19–36.

Arlinghaus, K. Recognizing brain injury in the returning soldier. Presentation at the North American Brain Injury Society Conference, San Antonio, Tex., September 28, 2007.

Arroll, B., S. Macgillivray, S. Ogston, I. Reid, F. Sullivan, B. Williams, and I. Crombie. Efficacy and tolerability of tricyclic antidepressants and SSRIS compared with placebo for treatment of depression in primary care: A meta-analysis. *Annals of Family Medicine*, Vol. 3, 2005, pp. 449–456.

Arthur, D. C. Testimony nefore the Subcommittee on Military Personnel of the House Armed Services Committee, Regarding the Department of Defense Task Force on Mental Health. Washington, D.C.: House of Representatives, July 12, 2007.

Asch, S. M., E. A. McGlynn, M. M. Hogan, R. A. Haywa, P. G. Shekelle, L. V. Rubenstein, J. Keesey, J. L. Adams, and E. A. Kerr. Comparison of quality of care for patients in the Veterans Health Administration and patients in a national sample. *Annals of Internal Medicine*, Vol. 141, No. 12, 2004, pp. 938–945.

Atizado, A. Witness testimony at Hearing: Polytrauma Center Care and the Traumatic Brain Injury (TBI) Patient: How Seamless Is the Transition Between the U.S. Department of Veterans Affairs and the Department of Defense and Are Needs Being Met? Subcommittee on Health, the House Committee on Veterans Affairs, 110th Congress. Washington, D.C.: House of Representatives, March 15, 2007.

Azocar, F., B. Cuffel, W. Goldman, and L. McCarter. The impact of evidence-based guideline dissemination for the assessment and treatment of major depression in a managed behavioral health care organization. *Journal of Behavioral Health Services and Research*, Vol. 30, No. 1, 2003, pp. 109–118.

Baldwin, D. S. Serotonin noradrenaline reuptake inhibitors: A new generation of treatment for anxiety disorders. *International Journal of Psychiatry in Clinical Practice*, Vol. 10, 2006, pp. 12–15.

Bandura, A. *Social Foundations of Thought and Action: A Social Cognitive Theory*. Upper Saddle River, N.J.: Prentice-Hall Inc., 1986.

Bascetta, C. A. *VA and Defense Health Care: More Information Needed to Determine If VA Can Meet an Increase in Demand for Post-Traumatic Stress Disorder Services*. Washington, D.C.: Government Accountability Office, GAO-04-1069, 2004.

———. *DoD and VA Health Care—Challenges Encountered by Injured Service Members During Their Recovery Process*. Washington, D.C.: Government Accountability Office, GAO-07-606T, 2007.

Bay, E., B. M. Hagerty, and R. A. Williams. Depressive symptomatology after mild-to-moderate traumatic brain injury: A comparison of three measures. *Archives of Psychiatric Nursing*, Vol. 21, 2007, pp. 2–11.

Beach, S. R. H. *Marital and Family Processes in Depression: A Scientific Foundation for Clinical Practice.* Washington, D.C.: American Psychological Association, 2001.

Beardsley, R., G. Gardocki, D. Larson, and J. Hidalgo. Prescribing of psychotropic medication by primary care PCMs and psychiatrists. *Annual Review of Public Health*, Vol. 45, 1998, pp. 1117–1119.

Bech, P., P. Cialdella, M. C. Haugh, A. Hours, J. P. Boissel, M. A. Birkett, and G. D. Tollefson. Meta-analysis of randomised controlled trials of fluoxetine v. placebo and tricyclic antidepressants in the short-term treatment of major depression. *British Journal of Psychiatry*, Vol. 176, 2000, pp. 421–428.

Beck, J. S. Why distinguish between cognitive therapy and cognitive behaviour therapy? *The Beck Institute Newsletter*, February 2001.

Beck Institute Web site. As of March 9, 2008:
http://www.beckinstitute.com

Belasco, A. *The Cost of Iraq, Afghanistan, and Other Global War on Terror Operations Since 9/11.* Washington, D.C.: Congressional Research Service, 2007.

Belenky, G. Sleep, sleep deprivation, and human performance in continuous operations, 1997. As of January 24, 2008:
http://www.usafa.af.mil/jscope/JSCOPE97/Belenky97/Belenky97.htm

Ben-Yishay, Y., S. M. Silver, E. Piasetsky, and J. Rattock. Relationship between employability and vocational outcome after intensive holistic cognitive rehabilitation. *Journal of Head Trauma Rehabilitation*, Vol. 2, 1987, pp. 35–48.

Berwick, D. A user's manual for the IOM's "quality chasm" report. *Health Affairs*, Vol. 21, No. 3, 2002, pp. 80–90.

Berwick, D. M. Continuous improvement as an ideal in health care. *New England Journal of Medicine*, Vol. 320, No. 1, 1989, pp. 53–56.

Bisson, J., P. Dix, A. Ehlers, J. Johnston, C. Jones, et al. Post-traumatic stress disorder: The management of PTSD in adults and children in primary and secondary care. National Clinical Practice Guideline Number 26. National Collaborating Centre for Mental Health, commissioned by the National Institute for Clinical Excellence. Gaskell and the British Psychological Society. The Royal College of Psychiatrists and the British Psychological Society. 2005.

Bisson, J., A. Ehlers, R. Matthews, S. Pilling, D. Richards, and S. Turner. Psychological treatments for chronic post-traumatic stress disorder: Systematic review and meta-analysis. *British Journal of Psychiatry*, Vol. 190, 2007, pp. 97–104.

Blackburn, J. M., K. M. Eunson, and S. Bishop. A two year naturalistic follow-up of depressed patients treated with cognitive therapy, pharmacotherapy, and a combination of both. *Journal of Affective Disorders*, Vol. 10, 1986, pp. 67–75.

Blake, C. Witness Testimony at Hearing: Specially Adaptive Housing, Subcommittee on Economic Opportunity, the House Committee on Veterans Affairs. Washington, D.C.: House of Representatives, June 7, 2007.

Bledsoe, B. E. Critical Incident Stress Management (CISM): Benefit or risk for emergency services? *Prehospital Emergency Care*, Vol. 7, 2003, pp. 272–279.

Blount, A. Introduction to integrated primary care. In A. Blount, ed., *Integrated Primary Care: The Future of Medical and Mental Health Collaboration.* New York: W. W. Norton, 1998, pp. 1–43.

Bradshaw, D., S. D. Franco, M. Toney, R. Labutta, and J. Ruiz. *Report to the Surgeon General: Traumatic Brain Injury Task Force,* May 15, 2007. As of March 12, 2008: http://www.armymedicine.army.mil/news/reports/TBITaskForceReportJanuary2008.pdf

Brain Trauma Foundation, American Association of Neurological Surgeons, and Congress of Neurological Surgeons. Guidelines for the management of severe traumatic brain injury, 3rd edition. *Journal of Neurotrauma,* Vol. 24, 2007, pp. i–S106.

Bray, R., L. Hourani, K. Olmstead, M. Witt, J. Brown, M. Pemberton, M. Marsden, B. Marriott, S. Scheffler, R. Vandermaas-Peeler, B. Weimer, S. Calvin, M. Bradshaw, K. Close, and D. Hayden. 2005 Department of Defense Survey of Health Related Behaviors Among Active Duty Military Personnel: A Component of the Defense Lifestyle Assessment Program (DLAP). Research Triangle Park, N.C.: Research Triangle Institute, 2006.

Britt, T. W., T. M. Greene-Shortridge, and C. A. Castro. The stigma of mental health problems in the military. *Military Medicine,* Vol. 172, 2007, pp. 157–161.

Brown, G. S., G. M. Burlingame, M. J. Lambert, E. Jones, and J. Vaccaro. Pushing the quality envelope: A new outcomes management system. *Psychiatric Services,* Vol. 52, No. 7, 2001, pp. 925–934.

Brown, J. VA Testimony before the House Veterans' Affairs Subcommittee on Oversight and Investigations, Regarding Efforts of the Department of Veterans Affairs (VA) Toward Effecting a Seamless Transition for Separating Service Members from the Department of Defense to VA, 109th Congress, Washington, D.C.: House of Representatives, May 19, 2005.

Bruner, E. F. *Military Forces: What Is the Appropriate Size for the United States?* Washington, D.C.: Congressional Research Service, 2006.

Bryant, R. A., A. G. Harvey, S. T. Dang, T. Sackville, and C. Basten. Treatment of acute stress disorder: A comparison of cognitive-behavioral therapy and supportive counseling. *Journal of Consulting and Clinical Psychology,* Vol. 66, 1998, pp. 862–866.

Bryant, R. A., M. L. Moulds, R. Guthrie, and R. D. V. Nixon. The additive benefit of hypnosis and cognitive-behavioral therapy in treating acute stress disorder. *Journal of Consulting and Clinical Psychology,* Vol. 73, 2005, pp. 334–340.

Bryant, R. A., M. L. Moulds, R. D. V. Nixon, J. Mastrodomenico, K. Felmingham, and S. Hopwood. Hypnotherapy and cognitive behaviour therapy of acute stress disorder: A 3-year follow-up. *Behaviour Research and Therapy,* Vol. 44, 2006, pp. 1331–1335.

Bullock, R., R. Chestnut, G. Clifton, J. Ghajar, D. Marion, and R. Narayan. Guidelines for the management of severe traumatic brain injury: Brain Trauma Foundation. *European Journal of Emergency Medicine,* Vol. 3, 1996, pp. 109–127.

Bullock, M. R., R. Chesnut, J. Ghajar, D. Gordon, R. Hartl, et al. Surgical management of TBI. *Neurosurgery,* Vol. 58, No. 3, March Supplement, 2006.

Burnam, M. A. Effect on clinical practice. In S. Feldman, ed., *Managed Behavioral Health Services: Perspectives and Practice.* Springfield, Ill.: Charles C. Thomas Publisher, 2003, pp. 24–60.

Butler, A. C., J. E. Chapman, E. M. Forman, and A. T. Beck. The empirical status of cognitive-behavioral therapy: A review of meta-analyses. *Clinical Psychology Review,* Vol. 26, 2006, pp. 17–31.

Cappa, S. F., T. Benke, S. Clarke, B. Rossi, B. Stemmer, and C. M. van Heugten. EFNS guidelines on cognitive rehabilitation: Report of an EFNS task force. *European Journal of Neurology: The Official Journal of the European Federation of Neurological Societies,* Vol. 10, 2003, pp. 11–23.

Cardenas, D. D., J. K. Haselkorn, J. M. McElligott, and S. M. Gnatz. A bibliography of cost-effectiveness practices in physical medicine and rehabilitation: AAPM&R white paper. *Archives of Physical Medicine and Rehabilitation*, Vol. 73, 2001, pp. 635–641.

Casacalenda, N., J. C. Perry, and K. Looper. Remission in major depressive disorder: A comparison of pharmacotherapy, psychotherapy and control conditions. *American Journal of Psychiatry*, Vol. 159, 2002, pp. 1354–1360.

Chang, B. S., and D. H. Lowenstein. Practice parameter: Antiepileptic drug prophylaxis in severe traumatic brain injury: Report of the Quality Standards Subcommittee of the American Academy of Neurology. *Neurology*, Vol. 60, 2003, pp. 10–16.

Chesnut, R. M., N. Carney, H. Maynard, N. C. Mann, P. Patterson, and M. Helfand. Summary report: Evidence for the effectiveness of rehabilitation for persons with traumatic brain injury. *Journal of Head Trauma and Rehabilitation*, Vol. 14, 1999, pp. 176–188.

The Chronic Care Model, Princeton, N.J.: Robert Wood Johnson Foundation, no date. As of March 13, 2008: http://www.improvingchroniccare.org

Chua, K. S., Y. S. Ng, S. G. Yap, and C. W. Bok. A brief review of traumatic brain injury rehabilitation. *Annals of the Academy of Medicine*, Singapore, Vol. 36, 2007, pp. 31–42.

Cicerone, K. D., C. Dahlberg, K. Kalmar, D. M. Langenbahn, J. F. Malec, T. F. Bergquist, T. Felicetti, J. T. Giacino, J. P. Harley, D. E. Harrington, J. Herzog, S. Kneipp, L. Laatsch, and P. A. Morse. Evidence-based cognitive rehabilitation: Recommendations for clinical practice. *Archives of Physical Medicine and Rehabilitation*, Vol. 81, 2000, pp. 1596–1615.

Cicerone, K. D., T. Mott, J. Azulay, and J. C. Friel. Community integration and satisfaction with functioning after intensive cognitive rehabilitation for traumatic brain injury. *Archives of Physical Medicine and Rehabilitation*, Vol. 85, 2004, pp. 943–950.

Clement, P. F., and J. E. Kennedy. Wechsler Adult Intelligence Scale–Third Edition: Characteristics of a military traumatic brain injury sample. *Military Medicine*, Vol. 168, No. 12, 2003, pp. 1025–1028.

Comper, P., S. M. Bisschop, N. Carnide, and A. Tricco. A systematic review of treatments for mild traumatic brain injury. *Brain Injury*, Vol. 19, 2005, pp. 863–880.

Cooke, R. S., B. P. McNicholl, and D. P. Byrnes. Early management of severe head injury in Northern Ireland. *Injury*, Vol. 26, 1995, pp. 395–397.

Cordova, J. V., L. Z. Warren, and C. B. Gee. Motivational interviewing as an intervention for at risk couples. *Journal of Marital and Family Therapy*, Vol. 27, No. 3, 2001, pp. 315–326.

Corrigan, P. W. How stigma interferes with mental health care. *American Psychologist*, Vol. 59, 2004, pp. 614–625.

Corrigan, P. W., F. E. Markowitz, and A. C. Watson. Structural levels of mental illness stigma and discrimination. *Schizophrenia Bulletin*, Vol. 30, No. 3, 2004, pp. 481–491.

Corrigan, P. W., and D. L. Penn. Lessons from social psychology on discrediting psychiatric stigma. *American Psychologist*, Vol. 54, 1999, pp. 765–766.

Corrigan, P. W., and A. C. Watson. The paradox of self-stigma and mental illness. *Clinical Psychology*, Vol. 9, 2002, pp. 35–53.

Courtois, C. A., and S. L. Bloom. Inpatient treatment. In E. B. Foa, T. M. Keane, and M. J. Friedman, eds., *Effective Treatments for PTSD*. New York: Guildford Press, 2000, pp. 342–326.

Cross, G. M. VA Testimony before a House Veterans Affairs Subcommittee on Oversight and Investigations Hearing, to Report the Progress Made by the Department of Veterans Affairs to Share Electronic Medical Records with the Department of Defense, 110th Congress. Washington, D.C.: House of Representatives, October 24, 2007.

———. VA Testimony before the House Veterans Subcommittee on Health, to Discuss Ongoing Efforts in the Veterans Health Administration to Improve the Quality of Care We Provide to Veterans Suffering from Post-Traumatic Stress Disorder and Traumatic Brain Injuries, 109th Congress. Washington, D.C.: House of Representatives, September 29, 2006.

Cuijpers, P., A. van Straten, and L. Warmerdam. Behavioral activation treatments of depression: A meta-analysis. *Clinical Psychology Review*, Vol. 27, No. 3, 2007a, pp. 318–326.

———. Problem solving therapies for depression: A meta-analysis. *European Psychiatry*, Vol. 22, 2007b, pp. 9–15.

Cuijpers, P., F. Smit, and A. van Straten. Psychological treatments of subthreshold depression: A meta-analytic review. *Acta Psychiatrica Scandinavica*, Vol. 115, 2007, pp. 434–441.

D'Zurilla, T. J., and A. Nezu. Social problem solving in adults. In P. C. Kendall, ed., *Advances in Cognitive-Behavioral Research and Therapy*, New York: Academic Press, 1982, pp. 202–274.

Davidson, P. R., and K. C. H. Parker. Eye movement desensitization and reprocessing (EMDR): A meta-analysis. *Journal of Consulting and Clinical Psychology*, Vol. 69, No. 2, 2001, pp. 305–316.

Davis, D. A., M. A. Thomson, A. D. Oxman, and R. B. Haynes. Changing physician performance: A systematic review of the effect of continuing education strategies. *Journal of the American Medical Association*, Vol. 274, 1995, pp. 700–705.

Davis, L. L., E. C. Frazier, R. B. Williford, and J. M. Newell. Long-term pharmacotherapy for post-traumatic stress disorder. *CNS Drugs*, Vol. 20, No. 6, 2006, pp. 465–476.

De Maat, S., J. Dekker, R. Schoevers, and F. De Jonghe. Relative efficacy of psychotherapy and pharmacotherapy in the treatment of depression: A meta-analysis. *Psychotherapy Research*, Vol. 16, 2006, pp. 566–578.

Defense and Veterans Brain Injury Center. *A Congressional Program for Servicemembers and Veterans with Traumatic Brain Injury and Their Families*, Informational Brochure, Washington, D.C., Walter Reed Army Medical Center, 2005.

Defense and Veterans Brain Injury Center, Working Group on the Acute Management of Mild Traumatic Brain Injury in Military Operational Settings. *Clinical Practice Guidelines and Recommendations*. December 22, 2006. As of March 13, 2008: http://www.pdhealth.mil/downloads/clinical_practice_guideline_recommendations.pdf

Defense Manpower Data Center. December 2005 Status of Forces Survey of Active-Duty Members: Tabulations of Responses. Arlington, Va.: Defense Manpower Data Center (DMDC), 2006.

Democratic staff of the House Committee on Veterans Affairs. Review of Capacity of Department of Veterans Affairs Readjustment Counseling Service Vet Centers, 2006.

Department of Defense. Military Health System Web site. As of March 6, 2008: http://www.health.mil

———. Department of Defense Survey of Health-Related Behaviors Among Active Duty Military Personnel: A Component of the Defense Lifestyle Assessment Program. 2005. As of March 13, 2008: http://www.ha.osd.mil/special_reports/2005_Health_Behaviors_Survey_1-07.pdf

Department of Defense Task Force on Mental Health. *An Achievable Vision: Report of the Department of Defense Task Force on Mental Health*. Falls Church, Va.: Defense Health Board, June 2007a.

————. *The Department of Defense Plan to Achieve the Vision of the DoD Task Force on Mental Health: Report to Congress.* Washington, D.C., September 2007b.

Department of Veterans Affairs. Screening and evaluation of possible traumatic brain injury in Operation Enduring Freedom (OEF) and Operation Iraqi Freedom (OIF) veterans. VHA Directive 2007-013, 2007.

————. Veterans Health Initiative: Traumatic Brain Injury—Independent Study Course. Washington D.C.: Department of Veterans Affairs, Employee Education System, 2004. As of March 13, 2008:
http://www1.va.gov/vhi/docs/TBI.pdf

————. Office of the Inspector General, Healthcare Inspection: Health Status of and Services for Operation Enduring Freedom/Operation Iraqi Freedom Veterans after Traumatic Brain Injury Rehabilitation, 2006a.

————. Office of Public Health and Environmental Hazards, Analysis of VA Health Care Utilization Among Southwest Asian War Veterans Combined—Operation Iraqi Freedom Operation Enduring Freedom, 2006b.

————. About VHA–Health Care–Veterans Health Administration, August 29, 2007a. As of March 13, 2008:
http://www1.va.gov/health/gateway.html

————. About Health Services Research and Development (HSR&D). As of March 13, 2008:
http://www.hsrd.research.va.gov/about/

————. Health Services Research and Development (HSR&D) Centers of Excellence. December 14, 2007b. As of March 13, 2008:
http://www.hsrd.research.va.gov/about/centers/centers_of_excellence.cfm

————. National Center for PTSD Web site, June 19, 2007c. As of March 13, 2008:
http://www.ncptsd.va.gov/ncmain/

————. National Center for PTSD, Fact Sheet: "Screening for PTSD in a Primary Care Setting." May 22, 2007d. As of March 13, 2008:
http://www.ncptsd.va.gov/ncmain/ncdocs/fact_shts/
fs_screen_disaster.html?opm=1&rr=rr62&srt=d&echorr=true

————. National Center for Veterans Analysis and Statistics, VA Stats at a Glance, October 25, 2007e. As of March 13, 2008:
http://www1.va.gov/vetdata/docs/4x6_fall07_sharepoint.pdf

————. Northeast Program Evaluation Center. The Long Journey Home XV: Treatment of Posttraumatic Stress Disorder in the Department of Veterans Affairs: Fiscal Year 2006 Service Delivery and Performance. In Northeast Program Evaluation Center Department of Veterans Affairs, VA Connecticut Healthcare System, ed., West Haven, Conn., 2007f.

————. Office of Research and Development, Health Services Research and Development Service, Improving Treatment for Depression in Primary Care: Translating Initiatives for Depression into Effective Solutions (TIDES), June 2007g. As of March 13, 2008:
http://www.hsrd.research.va.gov/queri/impact_updates/MH.pdf

————.Office of Research and Development, Health Services Research and Development Service QUERI Fact Sheet: Mental Health, Little Rock, Ark.: U.S. Veterans Affairs, 2007h.

————. Task Force on Returning Global War on Terror Heroes, Report to the President, April 19, 2007i. As of March 13, 2008:
http://www1.va.gov/taskforce/docs/GWOT_TF_Report_042407.pdf

————. VA Announces $4.7 Million to Help Caregivers. December 6, 2007j. As of March 13, 2008:
http://www1.va.gov/opa/pressrel/pressrelease.cfm?id=1428

————. VA Health Care Eligibility and Enrollment, Fact Sheet 164-2: Enrollment Priority Groups, March 2007k. As of March 13, 2008:
http://www.va.gov/healtheligibility/Library/pubs/EPG/

————. VA Health Care Eligibility and Enrollment, 2007l. As of March 13, 2008:
http://www.va.gov/healtheligibility/

————. VA Polytrauma System of Care, Frequently Asked Questions, April 9, 2007m. As of March 13, 2008:
http://www.polytrauma.va.gov/faq.asp?FAQ#FAQ1

Department of Veterans Affairs and Department of Defense. The Management of Major Depressive Disorder Working Group. VA/DoD clinical practice guideline for the management of major depressive disorder in adults (v. 2.0). 2000.

————. The Management of Post Traumatic Stress Working Group. VA/DoD clinical practice guideline for the management of post-traumatic stress (v. 1.0). 2004.

Depression Guideline Panel. *Depression in Primary Care, Vol. 2. Treatment of Major Depression.* Rockville, Md.: U.S. Department of Health and Human Services, Public Health Service, Agency for Health Care Policy and Research, Clinical Practice Guideline No. 5, AHCPR Publication No. 93-0551, 1993.

DeRubeis, R. J., S. D. Hollon, J. D. Amsterdam, R. C. Shelton, P. R. Young, R. M. Salomon, J. P. O'Reardon, M. L. Lovett, M. M. Gladis, L. L. Brown, and R. Gallop. Cognitive therapy vs medications in the treatment of moderate to severe depression. *Archives of General Psychiatry,* Vol. 62, 2005, pp. 409–416.

Dietrich, A. J., T. E. Oxman, J. W. Williams, Jr., K. Kroenke, H. C. Schulberg, M. Bruce, and S. L. Barry. Going to scale: Re-engineering systems for primary care treatment of depression. *Annals of Family Medicine,* Vol. 2, No. 4, 2004, pp. 301–304.

Dimidjian, S., S. D. Hollon, K. S. Dobson, K. B. Schmaling, R. J. Kohlenberg, M. E. Addis, R. Gallop, J. B. McGlinchey, D. K. Markley, J. K. Gollan, D. C. Atkins, D. L. Dunner, and N. S. Jacobson. Randomized trial of behavioral activation, cognitive therapy, and antidepressant medication in the acute treatment of adults with major depression. *Journal of Consulting and Clinical Psychology,* Vol. 74, 2006, pp. 658–670.

Druss, B. Improving medical care for persons with serious mental illness: Challenges and solutions. *Journal of Clinical Psychiatry,* Vol. 68, Suppl. 4, 2007, pp. 40–44.

Dwight-Johnson, M., C. D. Sherbourne, D. Llao, and K. B. Wells. Treatment preferences among depressed primary care patients. *Journal of General Internal Medicine,* Vol. 15, 2000, pp. 527–534.

Ehlers, A., and D. M. Clark. Early psychological interventions for adult survivors of trauma: A review. *Biological Psychiatry,* Vol. 53, 2003, pp. 817-826.

Eisen, S. V., B. Clarridge, V. Stringfellow, J. A. Shaul, and P. D. Cleary. Toward a national report card: Measuring consumer experiences with behavioral health services. In B. Dicky and L. Seder, eds., *Achieving Quality in Psychiatric and Substance Abuse Practice: Concepts and Case Reports.* Washington, D.C.: APA Press, 2001, pp. 115–134.

Elkin, I., R. D. Gibbons, T. Shea, S. M. Sotsky, J. T. Watkins, P. A. Pilkonis, and D. Hedeker. Initial severity and differential treatment outcome in the National Institute of Mental Health Treatment of Depression Collaborative Research Program. *Clinical Psychology,* Vol. 63, 1995, pp. 841–847.

Elkin, I., M. T. Shea, J. T. Watkins, S. D. Imber, S. M. Sotsky, J. F. Collins, D. R. Glass, P. A. Pilkonis, W. R. Leber, J. P. Docherty, S. J. Fiester, and M. B. Parloff. National Institute of Mental Health Treatment of Depression Collaborative Research Program: General effectiveness of treatments. *Archives of General Psychiatry*, Vol. 46, 1989, pp. 971–982.

Embrey, Ellen. Testimony to House Committee on Veterans Affairs Subcommittee on Health, February, 27, 2002.

Engel, C. C., T. Oxman, C. Yamamoto, D. Gould, S. Barry, P. Stewart, K. Kroenke, J. Williams, and A. J. Dietrich. RESPECT-Mil: Feasibility of a systems-level collaborative care approach to depression and post-traumatic stress disorder in military primary care. *Journal of Military Medicine*, in press.

Ernst, Ed. Herbal remedies for depression and anxiety. *Advances in Psychiatric Treatment*, Vol. 13, 2007, pp. 312–316.

Ernst, E., J. I. Rand, and C. Stevinson. Complementary therapies for depression. *Archives of General Psychiatry*, Vol. 55, 1998, pp. 1026–1032.

Evans, M. D., S. D. Hollon, R. J. DeRubeis, J. M. Piasecki, M. W. Grove, M. J. Garvey, and V. B. Tuason. Differential relapse following cognitive therapy and pharmacotherapy for depression. *Archives of General Psychiatry*, Vol. 49, 1992, pp. 802–808.

Evans, R. W. The postconcussion syndrome and the sequelae of mild head injury. *Neurologic Clinics*, Vol. 10, 1992, pp. 815–847.

Fann, Jesse R., Wayne J. Katon, Jay M. Uomoto, and Peter C. Esselman. Psychiatric disorders and functional disability in outpatients with traumatic brain injuries. *American Journal of Psychiatry*, Vol. 152, No. 10, 1995, pp. 1493–1499.

Fann, J. R., J. M. Uomoto, and W. J. Katon. Cognitive improvement with treatment of depression following mild traumatic brain injury. *Psychosomatics*, Vol. 42, 2001, pp. 48–54.

Feeley, William F., Deputy Under Secretary for Health for Operations and Management. Testimony before the Subcommittee on Health, Committee on Veterans Affairs, September 25, 2007. As of March 13, 2008:
http://www.va.gov/OCA/testimony/hvac/070925WF.asp

Feijo de Mello, M., J. de Jesus Mari, J. Bacaltchuk, H. Verdeli, and R. Neugebauer. Systematic review of research findings on the efficacy of interpersonal therapy for depressive disorders. *European Archives of Psychiatry and Clinical Neuroscience*, Vol. 255, 2005, pp. 75–82.

Feldman, S. Choices and challenges. In S. Feldman, ed., *Managed Behavioral Health Services: Perspectives and Practice*, Springfield, Ill.: Charles C. Thomas Publisher, 2003, pp. 3–23.

Ferguson, J. M., R. K. Shrivastava, S. M. Stahl, J. T. Hartford, F. Borian, J. Ieni, R. D. McQuade, and D. Jody. Reemergence of sexual dysfunction in patients with major depressive disorder: Double-blind comparison of nefazodone and sertraline. *Journal of Clinical Psychiatry*, Vol. 62, No. 1, 2001, pp. 24–29.

Figiel, G. S., C. Epstein, W. M. McDonald, J. Amazon-Leece, L. Figiel, A. Saldivia, and S. Glover. The use of rapid-rate transcranial magnetic stimulation (rTMS) in refractory depressed patients. *Journal of Neuropsychiatry and Clinical Neuroscience*, Vol. 10, 1998, pp. 20–25.

Fincham, F. D., S. R. H. Beach, G. T. Harold, and L. N. Osborne. Marital satisfaction and depression: Different causal relationships for men and women? *Psychological Science*, Vol. 8, No. 5, 1997, pp. 351–357.

Fink, M., and M. A. Taylor. Electroconvulsive therapy: Evidence and challenges. *Journal of the American Medical Association*, Vol. 298, No. 3, 2007, pp. 330–332.

Foa, E. B. Psychosocial treatment of posttraumatic stress disorder. *Journal of Clinical Psychiatry*, Vol. 61, Suppl. 5, 2000, pp. 43–51.

Foa, E. B., T. M. Keane, and M. J. Friedman. *Effective Treatments for PTSD*. New York: Guildford Press, 2000a.

———. Guidelines for treatment of PTSD. *Journal of Traumatic Stress*, Vol. 13, 2000b, pp. 539–588.

Forbes, D., A. J. Phelps, A. F. McHugh, P. Debenham, M. Honwood, and M. Creamer. Imagery rehearsal in the treatment of posttraumatic nightmares in Australian veterans with chronic combat-related PTSD: 12-month follow-up data. *Journal of Traumatic Stress*, Vol. 16, No. 5, 2003, pp. 509–513.

Force Health Protection and Readiness (FHP&R) Military Mental Health. "Sustaining the Mental Health and Well Being of the Military Community." February 2007. As of March 13, 2008: http://fhp.osd.mil/mmh/docs/mh_white_paper.doc.

Fortney, J. C., J. M. Pyne, M. J. Edlund, D. K. Williams, D. E. Robinson, D. Mittal, and K. L. Henderson. A randomized trial of telemedicine-based collaborative care for depression. *Journal of General Internal Medicine*, Vol. 22, 2007, pp. 1086–1093.

Foster, Tech. Sgt. Sabrina. Warriors with mild to moderate injuries stay near the fight. November 20, 2007. As of March 13, 2008: http://www.af.mil/news/story.asp?id=123076460 (as January 28, 2008).

Foy, D. W., S. M. Glynn, P. P. Schnurr, M. K. Jankowski, M. S. Wattenberg, D. S. Weiss, C. R. Marmar, and F. D. Gusman. Group therapy. In E. B. Foa, T. M. Keane and M. J. Friedman, eds., *Effective Treatments for PTSD*, New York: Guildford Press, 2000, pp. 155–175.

Frame, R. VA Readjustment Counseling Services (Vet Ccenters) Support for Reserve Marines and Their Families. Marine Corps Combat/Operational Stress Control Conference, June 18–19, 2007.

Freemantle, N., E. L. Harvey, F. Wolf, J. M. Grimshaw, R. Grilli, and L. A. Bero. Printed educational materials: Effects on professional practice and health care outcomes. *Cochrane Database of Systematic Reviews*, Vol. 2, 2000.

Friedman, M. A., J. B. Detweiler-Bedell, H. E. Leventhal, R. Horne, G. I. Keitner, and I. W. Miller. Combined psychotherapy and pharmacotherapy for the treatment of major depressive disorder. *Clinical Psychology: Science and Practice*, Vol. 11, 2004, pp. 47–68.

Gabriel, E. J., J. Ghajar, A. Jogoda, P. T. Pons, T. Scaelea, and B. C. Walters. *Guidelines for Prehospital Management of Traumatic Brain Injury*. New York: Brain Trauma Foundation, 2000.

GAO. *Defense Health Care: Oversight of the TRICARE Civilian Provider Network Should Be Improved*. Washington, D.C.: U.S. Government Accountability Office, 2003.

———. *Defense Health Care: Access to Care for Beneficiaries Who Have Not Enrolled in TRICARE's Managed Care Option*. Washington, D.C.: U.S. Government Accountability Office, 2006a.

———. *Posttraumatic Stress Disorder: DoD Needs to Identify the Factors Its Providers Use to Make Mental Health Evaluation Referrals for Service Members*. Washington, D.C., GAO-06-397, 2006b. As of March 2, 2008: http://www.gao.gov/highlights/d06397high.pdf

———. *Military Health: Increased TRICARE Eligibility for Reservists Presents Educational Challenges*. Washington, D.C.: U.S. Government Accountability Office, 2007a.

———. *Preliminary Observations on Efforts to Improve Health Care and Disability Evaluations for Returning Service Members: Statements of John H. Pendleton and Daniel Bertoni*. Washington, D.C.: U.S. Government Accountability Office, 185, 2007b.

———. *VA and DoD Health Care: Efforts to Provide Seamless Transition of Care for OEF and OIF Service Members and Veterans*. Washington, D.C.: U.S. Government Accountability Office, 2006c.

———. *Veterans' Disability Benefits: Long-Standing Claims Processing Challenges Persist, statement of Daniel Bertoni, Acting Director, Education, Workforce, and Income Security*. Washington, D.C.: U.S. Government Accountability Office, March 7, 2007c.

Gaskin, T. U.S. Marine Corps Combat/Operational Stress Control Program Update. 2007. As of March 13, 2008:
http://www.manpower.usmc.mil/cosc

Gellatly, J., P. Bower, S. Hennessy, D. Richards, S. Gilbody, and K. Lovell. What makes self-help interventions effective in the management of depressive symptoms? Meta-analysis and meta-regression. *Psychological Medicine*, Vol. 37, 2007, pp. 1217–1228.

George, D. S. Iraq war may add stress for past vets: Trauma disorder claims at new high. *Washington Post*, June 20, 2006.

George, K. Witness testimony at hearing "Polytrauma Center Care and the Traumatic Brain Injury (TBI) Patient: How Seamless Is the Transition Between the U.S. Department of Veterans Affairs and the Department of Defense and Are Needs Being Met?" Subcommittee on Health, the House Committee on Veterans Affairs, 110th Congress, March 15, 2007.

Gerber, P. D., J. Barrett, J. Barrett, E. Manheimer, R. Whiting, and R. Smith. Recognition of depression by internists in primary care: A comparison of internist and "gold standard" psychiatric assessments. *Journal of General Internal Medicine*, Vol. 4, No. 1, 1989, pp. 7–13.

Gerrity, M. S., J. W. Williams, A. J. Dietrich, and A. L. Olson. Identifying physicians likely to benefit from depression education: A challenge for health care organizations. *Medical Care*, Vol. 39, No. 8, 2001, pp. 856–866.

Gershon, A. A., P. N. Dannon, and L. Grunhaus. Transcranial magnetic stimulation in the treatment of depression. *American Journal of Psychiatry*, Vol. 160, 2003, pp. 835–845.

Gilbody, S., P. Bower, J. Fletcher, D. Richards, and A. J. Sutton. Collaborative care for depression: A cumulative meta-analysis and review of longer-term outcomes. *Archives of Internal Medicine*, Vol. 166, 2006, pp. 2314–2321.

Gilbody, S., P. Whitty, J. Grimshaw, and R. Thomas. Educational and organizational interventions to improve the management of depression in primary care: A systematic review. *Journal of the American Medical Association,* Vol. 289, No. 23, 2003, pp. 3145–3151.

Goldman, W., J. McCulloch, and B. Cuffel. A four-year study of enhancing outpatient psychotherapy in managed care. *Psychiatric Services*, Vol. 54, No. 1, 2003, pp. 41–49.

Grady, D. Struggling back from war's once-deadly wounds. *New York Times*, January 22, 2006.

Grieger, T. A., T. T. Kolkow, J. L. Spira, and J. S. Morse. Posttraumatic stress disorder and depression in health care providers returning from deployment to Iraq and Afghanistan. *Military Medicine*, Vol. 172, No. 5, 2007, pp. 451–455.

Grol, R., and J. Grimshaw. Evidence-based implementation of evidence-based medicine. *Joint Commission Journal on Quality Improvement*, Vol. 25, No. 10, 1999, pp. 503–513.

Gunnell, D., J. Saperia, and D. Ashby. Selective serotonin reuptake inhibitors (SSRIs) and suicide in adults: Meta-analysis of drug company data from placebo controlled, randomised controlled trials submitted to the MHRA's safety review. *British Medical Journal*, Vol. 330, 2005, pp. 1–5.

Hagan, C., D. Malkmus, P. Durham, and K. Bowman. Levels of cognitive functioning. In *Rehabilitation of the Head Injured Adult: Comprehensive Physical Management*, Downey, Calif.: Professional Staff Association of Rancho Los Amigos Hospital, 1979.

Hamblen, J. L., L. E. Gibson, K. T. Mueser, and F. H. Norris. Cognitive behavioral therapy for prolonged postdisaster distress. *Journal of Clinical Psychology*, Vol. 62, August 2006, pp. 1043–1052.

Harris, O. A., J. M. Colford, Jr., M. C. Good, and P. G. Matz. The role of hypothermia in the management of severe brain injury: A meta-analysis. *Archives of Neurology*, Vol. 59, July 2002, pp. 1077–1083.

Hegel, M. T., J. Ünützer, L. Tang, P. A. Arean, W. Katon, P. H. Noel, J. W. Williams, Jr., and E. H. Lin. Impact of comorbid panic and posttraumatic stress disorder on outcomes of collaborative care for late-life depression in primary care. *American Journal of Geriatric Psychiatry*, Vol. 13, No. 1, 2005, pp. 48–58.

Helmick, K., K. Guskiewicz, J. Barth, R. Cantu, J. P. Kelly, E. McDonald, S. Flaherty, J. Bazarian, J. Bleiberg, T. Carter, J. Cooper, et al. Defense and Veterans Brain Injury Center Working Group on the Acute Management of Mild Traumatic Brain Injury in Military Operational Settings. Clinical Practice Guideline and Recommendations. December 22, 2006. As of March 13, 2008: http://www.dvbic.org/pdfs/clinical_practice_guideline_recommendations.pdf

Helmus, T. C., and R. W. Glenn. *Steeling the Mind: Combat Stress Reactions and Their Implications for Urban Warfare*. Santa Monica, Calif.: RAND Corporation, 2005. As of March 13, 2008: http://www.rand.org/pubs/monographs/MG191

High, W. M., C. Boake, and L. D. Lehmkuhl. Critical analysis of studies evaluating the effectiveness of rehabilitation after traumatic brain injury. *Journal of Head Trauma Rehabilitation*, Vol. 10, No. 1, 1995, pp. 14–26.

High, W. M., T. Roebuck-Spencer, A. M. Sander, M. A. Struchen, and M. Sherer. Early versus later admission to postacute rehabilitation: Impact on functional outcome after traumatic brain injury. *Archives of Physical Medicine and Rehabilitation*, Vol. 87, No. 3, 2006, pp. 334–342.

Hoge, C. W., J. L. Auchterlonie, and C. S. Milliken. Mental health problems, use of mental health services, and attrition from military service after returning from deployment to Iraq or Afghanistan. *Journal of the American Medical Association*, Vol. 295, No. 9, 2006, pp. 1023–1032.

Hoge, C. W., C. A. Castro, S. C. Messer, D. McGurk, D. I. Cotting, and R. L. Koffman. Combat duty in Iraq and Afghanistan, mental health problems, and barriers to care. *New England Journal of Medicine*, Vol. 351, No. 1, 2004, pp. 13–22.

Hoge, C. W., D. McGurk, J. L. Thomas, A. L. Cox, C. C. Engel, and C. A. Castro. Mild traumatic brain injury in U.S. soldiers returning from Iraq. *New England Journal of Medicine*, Vol. 358, No. 5, 2008, pp. 453–463.

Hollon, S. D., M. E. Thase, and J. C. Markowitz. Treatment and prevention of depression. *Psychological Science in the Public Interest*, Vol. 3, No. 2, 2002, pp. 39–77.

Hosek, J., J. Kavanagh, and L. Miller. *How Deployments Affect Service Members*. Santa Monica, Calif.: RAND Corporation, MG-432-RC, 2006. As of March 13, 2008: http://www.rand.org/pubs/monographs/MG432/

Hull, A., and D. Priest. Little relief on Ward 53. *Washington Post*, June 18, 2007, p. A01.

Humphreys, L., J. Westerink, L. Giarratano, and R. Brooks. An intensive treatment program for chronic posttraumatic stress disorder: 2-year outcome data. *Australian and New Zealand Journal of Psychiatry*, Vol. 33, No. 6, 1999, pp. 848-854.

Hunter, C. L., C. M. Hunter, E. T. West, M. H. Kinder, and D. W. Carroll. Recognition of depressive disorders by primary care providers in a military medical setting. *Military Medicine*, Vol. 167, No. 4, 2002, pp. 308–311.

Improving Chronic Illness Care Evaluation (ICICE) Web site. As of March 4, 2008: http://www.rand.org/health/projects/icice

Improving Chronic Illness Care (ICIC) Web site. As of March 4, 2008: http://www.improvingchroniccare.org

Independent Review Group. *Rebuilding the Trust: Rehabilitative Care and Administrative Processes at Walter Reed Army Medical Center and National Naval Medical Center.* Arlington, Va., 2007.

Institute of Medicine. *Crossing the Quality Chasm: A New Health System for the 21st Century.* Washington, D.C.: National Academy Press, 2001.

———. Committee on Crossing the Quality Chasm: Adaptation to Mental Health and Addictive Disorders, *Improving the Quality of Health Care for Mental and Substance-Use Conditions: Quality Chasm Series.* Washington, D.C.: National Academies Press, 2006.

———. Committee on Monitoring Access to Personal Health Care Services. *Access to Health Care in America.* Washington, D.C.: National Academy Press, 1993.

———. Committee on Treatment of Posttraumatic Stress Disorder, Board on Population Health and Public Health Practice. *Treatment of Posttraumatic Stress Disorder: An Assessment of the Evidence.* Washington, D.C.: National Academies Press, 2007.

Jacobson, N. S., and A. Christensen. *Integrative Couple Therapy: Promoting Acceptance and Change.* New York: Norton, 1996.

Jane-Llopis, E., C. Hosman, R. Jenkins, and P. Anderson. Predictors of efficacy in depression prevention programmes: Meta-analysis. *British Journal of Psychiatry*, Vol. 183, 2003, pp. 384–397.

Jarrett, R. B., M. Schaffer, D. McIntire, A. Witt-Browder, D. Kraft, and R. C. Risser. Treatment of atypical depression with cognitive therapy or phenelzine: A double-blind, placebo-controlled trial. *Archives of General Psychiatry*, Vol. 56, 1999, pp. 431–437.

Jay, G. W., R. S. Goka, and A. H. Arakaki. Minor traumatic brain injury: Review of clinical data and appropriate evaluation and treatment. *Journal of Insurance Medicine*, Vol. 27, 1996, pp. 262–282.

Jha, A. K., J. B. Perlin, K. W. Kizer, and R. A. Dudley. Effect of the transformation of the veterans affairs health care system on the quality of care. *New England Journal of Medicine*, Vol. 348, 2003, pp. 2218–2227.

Jha, A. K., S. M. Wright, and J. B. Perlin. Performance measures, vaccinations, and pneumonia rates among high-risk patients in veterans administration health care. *American Journal of Public Health*, Vol. 97, No. 12, 2007, pp. 2167–2172.

Johnson, S. J., M. D. Sherman, J. S. Hoffman, L. C. James, P. L. Johnson, J. E. Lochman, T. N. Magee, and D. Riggs, *The Psychological Needs of U.S. Military Service Members and Their Families: A Preliminary Report.* American Psychological Association Presidential Task Force on Military Deployment Services for Youth, Families, and Servicemembers, 2007.

Joint Theater Trauma System (JTTS). Clinical practice guidelines for in-theatre management of mild traumatic brain injury (concussion). Updated August 2006. As of Maech 13, 2008: http://www.pdhealth.mil/TBI.asp

Jones, E., N. T. Fear, and S. Wessely. Shell shock and mild traumatic brain injury: A historical review. *American Journal of Psychiatry*, Vol. 164, No. 11, 2007, pp. 1641–1645.

Jones, J. H., S. L. Viola, M. M. LaBan, W. G. Schynoll, and R. L. Krome. The incidence of post minor traumatic brain injury syndrome: A retrospective survey of treating physicians. *Archives of Physical Medicine and Rehabilitation*, Vol. 73, 1992, pp. 145–146.

Kang, H. K. VA Facility Specific OIF/OEF Veterans Coded with Potential PTSD Through 3rd Quarter FY 2006, 2006.

Katon, W., P. Robinson, M. Von Korff, E. Lin, T. Bush, E. Ludman, G. Simon, and E. Walker. A multifaceted intervention to improve treatment of depression in primary care. *Archives of General Psychiatry*, Vol. 53, No. 10, 1996, pp. 924–932.

Katon, W. J., P. Roy-Byrne, J. Russo, and D. Cowley. Cost-effectiveness and cost offset of a collaborative care intervention for primary care patients with panic disorder. *Archives of General Psychiatry*, Vol. 59, No. 12, 2002, pp. 1098–1104.

Katon, W., and H. Schulberg. Epidemiology of depression in primary care. *General Hospital Psychiatry*, Vol. 14, 1992, pp. 237–247.

Katon, W., J. Ünützer, M. Y. Fan, J. W. Williams, Jr., M. Schoenbaum, E. H. Lin, et al. Cost-effectiveness and net benefit of enhanced treatment of depression for older adults with diabetes and depression. *Diabetes Care*, Vol. 29, No. 2, 2006, pp. 265–270.

Katon, W., M. Von Korff, E. Lin, and G. Simon. Rethinking practitioner roles in chronic illness: The specialist, primary care physician, and the practice nurse. *General Hospital Psychiatry*, Vol. 23, No. 3, 2001, pp. 138–144.

Katon, W., M. Von Korff, E. Lin, G. Simon, E. Walker, J. Ünützer, et al. Stepped collaborative care for primary care patients with persistent symptoms of depression: A randomized trial. *Archives of General Psychiatry*, Vol. 56, No. 12, 1999, pp. 1109–1115.

Katon, W., M. Von Korff, E. Lin, E. Walker, G. Simon, T. Bush, P. Robinson, and J. Russo. Collaborative management to achieve treatment guidelines. Impact on depression in primary care. *Journal of American Medical Association*, Vol. 273, No. 13, 1995, pp. 1026–1031.

Kay, T., D. E. Harrington, R. Adams, and T. Anderson. Definition of mild traumatic brain injury. *Journal of Head Trauma and Rehabilitation*, Vol. 8, 1993, pp. 86–87.

Keane, T. M., A. D. Marshall, and C. T. Taft. Posttraumatic stress disorder: Etiology, epidemiology, and treatment outcome. *Annual Review of Clinical Psychology*, Vol. 2, 2006, pp. 161–197.

Kellner, C. H., R. G. Knapp, G. Petrides, T. A. Rummans, M. M. Husain, K. Rasmussen, M. Mueller, H. J. Bernstein, K. O'Connor, G. Smith, M. Biggs, S. H. Bailine, C. Malur, E. Yim, S. McClintock, S. Sampson, and M. Fink. Continuation electroconvulsive therapy vs pharmacotherapy for relapse prevention in major depression: A multisite study from the Consortium for Research in Electroconvulsive Therapy (CORE). *Archives of General Psychiatry*, Vol. 63, 2006, pp. 1337–1344.

Kennedy, S. H., H. F. Anderson, and R. W. Lam. Efficacy of escitalopram in the treatment of major depressive disorder compared with conventional selective serotonin reuptake inhibitors and venlafaxine XR: A meta analysis. *Journal of Psychiatry and Neuroscience*, Vol. 31, No. 2, 2006, pp. 122–131.

Kerr, E. A., R. B. Gerzoff, S. L. Krein, J. V. Selby, J. D. Piette, J. D. Curb, W. H. Herman, D. G. Marrero, K. M. V. Narayan, M. M. Safford, T. Thompson, and C. M. Mangione. Diabetes care quality in the veterans affairs health care system and commercial managed care: The triad study. *Annals of Internal Medicine*, Vol. 141, No. 4, 2004, pp. 272–281.

Kessler, R. C., P. A. Berglund, M. L. Bruce, J. R. Koch, E. M. Laska, P. J. Leaf, R. W. Manderscheid, R. A. Rosenheck, E. E. Walters, and P. S. Wang. The prevalence and correlates of untreated serious mental illness. *Health Services Research*, Vol. 36, 2001, pp. 987–1007.

Kilbourne, A. M., H. A. Pincus, K. Schutte, J. E. Kirchner, G. L. Haas, and E. M. Yano. Management of mental disorders in VA primary care practices. *Administration and Policy in Mental Health*, Vol. 33, 2006, pp. 208–214.

Kirchner, J. E., G. M. Curran, and M. S. Aikens. Detecting depression in VA primary care clinics. *Psychiatric Services*, Vol. 55, 2004, p. 350.

Kirklady, R. D., and L. L. Tynes. Best practices: Depression screening in a VA primary care clinic. *Psychiatric Services*, Vol. 57, 2006, pp. 1694–1696.

Kirsch, I., A. Capafons, E. Cardena, and S. Amigo. *Clinical Hypnosis and Self-Regulation Therapy: A Cognitive-Behavioral Perspective*, Washington D.C.: American Psychological Association, 1998.

Kizer, K. W. *Vision for Change: A Plan to Restructure the Veterans Health Administration*. Washington, D.C.: Department of Veterans Affairs, 1995.

Knuth, T., P. B. Letarte, G. Ling, L. E. Moores, P. Rhee et al. *Guidelines for the Field Management of Combat-Related Head Trauma*. New York: Brain Trauma Foundation, 2005.

Koffman, R. L. Navy Combat/Operational Stress Control (COSC) Update. 2007.

Korsen, N., P. Scott, A. J. Dietrich, and T. Oxman. Implementing an office system to improve primary care management of depression. *Psychiatry Quarterly*, Vol. 74, No. 1, 2003, pp. 45–60.

Kozel, F. A., Z. Nahas, C. deBrux, M. Molloy, J. P. Lorberbaum, D. Bohning, S. C. Risch, and M. S. George. How coil-cortex distance relates to age, motor threshold, and antidepressive response to repetitive transcranial magnetic stimulation. *Journal of Neuropsychiatry and Clinical Neuroscience*, Vol. 12, 2000, pp. 376–384.

Krakow, B., M. Hollifield, L. Johnston, M. Koss, R. Schrader, T. D. Warner, D. Tandberg, J. Lauriello, L. McBride, and L. Cutchen. Imagery rehearsal therapy for chronic nightmares in sexual assault survivors with posttraumatic stress disorder a randomized controlled trial. *Journal of the American Medical Association*. Vol. 286, No. 5, 2001, pp. 537–545.

Krakow, B., R. Kellner, D. Pathak, and L. Lambert. Imagery rehearsal treatment for chronic nightmares. *Behaviour Research and Therapy*, Vol. 33, No. 7, 1995, pp. 837-843.

Kudler, H. S., A. S. Blank, Jr., and J. L. Krupnick. Psychodynamic therapy. In E. B. Foa, T. M. Keane and M. J. Friedman, eds., *Effective Treatments for PTSD*, New York: Guildford Press, 2000, pp. 339–341.

Labuc, S. Cultural and societal factors in military organizations. In R. Gal and D. Mangelsdorff, eds., *The Handbook of Military Psychology*, New York: P. Wiley, 1991, pp. 471–489.

Langhorne, P., and P. Duncan. Does the organisation of post-acute stroke care really matter? *Stroke*, Vol. 32, 2001, pp. 268–274.

Leichsenring, F., S. Rabung, and E. Leibing. The efficacy of short-term psychodynamic psychotherapy in specific psychiatric disorders: A meta-analysis. *Archives of General Psychiatry*, Vol. 61, No. 12, 2004, pp. 1208–1216.

Leininger, B. E., S. E. Gramling, A. D. Farrell, J. S. Kreutzer, and E. A. Peck. Neuropsychological deficits in symptomatic minor head injury patients after concussion and mild concussion. *Journal of Neurology, Neurosurgery, and Psychiatry*, Vol. 53, 1990, pp. 293–296.

Leslie, D. L., and R. A. Rosenheck. Comparing quality of mental health care for public-sector and privately insured populations. *Psychiatric Services*, Vol. 51, No. 5, 2000, pp. 650–655.

Lester, H., and L. Gask. Delivering medical care for patients with serious mental illness or promoting a collaborative model of recovery? *British Journal of Psychiatry*, Vol. 188, No. 5, 2006, pp. 401–402.

Lester, H. E., J. Q. Tritter, and H. Sorohan. Patients' and health professionals' views on primary care for people with serious mental illness: Focus group study. *British Medical Journal*, Vol. 330, No. 7500, 2005, pp. 1122–1127.

Levin, H. S., S. Mattis, and R. M. Ruff. Neurobehavioral outcome following minor head injury: Three-center study. *Journal of Neurosurgery*, Vol. 66, 1987, pp. 234–243.

Lewin, W., T. F. D. Marshall, and A. H. Roberts. Long-term outcome after severe head injury. *British Medical Journal*, Vol. 2, 1979, pp. 1533–1537.

Lin, E. H., W. J. Katon, G. E. Simon, M. Von Korff, T. M. Bush, C. M. Rutter, et al. Achieving guidelines for the treatment of depression in primary care: Is physician education enough? *Medical Care*, Vol. 35, No. 8, 1997, pp. 831–842.

Link, B. G. Mental patient status, work, and income: An examination of the effects of a psychiatric label. *American Sociological Review*, Vol. 47, 1982, pp. 202–215.

Link, B. G., and Jo C. Phelan. Conceptualizing stigma. *Annual Review of Sociology*, Vol. 27, 2001, pp. 363–385.

Link, B. G., Jo C. Phelan, M. Bresnahan, A. Stueve, and B. A. Pescosolido. Public conceptions of mental illness: Labels, causes, dangerousness, and social distance. *American Journal of Public Health*, Vol. 89, 1999, pp. 1328–1333.

Lobatz, M., J. Martinez, and D. Romito. *Impact of Treating Combat Injured Military Personnel in a Community Hospital's Brain Injury Day Treatment Program*. Encinitas, Calif.: Scripps Memorial Hospital, 2007.

Lomas, J., and R. B. Haynes. A taxonomy and critical review of tested strategies for the application of clinical practice recommendations: From "official" to "individual" clinical policy. *American Journal of Preventive Medicine*, Vol. 4, No. 4, Supplement, 1988, pp. 77–94.

Lorge, E. M. Army study finds delayed combat stress reporting. Army News Service, 2007. As of March 13, 2008: http://www.army.mil/-news/2007/11/14/6090-army-study-finds-delayed-combat-stress-reporting/

Malec, J. F., and J. S. Basford. Postacute brain injury rehabilitation. *Archives of Physical Medicine and Rehabilitation*, Vol. 77, 1996, pp. 198–207.

Mark, M., S. Rabin, I. Modai, M. Kotler, and H. Hermesh. A combined clinical approach to treating and understanding prolonged combat stress reaction. *Military Medicine*, Vol. 161, No. 12, 1996, pp. 763–765.

Marshall, R. D., J. H. Câarcamo, C. Blanco, and M. Liebowitz. Trauma-focused psychotherapy after a trial of medication for chronic PTSD: Pilot observations. *American Journal of Psychotherapy*, Vol. 57, 2003, pp. 374–383.

Maugh II, T. H. Iraq war veterans often delay mental reactions. *Los Angeles Times*, December 19, 2007.

Mauksch, L. B., S. M. Tucker, W. J. Katon, J. Russo, J. Cameron, E. Walker, and R. Spitzer. Mental illness, functional impairment, and patient preferences for collaborative care in an uninsured, primary care population. *Journal of Family Practice*, Vol. 50, No. 1, 2001, pp. 41–47.

Maze, R. Disability pay can depend on where you live. *Army Times*, November 30, 2007.

McDermut, W., I. W. Miller, and R. A. Brown. The efficacy of group psychotherapy for depression: A meta-analysis and review of the empirical research. *Clinical Psychology: Science and Practice*, Vol. 8, 2001, pp. 98–116.

McGlynn, E. A., S. M. Asch, J. Adams, J. Keesey, J. Hicks, A. DeCristofaro, and E. A. Kerr. The quality of health care delivered to adults in the United States. *New England Journal of Medicine*, Vol. 348, No. 26, 2003, pp. 2635–2645.

McKaughan, J. Interview with Major General Elder Granger. 2007. As of March 13, 2008: http://www.military-medical-technology.com/print_article.cfm?DocID=1882

McQueen, L., B. S. Mittman, and J. G. Demakis. Overview of the Veterans Health Administration (VHA) Quality Enhancement Research Initiative (QUERI). *Journal of the American Medical Informatics Association*, Vol. 11, No. 5, 2004, pp. 339–343.

Mead, D. E. Marital distress, co-occurring depression, and marital therapy: A review. *Journal of Marital and Family Therapy*, Vol. 28, 2002, pp. 299–314.

Medical Service Corps. Completed Issues and Initiatives: Special Pays, 2002. As of March 13, 2008: http://medicalservicecorps.amedd.army.mil/leadership_initiative/issues_and_initiatives/special_pays.htm

Menchola, M., H. S. Arkowitz, and B. L. Burke. Efficacy of self-administered treatments for depression and anxiety. *Professional Psychology: Research and Practice*, Vol. 38, 2007, pp. 421–429.

Meredith, L. S., M. Jackson-Triche, N. Duan, L. V. Rubenstein, P. Camp, and K. B. Wells. Quality improvement for depression enhances long-term treatment knowledge for primary care clinicians. *Journal of General Internal Medicine*, Vol. 15, No. 12, 2000, pp. 868–877.

Meredith. L. S., P. Mendel, M. Pearson, S. Y. Wu, G. Joyce, J. B. Straus, G. Ryan, E. Keeler, and J. Ünützer. Implementation and maintenance of quality improvement for treating depression in primary care. *Psychiatric Services*, Vol. 57, 2006, pp. 48–55.

Meredith, L. S., A. M. Parker, E. B. Beckjord, S. Gaillot, M. M. Trivedi, and M. E. Vaiana. *Post-Deployment Stress: What Families Should Know, What Families Can Do*. Santa Monica, Calif.: RAND Corporation, CP-535, 2008a.

Meredith, L. S., A. M. Parker, E. B. Beckjord, S. Gaillot, M. M. Trivedi, and M. E. Vaiana. *Post-Deployment Stress: What You Should Know, What You Can Do*. Santa Monica, Calif.: RAND Corporation, CP-534, 2008b.

Mericle, E. W. The psychiatric and the tactical situations in an armored division. *Bulletin of the United States Army Medical Department*, Vol. 6, No. 3, 1946, pp. 325–334.

Military.com. Air Force Palace HART Program, week of September 10, 2007a. As of March 13, 2008: http://www.military.com/military-report/air-force-palace-hart-program

———. Bonus for Clinical Psychology Officers, week of December 17, 2007b. As of March 13, 2008: http://www.military.com/military-report/bonus-for-clinical-psychology-officers

Milliken, C. S., J. L. Auchterlonie, and C. W. Hoge. Longitudinal assessment of mental health problems among Active and Reserve Component soldiers returning from the Iraq war. *Journal of the American Medical Association*, Vol. 298, 2007, pp. 2141–2148.

Ministry of Health [Singapore]. *Health Facts Singapore*. No date. As of March 13, 2008: http://www.moh.gov.sg/mohcorp/statistics.aspx?id=240

Mojtabi, R., R. Rosenheck, R. J. Wyatt, and E. Susser. Transition to VA outpatient mental health service among severely mentally ill patients discharged from the armed services. *Psychiatric Services*, Vol. 54, No. 3, 2003, pp. 383–388.

Monson, C. M., P. P. Schnurr, P. A. Resick, M. J. Friedman, Y. Young-Xu, and S. P. Stevens. Cognitive processing therapy for veterans with military-related posttraumatic stress disorder. *Journal of Consulting and Clinical Psychology*, Vol. 74, No. 5, 2006, pp. 898–907.

Mynors-Wallis, L. M., D. H. Gath, A. R. Lloyd-Thomas, and D. Tomlinson. Randomised controlled trial comparing problem solving treatment with amitriptyline and placebo for major depression in primary care. *British Medical Journal*, Vol. 310, 1995, pp. 441–445.

National Alliance on Mental Illness Web site, Transcranial magnetic stimulation page. As of March 10, 2008: http://www.nami.org/Content/ContentGroups/Helpline1/Transcranial_Magnetic_Stimulation_ (rTMS).htm

National Association of Cognitive-Behavioral Therapists Web site. As of March 8, 2008: http://www.nacbt.org

National Committee for Quality Assurance (NCQA). *The State of Health Care Quality*. Washington, D.C., 2007.

National Defense Research Institute. *Sexual Orientation and U.S. Military Personnel Policy: Options and Assessment*. Santa Monica, Calif.: RAND Corporation, 1993. As of March 13, 2008: http://www.rand.org/pubs/monograph_reports/MR323/

National Guideline Clearinghouse. Traumatic brain injury: Diagnosis, acute management and rehabilitation. Unpublished, 2007.

National Institute for Health and Clinical Excellence. *Clinical Guideline 26, Post-Traumatic Stress Disorder (PTSD): The Management of PTSD in Adults and Children in Primary and Secondary Care*, London: National Institute for Clinical Excellence, 2005.

Noy, S. Stress and personality as factors in the causation and prognosis of combat reactions. In G.L. Belenky, ed., *Contemporary Studies in Combat Psychiatry*. Westport, Conn.: Greenwood Press, 1987, pp. 21–30.

O'Hara, M. W., Gorman, L. L., and Wright, E. J. Description and Evaluation of the Iowa Depression Awareness, Recognition, and Treatment Program. *American Journal of Psychiatry*, Vol. 153, 1996, pp. 645–649.

Okie, S. Traumatic brain injury in the war zone. *New England Journal of Medicine*, Vol. 352, 2005, pp. 2043–2047.

Olfson, M., Marcus, S. C., Druss, D., Elinson, L., Tanielian, T., and Pincus, H. A. National trends in the outpatient treatment of depression. *Journal of the American Medical Association*, Vol. 287, 2002, pp. 203–209.

Ommaya, A. K., A. K. Ommaya, A. L. Dannenberg, and A. M. Salazar. Causation, incidence, and costs of traumatic brain injury in the U.S. military medical system. *Journal of Trauma*, Vol. 40, No. 2, 1996, pp. 211–217.

Oslin, D. W., J. Ross, S. Sayers, J. Murphy, V. Kane, and I. R. Katz. Screening, assessment, and management of depression in VA primary care clinics. The Behavioral Health Laboratory. *Journal of General Internal Medicine*, Vol. 21, 2006, pp. 46–50.

Pach, M. J. Traumatic Brain Injury Task Force Visits Fort Carlson. U.S. Army News Release, 2007. As of March 13, 2008:

http://www.army.mil/-news/2007/03/05/2124-traumatic-brain-injury-task-force-visits-fort-carson/index.html

Pampallona, S., P. Bollini, G. Tibaldi, B. Kupelnick, and C. Munizza. Combined psychotherapy and psychological treatment for depression: A systematic review. *Archives of General Psychiatry*, Vol. 61, 2004, pp. 714–719.

Parker, L. E., E. de Pillis, A. Altschuler, L. V. Rubenstein, L. S. Meredith, and N. Gordon. Balancing participation and expertise: A comparison of locally and centrally managed quality improvement within primary care practices. *Qualitative Health Research*, Vol. 17, 2007, pp. 1268–1279.

Parry, G., J. Cape, and S. Pilling. Clinical practice guidelines in clinical psychology and psychotherapy. *Clinical Psychology and Psychotherapy*, Vol. 10, No. 6, 2003, pp. 337–351.

Penk, W., and R. B. Flannery, Jr. Psychosocial rehabilitation. In E. B. Foa, T. M. Keane and M. J. Friedman, eds., *Effective Treatments for PTSD*. New York: Guildford Press, 2000, pp. 347–349.

Perkins, B. R., and C. C. Rouanzoin. A critical evaluation of current views regarding eye movement desensitization and reprocessing (EMDR): Clarifying points of confusion. *Journal of Clinical Psychology*, Vol. 58, No. 1, 2002, pp. 77–97.

Perlin, J. B., R. M. Kolodner, and R. H. Roswell. The Veterans Health Administration: Quality, value, accountability, and information as transforming strategies for patient-centered care. *HealthcarePapers*, Vol. 5, 2005, pp. 10–24.

Petrides, G., M. Fink, M. M. Husain, et al. ECT remission rates in psychotic versus non-psychotic depressed patients: A report from CORE. *Journal of ECT*, Vol. 17, 2001, pp. 244–253.

Pitman, R. K., K. M. Sanders, R. M. Zusman, A. R. Healy, F. Cheema, N. B. Lasko, L. Cahill, and S. P. Orr. Pilot study of secondary prevention of posttraumatic stress disorder with propranolol. *Biological Psychiatry*, Vol. 51, No. 2, 2002, pp. 189–192.

Powell, J., J. Heslin, and R. Greenwood. Community based rehabilitation after severe traumatic brain injury: A randomized controlled trial. *Journal of Neurology, Neurosurgery and Psychiatry*, Vol. 72, No. 2, 2002, pp. 193–202.

President's Commission on Care for America's Returning Wounded Warriors (PCCWW). *Serve, Support, Simplify: Report of the President's Commission on Care for America's Returning Wounded Warriors*, Washington, D.C.: The President's Commission on Care, 2007a.

―――. *Serve, Support, Simplify: Report of the President's Commission on Care for America's Returning Wounded Warriors, Subcommittee Reports and Survey Findings*. Washington, D.C.: The President's Commission on Care, 2007b.

Prigatano, G. P., P. S. Klonoff, K. P. O'Brien, I. M. Altman, K. Amin, D. Chiapello, J. Shepherd, M. Cunningham, and M. Mora. Productivity after neuropsychologically oriented milieu rehabilitation. *Journal of Head Trauma Rehabilitation*, Vol. 9, No. 1, 1994, pp. 91–102.

Prince, S. E., and N. S. Jacobsen. A review and evaluation of marital and family therapies for affective disorders. *Journal of Marital and Family Therapy*, Vol. 21, No. 4, 1995, pp. 377–401.

Quitkin, Frederic M., Bonnie P. Taylor, and Charlotte Kremer. Does mirtazapine have a more rapid onset than SSSRIs? *Journal of Clinical Psychiatry*, Vol. 62, No. 5, 2001, pp. 358–361.

Raskind, M. A., E. R. Peskind, D. J. Hoff, K. L. Hart, H. A. Holmes, D. Warren, J. Shofer, J. O'Connell, F. Taylor, C. Gross, K. Rohde, and M. E. McFall. A parallel group placebo controlled study of prazosin for trauma nightmares and sleep disturbance in combat veterans with post-traumatic stress disorder. *Biological Psychiatry*, Vol. 61, 2007, pp. 928–934.

Regan, T. Report: High survival rate for US troops wounded in Iraq. *Christian Science Monitor*, November 29, 2004.

Regier, D. A., R. M. A. Hirschfeld, F. K. Goodwin, J. D. Burke, Jr., J. B. Lazar, and I. I. Judd. The NIMH Depression Awareness, Recognition, and Treatment Program: Structure, aims, and scientific basis. *American Journal of Psychiatry*, Vol. 145, 1988, pp. 1352–1357.

Resick, P. A., P. Nishith, T. L. Weaver, M. C. Astin, and C. A. Feuer. A comparison of cognitive-processing therapy with prolonged exposure and a waiting condition for the treatment of chronic posttraumatic stress disorder in female rape victims. *Journal of Consulting and Clinical Psychology*, Vol. 70, No. 4, 2002, pp. 867–879.

Riggs, D. S. Marital and family therapy. In E. B. Foa, T. M. Keane and M. J. Friedman, eds., *Effective Treatments for PTSD*. New York: Guildford Press, 2000, pp. 354–355.

Rix, S., E. S. Paykel, P. Lelliott, A. Tylee, P. Freeling, L. Gask, and D. Hart. Impact of a national campaign on GP education: An evaluation of the Defeat Depression campaign. *British Journal of General Practice*, Vol. 49, 1999, pp. 99–102.

Roberts, I. Aminosteroids for acute traumatic brain injury. *Cochrane Database of Systematic Reviews*, Vol. 4, 2000, p. CD001527.

Rochlen, A. B., R. A. McKelley, and K. A. Pituch. A preliminary examination of the "Real Men. Real Depression" campaign. *Psychology of Men and Masculinity*, Vol. 7, 2006, pp. 1–13.

Rochlen, A. B., M. R. Whilde, and W. D. Hoyer. Real Men. Real Depression: Overview, theoretical implications, and research considerations. *Psychology of Men and Masculinity*, Vol. 6, 2005, pp. 186–194.

Rollman, B. L., B. H. Belnap, S. Mazumdar, P. R. Houck, F. Zhu, W. Gardner, C. F. Reynolds III, H. C. Schulberg, and M. K. Shear. A randomized trial to improve the quality of treatment for panic and generalized anxiety disorders in primary care. *Archives of General Psychiatry*, Vol. 62, No. 12, 2005, pp. 1332–1341.

Rollman, B. L., B. H. Hanusa, H. J. Lowe, T. Gilbert, W. N. Kapoor, and H. C. Schulberg. A randomized trial using computerized decision support to improve treatment of major depression in primary care. *Journal of General Internal Medicine*, Vol. 17, No. 7, 2002, pp. 493–503.

Rosenheck, R. Appendix C, Mental and Substance-Use Health Services for Veterans: Experience with Performance Evaluation in the Department of Veterans Affairs. In Prepared for the Institute of Medicine Committee on Crossing the Quality Chasm: Adaptation to Mental Health and Addictive Disorders, ed., *Improving the Quality of Health Care for Mental and Substance-Use Conditions*, Washington, D.C.: National Academies Press, 2006.

Rosenheck, R. A., and A. F. Fontana. Recent trends in VA treatment of post-traumatic stress disorder and other mental disorders. *Health Affairs* (Project Hope), Vol. 26, 2007, pp. 1720–1727.

Rothbaum, B. O., E. A. Meadows, P. A. Resick, and D. W. Foy. Cognitive behavioral therapy. In E. B. Foa, T. M. Keane, and M. J. Friedman, eds., *Effective Treatments for PTSD*, New York: Guildford Press, 2000, pp. 60–83.

Rowan, A. B., and R. L. Campise. A multisite study of Air Force outpatient behavioral health treatment-seeking patterns and career impact. *Military Medicine*, Vol. 171, 2006, pp. 1123–1127.

Roy-Byrne, P. P., W. Katon, D. S. Cowley, and J. Russo. A randomized effectiveness trial of collaborative care for patients with panic disorder in primary care. *Archives of General Psychiatry*, Vol. 58, No. 9, 2001, pp. 869–876.

Rubenstein, L. V., E. Chaney, J. J. Williams, and M. Gerrity. Collaborative treatment for depression. Veterans Administration practice matters. *Veterans Administration Practice Matters*, Vol. 9, 2004, pp. 1–6.

Rubenstein, L. V., M. Jackson-Triche, J. Ünützer, J. Miranda, K. Minnium, M. L. Pearons, et al. Evidence-based care for depression in managed primary care practices. *Health Affairs*, Vol. 18, 1999, pp. 89–105.

Rubenstein, L. V., L. S. Meredith, L. E. Parker, N. P. Gordon, S. C. Hickey, C. Oken, and M. L. Lee. Impacts of evidence-based quality improvement on depression in primary care: A randomized experiment. *Journal of General Internal Medicine*, Vol. 21, No. 10, 2006, pp. 1027–1035.

Rubenstein, L. V., B. S. Mittman, E. M. Yano, and C. D. Mulrow. From understanding health care provider behavior to improving health care: The QUERI framework for quality improvement. *Quality Enhancement Research Initiative. Medical Care*, Vol. 38, No. 6, Suppl. 1, 2000, pp. 129–141.

Rubenstein, L. V., L. E. Parker, L. S. Meredith, A. Altschuler, E. de Pillis, J. Hernandez, et al. Understanding team-based quality improvement for depression in primary care. *Health Services Research*, Vol. 37, 2002, pp. 1009–1029.

Rush, A. J., R. Armitage, J. C. Gillin, K. A. Yonkers, A. Winokur, H. Moldofsky, G. W. Vogel, S. B. Kaplita, J. B. Fleming, J. Montplaisir, M. K. Erman, B. J. Albala, and R. D. McQuade. Comparative effects of nefazodone and fluoxetine on sleep in outpatients with major depressive disorder. *Biological Psychiatry*, Vol. 44, No. 1, 1998, pp. 3–14.

Rush, A. J., M. H. Trivedi, S. R. Wisniewski, A. A. Nierenberg, J. W. Stewart, D. Warden, G. Niederehe, M. E. Thase, P. W. Lavori, B. D. Lebowitz, P. J. McGrath, J. F. Rosenbaum, H. A. Sackeim, D. J. Kupfer, J. Luther, and M. Fava. Acute and longer-term outcomes in depressed outpatients requiring one or several treatment steps: A STAR*D Report. *American Journal of Psychiatry*, Vol. 163, No. 11, 2006, pp. 1905–1917.

Russell, M. C., *Military Mental Health Care and the Global War on Terrorism: A Critical Analysis from the Field Part Two: Meeting the Mental Health Need*. Yokosuka, Japan: Naval Hospital, 2007.

Russell, M., and S. M. Silver. Training needs for the treatment of combat-related posttraumatic stress disorder: A survey of Department of Defense clinicians. *Traumatology*, Vol. 13, No. 3, 2007, p. 4.

Russell, Mark C., Steven M. Silver, Susan Rogers, and Jolee N. Darnell. Responding to an identified need: A joint Department of Defense/Department of Veterans Affairs training program in eye movement desensitization and reprocessing (EMDR) for clinicians providing trauma services. *International Journal of Stress Management*, Vol. 14, 2007, pp. 61–71.

Rutherford, W. Symptoms at one year following concussion from minor head injuries. *Injury*, Vol. 10, 1989, pp. 225–230.

Sackeim, H. A., R. F. Haskett, B. H. Mulsant, et al. Continuation pharmacotherapy in the prevention of relapse following electroconvulsive therapy: a randomized controlled trial. *Journal of the American Medical Association*, Vol. 285, 2001, pp. 1299–1307.

Sammons, M. T. Psychology in the public sector: Addressing *the Psychological Effects of Combat* in the US Navy. American Psychologist, Vol. 60, 2005, pp. 899–909.

Sander, A. M., T. M. Roebuck, M. A. Struchen, and M. Sherer. Long-term maintenance of gains obtained in post-acute rehabilitation by persons with TBI. *Journal of Head Trauma Rehabilitation*, Vol. 16, 2001, pp. 356–373.

Schierhout, G., and I. Roberts. Anti-epileptic drugs for preventing seizures following acute traumatic brain injury. *Cochrane Database of Systematic Reviews*, Vol. 4, 2001.

Schnurr, P. P., M. J. Friedman, D. W. Foy, M. T. Shea, F. Y. Hsieh, P. W. Lavori, S. M. Glynn, M. Wattenberg, and N. C. Bernardy. Randomized trial of trauma-focused group therapy for posttraumatic stress disorder: Results from a Department of Veterans Affairs cooperative study. *Archives of General Psychiatry*, Vol. 60, No. 5, 2003, p. 481.

Schoenbaum, M., J. Ünützer, C. D. Sherbourne, N. Duan, L. V. Rubenstein, J. Miranda, L. S. Meredith, M. F. Carney, and K. Wells. Cost-effectiveness of practiced-initiated quality improvement for depression: Results of a randomized controlled trial. *Journal of American Medical Association*, Vol. 286, No. 11, 2001, pp. 1325–1330.

Schraa, J., K. Arlinghaus, D. Cooper, and P. Fitzpatrick. Panel Session: "Returning veterans with TBI," at the North American Brain Injury Society Conference on September 28, 2007, San Antonio, Tex.

Scott, S. G., H. G. Belanger, R. D. Vanderploeg, J. Massengale, and J. Scholten. Mechanism of injury approach to evaluating patients with blast-related polytrauma. *Journal of the American Osteopathic Association*, Vol. 106, 2006, pp. 265–270.

Seaton, D. Presentation: "Implications of Life Long Planning for Individuals with Brain Injuries" at the North American Brain Injury Society Conference on September 28, 2007, San Antonio, Tex.

Seedat, S., C. Lochner, B. Vythilingum, and D. Stein. Disability and quality of life in post-traumatic stress disorder: Impact of drug treatment. *PharmacoEconomics*, Vol. 24, No. 10, 2006, pp. 989–998.

Shalev, A. Y., M. J. Friedman, E. B. Foa, and T. M. Keane. Integration and summary. In E. B. Foa, T. M. Keane and E. B. Foa, eds., *Effective Treatments for PTSD*, New York: Guildford Press, 2000, pp. 359–379.

Sherbourne, C. D., K. B. Wells, N. Duan, J. Miranda, J. Ünützer, L. Jaycox, M. Schoenbaum, L. S. Meredith, and L. V. Rubenstein. Long-term effectiveness of disseminating quality improvement for depression in primary care. *Archives of General Psychiatry*, Vol. 58, No. 7, Jul 2001, pp. 696–703.

Sherman, J. J. Effects of psychotherapeutic treatments for PTSD: A meta-analysis of controlled clinical trials. *Journal of Traumatic Stress*, Vol. 11, No. 3, 1998, pp. 413–435.

Shiel, A., J. P. S. Burn, D. Henry, J. Clark, B. A. Wilson, M. E. Burnett, and D. L. McLellan. The effects of increased rehabilitation therapy after brain injury: results of a prospective controlled trial. *Clinical Rehabilitation*, Vol. 15, 2001, pp. 501–514.

Sigford, B. Testimony at Hearing "Polytrauma Center Care and the Traumatic Brain Injury (TBI) Patient: How Seamless Is the Transition Between the U.S. Department of Veterans Affairs and the Department of Defense and Are Needs Being Met?" Subcommittee on Health, the House Committee on Veterans Affairs, 110th Congress, 2007.

Simon, G. E., and M. Von Korff. Recognition, management, and outcomes of depression in primary care. *Archives of Family Medicine*, Vol. 4, 1995, pp. 99–105.

Simon, G. E., E. J. Ludman, J. UnèUtzer, M. S. Bauer, B. Operskalski, and C. Rutter. Randomized trial of a population-based care program for people with bipolar disorder. *Psychological Medicine*, Vol. 35, No. 1, 2005, pp. 13–24.

Sirey, J. A., M. L. Bruce, G. S. Alexopoulos, D. A. Perlick, P. Raue, S. J. Friedman, and B. S. Meyers. Perceived stigma as a predictor of treatment discontinuation in young and older outpatients with depression. *American Journal of Psychiatry*, Vol. 158, 2001, pp. 479–481.

Smit, F., G. Willemse, M. Koopmanschap, S. Onrust, P. Cuijpers, and A. Beekman. Cost effectiveness of preventing depression in primary care patients. *British Journal of Psychiatry*, Vol. 188, No. 4, 2006, pp. 330–336.

Solomon, Z., M. Mikulincer, and R. Benbenishty. Combat stress reaction: Clinical manifestations and correlates. *Military Psychology*, Vol. 1, 1989, pp. 35–47.

Solomon, Z., M. Mikulincer, and S. E. Hobfoll. Effects of social support and battle intensity on loneliness and breakdown during combat. *Journal of Personality and Social Psychology*, Vol. 51, No. 6, 1986, pp. 1269–1276.

Spotswood, S. Congress Concerned Some Vets May Slip Through Cracks. 2007. As of March 13, 2008:
http://www.usmedicine.com/article.cfm?articleID=1535&issueID=98

Stecker, T., J. C. Fortney, F. Hamilton, and I. Ajzen. An assessment of beliefs about mental health care among veterans who served in Iraq. *Psychiatric Services*, Vol. 58, No. 10, October 2007, pp. 1358–1361.

Stochetti, N., A. Furlan, and F. Volta. Hypoxemia and Arterial hypotension at the accident scene in head injury, *Journal of Trauma*, Vol. 40, 1996, pp. 764–767.

Stouffer, S. A., and A. A. Lumsdaine. *The American Soldier, Combat, and Its Aftermath.* New York: John Wiley & Sons, Inc., 1965.

Taylor, D. P., R. B. Carter, A. S. Eison, U. L. Mullins, H. L. Smith, J. R. Torrente, R. N. Wright, and F. D. Yocca. Pharmacology and neurochemistry of nefazodone, a novel antidepressant drug. *Journal of Clinical Psychiatry*, Vol. 56, 1995, pp. 3–11.

Taylor, F., P. Martin, C. T. J. Williams, T. A. Mellman, C. Gross, E. R. Peskind, and M. A. Raskind. Prazosin effects on objective sleep measures and clinical symptoms in civilian trauma posttraumatic stress disorder: A placebo-controlled study. *Journal of Biological Psychiatry*, Vol. 63, No. 6, 2007, pp. 629–632.

Teicher, M. T., C. Glod, and J. O. Cole. Emergence of intense suicidal preoccupation during fluoxetine treatment. *American Journal of Psychiatry*, Vol. 147, 1990, pp. 207–210.

Temkin, N. R., S. S. Dikmen, and H. R. Winn. Posttraumatic seizures. In H. M. Eisenberg and E. F. Aldrich, eds., *Management of Head Injury*, Philadelphia: W.B. Saunders, 1991, pp. 425–435.

Terrio, H., A. Prowell, and L. Brenner. Fort Carson Soldier Readiness Center (SRC): Collaborative Interdisciplinary Efforts Aimed at Establishing Evidence-Based Best Practices. 2007.

Thase, M. E., A. R. Entsuah, and R. L. Rudolph. Remission rates during treatment with venlafaxine or selective serotonin reuptake inhibitors. *British Journal of Psychiatry*, Vol. 178, 2001, pp. 234–241.

Thompson, C., A. L. Kinmonth, L. Stevens, R. C. Peveler, A. Stevens, K. J. Ostler, R. M. Pickering, N. G. Baker, A. Henson, J. Preece, D. Cooper, and M. J. Campbell. Effects of a clinical-practice guideline and practice-based education on detection and outcome of depression in primary care: Hampshire Depression Project Randomised Controlled Trial. *Lancet*, Vol. 355, No. 9199, 2000, pp. 185–191.

Thompson, W. Biofeedback relaxation training: A rediscovered mind-body tool in public health. *American Journal of Health Studies*, Vol. 19, 2004, pp. 185–194.

Tiersky, L. A., V. Anselmi, M. V. Johnston, J. Kurtyka, E. Roosen, T. Schwartz, and J. Deluca. A trial of neuropsychologic rehabilitation in mild-spectrum traumatic brain injury. *Archives of Physical Medicine and Rehabilitation*, Vol. 86, 2005, pp. 1565–1574.

TRICARE. TRICARE: The Basics, 2003.

———. Evaluation of the TRICARE Program: FY07 Report to Congress, TRICARE, 2007.

Trudel, T. M. Presentation: "Post-traumatic Stress Disorder and TBI" at the North American Brain Injury Society Conference on September 29, 2007a, San Antonio, Tex.

———. Testimony at Hearing "Polytrauma Center Care and the Traumatic Brain Injury (TBI) Patient: How Seamless Is the Transition Between the U.S. Department of Veterans Affairs and the Department of Defense and Are Needs Being Met?" Subcommittee on Health, the House Committee on Veterans Affairs, 110th Congress, 2007b.

Trudel, T. M., F. D. Nidiffer, and J. T. Barth. Community integrated brain injury rehabilitation: Treatment models and challenges for civilian, military, and veteran populations. *Journal of Rehabilitation Research and Development*, Vol. 44, No. 7, 2007, pp. 1007–1016.

Turner-Stokes, L. The effectiveness of rehabilitation: A critical review of the evidence. *Clinical Rehabilitation*, Vol. 13, Suppl., 1999.

Turner-Stokes, L., P. B. Disler, A. Nair, and D. T. Wade. Multi-disciplinary rehabilitation for acquired brain injury in adults of working age. *Cochrane Database of Systematic Reviews*, Vol. 3, 2007.

Turner-Stokes, L., and D. Wade. Rehabilitation following acquired brain injury: Concise guidance. *Clinical Medicine*, Vol. 4, 2004, pp. 61–65.

U.S. Army Surgeon General and HQDA G1. Operation Advisory Team Report, 2003.

U.S. Department of the Army, Office of the Surgeon General, Mental Health Advisory Team (MHAT). *Operation Iraqi Freedom (OIF), MHAT Report*. U.S. Army Surgeon General and HQDA G-1, December 16, 2003.

U.S. Department of the Army, Office of the Surgeon General, Mental Health Advisory Team (MHAT-II). *Operation lraqi Freedom (OIF-II), MHAT-II Report*. U.S. Army Surgeon General, January 30, 2005.

U.S. Department of the Army, Office of the Surgeon, Multinational Force–Iraq and Office of the Surgeon General, U.S. Army Medical Command, Mental Health Advisory Team (MHAT-III). *Operation Iraqi Freedom 04-06, MHAT-III Report*. May 29, 2006a.

U.S. Department of the Army, Office of the Surgeon, Multinational Force–Iraq and Office of the Surgeon General, U.S. Army Medical Command, Mental Health Advisory Team (MHAT-IV). *Operation Iraqi Freedom 05-07, MHAT-IV Report*. November 17, 2006b.

U.S. Department of the Army. U.S. Army Wounded Warrior Program: We will never leave a fallen comrade (mission page). 2007. As of March 13, 2008:
http://aw2portal.com/Mission.aspx

———. Report to the Surgeon General Traumatic Brain Injury (TBI) Taskforce, Washington, D.C., 2008.

U.S. Marine Corps. Marine for Life Injured Support Program Announces Initial Operational Capability. 2005. As of March 13, 2008:
http://www.usmc.mil/maradmins/maradmin2000.nsf/0/
41a98930832be6e485257020007c79cc?OpenDocument&Highlight=2,262%2F05

U.S. Navy. Naval Hospital Oak Harbor Opens Deployment Health Clinic. Unpublished, 2007a.

———. Safe Harbor—Severely Injured Support. 2007b. As of March 13, 2008:
http://www.npc.navy.mil/CommandSupport/SafeHarbor/

University of Michigan School of Business. American Customer Satisfaction Index, 2004. As of March 13, 2008:
http://www.theacsi.org/index.php?option=com_content&task=view&id=152

Ünützer, J., D. Powers, W. Katon, and C. Langston. From establishing an evidence-based practice to implementation in real-world settings: Impact as a case study. *Psychiatric Clinics of North America*, Vol. 28, No. 4, 2005, pp. 1079–1097.

van Emmerik, A. A. P., J. H. Kamphuis, A. M. Hulsbosch, and P. M. G. Emmelkamp. Single session debriefing after psychological trauma: A meta-analysis. *The Lancet*, Vol. 360, No. 9335, 2002, pp. 766–771.

van Etten, M. L., and S. Taylor. Comparative efficacy of treatments for post-traumatic stress disorder: A meta-analysis. *Clinical Psychology and Psychotherapy*, Vol. 5, 1998, pp. 126–144.

Vander Laan, R., C. Brandys, I. Sullivan, and C. Lemsky. Integration through a city-wide brain injury network and best practices project. *NeuroRehabilitation*, Vol. 16, 2001, pp. 17–26.

Veterans Health Administration. VA/DoD Clinical Practice Guideline for the Management of Major Depressive Disorder (Version 1.0). Washington, D.C.: Department of Defense, 2004.

———. Va/DoD Joint Executive Council FY 2005 Annual Report. Washington, D.C.: Veterans Health Administration, 2006.

Veterans Health Initiative: Traumatic Brain Injury—Independent Study Course. Washington, D.C.: Department of Veterans Affairs, 2004. As of March 12, 2008: http://www1.va.gov/vhi/docs/TBI.pdf

Vittengl, J. R., L. A. Clark, T. W. Dunn, and R. B. Jarrett. Reducing relapse and recurrence in unipolar depression: A comparative meta-analysis of cognitive-behavioral therapy's effects. *Journal of Consulting and Clinical Psychology*, Vol. 75, No. 3, 2007, pp. 475–488.

Von Korff, M., J. Gruman, J. Schaefer, S. J. Curry, and E. H. Wagner. Collaborative management of chronic illness care. *Annals of Internal Medicine*, Vol. 127, No. 12, 1997, pp. 1097–1102.

Voogt, R. Pre-Conference Workshop: "Brain Injury and the Returning Veteran. Long-Term Consequences," at the North American Brain Injury Society Conference on September 27, 2007, San Antonio, Tex.

Wagner, E. H., B. T. Austin, and M. Von Korff. Organizing care for patients with chronic illness. *Milbank Quarterly*, Vol. 74, 1996, pp. 511–544.

Wagner, E. H., R. E. Galsgow, C. Davis, A. E. Bonomi, L. Provost, D. McCulloch, P. Carver, and C. Sixta. Quality improvement in chronic illness care: A collaborative approach. *Joint Commission Journal on Quality Improvement*, Vol. 27, No. 2, 2001, pp. 63–80.

Wang, P. S., P. Berglund, M. Olfson, H. A. Pincus, K. B. Wells, and R. C. Kessler. Failure and delay in initial treatment contact after first onset of mental disorders in the National Comorbidity Survey Replication. *Archives of General Psychiatry*, Vol. 62, 2005, pp. 603–613.

Wang, P. S., M. Lane, M. Olfson, H. A. Pincus, K. B. Wells, and R. C. Kessler. Twelve-month use of mental health services in the United States: Results from the National Comorbidity Survey Replication. *Archives of General Psychiatry*, Vol. 62, No. 6, 2005, pp. 629–640.

Wang, P. S., G. E. Simon, J. Avorn, F. Azocar, E. J. Ludman, J. McCulloch, M. Z. Petukhova, and R. C. Kessler. Telephone screening, outreach, and care management for depressed workers and impact on clinical and work productivity outcomes. *Journal of the American Medical Association*, Vol. 298, No. 12, September 26, 2007, 179, pp. 1401–1411.

Warden, D. Military TBI during the Iraq and Afghanistan wars. *Journal of Head Trauma and Rehabilitation*, Vol. 21, September–October 2006, pp. 398–402.

Weissman, M. M., and J. C. Markowitz. Interpersonal psychotherapy: Current status. *Archives of General Psychiatry*, Vol. 51, 1994, pp. 599–606.

Wells, K. B. The design of Partners in Care: Evaluating the cost-effectiveness of improving care for depression in primary care. *Social Psychiatry and Psychiatric Epidemiology*, Vol. 34, 1999, No. 1, pp. 20–29.

Wells, K. B., C. Sherbourne, J. Miranda, L. Tang, B. Benjamin, and N. Duan. The cumulative effects of quality improvement for depression on outcome disparities over 9 years: Results from a randomized, controlled group-level trial, *Medical Care*, Vol. 45, No. 11, November 2007, pp. 1052–1059.

Wells, K. B., C. Sherbourne, M. Schoenbaum, N. Duan, L. S. Meredith, J. Ünützer, J. Miranda, M. F. Carney, and L. V. Rubenstein. Impact of disseminating quality improvement programs for depression to managed primary care: A randomized controlled trial. *Journal of the American Medical Association*, Vol. 282, 2000, pp. 212–220.

Whyte, J., T. Hart, A. Laborde, and M. Rosenthal. Rehabilitation of the patient with traumatic brain injury. In J. A. DeLisa, B. M. Gans, and N. E. Walsh, eds., *Physical Medicine and Rehabilitation: Principles and Practice*. Philadelphia, Pa.: Lippincott Williams and Wilkind, 2005, pp. 1680–1693.

Williams, J. W., C. D. Mulrow, E. Chiquette, P. H. Noël, C. Aguilar, and J. Cornell. A systematic review of newer pharmacotherapies for depression in adults: Evidence report summary. *Annals of Internal Medicine*, Vol. 132, No. 9, 2000, pp. 743–756.

Willis, C., S. Lybrand, and N. Bellamy. Excitatory amino acid inhibitors for traumatic brain injury. *Cochrane Database of Systematic Reviews*, No. 4, 2007.

Wilson, E. $50 million rehabilitation center opens on Fort Sam Houston. Army News Service, 2007. As of March 13, 2008:
http://www.army.mil/-news/2007/01/30/1570-50-million-rehabilitation-center-opens-on-fort-sam-houston/

Wood, R., J. McCrea, L. Wood, and R. Merriman. Clinical and cost effectiveness of post-acute neurobehavioral rehabilitation. *Brain Injury*, Vol. 13, 1999, pp. 69–88.

Wright, D. W., A. L. Kellermann, V. S. Hertzberg, P. L. Clark, M. Frankel, F. C. Goldstein, J. P. Salomone, L. L. Dent, O. A. Harris, D. S. Ander, D. W. Lowery, M. M. Patel, D. D. Denson, A. B. Gordon, M. M. Wald, S. Gupta, S. W. Hoffman, and D. G. Stein. ProTEConn.: A randomized clinical trial of progesterone for acute traumatic brain injury. *Annals of Emergency Medicine*, Vol. 49, April 2007, pp. 391–402.

Yablon, S. A. Posttraumatic seizures. *Archives of Physical Medicine and Rehabilitation*, Vol. 74, 1993, pp. 983–1001.

Yu, W., A. Ravelo, T. H. Wagner, C. S. Phibbs, A. Bhandari, S. Chen, and P. G. Barnett. Prevalence and costs of chronic conditions in the VA health care system. *Medical Care Research and Review*, Vol. 60, 2003, pp. 146S–147S.

Zatzick, D., P. Roy-Byrne, J. Russo, F. Rivara, R. Droesch, A. Wagner, C. Dunn, G. Jurkovich, E. Uehara, and W. Katon. A randomized effectiveness trial of stepped collaborative care for acutely injured trauma survivors. *Archives of General Psychiatry*, Vol. 61, No. 5, 2004, pp. 498–506.

Zatzick, D. F., P. Roy-Byrne, J. E. Russo, F. P. Rivara, A. Koike, G. J. Jurkovich, and W. Katon. Collaborative interventions for physically injured trauma survivors: A pilot randomized effectiveness trial. *General Hospital Psychiatry*, Vol. 23, No. 3, 2001, pp. 114–123.

Zoroya, G. Troops cheat on brain-injury tests to stay with units. *USA Today*, November 7, 2007, p. 16A.

Zwerdling, D. Soldiers say Army ignores, punishes mental anguish. 2007a. As of March 13, 2008: http://www.npr.org/templates/story/story.php?storyId=6576505

Zwerdling, D. Army dismissals for mental health, misconduct rise. 2007b. As of March 13, 2008: http://www.npr.org/templates/story/story.php?storyId=16330374

Part VI: Conclusions and Recommendations

This monograph sought to understand the prevalence, costs, and systems of care for post-traumatic stress disorder (PTSD), major depression, and traumatic brain injury (TBI) among servicemembers who deployed to Afghanistan and Iraq in support of Operations Enduring Freedom (OEF) and Iraqi Freedom (OIF). Part II summarized our efforts to identify the nature and scope of the mental health and cognitive problems that OEF/OIF veterans face; we examined the prevalence of post-traumatic stress disorder, major depression, and traumatic brain injury. Part III described the short- and long-term consequences of these problems in terms of outcomes such as suicide, homelessness, work productivity, and marital/family relations. Part IV provided results from our work to estimate the economic costs associated with these conditions, and Part V assessed the systems of care available to address these issues among military servicemembers and veterans.

In Part VI, we provide an overview of the study and describe our key findings, present general conclusions stemming from these findings, and offer recommendations for improving policy and enhancing services to meet the evolving needs of veterans with psychological and cognitive injuries.

CHAPTER EIGHT

Treating the Invisible Wounds of War: Conclusions and Recommendations

Terri Tanielian, Lisa H. Jaycox, Terry L. Schell, Grant N. Marshall, and Mary E. Vaiana

Throughout its history, the United States has striven to recruit, prepare, and sustain an armed force with the capacity and capability to defend the nation. The Department of Defense (DoD), through the Secretary of Defense and the Services, bears the responsibility for ensuring that the force is ready and deployable to conduct and support military operations.

The nation has committed not only to compensating military servicemembers for their duty but also to addressing and providing compensation, benefits, and medical care for any Service-connected injuries and disabilities. For those who suffer injuries but remain on active duty, benefits and medical care are typically provided through DoD, which remains their employer. Veterans who have left the military may be eligible for health care and other benefits (disability, vocational training), as well as memorial and burial services, through the Department of Veterans Affairs (VA).

Safeguarding mental health is an integral part of the national responsibility to recruit, prepare, and sustain a military force and to address Service-connected injuries and disabilities. Safeguarding mental health is also critical for compensating and honoring those who have served the nation. The Departments of Defense and Veterans Affairs are primarily responsible for these critical tasks; however, other federal agencies (e.g., the Department of Labor) and states also play important roles in ensuring that the military population is not only ready as a national asset but also valued as a national priority.[1] Our research has focused mainly on services available through DoD and the VA; however, where applicable, we also refer to state programs and other resources.

---

[1] In March 2007, the President not only tasked the Secretaries of Defense and Veterans Affairs with making improvements to address the systemic failures in caring for the wounded, he also created an interagency task force that also included, at a minimum, the Secretaries of Labor, Health and Human Services, Housing and Urban Development, and Education; the Director of the Office of Management and Budget; and the Administrator of the Small Business Administration ("Executive Order Establishing Task Force; Executive Order 13426—Establishing a Commission on Care for America's Returning Wounded Warriors and a Task Force on Returning Global War on Terror Heroes," 2007, Appendix A). Indeed, the obligation for care of veterans does not stop at the federal level. Each of the states has a division of veterans' affairs, and since the inception of the Global

With the United States still involved in military operations in Afghanistan and Iraq, psychological and cognitive injuries among those deployed in support of Operations Enduring Freedom (OEF) and Iraqi Freedom (OIF) are of growing concern. Most servicemembers return home from deployment without problems and successfully readjust to ongoing military employment or work in civilian settings. But others return with mental health conditions, such as post-traumatic stress disorder (PTSD) or major depression, and some have suffered a traumatic brain injury (TBI), such as a concussion, leaving a portion of sufferers with cognitive impairments.

Despite widespread policy interest and a firm commitment from the Departments of Defense and Veterans Affairs to address these injuries, fundamental gaps remain in our knowledge about the mental health and cognitive needs of U.S. servicemembers returning from Afghanistan and Iraq, the adequacy of the care system available to meet those needs, the experience of servicemembers who are in need of treatment, and the factors affecting whether injured servicemembers and veterans seek care. RAND undertook this comprehensive study to address these gaps and make these conditions and their consequences visible.

We focused on three major conditions—post-traumatic stress disorder, major depression, and traumatic brain injury—because there are obvious mechanisms that link each of these conditions to specific experiences in war. Unfortunately, these conditions are often invisible to the eye. Unlike physical wounds of war that maim or disfigure, these conditions remain invisible to other servicemembers, family members, and society in general. All three conditions affect mood, thoughts, and behavior, yet these conditions often go unrecognized or unacknowledged. In addition, the effects of traumatic brain injury are still poorly understood, leaving a substantial gap in knowledge about the extent of the problem and its effective treatment.

The study was guided by a series of overarching questions:

- **Prevalence:** What is the scope of mental health and cognitive conditions that troops face when returning from deployment to Afghanistan and Iraq?
- **Costs:** What are the costs of these conditions, including treatment costs and costs stemming from lost productivity and other consequences? What are the costs and potential savings associated with different levels of medical care—including proven, evidence-based care; usual care; and no care?
- **The care system:** What are the existing programs and services to meet the health-related needs of servicemembers and veterans with post-traumatic stress disorder, major depression, or traumatic brain injury? What are the gaps in the programs and services? What steps can be taken to close the gaps?

War on Terror, several states have expanded health care access, educational benefits, and job support programs (see the National Governors Association Web site).

To answer these questions, we designed a series of data-collection activities to accomplish four aims:

1. Identify and assess current mental health and cognitive conditions among military servicemembers who served in Afghanistan or Iraq.
2. Identify the short- and long-term consequences of untreated psychological and cognitive injuries (e.g., PTSD, major depression, TBI).
3. Document and assess the availability, accessibility, and capacity of existing programs and services to meet short- and long-term mental health and cognitive needs, as well as brain injuries, in injured servicemembers.
4. Evaluate aids and barriers to seeking care and to using services.

Key Findings

Prevalence of Mental Health Conditions and TBI

- *Most servicemembers return home from war without problems and readjust successfully, but some have significant deployment-related mental health problems.*

To examine the prevalence of PTSD, major depression, and TBI among OEF/OIF veterans, we reviewed the first wave of studies that estimate the extent of these problems among servicemembers deployed to Afghanistan and Iraq. More than a dozen studies described the possible prevalence of PTSD and major depression, but there was very limited information about the extent of cognitive impairments following TBI events. The studies we reviewed and our own data (see Part II) suggest that, although most servicemembers are returning from combat free from any of these conditions, 5 to 15 percent of them may be returning with PTSD, and 2 to 14 percent with major depression. Very little is known about the number who experienced a traumatic brain injury or who are currently suffering from problems related to such an injury. The data are scant at present, and estimates range widely.

Several themes emerge from the currently available literature. Many studies have used common screening tools, facilitating comparisons across studies. But, regardless of the sample, measurement tool, or time of assessment, servicemembers who had been in combat and had been wounded had a heightened risk of having a mental health condition, mostly PTSD. When comparisons are available, servicemembers deployed to Iraq appear to be at higher risk for PTSD than those deployed to Afghanistan. These findings may help to identify which servicemembers will be most at risk for mental health problems upon redeployment, but they offer limited guidance for understanding specific mental health treatment needs among the entire deployed population. Thus, despite many strengths in the studies reviewed, the studies' limitations call for additional data collection within the post-deployed population.

We identified three important data gaps with respect to generalizability, scope, and availability of information on traumatic brain injury in the existing studies of OEF/OIF veterans:

First, these studies relied on surveys of relatively narrow groups (e.g., combat units, active duty units, Army), making it difficult to generalize findings to all deployed servicemembers, since information about other components and Service branches is weaker or nonexistent. Although the Army has accounted for the majority of the ground forces in OEF/OIF, data that generalize to the entire deployed population would help in planning efforts to address the full array of mental health and cognitive conditions post-deployment across Service branches and components.

Second, very limited research examined associations between deployment experiences and subsequent mental health problems—knowledge that is essential if we wish to understand how we can intervene earlier or mitigate the consequences of combat exposure.

Third, there is limited research on the prevalence of TBI and its long-term effects on functioning.

To address some of the gaps in knowledge in the existing prevalence literature, we conducted a telephone survey of 1,965 servicemembers from 24 geographic areas who had been deployed to Afghanistan or Iraq as part of OEF or OIF. The survey was designed to capture a wide range of deployed servicemembers across branches of Service, rank, military occupational specialty, and geographic regions. (Details of our methods and analysis can be found in Part II.)

- *Current rates of exposure to combat trauma and mental health conditions among returning veterans are relatively high.*

Rates of exposure to specific types of combat trauma ranged from 5 to 50 percent, with high levels of exposure reported for many traumatic events. Vicariously experienced traumas (e.g., having a friend who was seriously wounded or killed) were the most frequently mentioned. Direct injuries were reported by 10 to 20 percent of the sample. A substantial number of previously deployed personnel are currently affected[2] by PTSD (14 percent) and major depression (14 percent), or report having experienced a probable TBI (19 percent). However, it is not possible to know from the survey the severity of the TBI or whether there is any ongoing functional impairment from the injury.

Assuming that the prevalence found in this study is representative of the 1.64 million individuals who had been deployed to Afghanistan and Iraq as of October 2007, we estimate that approximately 300,000 individuals currently suffer from PTSD

---

[2]   As defined by presence of symptoms in the previous 30 days for PTSD and in the previous 14 days for depression.

or major depression and that 320,000 veterans may have experienced a probable TBI during deployment. About one-third (31 percent) of those previously deployed have at least one of these three conditions, and about 5 percent report symptoms consistent with PTSD and major depression, as well as reporting a probable TBI.

- *Some groups are at higher risk for these conditions.*

We identified several groups that are at increased risk for current PTSD and major depression. Higher rates of PTSD and major depression are found among Army soldiers and marines, and among servicemembers who are not on active duty (e.g., those in the Reserve Component, as well as those who have been discharged or retired from the military). In addition, enlisted personnel, women, and Hispanics are more likely than their counterparts to meet screening criteria for PTSD and major depression. Finally, individuals with more-lengthy deployments (i.e., 12 to 15 months) and more-extensive exposure to combat trauma are at greater risk of suffering from current PTSD and major depression. Exposure to specific combat traumas was the single-best predictor for both PTSD and major depression. Examination of rates of these conditions within the group of veterans who reported no exposure to combat-related situations showed very low rates (2, 3, and 1 percent for probable PTSD, depression, and TBI, respectively). When we used statistical techniques to control for the effects of different trauma exposure, enlisted personnel, women, Reserve members/National Guard, Hispanics, and older military servicemembers continued to show an increased risk for mental health problems.

Similarly, we found several groups to be at high risk of reporting a probable TBI, particularly soldiers, marines, enlisted servicemembers, and those with extensive combat exposures. Here again, combat exposure was the best predictor of probable TBI.

- *There is a large gap in care for these disorders: The need for treatment is high, but few receive adequate services.*

Our survey also assessed *use of health care* (seeing a physician or other provider) for these three conditions. Servicemembers and veterans with probable PTSD or major depression seek care at about the same rate as the civilian population, and, just as in the civilian population, many of the afflicted individuals were not receiving treatment. Among those who met diagnostic criteria for PTSD or major depression, only 53 percent had seen a physician or mental health provider to seek help for a mental health problem in the past 12 months. Of those who sought medical care, just over half received minimally adequate treatment (see Chapter Four). The gap in care was even higher for TBI: 57 percent of those who reported experiencing a probable TBI were never evaluated by a physician for a brain injury.

Survey respondents identified many barriers that inhibit their getting treatment for mental health problems. In general, respondents were concerned that if they received treatment, it would not be kept confidential and would constrain future job assignments and career advancement. About 45 percent were concerned that drug therapies for mental health problems may have unpleasant side effects, and about one-quarter thought that even good mental health care was not very effective. Logistical barriers to mental health treatment, such as time, money, and access, were mentioned less frequently but may still be important barriers for many individuals. At the same time, it is possible that many servicemembers and veterans do not seek treatment because they may perceive little or no benefit.

These survey data, combined with the results of our literature review, suggest the following conclusions:

- Most published studies of mental health conditions among military servicemembers and veterans to date have systematically excluded or underrepresented individuals who have separated from a Service or serve in the Reserve Component. Yet, our survey found these individuals to be at significantly higher risk for mental health problems than those currently on active duty.
- Major depression is often not considered a combat injury; however, our data suggest that it is highly associated with combat trauma and warrants closer attention.
- About half of individuals with a probable diagnosis of PTSD or major depression had sought help from a health professional, but most did not get minimally adequate treatment (defined as [1] taking a prescribed medication for as long as the doctor wanted and having at least four visits with a doctor or therapist in the past 12 months or [2] having had at least eight visits with a mental health professional in the past 12 months, with visits averaging at least 30 minutes). Thus, by increasing the rate of effective treatment utilization, we can reduce the number of individuals who otherwise would have persistent PTSD or depression.
- Many of the most commonly identified barriers to getting needed mental health treatment could be reduced if servicemembers had access to confidential treatment.
- Access to both medications and psychotherapies is necessary, since many servicemembers and veterans have concerns about the side effects of medications.

We now consider the potential long-term consequences associated with these injuries.

Long-Term Consequences of Mental Health and Cognitive Conditions

- *PTSD, major depression, and TBI can have long-term, cascading consequences.*

Research conducted in both military and civilian populations on the long-term effects of PTSD, depression, or TBI suggests that, unless treated, each of these conditions has implications that are wide-ranging and negative for those afflicted. Thus, the effects of post-combat mental health and cognitive conditions can be compared to ripples spreading outward on a pond. However, whereas ripples diminish over time, the consequences of mental health conditions may grow more severe, especially if left untreated.

An individual with any one of these conditions is more likely to have other psychiatric problems (e.g., substance use) and to attempt suicide. Those afflicted are also more likely to have higher rates of unhealthy behaviors (e.g., smoking, overeating, unsafe sex); higher rates of physical health problems and mortality; a tendency to miss more days of work and report being less productive while at work; and a greater likelihood of being unemployed. Suffering from these conditions can also impair personal relationships, disrupt marriages, aggravate difficulties with parenting, and cause problems in children that extend the costs of combat experiences across generations. There is also a possible connection between having one of these conditions and being homeless (see Chapter Five).

In Chapter Five, we presented a framework to help clarify how a mental health or cognitive condition (i.e., impaired emotional and cognitive functioning) has both short-term and long-term effects. The condition can have immediate consequences for the individual (e.g., additional psychiatric problems, poor health-maintenance behaviors), which themselves accumulate and contribute to additional problems (e.g., with physical health, work performance, and interpersonal relationships). The likelihood that the condition will trigger a negative cascade of consequences over time is greater if the initial symptoms of the condition are more severe and the afflicted individual has other sources of vulnerability (e.g., unstable family relationships, low socioeconomic status [SES], a prior history of psychopathology).

The studies we reviewed support this framework. They consistently show that individuals afflicted with one of these conditions experience worse consequences when they must simultaneously confront other sources of stress. In contrast, other sources of strength (e.g., supportive family relationships, high SES, high education) may serve as buffers, even for those whose symptoms are relatively severe.

The extant literature clearly documents that there are long-term negative repercussions of having these conditions if they remain untreated. Thus, efforts to identify and treat these conditions should be made as early as possible. Early interventions are likely to pay long-term dividends in improved outcomes for years to come; so, it is critical to help servicemembers and veterans seek and receive treatment. The literature also clearly indicates that individuals who have more resources (social, financial, educational) fare better; thus, policies that promote resilience by providing such resources could be as effective as programs that target the symptoms of these conditions directly.

Costs

To understand the long-term consequences of these conditions in economic terms, we developed a microsimulation model. Using data from the literature (which had limited information on specific populations and costs), we estimated the costs associated with mental health conditions (PTSD and major depression) for a hypothetical cohort of military personnel deployed to Afghanistan and Iraq. Then, we calculated the costs across the deployed population, based on an approximation for the whole distribution of the deployed population, using publicly available data on the proportion of those returning from deployment, by rank (see *Medical Surveillance Monthly Report* [2007]).

We defined *costs* in terms of lost productivity, treatment, and suicide attempts and completions, and we estimated costs over a two-year period (see Chapter Six). For each condition, we generated two estimates—one that included the medical costs and the value of lives lost to suicide, and one that excluded such costs. We were unable to estimate the costs associated with homelessness, domestic violence, family strain, and substance abuse, because there are no good data available to create credible dollar figures for these outcomes. However, if figures for these consequences were available, the costs of having these conditions would be higher. Our estimates represent costs incurred within the first two years of returning home from deployment, so they accrue at different times for different personnel. For servicemembers who returned more than two years ago and have not redeployed, these costs have already been incurred. However, these calculations omit costs for servicemembers who may deploy in the future, and they do not include costs associated with chronic or recurring cases that linger beyond two years. More details on the model assumptions and parameters can be found in Part IV (Chapter Six). Below, we briefly summarize the findings from our model, first for PTSD and major depression, then for TBI. All costs for PTSD and depression represent two-year post-deployment costs and are shown in 2007 dollars. Costs for TBI are one-year costs based on documented cases of TBI in 2005, inflated to 2007 dollars.

- *Estimates of the cost of a condition for two years post-deployment range from $5,904 to $25,757 per case for major depression and PTSD.*

Our microsimulation model predicts that two-year post-deployment costs to society resulting from PTSD and major depression for 1.6 million deployed servicemembers could range from $4.0 billion to $6.2 billion, depending on how we account for the costs of lives lost to suicide. For PTSD, average costs per case over two years range from $5,904 to $10,298; for depression, costs range from $15,461 to $25,757; and for PTSD and major depression together, costs range from $12,427 to $16,884. The majority of the costs were due to lost productivity. Because these numbers do not account for future costs that may be incurred if additional personnel deploy and because they are limited to two years following deployment, they underestimate total future costs to society.

- *Provision of proven (evidence-based) care will save money or pay for itself.*

The costs associated with PTSD and major depression are high, but savings can be attained if evidence-based treatments are provided to a higher percentage of the population suffering from these conditions. Providing evidence-based care to every individual with the condition would increase treatment costs over what is now being provided (a mix of no care, usual care, and evidence-based care), but these costs can be offset over time through increased productivity and lower incidence of suicide. Projected cost savings are highest for those with major depression; for those with PTSD or co-morbid PTSD and depression, the finding that evidence-based treatment saves money is sensitive to whether or not we include the cost of lives lost to suicide in our estimates.

Given that costs of problems related to mental health, such as homelessness, domestic violence, family strain, and substance abuse, are not factored into our economic models and would add substantially to the costs of illness, we may have underestimated the amount saved by providing evidence-based care. However, a caveat is that we did not consider additional implementation and outreach costs (over and above the day-to-day costs of care) that might be incurred if DoD and the VA attempted to expand evidence-based treatment beyond their current capacity.

- *Estimates of the cost of mild TBI range from $25,572 to $30,730 per case in 2005 ($27,259 to $32,759 in 2007 dollars); estimates of moderate or severe TBI costs range from $252,251 to $383,221 per case in 2005 ($268,902 to $408,519 in 2007 dollars).*

Given the dearth of literature on TBI-related costs and the effect of treatment on TBI, we conducted a prevalence-based cost-of-illness analysis. Because there is a high level of uncertainty around many of the parameters needed, we developed different assumptions and generated estimates for both a low-cost scenario and a high-cost scenario. We estimated that the cost of deployment-related TBI ranged from $90.6 million to $135.4 million in 2005 ($96.6 to $144.4 million in 2007 dollars), based on a total of 609 diagnosed cases of TBI reported in 2005. On a per-case basis, this translates to a range of from $158,385 in the low-cost scenario to $236,655 in the high-cost scenario, in 2007 dollars. These costs are applicable to servicemembers who have accessed the health care system and received a diagnosis of TBI; they do not reflect costs for all individuals who have met screening criteria for probable TBI.

Costs and cost drivers vary substantially by severity of the injury. The one-year per-case costs for mild TBI range from $27,259 to $32,759 in 2007 dollars. Productivity losses account for 47 to 57 percent of total costs, whereas treatment accounts for 43 to 53 percent in these estimates. Costs are much higher for moderate to severe cases, with per-case costs ranging from $268,902 to $408,519 in 2007 dollars. In moderate-to-severe cases, TBI-related death is the largest cost component (70 to 80 percent of total costs); productivity losses account for only 8 to 13 percent, and treatment costs, 7 to 10 percent. Suicide, which we consider separately from TBI-related death, can account for up to 12 percent of total costs.

We estimated the total cost of deployment-related TBI by applying an adjusted per-case cost for 2005 to the total number of TBI cases reported in *Serve, Support, Simplify: The Report of the President's Commission on Care for America's Returning Wounded Warriors* (President's Commission on Care for America's Returning Wounded Warriors, 2007, p. 2). From this calculation, we estimated that one-year costs for diagnosed TBI range between $591 million and $910 million. As with the cost estimates for PTSD and major depression, these figures underestimate the total costs that will accrue in the future, both because they are one-year costs and because they do not account for TBI cases that may occur as the conflicts continue.

• *Lost productivity is a key cost driver for major depression, PTSD, and mild TBI.*

To date, other estimates of the costs associated with war have not always included those related to productivity; however, our model demonstrates that reduced productivity is a key cost driver. Thus, future efforts to tally the costs of mental health conditions should consider how the condition affects an individual's productivity (see Chapter Six). Supporting such efforts will require better information about how these conditions affect labor-market outcomes over both the short term and the long term, particularly for PTSD, for which current evidence is scant. Additional data on career labor-force transitions (within DoD and from DoD to civilian jobs) and participation could help refine our cost estimates.

Systems of Care

Our cost estimates and review of the literature suggest that providing care to servicemembers and veterans afflicted with PTSD, major depression, and TBI can help mitigate long-term consequences and offset the costs associated with these conditions. We examined the existing programs to determine whether there were sufficient resources to meet the needs of the afflicted population. We drew on existing documents and descriptions of programs, as well as interviews with key personnel and administrators of such programs within the Departments of Defense and Veterans Affairs. We included information from focus groups that we conducted with military servicemembers to understand their perspective as consumers of these health services. We also drew lessons from the broader general health and mental health services research field to provide a framework for understanding and illuminating both gaps in care and promising approaches for improving access and quality.

We integrated information from all of these sources to identify gaps in access and quality that must be addressed if the nation is to honor its commitment to provide care and support for service-related injuries and disabilities. Chapter Seven of this monograph provides additional details of our analysis, including a summary of the available information on the efficacy and effectiveness of treatments for PTSD, major depression, and TBI.

Below, we summarize our findings about the systems of care for post-deployment mental health and cognitive conditions. Since mental health conditions and cognitive problems related to TBI are, for the most part, handled in different systems of care, we consider each in turn.

- *Many mental health services are available for active duty personnel, but gaps and barriers are substantial.*

U.S. military personnel have several options when seeking help for mental health problems, including U.S. military chaplains, mental health practitioners embedded in operational units, counseling offered in community service programs, and mental health services provided by Military Treatment Facilities (MTFs) within both specialty mental health and primary care settings. The Department of Defense has also implemented innovations, such as collaborative care models (e.g., RESPECT-Mil) that bring mental health services into primary care settings. Additionally, information and counseling are available through Military OneSource, and a range of health and specialty mental health services is also available from TRICARE civilian network providers.

For active duty personnel and retired military with continued TRICARE coverage, efforts to expand the capacity to treat mental health and cognitive problems are under way (including the hiring and training of additional providers), but significant gaps in access and quality of care remain, owing both to structural aspects of the health care system (availability of providers, wait times, etc.) and to personal and cultural factors that may limit care-seeking.

Improving the efficiency and transparency of the system would address gaps in service use. For example, one strategy would be to reconsider policies that limit the scope of practice for military community-service program counselors so that they can provide evidence-based counseling to those afflicted with PTSD and major depression. Expanding training on evidence-based mental health treatments for these providers could aid early-intervention efforts. At the same time, increased reimbursement rates for TRICARE providers could help to increase the availability of civilian providers.

However, even if adequate capacity to provide high-quality mental health services were provided, policies and cultural issues make servicemembers hesitant to seek care. As noted earlier, many individuals in our survey and also in our focus groups reported concern that using mental health services would diminish their employment and military-career prospects. DoD is undertaking major efforts to overcome cultural and attitudinal barriers to getting help for mental health issues (see Chapter Seven), including providing educational efforts aimed at raising awareness among military leaders and embedding mental health professionals into line units. These initiatives can help ensure that servicemembers are aware of the benefits of mental health care, but they do not address concerns about negative career consequences. In addition to educational efforts, institutional barriers, such as the required disclosure of use of mental health services, must be addressed if gaps in access and use are to be closed.

To reduce such barriers, DoD should consider providing access to off-the-record, confidential counseling—"safe" counseling. Providing access to "safe" mental health services would require the development of guidelines for command notification; however, the guidelines could be limited and transparent to servicemembers, thereby preserving trust that negative career consequences can be avoided. "Safe" counseling services in garrison could support and supplement mental health providers embedded in units to provide evidence-based psychotherapies for PTSD and major depression and to counsel for a broader range of emotional and situational problems, with confidentiality explicitly ensured and clearly communicated to the servicemember. In addition, it may be possible to harness the powerful buffering effect of social support from peers to help stem or even reverse the development of mental health problems, following recently developed models that engage noncommissioned officers in support of mental health issues in combat zones.

- *Attention to quality of mental health treatment within DoD is needed; the VA offers a promising model.*

Although DoD undertakes significant efforts to monitor quality and consumer satisfaction, it has not developed an infrastructure to routinely measure processes or outcomes of mental health care and has not examined the quality of its usual-care services. Thus, quality in many sectors of the care system is unknown. At the same time, efforts to train providers in evidence-based practices are under way but have not yet been integrated into larger system redesign for sustainability. The VA, which has focused on performance measurement and quality-of-care improvement for over a decade, can provide a model for DoD, particularly in informing efforts within the newly created Defense Center of Excellence for Psychological Health and Traumatic Brain Injury (see Chapter Seven). Quality monitoring for psychotherapy delivered to military personnel and veterans has been particularly lacking, as it is in the civilian sector, and should be addressed.

- *The VA faces challenges in providing access to mental health care for veterans and deactivated Reservists and Guard personnel.*

Because the VA operates within a fixed budget and uses a priority system to guide access, veterans from different eras are competing for treatment and support service programs within a system of limited resources. In addition, younger veterans report that they feel uncomfortable and out of place in VA facilities, in which many patients are much older and have different types of health care issues. This disconnect suggests a need for some VA facilities to make special efforts to accommodate the younger generation of veterans. Geographical dispersion of individuals limits access as well. New approaches to reaching Afghanistan and Iraq veterans are likely to involve both marketing and system redesign. Additional data and analyses will be needed to inform capacity requirements, in addition to understanding the need for services (as might be accomplished with prevalence studies) and types of services offered within each system of care. For example, additional analyses of the number of trained providers available and current utilization at the local level are needed.

In addition, OEF/OIF veterans will need better access to mental health services beyond the VA health care system. Further expansion of Vet Centers (VA-run centers that offer benefits and supportive counseling) could broaden access, particularly for veterans in underserved areas. Networks of community-based mental health specialists (available through private, employer-based insurance, including TRICARE) may also provide an important opportunity to build capacity. However, taking advantage of this opportunity will require critical examination of the TRICARE reimbursement rates, which may limit network participation. Determining the best option for expanding services will require additional study. Furthermore, the quality of these services would need to be ensured.

- *The VA is a leader in assessment of health care quality and improvement, but Vet Centers and community providers, including those within TRICARE, still need evaluation.*

A congressionally mandated and independent study of the VA's mental health care services is under way and will be released soon.[3] It is likely to point to areas in which the VA can serve as a model of quality improvement for DoD and the nation, suggesting areas to target for future quality-improvement efforts. Approaches to assessment include examining administrative and claims data and collecting consumer-satisfaction survey data related to mental health services within the TRICARE network. But performance monitoring among general community providers is difficult. Approaches to ensure quality of services and to inform consumers about beneficial services would be helpful.

- *The science of treating traumatic brain injury is young.*

In the newly emerging field of medical care for combat-related TBI, a key gap is knowledge. Continued research on what treatment and rehabilitation are most effec-

---

[3]   See Department of Veterans Affairs (2006). This evaluation should fulfill the ongoing requirements of P.L. 103-62, the Government Performance and Results Act of 1993; Title 38, §527, Evaluation and Data Collection; and 38 CFR §1.15, Standards for Program Evaluation.

tive is urgently needed, as is information on how to identify those in need of care and the level of their impairments.

- *The difficulty of identifying those with lasting effects from mild TBI hampers care.*

For mild TBI, in which cognitive deficits are less common and more transient (see Chapters One and Seven), gaps in access to services arise from poor documentation of blast exposure and failure to identify individuals with probable TBI, including inconsistent screening practices, personal attitudes and military cultural factors, the overlap of symptoms with acute stress reactions and PTSD symptoms, and possible delayed emergence of symptoms. Materials (e.g., fact sheets, resource guides) developed for more-severe brain injury can misguide or unnecessarily stigmatize or alarm those with mild TBI.

The Defense Veterans Brain Injury Center, now reorganized under the Defense Center of Excellence, is increasing its outreach and training to meet the need for more-accurate materials. Strategies to better educate the military community, service providers, and families about mild TBI will complement screening efforts.

- *The complex health care needs of military servicemembers with more-severe injuries require coordination of services.*

Those severely wounded in OEF/OIF face different kinds of gaps in care. Their injuries typically involve complex needs for treatment, and supportive and rehabilitative services, and these needs change over time. Particularly problematic, and the focus of joint VA and DoD efforts, are transitions from the DoD acute care health system to the specialized Polytrauma Services within the VA health care system.

Work is under way to address these issues. However, principles of patient-centered care and collaborative care could appropriately be applied to the complex needs of TBI patients. Widely applied and evaluated in civilian-sector primary care, these approaches organize care around patients' specific needs and preferences. They are particularly relevant for moderate to severe TBI, for which coordination of care to ensure access to needed services is also critical for more seriously injured personnel.

The VA has announced plans to rapidly hire and expand capacity to provide care coordination, and over the past year the Defense Veterans Brain Injury Center implemented a TBI-specific care coordinator system for those who have been medically evacuated from a war zone. Evaluating the effectiveness of care coordinators will be important. Key challenges to expanding DoD and VA capacity to meet the needs of those with TBI are hiring qualified staff and providing appropriate training in and supervision and oversight of their work. The training of recovery coordinators will be critical, as will training for those providing evaluation, medical, and rehabilitative services.

Strengths and Limitations

Both the strengths and limitations of our study approach should be considered alongside the recommendations stemming from this work. Our *survey* was conducted independently and was population-based; thus, it provides estimates not previously available, obtained from populations not included in prior reports. Because it was conducted independently of the military and VA, it may contain a smaller potential for bias in reporting than do surveys that are linked to an individual in military records. However, the telephone-survey methodology limited respondents to those with a land-based telephone and those who lived in proximity to a military base. We used standard statistical methods to partially account for these limitations (see Chapter Four). Nevertheless, certain groups are underrepresented in our sample, and thus the overall results may not accurately generalize to the entire deployed population.

Our *estimation of costs* for PTSD and major depression was based on a state-of-the-art microsimulation model, adding valuable information to other cost estimates. However, scant research was available for some cost-estimate parameters associated with mental health conditions, and we were unable to use the modeling approach for TBI because of the absence of relevant research. These cost estimates are unavoidably imprecise, owing to uncertainty in estimates of prevalence rates, individuals' willingness to seek care, treatment efficacy, the effect of mental health conditions on productivity, and other estimates used to parameterize our model. Nevertheless, all of the parameters used in our model are grounded on prior literature, and we have done our best to be conservative in generating the cost predictions.

Finally, our *review of the programs* now available to OEF/OIF veterans applied a health services model, bringing to bear a focus on access and quality that has been missing from examinations of these systems of care. In our analyses, we focused on three specific mental health and cognitive conditions that affect servicemembers and veterans post-deployment, the costs associated with addressing those conditions, and the services available post-deployment to assist in recovery. The delivery of post-deployment services is part of a larger continuum of ensuring the health of servicemembers, which includes pre-deployment screenings, education, and trainings about the potential effects of combat and deployment. It was beyond the scope of this study to fully assess the adequacy of pre-deployment screenings and training/education programs. However, these programs do require more in-depth analyses to determine their effectiveness. Our findings offer guidance at the system level for improving post-deployment services for those in need following deployment, regardless of the individual's pre-deployment experiences. We also did not comprehensively examine issues affecting determination of service-related injuries or disability determination, both of which are critical for determining eligibility for care within the VA. Finally, we relied solely on publicly available information, because requests for official data were still under review at the time of this writing.

Recommendations

Concern about the invisible wounds of war is increasing, and many efforts to identify and treat those wounds are already under way. Our data show that these mental health and cognitive conditions are widespread; in a cohort of otherwise-healthy, young individuals, they represent the primary type of morbidity or illness for this population in the coming years. What is most worrisome is that these problems are not yet fully understood, particularly TBI, and systems of care are not yet fully available to assist recovery for any of the three conditions. Thus, these invisible wounds of war require special attention and high priority. An exceptional effort will be required to ensure that they are appropriately recognized and treated.

Looking across the dimensions of our analysis, we offer four specific recommendations that we believe would improve the understanding and treatment of PTSD, major depression, and TBI among military veterans. We briefly describe each recommendation and then discuss some of the issues that would need to be addressed for its successful implementation. We believe that efforts to address these recommendations should be standardized to the greatest extent possible *within DoD* (across Service branches, with appropriate guidance from the Assistant Secretary of Defense for Health Affairs), *within the VA* (across health care facilities and Vet Centers), and *across these systems* and extended *into the community-based civilian sector*. These policies and programs must be consistent within and across these sectors in order to have the intended effect on care-seeking and improvements in quality of care for our nation's veterans.

1. **Increase the cadre of providers who are trained and certified to deliver proven (evidence-based) care, so that capacity is adequate for current and future needs.**

There is substantial unmet need for treatment of PTSD and major depression among military servicemembers following deployment. Both DoD and the VA have had difficulty in recruiting and retaining appropriately trained mental health professionals to fill existing *or* new slots. With the possibility of more than 300,000 new cases of mental health conditions among OEF/OIF veterans, a commensurate increase in treatment capacity is needed. Increased numbers of trained and certified professionals are needed to provide high-quality care (evidence-based, patient-centered, efficient, equitable, and timely care) in all sectors, both military and civilian, serving previously deployed personnel. Although the precise increase of newly trained providers is not yet known, it is likely to number in the thousands. These would include providers not just in specialty mental health settings but also embedded in settings such as primary care, where servicemembers already are served. Stakeholders consistently referred to challenges in hiring and retaining trained mental health providers. Determining the exact number of providers will require further analyses of demand projections over time, taking into account the expected length of evidence-based treatment and desired utilization rates.

Additional training in evidence-based approaches for trauma will also be required for tens of thousands of existing providers. Moreover, since there is already an increased need for services, the required expansion in trained providers is already several years overdue.

This large-scale training effort necessitates substantial investment immediately. Such investment could be facilitated by several strategies, including the following:

- Adjustment of financial reimbursement for providers to offer appropriate compensation and incentives to attract and retain highly qualified professionals and ensure motivation for delivering quality care.
- Development of a certification process to document the qualifications of providers. To ensure that providers have the skills to implement high-quality therapies, substantial change from the status quo is required. Rather than rely on a system in which any licensed counselor is assumed to have all necessary skills regardless of training, certification should confirm that a provider is trained to use specific evidence-based treatment for specific conditions. Providers would also be required to demonstrate requisite knowledge of unique military culture, military employment, and issues relevant to veterans (gained through their prior training and through the new training/certification we are recommending).
- Expansion of existing training programs for psychiatrists, psychologists, social workers, marriage and family therapists, and other counselors. Programs should include training in specific therapies related to trauma and to military culture.
- Establishment of regional training centers for joint training of DoD, VA, and civilian providers in evidence-based care for PTSD and major depression. The centers should be federally funded, possibly outside of DoD and VA budgets. This training could occur in coordination with or through the Department of Health and Human Services. Training should be standardized across training centers to ensure both consistency and increase fidelity in treatment delivery.
- Linkage of certification to training to ensure that providers not only receive required training but also are supervised and monitored to verify that quality standards are met and maintained over time.
- Retraining or expansion of existing providers within DoD and the VA (e.g., military community-service program counselors) to include delivery or support of evidence-based care.
- Evaluation of training efforts as they are rolled out, so that we understand how much training is needed and of what type, thereby ensuring delivery of effective care.

2.   Change policies to encourage active duty personnel and veterans to seek needed care.

Creating an adequate supply of well-trained professionals to provide care is but one facet of ensuring access to care. Strategies must also increase demand for necessary services. Many servicemembers are reluctant to seek services for fear of negative career repercussions. Policies must be changed so that there are no perceived or real adverse career consequences for individuals who seek treatment, except when functional impairment (e.g., poor job performance or being a hazard to oneself or others) compromises fitness for duty. Primarily, such policies will require creating new ways for servicemembers and veterans to obtain treatments that are confidential, to operate in parallel with existing mechanisms for receiving treatment (e.g., command referral, unit-embedded support, or self-referral).

We are not suggesting that the confidentiality of treatment should be absolute; both military and civilian treatment providers already have a legal obligation to report to authorities/commanders any patients that represent a threat to themselves or others. However, information about being in treatment is currently available to command staff, even though treatment itself is not a sign of dysfunction or poor job performance and may not have any relationship to deployment eligibility. Providing an option for confidential treatment has the potential to increase total-force readiness by encouraging individuals to seek needed health care before problems accrue to a critical level. In this way, mental health treatment would be appropriately used by the military as a tool to avoid or mitigate functional impairment, rather than as evidence of functional impairment. We believe that this option would ultimately lead to better force readiness and retention, and thus be a beneficial change for both the organization and the individual.

This recommendation would require resolving many practical challenges, but it is vital for addressing the mental health problems of servicemembers who, out of concern for their military careers, are not seeking care. Specific strategies for facilitating care-seeking include the following:

- Developing strategies for early identification of problems that can be confidential, so that problems are recognized and care sought early before the problems lead to impairments in daily life, including job function or eligibility for deployment.
- Developing ways for servicemembers to seek mental health care voluntarily and off-the-record, including ways to allow servicemembers to seek this care off-base if they prefer and ways to pay for confidential mental health care (that is not necessarily tied to an insurance claim from the individual servicemember). Thus, the care would be offered to military personnel without mandating disclosure, unless the servicemember chooses to disclose use of mental health care or there is a command-initiated referral to mental health care.

- Separating the system for determining deployment eligibility from the mental health care system. This may require the development of new ways to determine fitness for duty and eligibility for deployment that do not include information about mental health service use.
- Making the system transparent to servicemembers so that they understand how information about mental health services is and is not used. This may help mitigate servicemembers' concerns about detriments to their careers.

3. Deliver proven, evidence-based care to servicemembers and veterans whenever and wherever services are provided.

Our extensive review of the scientific literature documented that treatments for PTSD and major depression vary substantially in their effectiveness. In addition, the recent report from the Institute of Medicine shows reasonable evidence for treatments for PTSD among military servicemembers and veterans (Institute of Medicine, 2007). Our evaluation shows that the most effective treatments are being delivered in some sectors of the care system for military personnel and veterans, but that gaps remain in systemwide implementation. Delivery of evidence-based care to all veterans with PTSD or major depression would pay for itself, or even save money, by improving productivity and reducing medical and mortality costs within only two years. Providing evidence-based care is not only the humane course of action but also a cost-effective way to retain a ready and healthy military force for the future. Providing one model, the VA is at the forefront of trying to ensure that evidence-based care is delivered to its patient population, but the VA has not yet fully evaluated the success of its efforts across the entire system.

We suggest requiring all providers who treat military personnel to use treatment approaches empirically demonstrated to be effective. This requirement would include uniformed providers in theater and embedded in active duty units; primary and specialty care providers within military and VA health care facilities and Vet Centers; and civilian providers. Evidence-based approaches to resilience-building and other programs need to be enforced among informal providers, including promising prevention efforts pre-deployment, noncommissioned officer support models in theater, and the work of chaplains and family-support providers. Such programs could bolster resilience before mental health conditions develop, or help to mitigate the long-term consequences of mental health conditions.

The goal of this requirement is not to stifle innovation or prevent tailoring of treatments to meet individual needs, but to ensure that individuals who have been diagnosed with PTSD or major depression are provided the most effective evidence-based treatment available.

Some key transformations may be required to achieve this needed improvement in the quality of care:

- The "black box" of psychotherapy delivered to veterans must be made more transparent, making providers accountable for the services they are providing. Doing so might require that TRICARE and the VA implement billing codes to indicate the specific type of therapy delivered, documentation requirements (i.e., structured medical note-taking that needs to accompany billing), and the like.
- TRICARE and the VA should require that all patients be treated by therapists who are certified to handle the diagnosed disorders of that patient.
- Veterans should be empowered to seek appropriate care by being informed about what types of therapies to expect, the benefits of such therapies, and how to evaluate for themselves whether they are receiving quality care.
- A monitoring system could be used to ensure sustained quality and coordination of care and quality improvement. Transparency, accountability, and training/certification, as described above, would facilitate ongoing monitoring of effectiveness that could inform policymaking and form the basis for focused quality-improvement initiatives (e.g., through performance measurement and evaluation). Additionally, linking performance measurements to reimbursement and incentives for providers may also promote delivery of quality care.

4. Invest in research to close information gaps and plan effectively.

In many respects, this study raises more research questions than it provides answers. Better understanding is needed of the full range of problems (emotional, economic, social, health, and other quality-of-life deficits) that confront individuals with post-combat PTSD, major depression, and TBI. This knowledge is required both to enable the health care system to respond effectively and to calibrate how disability benefits are ultimately determined. Greater knowledge is needed to understand who is at risk for developing mental health problems and who is most vulnerable to relapse, and how to target treatments for these individuals.

We need to be able to accurately measure the costs and benefits of different treatment options so that fiscally responsible investments in care can be made. We need to document how these mental health and cognitive conditions affect families of servicemembers and veterans so that appropriate support services can be provided. We need sustained research into the effectiveness of treatments, particularly treatments that can improve the functioning of individuals who do not improve from the current evidence-based therapies. Finally, we need research that evaluates the effects of policy changes implemented to address the injuries of OEF/OIF veterans, including how such changes affect the health and well-being of the veterans, the costs to society, and the state of military readiness and effectiveness.

Addressing these vital questions will require a substantial, coordinated, and strategic research effort. We see the need for several types of studies to address these information gaps. A coordinated federal research agenda on these issues within the veterans' population is needed. Further, to adequately address knowledge gaps will require funding mechanisms that encourage longer-term research that examines a broader set of issues than can be financed within the mandated priorities of an existing funder or agency. Such a research program would likely require funding in excess of that currently devoted to PTSD and TBI research through DoD and the VA, and would extend to the National Institutes of Health, the Substance Abuse and Mental Health Services Administration, the Centers for Disease Control and Prevention, and the Agency for Healthcare Research and Quality. These agencies have limited research activities relevant to military and veteran populations, but these populations have not always been prioritized within their programs.

Initial strategies for implementing this national research agenda include the following:

- Launch a large, longitudinal study on the natural course of these mental health and cognitive conditions among OEF/OIF veterans, including predictors of relapse and recovery. Ideally, such a study would gather data pre-deployment, during deployment, and at multiple time points post-deployment. The study should be designed so that its findings can be generalized to all deployed servicemembers while still facilitating identification of those at highest risk, and it should focus on the causal associations between deployment and mental health conditions. A longitudinal approach would also make it possible to evaluate how use of health care services affects symptoms, functioning, and outcomes over time; how TBI and mental health conditions affect physical health, economic productivity, and social functioning; and how these problems affect the spouses and children of servicemembers and veterans. These data would greatly inform how services are arrayed to meet evolving needs within this population of veterans. They would also afford a better understanding of the costs of these conditions and the benefits of treatment so that the nation can make fiscally responsible investments in treatment and prevention programs. Some ongoing studies are examining these issues (Smith et al., 2008; Vasterling et al., 2006); however, they are primarily designed for different purposes and thus can provide only partial answers.
- Continue to aggressively support research to identify the most effective treatments and approaches, especially for TBI care and rehabilitation. Although many studies are already under way or under review (as a result of the recent congressional mandate for more research on PTSD and TBI), an analysis that identifies priority-research needs within each area could add value to the current programs by informing the overall research agenda and creating new program opportunities in areas in which research may be lacking or needed. More research is also needed to evaluate innovative treatment methods, since not all individuals benefit from the currently available treatments.

- Evaluate new initiatives, policies, and programs. Many new initiatives and programs designed to address psychological and cognitive injuries have been put into place, ranging from screening programs and resiliency training, to use of care managers and recovery coordinators, to implementation of new therapies. Each of these initiatives and programs should be carefully evaluated to ensure that it is effective and is improving over time. Only programs that demonstrate effectiveness should be maintained and disseminated.

Treating the Invisible Wounds of War

Addressing PTSD, depression, and TBI among those who deployed to Afghanistan and Iraq should be a national priority. But it is not an easy undertaking. The prevalence of these injuries is relatively high and may grow as the conflicts continue. And long-term negative consequences are associated with these injuries if they are not treated with evidence-based, patient-centered, efficient, equitable, and timely care. The systems of care available to address these injuries have been improved significantly, but critical gaps remain.

The nation must ensure that quality care is available and provided to its military veterans now and in the future. As a group, the veterans returning from Afghanistan and Iraq are predominantly young, healthy, and productive members of society. However, about a third are currently affected by PTSD or depression, or report exposure to a possible TBI while deployed. Whether the TBIs will translate into any lasting impairments is unknown. In the absence of knowing, these injuries cause great concern for servicemembers and their families. These veterans need our attention now, to ensure a successful adjustment post-deployment and a full recovery.

Meeting the goal of providing quality care for these servicemembers will require system-level changes, which means expanding our focus to consider issues not just within DoD and the VA, from which the majority of veterans will receive benefits, but across the overall U.S. health care system, where veterans may seek care through other, employer-sponsored health plans and in the public sector (e.g., Medicaid). System-level changes are essential if the nation is to meet not only its responsibility to recruit, prepare, and sustain a military force but also its responsibility to address Service-connected injuries and disabilities.

References

Department of Veterans Affairs, Office of Policy, Planning, and Preparedness. *Evaluation of Services for Seriously Mentally Ill Patients in the Veterans Health Administration of the Department of Veterans Affairs, Revised Statement of Work*. Washington, D.C., March 2006.

"Executive Order Establishing Task Force; Executive Order 13426—Establishing a Commission on Care for America's Returning Wounded Warriors and a Task Force on Returning Global War on Terror Heroes." *Federal Register*, March 8, 2007, Appendix A. As of December 31, 2007: http://www1.va.gov/taskforce/

Institute of Medicine, Committee on Treatment of Posttraumatic Stress Disorder, Board on Population Health and Public Health Practice. *Treatment of Posttraumatic Stress Disorder: An Assessment of the Evidence*. Washington, D.C.: National Academies Press, 2007.

Medical Surveillance Monthly Report (MSMR): A Publication of the Armed Forces Health Surveillance Center, Vol. 14, No. 6, September–October 2007.

National Governors Association Web site. As of January 17, 2008: http://www.nga.org/

President's Commission on Care for America's Returning Wounded Warriors. *Serve, Support, Simplify: Report of the President's Commission on Care for America's Returning Wounded Warriors*. July 2007.

Smith, T. C., M. A. K. Ryan, D. L. Wingard, D. J. Slymen, J. F. Sallis, and D. Kritz-Silverstein. New onset and persistent symptoms of post-traumatic stress disorder self reported after deployment and combat exposures: Prospective population based US military cohort study. *British Medical Journal*, January 15, 2008.

Vasterling, J. J., S. P. Proctor, P. Amoroso, R. Kane, T. Heeren, and R. F. White. Neuropsychological outcomes of Army personnel following deployment to the Iraq war. *Journal of the American Medical Association*, Vol. 296, No. 5, August 2, 2006, pp. 519–529. As of March 11, 2008: http://www.ncbi.nlm.nih.gov/entrez/query.fcgi?cmd=Retrieve&db=PubMed&dopt=Citation&list_uids=16882958